MARRIAGE NOTICES
FROM EXTANT ISSUES OF THE
Rockingham Register
HARRISONBURG, VIRGINIA
1822–1870

I0093469

Dorothy A. Boyd-Rush, Ph.D.

HERITAGE BOOKS
2011

HERITAGE BOOKS

AN IMPRINT OF HERITAGE BOOKS, INC.

Books, CDs, and more—Worldwide

For our listing of thousands of titles see our website
at
www.HeritageBooks.com

Published 2011 by
HERITAGE BOOKS, INC.
Publishing Division
100 Railroad Ave. #104
Westminster, Maryland 21157

International Standard Book Numbers
Paperbound: 978-1-55613-822-5
Clothbound: 978-0-7884-8931-0

DEDICATION

This book would not have become a reality without the unfailing encouragement of my husband, my mother, and my uncle.

CONTENTS

According to the best available evidence,[1] the <u>Rockingham Weekly Register</u> began publication in Harrisonburg, Virginia, in July of 1822. Prior to 1870, it underwent a number of minor name changes, including <u>Rockingham Register and Valley Advertiser</u>, <u>Rockingham Register and Virginia Advertiser</u>, <u>Rockingham Register and Advertiser</u>, <u>The Rockingham Register</u>, <u>Rockingham Register</u>, and <u>Rockingham Register & Advertiser</u>. At an early date, however, the newspaper came to be generally referred to simply as the <u>Rockingham Register</u>.

The <u>Register</u> from its inception until well after 1870 usually consisted of four pages and appeared weekly. Understandably, during the early 1860's, largely due to war time shortages of paper, it occasionally was not published or appeared in an abbreviated format.

Throughout the period covered by this book, the <u>Rockingham Register</u> was respected as an important regional newspaper, not simply as a "local" publication. It circulated widely throughout the Shenandoah Valley and in parts of what is today West Virginia.

The marriage notices extracted for

---

[1]The earliest extant issue of the <u>Register</u> is dated Saturday, 5 October 1822. The partial masthead indicates that it is vol. 1, no. 1[torn]. The next existing issue bears the date Saturday, 1 December 1822. It is identified as vol. 1, no. 22. Thus, it can be reasonably argued that the first issue published by Lawrence Wartmann bore the date of Saturday, 27 July 1822.

publication in this volume are drawn from all extant issues of the <u>Register</u> for the period 1822 until 1870. They predictably incorporate information on the marriages that took place in the Shenandoah Valley and immediately beyond, but they also convey information not usually found in courthouse records and report valuable information on those who had "gone west" - making this volume a veritable treasure trove of data on the families who either lived in or passed through the Valley of Virginia in the nineteenth century.

The early, extant issues of the <u>Rockingham</u> <u>Register</u> are widely dispersed. Many have totally disappeared. Some that survive are in the collections of major research institutions, i.e., the University of Virginia and Duke University. Others are in the hands of private collectors, local family members, and/or historical societies. All have my sincere thanks for kindly allowing me to have access to their holdings.

Dorothy A. Boyd-Rush, Ph.D.

ABBOTT: In Strasburg, on the 20th ult., by Rev. Wm. Rusmisell, W.B. ABBOTT, of Frederick county, and Miss C. Virginia KEISTER, of Shenandoah.
Rockingham Register and Advertiser, 11 July 1867 (Thursday), p. 2, c. 6.

ABNEY: On the 30th ult., by Rev. Geo. B. Taylor, Mr. U.V. ABNEY and Miss M.E. BLEDSOE, all of Staunton.
Rockingham Register and Advertiser, 9 November 1860 (Friday), p. 2, c. 6.

ACKER: See entry for CUNNINGHAM.

ACKER: See entry for MORRIS.

ACKER: On Tuesday morning, the 17th inst., by Rev. Jacob Miller, Isaac ACKER and Mrs. Sallie SHOUP, widow of the late Capt. J.C. SHOUP, all of Rockingham county.
Rockingham Register, 26 November 1868 (Thursday), p. 2, c. 5.

ACKERMAN: On the 5th inst., by Elder Henry Jennings, Philip ACKERMAN and Mrs. Elizabeth STINEHARDT, all of Edinburg.
Rockingham Register, 23 April 1868 (Thursday), p. 2, c. 5.

ACREY: On the 10th inst., near Franklin, by Rev. M. Beverly, Daniel H. ACREY and Mary A. HEDRICK, all of Pendleton.
Rockingham Register and Advertiser, 31 January 1867 (Thursday), p. 3, c. 2.

ACUFF: See entry for REEDY.

ADAIR: See entry for BEARD.

ADAMS: See entry for FUNK.

ADAMS: See entry for GANES.

ADAMS: See entry for MUMAW.

ADAMS: On the 15th inst., at the residence of Peter Dinkle, Mr. Joseph A. ADAMS, of Taylorsville, Tennessee, and Miss Susan KRICKENBERGER, formerly of Rockingham county, Va.
Rockingham Register and Advertiser, 27 September 1861 (Friday), p. 3, c. 3.

ADAMS: In Lexington, Va., on Wednesday morning, May 30th, at the residence of

the bride's father, by the Rev. F.C. Tebbs, Mr. Robert S. ADAMS, of Warrenton, Va., and Miss Julia A., daughter of Charles CHAPIN, Esq., Clerk of the Rockbridge county Court.
Rockingham Register and Advertiser, 15 June 1860 (Friday), p. 2, c. 5.

ADAMS: On Sunday, July 5, by Rev. Joseph Funkhouser, Mr. Thomas F. ADAMS, of Loudoun [sic] county, Va., and Miss Frances J., daughter of Mr. Nimrod DOVE, of Rockingham.
The Rockingham Register, 10 July 1863 (Friday), p. 2, c. 5.

ADREW: See entry for FRANKUM.

AGNER: See entry for UPDIKE.

AGNER: On the 5th ult., by Rev. A.L. Hogshead, Mr. Thos. B. AGNER and Miss Martha E., daughter of Peachy SHELTMAN, all of Rockbridge.
Rockingham Register and Advertiser, 19 January 1866 (Friday), p. 3, c. 2.

AGNOR: See entry for PARKS.

AILER: See entry for BOSSERMAN.

AKENS: On the 21st inst., in the Clerk's Office of the Circuit Court of Augusta, by the Rev. J.I. Miller, Benj. AKENS and Mrs. Francis WISEMAN, both of Augusta.
Rockingham Register and Advertiser, 28 March 1867 (Thursday), p. 2, c. 6.

ALBERT: See entry for BURNER.

ALBERT: On the 27th January, by Elder John Pirkey, Mr. Geo. H. ALBERT, of Frederick, and Miss Lucy Ellen SHOTTS.
Rockingham Register and Advertiser, 4 February 1859 (Friday), p. 2, c. 5.

ALBERT: On Wednesday, the 17th inst., by Rev. Joseph Wheeler, at the residence of Richard Hawkins, Esq., Colonel H.S.G.T. ALBERT, of Woodstock, Va., and Miss Harriet J. BLACK, of Staunton.
The Rockingham Register, 20 February 1863 (Friday), p. 2, c. 3.

ALBERT: On Wednesday evening, November 7, in the M.E. Church, in Woodstock, by Rev. Jno. P. Hyde, James ALBERT and Miss

Jennie A. GILLOCK, all of Woodstock.
Rockingham _Register_ and _Advertiser_, 15
November 1866 (Thursday), p. 2, c. 5.

ALBURTIS: On the 13th inst., by the Rev.
John Winter, Samuel ALBURTIS, E s q . ,
Editor of the _Virginia Republican_, to
Miss Susan M., daughter of Mr. Ezekiel
SHOWERS, of Martinsburg, Va.
Rockingham _Register_ and _Valley
Advertiser_, 20 March 1847 (Saturday), p.
3, c. 1.

ALDER: See entry for RHODES.

ALDRIDGE: See entry for CLINE.

ALEXANDER: See entry for JOHNSTON.

ALEXANDER: See entry for LANDES.

ALEXANDER: See entry for MUDDEMAN.

ALEXANDER: On the 30th ult., at Glenmoon,
the residence of the bride's father, by
Rev. Jas. Beatty, Edgar S. ALEXANDER, of
Moorefield,   W.Va.,   and   Miss   R.L.
CUNNINGHAM.
Rockingham _Register_ and _Advertiser_, 8
November 1866 (Thursday), p. 3, c. 4.

ALEXANDER: On the 24th inst., by Rev. T.D.
Bell,   James   A.   ALEXANDER,   M.D.,   of
Highland   county,   and   Miss   Sallie   E.,
daughter of Mr. M. CASLER, of Rockingham.
Rockingham _Register_ and _Advertiser_, 27
April 1866 (Friday), p. 2, c. 2.

ALEXANDER: On the 6th of September, by the
Rev. W.W. Trimble, Mr. Jno. F. ALEXANDER
and Miss B.A., daughter of John SILVEY,
of Augusta county.
Rockingham _Register_ and _Advertiser_, 25
October 1866 (Thursday), p. 3, c. 3.

ALEXANDER: On the 23rd ult., by Rev. Isaac
Long, Peter ALEXANDER and Miss Harriett,
daughter   of   Geo.   HAYNES,   all   of
Rockingham county.
Rockingham _Register_ and _Advertiser_,
13 September 1866 (Thursday), p. 2, c. 5.

ALEXANDER: On the 21st of February, by Rev.
C. Beard, Robert C. ALEXANDER and   Miss
Mary   Susan   JORDAN,   both   of   Augusta
county.
Rockingham _Register_ and _Advertiser_, 7

March 1867 (Thursday), p. 3, c. 3.

ALGER: See entry for BUTLER.

ALLEBAUGH: See entry for ROGERS.

ALLEBAUGH: See entry for ROLER.

ALLEBAUGH: See entry for WILSON.

ALLEN: See entry for CHERRYHOLMES.

ALLEN: See entry for GROVE.

ALLEN: See entry for JOHNSON.

ALLEN: See entry for LARKINS.

ALLEN: See entry for RIDDLE.

ALLEN: See entry for RYAN.

ALLEN: See entry for SNYDER.

ALLEN: See entry for SPENGLER.

ALLEN: See entry for WUNDER.

ALLEN: On the 28th ult., by Rev. G.H. Martin, Henry C. ALLEN and Miss Julia McKay, daughter of John GATEWOOD, Esq., all of Woodstock, Va.
Rockingham Register and Advertiser, 7 February 1867 (Thursday), p. 3, c. 3.

ALLEN: On the 22nd ult., Linden E. ALLEN and Miss Fannie M. MOORE.
Rockingham Register, 8 December 1870 (Thursday), p. 2, c. 4.

ALLEN: On the 24th of December, by Rev. J.A. Snyder, Reuben E. ALLEN and Miss Louisa BOWEN, all of Shenandoah county.
Rockingham Register, 14 January 1869 (Thursday), p. 3, c. 3.

ALLEN: On the 29th ult., by Rev. John P. Hyde, Reuben S. ALLEN and Miss Ellen HAUN, all of Shenandoah county.
Rockingham Register and Advertiser, 8 November 1866 (Thursday), p. 3, c. 4.

ALLEN: On the 26th ult., by Rev. P. Fletcher, at the residence of the bride's father, S. Brown ALLEN and Miss Mary S., daughter of John HAMILTON, Esq., of Augusta.
Rockingham Register, 4 November 1869 (Thursday), p. 2, c. 4.

ALLEN: On Sunday, the 31st of December, by Rev. Isaac Long, Thomas H. ALLEN, C.S.A., late of Tennessee, and Miss Mary C., daughter of Howard CAMPBELL, of Rockingham county.
Rockingham Register and Advertiser, 19

January 1866 (Friday), p. 3, c. 2.

ALLEN: On the 21st of February, by Rev. J.E. Armstrong, Tipten W. ALLEN, of Shenandoah county, and Mrs. Mary B. PATTERSON, of Augusta county.

Rockingham Register and Advertiser, 7 March 1867 (Thursday), p. 3, c. 3.

ALLEN: At Fruit Hill, near Chillicothe, Ohio, on Monday evening, the 12th inst., by the Rev. James B. Britton, the Hon. William ALLEN, of the United States Senate, to Mrs. Effie McARTHUR COONES, daughter of the late Governor McARTHUR. Fourteen years ago, Mr. ALLEN was a suitor of this lady, but the match was broken off, in consequence of the young lover's beating his intended father-in-law, in a contest for a seat in Congress, by one vote. The lady married another man, and afterwards became a widow, which furnished an opportunity for a renewal of the engagement, which this time has resulted more happily.

Rockingham Register and Valley Advertiser, 31 May 1845 (Saturday), p. 3, c. 2.

ALLISON: See entry for BAKER.

ALLISON: See entry for CARSON.

ALLPOORT: On Thursday, the 10th of January, by Rev. Jos. Funkhouser, Esq., Robert C. ALLPOORT and Miss Sarah C., daughter of Michael BAZZLE, all of Rockingham county.

Rockingham Register and Advertiser, 19 January 1866 (Friday), p. 3, c. 2.

ALMARODE: See entry for BAILY.

ALMARODE: See entry for HEIZER.

ALMARODE: On the 5th inst., in Staunton, by Rev. Wm. E. Baker, George D. ALMARODE and Miss Sue J. WHITESELL, all of Augusta county.

Rockingham Register, 12 November 1868 (Thursday), p. 3, c. 3.

ALMARODE: On the 15th of November, by Rev. Wm. S. McClanahan, John W. ALMARODE to Miss Estaline M. TAYLOR, both of Augusta county.

5

Rockingham <u>Register</u> and <u>Advertiser</u>, 28
December 1860 (Friday), p. 1, c. 5.
ALMON: On the 7th of March, at the Wesleyan
    Female Institute, by Rev. W.S. Baird, Mr.
    Jas. L. ALMON and Miss Eliza J. SULLIVAN,
    all of Augusta county.
Rockingham <u>Register</u> and <u>Advertiser</u>, 16
March 1866 (Friday), p. 3, c. 4.
ALMOND: See entry for LOCKE.
ALMOND: On the 24th ult., near McGaheysville,
    by Rev. I. Conder, C.C. ALMOND, of
    Spottsylvania county, and Miss Annie E.
    KIGER, of Rockingham.
Rockingham <u>Register</u>, 3 March 1870
(Thursday), p. 2, c. 5.
ALTAFFER: See entry for GILKESON.
ALTAFFER: On Tuesday last, by the Rev. Mr.
    Morgan, Mr. John ALTAFFER to Miss Ellvina
    HARRELL, both of this place.
Rockingham <u>Weekly</u> <u>Register</u>, 15 February
1823 (Saturday), p. 3, c. 2.
ALTHER: See entry for GRIFFITH.
AMBROSE: See entry on HENRIETTA.
AMBROSE: See entry for KOONS.
AMISS: See entry for AMISS.
AMISS: At the residence of the bride's uncle,
    R.H. SPINDLE, Esq., Waverlie [sic], Va.,
    on Thursday, January the 27th, by Rev.
    W.P. Twyman, Dr. J.B. AMISS, of
    Rockingham, formerly of Rappahannock, and
    Miss A. Jennie, daughter of the late Col.
    THROOP, of Kentucky.
Rockingham <u>Register</u> and <u>Advertiser</u>, 4
February 1859 (Friday), p. 2, c. 5.
AMISS: On Wednesday evening of last week, at
    the residence of the bride's mother, near
    Harrisonburg, by Rev. J. Rice Bowman,
    Joseph B. AMISS, of Front Royal, Warren
    county, Va., and Miss Jennie M., daughter
    of Mrs. Kitty AMISS, of this vicinity.
Rockingham <u>Register</u>, 23 April 1868
(Thursday), p. 2, c. 5.
AMMON: See entry for MELHORN.
AMMON: On Thursday the 15th of February, by
    Rev. Isaac Long, Yelverton C. AMMON,
    Esq., former sheriff of Rockingham

6

county, and Miss Margaret A., daughter of
Smith SAMPSON, all of Rockingham county.
Rockingham Register and Advertiser, 23
February 1866 (Friday), p. 2, c. 4.

ANDERSON: See entry for ARNOLD.

ANDERSON: See entry for CAUFFMAN.

ANDERSON: See entry for CLATTERBAUGH.

ANDERSON: See entry for FAUVER.

ANDERSON: See entry for HUFFMAN.

ANDERSON: See entry for SUTHERLAND.

ANDERSON: See entry for WHITMER.

ANDERSON: On the 16th of August, at the
residence of Daniel Fishburn, by the Rev.
R.C. Walker, A.T. ANDERSON and Miss
Columbia V. CROSBY, all of Augusta
county.
Rockingham Register and Advertiser, 30
August 1866 (Thursday), p. 2, c. 4.

ANDERSON: On the 23rd ult., by Rev. P.
Miller, Alfred E. ANDERSON and Miss
Jemima BUMGARNER, all of Hampshire
county.
Rockingham Register, 20 January 1870
(Thursday), p. 2, c. 5.

ANDERSON: At the residence of the bride's
parents, in the city of Richmond, at 7
o'clock in the morning, on the 17th
inst., by Rev. Mr. Baker, C.W. ANDERSON,
of Nottoway county, and Miss Bettie V.,
daughter of J. P. EFFINGER, Esq.,
formerly of Harrisonburg, Rockingham
county.
Rockingham Register, 25 November 1869
(Thursday), p. 2, c. 3.

ANDERSON: On the 24th of September, by Rev.
R.C. Walker, Edward M. ANDERSON and Miss
Hannah, daughter of John JONES, dec'd,
all of Augusta county.
Rockingham Register, 29 October 1868
(Thursday), p. 3, c. 3.

ANDERSON: At "Locust Lawn," the residence of
the bride's father, on the 7th inst., by
the Rev. Dr. Kirkpatrick, Mr. James D.
ANDERSON to Miss M. Hanna BUCHANAN, all
of Rockbridge, Va.
Rockingham Register and Advertiser, 22

November 1866 (Thursday), p. 3, c. 3.

ANDERSON: On the 28th of June, by Rev. J.I. Miller, Nathan H. ANDERSON and Miss Maggie M. JAMISON, both of Staunton.

Rockingham Register and Advertiser, 5 July 1866 (Thursday), p. 3, c. 5.

ANDERSON: On the 16th inst., at Trinity Church, Staunton, by Rev. J.C. Wheat, R.H. ANDERSON, of Richmond, and Miss Rebecca C., daughter of Col. Chas. LEWIS, of Rockingham.

Rockingham Register and Advertiser, 25 October 1866 (Thursday), p. 3, c. 3.

ANDES: See entry for LINAWEAVER.

ANDREW: See entry for DICE.

ANDREW: In Pocahontas county, W.Va., on the 7th of January, by Rev. M.D. Dunlap, John H. ANDREW, of Augusta, and Miss Josephine, daughter of Wm. P. McCALL, of Rockingham county.

Rockingham Register and Advertiser, 19 January 1866 (Friday), p. 3, c. 2.

ANDREWS: On the 26th of December, by Rev. John Pinkerton, Nelson ANDREWS, of Harrisonburg, and Miss Christiana S., daughter of John EARHART, Esq., of Augusta county.

Rockingham Register and Advertiser, 6 February 1868 (Thursday), p. 2, c. 4.

ANDRICK: See entry for McWAY.

ANDRICK: On the 10th inst., by Rev. J.W. Hoffmeier, Mr. George ANDRICK to Miss Elizabeth, daughter of Mr. David MUMAW, all of Shenandoah county.

Rockingham Register and Valley Advertiser, 19 April 1845 (Saturday), p. 3, c. 1.

ANTHONY: See entry for BRIGHT.

ANTHONY: On the 24th of April, at Antioch Church, by Rev. A.J. Kibler, Mr. James ANTHONY and Miss Elizabeth Catharine BOWMAN, all of Rockingham county.

The Rockingham Register, 29 April 1864 (Friday), p. 2, c. 5.

ANTHONY: On the 26th of February, 1863, by Rev. J.W. Howe, Mr. John B. ANTHONY, of

8

Bath county, Va., and Mrs. Sophia M. BEARD of Rockingham.

The Rockingham Register, 13 March 1863 (Friday), p. 2, c. 5.

ARBOGAST: See entry for CLARK.

ARBOGAST: See entry for SHUEY.

ARBOGAST: See entry for TARLETON.

ARBOGAST: Near the Hot Springs, on the 21st inst., by Rev. L.D. Nixon, Mr. B.A. ARBOGAST, of Pocahontas, to Miss Margaret J., daughter of John McELWEE, Esq., of Bath.

Rockingham Register and Advertiser, 31 August 1860 (Friday), p. 2, c. 4.

ARBOGAST: At Traveler's Repose, on Thursday, 5th ult., by Rev. Wm. Price, George Washington ARBOGAST, son of Wm. ARBOGAST, dec'd, of Green Bank, and Miss Adaline Ellen, daughter of Jacob S. SLAVEN, dec'd, all of Pocahontas county.

Rockingham Register and Advertiser, 4 May 1860 (Friday), p. 2, c. 4.

ARBOGAST: On the 4th inst., at Greenbank, Pocahontas county, by Rev. S.B. Dolly, Maj. J.C. ARBOGAST and Miss Sallie J. BEARD, all of Pocahontas county.

The Rockingham Register, 13 March 1863 (Friday), p. 2, c. 5.

ARBUCKEL: On the 8th inst, near Mt. Solon, Augusta county, by Rev. John Pinkerton, John D. ARBUCKEL, of Greenbrier county, W.Va., and Miss M. Lizzie, daughter of Rev. J.A. VAN LEAR, dec'd.

Rockingham Register, 16 December 1869 (Thursday), p. 2, c. 5.

AREHART: See entry for BRENNER.

AREHART: See entry for BROCK.

AREHART: See entry for CLEMMER.

AREHART: See entry for FITSMOYERS.

AREHART: On the 11th inst., by Rev. S. Henkel, Captain Geo. AREHART and Miss Sarah, eldest daughter of John BOWMAN, Esq., all of Rockingham.

Rockingham Register and Advertiser, 26 August 1859 (Friday), p. 2, c. 5.

AREHART: On the 6th inst., by Rev. J.

Stirewalt, Mr. Wm. H. AREHART and Miss
Lizzie A. HINEGARDNER, near Rader's
Church, all of Rockingham.
Rockingham Register and Advertiser, 20
February 1868 (Thursday), p. 2, c. 6.

AREHEART: See entry for ENGLEMAN.

AREY: See entry for TROUT.

AREY: On the 30th of April, by Rev. J.C.
Hensell, Geo. F. AREY, of Augusta county,
and Miss Amanda V., youngest daughter of
Harvey LIGHT, of Rockingham county.
Rockingham Register, 7 May 1868
(Thursday), p. 2, c. 4.

AREY: On the 18th inst., at the residence of
the bride's father, by Rev. Thos. E.
Carson, John W. AREY and Miss Lou C.
WHEELER, both of Augusta.
Rockingham Register, 26 November 1868
(Thursday), p. 2, c. 5.

AREY: On the 31st of October, at Mt. Clinton,
by Rev. T.D. Bell, Mr. William AREY and
Miss Lydia A., daughter of Mr. Joseph
BURKHOLDER.
Rockingham Register and Advertiser, 22
November 1866 (Thursday), p. 3, c. 3.

ARGABRIGHT: On the 6th inst., by Rev. Joseph
Funkhouser, John ARGABRIGHT, of Augusta
county, and Miss Matilda J. KNICELY, of
Rockingham.
Rockingham Register and Advertiser, 13
June 1867 (Thursday), p. 2, c. 6.

ARGABRIGHT: On the 16th of September, by Rev.
Frederick Miller, Philip R. ARGABRIGHT
and Miss Samantha Jane ARMENTROUT, all of
Rockingham county.
Rockingham Register, 30 September 1869
(Thursday), p. 2, c. 4.

ARGEBRIGHT: See entry for HAMMOND.

ARGENBRIGHT: See entry for BAUSERMAN.

ARGENBRIGHT: See entry for OREBAUGH.

ARGENBRIGHT: See entry for WRIGHT.

ARGENBRIGHT: On the 5th inst., at Elizabeth
Furnace, by Rev. H. Getzendanner, James
A. ARGENBRIGHT and Miss Elizabeth WARD,
all of Augusta county.
Rockingham Register, 16 April 1868

(Thursday), p. 2, c. 5.

ARGENBRIGHT: On the 30th ult., by Rev. T. Brashear, Mr. James S. ARGENBRIGHT and Miss Rachel BOWERS, all of Augusta county.
Rockingham Register and Advertiser, 4 February 1859 (Friday), p. 2, c. 5.

ARGENBRIGHT: On the 15th inst., at the house of the bride, by Rev. J.I. Miller, John D. ARGENBRIGHT and Henrietta V. ZIMMERMAN, all of Augusta county.
Rockingham Register, 22 October 1868 (Thursday), p. 3, c. 3.

ARGENBRIGHT: On Wednesday the 26th of February, 1868, by Rev. John L. Clarke, at the residence of the bride's father, in Staunton, T.N. ARGENBRIGHT, of the Spectator, and Miss Virginia, only daughter of Dr. S.D. HOPKINS, formerly of Albemarle.
Rockingham Register and Advertiser, 19 March 1868 (Thursday), p. 2, c. 4.

ARION: In Carroll county, Indiana, on the 8th inst., by the Rev. Dl. Neher, Mr. John ARION, formerly of this county, to Miss Susannah, only daughter of John G. and Maria NEHER.
Rockingham Register and Advertiser, 13 February 1857 (Friday), p. 2, c. 5.

ARION: Near Timberville, on the 23rd of December, by Rev. John Kline, Mr. John ARION, of Smith's Creek, and Miss Rebecca, daughter of David KLINE, all of Rockingham.
Rockingham Register and Advertiser, 21 January 1859 (Friday), p. 3, c. 5.

ARMENTROUT: See entry for ARGABRIGHT.
ARMENTROUT: See entry for ARMENTROUT (3).
ARMENTROUT: See entry for DARRER.
ARMENTROUT: See entry for EARMAN.
ARMENTROUT: See entry for GLOVIER.
ARMENTROUT: See entry for HAINES.
ARMENTROUT: See entry for HASLER.
ARMENTROUT: See entry for HOSLER.
ARMENTROUT: See entry for KOONTZ.
ARMENTROUT: See entry for SHAFER.

ARMENTROUT: See entry for WHITMORE.

ARMENTROUT: On the 31st of July, 1862, by Rev. J.W. Howe, Mr. B.F. ARMENTROUT and Miss Mary J. HENTON, all of this county. Rockingham Register and Virginia Advertiser, 22 August 1862 (Friday), p. 2, c. 3.

ARMENTROUT: In Staunton, on the 2nd of August, by the Rev. G.B. Taylor, Charles E. ARMENTROUT and Mrs. Cordelia A. LAYNE. Rockingham Register and Advertiser, 30 August 1866 (Thursday), p. 2, c. 4.

ARMENTROUT: On the 1st of March, by Rev. Joseph Funkhouser, at the residence of David Flook, Daniel ARMENTROUT and Miss Elizabeth O'ROARK, all of Rockingham county. Rockingham Register and Advertiser, 9 March 1866 (Friday), p. 2, c. 3.

ARMENTROUT: On the 26th of January, 1865, by Rev. J. Stirewalt, Mr. Geo. D. ARMENTROUT and Miss Amanda LUTHOLTZ, all of Rockingham county, Va. Rockingham Register and Advertiser, 17 February 1865 (Friday), p. 2, c. 4.

ARMENTROUT: On Tuesday the 10th inst., by Rev. A. Poe Boude, Harrison B. ARMENTROUT and Miss Eliza A., daughter of Silum SELLERS, all of Rockingham county. Rockingham Register and Advertiser, 12 December 1867 (Thursday), p. 3, c. 2.

ARMENTROUT: At the residence of the bride's father, in Winchester, on the 5th inst., by Rev. W.G. Eggleston, James A. ARMENTROUT, of Staunton, to Miss Mattie E., daughter of Mr. Michael PRICE, formerly of Harper's Ferry. Rockingham Register & Advertiser, 22 October 1865 (Friday), p. 3, c. 4.

ARMENTROUT: On the 1st inst., by the Rev. Daniel Feete, Mr. Jeremiah ARMENTROUT and Miss Sarah J. MILLER, all of this county. Rockingham Register and Valley Advertiser, 17 April 1847 (Saturday), p. 3, c. 7.

ARMENTROUT: On Thursday, November 2nd, by

Rev. Jos. Funkhouser, Mr. John A. ARMENTROUT and Miss Lucy Jane, daughter of Mr. John J. MARTZ, all of Rockingham county.

Rockingham Register & Advertiser, 10 November 1865 (Friday), p. 2, c. 4.

ARMENTROUT: On the 19th of March, by Rev. Jos. Funkhouser, John H. ARMENTROUT and Miss Mary, daughter of Henry ROGERS, all of Rockingham.

Rockingham Register, 26 March 1868 (Thursday), p. 2, c. 4.

ARMENTROUT: On the 14th inst., at the residence of the bride's father, by Rev. A. Poe Boude, John W. ARMENTROUT and Miss Agnes Virginia, daughter of James BAKER, all of Rockingham county.

Rockingham Register and Advertiser, 28 February 1867 (Thursday), p. 2, c. 6.

ARMENTROUT: At Falls Church, Va., the residence of the bride's brother, on Thursday, the 22nd inst., by Rev. A.B. Dolly, John W. ARMENTROUT and Miss Mattie DOLLY, all of Pendleton county, W.Va.

Rockingham Register, 29 October 1868 (Thursday), p. 3, c. 3.

ARMENTROUT: On Sunday, the 24th inst., by the Rev. Joseph Funkhouser, Mr. Joseph ARMENTROUT and Miss Frances, daughter of Mr. Joseph ARMENTROUT, all of Smith's Creek, Rockingham county.

Rockingham Register and Advertiser, 29 July 1859 (Friday), p. 3, c. 2.

ARMENTROUT: On Sunday last, the 14th inst., by the Rev. Peter Shickel, Mr. Peter W. ARMENTROUT and Miss Phebe Ann ARMENTROUT, all of Rockingham county.

Rockingham Register, 20 February 1841 (Saturday), p. 3, c. 2.

ARMENTROUT: On Sunday the 14th of August, by Rev. Jacob Miller, Riley ARMENTROUT and Mrs. Elizabeth ARMENTROUT, all of Rockingham county.

Rockingham Register, 18 August 1870 (Thursday), p. 3, c. 3.

ARMENTROUT: On Thursday, the 25th of March,

by Rev. J. C. Hensell, Mr. Stephen ARMENTROUT and Miss Hetty J. RIDDLE, all of Rockingham county.

The Rockingham Register, 1 April 1864 (Friday), p. 2, c. 6.

ARMENTROUT: In this place on Monday evening last, by the Rev. J.W. Stine, Mr. William ARMENTROUT and Miss Samantha PRICE - all of Rockingham county.

Rockingham Register, 15 January 1842 (Saturday), p. 3, c. 1.

ARMSTEAD: See entry for CAMPBELL.

ARMSTRONG: See entry for BROWN.

ARMSTRONG: See entry for CRAWFORD.

ARMSTRONG: See entry for KIRACOFE.

ARMSTRONG: See entry for STEVENS.

ARMSTRONG: On the 16th of February, near Farmington, W.Va., by Rev. T.M. Williams, E. Jones ARMSTRONG, of Luray, Page county, Va., and Miss Mary E. MARTIN, of Marion county, W.Va.

Rockingham Register, 4 March 1869 (Thursday), p. 2, c. 4.

ARMSTRONG: On the 20th ult., near Doe Hill, by Rev. W.T. Price, William ARMSTRONG and Miss Sarah, daughter of Townsend PRICE, all of Highland county.

Rockingham Register and Advertiser, 6 September 1866 (Thursday), p. 2, c. 5.

ARNALL: See entry for WOODWARD.

ARNOLD: On the 23rd of December, by Rev. J.R. Graham, Dr. Jacob W. ARNOLD, of Rockbridge county, and Miss Sarah W., fourth daughter of Lloyd LOGAN, of Winchester, Va.

Rockingham Register, 14 January 1869 (Thursday), p. 3, c. 3.

ARNOLD: By the Rev. Peter Miller, January 11th, Mr. Lem. S. ARNOLD and Miss Nancy C. ANDERSON, all of Hampshire county.

Rockingham Register and Advertiser, 9 February 1866 (Friday), p. 3, c. 3.

ARTHUR: On the 30th ult., by Rev. John M. Clymer, Wm. Smith ARTHUR, Esq., and Miss Mary E. IRWIN, all of Woodstock.

Rockingham Register and Advertiser, 15

14

June 1860 (Friday), p. 2, c. 5.

ARTZ: See entry for MILLER.

ARTZ: On the 21st ult., by Rev. Thomas Miller, Henry ARTZ and Miss Amanda LAYMAN, all of Shenandoah.
Rockingham Register and Advertiser, 5 December 1867 (Thursday), p. 2, c. 5.

ASHBY: See entry for YAGER.

ASHBY: On the 20th inst., at the residence of the bride's father, by the Rev. R.C. Walker, John A. ASHBY, formerly of Clarke county, and Miss Nannie V. ROUDABUSH, of Augusta.
Rockingham Register and Advertiser, 27 June 1867 (Thursday), p. 2, c. 6.

ASHENFELTER: See entry for PENCE.

ASHENFELTER: On the 14th of November, by Rev. Jacob Miller, John T. ASHENFELTER and Miss Elizabeth Ann, daughter of James MAUCK, all of Rockingham county.
Rockingham Register, 24 November 1870 (Thursday), p. 2, c. 4.

ATCHISON: See entry for BEERY.

ATCHISON: See entry for WILLIAMS.

ATKINS: On the 14th inst., near Cross Keys, by Rev. Fred. Miller, John T. ATKINS, of Rappahannock county, and Miss Agnes Ann Elizabeth SHOWALTER, of Rockingham county.
Rockingham Register and Advertiser, 30 August 1866 (Thursday), p. 2, c. 4.

ATKINSON: See entry for BAKER.

ATKINSON: See entry for YOUNG.

ATWOOD: See entry for THORNHILL.

ATWOOD: On the 28th ult., by Rev. E.L. Kreglo, Mr. Thomas S. ATWOOD and Miss Ann Catharine, daughter of James MILLS, Esq., all of Page county.
Rockingham Register and Advertiser, 13 January 1860 (Friday), p. 2, c. 6.

AUCHINCLOES: At the University of Virginia, on the 5th ult., by Rev. R.K. Meade, Henry B. AUCHINCLOES, Esq., of New York, and Miss Mary CABELL.
Rockingham Register and Advertiser, 4 January 1861 (Friday), p. 3, c. 4.

AVERITT: On the 26th ult., in Christ Church, Winchester, by Rev. Mr. Meredith, Rev. Jas. A. AVERITT, of Alabama, and Miss Mary L.D., daughter of Phillip WILLIAMS, Esq., of the former place.
Rockingham Register and Advertiser, 14 March 1862 (Friday), p. 3, c. 2.

AVIS: At Emanuel Church, in Harrisonburg, on Wednesday morning, November 16th, by Rev. A.W. Weddell, Braxton D. AVIS and Miss Harriet E., daughter of Henry C. WILSON, dec'd, all of Harrisonburg.
Rockingham Register, 17 November 1870 (Thursday), p. 2, c. 3.

AVIS: In Fredericksburg, Va., on the 26th inst., Dr. James L. AVIS, of this place, formerly of Charlestown, W.Va., and Miss Sophie V. MITCHELL, of Fredericksburg.
Rockingham Register, 28 October 1869 (Thursday), p. 2, c. 3.

AYERS: On the 15th ult., by Rev. Jas. W. Wolff, Mr. S.P. AYERS and Miss Angeline E. RHEA, all of Bath.
Rockingham Register and Advertiser, 14 December 1860 (Friday), p. 2, c. 6.

AYERS: On the 23rd ult., by Rev. E.M. Peterson, in the city of Staunton, W.P. AYERS, of Charlottesville, and Miss Catherine E. TURNER, of Henrico county.
Rockingham Register and Advertiser, 2 May 1867 (Thursday), p. 2, c. 6.

AYERS: Near Goshen, Va., on the 28th of February, by Rev. S.P. Huff, Mr.Wm. L. AYERS and Miss Mary L. DILL.
Rockingham Register and Advertiser, 9 March 1860 (Friday), p. 3, c. 2.

AYERS: On the 27th ult., by Rev. Wm. E. Baker, Wm. L. AYERS and Miss Isabella D. McLAUGHLIN, all of Staunton.
Rockingham Register and Advertiser, 4 April 1867 (Thursday), p. 3, c. 4.

- B -

BACKENSTO: See entry for PLECKER.
BADER: See entry for BARR.

16

BAENNER: See entry for DRIVER.

BAER: See entry for CEASE.

BAER: See entry for LANGDON.

BAGBY: On the 21st ult., by Rev. J.R. Wheeler, Mr. Chapman BAGBY and Miss Theresa HUMPHREYS, all of Staunton. Rockingham Register and Advertiser, 11 January 1861 (Friday), p. 3, c. 4.

BAGGS: See entry for MILLER.

BAILEY: See entry for HATCHER.

BAILEY: See entry for HENEBERGER.

BAILEY: See entry for PAYTON.

BAILEY: See entry for SHAFFER.

BAILEY: By the Rev. W.G. Campbell, on the 25th ult., Mr. Charles E. BAILEY, of Charlottesville, and Miss Fannie E. BASHAW, of Augusta. Rockingham Register and Advertiser, 4 January 1861 (Friday), p. 3, c. 4.

BAILEY: On the __th [torn] ult., by the Rev. John A. Van Lear, Mr. George BAILEY to Miss Elizabeth, daughter of Mr. John KARICOFE, Sr., all of Augusta county. Rockingham Register and Valley Advertiser, 4 November 1848 (Saturday), p. 3, c. 2.

BAILEY: At Mr. Daniel Shaw's, near Sherando, on the 24th ult., by Rev. W.R. Stringer, Geo. W. BAILEY to Miss Rebecca B. SHAW, all of Augusta. Rockingham Register and Advertiser, 3 January 1867 (Thursday), p. 3, c. 3.

BAILEY: On the 26th ult., by Rev. J.S. Blain, Mr. H.H. BAILEY, of St. Louis, Mo., and Miss Ann RUTLEDGE, near Deerfield, Augusta county, Va. Rockingham Register and Advertiser, 10 February 1860 (Friday), p. 2, c. 5.

BAILEY: On the 25th of March, by Rev. Isaac Long, Wm. BAILEY and Miss Sarah Jane, daughter of John BONTS, all of Rockingham county. Rockingham Register, 20 May 1869 (Thursday), p. 2, c. 3.

BAILY: See entry for HOUFF.

BAILY: On the 30th of May, by Rev. A.A.J.

Bushong, Jacob H. BAILY and Mrs. M.S. ALMARODE, all of Augusta county.
Rockingham Register, 11 June 1868 (Thursday), p. 2, c. 5.

BAILY: In Washington city, on the 29th December, 1859, Mr. Perry BAILY and Miss Clarinda BURAKER, all of Page county.
Rockingham Register and Advertiser, 27 January 1860 (Friday), p. 2, c. 6.

BAIN: See entry for PARKER.
BAKER: See entry for ARMENTROUT.
BAKER: See entry for BERRY.
BAKER: See entry for CARPENTER.
BAKER: See entry for CRAWN.
BAKER: See entry for FRAVEL.
BAKER: See entry for HALL.
BAKER: See entry for HARTMAN.
BAKER: See entry for HOCKMAN.
BAKER: See entry for HUNTON.
BAKER: See entry for LEWIS.
BAKER: See entry for LONG.
BAKER: See entry for NISWANDER.
BAKER: See entry for POINDEXTER.
BAKER: See entry for ROBINSON.
BAKER: See entry for SMALS.
BAKER: See entry for SWARTZ.

BAKER: At Union Station Church, on the 16th inst., D.G. BAKER, Esq., and Miss Flora, daughter of H.A. ATKINSON, Esq., both of Richmond.
Rockingham Register, 23 July 1868 (Thursday), p. 3, c. 4.

BAKER: On the 13th inst., by Rev. J.H. Hunton, Mr. Ephraim BAKER and Miss Rebecca EVERLY, all of Shenandoah county.
Rockingham Register and Advertiser, 28 January 1859 (Friday), p. 2, c. 6.

BAKER: At the American Hotel, in Harrisonburg, on the 26th ult., by Rev. George W. Holland, Jacob F. BAKER and Miss Belle C. BAYLEY, all of Rockingham county.
Rockingham Register, 3 June 1870 (Thursday), p. 3, c. 3.

BAKER: On the 19th inst., at the residence of the bride's father, near Dayton, by Rev.

Solomon Garber, John F. BAKER and Miss
Sallie E. KERLIN, all of Rockingham.
Rockingham Register, 30 June 1870
(Thursday), p. 2, c. 5.

BAKER: On the 27th ult., by Rev. Daniel
Thomas, Mr. John H. BAKER and Miss Ann B.
WINE, all of Rockingham.
Rockingham Register and Advertiser, 18
January 1861 (Friday), p. 3, c. 2.

BAKER: On the 20th inst., in Luray, Page
county, by Rev. E.R. Kreglo, Mr. John W.
BAKER and Miss Rachel B. WALTER, all of
Page.
Rockingham Register and Advertiser, 20
January 1860 (Friday), p. 2, c. 6.

BAKER: On the 23rd of October, by Rev. S.
Filler, at the residence of Mr. John
Showalter, near the Cross-Keys, Mr.
Philip BAKER and Mrs. Melvina WHITMORE,
all of this county.
Rockingham Register and Advertiser, 14
November 1856 (Friday), p. 2, c. 6.

BAKER: On the 30th of January, by the Rev.
Solomon Garber, Mr. Wm. H. BAKER and Miss
Mary E. COFFMAN, both of Dayton,
Rockingham county.
Rockingham Register and Advertiser, 24
February 1865 (Friday), p. 2, c. 5.

BAKER: On the Bridge, at Harper's Ferry, on
the 22nd ult., by Rev. Mr. Baker, Wm. H.
BAKER, formerly of Co. B, 12th Va.
Cavalry, and Miss Bettie E. ALLISON, of
Edinburg, Shenandoah county.
Rockingham Register and Advertiser, 7
November 1867 (Thursday), p. 2, c. 5.

BAKER: At the Clerk's office of Page county,
on the 20th ult., by J.W. Watson, Wm. S.
BAKER to Sarah E. EPPARD, all of Page
county.
Rockingham Register, 7 October 1869
(Thursday), p. 2, c. 3.

BALDWIN: See entry for STANLEY.

BALDWIN: On the 15th ult., near Mt. Crawford,
by Rev. Solomon Garber, Mr. Alexander F.
BALDWIN, of Louisiana, and Miss Elizabeth
STINEBUCK, of Rockingham.

<u>Rockingham</u> <u>Register</u> <u>and</u> <u>Advertiser</u>, 4
August 1865 (Friday), p. 3, c. 2.
BALDWIN: On the 15th inst., at Trinity
Church, in Staunton, by Rev. Jas. A.
Latane, James W. BALDWIN and Miss M.A.,
daughter of A.J. GARBER, Esq.
<u>Rockingham</u> <u>Register</u>, 24 March 1870
(Thursday), p. 3, c. 2.
BALL: See entry for RICE.
BALLEW: On the 28th ult., by Rev. Horatio
Thompson, near Old Providence Church,
John Dorsey BALLEW and Miss Catharine,
daughter of the late John LOTTS, of
Augusta county.
<u>Rockingham</u> <u>Register</u> <u>and</u> <u>Advertiser</u>, 7
March 1867 (Thursday), p. 3, c. 3.
BALTHIS: See entry for HARTSHORN.
BALTZEL: On the 17th inst., by Rev. J.
Markwood, Rev. Isaiah BALTZEL, of the
Virginia Conference of the United
Brethren in Christ, to Miss Cecelia
JAMES, of Mt. Jackson, Shenandoah county.
<u>Rockingham</u> <u>Register</u> <u>and</u> <u>Advertiser</u>, 25
February 1859 (Friday), p. 2, c. 5.
BANE: See entry for TURNER.
BARAX: See entry for FISHBACK.
BARB: See entry for BOWERS.
BARB: See entry for MUMAW.
BARB: See entry for NESSELRODT.
BARB: On the 12th inst., by Rev. Levi Keller,
Noah BARB and Sarah HEPNER, of Shenandoah
county.
<u>Rockingham</u> <u>Register</u>, 28 April 1870
(Thursday), p. 3, c. 3.
BARBEE: See entry for JOHNSON.
BARCLAY: See entry for PATTON.
BARE: See entry for HOUSEMAN.
BARE: See entry for LINDIN.
BARE: See entry for RALSTON.
BARE: On the 9th inst., at the American
Hotel, Staunton, by the Rev. Wm. E.
Baker, Mr. Noah F. BARE, of Rockingham,
and Miss M.E. PULLENS, of Augusta county.
<u>Rockingham</u> <u>Register</u> <u>and</u> <u>Advertiser</u>, 17
February 1860 (Friday), p. 2, c. 4.
BARER: On Thursday, the 20th inst., by the

Rev. J.C. Hensell, Mr. Isaac H. BARER to Miss Elizabeth S., eldest daughter of John F. and Lucy CRAWN, all of Rockingham.

Rockingham Register and Advertiser, 28 December 1860 (Friday), p. 1, c. 5.

BARER: On the 3rd inst., by Rev. Jacob Wine, Samuel BARER and Miss Anna C. FRY, both of Shenandoah county.

Rockingham Register, 24 February 1870 (Thursday), p. 2, c. 5.

BARGELT: On Thursday of last week, by Rev. F.H. Richey, Mr. Wm. BARGELT to Miss Catharine FRAVEL, all of Woodstock.

Rockingham Register and Valley Advertiser, 3 November 1849 (Saturday), p. 2, c. 7.

BARGER: See entry for FREED.

BARK: See entry for DEAN.

BARKER: See entry for RICE.

BARNS: See entry for WIGGONTON.

BARR: See entry for DELLINGER.

BARR: On the 20th inst., by Rev. J.M. Clymer, Anderson BARR and Miss Sarah E. KIBLER, all of Shenandoah.

Rockingham Register and Advertiser, 31 October 1867 (Thursday), p. 2, c. 6.

BARR: On the 4th inst., at "Rose Hill," the residence of A.D. Armentrout, by Rev. Joseph Holcomb, Mr. Benjamin BARR and Miss Jennie EATON, all of Rockingham county.

Rockingham Register, 11 June 1868 (Thursday), p. 2, c. 5.

BARR: On the 27th ult., by Elder Henry Jennings, Mr. Jas. W. BARR and Miss Rebecca Ann BADER, all of this county.

Rockingham Register and Advertiser, 5 October 1860 (Friday), p. 2, c. 3.

BARRACK: See entry for PERKINS.

BARROW: See entry for MILBUN.

BARRY: See entry for BROWN.

BARTIN: On Thursday, the 7th inst., by Elder Henry Jennings, Alexander BARTIN and Miss Eliza E. THOMPSON, of Shenandoah county.

Rockingham Register, 21 April 1870

21

(Thursday), p. 3, c. 3.

BARTLEY: See entry for RAMSEY.

BARTLEY: At the Virginia Hotel, on the 19th
ult., by Rev. John L. Clark, Henry B.
BARTLEY and Miss Jane LAYTON, all of
Augusta county.
Rockingham Register and Advertiser, 4
July 1867 (Thursday), p. 2, c. 6.

BASEL: See entry for HAUGHEY.

BASEY: See entry for WHITMORE.

BASFORD: See entry for HAYNES.

BASH: On the 20th ult., by Elder F. M. Perry,
Henry BASH and Miss Sarah E. JUDD, all of
Page county.
Rockingham Register, 3 February 1870
(Thursday), p. 3, c. 4.

BASHAW: See entry for BAILEY.

BASKIN: See entry for KEE.

BATEMAN: See entry for COLLIER.

BATEMAN: See entry for EUTZLER.

BATEMAN: On the 21st of April, by Rev. Isaac
Long, Harrison BATEMAN and Miss
Elizabeth, daughter of Rob't HOOK, all of
Rockingham county.
Rockingham Register, 30 April 1868
(Thursday), p. 2, c. 6. Repeated, 7 May
1868 (Thursday), p. 2, c. 4. In the
latter, the bride's name is given as
Rebecca HOOK.

BATEMAN: On the 22nd of October, by Rev. Wm.
J. Miller, James BATEMAN and Miss Mary
POWELL, all of Rockingham.
Rockingham Register, 5 November 1868
(Thursday), p. 3, c. 3.

BATEMAN: On the 9th inst., by Rev. J.B.
Houck, Mr. Joseph BATEMAN and Miss
Emilina, daughter of Mr. Jacob ROUDABUSH,
all of Page county.
Rockingham Register and Virginia
Advertiser, 21 December 1855 (Friday), p.
2, c. 8.

BATEMAN: In Port Republic, on Thursday the
29th of October, by Rev. J.F. Liggett,
William Harrison BATEMAN and Miss Anna
Etta, daughter of William MOORE, all of
Rockingham county.

22

Rockingham Register, 19 November 1868 (Thursday), p. 2, c. 5.

BATIS: See entry for MYERS.

BAUGH: See entry for CASLER.

BAUGHER: See entry for GLEN.

BAUGHER: See entry for MOYERS.

BAUGHER: On the 17th inst., by Rev. H.A. Gaver, Geo. T. BAUGHER and Miss Bettie M. DUFF, all of Rockingham county.
Rockingham Register and Advertiser, 24 January 1867 (Thursday), p. 2, c. 4.

BAUGHER: On the 15th of November, by the Rev. Isaac Long, Jeremiah BAUGHER and Miss Mary Ann SULLIVAN, formerly of Greene county, Va.
Rockingham Register and Advertiser, 22 November 1866 (Thursday), p. 3, c. 3.

BAUGHER: On the 29th of January, by Rev. Isaac Long, Joseph W. BAUGHER and Mrs. Julia WYANT, all of Rockingham.
Rockingham Register and Advertiser, 21 February 1867 (Thursday), p. 3, c. 2.

BAUGHMAN: See entry for SENGER.

BAUGHMAN: By Rev. P. Miller, November 18th, John N. BAUGHMAN and Miss Sophia DAY, all of Hardy county, W.Va.
Rockingham Register, 9 December 1869 (Thursday), p. 3, c. 2.

BAUSERMAN: See entry for CULLERS.

BAUSERMAN: See entry for HOTTEL.

BAUSERMAN: See entry for SCHMUCKER.

BAUSERMAN: On the 29th of April, by Rev. Jacob Funkhouser, George W. BAUSERMAN and Sarah J. ARGENBRIGHT, all of Rockingham county.
Rockingham Register and Virginia Advertiser, 11 May 1855 (Friday), p. 3, c. 3.

BAXTER: See entry for BEAM.

BAXTER: See entry for MILLER.

BAXTER: See entry for PENCE.

BAXTER: See entry for RHODES.

BAXTER: See entry for RINEHART.

BAYLEY: See entry for BAKER.

BAYLEY: On the 19th of May, by Rev. Joseph Early, Mr. John BAYLEY and Miss Elizabeth

DONSON, all of Rockingham county.
Rockingham Register and Advertiser, 5
July 1861 (Friday), p. 3, c. 3.

BAYLOR: See entry for EICHELBERGER.

BAYLOR: See entry for McCUTCHEN.

BAYLOR: On the 22nd ult., by Rev. Mr. Ewing,
Geo. Milton BAYLOR and Miss Lizzie C.
HOOVER, all of Augusta.
Rockingham Register, 6 January 1870
(Thursday), p. 3, c. 3.

BAYLOR: On the 28th of December, by Rev.
Jacob Thomas, Mr. James R. BAYLOR, of
Augusta county, and Miss Susan Harriet,
daughter of Wm. H. VAN PELT, all of
Rockingham county.
Rockingham Register and Advertiser, 12
January 1866 (Friday), p. 1, c. 3.

BAYLOR: On the 9th inst., by Rev. J. Lantz,
John M. BAYLOR, of Middlebrook. to Miss
Trusie E. CLEMMER, all of Augusta.
Rockingham Register, 23 September 1869
(Thursday), p. 2, c. 3.

BAZZEL: On the 31st of January, by the Rev.
J.L. Blakemore, Mr. Reuben B. BAZZEL and
Miss Sarah C. HORN, all of Augusta.
Rockingham Register and Advertiser, 1
March 1861 (Friday), p. 3, c. 3.

BAZZLE: See entry for ALLPOORT.

BAZZLE: On the 2nd inst., by Rev. Jacob
Miller, at the residence of W.C. Simmers,
Andrew BAZZLE and Miss Mary E. SIMMERS,
all of Rockingham county.
Rockingham Register, 9 June 1870
(Thursday), p. 3, c. 4.

BAZZLE: On the 8th inst., near Tenth Legion,
by Rev. Jos. Funkhouser, Wm. A. BAZZLE
and Mrs. Hannah PICKERING, all of
Rockingham county.
Rockingham Register and Advertiser, 15
November 1866 (Thursday), p. 2, c. 5.

BEACH: See entry for BEACH.

BEACH: See entry for BOWERS.

BEACH: On the 26th ult., by Rev. F.M. Perry,
Elijah BEACH and Miss Sarah BEACH, all of
Page county.
Rockingham Register, 10 December 1868

24

(Thursday), p. 3, c. 3.

BEALL: See entry for TEECH.

BEALL: At Court street Church, Lynchburg, by Rev. Dr. J.E. Edwards, Wednesday, June 17, Henry D. BEALL, Esq., of Winchester, Junior Editor of the Times, and Miss Nannie V., daughter of H.H. LEWIS, Esq., of Lynchburg.
Rockingham Register, 25 June 1868 (Thursday), p. 2, c. 6.

BEAM: See entry for PICKERING.

BEAM: On Thursday, December 31, by Rev. Joseph Funkhouser, Mr. Benjamin BEAM and Miss Susannah, daughter of Mr. Jacob BAXTER, all of Rockingham county.
Rockingham Register and Advertiser, 8 January 1858 (Friday), p. 3, c. 1.

BEAM: On the 17th inst., by Rev. Jacob Stirewalt, Jacob BEAM and Miss Mary E., daughter of Curtis YATES, Esq., all of Rockingham county.
Rockingham Register and Advertiser, 24 October 1867 (Thursday), p. 2, c. 7. Repeated, 31 October 1867 (Thursday), p. 2, c. 6. The latter is given here.

BEAM: On the 1st inst., by Rev. S. Henkel, Wm. BEAM and Mary J. WEAN, of Rockingham.
Rockingham Register and Advertiser, 15 April 1859 (Friday), p. 3, c. 1.

BEAN: See entry for FUNKHOUSER.

BEAN: See entry for GAW.

BEAN: See entry for SWISHER.

BEANE: See entry for ROLFE.

BEAR: See entry for BERRY.

BEAR: See entry for CEASE.

BEAR: See entry for EFFINGER.

BEAR: See entry for FRAINUM.

BEAR: See entry for GORDON.

BEAR: See entry for PATTERSON.

BEAR: On the 19th inst., by Rev. T.D. Bell, Mr. Andrew J. BEAR and Miss Eliza, daughter of Mr. Robert S. GAINES, all of Rockingham county.
The Rockingham Register, 24 October 1862 (Friday), p. 2, c. 6.

BEAR: On Thursday evening, the 21st inst., by

the Rev. Henry Brown, Mr. Christian M.
BEAR to Miss Elizabeth RALSTON, all of
Rockingham.
Rockingham Register and Valley
Advertiser, 30 December 1843 (Saturday),
p. 4, c. 1.

BEAR: On the 11th ult., at Christ's Church,
Smithfield, Isle of Wight county, by Rev.
Geo. Easter, Henry A. BEAR, of
Rockingham, and Miss Bettie B., daughter
of the late Maj. Allen EDWARDS, of Isle
of Wight, Va. Both of the above parties
are mutes.
Rockingham Register, 10 September 1868
(Thursday), p. 2, c. 5.

BEAR: On the 30th ult., at the residence of
the bride's mother, [by] Rev. E.D.
Junkin, Madison H. BEAR, of Rockingham,
and Miss Sarah C. FIREBAUGH, of
Rockbridge county.
Rockingham Register, 6 August 1868
(Thursday), p. 3, c. 2.

BEARD: See entry for ANTHONY.
BEARD: See entry for ARBOGAST.
BEARD: See entry for CARRICOFF.
BEARD: See entry for COINER.
BEARD: See entry for ENSOR.
BEARD: See entry for HANSBERGER.
BEARD: See entry for KREBS.
BEARD: See entry for MONTGOMERY.
BEARD: See entry for TEAWALT.
BEARD: On the 25th December, 1860, at the
residence of the bride's father, by Rev.
J.P. Cummins, Dr. H.O. BEARD, late of
Augusta county, Va., and Miss Mary E.,
daughter of Mr. David NOEL, of Scioto
county, Ohio.
Rockingham Register and Advertiser, 8
February 1861 (Friday), p. 3, c. 4.

BEARD: At Johnson's Cross Road, Monroe
county, W.Va., on the 23rd of August, by
Rev. J.W. Ewan, Mr. J.D. BEARD, of
Augusta county, Va., and Miss Mary M.
JOHNSON, of Monroe county, W.Va.
Rockingham Register and Advertiser, 20
September 1866 (Thursday), p. 3, c. 4.

BEARD: On the 20th of October, at the residence of the bride's father, by the Rev. Daniel T. Colmick, Mr. Joseph BEARD, formerly of Mint Spring, Augusta county, and Lou C., daughter of Geo. W. LORENTZ, Esq., of Upshur county, West Va.
Rockingham Register & Advertiser, 22 December 1865 (Friday), p. 3, c. 2.

BEARD: On the 2nd inst., by the Rev. Peter Shickel, Mr. Levi BEARD and Miss Margaret SHUE, all of Augusta.
Rockingham Register and Valley Advertiser, 11 October 1845 (Saturday), p. 2, c. 6.

BEARD: At Fairfield, on the 27th of October, by Rev. Harvey Gilmore, Wm. A. BEARD and Mrs. Rachel E. ADAIR.
Rockingham Register, 12 November 1868 (Thursday), p. 3, c. 3.

BEARD: In Mt. Crawford, on the 11th inst., by Rev. T. Brashear, Mr. Wm. F. BEARD and Miss Martha MAY, all of this county.
Rockingham Register and Advertiser, 19 June 1857 (Friday), p. 3, c. 2.

BEASLEY: See entry for HARMON.

BEASLEY: See entry for ROACH.

BEASLEY: On the 16th of June, by Rev. Isaac Long, James J. BEASLEY and Miss Margaret WILLIAMS, all of Rockingham county, Va.
Rockingham Register, 21 July 1870 (Thursday), p. 3, c. 3.

BEASLY: See entry for WARBLE.

BEATLY: See entry for POE.

BEATTY: On Tuesday, the 12th inst., by Rev. C.L. Damron, at Millboro Springs, Geo. BEATTY, of Rockbridge county, and Miss Ann E. SIMPSON, of Bath county.
Rockingham Register and Advertiser, 21 November 1867 (Thursday), p. 2, c. 5.

BEATTY: By Rev. Samuel Brown, Capt. John BEATTY, formerly of Brownsburg, to Miss S. Law, eldest daughter of Wm. FRY, Esq., all of Millboro' Springs. [No date is given.]
Rockingham Register and Advertiser, 25 December 1857 (Friday), p. 3, c. 3.

27

BEATTY: Near Strasburg, on the 4th inst., Mr. Thomas K. BEATTY, of Frederick, and Miss Ann E. SHOWALTER, of Warren county.
Rockingham Register and Advertiser, 26 January 1866 (Friday), p. 3, c. 3.

BEAVER: See entry for SHANK.

BEAZELL: In the Presbyterian Church of Zionsville, Boon county, Missouri, at the dedication of the church, by Rev. J.S. Oeland, of Indianapolis, Ind., John S. BEAZELL and Miss Mollie P., daughter of Dr. John DILLARD, formerly of Rockingham county, Va.
Rockingham Register, 1 October 1868 (Thursday), p. 3, c. 3.

BEAZLEY: See entry for DAVIS.

BEAZLEY: See entry for RUNCLE.

BECK: See entry for PLANT.

BECK: At the residence of the bride's mother, in Harrisonburg, on Thursday evening last, by Rev. D.C. Irwin, Henry BECK, of Greensborough, Alabama, and Miss Lucy R., daughter of Hermann HELLER, dec'd, of Harrisonburg.
Rockingham Register and Advertiser, 23 March 1866 (Friday), p. 3, c. 3.

BECKLE: See entry for FIPER.

BECKNER: See entry for CARICKHOFF.

BEDINGER: See entry for MICHIE.

BEECH: See entry for SHENK.

BEELER: On the 19th inst., in Strasburg, by Rev. W. Rusmisell, Samuel A. BEELER, of Hagerstown, Maryland, and Miss Rachel L. FUNKHOUSER, of Shenandoah county.
Rockingham Register and Advertiser, 28 November 1867 (Thursday), p. 2, c. 6.

BEERY: See entry for BEERY.

BEERY: See entry for BOWERS.

BEERY: See entry for HAWSE.

BEERY: See entry for SHANK.

BEERY: See entry for ZIRKLE.

BEERY: On February 21st, by Rev. Timothy Funk, Mr. DeWitt C. BEERY and Miss Ann C., daughter of Christian BRUNK, all of Rockingham county.
Rockingham Register and Advertiser, 7

March 1867 (Thursday), p. 3, c. 3.

BEERY: On the 31st of December, by Rev. T.D. Bell, Mr. Henry C. BEERY and Miss Emma J. MURRAY, all of Rockingham.
Rockingham Register and Advertiser, 9 January 1868 (Thursday), p. 2, c. 4.

BEERY: On Thursday, the 8th inst., by Rev. A. Poe Boude, Isaac N. BEERY and Miss S. Jennie SWANK, all of Rockingham county.
Rockingham Register and Advertiser, 17 October 1867 (Thursday), p. 3, c. 3.

BEERY: On the 30th day of May, by the Rev. Jacob B. Houck, Mr. Jacob T. BEERY and Miss Isabella, daughter of Mr. Rodney ATCHISON, all of Rockingham county.
Rockingham Register and Valley Advertiser, 8 June 1850 (Saturday), p. 2, c. 7.

BERRY: On the 4th inst., by Rev. R.L. McCune, James BERRY, Esq., to Miss Julia A. KING, all of Augusta county.
Rockingham Register and Advertiser, 19 March 1858 (Friday), p. 3, c. 3.

BEERY: At Edom, February 28, by Rev. A.P. Boude, Mr. John C. BEERY and Miss Hannah M., daughter of Josiah BEERY, all of Rockingham county.
Rockingham Register and Advertiser, 7 March 1867 (Thursday), p. 3, c. 3.

BEERY: On the 1st of December, by Rev. Jacob Miller, John N. BEERY and Miss Bettie A., daughter of Philip McMULLIN, all of Rockingham.
Rockingham Register, 8 December 1870 (Thursday), p. 2, c. 4.

BEERY: On the 3rd inst., by Rev. Jacob Wine, Mr. Noah N. BEERY, of Rockingham, and Miss Kate V. NEFF, of Shenandoah.
Rockingham Register and Advertiser, 12 October 1860 (Friday), p. 2, c. 4.

BEGONE: On the 3rd inst., at the residence of Mr. L.F. Meyerhoeffer, by the Rev. S. Filler, Mr. George BEGONE and Miss Sarah Ann MEYERHOEFFER, all of this county.
Rockingham Register and Advertiser, 11 February 1859 (Friday), p. 3, c. 2.

BEGOON: On the 25th of March, by Rev. Geo. W. Holland, at the residence of the bride's father, near Cross Keys, Rockingham county, James A. BEGOON and Miss Elizabeth M., second daughter of Lewis MEYERHOEFFER, and grand-daughter of Rev. Michael MEYERHOEFFER, dec'd.

Rockingham Register, 1 April 1869 (Thursday), p. 3, c. 3.

BEHM: See entry for WILMER.

BEHM: On Thursday, the 26th of January, by Rev. Jno. W. Watson, Mr. James H. BEHM and Miss Caroline SOURS, all of Page county, Va.

Rockingham Register and Advertiser, 4 February 1859 (Friday), p. 2, c. 5.

BEIDLER: On the 15th inst., by Rev. S. Henkel, Daniel W. BEIDLER, of Page county, and Miss Mary Ellen, daughter of Edmond ROSENBERGER, Esq., of Rockingham county.

Rockingham Register, 24 September 1868 (Thursday), p. 3, c. 4.

BEIRNE: See entry for KINNEY.

BELL: On the morning of the 6th of May, in Staunton, Va., at the residence of the bride's father, by the Rev. Wm. E. Baker, Col. D. Ed. BELL, of the 18th Cavalry, C.S.A., of Hampshire county, W.Va., and Miss Minnie A., daughter of J. TIPPING, Esq., of Staunton.

Rockingham Register, 14 May 1868 (Thursday), p. 2, c. 5.

BELL: On the 12th ult., by Rev. John Pinkerton, near Spring Hill, Augusta county, Mr. Daniel M. BELL and Miss Susan V., daughter of Thos. MILLS, Esq.

Rockingham Register and Advertiser, 9 January 1868 (Thursday), p. 2, c. 4.

BELL: On Thursday, the 20th inst., by the Rev. Mr. See, Col. David S. BELL and Miss Elizabeth, daughter of John S. McCUE, of Augusta.

Rockingham Register and Advertiser, 28 January 1859 (Friday), p. 2, c. 6.

BELL: On the 5th inst., by Rev. Mr. Hickman,

Mr. Francis BELL, of Augusta county, to Miss Sarah J., daughter of Maj. James KENT, of Montgomery.
Rockingham Register and Virginia Advertiser, 14 December 1855 (Friday), p. 2, c. 8.

BELL: On November 22nd, at the residence of the bride's uncle, Cyrus BROWN, Esq., by Rev. Isaac Handy, Franklin BELL and Miss Esta C., daughter of Archie TROTTER, dec'd, all of this county.
Rockingham Register, 22 December 1870 (Thursday), p. 2, c. 4.

BELL: On the 9th ult., on Beaver Creek, by Rev. G.W. Stevenson, Mr. J.W. BELL, formerly of Loudon county, and Miss Mary E. MINNICK, of Rockingham county, Va.
Rockingham Register and Advertiser, 16 May 1867 (Thursday), p. 2, c. 5.

BELL: On the 14th inst., in the Clerk's Office of this county, by Rev. J. Rice Bowman, James W. BELL, Esq., and Miss Caroline J. COFFMAN, of Port Republic.
Rockingham Register and Advertiser, 17 October 1867 (Thursday), p. 3, c. 3.

BELL: At the First Presbyterian Church, in Nashville, Tennessee, June 16, 1868, by Rev. Dr. R.F. Bunting, Col. Wm. A. BELL, of Augusta county, Va., and Miss Elizabeth E. NOTTINGHAM, of Nashville.
Rockingham Register, 2 July 1868 (Thursday), p. 2, c. 4.

BELL: On the 16th inst., by Rev. H.H. Hawes, at the residence of Mr. George C. PATTERSON, father of the brides, Dr. Wm. J. BELL and Miss Mary A., and J.F. McCLUNG and Miss Maria Virginia, all of Augusta.
Rockingham Register and Advertiser, 24 October 1867 (Thursday), p. 2, c. 7.

BELLER: On the 11th ult., by Rev. Henry St. John Rinker, John R. BELLER and Miss Amanda C. FADELY, all of Shenandoah county.
Rockingham Register and Advertiser, 2 May 1867 (Thursday), p. 2, c. 6.

31

BELT: See entry for CLINEDINST.
BELT: See entry for HERRON.
BELVER: See entry for YATES.
BENNER: See entry for YOUNG.
BENNETT: See entry for KEAVALL.
BENNETT: See entry for POWERS.
BENNETT: See entry for STUART.
BENNETT: On the 15th of November, by the Rev. Jos. Funkhouser, Lewis BENNETT and Miss Sarah E., daughter of Samuel HANDLEY, all of Rockingham.
Rockingham Register and Advertiser, 22 November 1866 (Thursday), p. 3, c. 3.
BENNICK: In New Market, on the 22nd of December, by Rev. Socrates Henkel, Mr. John S. BENNICK, of Shenandoah county, and Miss Elizabeth E. WISE, of Rockingham county.
Rockingham Register and Advertiser, 9 January 1868 (Thursday), p. 2, c. 4.
BENNIEN: See entry for WHITMORE.
BENSON: See entry for TROUT.
BEOHM: See entry for RAU.
BEOHM: See entry for SHEETZ.
BEOUN: At St. James Church, Richmond, Va., June 7th, by Rev. J. Peterkin, Major Thomas L. BEOUN, of the late Confederate States Army, and Mary Norris, daughter of Colonel F. FONTAINE.
Rockingham Register and Advertiser, 14 June 1866 (Thursday), p. 3, c. 4.
BERKELEY: On the 28th ult., near Staunton, by Rev. Francis McFarland, Dr. Carter BERKELEY, of Prince William, formerly of Staunton, and Miss Lovie, second daughter of the late Wm. GILKESON, Esq.
Rockingham Register and Advertiser, 6 February 1868 (Thursday), p. 2, c. 4.
BERKELEY: In Alleghany county, Maryland, on Thursday the 30th ult., Rev. James BERKELEY, of the Methodist Episcopal Church, to Miss Ellen, daughter of Thomas CROMWELL, Esq., of that county.
Rockingham Register, 22 April 1837 (Saturday), p. 3, c. 3.
BERRY: See entry for FLICK.

BERRY: See entry for GOOD.
BERRY: See entry for HORTON.
BERRY: See entry for LAMB.
BERRY: See entry for LINDAMOOD.
BERRY: See entry for McNETT.
BERRY: See entry for MICHAEL.
BERRY: See entry for SHIFLET.
BERRY: Near Churchville, Augusta county, Va., May 26th, by Rev. P. Fletcher, Charles B. BERRY, M.D., and Miss Ella D. BEAR.
Rockingham Register, 3 June 1869 (Thursday), p. 3, c. 2.
BERRY: On the 10th inst., by Rev. Horatio Thompson, Mr. Chas. G. BERRY and Mary E. ROWAN, both of Augusta.
Rockingham Register and Advertiser, 25 February 1859 (Friday), p. 2, c. 5.
BERRY: On the 13th of November, by Rev. Isaac Kibler, Mr. D.N. BERRY, of Co. D, 10th Va. Infantry, and Miss Julia A. BAKER, all of this county.
The Rockingham Register, 2 December 1864 (Friday), p. 1, c. 4.
BERRY: On Tuesday, the 4th of March, by the Rev. Peter Shickle, Mr. Henry BERRY and Miss Susan Caroline SHEPHERD, all of Augusta county.
Rockingham Register and Valley Advertiser, 19 April 1845 (Saturday), p. 3, c. 1.
BERRY: In McGaheysville, October 24, by Rev. Wm. J. Miller, Henry BERRY, Sr., and Miss Elizabeth, daughter of Wm. R. BOWMAN, all of Rockingham county.
Rockingham Register, 4 November 1869 (Thursday), p. 2, c. 4.
BERRY: On the 11th inst., at the residence of the bride's father, in Greenville, by Rev. Wm. Pinkerton, J.W. BERRY and Miss Molly E. SHULTZ.
Rockingham Register, 20 January 1870 (Thursday), p. 2, c. 5.
BERTRAM: On Thursday, the 2nd inst., by the Rev. T.D. Bell, Mr. Peachy A. BERTRAM and Miss Amelia E., daughter of Mr. Daniel BOWMAN, all of Rockingham county.

Rockingham <u>Register</u> and <u>Advertiser</u>, 10
June 1859 (Friday), p. 3, c. 2.
BETHEL: See entry for VESS.
BETTS: See entry for SINE.
BEAVER: On the 5th inst., by John W. Watson,
    Rev. Aaron BEVER, of the Virginia Annual
    Conference M.E. Church, South, and Miss
    Clarisse Ann, eldest daughter of Capt.
    Henry WARREN, dec'd, of Page county.
    <u>Rockingham</u> <u>Register</u> and <u>Advertiser</u>, 20
    July 1860 (Friday), p. 2, c. 3.
BEX: See entry for McCOLLY.
BEYDLER: See entry for ROSENBERGER.
BEZANSON: See entry for SMITH.
BEZANSON: See entry for WILLIS.
BICKEL: See entry for NICEWANDER.
BICKLE: See entry for BIRTNIT.
BICKLE: On the 25th ult., by Rev. Mr.
    Preston, John A. BICKLE, of Staunton, and
    Miss Bettie N. LOCKRIDGE, of Rockbridge.
    <u>Rockingham</u> <u>Register</u> and <u>Advertiser</u>, 9
    August 1866 (Thursday), p. 3, c. 4.
BICKLE: On the 23rd ult., at the residence of
    the bride's father, near Staunton, by the
    Rev. H.H. Kennedy, Yeizer M. BICKLE to
    Miss Henrietta M., daughter of Maurice
    PARKER, Esq., both of Augusta.
    <u>Rockingham</u> <u>Register</u>, 1 December 1870
    (Thursday), p. 2, c. 4.
BIERLY: See entry for STONE.
BIERLY: On the 11th of June, by Rev. B.F.
    Moomaw, Rev. B.F. BIERLY, late of
    Rockingham county, and Miss Mary
    Elizabeth TROUT, of Roanoke county, Va.
    <u>The</u> <u>Rockingham</u> <u>Register</u>, 3 July 1863
    (Friday), p. 2, c. 5.
BIERLY: On the 29th ult., by the Rev. Daniel
    Feete, Mr. Peter BIERLY and Miss Laura E.
    WILLIAMS, all of Mt. Crawford, Rockingham
    county.
    <u>The</u> <u>Rockingham</u> <u>Register</u> and <u>Valley</u>
    <u>Advertiser</u>, 7 August 1852 (Saturday), p.
    2, c. 6.
BILLHIMER: See entry for BLOSE.
BILLHIMER: See entry for GREINER.
BILLHIMER: See entry for MILLER.

34

BILLHIMER: April 7th, by Rev. A.J. Kibler, Abram BILLHIMER and Miss Sarah JONES, all of Rockingham county.
Rockingham Register, 21 April 1870 (Thursday), p. 3, c. 3.

BILLHIMER: In Shenandoah, on the 22nd of February, by Rev. Henry Jennings, Mr. George BILLHIMER, of Rockingham, and Miss Catharine, daughter of Mr. John SPIGGLE, of Shenandoah.
The Rockingham Register, 25 March 1864 (Friday), p. 2, c. 7.

BILLHIMER: At the residence of the bride's parents, on the 1st inst., by Rev. Geo. H. Ray, Mr. John H. BILLHIMER and Miss Margaret Jane, daughter of Mr. Charles CHANDLER, all of this vicinity.
Rockingham Register and Advertiser, 9 November 1860 (Friday), p. 2, c. 6.

BIRD: See entry for BIRD.

BIRD: See entry for CAMPBELL.

BIRD: See entry for KENDRICK.

BIRD: See entry for PULLIN.

BIRD: See entry for STEPHENSON.

BIRD: At the residence of Alexander Gilmer, in Highland county, by Rev. J.W. Canter, on the 23rd ult., J.W. BIRD, of Highland, and Miss Pamela E. GILMER, of Rockingham.
Rockingham Register and Advertiser, 6 February 1868 (Thursday), p. 2, c. 4.

BIRD: On the 16th ult., by Rev. O.P. Wirgman, Mr. Jacob BIRD to Miss Matilda S., daughter of David H. BIRD, Esq., both of Highland county.
Rockingham Register and Virginia Advertiser, 11 April 1856 (Friday), p. 2, c. 8.

BIRD: On the 26th, by the Rev. John S. Fullen, at the residence of the bride, in Pendleton county, John BIRD, Esq., of Highland county, to Miss Elizabeth M. HINER.
Rockingham Register and Advertiser, 10 August 1860 (Friday), p. 2, c. 5.

BIRTNIT: On the 16th of July, in Staunton, by Rev. Geo. B. Taylor, Mr. Robert BIRTNIT and Miss Margaret BICKLE, all of that place.

Rockingham Register and Advertiser, 23 August 1861 (Friday), p. 3, c. 4.

BISHOP: See entry for CUPP.

BISHOP: See entry for SPITLER.

BISHOP: On the 12th inst., by Elder H. Jennings, Charles M. BISHOP, of Berkeley county, W.Va., and Miss Annie B. FRAVEL, of Shenandoah county.

Rockingham Register and Advertiser, 28 March 1867 (Thursday), p. 2, c. 6.

BISHOP: On the 20th ult., at the residence of the bride's father, by Rev. H.H. Forsyth, James M. BISHOP and Miss Teresa E. GLASS, both of Staunton.

Rockingham Register, 1 December 1870 (Thursday), p. 2, c. 4.

BITTLE: See entry for HOLLAND.

BIXLER: On the 27th of September, by Rev. R.H. Walton, at the residence of the bride's father, near Timberville, Morgan J. BIXLER and Miss Mary C. FULK, all of Rockingham.

Rockingham Register and Advertiser, 5 October 1860 (Friday), p. 2, c. 3.

BLACK: See entry for ALBERT.

BLACK: See entry for LOFTUS.

BLACK: On the 15th inst., by Rev. J.M. Shreckhise, Calvin M. BLACK and Miss Rachael J. GOLLADAY, all of Augusta.

Rockingham Register, 29 October 1868 (Thursday), p. 3, c. 3.

BLACK: In Dayton, on the 18th inst., by the Rev. J.M. Grabill, Mr. James BLACK and Miss Sarah F. TYLER, all of Rockingham.

Rockingham Register and Advertiser, 23 March 1860 (Friday), p. 2, c. 6.

BLACK: At Locust Hill, on Thursday morning, 17th inst., by Rev. C.S.M. See, Mr. Jas. T. BLACK and Miss M. Cornelia MOFFETT, of Augusta.

Rockingham Register and Advertiser, 25 November 1859 (Friday), p. 2, c. 4.

BLACK: On the 9th inst., near Keezletown, by Rev. T. Brashear, Mr. Joseph M. BLACK and

Miss Margaret C. CALDWELL.
Rockingham Register and Advertiser, 26
March 1858 (Friday), p. 3, c. 2.
BLACKWELL: See entry for MAGANN.
BLAGG: See entry for CUPP.
BLAIN: See entry for OAKS.
BLAIN: See entry for WALKER.
BLAIR: See entry for CULLUM.
BLAIR: See entry for DUNLAP.
BLAIR: On the 26th ult., by Rev. S.H. Mullan,
Dr. Matthew BLAIR and Miss Kate B. SMITH,
all of Harrison county, Va.
Rockingham Register and Advertiser, 17
August 1860 (Friday), p. 2, c. 5.
BLAKELEY: See entry for PENCE.
BLAKEMORE: See entry for CRIST.
BLAKEMORE: See entry for DEVER.
BLAKEMORE: See entry for HALL.
BLAKEMORE: See entry for LITTON.
BLAKEMORE: See entry for RIVERCOMB.
BLANTON: In the Presbyterian Church, in
Romney, on Tuesday evening, December 21,
by the Rev. W.M. Woodworth, Prof. Erastus
L. BLANTON, of Paris, Kentucky, to Miss
Anna M., daughter of John M. SNYDER, of
Romney.
Rockingham Register, 6 January 1870
(Thursday), p. 3, c. 3.
BLAZER: By the Rev. Mr. Bryant, on Thursday,
the 3rd inst., Mr. George BLAZER to the
amiable and much admired Miss Sarah
WHISLER, all of this county.
Rockingham Weekly Register, 5 October
1822 (Saturday), p. 3, c. 2.
BLEDSOE: See entry for ABNEY.
BLEDSOE: On the 11th inst., by Rev. J.L.
Clark, Rev. A.C. BLEDSOE, of the Virginia
Annual Conference, and Miss Annie M.
THURMOND, of Nelson county.
The Rockingham Register, 28 November 1862
(Friday), p. 2, c. 5.
BLEDSOE: In the Presbyterian Church, in
Staunton, on Thursday evening week last,
by the Rev. Mr. Baker, Mr. Thomas A.
BLEDSOE and Miss Mattie, daughter of John
WAYAT, Esq., all of   that place.

Rockingham Register and Advertiser, 21 January 1859 (Friday), p. 3, c. 5.

BLISS: On Tuesday the 16th inst., by Rev. T.D. Bell, Mr. Asahel BLISS and Miss Sarah Ann HOARD, - all of Rockingham county.

Rockingham Register and Advertiser, 26 November 1858 (Friday), p. 3, c. 2.

BLOCE: See entry for ROBERTS.

BLOSE: See entry for KIBLINGER.

BLOSE: See entry for YANCEY.

BLOSE: On the 1st inst., at the residence of the bride's mother, by Rev. J.C. Hensell, Mr. Wm. P. BLOSE and Miss Elizabeth, daughter of Mr. Joseph BILLHIMER, Jr., dec'd, all of Rockingham.

Rockingham Register and Advertiser, 9 November 1860 (Friday), p. 2, c. 6.

BLOSSER: See entry for EYE.

BLOSSER: See entry for JUDD.

BLOSSER: On the 10th inst., by Rev. Timothy Funk, Jacob H. BLOSSER and Miss Nancy Virginia, daughter of Branson M. PARROTT, all of Rockingham.

Rockingham Register and Advertiser, 17 October 1867 (Thursday), p. 3, c. 3.

BLY: See entry for LINN.

BLY: See entry for McFARLAND.

BLY: On the 26th of March, by the Rev. John Perkey, Mr. David H. BLY and Miss Angeline STEED, the former of Shenandoah and the latter of Warren county.

Rockingham Register and Advertiser, 20 April 1866 (Friday), p. 2, c. 3.

BODELL: In the Methodist Church, New Market, Va., on Tuesday, the 23rd day of February, Geo. M. BODELL and Miss Ella CLINEDINST, both of Shenandoah county.

Rockingham Register, 3 March 1870 (Thursday), p. 2, c. 5.

BODKIN: On the 8th inst., by Rev. Geo. A. Shuey, Jas. A. BODKIN and Miss Mary E. SHANK, all of Augusta county.

Rockingham Register and Advertiser, 20 April 1866 (Friday), p. 2, c. 3.

BOGGS: On the 26th of March, by Rev. J.

Beaty, Edmund W. BOGGS, of Pendleton county, and Miss Rebecca L. SHULTZ, of Hardy county.
Rockingham Register and Advertiser, 4 April 1867 (Thursday), p. 3, c. 4.

BOGGS: On Tuesday, the 24th ult., by Rev. S.H. Griffith, W.H. BOGGS and Miss Carrie H. McCOY, all of Franklin, Pendleton county, W.Va.
Rockingham Register, 10 December 1868 (Thursday), p. 3, c. 3.

BOLEN: See entry for MOORE.

BOLLINGER: By Elder George Shaver, May 12th, Adam BOLLINGER and Miss Margaret Jane ORNDORF, all of Shenandoah county.
Rockingham Register, 26 May 1870 (Thursday), p. 2, c. 6.

BOLTON: On the 24th of September, by Rev. W.R. Stringer, A.G. BOLTON and Miss Sarah C. TRUSLER, all of Staunton.
Rockingham Register, 8 October 1868 (Thursday), p. 3, c. 3.

BOLTON: On the 9th of January, by Rev. J.H. Temple, Mr. John A. BOLTON and Miss Lucy J. HINER, all of Pendleton county.
Rockingham Register and Advertiser, 21 February 1862 (Friday), p. 3, c. 2.

BOLTON: On Wednesday morning, the 26th, by the Rev. J.C. Hensell, Mr. Joseph V. BOLTON to Miss Lucy A.C. SHELTON, all of Rockingham.
Rockingham Register and Advertiser, 28 December 1860 (Friday), p. 1, c. 5.

BONER: See entry for CAMPBELL.

BONHAM: See entry for PERRY.

BONTS: See entry for BAILEY.

BOOKER: In Dayton, on the 21st of January, Mr. Wm. T. BOOKER, of Queen Ann county, Maryland, and Miss Maggie J., eldest daughter of Mr. John BUTLER, dec'd ....
The Rockingham Register, 5 February 1864 (Friday), p. 2, c. 6.

BOON: See entry for HEIRER.

BOONE: See entry for HAUPE.

BOONE: See entry for WALKER.

BOONE: On the 20th of December, by Rev. P.

Miller, Mr. Samuel L. BOONE and Mrs. Mary
LINK, all of Hardy county.
Rockingham Register and Advertiser, 10
February 1865 (Friday), p. 2, c. 2.

BOOTH: See entry for TEWALT.

BOOTON: On Thursday morning, the 18th inst.,
at the residence of the bride's father,
Elder John CLARK, by Elder Wm. C. Lauck,
Wm. C. BOOTON, of Kentucky, and Miss Mary
A. CLARK, of Warren county, Va.
Rockingham Register, 25 November 1869
(Thursday), p. 2, c. 3.

BOOZE: See entry for BYERLY.

BORDEN: See entry for KELLER.

BORDEN: See entry for SMITH.

BORDEN: On the 25th ult., at Mt. Olive, by
Rev. G.H. Martin, Ben. F. BORDEN and Miss
Sallie Kate PITMAN, both of Shenandoah
county.
Rockingham Register, 3 February 1870
(Thursday), p. 3, c. 4.

BORDEN: On the 20th of November, at the
German Reformed Parsonage, in Woodstock,
by Rev. G.H. Martin, Mr. Hampson BORDEN
and Miss Elizabeth HAMMAND, all of
Shenandoah county.
Rockingham Register and Advertiser, 13
December 1866 (Thursday), p. 2, c. 5.

BORROW: See entry for KRAUSE.

BORTON: See entry for LONG.

BORUM: See entry for WILSON.

BORUM: At the residence of Col. Jacob
Sencindiver, by Rev. D. Shoaf, Richard H.
BORUM, of Shenandoah county, Va., and
Miss Susan C. SENCINDIVER, of Berkeley
county, W.Va.
Rockingham Register and Advertiser, 14
February 1867 (Thursday), p. 2, c. 6.

BOSSERMAN: On the 15th inst., by Rev. Geo. A.
Shuey, Mr. G.W. BOSSERMAN and Miss Sarah
C. AILER, all of Augusta county.
Rockingham Register and Advertiser, 23
March 1860 (Friday), p. 2, c. 6.

BOSTON: See entry for DOVEL.

BOTKIN: On the 6th inst., on South River, in
Pendleton county, by Rev. J.H. Temple, at

the residence of the bride's mother, Mrs. Jane DYER, Mr. John A. BOTKIN and Miss Rachel E. DYER.
Rockingham Register and Advertiser, 21 February 1862 (Friday), p. 3, c. 2.

BOTKIN: On the 17th ult., by the Rev. John S. Pullen, Mr. Wm. BOTKIN, late of Indiana, to Mrs. Emeline MORTON, widow of Wm. MORTON, dec'd, and daughter of Jas. STUART, dec'd, all of Highland.
Rockingham Register and Advertiser, 29 April 1859 (Friday), p. 3, c. 2.

BOTT: In Woodstock, Va., on the 1st of December, by Elder E. Jennings, Capt. Charles E. BOTT, of Shenandoah county, and Miss Emma V. PRITCHARD, of Winchester, Va.
The Rockingham Register and Advertiser, 16 December 1864 (Friday), p. 2, c. 1.

BOTT: On the 12th inst., by Rev. Samuel Shaver, Mr. Joseph BOTT and Miss Mary A. CONNER, all of Shenandoah county.
Rockingham Register & Advertiser, 27 October 1865 (Friday), p. 2, c. 3.

BOTTS: See entry for LEWIS.

BOTTS: At "Lewiston," the residence of the bride's father, near Port Republic, on Thursday morning, the 23rd inst., by Rev. J.C. Wheat, Beverly BOTTS, son of John Minor BOTTS, of Culpeper county, Va., and Miss Lottie, daughter of Gen. S.H. LEWIS, of Rockingham county.
Rockingham Register and Advertiser, 30 May 1867 (Thursday), p. 3, c. 3.

BOUDE: On Wednesday, August 23rd, by Rev. J.S. Martin, Rev. A. Poe BOUDE, of the Baltimore Annual Conference, to Miss Lou Lee PLUNKETT, of Lexington, Va.
Rockingham Register & Advertiser, 1 September 1865 (Friday), p. 2, c. 4.

BOWCOCK: On Wednesday, the 20th of April, by the Rev. J.C. Hensel, Mr. Jesse L. BOWCOCK, son of Mr. J.J. BOCOCK [sic], of Albemarle county, Va., and Miss Maggie, daughter of Mr. Porterfield RIPPETOE, of Rockingham county, Va.

Rockingham Register and Advertiser, 6 May 1859 (Friday), p. 3, c. 2.
BOWCOCK: On the 29th ult., at Trinity Church, by Rev. J.A. Latane, Mr. John Q. BOWCOCK, of Albemarle county, to Miss Mary R.S., daughter of the late Major Robert S. BROOKE, of Staunton.

Rockingham Register, 7 May 1868 (Thursday), p. 2, c. 4.
BOWEN: See entry for ALLEN.
BOWEN: On the 27th ult., at Glen Home, the residence of Mr. Robinson Stuart, Major Thomas P. BOWEN, of Tazewell county, and Miss M. Gussie STUART, of Greenbrier county.

Rockingham Register and Advertiser, 5 July 1866 (Thursday), p. 3, c. 5.
BOWER: In Harrisonburg, on Wednesday, May 27th, by Rev. T.U. Dudley, James R. BOWER, Esq., of Bedford county, and Miss Mary Scott, eldest daughter of the late Capt. Elverton A. SHANDS, of Harrisonburg, Va.

Rockingham Register, 4 June 1868 (Thursday), p. 2, c. 3.
BOWERS: See entry for ARGENBRIGHT.
BOWERS: See entry for BUCHANAN.
BOWERS: See entry for CRAIG.
BOWERS: See entry for GETE.
BOWERS: See entry for JONES.
BOWERS: See entry for RITENOUR.
BOWERS: See entry for RUDOLPH.
BOWERS: See entry for WISE.
BOWERS: On the 19th inst., by Rev. J.P. Hyde, Elijah BOWERS and Miss Anna BEACH, all of Shenandoah county.

Rockingham Register and Advertiser, 30 January 1868 (Thursday), p. 2, c. 4.
BOWERS: On the 17th ult., by Elder H. Jennings, Ezra BOWERS and Miss Sarah A. BROMBACH, all of Shenandoah.

Rockingham Register and Advertiser, 7 June 1866 (Thursday), p. 3, c. 3.
BOWERS: On the 21st of December, at the residence of Mr. John J. Davis, by Rev. R.N. Pool, Mr. Jacob P. BOWERS, of

Rockingham county, and Miss Sallie M. WOLF, of Albemarle county, Va.

Rockingham Register and Advertiser, 12 January 1866 (Friday), p. 2, c. 3.

BOWERS: On the 6th of March, by Rev. Benj. Bowman, Mr. John W. BOWERS, of Berkeley county, Va., and Miss Barbara BEERY, of Rockingham.

The Rockingham Register, 18 March 1864 (Friday), p. 2, c. 7.

BOWERS: On the 24th ult., by Rev. H. Wetzel, Joseph BOWERS and Mrs. Elizabeth BARB, all of Shenandoah.

Rockingham Register, 8 July 1869 (Thursday), p. 2, c. 5.

BOWERS: On the 27th of November, 1862, at Lantz's Mill, Shenandoah county, by Rev. W.H. Cone, Mr. Philip BOWERS and Miss Isabella COFFELT, all of that county.

The Rockingham Register, 5 December 1862 (Friday), p. 2, c. 5.

BOWERS: On the 25th of November, by Rev. P. Miller, Mr. Strium BOWERS, of Shenandoah county, Va., and Miss Amanda HEISHMAN, of Hardy county, W.Va.

Rockingham Register, 9 December 1869 (Thursday), p. 3, c. 2.

BOWERS: On the 31st ult., by Rev. Thos. Hildebrand, T. Page BOWERS, of Strasburg, and Miss M.E. DUFFEY, of Moorefield.

Rockingham Register and Advertiser, 16 January 1868 (Thursday), p. 2, c. 5.

BOWERS: Near Timberville, Rockingham county, on the 31st ult., by Rev. S. Henkel, Mr. Wm. F. BOWERS and Miss Mary C. RITCHIE.

The Rockingham Register, 15 April 1864 (Friday), p. 2, c. 4.

BOWERS: On the 24th ult., at the residence of the bride's father, by Rev. H. Tallhelm, Mr. William T. BOWERS and Miss Catharine A.E. SHEETS, all of Augusta.

Rockingham Register, 7 January 1869 (Thursday), p. 3, c. 3.

BOWLES: See entry for KICE.

BOWLES: At Mrs. Hupp's, in New Market, on the 6th inst., by Rev. S. Henkel, Miss

Isabella SWARTZ and J.A. BOWLES, all of New Market.
Rockingham Register and Advertiser, 20 February 1868 (Thursday), p. 2, c. 6.

BOWLS: See entry for HARDY.
BOWMAN: See entry for ANTHONY.
BOWMAN: See entry for AREHART.
BOWMAN: See entry for BERRY.
BOWMAN: See entry for BERTRAM.
BOWMAN: See entry for BROCK.
BOWMAN: See entry for CRABILL.
BOWMAN: See entry for FAUGHT.
BOWMAN: See entry for GRANDSTAFF.
BOWMAN: See entry for GROVENSTINE.
BOWMAN: See entry for HALL.
BOWMAN: See entry for KING.
BOWMAN: See entry for LINDAMOOD.
BOWMAN: See entry for LINTHICUM.
BOWMAN: See entry for McCLANNAHAN.
BOWMAN: See entry for MATTHIAS.
BOWMAN: See entry for MOOMAW.
BOWMAN: See entry for MOORE.
BOWMAN: See entry for PENCE.
BOWMAN: See entry for PENNYBACKER.
BOWMAN: See entry for SHANK.
BOWMAN: See entry for SPIGLE.
BOWMAN: See entry for STICKLEY.
BOWMAN: See entry for WEAN.
BOWMAN: On the 31st ult., by Rev. H. St. J. Rinker, Andrew J. BOWMAN and Miss Mary J. ROSENBERGER, all of Shenandoah county.
Rockingham Register and Advertiser, 21 November 1867 (Thursday), p. 2, c. 5.
BOWMAN: On Thursday, the 19th of January, by Rev. Jacob Miller, Mr. Benj. BOWMAN and Miss Catharine A., daughter of Willis DEBARD, dec'd, all of Rockingham.
Rockingham Register and Advertiser, 27 January 1860 (Friday), p. 2, c. 6.
BOWMAN: By Elder Henry Jennings, on Thursday, the 7th inst., Daniel A. BOWMAN and Mrs. Milly A. COFFMAN, of Shenandoah county.
Rockingham Register, 21 April 1870 (Thursday), p. 3, c. 3.
BOWMAN: On the 27th of December, by Rev. Solomon Garber, Mr. David BOWMAN and Miss

Susannah, daughter of John HETTRICK, all of Rockingham.

The Rockingham Register, 8 January 1864 (Friday), p. 2, c. 5.

BOWMAN: On the 30th of January, at the residence of the bride's father, by Rev. J. Hensell, Ephraim BOWMAN and Miss Mary E., daughter of Reuben HUFFMAN, Esq., all of Rockingham county.

Rockingham Register and Advertiser, 6 February 1868 (Thursday), p. 2, c. 4.

BOWMAN: On the 12th ult., by Rev. S. Henkel, Franklin M. BOWMAN, of Rockingham, and Miss Annie Rebecca, daughter of Nicholas KIPPS, of Shenandoah.

Rockingham Register and Advertiser, 3 October 1867 (Thursday), p. 2, c. 6.

BOWMAN: On the 27th ult., on the Bridge at Harper's Ferry, by Rev. J.A. McFaden, Henry BOWMAN and Annie F. HOLMES, both of Shenandoah.

Rockingham Register, 10 February 1870 (Thursday), p. 2, c. 5.

BOWMAN: On the 15th inst., by Rev. H. St. John Rinker, Isaiah BOWMAN and Miss Annie FRAVEL, all of Shenandoah.

Rockingham Register and Advertiser, 22 November 1866 (Thursday), p. 3, c. 3. Repeated, 6 December 1866 (Thursday), p. 3, c. 2. The latter gives the date as "the 13th ult."

BOWMAN: On the 28th ult., at Grassy Dale, near Middletown, by Rev. P.S. Davis, J.W. BOWMAN, of Rockingham, and Miss Eliza TABLER, of Frederick county.

Rockingham Register and Advertiser, 12 June 1857 (Friday), p. 3, c. 2.

BOWMAN: On Thursday evening, the 4th inst., by the Rev. William Bryan, Mr. Jacob BOWMAN to Miss Barbara MOYERS, all of this county.

Rockingham Weekly Register, 11 August 1825 (Thursday), p. 3, c. 4.

BOWMAN: On Thursday, the 29th of November, by the Rev. Benjamin Bowman, Mr. Jacob BOWMAN to Mrs. Mary DELOARD, all of this

county.

Rockingham <u>Register</u> <u>and</u> <u>Virginia</u>
<u>Advertiser</u>, 14 December 1855 (Friday), p.
2, c. 8.

BOWMAN: On the 21st ult., by Rev. Jacob Wine,
John BOWMAN and Matilda ESTEP, all of
Shenandoah county.

Rockingham <u>Register</u>, 7 April 1870
(Thursday), p. 2, c. 5. Repeated, 14
April 1870 (Thursday), p. 2, c. 6.

BOWMAN: On the 1st day of November, by Rev.
J.C. Hensell, John S. BOWMAN and Miss
Elizabeth, second daughter of Mr. Emanuel
ROLLER, all of Rockingham county.

Rockingham <u>Register</u> <u>and</u> <u>Advertiser</u>, 15
November 1866 (Thursday), p. 2, c. 5.

BOWMAN: In Frederick city, Md., on Wednesday,
the 3rd of June, by Rev. Michael H.
BOWMAN and Miss Mary M., only daughter of
Christian SITES, both of Linvill's [<u>sic</u>]
Creek, Rockingham county, Va.

Rockingham <u>Register</u>, 11 June 1868
(Thursday), p. 2, c. 5.

BOWMAN: On the 23rd of November, by Rev. L.A.
Cutler, Capt. N.W. BOWMAN, of Rockingham,
and Miss Laura A. JONES, of Orange
county, Va.

Rockingham <u>Register</u>, 8 December 1870
(Thursday), p. 2, c. 4.

BOWMAN: On Thursday, the 26th of December,
1861, by Rev. Daniel Thomas, Mr. Samuel
BOWMAN and Mrs. Sarah E. SHULL, all of
Rockingham county.

Rockingham <u>Register</u> <u>and</u> <u>Advertiser</u>, 10
January 1862 (Friday), p. 3, c. 2.

BOWMAN: On Thursday the 12th inst., Capt.
Samuel BOWMAN and Miss Ellen, daughter of
Mr. Ferdiman SCHMUCKER, all of Shenandoah
county.

Rockingham <u>Register</u> <u>&</u> <u>Advertiser</u>, 27
October 1865 (Friday), p. 2, c. 3.

BOWYER: On the 12th ult., by Rev. W.M. Ervin,
Mr. Washington Cicero BOWYER to Miss Mary
Jane, daughter of Wm. LOWRY, Esq., both
of Highland county.

Rockingham <u>Register</u> <u>and</u> <u>Virginia</u>

<u>Advertiser</u>, 11 April 1856 (Friday),
p. 2, c. 8.

BOWYERS: See entry for CLOUGH.

BOX: On Saturday evening last, in
Harrisonburg, by Rev. H. Hoffman, Mr.
Caleb W. BOX, Confederate soldier, of
Beaufort, S.C., and Miss Anne R.,
daughter of Mr. Wm. PAYNE, of this place.
<u>The</u> <u>Rockingham</u> <u>Register</u>, 27 March 1863
(Friday), p. 2, c. 6.

BOX: On the 16th inst., by Rev. Timothy Funk,
Jerry Franklin BOX, of Blount county,
Alabama, and Miss Barbara E., daughter of
Henry FURR, dec'd, of Rockingham county.
<u>Rockingham</u> <u>Register</u> <u>and</u> <u>Advertiser</u>, 27
September 1866 (Thursday), p. 3, c. 3.

BOYD: See entry for TODD.

BOYD: On Thursday last, the 20th ult., by
Rev. Samuel Kepler, C.W. BOYD and Miss
Virginia, daughter of Col. A.J. VAN PELT,
all of Harrisonburg.
<u>Rockingham</u> <u>Register</u> <u>and</u> <u>Advertiser</u>, 5
March 1868 (Thursday), p. 2, c. 4.

BOYD: At the residence of the bride's father,
near Front Royal, on the 23rd October, by
Rev. Mr. Ritchie, H.P. BOYD, Esq., and
Miss L.O., daughter of Col. Isaac N.
KING, all of Warren county, Va.
<u>Rockingham</u> <u>Register</u> <u>and</u> <u>Advertiser</u>, 21
November 1867 (Thursday), p. 2, c. 5.

BOYD: On the 6th inst., by Rev. J. Pinkerton,
Captain James BOYD, of San Saba, Texas,
and Miss Mary E. SHEETS, of Augusta
county.
<u>Rockingham</u> <u>Register</u>, 14 January 1869
(Thursday), p. 3, c. 3.

BOYD: On the 10th inst., at New Hope, by Rev.
John H. Taylor, W.S. BOYD and Miss Eddie
G. ROTHWELL, both of Augusta.
<u>Rockingham</u> <u>Register</u>, 17 March 1870
(Thursday), p. 2, c. 4.

BOYER: See entry for STICKLEY.

BOYER: On the 15th inst., by Rev. L. Keller,
John D. BOYER and Miss Rebecca
COVERSTONE, all of Shenandoah county.
<u>Rockingham</u> <u>Register</u> <u>and</u> <u>Advertiser</u>, 30

January 1868 (Thursday), p. 2, c. 4.

BOYERS: On the 27th ult., by Rev. H.A. Bovey, Mr. Geo. BOYERS and Miss Lucy F. DOWELLE, all of Rockingham.

Rockingham Register, 17 June 1869 (Thursday), p. 2, c. 6.

BOYLAN: On the 27th of February, at the residence of the bride's father, J.G. SPRINKEL, Esq., by Rev. A.P. Boude, Capt. Frank BOYLAN and Miss Sallie A. SPRINKEL, of this place.

Rockingham Register and Advertiser, 2 March 1866 (Friday), p. 3, c. 3.

BOZARTH: See entry for RITCHIE.

BRADBURN: On January 15, 1867, by Rev. Christian Hartman, John T. BRADBURN and Miss Maggie J.B., daughter of Wm. HIDEN, all of Cub Run, Rockingham county.

Rockingham Register and Advertiser, 24 January 1867 (Thursday), p. 2, c. 4.

BRADLEY: On the 19th ult., by Elder A.C. Booton, Mr. Benj. F. BRADLEY and Miss Mary A. STRICKLER, all of Page county.

Rockingham Register and Advertiser, 18 May 1860 (Friday), p. 3, c. 4.

BRADSHAW: October 26th, by Rev. T.D. Bell, Lieut. Thomas S. BRADSHAW, of Missouri, and Miss Nannie Kate, daughter of Mr. Archibald HOPKINS, Jr., of Rockingham.

Rockingham Register & Advertiser, 3 November 1865 (Friday), p. 2, c. 2.

BRADY: See entry for DOOM.

BRADY: On the 19th inst., by Rev. George V. Leech, Mr. George M. BRADY and Miss Martha V. PARR.

The Rockingham Register, 27 February 1863 (Friday), p. 2, c. 5.

BRAGONIER: See entry for MOORE.

BRAGONIER: At Millwood, Rappahannock county, on the 28th ult., by Rev. L.H. Graybill, Robert C. BRAGONIER, Esq., and Miss Fannie, daughter ofJos. REID, Esq., both of Virginia.

Rockingham Register, 11 November 1869 (Thursday), p. 3, c. 3.

BRAMHAM: See entry for PEYTON.

BRANHAM: January 30th, by Rev. Jos. Early, Mr. James BRANHAM and Miss Elizabeth, daughter of Mr. Andrew SWITZER, all of Rockingham county, Va.
Rockingham Register and Advertiser, 7 February 1862 (Friday), p. 2, c. 6.

BRANNAN: At the Louisa Hotel, Louisa C.H., Va., on the 26th of December, by Rev. Wm. McK. Ward, Mr. Wm. F. BRANNAN, of Fluvanna county, and Miss Mildred A. TATE, of Louisa county, Va.
Rockingham Register and Virginia Advertiser, 22 February 1856 (Friday), p. 2, c. 8.

BRANNER: See entry for PUGH.

BRANNER: See entry for ZIRKLE.

BRANSON: See entry for CHRISMAN.

BRANTNER: See entry for SNYDER.

BRATTON: See entry for McDANNALD.

BRATTON: On the 5th inst., by Rev. Samuel BROWN, Mr. Jas. L. BRATTON and Miss Mary Moore, daughter of the officiating minister, all of Bath county.
Rockingham Register and Advertiser, 13 May 1859 (Friday), p. 3, c. 4.

BRECKENBAUGH: In Trinity Church, Shepherdstown, W.Va., on the 19th ult., by Rev. W.C. Andrews, Dr. John M. BRECKENBAUGH, of Sharpsburg, Md., and Miss Nannie, daughter of the late Rev. Robert DOUGLAS.
Rockingham Register, 10 December 1868 (Thursday), p. 3, c. 3.

BRECKINRIDGE: On the 27th ult., at the residence of Major John Copeland,by the Rev. Mr. Tinsley, Col. Cary BRECKINRIDGE, of Botetourt county, and Miss Mary Virginia CALDWELL, of Greenbrier county.
Rockingham Register and Advertiser, 5 July 1866 (Thursday), p. 3, c. 5.

BREDEN: On Sunday, the 8th inst., by the Rev. Isaac Long, Mr. John Calvin BREDEN and Miss Susanna LINDAMOOD, all of Rockingham county.
The Rockingham Register, 20 February 1863

(Friday), p. 2, c. 3.

BREEDEN: See entry for BREEDEN.

BREEDEN: See entry for LAFFERTY.

BREEDEN: See entry for LAMB.

BREEDEN: See entry for ROWEN.

BREEDEN: At Shenandoah Iron Works, on the 26th of December, by Rev. A. Poe Boude, Alexander BREEDEN and Miss Martha Ann Susan, daughter of Wm. MEADOWS, all of Rockingham county.
Rockingham Register, 7 January 1869 (Thursday), p. 3, c. 3.

BREEDEN: On the 12th ult., by Rev. A.A. Bushong, Joseph BREEDEN and Miss Sarah A. BUCHANAN.
Rockingham Register, 6 January 1870 (Thursday), p. 3, c. 3.

BREEDEN: In McGaheysville, on the 7th inst., by Rev. J.B. Houck, Mr. Robert BREEDEN and Miss Mary BREEDEN, all of Rockingham.
Rockingham Register and Advertiser, 12 June 1857 (Friday), p. 3, c. 2.

BREEDLOVE: On the 28th ult., by Elder G.W. Wood, Lafayette W. BREEDLOVE and Miss Annie SHOMO, all of Page county.
Rockingham Register and Advertiser, 26 December 1867 (Thursday), p. 2, c. 6.

BREEN: On Wednesday, the 19th inst., at the Methodist Parsonage in Harrisonburg, by Rev. T. Hildebrand, Mr. James C. BREEN, of the Valley Rangers, and Miss Mary J., daughter of Capt. Addison HARPER, all of Rockingham county.
Rockingham Register and Advertiser, 28 March 1862 (Friday), p. 3, c. 2.

BREITT: On Monday the 27th ult., by the Rev. W. Burgess, Mr. Levoy O. BREITT, of this county, to Miss Elizabeth Jane WALKER, of Augusta county.
Rockingham Register and Valley Advertiser, 8 June 1850 (Saturday), p. 2, c. 7.

BRENEMAN: See entry for RITCHIE.

BRENEMAN: On the 24th of December, by Rev. Solomon Garber, Mr. Melchor BRENEMAN and Miss Elizabeth J., daughter of David

50

SHANK, all of Rockingham county.
The Rockingham Register, 8 January 1864
(Friday), p. 2, c. 5.

BRENNEMAN: See entry for SPRINKLE.

BRENNEMAN: On the 1st day of September, by
Rev. Jacob Miller, Peter BRENNEMAN and
Miss Barbara Ann, daughter of Samuel
NIESWANDER, all of Rockingham.
Rockingham Register, 15 September 1870
(Thursday), p. 3, c. 3.

BRENNER: On the 30th March, by Rev. S.
Henkel, Josiah BRENNER, of Shenandoah,
and Miss Elizabeth AREHART, of this
county.
Rockingham Register and Advertiser, 7
April 1865 (Friday), p. 2, c. 5.
Repeated, 14 April 1865 (Friday), p. 2,
c. 5.

BRENNER: On the 26th inst., by Rev. S.
Henkel, Mr. Philip BRENNER and Miss Mary
Ann ESTEP, all of Shenandoah.
Rockingham Register and Advertiser, 3
February 1865 (Friday), p. 1, c. 2.

BRENT: See entry for SNOWDEN.

BREWER: See entry for PRICE.

BRICKER: In Bridgewater, the 12th inst., by
the Rev. G.W. Statton, Mr. Abner BRICKER
and Miss Margaret A.B. WILHITE, all of
Rockingham county.
Rockingham Register and Advertiser, 19
August 1859 (Friday), p. 2, c. 5.

BRICKER: On the 15th of November, by Rev.
Solomon Garber, Geo. W. BRICKER and Miss
Lydia, daughter of Jacob SHEETS, dec'd,
all of Rockingham.
Rockingham Register and Advertiser, 6
December 1866 (Thursday), p. 3, c. 2.

BRICKER: On the 6th inst., by Rev. Solomon
Garber, at the residence of the
officiating minister, John W. BRICKER,
formerly of Page county,and Miss Mary J.
HAUS, of Rockingham county.
Rockingham Register and Advertiser, 6
February 1868 (Thursday), p. 2, c. 5.

BRIDGE: At Mr. Daniel Shaw's, near Sherando,
on the 24th ult., by Rev. W.R. Stringer,

Jesse R. BRIDGE and Miss Elizabeth E. TREVEY, all of Augusta county.
Rockingham Register and Advertiser, 3 January 1867 (Thursday), p. 3, c. 3.

BRIDGES: See entry for CONRAD.

BRIDGES: See entry for WELSH.

BRIGHT: See entry for FRY.

BRIGHT: See entry for SHANK.

BRIGHT: On the 9th of April, by Rev. A.J. Kibler, John R. BRIGHT and Katy GLOVIER, all of Rockingham county.
Rockingham Register and Advertiser, 28 April 1865 (Friday), p. 2, c. 5.

BRIGHT: On the 14th inst., by the Rev. Mr. Howe, Mr. Thos. BRIGHT, of Bath, and Miss M.J. ANTHONY, near Deerfield, Augusta.
Rockingham Register and Advertiser, 24 February 1860 (Friday), p. 2, c. 4.

BRIGHTMAN: On Tuesday, the 11th of May, in Charlottesville, Va., by Rev. Mr. Edwards, John C. BRIGHTMAN, printer, formerly of Harrisonburg, assistant foreman in the *Chronicle* office, and Miss Jennie A. WINGFIELD, of Charlottesville.
Rockingham Register, 20 May 1869 (Thursday), p. 2, c. 3.

BRIGHTWELL: See entry for JOHNSON.

BRILL: See entry for PARK.

BRILL: On the 20th ult., by Rev. Peter Miller, Mr. Amos T. BRILL and Miss Elizabeth COLE, of Hampshire.
Rockingham Register and Advertiser, 11 January 1861 (Friday), p. 3, c. 4.

BRILL: On the 22nd ult., on Naked Creek, by the Rev. Daniel Feete, Mr. George BRILL, of Rockingham, and Miss Margaret E., daughter of Mr. Richard PICKERING of Page county.
The Rockingham Register and Valley Advertiser, 7 August 1852 (Saturday), p. 2, c. 6.

BROADDUS: At Locust Grove, near Charlottesville, on Tuesday morning last, by Rev. Wm. F. Broaddus, Rev. John A. BROADDUS and Miss Charlotte Ellen, eldest daughter of the late Mr. George SINCLAIR.

Rockingham Register and Advertiser, 14
January 1859 (Friday), p. 3, c. 3.
Repeated, 17 June 1859 (Friday), p. 3, c.
3. The second notice simply gives the
date as "4th inst."
BROBECK: On the 16th inst., by Rev. J.W.
Wolff, Mr. Philip BROBECK and Miss
Elizabeth FISHER, all of Shenandoah.
Rockingham Register and Advertiser, 23
March 1860 (Friday), p. 2, c. 6.
BROCK: See entry for MORRIS.
BROCK: See entry for STERN.
BROCK: On the 12th inst., by Rev. T.D. Bell,
Charles J. BROCK and Miss Henrietta S.,
youngest daughter of Derrick PENNYBACKER,
Esq., all of Rockingham county.
Rockingham Register and Advertiser, 21
March 1867 (Thursday), p. 2, c. 5.
BROCK: On the 8th of January, by Rev. Jacob
Wine, Mr. Godfrey BROCK and Miss
Elizabeth, daughter of Mr. George
AREHART, all of Rockingham county.
The Rockingham Register, 15 January 1864
(Friday), p. 2, c. 6.
BROCK: On Thursday evening, the 4th inst., by
the Rev. C.W. Petherbridge, Capt. John P.
BROCK to Miss Caroline A., daughter of
Col. Abraham LINCOLN, dec'd, all of
Rockingham county.
Rockingham Register and Valley
Advertiser, 13 September 1851 (Saturday),
p. 2, c. 7.
BROCK: On the morning of the 21st inst., near
Timberville, by Rev. H. St. J. Rinker,
Michael BROCK and Miss Rebecca BOWMAN,
all of Rockingham.
Rockingham Register, 25 June 1868
(Thursday), p. 2, c. 6.
BROCKENBROUGH: On the 29th ult., at
Providence, Mo., Willoughby N.
BROCKENBROUGH, of Lexington, Mo., and
Miss Alica P. THOMAS, of St. Louis.
Rockingham Register, 26 November 1868
(Thursday), p. 2, c. 5.
BROILS: Near New Market, Va., on the 7th
inst., by Rev. J.P. Cline, Mr. James

53

BROILS and Lucy A. ROSSER.
Rockingham Register and Advertiser, 17
February 1865 (Friday), p. 2, c. 4.
BROMBACH: See entry for BOWERS.
BROOK: See entry for WHITE.
BROOKE: See entry for BOWCOCK.
BROOKS: See entry for FULLER.
BROOKS: See entry for RICHARDSON.
BROOKS: See entry for WALKER.
BROOKS: On the 12th ult., by the Rev. T.
Ellison, Mr. Abraham BROOKS & Miss Mary
GREEN, all of Braxton county, Va.
Rockingham Register and Virginia
Advertiser, 11 May 1855 (Friday), p. 3,
c. 3.
BROOKS: On the 24th ult., by Rev. H. Wetzel,
Hezikiah BROOKS and Miss Mary E.
McKELVEY, all of Shenandoah.
Rockingham Register and Advertiser, 7
November 1867 (Thursday), p. 2, c. 5.
BROOKS: On the 29th ult., at Churchville, by
Rev. J.J. Engle, Jas. W. BROOKS and Miss
S.A. FAUBER, all of Augusta.
Rockingham Register, 6 May 1869
(Thursday), p. 2, c. 3.
BROWER: See entry for STONE.
BROWN: See entry for BRATTON.
BROWN: See entry for BROWN.
BROWN: See entry for DUNLAP.
BROWN: See entry for GIFFIN.
BROWN: See entry for HARRIS.
BROWN: See entry for HORDE.
BROWN: See entry for KELLER.
BROWN: See entry for KENEEDY.
BROWN: See entry for KING.
BROWN: See entry for LAFFERTY.
BROWN: See entry for LONGAKER.
BROWN: See entry for MILLER.
BROWN: See entry for PELTER.
BROWN: See entry for POINTS.
BROWN: See entry for PRATT.
BROWN: See entry for RICHARDSON.
BROWN: See entry for RILEY.
BROWN: See entry for SHEETS.
BROWN: See entry for SHOWALTER.
BROWN: See entry for SHUEY.

BROWN: See entry for STOGDALE.

BROWN: See entry for WILSON.

BROWN: On Thursday, the 5th of November, in Bridgewater, by Rev. J.J. Lafferty, Chaplain of the 16th Regiment, Mr. Bernard S. BROWN, of Rockingham, and Miss Bettie A., daughter of Col. Edward J. ARMSTRONG, formerly of Prunty-Town, Taylor county, Va.
The Rockingham Register, 20 November 1863 (Friday), p. 2, c. 6.

BROWN: On the 2nd inst., at the residence [of] Col. W.J. Anderson, Fort Valley, Ga., by Rev. Mr. Russell, E.M. BROWN, formerly of Staunton, to Miss Mattie BARRY, of Ga.
Rockingham Register, 18 November 1869 (Thursday), p. 3, c. 2.

BROWN: At the residence of the bride's father, in Harrisonburg, on Thursday the 3rd of July, by Rev. H. Hoffman, Mr. Francis M. BROWN, of Charleston, S.C., and Miss Sarah Jane, daughter of Mr. Henry BUTLER, of this place.
Rockingham Register and Virginia Advertiser, 11 July 1862 (Friday), p. 2, c. 6.

BROWN: On the 22nd of September, by Rev. Jacob Spitzer, Mr. Franklin BROWN and Miss Phoebe Jane, daughter of Mr. John TURNER, all of Rockingham county.
The Rockingham Register, 17 October 1862 (Friday), p. 2, c. 7.

BROWN: On the 24th inst., by Rev. G.W. Stevenson, at the residence of the bride's mother, in Sangersville, G. Henry BROWN and Miss M. Virginia BROWN, all of Augusta.
Rockingham Register and Advertiser, 31 January 1867 (Thursday), p. 3, c. 2.

BROWN: At the residence of Mr. David Polmer, by the Rev. J.H. Crawford, Mr. Henry BROWN to Miss Hetty M. COALTER, all of Augusta.
Rockingham Register and Advertiser, 30 March 1860 (Friday), p. 2, c. 4.

BROWN: At Strasburg, Va., on the 14th inst., by Rev. J.A. Snyder, Mr. J.Y. BROWN and Miss Elizabeth R. YOST, both of Strasburg.
Rockingham Register and Advertiser, 29 June 1860 (Friday), p. 2, c. 5.

BROWN: On the 20th ult., by Rev. John L. Clarke, Jacob BROWN and Miss Lucy A. RILEY, all of Augusta county.
Rockingham Register, 12 November 1868 (Thursday), p. 3, c. 3.

BROWN: On the 21st inst., at the Union Hotel, in Luray, by Rev. J.W. Watson, Mr. James R. BROWN, of Culpeper, and Miss Sarah J., daughter of John KITE, Esq., of Page.
Rockingham Register and Advertiser, 6 May 1859 (Friday), p. 3, c. 2.

BROWN: On the 17th inst., by Rev. Joseph Funkhouser, John M. BROWN and Miss Emma C. LISKEY, all of Rockingham county.
Rockingham Register, 19 August 1869 (Thursday), p. 3, c. 2.

BROWN: At the residence of the bride's father, on the 12th inst., by Rev. Wm. Hirst, Rev. Peyton BROWN, of the Baltimore Conference, and Miss Henrietta H., daughter of Noah DORSEY, Esq., of Anne Arundel county, Md.
Rockingham Register and Advertiser, 28 January 1859 (Friday), p. 2, c. 6.

BROWN: On the morning of July 26th, 1860, at Monterey, Highland county, Va., by Rev. Wm. T. Price, S.W. [or B.] BROWN, M.D., to Miss Mary, eldest daughter of William W. FLEMING, Esq., of Highland.
Rockingham Register and Advertiser, 10 August 1860 (Friday), p. 2, c. 5. Repeated, 31 August 1860 (Friday), p. 2, c. 4. The above is a combination of the two.

BROWN: On the 13th inst., by Rev. Horatio Thompson, D.D., Mr. Stuart S. BROWN and Miss Isabella F. McCUTCHAN, all of Augusta county.
Rockingham Register and Advertiser, 28 October 1859 (Friday), p. 2, c. 6.

BROWN: On Tuesday evening last, at the residence of the bride's father, by Rev. J.C. Hensel, Dr. T.H. BROWN, of Mt. Crawford, formerly of Albemarle county, and Miss Elizabeth E., daughter of Mr. Wm. CARPENTER, of Rockingham county. Rockingham Register and Advertiser, 25 May 1860 (Friday), p. 2, c. 5.

BROWN: On the 9th of April, by Rev. John W. Wolff, Mr. Thomas BROWN and Miss Margaret COLLIN, all of this county. Rockingham Register and Advertiser, 12 June 1857 (Friday), p. 3, c. 2.

BROWN: On Thursday morning last, at Trinity Church, Staunton, by Rev. J.A. Latane, Dr. Thomas E. BROWN, of Abingdon, and Miss Cornelia Bernard, youngest daughter of the late John Howe PEYTON, of Staunton. Rockingham Register, 15 October 1868 (Thursday), p. 2, c. 3.

BROWN: On the 28th ult., by Rev. Geo. H. Ray, Mr. William G. BROWN, of Staunton, and Miss Mary A., daughter of Charles HARDY, Esq., of Winchester. Rockingham Register and Advertiser, 7 January 1859 (Friday), p. 3, c. 1.

BROWNING: See entry for STICKLEY.

BROWNLEE: See entry for MILLER.

BRUBAKER: See entry for KITE.

BRUBAKER: See entry for MILLER.

BRUBAKER: See entry for PRICE.

BRUBAKER: On the 27th ult., by Rev. Wm. C. Lauck, Abram BRUBAKER and Miss Sallie, daughter of Philip LONG, all of Page county. Rockingham Register, 10 December 1868 (Thursday), p. 3, c. 3.

BRUBAKER: On Thursday evening, March 29th, by Elder Philip McInturf, Daniel R. BRUBAKER and Miss Fannie E., daughter of Henry GANDER, all of Page county. Rockingham Register and Advertiser, 6 April 1866 (Friday), p. 3, c. 3.

BRUBAKER: On the 9th of December last, by the Rev. Madison M. Bowman, Mr. John

BRUBAKER, of Greene county, Tenn., and Miss Anna, daughter of Samuel MILLER, of Washington county, Tenn., formerly of Rockingham county.
Rockingham Register and Advertiser, 14 January 1859 (Friday), p. 3, c. 3.

BRUBECK: On the 17th inst., by Rev. X.J. Richardson, Mr. John BRUBECK, Jr., to Miss Fanny R. RUSMISELL, all of Augusta county.
Rockingham Register and Advertiser, 25 December 1857 (Friday), p. 3, c. 3.

BRUBECKER: On the 28th of January, by the Rev. J.W. Howe, Mr. Thomas BRUBECKER, of Page county, and Miss Pheby E. HUFFMAN, of Rockingham.
The Rockingham Register, 26 February 1864 (Friday), p. 2, c. 4.

BRUBUCK: See entry for ELBURN.

BRUCE: See entry for HARPER.

BRUCE: On the 22nd inst., by Elder P.W. Yates, Rob't N. BRUCE, of Sperryville, and Miss Mary C. ROTHGEB, all of Page county.
Rockingham Register, 29 October 1868 (Thursday), p. 3, c. 3.

BRUFFEY: Dr. John W. BRUFFEY, of Catawba, Roanoke county, Va., and Miss Lilu M. CRAWFORD, of Lynchburg, Va.
Rockingham Register, 10 February 1870 (Thursday), p. 2, c. 5.

BRUMBACH: At the residence of John Reeser, on Thursday, the 31st of March, by Elder R.C. Cave, Isaac BRUMBACH and Miss Pamley SHIP, all of Shenandoah county.
Rockingham Register, 14 April 1870 (Thursday), p. 2, c. 6.

BRUMBACK: See entry for STRADERMAN.

BRUNK: See entry for BEERY.

BRUNK: On Thursday, the 2nd inst., by Rev. Solomon Garber, Abraham D. BRUNK and Miss Frances LOOKER, all of Rockingham.
Rockingham Register and Advertiser, 9 August 1866 (Thursday), p. 3, c. 4.

BRUNK: On the 1st of March, by Rev. Jacob Miller, Michael E. BRUNK and Miss Rebecca

J., daughter of Geo. HOGAN, all of Rockingham.

Rockingham Register and Advertiser, 24 March 1865 (Friday), p. 2, c. 3.

BRYAN: See entry for KELLY.

BRYAN: See entry for WALLACE.

BRYAN: See entry for WHEELER.

BRYAN: See entry for WINDLE.

BRYAN: On the 24th of April, by Rev. Timothy Funk, Jeremiah H. BRYAN and Miss Mary F., daughter of John FRIDLEY, all of Rockingham county.

Rockingham Register and Advertiser, 2 May 1867 (Thursday), p. 2, c. 6.

BRYAN: By Rev. D.C. Irwin, at Hill's Hotel, October 29th, Mr. Peter BRYAN, of Indiana, and Miss Sarah Ann SHOWALTER, of Augusta county.

Rockingham Register and Advertiser, 2 November 1860 (Friday), p. 2, c. 5.

BRYANT: See entry for MAHONE.

BRYANT: On the 28th ult., at the residence of the bride's mother, near Keezeltown [sic], by Rev. H.A. Bovey, John W. BRYANT and Miss Amantha C. GAITHER, all of Rockingham county, Va.

Rockingham Register, 4 November 1869 (Thursday), p. 2, c. 4.

BRYSON: On Tuesday, September 13th, at the residence of the bride's father, on Back Creek, Bath county, by J.E. Wasson, Mr. John R. BRYSON, of Staunton, and Miss Medorah, second daughter of Capt. H.S. WADE, of Bath county.

Rockingham Register and Advertiser, 7 October 1859 (Friday), p. 2, c. 4.

BUCHANAN: See entry for ANDERSON.

BUCHANAN: See entry for BREEDEN.

BUCHANAN: On the 29th ult., by the Rev. J.H. Crawford, Mr. Samuel A. BUCHANAN and Miss Catharine A.V. BOWERS, all of Augusta.

Rockingham Register and Advertiser, 10 June 1859 (Friday), p. 3, c. 2.

BUCHANAN: On the 28th ult., by Rev. R. Lewis McClune, Mr. Wm. A. BUCHANAN and Mrs. Jane SMITH, all of Augusta county, Va.

Rockingham *Register* and *Advertiser*, 5 August 1859 (Friday), p. 3, c. 2.

BUCHER: See entry for MANUEL.

BUCHER: In Harrisonburg, November 17th, by Rev. G.W. Holland, Wm. BUCHER and Miss Laura, only daughter of Samuel HOCKMAN, dec'd, of Warren county.
Rockingham *Register*, 24 November 1870 (Thursday), p. 2, c. 4.

BUCK: See entry for BUCK.

BUCK: See entry for GRANDSTAFF.

BUCK: See entry for LEHEW.

BUCK: On the 2nd inst., by the Rev. Mr. Lauck, Mr. John N. BUCK, Merchant of Front Royal, to Miss Amelia A., daughter of the late Mr. John L. BUCK, of Warren county.
Rockingham *Register* and *Valley* *Advertiser*, 3 November 1849 (Saturday), p. 2, c. 7.

BUCKLEY: On the 3rd inst., by Rev. T.D. Bell, Chancelor Benjamin C. BUCKLEY of Mississispi and Miss Margaret Ann, daughter of Mr. George CHRISMAN, of this county.
Rockingham *Register* and *Virginia* *Advertiser*, 18 July 1856 (Friday), p. 2, c. 8.

BUCKNER: See entry for SMITH.

BULL: On the 3rd inst., by Rev. Jacob Stirewalt, Mr. William BULL and Miss Seanah COOK, both of Rockingham.
Rockingham *Register* and *Advertiser*, 18 March 1859 (Friday), p. 3, c. 1.

BUMGARDNER: See entry for SPROUL.

BUMGARDNER: See entry for WOODDELL.

BUMGARDNER: On the 29th of December, by Rev. James Murray, Jacob A. BUMGARDNER and Miss Sarah M. McGILVRAY, all of Augusta county.
Rockingham *Register*, 14 January 1869 (Thursday), p. 3, c. 3.

BUMGARNER: See entry for ANDERSON.

BUMGARNER: On Sunday morning last, by Elder Jennings, Mr. Joseph F. BUMGARNER and Miss Fannie M., daughter of Elder

Christopher KEYSER, all of Rockingham
county.
Rockingham Register and Advertiser, 17
October 1856 (Friday), p. 2, c. 5.
BUMPHRY: See entry for LANDIS.
BUNCH: See entry for WRIGHT.
BURACKER: See entry for BAILY.
BURACKER: See entry for SIBERT.
BURDETT: See entry for LAMBERT.
BURGESS: See entry for VALENTINE.
BURGESS: See entry for WRIGHT.
BURGESS: On the 23rd ult., by the Rev. J.C.
Hensell, James W. BURGESS and Miss
Lucinda J. SHEETS, all of Mt. Crawford,
Rockingham county, Va.
Rockingham Register and Advertiser, 2
March 1866 (Friday), p. 3, c. 3.
BURGESS: On Tuesday the 2nd inst., by Rev.
Wm. S. White, D.D., Mr. Morgan G. BURGESS
and Miss Ann Ellen CLOWES, all of
Lexington, Va.
The Rockingham Register, 12 December 1862
(Friday), p. 2, c. 5.
BURK: See entry for McCAULEY.
BURKE: See entry for CONWAY.
BURKE: See entry for ERGENBRIGHT.
BURKE: In McGaheysville, on the 10th of
March, by Rev. Isaac Long, Harvey BURKE
and Miss Caroline CRAWFORD, all of
Rockingham county.
Rockingham Register and Advertiser, 30
March 1866 (Friday), p. 2, c. 3.
BURKE: In Edinburg, on Thursday, June 14th,
by Elder Henry Jennings, JohnBURKE, aged
90 years, and Miss Susan PENCE, aged 50
years, all of Shenandoah county.
Rockingham Register and Advertiser, 5
July 1866 (Thursday), p. 3, c. 5.
BURKEHOLDER: See entry for MYERS.
BURKETT: See entry for ROOTS.
BURKETT: On the 1st day of January, in New
Market, by Rev. S. Henkel, Mr. Wm. H.H.
BURKETT, of Ohio county, Va., and Miss
Caroline F. HUPP, of New Market.
The Rockingham Register, 6 February 1863
(Friday), p. 2, c. 5.

BURKHOLDER: See entry for AREY.

BURKHOLDER: See entry for RICE.

BURKHOLDER: See entry for SAMUELS.

BURKHOLDER: On the Bridge at Harpers Ferry, on the 25th inst. [sic, ult.], by the Rev. T.H.W. Monroe, Mr. Alexander BURKHOLDER to Miss Harriet P. PENN, both of Botetourt county, Va.
Rockingham Register and Valley Advertiser, 3 November 1849 (Saturday), p. 2, c. 7.

BURKHOLDER: On the 6th of February, by the Rev. Jacob Miller, Mr. Henry BURKHOLDER and Miss Mary A. SHANK, all of this county.
Rockingham Register and Advertiser, 7 March 1862 (Friday), p. 3, c. 2.

BURKHOLDER: On January 24th, by Rev. Jacob Miller, Jacob BURKHOLDER and Miss Sarah Ann WEBB, all of Rockingham county.
Rockingham Register and Advertiser, 31 January 1867 (Thursday), p. 3, c. 2.

BURKHOLDER: On the 3rd inst., by Rev. N.J. Miller, Mr. John BURKHOLDER and Miss Nancy, daughter of ____ GAINES, dec'd, all of this place.
Rockingham Register & Advertiser, 8 September 1865 (Friday), p. 3, c. 2.

BURKHOLDER: On the 19th inst., at the residence of the bride's father, by Rev. Mr. Stringer, Mr. Jno. W. BURKHOLDER and Miss Virginia F. VINES, all of Augusta county.
Rockingham Register and Advertiser, 28 June 1866 (Thursday), p. 2, c. 5.

BURKHOLDER: On the evening of the 27th ult., at the residence of the bride's father, by the Rev. Dr. N.W. Calhoun, Mr. Newt. M. BURKHOLDER and Miss Samuella A., daughter of Dr. Reuben MOORE, all of Rockingham county, Va.
Rockingham Register and Advertiser, 7 July 1865 (Friday), p. 2, c. 4.

BURNER: See entry for BUSHONG.

BURNER: See entry for CALVIN.

BURNER: See entry for COHNE.

BURNER: See entry for O'NEAL.

BURNER: On the 11th ult., by Rev. G. Stevenson, A. BURNER, of Pocahontas county, W.Va., and Miss Virginia CLARK, of Augusta county.
Rockingham Register and Advertiser, 20 September 1866 (Thursday), p. 3, c. 4.

BURNER: On the 24th ult., by Elder Z.J. Compton, Casper W. BURNER and Miss Elzorah, daughter of John H. KEYSER, of Page county.
Rockingham Register, 10 March 1870 (Thursday), p. 2, c. 4.

BURNER: At Mr. Ed. Locke's, in Luray, on the 23rd ult., by Elder Wm. Locke, Christian BURNER, of Rockingham, and Miss Sallie SHUFF, of Page ....
Rockingham Register and Advertiser, 5 March 1868 (Thursday), p. 2, c. 4.

BURNER: On the 16th ult., in Page county, by Rev. J.W. Watson, Israel B.BURNER, formerly of Shenandoah county, and Miss Martha CULLERS, of Page county.
Rockingham Register and Advertiser, 3 October 1867 (Thursday), p. 2, c. 6.

BURNER: On the 9th inst., by Rev. John M. Clymer, Lemuel BURNER and Miss Mollie C. ALBERT, all of Shenandoah.
Rockingham Register, 17 December 1868 (Thursday), p. 3, c. 2.

BURNETT: On Wednesday evening, the 12th inst., at the Episcopal Church, in Staunton, by Rev. J.A. Latane, Mr. William A. BURNETT and Miss Kate, daughter of Samuel M. WOODWARD, all of Staunton, Va.
The Rockingham Register, 21 November 1862 (Friday), p. 2, c. 5.

BURNS: See entry for CROSS.

BURNS: See entry for DAGGY.

BURNSIDE: See entry for ECHORD.

BURROUGH: See entry for PAULSEL.

BURRUSS: See entry for LACKEY.

BURTON: On Tuesday, the 7th inst., at the Presbyterian Church at Harpers-Ferry, by the Rev. Charles White, James H. BURTON,

Chief Engineer of the Royal Small Arms Manufactory at Enfield Lock, Middlesex, England, and Eugenia Harper, daughter of George MAUZY, Esq.

Rockingham Register and Advertiser, 24 June 1859 (Friday), p. 2, c. 4.

BURWELL: See entry for WADDELL.

BUSH: See entry for ROOT.

BUSH: See entry for SMITH.

BUSH: On the 2nd inst., near Pleasant Grove, by Rev. A.A.P. Neil, Charles R. BUSH to Miss Virginia PIERCE, of Augusta.

Rockingham Register, 23 September 1869 (Thursday), p. 2, c. 3.

BUSHNELL: See entry for PEALE.

BUSHONG: On the 11th inst., by Rev. S. Henkel, Mr. Abraham BUSHONG and Miss Catharine J., eldest daughter of Levi RYMAN, all of Rockingham.

Rockingham Register and Advertiser, 26 October 1860 (Friday), p. 2, c. 6.

BUSHONG: On the 6th inst., by Rev. J.W. Wolff, Mr. Calvin BUSHONG and Miss Susan F., daughter of Mr. Jacob COPP, of the vicinity of Woodstock.

Rockingham Register and Advertiser, 15 March 1861 (Friday), p. 2, c. 4.

BUSHONG: At the residence of the bride's father, in Woodstock, on the 14th inst., by Rev. Mr. ____, E.D. BUSHONG and Miss Bessie C. BURNER, all of Shenandoah county.

Rockingham Register and Advertiser, 22 November 1866 (Thursday), p. 3, c. 3.

BUSHONG: On the 12th inst., by Rev. John Pirkey, Mr. James H. BUSHONG and Miss Mary E. MORT, all of Shenandoah county.

Rockingham Register & Advertiser, 27 October 1865 (Friday), p. 2, c. 3.

BUSHONG: Near New Market, on Thursday, the 22nd ult., by Rev. J.P. Cline, Jesse BUSHONG and Bettie J., youngest daughter of Mr. Geo. ZIRKLE.

Rockingham Register and Advertiser, 13 April 1860 (Friday), p. 2, c. 5.

BUSHONG: On the 21st ult., by Rev. G.H.

Martin, Mark A. BUSHONG and Miss Fannie A. COFFMAN, all of Shenandoah.
Rockingham Register and Advertiser, 4 October 1866 (Thursday), p. 2, c. 5.

BUTCHER: See entry for VINCENT.

BUTCHER: In Bridgewater, on the 29th ult., by Rev. Wm. H. Dinkel, Eli E. BUTCHER, of Frederick county, Va., and Miss Eliza A. POOL, of Rockingham.
Rockingham Register and Advertiser, 6 February 1868 (Thursday), p. 2, c. 4.

BUTLER: See entry for BOOKER.

BUTLER: See entry for BROWN.

BUTLER: See entry for EMSWILER.

BUTLER: See entry for SMITH.

BUTLER: On the 27th September, by the Rev. T.A. Morgan, Mr. Raphael BUTLER and Miss Susannah HEFNER, all of Rockingham.
Rockingham Register and Valley Advertiser, 13 October 1849 (Saturday), p. 2, c. 5.

BUTLER: On the 11th inst., by Rev. J.E. Wasson, S.S. BUTLER and Miss M. ALGER, all of Page county.
Rockingham Register, 25 November 1869 (Thursday), p. 2, c. 3.

BUTTERLY: On the 27th ult., by Rev. G.G. Brooke, Mr. John P. BUTTERLY, of Boston, and Miss Ann Maria GROVE, of Staunton.
Rockingham Register and Advertiser, 14 January 1859 (Friday), p. 3, c. 3.

BYERLEY: On the 13th inst., in Bridgewater, by Rev. Solomon Garber, Mr. Daniel W. BYERLEY and Miss Mary V. GRIMSLEY, all of Rockingham.
Rockingham Register and Advertiser, 21 June 1861 (Friday), p. 3, c. 3.

BYERLY: See entry for LEWIS.

BYERLY: See entry for SAUFLY.

BYERLY: On the 14th inst., by Rev. Solomon Garber, Jacob P. BYERLY and Miss Isabella, daughter of John THUMA, all of Rockingham county.
Rockingham Register and Advertiser, 21 March 1867 (Thursday), p. 2, c. 5.

BYERLY: In Davidson county, N.C., Mr. Joseph

BYERLY, aged 70 years, to widow RICHARDS, aged 60. Forty-four years ago, this lady acted as Bridesmaid on the occasion of Mr. B.'s marriage to his first wife.
Rockingham Register, 14 February 1835 (Saturday), p. 1, c. 4.

BYERLY: On the 24th of December, by the Rev. H. Hoffman, Mr. Jos. C. BYERLY and Miss H.V. CONNER, all of Rockingham.
Rockingham Register and Advertiser, 1 March 1861 (Friday), p. 3, c. 3.

BYERLY: On the 17th ult., by the Rev. P. Shickel, Samuel D. BYERLY and Miss Elizabeth S. BOOZE, all of Botetourt county.
Rockingham Register and Advertiser, 5 July 1866 (Thursday), p. 3, c. 5.

BYERLY: In Port Republic, Rockingham county, on the 23rd inst. [sic, ult.], by Rev. J.F. Liggett, Dr. William H. BYERLY, of Spring Hill, Augusta county, to Miss Annie Lee RYAN, of Shenandoah.
Rockingham Register, 1 December 1870 (Thursday), p. 2, c. 4.

BYERS: See entry for KEISTER.

BYERS: On the 12th inst., by Rev. Wm. Brown, Samuel BYERS, Esq., to Miss Sarah C., daughter of Samuel CLINE, Esq., of Augusta.
Rockingham Register and Advertiser, 27 January 1860 (Friday), p. 2, c. 6.

BYRD: See entry for HAYS.

BYRD: See entry for WARTMANN.

BYRD: On the 26th of January, at the residence of the bride's father, in Port Republic, by Rev. Jno. P. Hyde, Mr. Daniel M. BYRD, of Shenandoah county, and Miss Kate REATON, of Rockingham county.
The Rockingham Register, 5 February 1864 (Friday), p. 2, c. 6.

BYRD: In Texas, on the 15th ult., by Rev. C.J. Bradley, Mr. John E. BYRD, formerly of Harrisonburg, and Miss Lydia J. GORDON, formerly of Rockingham [county], Va.
Rockingham Register and Advertiser, 8

June 1860 (Friday), p. 2, c. 5.

BYRD: On Thursday, the 1st inst., by Rev. J.C. Hensell, Mr. Joseph BYRD, merchant of Bridgewater, to Miss Sarah J., eldest daughter of Mr. Emanuel WISE, all of Rockingham.
Rockingham Register and Advertiser, 16 April 1858 (Friday), p. 3, c. 2.

BYRD: On the 6th inst., near Dayton, by Rev. Wm. H. Dinkel, Levi S. BYRD and Miss M. Fannie McLEOD, all of Rockingham county.
Rockingham Register, 13 May 1869 (Thursday), p. 3, c. 3.

BYRD: On the 20th inst., by Rev. J. Ryder, W.E. BYRD, of Bath, and Miss Mary J. WALTON, of Alleghany [sic].
Rockingham Register and Advertiser, 9 March 1866 (Friday), p. 2, c. 3.

- C -

CABELL: See entry for AUCHINCLOES.

CALDWELL: See entry for BLACK.

CALDWELL: See entry for BRECKINRIDGE.

CALDWELL: See entry for RICHMOND.

CALDWELL: On Sunday, the 30th of August, at Beaver Creek Church, by Rev. George Wine, Benjamin F. CALDWELL and Miss Mary E., daughter of Charles POLLARD, dec'd, all of Rockingham county.
Rockingham Register, 3 September 1868 (Thursday), p. 2, c. 4.

CALDWELL: At Rose Hill, near Charlottesville, Tuesday morning, October 5th, by Rev. J.C. Long, Henry CALDWELL and Miss Rosa D. POOL, both of Greenbrier county, W.Va.
Rockingham Register, 14 October 1869 (Thursday), p. 2, c. 2.

CALDWELL: On the morning of the 7th ult., by the Rev. Thomas Owen, Mr. James S.W. CALDWELL to Miss Edmonia Virginia, only child of Major Edmund RICHMOND; and, on the evening of the same day, the parents of this young and interesting couple, Maj. Edmund RICHMOND and Mrs. Lydia E. CALDWELL, sister of the late ex-President

James K. POLK, were joined in marriage by the Rev. Arthur Davis, all of Haywood county, Tennessee.

Rockingham Register and Valley Advertiser, 13 October 1849 (Saturday), p. 2, c. 5.

CALDWELL: On the 18th ult., by Rev. C.H. Read, Miss Ella F. TEMPLE, of Richmond, Va., and Wm. B. CALDWELL, Esq., of Greenbrier.

Rockingham Register and Advertiser, 9 November 1860 (Friday), p. 2, c. 6.

CALDWELL: On the 6th ult., at the residence of the bride's father, by Rev. Wm. J. Richardson, Mr. Will [torn] M. CALDWELL, of Richmond city, to Miss Fan [torn] C. WITHROW, of Waynesboro, Va.

Rockingham Register and Advertiser, 15 March 1861 (Friday), p. 2, c. 4.

CALE: See entry for KOOGLAR.

CALE: On the 3rd inst., by Rev. J.H. Crawford, Mr. Wm. H. CALE and Miss Sarah F. MORGAN, all of Middlebrook, Augusta.

Rockingham Register and Advertiesr, 11 January 1861 (Friday), p. 3, c. 4.

CALHOON: On the 2nd inst., by Rev. W.A. Jackson, Capt. John C. CALHOON and Miss Berlinda C. LOUGH, both of Pendleton county, Va.

Rockingham Register and Advertiser, 17 May 1861 (Friday), p. 3, c. 3.

CALHOUN: See entry for LUNSFORD.

CALHOUN: See entry for WALTERS.

CALLISON: See entry for GILMER.

CALLISON: On the 10th inst., by Rev. Horatio Thompson, D.D., at Cherry Lane, Rockbridge county, Va., Mr. Jno. CALLISON and Miss Archie C. CARSON.

Rockingham Register and Advertiser, 25 February 1859 (Friday), p. 2, c. 5.

CALVERT: See entry for KIRKER.

CALVERT: See entry for SNYDER.

CALVERT: See entry for WESCOTT.

CALVERT: On Thursday, the 15th inst., by Rev. J.R. Stringer, at the residence of the bride's parents, near Mt. Jackson, E.S.

CALVERT and Miss Maria HUFFMAN.
Rockingham Register, 22 December 1870
(Thursday), p. 2, c. 4.
CALVERT: In Emanuel's Church, New Market,
Va., on the 11th inst., at 7 o'clock
P.M., by Rev. S. Henkel, Miss Annie M.
CLINEDINIST and Geo. R. CALVERT, Esq.,
Editor of the Shenandoah Valley.
Rockingham Register and Advertiser, 20
February 1868 (Thursday), p. 2, c. 6.
CALVIN: On the 9th inst., by Elder John
Pirkey, Obediah CALVIN and Miss Mary
BURNER, all of Shenandoah.
Rockingham Register, 19 November 1868
(Thursday), p. 2, c. 5.
CAMDEN: See entry for DINKLE.
CAMERON: See entry for COCHRAN.
CAMERON: See entry for McCLELLAN.
CAMERON: See entry for SHERRARD.
CAMERON: See entry for SWATSLEY.
CAMERON: See entry for WHITE.
CAMPBELL: See entry for ALLEN.
CAMPBELL: See entry for CANTER.
CAMPBELL: See entry for HULL.
CAMPBELL: See entry for MOSINGO.
CAMPBELL: See entry for NISEWANDER.
CAMPBELL: See entry for PATTERSON.
CAMPBELL: At the residence of the bride's
father, on Tuesday, the 23rd of July, by
Rev. ____, Brown CAMPBELL and Miss Amanda
FLEISHER, all of Highland county.
Rockingham Register and Advertiser, 1
August 1867 (Thursday), p. 2, c. 6.
CAMPBELL: On the 16th ult., by Rev. W.T.
Price, David H. CAMPBELL and Miss Eliza
DEVIER, all of Highland.
Rockingham Register, 4 March 1869
(Thursday), p. 2, c. 4.
CAMPBELL: At the parsonage of Dr. Huston, in
Baltimore, by Rev. Dr. Huston, on the
17th of November, James B. CAMPBELL and
Miss Jennie R. VAN PELT, all of Augusta.
Rockingham Register, 17 December 1868
(Thursday), p. 3, c. 2.
CAMPBELL: At the residence of the bride's
father, in Greenville, on the 1st inst.,

by Rev. H.A. Gaver, Mr. Jas. H. CAMPBELL, of Rockbridge, and Miss Anna HUTCHESON. *Rockingham Register and Advertiser*, 16 March 1866 (Friday), p. 3, c. 4.

CAMPBELL: On the 17th inst., in Bridgewater, by Rev. Thos. Hildebrand, Mr. James R. CAMPBELL, of Frederick county, Va., and Miss Sarah Jane, daughter of Mr. Peter SNYDER, of Bridgewater, Rockingham county, Va.
The Rockingham Register, 25 December 1863 (Friday), p. 2, c. 6.

CAMPBELL: On the 15th inst., by Rev. Horatio Thompson, D.D., James W. CAMPBELL and Miss Virginia DEMASTERS, all of Augusta. *Rockingham Register and Advertiser*, 31 October 1867 (Thursday), p. 2, c. 6.

CAMPBELL: On the 13th ult., by Rev. John S. Pullen, John A. CAMPBELL and Mary F. ARMSTEAD, all of Highland county.
Rockingham Register and Advertiser, 18 October 1866 (Thursday), p. 2, c. 4.

CAMPBELL: On the 26th inst., at the Virginia Hotel, by Rev. G.G. Brooke, Mr. Lafayette CAMPBELL, formerly of Madison county, and Miss Sallie TALLEY, of Augusta county. *Rockingham Register and Advertiser*, 30 September 1859 (Friday), p. 2, c. 4.

CAMPBELL: On the morning of the 9th inst., at Williamsville, Bath county, Va., by Rev. W.T. Price, Rollin CAMPBELL, Esq., of Highland, and Miss Louisa, daughter of Reuben H. ROGERS, of Bath.
Rockingham Register and Advertiser, 20 May 1859 (Friday), p. 2, c. 6.

CAMPBELL: On Tuesday, November 15th, by the Rev. J.E. Wasson, Thomas CAMPBELL, Esq., of Highland, to Mrs. Mary J. BONER, of Bath.
Rockingham Register and Advertiser, 9 December 1859 (Friday), p. 2, c. 5.

CAMPBELL: In Highland county, Va., on the 22nd ult., at the residence of the bride's father, by Rev. J.W. Canter, Mr. Vernon CAMPBELL and Miss Bettie A. BIRD, all of Highland county.

Rockingham Register and Advertiser, 29
June 1860 (Friday), p. 3, c. 2.
CANTER: On the 20th ult., by Rev. Mr. Graham,
Rev. J.W. CANTER, of the Baltimore
Conference, and Mrs. Mattie CAMPBELL, of
Highland.
Rockingham Register and Advertiser, 18
January 1861 (Friday), p. 3, c. 2.
CAPLINGER: See entry for DOVE.
CAPLINGER: See entry for LENTZ.
CAPLINGER: In Germany, Brock's Gap, on the
25th ult., Mr. Jackson CAPLINGER and Miss
Elizabeth LEUTZ, all of Rockingham.
Rockingham Register and Advertiser, 7
December 1860 (Friday), p. 2, c. 6.
CARACOFE: See entry for LAMBERT.
CARDEN: On the 9th inst., by Rev. T.D. Bell,
Peter S. CARDEN, M.D., of Halifax county,
and Miss Maria L., daughter of Mr. David
S. JONES, of Harrisonburg.
Rockingham Register & Advertiser, 17
November 1865 (Friday), p. 2, c. 4.
CARDER: On the 24th ult., by Rev. John W.
Watson, Joshua W. CARDER and Miss Sabina
J., daughter of Harrison STRICKLER,
dec'd, of Page county.
Rockingham Register, 13 August 1868
(Thursday), p. 2, c. 5.
CARICKHOFF: On the 27th ult., by the Rev. P.
Shickel, Mr. George CARICKHOFF, formerly
of Rockingham, and Miss Martha S.
BECKNER, of Botetourt.
Rockingham Register and Advertiser, 28
September 1860 (Friday), p. 2, c. 4.
CARL: See entry for WHITMER.
CARPENTER: See entry for BROWN.
CARPENTER: See entry for CROPP.
CARPENTER: See entry for EARMAN.
CARPENTER: See entry for LACKIE.
CARPENTER: See entry for READ.
CARPENTER: See entry for ROLLER.
CARPENTER: At the parsonage of the M.E.
Church, South, in Woodstock, on Tuesday,
the 28th of October, by Rev. J.W. Wolfe,
Crawford H. CARPENTER, of Pocahontas
county, W.Va., and Miss Sallie E. BAKER,

of Shenandoah.

Rockingham Register, 4 November 1869 (Thursday), p. 2, c. 4.

CARPENTER: On Thursday morning last, 7th inst., at the residence of the bride's father, by Rev. C. White, Dr. George H. CARPENTER to Miss Hannah Susan HEISKELL, all of Hardy county.

Rockingham Register, 14 October 1869 (Thursday), p. 2, c. 2.

CARPENTER: On Wednesday evening, the 16th inst., by Rev. J.C. Hensell, Mr. John CARPENTER, of Rockland, and Mrs. Mary Ann LAMB, all of Rockingham.

Rockingham Register and Advertiser, 25 February 1859 (Friday), p. 2, c. 5.

CARPENTER: On Thursday, the 8th inst., by Rev. J.C. Hensell, John H. CARPENTER and Miss Sallie E., daughter of John K. MOORE, all of Rockingham.

Rockingham Register and Advertiser, 17 October 1867 (Thursday), p. 3, c. 3.

CARPENTER: On the 14th inst., at Mr. S. Crickenberger's, by Rev. J.C. Hensell, John Wesley CARPENTER, of Rockingham county, and Miss Mary E., daughter of the late Philip and Sophia MILLER.

Rockingham Register, 21 May 1868 (Thursday), p. 2, c. 5.

CARPENTER: On the 16th ult., at the residence of the bride's father, by the Rev. J.D. Gray, Mr. R.L. CARPENTER, formerly of Rockingham county, and Miss Mary A., daughter of H.C. RODGERS, Esq., of St. Clair county, Illinois.

Rockingham Register and Advertiser, 9 March 1860 (Friday), p. 3, c. 2. Repeated, 16 March 1860 (Friday), p. 2, c. 5.

CARPENTER: On the 1st inst., by Rev. Levi Keller, Robert A. CARPENTER and Miss Georgianna UTZ, both of Madison county, Va.

Rockingham Register and Advertiser, 23 March 1866 (Friday), p. 3, c. 3.

CARPENTER: On Thursday the 25th of January,

by the Rev. J.C. Hensell, Mr. Wm. J. CARPENTER and Miss Cornelia A., eldest daughter of Martin WHITMORE, Esq., all of Rockingham county.
Rockingham Register and Advertiser, 9 February 1866 (Friday), p. 3, c. 3.

CARPER: See entry for CLINEDINST.

CARR: On the 29th of December, 1864, by Rev. Jacob Wine, David CARR and Leannah HOTTINGER, all of Shenandoah county.
Rockingham Register and Advertiser, 27 January 1865 (Friday), p. 1, c. 3.

CARR: On the 18th of October, at the residence of the bride's father, by Rev. W.C. Barrett, Wm. H. CARR, recently of Loudoun county, Va., but now of Milton, Missouri, and Miss M.M., daughter of Mr. Kit PERKINS, of Clinton county, Missouri.
Rockingham Register and Advertiser, 8 November 1866 (Thursday), p. 3, c. 4.

CARRECOFE: On the 21st ult., by the Rev. John D. Freed, Mr. Lewis CARRECOFE, of Rockingham, and Miss Rebecca J. PRIEST, of Pendleton county, Va.
Rockingham Register and Advertiser, 17 February 1860 (Friday), p. 2, c. 4.

CARREL: See entry for LEEDY.

CARRICOFF: On the 18th inst., by the Rev. T. Brashear, Mr. James M. CARRICOFF, of Rockingham, and Miss Ann Elizabeth BEARD, of Augusta.
Rockingham Register and Advertiser, 21 January 1859 (Friday), p. 3, c. 5.

CARRIER: See entry for COAKLEY.

CARRIER: See entry for HALTERMAN.

CARRIER: See entry for HARRISON.

CARRIER: See entry for RHODES.

CARRIER: See entry for RYMAN.

CARRIER: See entry for THOMPSON.

CARRIER: On the 2nd inst., at the residence of Rev. John Tamkins, Mr. Andrew CARRIER and Miss Susan C. GUY, all of Rockingham.
Rockingham Register and Advertiser, 14 December 1860 (Friday), p. 2, c. 6.

CARRIER: On Wednesday last, by the Rev. G.W. Holland, Mr. John CARRIER, of Leesburg,

Tennessee, and Miss Rachel DEVER, of Rockingham.
Rockingham Register and Advertiser, 7 June 1861 (Friday), p. 3, c. 2.

CARRIER: On Sunday morning, the 20th inst., by Rev. Jacob Miller, Mr. Jos. A.W. CARRIER and Miss Mary J. FULK, all of Rockingham county.
The Rockingham Register, 25 March 1864 (Friday), p. 2, c. 7.

CARRIER: On Wednesday morning last, in Keezeltown [sic], by the Rev. A. Poe Boude, Moses CARRIER and Mrs. Rebecca NICHOLAS, all of Rockingham county.
Rockingham Register and Advertiser, 2 May 1867 (Thursday), p. 2, c. 6.

CARRINGTON: See entry for COCHRAN.

CARRINGTON: See entry for PHELPS.

CARRINGTON: See entry for THOMPSON.

CARROL: See entry for REEVES.

CARROL: On the 7th inst., by Rev. A.J. Kibler, Benj. J. CARROL and Miss Lucy C. WHITLOCK, all of Rockingham.
Rockingham Register, 25 November 1869 (Thursday), p. 2, c. 3.

CARROLL: At Crab Bottom, on the 3rd ult., by the Rev. Stephen Smith, John D. CARROLL and Miss Mary A.J. CHEW, all of Highland county.
Rockingham Register and Advertiser, 18 July 1867 (Thursday), p. 2, c. 6.

CARROLL: On the morning of the 19th inst., by the Rev. Geo. G. Brooke, John M. CARROLL and Mary C. SIMPSON, all of Staunton.
Rockingham Register and Advertiser, 27 May 1859 (Friday), p. 2, c. 6.

CARSON: See entry for CALLISON.

CARSON: On the 24th of November, 1869, at the residence of Col. John McKemy, Rockbridge county, Va., by Rev. J.L. Hemphill, John Hawpe CARSON and Miss Senie A. NELSON.
Rockingham Register, 9 December 1869 (Thursday), p. 3, c. 2.

CARSON: On the 25th of January, at Mint Spring, by Rev. James Murray, Jos. CARSON and Miss Lavalette SWINK, both of

Augusta.

Rockingham Register, 10 February 1870 (Thursday), p. 2, c. 5.

CARSON: On the 15th inst., in Staunton, at the Virginia Hotel, by Rev. Wm. E. Baker, R.N. CARSON and Miss Amanda C. MEEK, both of Augusta county.

Rockingham Register, 23 December 1869 (Thursday), p. 3, c. 2.

CARSON: At Richmond, Va., on Tuesday, the 3rd inst., by Rev. Thomas E. Carson, Rev. Theodore M. CARSON, of the Baltimore Annual Conference, and Miss V. Ellen, youngest daughter of the late William ALLISON, of that city.

Rockingham Register and Advertiser, 20 July 1860 (Friday), p. 2, c. 3.

CARTER: See entry for COPENHANER.

CARTER: See entry for COX.

CARTER: See entry for HALL.

CARTER: See entry for MARTZ.

CARTER: At the residence of G.W. Cook, in Louisa county, on the 22nd of January, by the Rev. Mr. Hawkins, C.H. CARTER, of Louisa county, and Miss Jennie, daughter of John R. O'NEALE, Esq., of Culpeper county, Va.

Rockingham Register and Advertiser, 28 February 1867 (Thursday), p. 2, c. 6.

CARTER: On Thursday evening, the 3rd inst., by Rev. J.C. Hensell, Mr. Henry CARTER and Miss Mary E.; and, Mr. George W. ROBERTSON and Miss Eliza J., both daughters of Daniel MAY, of Mt. Crawford.

The Rockingham Register, 11 March 1864 (Friday), p. 2, c. 6.

CARWELL: On the 13th of September, by Rev. W.S. McClanahan, Mr. Jacob B. CARWELL and Miss Eliza HUTCHENS, all of Augusta county.

Rockingham Register and Advertiser, 20 September 1866 (Thursday), p. 3, c. 4.

CASEBEERE: See entry for RHODES.

CASKIE: See entry for LONDON.

CASLER: See entry for ALEXANDER.

CASLER: At the residence of E.W. Pollard, in

75

Dayton, on Thursday evening, the 15th inst., by Rev. R.N. Pool, John O. CASLER and Miss Martha E. BAUGH, all of Rockingham county.

Rockingham Register and Advertiser, 22 November 1866 (Thursday), p. 3, c. 3.

CASSADAY: On January 24, by Rev. Solomon Garber, Hugh CASSADAY, of Augusta county, and Miss Mary, daughter of Jas. KEATON, of Rockingham.

Rockingham Register and Advertiser, 7 February 1867 (Thursday), p. 3, c. 3.

CASTLEMAN: At Clear Springs in Frederick county, on the 4th inst., by the Rev. Mr. Lacy, Mr. Wm. CASTLEMAN, of Mississippi, to Miss Juliet V., youngest daughter of the late Moses SHEPHERD.

Rockingham Register and Valley Advertiser, 13 October 1849 (Saturday), p. 2, c. 5.

CATLETT: See entry for COLEMAN.

CATON: See entry for RODGERS.

CAUFFMAN: At Northwood, Albemarle county, by Rev. D.C.T. Davis, on the 5th inst., Samuel J. CAUFFMAN, of Rockingham, and Miss Lucy Page ANDERSON.

Rockingham Register, 19 August 1869 (Thursday), p. 3, c. 2.

CAUFMAN: In Staunton, on the 23rd inst., by Rev. G.B. Taylor, Mr. A.B. CAUFMAN to Miss Martha HUFF.

Rockingham Register and Advertiser, 31 August 1860 (Friday), p. 2, c. 4.

CAVE: See entry for DRUMHELLER.

CAVE: See entry for KEEWRIGHT.

CAVE: See entry for VAN ORY.

CAVE: On the 29th ult., near Bridgewater, by Rev. Solomon Garber, Marcellus W. CAVE and Miss Maggie V., daughter of John FLEMING, all of Rockingham ....

Rockingham Register, 6 May 1869 (Thursday), p. 2, c. 3.

CAVE: On the 30th ult., at the Episcopal Methodist Parsonage, in Woodstock, by Rev. John P. Hyde, Noah A. CAVE and Miss Sarah C. SMITH, all of Shenandoah county.

Rockingham <u>Register</u> <u>and</u> <u>Advertiser</u>, 8
November 1866 (Thursday), p. 3, c. 4.

CEASE: On the 15th inst., by Rev. E.F. Busey,
Erasmus P. CEASE and Miss Sallie A.,
daughter of Washington SWINK, all of
Augusta county.

Rockingham <u>Register</u> <u>and</u> <u>Advertiser</u>, 24
January 1867 (Thursday), p. 2, c. 4.

CEASE: On the 17th of May, 1866, by Rev. J.W.
Howe, Henry P. CEASE, of Staunton, and
Miss Mollie A.F. BEAR, of Rockingham.

Rockingham <u>Register</u> <u>and</u> <u>Advertiser</u>, 31
May 1866 (Thursday), p. 3, c. 5.

CEASE: On Thursday evening, the 7th inst., by
Rev. George W. Shuey, John W. CEASE, of
Staunton, to Miss Eliza A. BAER, of
Churchville.

Rockingham <u>Register</u> <u>and</u> <u>Advertiser</u>, 14
March 1867 (Thursday), p. 3, c. 5.

CEASE: On the 6th inst., by Rev. John
Pinkerton, at the residence of the
bride's father, in Mt. Solon, Mr. Magnus
S. CEASE and Miss Ella R., daughter of
Lorenzo SIBERT, Esq.

Rockingham <u>Register</u> <u>and</u> <u>Advertiser</u>, 21
February 1862 (Friday), p. 3, c. 2.

CEASE: On the 8th of January, in Harrison
county, W.Va., by Rev. Mr. Helmick, N.K.
CEASE, of Staunton, and Miss Helen T.
JOHNSON, recently of Holmes county,
Mississippi.

Rockingham <u>Register</u> <u>and</u> <u>Advertiser</u>, 7
March 1867 (Thursday), p. 3, c. 3.

CHADDUCK: At Wm. KIBLER's, Springfield, Page
county, Va., on the 6th inst., by the
Rev. J.E. Wasson, Charles T. CHADDUCK and
Miss Emma E. KIBLER.

Rockingham <u>Register</u>, 20 January 1870
(Thursday), p. 2, c. 5.

CHAMBERS: See entry for HEISKELL.

CHAMBERS: On the 9th of March, by Rev. S.
Garber, J.R. CHAMBERS, of Weeks [<u>sic</u>]
county, N.C., and Miss M. A. HENTON, of
Rockingham county, Va.

Rockingham <u>Register</u> <u>and</u> <u>Advertiser</u>, 24
March 1865 (Friday), p. 2, c. 3.

CHANDLER: See entry for BILLHIMER.
CHANDLER: See entry for EARMON.
CHANDLER: See entry for LANDES.
CHANDLER: On the 28th of January, by Rev.
   Solomon Garber, Richard C. CHANDLER and
   Miss Elizabeth, daughter of Wm. A. VIGER,
   of Augusta county.
   Rockingham Register and Advertiser, 7
   February 1867 (Thursday), p. 3, c. 3.
CHANDLER: In Harrisonburg, on the 20th inst.,
   by Rev. P.M. Custer, St. Clair H.
   CHANDLER and Miss Maggie E. MILLER, all
   of Rockingham county.
   Rockingham Register and Advertiser, 27
   June 1867 (Thursday), p. 2, c. 6.
CHAPIN: See entry for ADAMS.
CHAPLAIN: See entry for HANEY.
CHAPLIN: See entry for SIMPSON.
CHAPMAN: See entry for LEE.
CHAPMAN: See entry for McGUIRE.
CHAPMAN: See entry for SHERMAN.
CHAPMAN: At Hill's Hotel, in Harrisonburg, on
   the 30th of December, by Rev. J.A. Bovey,
   Mr. James M. CHAPMAN and Miss Lydia A.
   O'ROARK.
   Rockingham Register and Advertiser, 7
   January 1859 (Friday), p. 3, c. 1.
CHAPMAN: At the residence of the bride's
   father, on the 11th inst., by Rev. Jos.
   Funkhouser, T.H. CHAPMAN and Miss Martha
   J. SPRINKLE, all of Rockingham county.
   Rockingham Register, 18 June 1868
   (Thursday), p. 3, c. 5.
CHARLTON: On Sunday evening, the 15th inst.,
   at the residence of Mr. Samuel
   Vanderslice, at Lexington, by Rev. Wm. S.
   White, Mr. Samuel C. CHARLTON and Miss
   Sallie, daughter of ____ LANKFORD, of
   Atlanta, Georgia.
   The Rockingham Register, 27 November 1863
   (Friday), p. 2, c. 5.
CHERRYHOLMES: In Woodstock, Va., on the 15th
   [1st] inst., at the residence of the
   bride's mother, by the Rev. J.M. Clymer,
   F.H. CHERRYHOLMES, of Rockingham county,
   and Miss S.E. [F.] ALLEN, of Shenandoah

county.

Rockingham *Register* and *Advertiser*, 9
March 1866 (Friday), p. 2, c. 3.
Repeated, 23 March 1866 (Friday), p. 3,
c. 3. The above is a combination of the
two with the divergent information from
the first appearing in brackets.

CHESHIRE: November 9th, by Rev. P. Miller, in
North River Meeting House, Uriah B.
CHESHIRE and Miss Emma WILSON, all of
Hampshire county.

Rockingham *Register*, 9 December 1869
(Thursday), p. 3, c. 2.

CHEW: See entry for CARROLL.

CHEWING: See entry for WALLACE.

CHEWNING: On the 15th December, 1859, by Rev.
W.T. Richardson, Mr. T.J. CHEWNING and
Miss A.E. KING, all of Augusta.

Rockingham *Register* and *Advertiser*, 24
February 1860 (Friday), p. 2, c. 4.

CHICK: On the 28th ult., by Rev. H. Wetzel,
Joseph B. CHICK and Miss Eliza FOLTZ, all
of Shenandoah county.

Rockingham *Register* and *Advertiser*, 4
October 1866 (Thursday), p. 2, c. 5.

CHILCOTT: See entry for LITTEN.

CHILDRESS: Near Fishersville, on the 9th
inst., by Rev. W.R. Stringer, Wm.
CHILDRESS and Miss E. Mildred MARION, all
of Augusta.

Rockingham *Register*, 23 April 1868
(Thursday), p. 2, c. 5.

CHRISMAN: See entry for BUCKLEY.

CHRISMAN: See entry for MOORE.

CHRISMAN: On the 25th of September, by the
Rev. Thos. Miller, Mr. Adam CHRISMAN and
Miss Sarah C. HOTTEL, all of Shenandoah
county.

Rockingham *Register* & *Advertiser*, 27
October 1865 (Friday), p. 2, c. 3.

CHRISMAN: In Harrisonburg, on Wednesday the
13th inst., by Rev. J.R. Bowman, Maj.
Geo. CHRISMAN and Miss Lucy Gilmer,
daughter of the late Robert GRATTAN, all
of Rockingham county.

Rockingham *Register* and *Advertiser*, 21

November 1867 (Thursday), p. 2, c. 5.

CHRISMAN: On the 10th inst., by Elder Joshua Jennings, Mr. Isaac CHRISMAN to Miss Catharine BRANSON, all of Hardy county. The Rockingham Register and Valley Advertiser, 26 June 1852 (Saturday), p. 2, c. 5.

CHRISMAN: At the residence of the bride's father, in Nelson county, Va., on the 28th of May, by Rev. Mr. Slaughter, Mr. Wm. J. CHRISMAN, of Rockingham, and Miss Jane G., daughter of Mr. T.R. GILES, of Nelson. Rockingham Register and Advertiser, 2 June 1865 (Friday), p. 2, c. 4.

CHRIST: See entry for McCUTCHEN.

CHRISTIE: On Wednesday evening last, in the M.E. Church, in this place, by the Rev. John Thrush, Mr. George S. CHRISTIE and Mrs. Margaret C. WILSON, all of this place. Rockingham Register and Advertiser, 14 November 1856 (Friday), p. 2, c. 6.

CLADEBUCK: See entry for MINNICK.

CLAPPER: See entry for PETRIE.

CLARK: See entry for BOOTON.

CLARK: See entry for BURNER.

CLARK: See entry for DARNEILE.

CLARK: See entry for OSBORN.

CLARK: On the 5th inst., by the Rev. J.W. Start, Mr. Erasmus D. CLARK, of Mt. Crawford, and Miss Leah F. ARBOGAST, of Crab Bottom, Highland county, Va. Rockingham Register and Valley Advertiser, 29 May 1852 (Saturday), p. 2, c. 6.

CLARK: At the Virginia Hotel, in Staunton, on the 15th inst., by Rev. B. Baker, Jas. D. CLARK and Susan ROPER. Rockingham Register and Advertiser, 31 August 1860 (Friday), p. 2, c. 4.

CLARKE: See entry for GILBERT.

CLARKE: On the 21st September, by Rev. Wm. E. Baker, Mr. Denvy N. CLARKE, of Pocahontas, and Miss Mary S. LOVERIDGE, of Augusta.

Rockingham Register and Advertiser, 30
September 1859 (Friday), p. 2, c. 4.
CLARKE: On the 28th of October, at Mt.
Crawford, by Rev. Solomon Garber,
Pleasant A. CLARKE, Jr., and Miss
Caroline M., daughter of Daniel MAY,
dec'd, all of Rockingham county.
Rockingham Register, 12 November 1868
(Thursday), p. 3, c. 3.
CLARKE: On Tuesday morning last, by the Rev.
B.M. Smith, Mr. Samuel E. CLARKE and Miss
Anna A., daughter of Wm. RUFF, Esq., all
of Staunton, Va.
Rockingham Register and Valley
Advertiser, 13 October 1849 (Saturday),
p. 2, c. 5.
CLARY: At the Presbyterian Parsonage, in this
place, on Wednesday evening, the 15th
inst., by Rev. J.R. Bowman, Chas. W.
CLARY and Miss Virginia, daughter of Mrs.
Martha KEENAN, all of Harrisonburg.
Rockingham Register, 23 June 1870
(Thursday), p. 2, c. 4.
CLARY: At the old School Presbyterian
Parsonage, in Harrisonburg, on Tuesday
evening last, by Rev. D.C. Irwin, Mr.
James O.A. CLARY and Miss Mollie E.,
daughter of Mr. Jefferson HERN, all of
Harrisonburg.
Rockingham Register & Advertiser, 6
October 1865 (Friday), p. 2, c. 2.
CLARY: On the 30th of January, at
Summerfield, Alabama, by Rev. Mr. Baker,
John W. CLARY, of Harrisonburg, Va., and
Mrs. Alice A. RICHARDSON, daughter of the
late Wm. C. HARRISON, of the above named
place.
Rockingham Register and Advertiser, 14
February 1867 (Thursday), p. 2, c. 6.
CLATTERBAUGH: On the 27th of May, by Rev.
J.M. Shreckhise, Samuel C. CLATTERBAUGH
and Miss Nany ANDERSON, all of
Rockbridge.
Rockingham Register, 3 June 1869
(Thursday), p. 3, c. 2.
CLATTERBUCK: See entry for KOONTZ.

81

CLATTERBUCK: See entry for MOOHENY.

CLATTERBUCK: On the 25th of January, at Abraham Miller's, near Cross Keys, Rockingham county, by Rev. Isaac Long, William CLATTERBUCK and Miss Lucy Jane EARMON, all of this county.
Rockingham Register and Advertiser, 9 February 1866 (Friday), p. 3, c. 3.

CLAYTON: See entry for RUSMISEL.

CLEARY: At St. Francis Church, August 4th, by Rev. Father Weed, Judge Nick CLEARY, of Washington, D.C., and Miss Catharine McMAHON, of Staunton.
Rockingham Register, 13 August 1868 (Thursday), p. 2, c. 5.

CLEEK: See entry for RIVERCOMB.

CLEEK: See entry for SINDSON.

CLEEK: See entry for WALLACE.

CLEEK: On the 26th ult., by Rev. W.T. Price, on Back Creek, George W. CLEEK and Miss Malcena, eldest daughter of Jacob LIGHTNER, all of Bath county.
Rockingham Register and Advertiser, 5 December 1867 (Thursday), p. 2, c. 5.

CLEEK: On Tuesday, September 29th, at the residence of the bride's aunt, by Rev. Wm. Price, John CLEEK, Jr., of Bath, and Miss Kate M. MYERS, of Highland county.
Rockingham Register, 29 October 1868 (Thursday), p. 3, c. 3.

CLEM: See entry for COVERSTONE.

CLEM: See entry for CRISMAN.

CLEM: On the 11th inst., by Rev. J.P. Cline, Mr. David CLEM, of Shenandoah county, and Miss Polly Ann, daughter of Jacob STROLE, Esq., of Page.
Rockingham Register and Valley Advertiser, 29 May 1852 (Saturday), p. 2, c. 6.

CLEM: On the 7th inst., by Rev. J.W. Watson, David B. CLEM and Miss Sarah GROVE, all of Page county.
Rockingham Register and Advertiser, 14 November 1867 (Thursday), p. 2, c. 6.

CLEM: On the 14th inst., by Rev. A.A.P. Neel, Hiram C. CLEM and Miss Adaline KOONTZ, all of Shenandoah county.

Rockingham Register and Advertiser, 28 February 1867 (Thursday), p. 2, c. 6.

CLEM: On the 11th inst., by Rev. S. Henkel, Mr. William CLEM and Miss Helena, youngest daughter of Michael NEASE, dec'd, all of Shenandoah.

Rockingham Register and Advertiser, 26 August 1859 (Friday), p. 2, c. 5.

CLEMENTS: See entry for SAUM.

CLEMENTS: On the 19th inst., by Rev. Wm. E. Baker, Mr. Wilson J. CLEMENTS and Miss Betsy A. THOMPSON, both of Augusta county.

Rockingham Register and Advertiser, 28 December 1860 (Friday), p. 1, c. 5.

CLEMER: See entry for GORDON.

CLEMMER: See entry for BAYLOR.

CLEMMER: See entry for McGUFFIN.

CLEMMER: Near Middlebrook, on the 7th inst., by Rev. John M. Schreckhise, Henry C. CLEMMER and Miss Mary M. AREHART, both of Augusta.

Rockingham Register and Advertiser, 21 November 1867 (Thursday), p. 2, c. 5.

CLEMMER: On the 24th of March, by Rev. A.A.J. Bushong, J.H. CLEMMER and Miss S. Jennie, daughter of Mr. Adam SNIDER, both of Augusta.

Rockingham Register, 21 April 1870 (Thursday), p. 3, c. 3.

CLENDENEN: On the 15th ult., by Rev. J.W. Canter, Charles CLENDENEN and Miss Mary TUMBLINSON, all of Highland county.

Rockingham Register, 8 October 1868 (Thursday), p. 3, c. 3.

CLEVELAND: On the 22nd inst., by Rev. Dr. Broadus, R.W. CLEVELAND, of Staunton, and Miss Alice M. TROWERS, of Charlottesville.

Rockingham Register and Advertiser, 30 January 1868 (Thursday), p. 2, c. 4.

CLICK: See entry for MILLER.

CLICK: See entry for WETZEL.

CLICK: On Thursday the 19th inst., by Rev. Daniel Thomas, Christian C. CLICK and

Miss Sarah F., daughter of Rev. Jacob THOMAS, all of Rockingham county.
Rockingham Register and Advertiser, 26 December 1867 (Thursday), p. 2, c. 6.

CLICK: On the 18th inst., by Rev. Jacob Miller, Martin CLICK and Miss Matilda Catharine TURNER, all of Rockingham county.
Rockingham Register and Advertiser, 25 October 1866 (Thursday), p. 3, c. 3.

CLINE: See entry for BYERS.

CLINE: See entry for COLE.

CLINE: See entry for CRIST.

CLINE: See entry for HIT.

CLINE: See entry for LAM.

CLINE: See entry for MILLER.

CLINE: See entry for SITES.

CLINE: See entry for ZIMMERMAN.

CLINE: On the 27th of November, at the residence of the bride's father, near Timberville, by Rev. Jacob Miller, David C. CLINE and Miss Mary E., daughter of John W. DRIVER, all of Rockingham.
Rockingham Register, 8 December 1870 (Thursday), p. 2, c. 4.

CLINE: In Fannin county, Texas, on the 15th of November last, by D. Chadwell, Esq., Mr. Ezra S. CLINE, formerly of Shenandoah county, and Miss Lizzie J. ALDRIDGE.
Rockingham Register and Advertiser, 25 January 1861 (Friday), p. 3, c. 1.

CLINE: On the 4th inst., by Rev. Jacob Miller, at the residence of the bride's parents, Jacob CLINE and Miss Bettie, daughter of John D. MILLER, all of Linvill's Creek, Rockingham county.
Rockingham Register, 12 May 1870 (Thursday), p. 3, c. 3.

CLINE: On the 26th of May, by the Rev. John Harshberger, Mr. John CLINE and Miss Elizabeth ROSS, all of Rockingham.
Rockingham Register and Advertiser, 24 June 1859 (Friday), p. 2, c. 4.

CLINE: On the 24th of December, by Rev. Jacob Thomas, John W. CLINE and Miss Sarah V. ZIMMERMAN.

Rockingham Register, 7 January 1869 (Thursday), p. 3, c. 3.

CLINE: On the 24th of August, by the Rev. Solomon Garber, Mr. Martin P. CLINE and Miss Susan A., daughter of Rev. Jacob MILLER, all of this county.

Rockingham Register & Advertiser, 8 September 1865 (Friday), p. 3, c. 2.

CLINE: On the 28th of May, by Rev. Isaac Long, Michael CLINE and Sarah J. GOOD, all of Rockingham county.

Rockingham Register, 11 June 1868 (Thursday), p. 2, c. 5.

CLINE: On the 6th inst., by Rev. A.J. Snyder, Dr. P.M. CLINE and Miss Amanda E., daughter of Capt. David NEFF, all of Shenandoah county.

Rockingham Register and Advertiser, 21 March 1867 (Thursday), p. 2, c. 5.

CLINE: On the 22nd inst., by Rev. Isaac Long, Samuel CLINE, Jr., and Miss Mary B. HUFF, all of Augusta county.

The Rockingham Register, 30 January 1863 (Friday), p. 2, c. 4.

CLINE: At the Lutheran Parsonage, near Capon Springs, on the 7th inst., by Rev. P. Miller, Mr. Stephen CLINE, of Hampshire, and Miss Mary Jane CONRAD, of Hardy county.

Rockingham Register and Advertiser, 29 March 1861 (Friday), p. 3, c. 1.

CLINE: In Hartford, Connecticut, on the 21st of December, 1869, by Rev. J.W. Burton, Dr. Wm. N. CLINE, of Quincey, Ill., formerly of Harrisonburg, Va., and Mrs. Jane Spencer TALCOTT, of Hartford.

Rockingham Register, 3 February 1870 (Thursday), p. 3, c. 4.

CLINEDINIST: See entry for CALVERT.

CLINEDINST: See entry for BODELL.

CLINEDINST: See entry for HITE.

CLINEDINST: See entry for HOFFMAN.

CLINEDINST: See entry for RICE.

CLINEDINST: See entry for TROUT.

CLINEDINST: Near Edinburg, Shenandoah county, by Elder Henry Jennings, Augustus

CLINEDINST and Miss Teany COFFMAN.
Rockingham Register and Advertiser, 16
May 1867 (Thursday), p. 2, c. 5.
CLINEDINST: On the 28th ult., by Rev. D.
Feete, Mr. Barnett M. CLINEDINST and Miss
Carrie M. SOUTH, all of Woodstock.
Rockingham Register and Advertiser, 7
January 1859 (Friday), p. 3, c. 1.
CLINEDINST: On Elk Run, Rockingham county,
Va., on the 16th inst., by Rev. S.
Henkel, Mrs. Caroline S. KITE, of
Rockingham, and Jacob CLINEDINST, of New
Market.
Rockingham Register and Advertiser, 30
May 1867 (Thursday), p. 3, c. 3.
CLINEDINST: On the 29th of January, by Rev.
G.H. Martin, James A. CLINEDINST, of
Woodstock, and Miss Sallie A. BELT,
formerly of Frederick county, late of
Woodstock, Va.
Rockingham Register and Advertiser, 7
February 1867 (Thursday), p. 3, c. 3.
CLINEDINST: At the residence of Mr. Jacob
Clinedinst, in New Market, on the morning
of the 5th inst., by Rev. S. Henkel, Mr.
Wm. CLINEDINST, of Centreville, Indiana,
and Miss Martha RUMBAUGH, of New Market.
Rockingham Register and Advertiser, 15
April 1859 (Friday), p. 3, c. 1.
CLINEDINST: On the 9th of February, 1865, by
Elder H. Jennings, Mr. Wm. R. CLINEDINST
to Miss Mary C., daughter of Henry
CARPER, all of Stony Creek, Shenandoah
county.
Rockingham Register and Advertiser, 24
February 1865 (Friday), p. 2, c. 5.
CLINEDIST: See entry for SOMMERS.
CLORE: On the 13th inst., by Rev. John
Bemick, at Columbia Mills, James O.
CLORE, of Madison county, and Miss Annie
V., daughter [of] Noah KITE, Esq., of
Page county.
Rockingham Register, 22 October 1868
(Thursday), p. 3, c. 3.
CLOUD: See entry for DARNELL.
CLOUDAS: In this place, on Tuesday evening

last, by Rev. A. Poe Boude, Capt. Pitt CLOUDAS, of Cillicothe, Missouri, late of the Confederate States Army, and Miss A. Virginia, second daughter of Robert H. SMITH, dec'd, of Harrisonburg, Va. Rockingham Register and Advertiser, 6 December 1866 (Thursday), p. 3, c. 2.

CLOUGH: At Bridgewater, Massachusetts, Mr. Benjamin CLOUGH, of Sanbornton, to Miss Caroline BOWYERS.   Both deaf and dumb. The scene was a novel one.   The marriage ceremony was performed in writing; it being presented, each assented, and they were pronounced married,agreeably to the laws of the state. Rockingham Register, 30 November 1833 (Saturday), p. 3, c. 2.

CLOWER: On Tuesday morning last, by the Rev. Silas Billings, Mr. John G. CLOWER to Miss Leah, daughter of Dr. John G. SHMITT, all of Shenandoah county. Rockingham Register and Valley Advertiser, 19 April 1845 (Saturday), p. 3, c. 1.

CLOWES: See entry for BURGESS.

CLOWSER: See entry for HAINES.

COAKLEY: See entry for FAIRBURN.

COAKLEY: See entry for KIRACOFE.

COAKLEY: See entry for NICELY.

COAKLEY: On Sunday, May 24, by Rev. Daniel Thomas, Mr. Fielding H. COAKLEY and Miss Julia Ann, daughter of Abraham CARRIER, dec'd, all of Rockingham county. The Rockingham Register, 19 June 1863 (Friday), p. 2, c. 5.

COAKLEY: On the 8th of February, by Rev. Jacob Thomas, Geo. W. COAKLEY and Miss Elizabeth, daughter of Harrison GRADY, all of this county. Rockingham Register and Advertiser, 16 March 1866 (Friday), p. 3, c. 4.

COAKLEY: Near the Mole Hill, on Sunday morning last, by Rev. Jacob Miller, Walter T. COAKLEY and Miss Caroline A., daughter of Philip MILLER, all of Rockingham county.

Rockingham Register, 4 June 1868
(Thursday), p. 2, c. 3.

COALTER: See entry for BROWN.

COALTER: See entry for KEADLE.

COARSEY: On the 4th inst., by Rev. John S.
Blain, Dr. J.W. COARSEY and Miss Irene
PAULEY, all of Augusta.
Rockingham Register and Advertiser, 21
October 1859 (Friday), p. 2, c. 5.

COATS: On the 19th inst., by Rev. ____,
Nathaniel COATS and Miss Elizabeth
GENTRY, all of this county.
Rockingham Register and Advertiser, 30
May 1867 (Thursday), p. 3, c. 3.

COCHENOUR: See entry for FELLER.

COCHRAN: See entry for COCHRAN.

COCHRAN: On the 20th inst., by Rev. C.S.M.
See, B.F. COCHRAN, Esq., and Mary,
daughter of Dr. I.N. HALL, all of Augusta
county.
Rockingham Register, 28 May 1868
(Thursday), p. 2, c. 6.

COCHRAN: On the 18th ult., in
Charlottesville, by Rev. Mr. Annan, Mr.
Howe Peyton COCHRAN and Miss Nancy L.,
daughter of Mrs. Geo. CARRINGTON.
Rockingham Register and Advertiser, 4
January 1861 (Friday), p. 3, c. 4.

COCHRAN: On the 22nd ult., at Loch Willow, by
the Rev. Dr. Hendren, John B. COCHRAN,
Esq., of Kentucky, to Miss Magdalen M.,
daughter of James A. COCHRAN, Esq., of
this county.
Rockingham Register and Virginia
Advertiser, 7 December 1855 (Friday), p.
3, c. 5.

COCHRAN: On the 14th inst., by Rev. W.E.
Baker, at the residence of C.C.
Francisco, Esq., Rob't COCHRAN, of
Culpeper, formerly of Augusta, and Miss
Sallie C. FRANCISCO, of Augusta.
Rockingham Register and Advertiser, 23
May 1867 (Thursday), p. 2, c. 6.

COCHRAN: On Thursday, January 6th, by Rev.
Dr. White, William B. COCHRAN, of
Augusta, and Miss Margaret M., daughter

of Col. Warwick CAMERON, of Rockbridge.
Rockingham Register and Advertiser, 21
January 1859 (Friday), p. 3, c. 5.

COCHRANE: On the 4th inst., at the residence
of Col. J.B. Baldwin, by Rev. James A.
Latane, Capt. Geo. M. COCHRANE and Miss
Margaret Lynn PEYTON, both of Staunton.
Rockingham Register and Advertiser, 11
October 1866 (Thursday), p. 3, c. 4.

COCK: On the 5th of February, in the Church,
at Hermitage, Mo., by the Rev. Mr.
Millar, Mr. Archibald COCK, of Benton
county, Mo., and Miss Sarah M. EFFINGER,
of Hickory county, Mo., and formerly of
this place.
Rockingham Register and Advertiser, 16
March 1860 (Friday), p. 2, c. 5.

COCKRELL: See entry for WUNDER.
COFFELT: See entry for BOWERS.
COFFELT: See entry for COFFMAN.
COFFELT: See entry for HOOVER.
COFFELT: See entry for LAUGHLIN.
COFFMAN: See entry for BAKER.
COFFMAN: See entry for BELL.
COFFMAN: See entry for BOWMAN.
COFFMAN: See entry for BUSHONG.
COFFMAN: See entry for CLINEDINST.
COFFMAN: See entry for COFFMAN (2).
COFFMAN: See entry for GARBER.
COFFMAN: See entry for GARDNER.
COFFMAN: See entry for KNIPPLE.
COFFMAN: See entry for LENTZ.
COFFMAN: See entry for MAPHIS.
COFFMAN: See entry for MILLER.
COFFMAN: See entry for NISWANDER.
COFFMAN: See entry for RUPERT.
COFFMAN: See entry for SHEPP.
COFFMAN: See entry for SNARR.
COFFMAN: See entry for WINE.

COFFMAN: By Rev. G.H. Martin, near Woodstock,
on the 29th of November, Mr. Adam A.
COFFMAN and Miss Lydia COOK, all of
Shenandoah county.
Rockingham Register and Advertiser, 13
December 1866 (Thursday), p. 2, c. 5.

COFFMAN: At Bridgewater, on the 20th of

December, by Rev. Geo. V. Leech,
Christian COFFMAN, Esq., of Augusta, and
Miss Catharine COLEY, of Rockingham.
Rockingham Register and Advertiser, 28
December 1860 (Friday), p. 1, c. 5.

COFFMAN: On the 21st inst., by Rev. L.D.
Brown, Mr. David COFFMAN to Miss Eliza
HEISEY, all of Shenandoah county.
The Rockingham Register and Valley
Advertiser, 22 November 1851 (Saturday),
p. 3, c. 1.

COFFMAN: On the 12th inst., at Cherry-Grove,
near Port Republic, by Rev. Mr. Baird,
DeWitt COFFMAN, Esq., and Christiana V.,
daughter of Stephen HARNSBERGER, Esq.,
all of this county.
Rockingham Register and Virginia
Advertiser, 21 December 1855 (Friday), p.
2, c. 8.

COFFMAN: Near Orange Court House, on the 17th
of October, by Elder E.G. Ship, Mr. E.G.
COFFMAN, of Rockingham county, and Miss
Bettie G., daughter of David HEATWOLE, of
Orange county, formerly of Rockingham.
Rockingham Register and Virginia
Advertiser, 8 November 1861 (Friday), p.
2, c. 2.

COFFMAN: On the 17th inst., near Forestville,
by Rev. H. St. J. Rinker, Erasmus COFFMAN
and Miss Maggie EATON, all of Shenandoah
county.
Rockingham Register and Advertiser, 27
September 1866 (Thursday), p. 3, c. 3.

COFFMAN: On the 30th ult., by Rev. Whetzel,
Henry H. COFFMAN and Miss Rebecca HOTTLE,
all of Rockingham county.
Rockingham Register and Advertiser, 13
September 1866 (Thursday), p. 2, c. 5.

COFFMAN: On the 9th inst., in Dayton, by Rev.
J.E. Armstrong, Hiram COFFMAN and Mrs.
Margaret C. MESSICK, all of Rockingham
county.
Rockingham Register and Advertiser, 13
September 1866 (Thursday), p. 2, c. 5.

COFFMAN: On the 2nd inst., by Rev. J.N.
Fallansbee, J.P. COFFMAN and Miss

Catharine M. CUPP, both of Augusta.
Rockingham Register, 11 November 1869
(Thursday), p. 3, c. 3.

COFFMAN: On the 12th inst., in Woodstock, by
Rev. J.P. Hyde, James J. COFFMAN and Miss
Ann E. COFFMAN, all of Shenandoah.
Rockingham Register and Advertiser, 26
December 1867 (Thursday), p. 2, c. 6.

COFFMAN: November 11th, near Dayton,
Rockingham county, by Rev. Jacob Thomas,
John S. COFFMAN and Miss Elizabeth J.,
daughter of John HEATWOLE, all of
Rockingham.
Rockingham Register, 18 November 1869
(Thursday), p. 3, c. 2.

COFFMAN: On the 12th inst., by Rev. H.
Shaull, at Lantz's Mill, John Wm. COFFMAN
and Miss Sallie B. HOLTZMAN, all of
Shenandoah.
Rockingham Register and Advertiser, 26
December 1867 (Thursday), p. 2, c. 6.

COFFMAN: On July 25th, by Rev. T.D. Bell, Mr.
Joseph S. COFFMAN, of Dayton, and Miss
Fanny H. COFFMAN, of Mt. Clinton.
Rockingham Register & Advertiser, 11
August 1865 (Friday), p. 2, c. 5.

COFFMAN: On the 25th of June, by Elder H.
Jennings, Mr. Samuel B. COFFMAN and Miss
Virginia F. FRY, all of Shenandoah
county.
Rockingham Register, 9 July 1868
(Thursday), p. 2, c. 5.

COFFMAN: On the 16th inst., by Elder Henry
Jennings, Samuel H. COFFMAN and Miss
Sarah V. COFFELT, all of Shenandoah
county.
Rockingham Register, 30 September 1869
(Thursday), p. 2, c. 4.

COFFMAN: On Sunday morning, the 26th inst.,
by Rev. Solomon Garber, Wm. T. COFFMAN
and Miss Eliza Ellen, daughter of Lanty
GOLDEN, all of Rockingham county.
Rockingham Register and Advertiser, 30
August 1866 (Thursday), p. 2, c. 4.

COHNE: On the 19th of March, by Rev. J.E.
Seneker, Mr. John W. COHNE, of Prussia,

and Miss Margaret, daughter of Wm. BURNER, of Rockingham county.
Rockingham Register and Advertiser, 31 March 1865 (Friday), p. 2, c. 3.

COINER: See entry for ENGLEMAN.

COINER: See entry for SHAVER.

COINER: See entry for SHEA.

COINER: See entry for ZIRKLE.

COINER: At New Market, Shenandoah county, Va., on the 13th of January, 1864, by Rev. S. Henkel, Lieut. Ellias COINER, Co. E, 1st Va. Cavalry, of Augusta county, Va., and Miss Anna E., youngest daughter of Thomas REID, Esq., of New Market.
The Rockingham Register, 22 January 1864 (Friday), p. 2, c. 5.

COINER: On the 3rd inst., by Rev. W.A. Gamewell, Mr. J.S. COINER, of Augusta, and Miss Sallie F. BEARD, of Columbia, S.C.
Rockingham Register and Advertiser, 18 January 1861 (Friday), p. 3, c. 2.

COINER: On the 15th inst., in Mt. Crawford, by Rev. J.C. Hensel, James D. COINER and Miss L. Carrie, youngest daughter of George KISER, all of Rockingham.
Rockingham Register and Advertiser, 23 May 1867 (Thursday), p. 2, c. 6.

COINER: On the 15th ult., near New Hope, by Rev. J.J. Engle, St. Clair COINER and Miss Sallie M. MOWRY, all of Augusta county.
Rockingham Register and Advertiser, 3 October 1867 (Thursday), p. 2, c. 6.

COLE: See entry for BRILL.

COLE: See entry for FISHER.

COLE: On the 8th ult., at the residence of the bride's father, by Rev. Jacob Wine, Abraham COLE and Miss Annie R. CLINE, all of Rockingham.
Rockingham Register and Advertiser, 2 February 1866 (Friday), p. 3, c. 2.

COLE: At the Law office of J.W.G. Smith, Esq., in Harrisonburg, on Thursday of last week, by Rev. Thomas Hildebrand, Mr. Jacob COLE, aged 75 years, and Miss

Elizabeth FAUGET, aged 52 years, both of Rockingham county.

Rockingham Register and Advertiser, 19 April 1861 (Friday), p. 2, c. 3.

COLEMAN: See entry for ROHR.

COLEMAN: See entry for TALLAFERRO.

COLEMAN: At Buckton, on the 26th of March, by Elder J. Pirkey, John T. COLEMAN and Mrs. Helen T. CATLETT, all of Warren county.

Rockingham Register, 23 April 1868 (Thursday), p. 2, c. 5.

COLEMAN: At Belle Isle, New Kent county, on the 25th ult., by the Rev. C.H. Read, D.D., Talbot B. COLEMAN, of Staunton, Va., and Miss Marcia A. GORDON, of New Kent county.

Rockingham Register and Advertiser, 3 January 1867 (Thursday), p. 3, c. 3.

COLEY: See entry for COFFMAN.

COLLEY: See entry for MAY.

COLLIER: See entry for LAWSON.

COLLIER: On the 15th inst., at Port Republic, by Rev. R. Smith, Andrew J. COLLIER to Martha J. BATEMAN, all of Rockingham county.

Rockingham Register and Advertiser, 25 January 1861 (Friday), p. 3, c. 1.

COLLIN: See entry for BROWN.

COLLINS: See entry for STEARNS.

COLLINS: See entry for WHOLEY.

COLLINS: On Thursday, 9th ult., near Greenville, Augusta county, by Rev. Geo. B. Taylor, Mr. James A. COLLINS, of Nelson county, and Miss Margaret E., daughter of J.A. SHIELDS, Esq.

Rockingham Register & Advertiser, 22 December 1865 (Friday), p. 3, c. 2.

COLLINS: On the 18th ult., by Elder Henry Jennings, John M. COLLINS and Miss Ozarina SINE, both of Shenandoah.

Rockingham Register and Advertiser, 6 April 1866 (Friday), p. 3, c. 3.

COLLINS: On the 19th ult., by the Rev. James Wanless, Mr. William COLLINS to Miss Sarah, daughter of Solomon VARNER, Esq., all of Pocahontas.

Rockingham Register and Valley Advertiser, 4 November 1848 (Saturday), p. 3, c. 2.

COLLINS: On the 29th of February, by Rev. Martin Garber, Wm. H. COLLINS and Miss Mary A. SMITH, all of Augusta county.
Rockingham Register and Advertiser, 19 March 1868 (Thursday), p. 2, c. 4.

COMER: See entry for GOOD.

COMER: See entry for KIBLER.

COMER: See entry for McCALLISTER.

COMER: See entry for MILLER.

COMER: On the 25th ult., by Elder C. Allemong, Mr. Jefferson COMER and Miss Clarinda CROFT, all of Page.
Rockingham Register and Advertiser, 9 November 1860 (Friday), p. 2, c. 6.

COMER: By Rev. T. Brashear, on the 28th ult., Mr. Joseph COMER and Miss Elisabeth J. WHISSEN, all of Shenandoah county.
Rockingham Register and Advertiser, 5 April 1861 (Friday), p. 2, c. 5.

COMER: On the 18th inst., by Rev. A.P. Boude, Wm. COMER and Miss Henrietta POWEL, all of Page county.
Rockingham Register, 25 November 1869 (Thursday), p. 2, c. 3.

COMPTON: See entry for JOHNSON.

COMPTON: On the 19th inst., by Rev. D.C. Irvin, Mr. Flemon W. COMPTON, of Tazewell county, and Miss Susan F. MESSERSMITH, of Rockingham county.
Rockingham Register & Advertiser, 27 October 1865 (Friday), p. 2, c. 3.

COMPTON: On the 23rd of November, by Rev. Mr. Hughes, of Martinsburg, Mr. Wm. B. COMPTON, of Harrisonburg, Va., and Kate M., daughter of Wm. KERR, Esq., of Marion county.
Rockingham Register & Advertiser, 8 December 1865 (Friday), p. 2, c. 4.

CONNER: See entry for BOTT.

CONNER: See entry for BYERLY.

CONNER: See entry for GARBER.

CONNER: See entry for LICHLITER.

CONNER: On Thursday evening, the 23rd ult.,

by Elder Wm. G. Proctor, Mr. Thomas CONNER, of Shenandoah, to Miss Ruth, daughter of Mr. John HIGGINS, of Rockingham.
Rockingham Register, 4 March 1837 (Saturday), p. 3, c. 3.

CONRAD: See entry for CLINE.

CONRAD: See entry for FAUNTLEROY.

CONRAD: See entry for GENTRY.

CONRAD: See entry for RIBBLE.

CONRAD: See entry for SUTLER.

CONRAD: By the Rev. Peter Miller, November 21st, Mr. Geo. CONRAD, of Hardy, to Miss Harriet ROSEBROUGH, of Hampshire county.
Rockingham Register and Advertiser, 9 February 1866 (Friday), p. 3, c. 3.

CONRAD: On the 3rd of September, by the Rev. A. Weller, Mr. Marion F. CONRAD, C.S.A., of Wirt county, Va., and Miss Elizabeth A. BRIDGES, of Shenandoah county.
The Rockingham Register, 11 September 1863 (Friday), p. 2, c. 3.

CONRAD: On Tuesday, the 10th inst., by the Rev. Philip Rescorl, Mr. Stephen CONRAD (son of John), to Miss Mary, daughter of Mr. Adam HANSBERGER, all of this county.
Rockingham Register, 14 February 1835 (Saturday), p. 3, c. 3.

CONRAD: On the 27th of September, at the residence of the bride's mother, in the city of Stillwater, by the Rev. Horace Hills, W.S. CONRAD, of Richmond, Va., and Miss Eliza C. McKUSICK, of Stillwater, Minnesota.
Rockingham Register, 14 October 1869 (Thursday), p. 2, c. 2.

CONTRI: In Richmond, Va., on Thursday evening, the 17th of March, 1864, by the Right Rev. Bishop McGill, Capt. I.G. CONTRI, of Gen. Morgan's staff, and Miss Virginia N., daughter of George N. SAUNDERS, of Kentucky.
The Rockingham Register, 15 April 1864 (Friday), p. 2, c. 4.

CONWAY: At the residence of the bride's father, in New Market, Va., February 1st,

95

by Rev. J.L. Stirewalt, Mr. John H. CONWAY and Miss Mildred BURKE.
Rockingham Register and Advertiser, 17 February 1865 (Friday), p. 2, c. 4.

CONWAY: At Blacksburg, Montgomery county, Va., on the 14th inst., by Rev. Wm. F. Wilhelm, Dr. W.B. CONWAY, of Weyer's Cave, and Miss Julia E., youngest daughter of the late Col. William THOMAS.
Rockingham Register, 22 December 1870 (Thursday), p. 2, c. 4.

COOK: See entry for BULL.
COOK: See entry for COFFMAN.
COOK: See entry for KAIN.
COOK: See entry for KIBBLINGER.
COOK: See entry for MILLER.
COOK: See entry for TANNER.
COOK: See entry for WELLER.
COOK: See entry for WISE.

COOK: On the 5th ult., at Christ Church, Washington, D.C., by the Rev. Mr. Olds, Mr. J. Faulkner COOK, of Washington, recently of the Black Horse Cavalry, C.S.A., to Miss Lucy C., daughter of Wm. Van Metre HENRY, Esq., of Warren county, Va.
Rockingham Register & Advertiser, 6 October 1865 (Friday), p. 2, c. 2.

COOK: On the 22nd ult., by Rev. T. Cotterell, Mr. Josiah COOK and Miss Lydia SHIREMAN, both of Hardy.
Rockingham Register and Advertiser, 11 January 1861 (Friday), p. 3, c. 4.

COOK: On Thursday evening, the 21st of December, near Sangersville, Augusta county, by Rev. Daniel Thomas, Mr. Samuel COOK, of Rockingham county, and Miss Mary Susan SHUE, of Augusta.
Rockingham Register and Advertiser, 12 January 1866 (Friday), p. 1, c. 3.

COOKE: At Millwood Church, on the 18th ult., by Rev. Joseph Jones, Maj. John Esten COOKE and Miss Mary Frances, daughter of the late Dr. Robert PAGE, of Saratoga, Clarke county.
Rockingham Register and Advertiser, 3

October 1867 (Thursday), p. 2, c. 6.

COOL: On the 28th of August, by Rev. Daniel
Thomas, Mr. Henry COOL and Mrs. Sarah A.
LEEDY, daughter of Henry WHISLER, all of
Rockingham.
Rockingham Register and Advertiser, 2
September 1859 (Friday), p. 2, c. 5.

COOLEY: On the 23rd inst., by Rev. Jos.
Funkhouser, Benjamin B. COOLEY, of
Frederick county, Va., and Miss Martha
Jane, daughter of Cyrus RHODES, Esq., of
Smith's Creek, Rockingham county.
Rockingham Register and Advertiser, 30
August 1866 (Thursday), p. 2, c. 4.

COONES: See entry for ALLEN.

COONTZ: See entry for O'BRIEN.

COOPER: See entry for PROCTOR.

COOTES: On Tuesday last, by the Rev. S.S.
Lambeth, Mr. B. Franklin COOTES, of
Harrisonburg, and Miss Mary E., daughter
of Jno. NEWTON, Esq., of Greenville,
Augusta county, Va.
Rockingham Register and Advertiser, 1
March 1861 (Friday), p. 3, c. 3.

COOTES: On Thursday morning, the 27th of
February, at Trevillian's, Louisa county,
Va., by the Rev. David Wood, Samuel
COOTES, Esq., of Rockingham, and Mrs.
Paulina C. NEFF, of first named place.
Rockingham Register and Valley
Advertiser, 8 March 1845 (Saturday), p.
3, c. 3.

COOTES: On the 15th of November, at the
residence of the bride's father, by Rev.
R.Y. Henly, Samuel COOTES, of Rockingham
county, Va., and Miss Bettie B. LYNE, of
King and Queen county, Va.
Rockingham Register, 24 November 1870
(Thursday), p. 2, c. 4.

COPENHANER: On the 22nd of January, by Rev.
Geo. B. Taylor, Mr. Thomas COPENHANER, of
Smythe county, to Miss Susan W. CARTER,
of Staunton.
Rockingham Register and Advertiser, 30
January 1868 (Thursday), p. 2, c. 4.

COPENHAVER: See entry for HOCKMAN.

97

COPELAND: On the 18th of February, by Rev. John Hutchens, Mr. Wm. COPELAND, of England, and Mrs. Mary E. GUTHRIE, of Augusta county.
Rockingham Register and Advertiser, 16 March 1866 (Friday), p. 3, c. 4.

COPP: See entry for BUSHONG.

COPP: See entry for LEE.

COPP: See entry for SHOKEY.

COPP: See entry for SMOOTZ.

COPP: See entry for WINDLE.

COPP: On the 29th of November, by Rev. G.H. Martin, Mr. Bernard COPP and Miss Mary Ellen LAYMAN, all of Shenandoah county.
Rockingham Register and Advertiser, 13 December 1866 (Thursday), p. 2, c. 5.

COPP: On the 18th inst., by Rev. Geo. Shaver, Mr. Jacob COPP to Miss Sarah GOCHENOUR, all of Shenandoah county.
Rockingham Register and Valley Advertiser, 3 November 1849 (Saturday), p. 2, c. 7.

COPP: On the 9th inst., by Rev. H. Wetzel, Mr. Jno. H. COPP and Mrs. Mary C. WARNER, all of Shenandoah county.
Rockingham Register and Advertiser, 20 April 1866 (Friday), p. 2, c. 3.

CORBEN: See entry for ZIRKLE.

CORBIN: See entry for SEIVER.

CORBIN: On the 20th day of July, by Rev. Jacob Miller, George CORBIN and Miss Permelia, daughter of Isaac SMITH, all of Rockingham.
Rockingham Register and Advertiser, 26 July 1866 (Thursday), p. 3, c. 2.

CORBIN: Near Mount Crawford, by Rev. J.M. Grabill, Mr. John S. CORBIN and Miss Elizabeth PAYNE, all of Rockingham county, Va.
Rockingham Register and Advertiser, 18 November 1859 (Friday), p. 2, c. 4.

CORDER: On Sabbath evening, 7th inst., at the residence of the bride's mother, by the Rev. J.C. Dice, B.F. CORDER and Miss Mary K. HYDER, all of Moorefield.
Rockingham Register, 18 November 1869

(Thursday), p. 3, c. 2.

CORNELL: On the 31st ult., by Rev. Thos. Hildebrand, Andrew CORNELL and Miss Virginia MORRISON, all of Moorefield, W.Va.
Rockingham Register and Advertiser, 16 January 1868 (Thursday), p. 2, c. 5.

CORNER: See entry for SPRINKEL.

CORRELL: See entry for EMSWILER.

COVERSTONE: See entry for BOYER.

COVERSTONE: On the 28th ult., by Rev. Levi Keller, in Powell's Fort, David COVERSTONE and Miss Nancy CLEM, all of Shenandoah.
Rockingham Register, 11 February 1869 (Thursday), p. 3, c. 3.

COWAN: See entry for MANNING (2).

COWAN: See entry for WEST.

COWELL: In Turleytown, on Thursday the 29th ult., by the Rev. John Kline, Mr. Andrew J. COWELL and Miss Maria C., eldest daughter of George MOORE, Esq.
Rockingham Register and Advertiser, 6 August 1858 (Friday), p. 3, c. 2.

COWGER: See entry for TALLEY.

COX: See entry for KOONTZ.

COX: See entry for REYNOLDS.

COX: See entry for WRIGHT.

COX: On the 19th of September, by Rev. C. Beard, Alexander H. COX and Miss Mary E. McCLURE, all of Augusta county.
Rockingham Register and Advertiser, 10 October 1867 (Thursday), p. 3, c. 3.

COX: At Waterford, on the 15th inst., by Rev. A. Neff, Henry C. COX, of Buckingham county, and Miss Sue R., daughter of Rev. John NEFF, of Shenandoah.
Rockingham Register, 24 September 1868 (Thursday), p. 3, c. 4.

COX: Near Lexington, on the 11th of September, by Rev. J.C. Richardson, Mr. Wm. COX and Miss Rebecca CARTER, all of Rockbridge county, Va.
Rockingham Register and Advertiser, 26 September 1856 (Friday), p. 2, c. 6.

COXON: See entry for STORY.

COYNER: See entry for DEDRICK.

COYNER: See entry for HANGER.

COYNER: See entry for ROWELL.

COYNER: On the 13th inst., at New Market, Charles COYNER, of Augusta, and Miss Sarah M., daughter of Solomon D. and Sarah HENKEL.
Rockingham Register, 28 April 1870 (Thursday), p. 3, c. 3.

COYNER: On the 25th of February, by Rev. Martin Garber, Wm. P. COYNER and Miss Sarah C. WHITESELL, all of Augusta county.
Rockingham Register and Advertiser, 19 March 1868 (Thursday), p. 2, c. 4.

CRABILL: See entry for FUNK.

CRABILL: See entry for NULL.

CRABILL: See entry for ROSENBERGER.

CRABILL: Near Strasburg, Shenandoah county, on the 29th of December, by Elder John Pirkey, Elias CRABILL, of Shenandoah, and Mrs. Elizabeth [Mollie] DREW, of Shenandoah county [of Missouri].
Rockingham Register, 7 January 1869 (Thursday), p. 3, c. 3. Repeated, 14 January 1869 (Thursday), p. 3, c. 3. The information in brackets comes from the first announcement.

CRABILL: On the 21st of April, in New Market, by Rev. J.A. Snyder, Joseph W. CRABILL and Miss Mary Susan RICE, all of Shenandoah.
Rockingham Register, 5 May 1870 (Thursday), p. 3, c. 2.

CRABILL: On the 15th inst., by Rev. John Pirkey, Mr. Obed H. CRABILL and Miss Annie BOWMAN, all of Strasburg, Va.
Rockingham Register & Advertiser, 27 October 1865 (Friday), p. 2, c. 3.

CRABILL: On the 26th ult., by Elder John Pirkey, Silas M. CRABILL and Miss Lucretia E. SMOOTZ, all of Shenandoah county.
Rockingham Register and Advertiser, 10 October 1867 (Thursday), p. 3, c. 3.

CRAIG: See entry for WEBB.

CRAIG: On Wednesday morning, the 14th inst., in Botetourt county, at the house of James Miller, Esq., by the Rev. Mr. Grasty, Benj. J. CRAIG, of Augusta county, and Miss Lizzie J., daughter of Mr. Geo. McCHESNEY, Esq., of Texas. Rockingham Register and Advertiser, 30 September 1859 (Friday), p. 2, c. 4.

CRAIG: On Thursday evening the 25th inst. [sic, ult.], by the Rev. Wm. Calhoun, Mr. May B. CRAIG to Miss Martha J., daughter of Col. Franklin McCUE, all of Augusta county. Rockingham Register and Valley Advertiser, 3 November 1849 (Saturday), p. 2. c. 7.

CRAIG: On the 5th ult., by Rev. H. Shaull, William H. CRAIG and Miss Lucinda BOWERS, all of Shenandoah county. Rockingham Register, 7 May 1868 (Thursday), p. 2, c. 4.

CRAUN See entry for KISER.

CRAUN: See entry for WHITMORE.

CRAUN: On the 10th inst., by Rev. Jos. Crickenberger, George A. CRAUN and Miss Amanda E., daughter of Waller ODER, Esq., all of Augusta county. Rockingham Register and Advertiser, 19 December 1867 (Thursday), p. 2, c. 6.

CRAWFORD: See entry for BRUFFEY.

CRAWFORD: See entry for BURKE.

CRAWFORD: See entry for DICKERSON.

CRAWFORD: See entry for LIFE.

CRAWFORD: See entry for LINDAMOOD.

CRAWFORD: See entry for McCAULEY.

CRAWFORD: See entry for MINOR.

CRAWFORD: See entry for MORRIS.

CRAWFORD: See entry for ROLER.

CRAWFORD: See entry for TAYLOR.

CRAWFORD: See entry for WESTON.

CRAWFORD: On the 6th inst., near Doe Hill, Highland county, by Rev. W.T. Price, A.A. CRAWFORD, of Augusta, and Miss Lucy, daughter of the late Josiah HINER, of Highland. Rockingham Register and Advertiser, 18

April 1867 (Thursday), p. 2, c. 6.

CRAWFORD: On the 6th inst., by Rev. John S. Blain, Mr. C.F. CRAWFORD and Miss Lizzie, daughter of Mr. S. MACKEY, near Deerfield, Augusta county.

Rockingham Register and Advertiser, 21 October 1859 (Friday), p. 2, c. 5.

CRAWFORD: On the 24th ult., near Mt. Sidney, James M. CRAWFORD and Miss Mary M. MILLER, all of Augusta.

Rockingham Register, 2 December 1869 (Thursday), p. 2, c. 3.

CRAWFORD: On the 26th of May, by Rev. Wm. Brown, James W. CRAWFORD, Esq., and Miss Caroline Y., daughter of George MESSERSMITH, Esq., all of Augusta county.

Rockingham Register and Advertiser, 12 June 1857 (Friday), p. 3, c. 2.

CRAWFORD: On the 23rd inst., at the residence of Mrs. Hettie Crawford, in this county, by Rev. Mr. Bowman, Jas. W. CRAWFORD, of Staunton, and Miss Cornelia, daughter of Mr. John MILLER, of Rockingham.

Rockingham Register and Advertiser, 31 January 1867 (Thursday), p. 3, c. 2.

CRAWFORD: In New Market, August 3rd, 1863, by Rev. Dr. Jno. P. Hyde, assisted by Rev. Julius Stirewalt, Lieut. John H. CRAWFORD, of Augusta county, to Mrs. Emily C. ZIRKLE, of Shenandoah county.

Rockingham Register, 7 August 1863 (Friday), p. 3, c. 3.

CRAWFORD: On the 3rd inst., by Rev. Mr. Crawford, Robert CRAWFORD and Miss Mary KENDRICK, all of Shenandoah.

Rockingham Register, 17 November 1870 (Thursday), p. 2, c. 3.

CRAWFORD: On Thursday evening of last week, at the Valley Hotel, in Staunton, by the Rev. T.M. Reese, Mr. William CRAWFORD to Miss Sarah ARMSTRONG, all of Augusta county.

Rockingham Register and Valley Advertiser, 8 June 1850 (Saturday), p. 2, c. 7.

CRAWFORD: At Variety Springs, on the 11th

inst., by the Rev. Geo. B. Taylor, Mr.
William T. CRAWFORD and Miss Elizabeth J.
WILLIAMS.
Rockingham Register and Advertiser, 9
January 1868 (Thursday), p. 2, c. 4.
CRAWN: See entry for BARER.
CRAWN: On the 3rd inst., at the house of Mr.
Josiah Neff, by the Rev. John Pinkerton,
Mr. Joseph H. CRAWN and Miss Maria C.
NEFF, all of Augusta county.
Rockingham Register and Advertiser, 11
November 1859 (Friday), p. 3, c. 1.
CRAWN: On Thursday, the 7th inst., at the
residence of Mr. Jacob Baker, by the Rev.
S. Filler, Mr. Samuel H. CRAWN, of
Augusta, and Miss Elizabeth, daughter of
Mr. Samuel BAKER, of Rockingham.
Rockingham Register and Advertiser, 22
April 1859 (Friday), p. 3, c. 1.
CREEL: See entry for MELLONEE.
CREIGH: See entry for WATKINS.
CREIGH: On the 14th inst., at the residence
of the bride's father, near Staunton, by
Rev. W.E. Baker, Mr. Cyrus CREIGH, of
Greenbrier county, and Miss Margaret,
daughter of Col. Wm. P. TATE.
Rockingham Register and Advertiser, 22
November 1866 (Thursday), p. 3, c. 3.
CREWS: On the 21st ult., by Rev. R.H.
Phillips, at the residence of Capt.
Balthis, in Staunton, Josiah S. CREWS, of
Danville, Va., and Miss Martha M. POTTER.
Rockingham Register and Advertiser, 5
July 1866 (Thursday), p. 3, c. 5.
CRICKENBERGER: On Thursday, the 3rd inst., by
Rev. Jos. Funkhouser, Mr. Wm. Anderson
CRICKENBERGER and Miss Josephine DAVIS,
all of Rockingham.
Rockingham Register and Advertiser, 11
May 1860 (Friday), p. 2, c. 6.
CRICKENBERGER: On the 28th of December, at
the residence of the bride's parents, by
the Rev. C.F. Fry, Zachary F.
CRICKENBERGER, of Albemarle, and Miss
Elizabeth F. KERBY, of this county.
Rockingham Register, 13 January 1870

103

(Thursday), p. 3, c. 4.

CRIGLER: On the 30th ult., in Hardy county, by Rev. Selestine Whitmore, John CRIGLER, of Pendleton county, and Miss Sarah WILSON.

Rockingham Register, 20 January 1870 (Thursday), p. 2, c. 5.

CRIGLER: On Thursday the 25th of September, by the Rev. J. Thrush, at that gentleman's residence, Mr. Zachariah CRIGLER and Miss Isabella C., daughter of Jacob ROHR, Sen., all of Harrisonburg.

Rockingham Register and Advertiser, 3 October 1856 (Friday), p. 2, c. 6.

CRISMAN: On the 1st inst., by Rev. J.D. Freed, Lewis CRISMAN and Miss Sarah E. CLEM, all of Shenandoah county.

Rockingham Register, 10 September 1868 (Thursday), p. 2, c. 5.

CRIST: See entry for HARRIS.

CRIST: On the 4th inst., by Rev. John Pinkerton, Lt. J.W. CRIST, Co. I, 5th Va. Infantry, and Miss Mary E., daughter of N.L. BLAKEMORE, Esq., Sangersville, Augusta county, Va.

Rockingham Register and Advertiser, 27 January 1865 (Friday), p. 1, c. 3.

CRIST: On the 9th inst., by Rev. T.D. Bell, Jacob CRIST and Miss Rebecca WAMPLER, all of Rockingham.

Rockingham Register and Advertiser, 17 January 1862 (Friday), p. 3, c. 1.

CRIST: On the 28th of February, by Rev. Jacob Wine, Mr. John W. CRIST and Miss Rebecca CLINE, all of this county.

Rockingham Register and Advertiser, 15 March 1861 (Friday), p. 2, c. 4.

CRIST: On Sunday morning, August 7th, by Rev. Jacob Miller, Mr. John W. CRIST and Miss Sarah, daughter of Michael and Milly SHOWALTER, all of Rockingham county.

The Rockingham Register, 19 August 1864 (Friday), p. 2, c. 3.

CRIST: On the 6th inst., by Rev. J.E. Armstrong, Joseph CRIST and Miss Nancy J. NEWMAN, all of Rockingham county.

Rockingham *Register* and *Advertiser*, 13 September 1866 (Thursday), p. 2, c. 5.

CRIST: At Harper's Ferry Bridge, on the 14th inst., by G.G. Baker, Joseph CRIST and Miss Bettie RITCHEY, both of Rockingham county.

Rockingham *Register*, 21 May 1868 (Thursday), p. 2, c. 5.

CRITES: On the 30th ult., in Moorefield, by Rev. Jno. C. Dice, Wm. CRITES and Miss Emily HUTTER.

Rockingham *Register*, 20 January 1870 (Thursday), p. 2, c. 5.

CRIZEE: On the 10th ult., at the residence of the bride's father, by Rev. Samuel Brown, Miss M.V. RUSH to Mr. John C. CRIZEE, all of Bath.

Rockingham *Register* and *Advertiser*, 2 December 1859 (Friday), p. 2, c. 5.

CROBARGER: See entry for KEISER.

CROFT: See entry for COMER.

CROFT: See entry for STANLEY.

CROMER: See entry for GILMER.

CROMER: See entry for KOONTZ.

CROMER: See entry for RITCHIE.

CROMER: See entry for SHAVER.

CROMER: See entry for SULLIVAN.

CROMER: On Thursday the 15th inst., by the Rev. Henry Brown, Mr. Levi CROMER, of Harrisonburg, and Miss Sarah, daughter of Jacob RALSTON, dec'd, of this county.

Rockingham *Register* and *Valley Advertiser*, 17 October 1846 (Saturday), p. 3, c. 1.

CROMWELL: See entry for BERKELEY.

CROPP: On Thursday evening, the 12th inst., by Rev. J.C. Hensell, Dr. Wm. W. CROPP and Miss Isabella, daughter of Mr. Geo. CARPENTER, of Rockingham.

Rockingham *Register* & *Advertiser*, 22 October 1865 (Friday), p. 3, c. 4.

CROPPER: See entry for McLOUD.

CROSBY: See entry for ANDERSON.

CROSBY: On Thursday, the 29th of January, by Rev. Mr. Wirgman, Mr. Amos CROSBY, Jr., of Churchville, to Miss Fannie, daughter of Capt. P.B. RODGERS, of Big Calf Pasture.

Rockingham Register and Advertiser, 13 February 1857 (Friday), p. 2, c. 5.

CROSBY: On the 30th ult., near Churchville, by Rev. J.W. Hott, James CROSBY and Miss Liza KOONTZ, all of Augusta county.

Rockingham Register, 6 January 1870 (Thursday), p. 3, c. 3.

CROSON: On the 12th inst., at the residence of the bride's father, near Sherando, Augusta county, by the Rev. John N. Lockridge, Franklin CROSON and Miss Sarah M. DRAWBONE, all of Augusta county.

Rockingham Register, 26 May 1870 (Thursday), p. 2, c. 6.

CROSS: See entry for HARLOW.

CROSS: On the 30th ult., near Lebanon, White Sulphur, by Rev. A.A.P. Neel, Thos. H. CROSS and Miss Winnie Matilda BURNS, all of Augusta county.

Rockingham Register and Advertiser, 6 February 1868 (Thursday), p. 2, c. 4.

CROSS: In Leesburg, Va., May 16, by Rev. J.A. Proctor, Rev. Wm. G. CROSS, of the Va. Annual Conference, and Miss Emily A. SAUNDERS, of Leesburg.

Rockingham Register and Advertiser, 24 May 1861 (Friday), p. 3, c. 2.

CROSSLEY: On the 10th inst., in Cumberland, by Rev. L.W. Matthews, John CROSSLEY, of Iowa, and Mrs. Ann C. HULL, of Hampshire county.

Rockingham Register and Virginia Advertiser, 27 May 1854 (Saturday), p. 2, c. 7.

CROUSEHORN: On Thursday, the 7th inst., by the Rev. J.C. Hensell, Mr. John CROUSEHORN and Miss Ann Eliza, eldest daughter of Mr. Samuel PLECKER, of Augusta.

Rockingham Register, 21 October 1869 (Thursday), p. 2, c. 3.

CRUM: At the residence of the bride's father, on Sunday the 21st inst., by the Rev. C.B. Hammack, Mr. John CRUM and Mrs.

Catherine THUMA, all of Augusta county.
Rockingham Register and Advertiser, 26 January 1866 (Friday), p. 3, c. 3.

CRUMPACKER: In Fayette county, Va., on the 13th inst., by Rev. John Thomas, Mr. Jacob CRUMPACKER, of Montgomery, Va., and Miss Susan V., daughter of Jacob SANGER, formerly of Augusta ....
Rockingham Register and Advertiser, 30 November 1860 (Friday), p. 3, c. 1.

CUBBAGE: See entry for HITT.

CUBBAGE: On the 11th inst. by Elder John Huffman, E. CUBBAGE and Miss P.A. SHORT, all of Page county.
Rockingham Register, 25 November 1869 (Thursday), p. 2, c. 3.

CULLARS: See entry for HOCKMAN.

CULLEN: See entry for RISER.

CULLEN: On the 9th inst., by the Rev. J.C. Hensell, Daniel C. CULLEN, of Augusta county, and Miss L.J.P., daughter of H.H. WYANT, of Rockingham county.
Rockingham Register, 23 June 1870 (Thursday), p. 2, c. 4.

CULLEN: On the 20th of September, at Pontiac, Ill., by Rev. John Manker, Mr. James K. CULLEN and Miss Christina L. HARSHBERGER, both formerly of Augusta county, Va.
Rockingham Register and Advertiser, 7 October 1859 (Friday), p. 2, c. 4.

CULLERS: See entry for BURNER.

CULLERS: See entry for FLAHERTY.

CULLERS: On Thursday, the 8th inst., by Elder Henry Jennings, Robert M. CULLERS, of Page county, and Miss Sarah E. BAUSERMAN, of Shenandoah.
Rockingham Register and Advertiser, 23 March 1866 (Friday), p. 3, c. 3.

CULLUM: On the 29th ult., by the Rev. Wm. H. Coffin, Rev. Jeremiah W. CULLUM, of the Methodist Episcopal Church, to Miss Margaret BLAIR, of Augusta county.
Rockingham Register, 18 April 1835 (Saturday), p. 3, c. 3.

CUMMINGS: See entry for CUMMINGS.

CUMMINGS: See entry for SMOOTZ.

CUMMINGS: On the 12th inst., in Harrisonburg, by Rev. T.D. Bell, James CUMMINGS, of Harrison county, W.Va., and Miss Elizabeth CUMMINGS, of Rockingham county. Rockingham Register and Advertiser, 26 December 1867 (Thursday), p. 2, c. 6.

CUMMINGS: See entry for FRANK.

CUMMONS: See entry for HUFF.

CUNINGHAM: At the residence of the bride's father, in Rappahannock county, on the 27th day of January, 1863, by Elder A.M. Grimsley, Daniel P. CUNINGHAM and Miss Martha HITT. The Rockingham Register, 20 February 1863 (Friday), p. 2, c. 3.

CUNNINGHAM: See entry for ALEXANDER.

CUNNINGHAM: See entry for TRUEHEART.

CUNNINGHAM: On the 23rd of December, by the Rev. Mr. Hazlup, Mr. Minor CUNNINGHAM to Miss Hattie, daughter of P.M. TAYLOR, of Grant county. Rockingham Register, 7 January 1869 (Thursday), p. 3, c. 3.

CUNNINGHAM: On the 27th of February, at the residence of the bride's father, on Linvill's Creek, Dr. W.W.J. CUNNINGHAM and Miss Amanda, daughter of Peter ACKER, all of Rockingham. Rockingham Register and Advertiser, 2 March 1866 (Friday), p. 3, c. 3.

CUNNINGHAM: On the 23rd of April, at the residence of the bride's father, in Rushville, by Rev. G.W. Stevenson, Mr. William A. CUNNINGHAM, of Highland county, and Miss Bettie M. KOOGLER, of Rockingham county. Rockingham Register and Advertiser, 16 May 1867 (Thursday), p. 2, c. 5.

CUPP: See entry for COFFMAN.

CUPP: See entry for CUPP.

CUPP: See entry for FIFER.

CUPP: See entry for SEAWRIGHT.

CUPP: By Elder A.C. Booton, on the 20th inst., Mr. Alfred CUPP and Miss Margaret A. PUMPHREY, all of Augusta county. Rockingham Register and Advertiser, 25

November 1859 (Friday), p. 2, c. 4.

CUPP: On the 30th ult., by Rev. John Pinkerton, Frederick CUPP and Miss Ellen J., daughter of Jacob STAUBUS, all of Augusta county.

Rockingham Register and Advertiser, 6 February 1868 (Thursday), p. 2, c. 4.

CUPP: In the Clerk's Office of Augusta county, on the 13th inst., by Rev. John L. Clarke, Henry CUPP and Mrs. Mary Jane CUPP, all of Augusta.

Rockingham Register and Advertiser, 16 May 1867 (Thursday), p. 2, c. 5.

CUPP: On the 30th ult., by the Rev. John Pinkerton, Mr. Joshua CUPP, of Rockingham county, to Mrs. Eliza J. BLAGG, of Augusta.

Rockingham Register and Advertiser, 6 January 1865 (Friday), p. 1, c. 2.

CUPP: On the 30th of August, by the Rev. George A. Shuey, Mr. William CUPP and Miss Susannah, daughter of Mr. George BISHOP, all of Augusta county.

Rockingham Register and Valley Advertiser, 13 October 1849 (Saturday), p. 2, c. 5.

CURRY: See entry for JAVINS.

CURRY: See entry for KOOGLER.

CURRY: See entry for LAMBERT.

CURRY: At Locust Willow Hotel, Bath county, by the Rev. J.W. Canter, Mr. Alexander CURRY to Miss Cynthia RANDULIFFE, all of Bath.

Rockingham Register and Advertiser, 10 August 1860 (Friday), p. 2, c. 5.

CURRY: On the 30th ult., by the Rev. John L. Blakemore, Mr. Thomas C. CURRY and Miss Martha Adaline, daughter of Mr. David RANKIN, all of Augusta county.

Rockingham Register and Valley Advertiser, 13 October 1849 (Saturday), p. 2, c. 5.

CURRY: Near Levelton, on Tuesday, the 21st of February last, by Rev. Jas. S. Gardner, Wm. CURRY, Esq., Clerk of Circuit and County Courts of Pocahontas, and Miss

Lucy, daughter of Capt. Joel HILL, of Little Levels, Pocahontas county, Va. *Rockingham Register and Advertiser*, 4 May 1860 (Friday), p. 2, c. 4.

CUSHING: See entry for YOUNT.

CUTHBERT: See entry for FETZER.

- D -

DABNEY: On the 7th of February, by Rev. Wm. McK. Ward, Robt. W. DABNEY, Esq., and Miss Mary Frances, daughter of Mr. Edmond NUCKALLS, all of Louisa county, Va. *Rockingham Register and Virginia Advertiser*, 22 February 1856 (Friday), p. 2, c. 8.

DAGGY: On the 27th of December, by the Rev. Jas. H. Wolff, Mr. John H. DAGGY to Miss Sarah D. BURNS, all of Bath county. *Rockingham Register and Advertiser*, 25 January 1861 (Friday), p. 3, c. 1.

DANGERFIELD: See entry for MASON.

DANGERFIELD: At the Old School Presbyterian Church, in Harrisonburg, on Wednesday evening of last week, by Rev. Mr. Latane, Capt. Foxhall A. DANGERFIELD, of the 11th Va. Cavalry, C.S.A., and Miss Henrietta H., daughter of Col. A.S. GRAY, of this place. *The Rockingham Register*, 13 November 1863 (Friday), p. 2, c. 6.

DANNER: See entry for HARRIS.

DANNER: See entry for WALTON.

DANNER: By Elder A.C. Booton, on the 13th inst., Mr. George Wilson DANNER and Miss Nancy Susan SMITH, both of Rockbridge county. *Rockingham Register and Advertiser*, 25 November 1859 (Friday), p. 2, c. 4.

DARFLINGER: On the 15th inst., by Rev. W.G. Coe, Jonas DARFLINGER and Miss Rachel FREDERICK, all of Warren county. *Rockingham Register and Advertiser*, 22 November 1866 (Thursday), p. 3, c. 3.

DARNEILE: On the 19th of November, in the Baptist Church at Scottsville, by Rev.

Chas. Wingfield, Mr. James M. DARNEILE and Mrs. Mary CLARK, widow of Dr. Geo. CLARK, dec'd, formerly of Harrisonburg.
Rockingham Register and Valley Advertiser, 30 December 1843 (Saturday), p. 4, c. 1.

DARNELL: On the 15th ult., by Rev. J.W. Watson, Mr. Alexander H. DARNELL and Miss Laura, daughter of Mordecai J. CLOUD, all of Page.
Rockingham Register and Advertiser, 2 November 1860 (Friday), p. 2, c. 5.

DARRER: On the 21st inst., at the American Hotel, Harrisonburg, by the Rev. T.D. Bell, Mr. George R. DARRER and Miss Isabella H. ARMENTROUT, all of Rockingham.
Rockingham Register and Advertiser, 29 June 1860 (Friday), p. 3, c. 2.

DASHIELL: On the 4th inst., at Union Church, Washington City, by Rev. John H. Dashiell, Rev. Robert L. DASHIELL, of the Baltimore Annual Conference, and Miss Mary Jane HANLY, of Washington.
Rockingham Register and Virginia Advertiser, 27 May 1854 (Saturday), p. 2, c. 7.

DAUGHERTY: See entry for MULLEN.

DAUGHERTY: On the 1st inst., by Rev. S.H. Griffith, James H. DAUGHERTY, of Moorefield, and Miss Mattie HOPKINS, of Pendleton county.
Rockingham Register, 16 April 1868 (Thursday), p. 2, c. 5.

DAUGHERTY: On Thursday, August 27th, by Rev. James H. Shreckhise, Wm. H. DAUGHERTY and Miss Mary C. WISEMAN, all of Augusta.
Rockingham Register, 3 September 1868 (Thursday), p. 2, c. 4.

DAVIDSON: See entry for SIBOLE.

DAVIES: Near Sangersville, on the 17th inst., by Rev. John Pinkerton, Wm. H. DAVIES, M.D., and Miss Margaret A., daughter of Mr. Henry PHILLIPS, of Augusta.
Rockingham Register and Advertiser, 31 October 1867 (Thursday), p. 2, c. 6.

DAVIS: See entry for CRICKENBERGER.
DAVIS: See entry for DETTOR.
DAVIS: See entry for DICE.
DAVIS: See entry for FLEISHER.
DAVIS: See entry for JACKSON.
DAVIS: See entry for KOONTZ.
DAVIS: See entry for MOFFETT.
DAVIS: See entry for WHITESELL.
DAVIS: October 24th, at Mt. Clinton, by Rev. T.D. Bell, Mr. F. Randolph DAVIS, of Hampshire county, and Miss Lydia K., daughter of Mr. David SHOWALTER, of Rockingham county.
Rockingham Register & Advertiser, 3 November 1865 (Friday), p. 2, c. 2.
DAVIS: On Thursday evening, the 11th inst., by Rev. A.G. Brown, Mr. Frank DAVIS and Miss Margaret, daughter of Mr. Nelson RODGERS, all of Harrisonburg.
Rockingham Register and Advertiser, 19 June 1857 (Friday), p. 3, c. 2.
DAVIS: On the 9th inst., by Rev. J.E. Armstrong, Henry J. DAVIS and Miss Mary HERNDON, all of Staunton.
Rockingham Register and Advertiser, 13 September 1866 (Thursday), p. 2, c. 5.
DAVIS: On Thursday, the 22nd day of September, by Rev. W.P. Twyman, Mr. John B. DAVIS and Miss Sallie E. SAMUELS, all of Page county.
Rockingham Register and Advertiser, 7 October 1859 (Friday), p. 2, c. 4.
DAVIS: At Houston, Miss., at the residence of Mrs. Baldwin, on the 5th inst., by Rev. W.A. Clarke, Gen. Reuben DAVIS, of Aberdeen, and Miss Sallie Virginia GARBER, late of Staunton, Va.
Rockingham Register and Advertiser, 27 June 1867 (Thursday), p. 2, c. 6.
DAVIS: At New Hope, on the 7th inst., by Rev. J.J. Engle, Capt. Robert C. DAVIS and Miss Elizabeth J. SCOTT, all of Augusta county.
Rockingham Register and Advertiser, 19 December 1867 (Thursday), p. 2, c. 6.
DAVIS: At Hill's Hotel, in this place, on

Thursday, the 20th inst., by Rev. A. Poe Boude, William H. DAVIS, of Page county, and Miss Louisa C. BEAZLEY, of Rockingham county.

Rockingham Register and Advertiser, 27 September 1866 (Thursday), p. 3, c. 3.

DAVIS: On the 4th of January, by Elder C. Allemong, Wm. R. DAVIS and Miss Virginia E. HENSLEY, both of Rockingham county.

Rockingham Register and Advertiser, 12 January 1866 (Friday), p. 2, c. 3.

DAY: See entry for BAUGHMAN.

DAY: See entry for SHIPP.

DAY: On the 20th ult., by Rev. W.W. Trimble, Mr. Geo. W. DAY and Miss Mary E., daughter of Levi WHITE, all of Rockbridge.

Rockingham Register and Advertiser, 11 January 1861 (Friday), p. 3, c. 4.

DEAN: On the 6th inst., by Rev. Jos. Funkhouser, Wm. DEAN and Miss Louisa L. GAITHER, all of Rockingham county.

Rockingham Register and Advertiser, 13 September 1866 (Thursday), p. 2, c. 5.

DEAN: On the 21st ult., by Rev. D. Feete, Mr. Zedekiah DEAN and Miss Martha BARK, all of Shenandoah.

Rockingham Register and Advertiser, 3 February 1860 (Friday), p. 2, c. 5.

DEANE: See entry for HENSLEY.

DEANERS: On the 26th inst., by the Rev. J.B. Houck, Mr. Michael DEANERS and Miss Leannah Frances SPITZER, all of Rockingham county.

Rockingham Register and Valley Advertiser, 29 May 1852 (Saturday), p. 2, c. 6.

DEARING: See entry for MONGER.

DEBARD: See entry for BOWMAN.

DECKER: See entry for GRAY.

DECKER: On the 11th of September, by the Rev. A.J. Coffman, Mr. And. J. DECKER and Miss Amanda SMITH, all of Page county.

Rockingham Register and Advertiser, 3 October 1856 (Friday), p. 2, c. 6.

DEDRICK: On the 8th inst., near Sherando,

Augusta county, by Rev. Mr. Wirgman, Mr.
James M. DEDRICK and Miss Rosannah
COYNER, all of Augusta county.
Rockingham Register and Advertiser, 16
September 1859 (Friday), p. 2, c. 4.
DEEHL: See entry for RETSEL.
DEELS: By Rev. I. Condor, on the 23rd ult.,
Adam DEELS and Miss Elizabeth HASLER, all
of Rockingham.
Rockingham Register, 7 April 1870
(Thursday), p. 2, c. 5.
DELAUGHTER: See entry for KNEFF.
DELAUGHTER: See entry for WEAVER.
DELAUTER: See entry for STRAWDERMAN.
DELLINGER: See entry for HELSLEY.
DELLINGER: See entry for ROLLER.
DELLINGER: See entry for WILKINS.
DELLINGER: On the 25th ult., by Rev. J.W.
Wolff, Mr. Geo. R. DELLINGER and Miss
Sarah E., daughter of the late Stephen
BARR, dec'd, all of Shenandoah.
Rockingham Register and Advertiser, 2
November 1860 (Friday), p. 2, c. 5.
DELLINGER: On the 30th ult., by Rev. John
Clymer, Geo. W. DELLINGER and Miss Annie
C. WYSMAN, both of Shenandoah county.
Rockingham Register, 13 January 1870
(Thursday), p. 3, c. 4.
DELLINGER: On Thursday, the 16th inst., by
Rev. Solomon Garber, Israel P. DELLINGER
and Miss Sarah Catharine, daughter of
Samuel HOOVER, dec'd, all of Rockingham
county.
Rockingham Register and Advertiser, 30
August 1866 (Thursday), p. 2, c. 5.
DELLINGER: On the 27th ult., by Rev. D.
Feete, Mr. John DELLINGER and Miss Jane
E., daughter of Jacob HOTTEL, all of
Shenandoah county.
Rockingham Register and Advertiser, 15
March 1861 (Friday), p. 2, c. 4.
DELLINGER: On the 17th, by the Rev. Joseph
Funkhouser, Mr. Joshua DELLINGER to Miss
Christiana NAUGLE, of Shenandoah county.
The Rockingham Register and Valley
Advertiser, 26 June 1852 (Saturday), p.

114

2, c. 5.

DELLINGER: On the 17th inst., by Rev. H. Wetzel, Mr. Philip C. DELLINGER and Miss Mary LUTZ, both of Shenandoah.
Rockingham Register, 31 March 1870 (Thursday), p. 3, c. 3.

DELOARD: See entry for BOWMAN.

DEMASTERS: See entry for CAMPBELL.

DENNETT: See entry for RUNCLE.

DENNETT: See entry for SCOTT.

DENNETT: On the 15th of November, by the Rev. Isaac Long, Geo. H. DENNETT and Miss Ellen, daughter of Jackson GARRISON, all of Rockingham.
Rockingham Register and Advertiser, 22 November 1866 (Thursday), p. 3, c. 3.

DENTON: On the 23rd of August, in Springfield, Illinois, by Rev. Wm. S. Prentice, Mr. Jackson DENTON, formerly of Rockingham county, Va., and Miss Mary E. PEEL, formerly of Lexington, Kentucky.
Rockingham Register and Advertiser, 14 September 1860 (Friday), p. 2, c. 5.

DENTON: April 10th, by the Rev. Jas. C. Hensell, James W. DENTON, of Rockingham, and Miss Elizabeth J., eldest daughter of George HERSH, of Augusta.
Rockingham Register, 21 April 1870 (Thursday), p. 3, c. 3.

DEPOY: On the 25th of March, by Rev. Jacob Miller, at the residence of Henry Hale, Mr. Charles DEPOY and Miss Elizabeth KESLER, all of Rockingham county.
Rockingham Register and Advertiser, 6 April 1866 (Friday), p. 3, c. 3.

DEPOY: On Thursday, the 6th inst., by Rev. Jacob Miller, Mr. Isaac DEPOY and Miss Jemima Jane, daughter of John WILLIAMS, dec'd, all of Rockingham county.
Rockingham Register and Advertiser, 14 October 1859 (Friday), p. 2, c. 3.

DEPUTY: See entry for DUNDORE.

DERROW: See entry for PENCE.

DERROW: On the 11th of November, by Rev. Isaac Long, Henry J. DERROW and Miss Mary S. HIGH, all of Rockingham.

November 1866 (Thursday), p. 3, c. 3.

DESHLER: See entry for LANE.

DESPER: On Thursday, the 2nd inst., by Rev.
G.G. Brooke, Mr. Joseph DESPER to Miss
Julia TISDALE - all of Augusta county.
Rockingham Register and Advertiser, 10
December 1858 (Friday), p. 3, c. 2.

DETAMORE: See entry for PRICE.

DETAMORE: On the 5th inst., by Rev. E. Welty,
Mr. John Wm. DETAMORE and Miss Susan M.
JARROLS, all of this county.
Rockingham Register and Advertiser, 8
January 1858 (Friday), p. 3, c. 1.

DETRICK: On the 22nd of December, 1859, by
Rev. Daniel Thomas, Mr. John G. DETRICK
and Miss Maria Jane, daughter of Mr.
Richard ROBINSON, all of Rockingham.
Rockingham Register and Advertiser, 13
January 1860 (Friday), p. 2, c. 6.

DETTOR: See entry for WARTMANN.

DETTOR: At the residence of the bride's
father, on the 12th inst., by Rev. S.F.
Butt, Allake DETTOR, of Albemarle county,
and Miss Sallie M. DAVIS, of Highland
county.
Rockingham Register and Advertiser, 21
March 1867 (Thursday), p. 2, c. 5.

DEVER: See entry for CARRIER.

DEVER: See entry for KILMER.

DEVER: See entry for PULLIN.

DEVER: On the 10th inst., by Rev. J.
Pinkerton, at the residence of the
bride's father, in Bridgewater, Lt. D.B.
DEVER, of Co. I, 1st Va. Cavalry, and
Miss Sarah E., daughter of Mr. John
DINKLE.
The Rockingham Register, 19 February 1864
(Friday), p. 2, c. 6.

DEVER: On the 9th inst., by Rev. John
Pinkerton, Mr. James A. DEVER and Miss
Mary J. BLAKEMORE, all of Rockingham.
The Rockingham Register, 22 April 1864
(Friday), p. 2, c. 6.

DEVER: On the 24th of December, at the
residence of the bride's father, by Rev.

116

John Pinkerton, Mr. John H. DEVER, C.S.A., of Rockingham county, and Miss Maggie J., daughter of William PHILIPS, of Augusta county.
The Rockingham Register, 8 January 1864 (Friday), p. 2, c. 5.

DeVERE: At Carlton, near Charlottesville, on Wednesday morning, the 21st, by the Rev. R.K. Meade, Prof. M. Schele DeVERE, of the University of Virginia, to Miss Lucy B., daughter of Alexander RIVES, Esq.
Rockingham Register and Advertiser, 30 March 1860 (Friday), p. 2, c. 4.

DEVERICKE: On the 26th ult., at Lebanon, White Sulphur Springs, by the Rev. Thomas Hildebrand, Mr. Thos. M. DEVERICKE, of Highland county, and Miss Mary M. RODGERS, of Augusta county.
Rockingham Register and Advertiser, 20 April 1866 (Friday), p. 2, c. 3.

DEVERS: On the 29th of December, by Rev. Jacob Miller, William DEVERS and Miss Sarah Frances, daughter of Abraham LIFE, all of Rockingham.
Rockingham Register and Advertiser, 9 January 1868 (Thursday), p. 2, c. 4.

DEVIER: See entry for CAMPBELL.

DEVIER: See entry for DEVIER.

DEVIER: See entry for MOORE.

DEVIER: On Thursday evening, the 27th of April, at the Metropolitan Hotel, Washington City, D.C., by Rev. C.C. Meador, Mr. Hiram K. DEVIER, of Warm Springs, Bath county, Va., and Miss Mary B., eldestdaughter of Derrick PENNYBACKER, Esq., of Rockingham county.
Rockingham Register and Advertiser, 4 May 1866 (Friday), p. 3, c. 2.

DEVIER: On the 23rd ult., near McDowell, Highland county, by Rev. W.T. Price, Lucius A. DEVIER, of Rockingham, and Miss Lucy Brandon, daughter of Ewing DEVIER, Esq., of Highland county.
Rockingham Register and Advertiser, 6 September 1866 (Thursday), p. 2, c. 5.

DEWER: See entry for HOTTEL.

DEYERLE: See entry for FORRER.

DICE: See entry for HARMON.

DICE: On Sunday evening, the 12th of May, by Rev. Isaac Soule, Mr. Franklin H. DICE, of Pendleton county, and Miss Mary A., daughter of Mr. Jacob ANDREW, dec'd, of Beaver Creek, Rockingham county.
Rockingham Register and Advertiser, 17 May 1861 (Friday), p. 3, c. 3.

DICE: On the 9th inst., by Rev. Mr. Freed, Mr. Geo. W. DICE, Jr., to Miss Sarah C. DAVIS, all of Pendleton county.
Rockingham Register and Advertiser, 21 October 1859 (Friday), p. 2, c. 5.

DICE: On Tuesday, the 18th inst., by the Rev. Abner W. Kilpatrick, Capt. John A. DICE, of Pendleton county, to Miss Eleanor, daughter of Mr. James FULTON, of this county.
Rockingham Register, 22 April 1837 (Saturday), p. 3, c. 3.

DICE: On the 14th inst., by Rev. G. Stevenson, at the residence of the bride's father, P.H. DICE, of Rockingham county, and Miss R.A. RIVERCOMB, of Sangersville, Augusta county.
Rockingham Register and Advertiser, 21 November 1867 (Thursday), p. 2, c. 5.

DICKENSON: On the 26th of May, by Rev. Samuel Brown, at the house of Capt. Andrew Sitlington, Mr. Joseph B. DICKENSON to Miss Margaret Ann SITLINGTON, all of Bath county.
Rockingham Register and Virginia Advertiser, 13 June 1856 (Friday), p. 2, c. 2.

DICKERSON: On the 29th ult., by Rev. J.C. Baker, H.B. DICKERSON, of Charlotte county, Va., and Miss Julia A. CRAWFORD, of Augusta county.
Rockingham Register and Advertiser, 7 June 1866 (Thursday), p. 3, c. 3.

DILL: See entry for AYERS.

DILLARD: See entry for BEAZELL.

DILLARD: On Thursday evening last, by the Rev. Jacob B. Houck, Mr. John DILLARD, of

Augusta, and Miss Sophronia, daughter of Mr. Peter IRICK, of Rockingham.
Rockingham Register and Valley Advertiser, 9 April 1842, p. 3, c. 1.

DILLER: See entry for SECRIST.

DINGES: On Tuesday, the 13th inst., at the residence of the bride's father, in Wardensville, Hardy county, W.Va., by Rev. C.L. Torreyson, Mr. David A. DINGES and Miss Mary Virginia, daughter of Hugh McKEEVER, Esq., all of Hardy county.
Rockingham Register, 6 May 1869 (Thursday), p. 2, c. 3.

DINGLEDINE: On Tuesday, the 16th of November, by Rev. Jacob Miller, Mr. John H. DINGLEDINE, of Shenandoah county, and Miss Mary K., daughter of Mr. J.J. MILLER, of Rockingham county.
Rockingham Register and Advertiser, 26 November 1858 (Friday), p. 3, c. 2.

DINGLEDINE: On the 27th of November, by the Rev. J.W. Howe, Mr. Philip DINGLEDINE and Miss Catharine V. MILLER, all of this county.
Rockingham Register and Advertiser, 13 December 1866 (Thursday), p. 2, c. 5.

DINKEL: See entry for FISHER.

DINKEL: See entry for HERRING.

DINKEL: See entry for PRIEST.

DINKEL: See entry for TUTWILER.

DINKEL: On Thursday, the 5th inst., by Rev. G.W. Statton, Mr. James M. DINKEL, of Saline county, Mo., and Miss Ann C. HINER, of Bridgewater, Rockingham county.
Rockingham Register and Advertiser, 13 May 1859 (Friday), p. 3, c. 4.

DINKLE: See entry for DEVER.

DINKLE: See entry for MESSERLY.

DINKLE: See entry for SMALS.

DINKLE: See entry for WINE.

DINKLE: On the 18th ult., by Rev. Wm. H. Dinkel, Jacob DINKLE and Miss Nancy W. CAMDEN, all of Rockingham.
Rockingham Register and Advertiser, 8 November 1866 (Thursday), p. 3, c. 4.

DINKLE: On the 18th of February, by Rev.

Thomas E. Carson, Joseph DINKLE and Miss Mary C., daughter of Col. Wm. F. PIFER, all of Bridgewater, Rockingham county. Rockingham Register, 4 March 1869 (Thursday), p. 2, c. 4.

DIRTING: See entry for YEW.

DIVELBISS: Near Greenville, Augusta county, on Thursday morning last, by Rev. J. McK. Riley, Mr. John A. DIVELBISS, formerly of Mercersburg, Pa., and Miss Julia A., daughter of David GROVE, dec'd, of Augusta county. Rockingham Register and Valley Advertiser, 3 November 1849 (Saturday), p. 2, c. 7.

DIXON: On the 21st inst., near Bridgewater, by Rev. Solomon Garber, Samuel M. DIXON and Mrs. Martha E. FRY, all of Rockingham county. Rockingham Register, 30 June 1870 (Thursday), p. 2, c. 5.

DIZARD: On horseback, in the streets of Huntersville, West Va., on the 22nd ult., by Rev. M.D. Dunlap, Asbury DIZARD, of Greenbrier county, and Miss Lizzie McCUTCHEN, of Pocahontas. Rockingham Register, 8 October 1868 (Thursday), p. 3, c. 3.

DODSON: On the 21st ult., by Rev. Henry St. J. Rinker, Mr. Charles F. DODSON and Miss Elizabeth F. FRY, all of Shenandoah county. Rockingham Register and Advertiser, 8 July 1859 (Friday), p. 2, c. 5.

DOFFENMOYER: See entry for SNYDER.

DOFFLEMOYER: On the 31st of December, by Rev. Solomon Garber, Jas. DOFFLEMOYER, formerly of Page county, and Miss Susan R., daughter of Tandy DOVEL, of Rockingham county. Rockingham Register, 14 January 1869 (Thursday), p. 3, c. 3.

DOLD: In Harrisonburg, on Wednesday, April 11th, by Rev. T.D. Bell, C.M. DOLD, of Rockbridge county, and Miss Emma, daughter of Henry OTT, Esq., of this place.

Rockingham _Register_ and _Advertiser_, 13
April 1866 (Friday), p. 3, c. 2.

DOLD: On the 27th of February, at the
residence of the bride's father, A.B.
IRICK, Esq., by Rev. D.C. Irwin, Dr. S.M.
DOLD and Miss Sallie IRICK, all of this
place.

Rockingham _Register_ and _Advertiser_, 2
March 1866 (Friday), p. 3, c. 3.

DOLL: Near Forestville, on the 9th ult., by
Rev. J.P. Cline, Mr. Isaac T. DOLL and
Miss Amanda, youngest daughter of the
late John SMOOTZ.

Rockingham _Register_ and _Advertiser_, 7
September 1860 (Friday), p. 2, c. 5.

DOLLY: See entry for ARMENTROUT.

DOLLY: In Bridgewater, on the 4th inst., by
Rev. J.N. Davis, Rev. Enoch B. DOLLY, of
the M.E. Church, and Miss Ann E.,
daughter of Samuel H. HUFFMAN.

Rockingham _Register_ and _Advertiser_, 7
October 1859 (Friday), p. 2, c. 4.

DONALDSON: See entry for MAGRUDER.

DONELEY: On the 24th ult., in Newtown, by the
Rev. John Allemong, Wm. J. DONELEY, of
Darien, Ga., and Miss Annie A., eldest
daughter of the late Simon LAUCK, of
Newtown.

Rockingham _Register_ and _Advertiser_, 7
November 1867 (Thursday), p. 2, c. 5.

DONSON: See entry for BAYLEY.

DOOLEY: At the residence of Maj. Elder in
Staunton, on Saturday morning, September
11th, by Rev. Father Weed, James H.
DOOLEY, of Richmond, Va., to Miss Sallie
O. MAY, formerly of Lunenburg.

Rockingham _Register_, 23 September 1869
(Thursday), p. 2, c. 3.

DOOM: On Friday, May 18th, by Rev. Geo.
Kramer, Kenton H. DOOM to Miss Araminta
BRADY, both of Staunton.

Rockingham _Register_, 27 May 1869
(Thursday), p. 2, c. 3.

DORMAN: See entry for GETTS.

DORSEY: See entry for BROWN.

DOUGLAS: See entry for BRECKENBAUGH.

DOUGLAS: See entry for ROGERS.

DOVAL: See entry for MAYES.

DOVAL: On the 27th ult., by Rev. J.W. Watson, Peter S. DOVAL and Miss E.S., daughter of Adam PETERFISH.
Rockingham Register and Advertiser, 18 November 1859 (Friday), p. 2, c. 4.

DOVE: See entry for ADAMS.

DOVE: See entry for FINK.

DOVE: On the 18th October, by Rev. Timothy Funk, Benjamin F. DOVE and Miss Sallie C. RALSTON, all of Rockingham county.
Rockingham Register and Advertiser, 1 November 1866 (Thursday), p. 3, c. 4.

DOVE: On Thursday, the 26th of April, by Rev. Joseph Funkhouser, Mr. Jacob DOVE and Miss Julia Ann, daughter of Jacob CAPLINGER, Esq., of Brock's Gap, Rockingham county.
Rockingham Register and Advertiser, 4 May 1860 (Friday), p. 2, c. 4.

DOVEL: See entry for DOFFLEMOYER.

DOVEL: See entry for DOVEL (2).

DOVEL: See entry for MILLER.

DOVEL: On Thursday the 11th inst., by Elder C. Allemong, Mr. Abraham DOVEL and Miss Elizabeth GROVE, all of Page county.
Rockingham Register and Advertiser, 26 January 1866 (Friday), p. 3, c. 3.

DOVEL: On the 8th of December, 1859, by Rev. John Kline, Mr. Daniel DOVEL, of Page county, and Miss Elizabeth, daughter of Rev. Abram KNOPP, of Rockingham.
Rockingham Register and Advertiser, 3 February 1860 (Friday), p. 2, c. 5.

DOVEL: On the 18th of January, by Elder C. Allemong, Daniel D. DOVEL and Miss Maria BOSTON, both of Rockingham county.
Rockingham Register and Advertiser, 17 February 1865 (Friday), p. 2, c. 4.

DOVEL: On the 19th inst., by Rev. J.W. Watson, Mr. David F. DOVEL and Miss Sarah J., daughter of George SUMMERS, Esq., all of Page county.
Rockingham Register & Advertiser, 29

September 1865 (Friday), p. 3, c. 3.

DOVEL: On the 26th day of July, 1866, by Rev. E.C. Alamong, Geo. A. DOVEL and Miss M.J. WOLFLY, both of Page county. Rockingham Register and Advertiser, 30 August 1866 (Thursday), p. 2, c. 4.

DOVEL: On the 19th inst., by Elder Philip McInturf, Mr. Harrison C. DOVEL and Mrs. Elizabeth HOLTZMAN, all of Page county. Rockingham Register & Advertiser, 29 September 1865 (Friday), p. 3, c. 3.

DOVEL: On the 21st ult., by Rev. V.T. Settle, Mr. James S. DOVEL, of Page, and Miss Clara V. DOVEL, of Rockingham. Rockingham Register and Advertiser, 2 March 1860 (Friday), p. 3, c. 2.

DOVEL: On the 13th inst., in Harrisonburg, by Rev. T.D. Bell, Mr. Jeremiah DOVEL and Miss Harriet SIGLER, all of Rockingham. Rockingham Register and Advertiser, 21 December 1860 (Friday), p. 2, c. 6.

DOVEL: On the 21st ult., at the residence of the groom's father, by Rev. Solomon Garber, Mr. Lucius B. DOVEL and Miss Cinderilla DOVEL, all of this county. Rockingham Register & Advertiser, 6 October 1865 (Friday), p. 2, c. 2.

DOVELL: See entry for DOVELL.

DOVELL: On Sunday morning, the 14th inst., at the residence of Mr. David Garber, by the Rev. J.C. Hensell, Mr. Tandy DOVELL, Jun., to Miss Mary Ann, daughter of John DOVELL, all of Rockingham county. Rockingham Register and Virginia Advertiser, 19 September 1862 (Friday), p. 2, c. 2.

DOWELLE: See entry for BOYERS.

DOWNEY: See entry for EVANS (2).

DOWNEY: On November 8th, at Variety Springs, Augusta county, by Rev. M.A. Taylor, A.F. DOWNEY, of Rockbridge, and Miss Mary E. SMELTZ, of Augusta. Rockingham Register, 24 November 1870 (Thursday), p. 2, c. 4.

DOYLE: On Thursday, the 26th ult., by Rev. G.G. Brooke, Allison DOYLE and Mary C.

ZOAN, all of Augusta county.
Rockingham Register and Advertiser, 4
November 1859 (Friday), p. 2, c. 6.
DOYLE: At the residence of G.G. Grattan,
Esq., on the 13th of September, 1870, by
Rev. J. Rice Bowman, Capt. Thos. DOYLE,
of Natchez, Mississippi, and Miss Louisa
M., of Harrisonburg, youngest daughter of
the   late   Maj.   R.   GRATTAN,   of
"Contentment," Rockingham county, Va.
Rockingham Register, 15 September 1870
(Thursday), p. 3, c. 3.
DRAKE: In the Episcopal Church, at Little
Washington, on Wednesday, the 15th inst.,
by Rev. Mr. Brown, D.W. DRAKE, of
Staunton, and Miss Kate Murat SLAUGHTER,
of Rappahannock county.
Rockingham Register, 23 April 1868
(Thursday), p. 2, c. 5.
DRAWBONE: See entry for CROSON.
DREW: See entry for CRABILL.
DRIVER: See entry for CLINE.
DRIVER: See entry for GARBER.
DRIVER: See entry for KARACOFE.
DRIVER: See entry for WAMPLER.
DRIVER: On the 27th of February, by Rev.
Jacob Wine, David J. DRIVER and Miss
Elizabeth EARLY, all of Rockingham
county.
Rockingham Register and Advertiser, 5
March 1868 (Thursday), p. 2, c. 4.
DRIVER: On Tuesday, the 11th of May, by Rev.
Jacob Thomas, Jacob DRIVER and Miss
Sarah, daughter of Wm. P. McCALL, both of
Augusta county.
Rockingham Register, 20 May 1869
(Thursday), p. 2, c. 3.
DRIVER: On the 19th of December, 1865, by
Rev. Jacob Miller, Mr. John C. DRIVER and
Miss Catharine BAENNER, all of Rockingham
county.
Rockingham Register and Advertiser, 12
January 1866 (Friday), p. 1, c. 3.
DRIVER: On the 18th inst., by Rev. J.
Stirewalt, John F. DRIVER and Miss
Catharine RIFE, all of Rockingham county.

Rockingham Register, 29 October 1868
(Thursday), p. 3, c. 3.

DRUMHELLER: Near Cline's Mill, on the 17th
inst., by Rev. A.A.P. Neel, Napoleon J.
DRUMHELLER and Miss Pennina E. GOLLADAY,
both of Augusta county.

Rockingham Register, 24 February 1870
(Thursday), p. 2, c. 5.

DRUMHELLER: On the 23rd of September, by Rev.
Isaac Long, Wm. P. DRUMHELLER, of Augusta
county, and Rowena S., daughter of Silas
CAVE, of Rockingham county.

Rockingham Register, 28 October 1869
(Thursday), p. 2, c. 3.

DRUMMOND: See entry for JENKINS.

DRUMMOND: See entry for ROOMBURG.

DUCKETT: See entry for HALL.

DUDLEY: See entry for KELLER.

DUDLEY: See entry for TREVY.

DUDLEY: See entry for TUTWILER.

DUDLEY: In Christ Church, Norfolk, on the 6th
inst., by Rev. O.S. Barten, Rev. T.U.
DUDLEY, Rector of Christ Church,
Baltimore, formerly of Harrisonburg, and
Virginia, second daughter of John H.
ROWLAND, Esq.

Rockingham Register, 15 April 1869
(Thursday), p. 2, c. 4.

DUEY: On the 27th of December, at Mt.
Crawford, by Rev. J.E. Chambliss, Geo. W.
DUEY and Miss Mary E. TURLEY, all of
Rockingham.

Rockingham Register, 7 January 1869
(Thursday), p. 3, c. 3.

DUFF: See entry for BAUGHER.

DUFFEY: See entry for BOWERS.

DULL: On the 28th ult., by Rev. Thomas L.
Preston, Alexander DULL and Miss Sarah F.
LIVICK.

Rockingham Register and Advertiser, 4
April 1867 (Thursday), p. 3, c. 4.

DULL: On the 3rd inst., by Rev. X.J.
Richardson, Mr. David DULL and Miss Anne
E. STOCKDALE, all of Augusta county.

Rockingham Register and Advertiser, 18
November 1859 (Friday), p. 2, c. 4.

DUNCAN: At the residence of the bride's father, in Harrisonburg, on Wednesday the 18th of December, by Rev. J.C. Hensel, Wm. B. DUNCAN, formerly of Cumberland county, Pa., and Miss Laura A., daughter of Jos. D. PRICE, Esq., of this place, formerly of Hagerstown, Maryland.
Rockingham Register and Advertiser, 9 January 1868 (Thursday), p. 2, c. 4.

DUNDORE: On Thursday, the 28th of February, by Rev. T.D. Bell, Mr. Jacob DUNDORE and Miss Mary DEPUTY, all of Rockingham.
Rockingham Register and Advertiser, 8 March 1861 (Friday), p. 3, c. 1.

DUNKAN: See entry for JUDD.

DUNLAP: See entry for GILES.

DUNLAP: On the 27th of March, by Rev. D.B. Ewing, James L. DUNLAP and Miss Mary A. KERR, both of Augusta.
Rockingham Register, 7 April 1870 (Thursday), p. 2, c. 5.

DUNLAP: On the 7th November, by Rev. J.I. Miller, John C. DUNLAP and Miss Theresa M. McCHESNEY, all of Augusta county.
Rockingham Register and Advertiser, 20 December 1866 (Thursday), p. 2, c. 5.

DUNLAP: On the 8th inst., by Rev. R. Walker, Robert B. DUNLAP and Miss Amelia M. MISH.
Rockingham Register and Advertiser, 23 March 1866 (Friday), p. 3, c. 3.

DUNLAP: On the 20th of March, by Rev. D.B. Ewing, Wm. B. DUNLAP and Miss Sarah C. BROWN, both of Augusta.
Rockingham Register, 7 April 1870 (Thursday), p. 2, c. 5.

DUNLAP: At the residence of the bride's father, near Newport, in Augusta county, by Rev. J.O. Miller, on Thursday, the 2nd inst., Wm. R. DUNLAP and Mrs. ____ BLAIR, all of Augusta.
Rockingham Register, 9 July 1868 (Thursday), p. 2, c. 5.

DUNN: See entry for PANNILL.

DUNN: By Rev. Horatio Thompson, D.D., on the 6th inst., Mr. S.H. DUNN, of Lynchburg, and Miss E.A. WHITE, of Rockbridge.

Rockingham Register and Advertiser, 11
January 1861 (Friday), p. 3, c. 4.
DUNNIVANT: On the 14th inst., by Rev. J.C.
Hensel, on Cub Run, John M. DUNNIVANT and
Miss Margaret Jane, second daughter of
William N. JORDAN, all of Rockingham.
Rockingham Register and Advertiser, 23
May 1867 (Thursday), p. 2, c. 6.
DUVALL: See entry for TWYMAN.
DUVALL: At "Linden," Spottsylvania county,
Va., the residence of the bride's father,
on the morning of the 9th inst., by Rev.
William Pleasant Twyman, of the Virginia
Conference, Edgar M. DUVALL, Esq., of
Georgetown, Kentucky, and Mrs. S.
Geraldine JERRELL, only daughter of Maj.
William T. CROPP.
Rockingham Register and Advertiser, 31
August 1860 (Friday), p. 2, c. 4.
DWYER: On the 2nd inst., at the residence of
the bride's father, the "Cedars," near
Harrisonburg, by Rev. D.C. Irwin, John
Henry DWYER and Ada, second daughter of
A. St. Clair SPRINKEL, Esq., all of this
place.
Rockingham Register and Advertiser, 4
April 1867 (Thursday), p. 3, c. 4.
DYER: See entry for BOTKIN.
DYER: See entry for HARDON.
DYER: See entry for MALLOW.
DYER: See entry for NEWMAN.
DYER: See entry for STROSNIDER.
DYER: On the 17th ult., ... Mr. James F.
DYER, of Company B, 11th Va. Cav., and
Miss Lydia F. ORNDOFF, of Hardy county,
Va.
Rockingham Register and Advertiser, 10
February 1865 (Friday), p. 2, c. 2.
DYER: On the 5th of January, by Rev. P.
Miller, Mr. John W. DYER, of Company F,
11th Va. Cavalry, and Miss Lydia H.
LANDACRE, of Hardy county.
Rockingham Register and Advertiser, 10
February 1865 (Friday), p. 2, c. 2.

- E -

EAGLE: See entry for Jones.

EARHART: See entry for ANDREWS.

EARHART: See entry for SPITLER.

EARLY: See entry for DRIVER.

EARLY: See entry for GARBER.

EARLY: By the Rev. Peter Miller, January 17th, Mr. James O. EARLY and Miss Rachel FRYE, all of Hardy county.
Rockingham Register and Advertiser, 9 February 1866 (Friday), p. 3, c. 3.

EARLY: On the 1st inst., by the Rev. J.C. Hensell, Mr. John B. EARLY and Miss Margaret E. MICHAEL, all of this county.
Rockingham Register & Advertiser, 6 October 1865 (Friday), p. 2, c. 2.

EARMAN: See entry for EARMAN.

EARMAN: See entry for GLEE.

EARMAN: On the 6th inst., by Rev. Wm. E. Baker, Mr. J.H. EARMAN and Miss Harriet M. HAGUE, all of Staunton.
Rockingham Register and Advertiser, 15 February 1861 (Friday), p. 2, c. 7.

EARMAN: On the 12th inst., by Rev. Joseph Funkhouser, James K. Polk EARMAN and Miss Margaret CARPENTER, all of Rockingham county.
Rockingham Register, 19 August 1869 (Thursday), p. 3, c. 2.

EARMAN: On Tuesday, the 13th inst., by Rev. J.C. Hensel, Mr. John B. EARMAN and Miss Mary Ann SITE, all of Rockingham.
Rockingham Register and Advertiser, 16 March 1860 (Friday), p. 2, c. 5.

EARMAN: On the 28th of June, by Rev. Jos. Funkhouser, Michael H. EARMAN and Miss Lucy Ann EARMAN, all of Rockingham county.
Rockingham Register and Advertiser, 12 July 1866 (Thursday), p. 3, c. 3.

EARMAN: On the 3rd inst., near Keezeltown, by Rev. Joseph Funkhouser, Thomas C. EARMAN and Miss Fannie E., daughter of Peter W. ARMENTROUT, all of Rockingham county.
Rockingham Register and Advertiser, 10 January 1867 (Thursday), p. 3, c. 2.

EARMON: See entry for CLATTERBUCK.

128

EARMON: On Sunday morning last, by Rev. J.W. Howe, Mr. Abram EARMON and Miss Elizabeth, daughter of Mr. Strother SHEETS, all of Rockingham county.
The Rockingham Register, 6 November 1863 (Friday), p. 2, c. 6.

EARMON: On the 14th inst., by Rev. Isaac Long, John H. EARMON and Miss Sarah A. CHANDLER, all of Rockingham county.
Rockingham Register, 21 May 1868 (Thursday), p. 2, c. 5.

EAST: On the 12th ult., by Rev. John Pinkerton, Col. S.A. EAST, of Rockbridge, and Miss Lucy V., daughter of Wm. HOWELL, of Long Glade, Augusta county.
Rockingham Register and Advertiser, 17 January 1867 (Thursday), p. 3, c. 3.

EASTHAM: See entry for EASTHAM.

EASTHAM: On Tuesday evening, the 11th inst., by Rev. S.S. Lambeth, at the residence of the bride's parents, Mr. C. Byrd EASTHAM and Miss Lucy E., daughter of George EASTHAM, Esq., all of Rockingham.
Rockingham Register and Advertiser, 14 June 1861 (Friday), p. 3, c. 3.

EASTMAN: See entry for EASTMAN.

EASTMAN: On Tuesday evening, December 29th, at Spring Lawn, the residence of the bride's father, by Rev. Jno. P. Hyde, Mr. Philip A. EASTMAN to Miss Annie B. EASTMAN, both of Rockingham county.
Rockingham Register and Advertiser, 6 January 1865 (Friday), p. 1, c. 2.

EATON: See entry for BARR.

EATON: See entry for COFFMAN.

EATON: Near McGaheysville, on Sunday, the 21st inst., by Rev. A. Poe Boude, Mr. James S. EATON and Miss Annie E. LEAP, all of this county.
Rockingham Register and Advertiser, 26 January 1866 (Friday), p. 3, c. 3.

EAVERS: On the 25th of February, by Rev. Daniel Thomas, Mr. Harvey EAVERS, of Rockingham, to Miss Daracha, daughter of Peter ZIMMERMAN, of Augusta county.
Rockingham Register and Advertiser, 19

March 1858 (Friday), p. 3, c. 3.

EBERT: See entry for GRABILL.

ECHARD: See entry for KOONTZ.

ECHARD: On the 12th inst., by Rev. A. Poe Boude, Jacob A. ECHARD and Miss Elizabeth KOONTZ, all of Rockingham.
Rockingham Register and Advertiser, 19 December 1867 (Thursday), p. 2, c. 6.

ECHERD: See entry for GILKISON.

ECHOLS: See entry for MILLER.

ECHORD: On the 29th ult., at the residence of Robert Cox, at Taylor Springs, in this county, by Rev. Henry Bovey, Silas C. ECHORD, of Augusta county, and Miss Phoeba C. BURNSIDE, of Rockingham.
Rockingham Register, 5 November 1868 (Thursday), p. 3, c. 3.

EDMONSON: On the 1st inst., at the residence of Mrs. Philisca Teaford, by Rev. J.L. Hemphill, Andrew EDMONSON, of Pocahontas, and Miss Julia A. TEAFORD, of Rockbridge.
Rockingham Register, 10 March 1870 (Thursday), p. 2, c. 4.

EDWARDS: See entry for BEAR.

EDWARDS: On the 19th inst., by Rev. T.D. Bell, at Mr. Jacob Lineweaver's, Mr. James A. EDWARDS and Miss Harriet E. SHANHOLTZ, of Hampshire county.
The Rockingham Register, 24 October 1862 (Friday), p. 2, c. 6.

EDWARDT: On the 20th ult., near Port Republic, by the Rev. G.W. Israel, Warner L. EDWARDT, Esq., of King William county, to Eliza Catharine, daughter of the late Wm. LEWIS, of this county.
Rockingham Register and Valley Advertiser, 5 September 1846 (Saturday), p. 2, c. 7.

EFFINGER: See entry for ANDERSON.

EFFINGER: See entry for COCK.

EFFINGER: See entry for JOHNSON.

EFFINGER: See entry for MASSIE.

EFFINGER: See entry for SHUE.

EFFINGER: On Monday evening last, at the residence of Philip Williams, Esq., in Winchester, by Rev. Dr. Boyd, Mr. Gerard

M. EFFINGER, of Harrisonburg, and Miss Bettie, daughter of Mr. Philip JONES, of Woodstock, Va.
Rockingham Register and Advertiser, 17 May 1861 (Friday), p. 3, c. 3.

EFFINGER: On Wednesday, January 6th, by Rev. C.H. Read, assisted by Rev. John E. Edwards, John Graham EFFINGER and Miss Sallie H., daugher of the late John JONES, of Richmond.
Rockingham Register, 13 January 1870 (Thursday), p. 3, c. 4.

EFFINGER: On Tuesday evening last, by Rev. T.D. Bell, Mr. John S. EFFINGER and Miss Bettie E., daughter of Mr. Andrew BEAR - all of this place.
Rockingham Register and Advertiser, 26 November 1858 (Friday), p. 3, c. 2.

EFFINGER: On the 21st of March, at the residence of Dr. F.A. Effinger, in Dallas county, Alabama, by Rev. W.J. Lowry, William H. EFFINGER, Esq., of Harrisonburg, Va., and Miss Emma E. HENDERSON, of Mississippi.
Rockingham Register and Advertiser, 6 April 1866 (Friday), p. 3, c. 3.

EGGLESTON: On the 22nd ult., at Mountain Home, Frederick county, by Rev. G.W. Eggleston, Robt. M. EGGLESTON and Miss Eliza Virginia, daughter of the late Maj. E.R. MUSE.
Rockingham Register, 8 October 1868 (Thursday), p. 3, c. 3.

EICHELBERGER: On Wednesday evening, the 26th ult., in the Lutheran Church, by Rev. J.B. Davis, Dr. Henry S. EICHELBERGER and Miss Susan C., daughter of Col. George BAYLOR, all of Staunton.
Rockingham Register and Advertiser, 4 November 1859 (Friday), p. 2, c. 6.

EICHELBERGER: At the residence of the bride's parents, in Harrisonburg, on Thursday evening, the 23rd of December, 1869, by Rev. Jas. S. Gardner, Lucien F. EICHELBERGER, printer, formerly of this place, but now of St. Louis, Mo., and

Miss Fannie Kate, daughter of S.P. REAMER, of this place.
Rockingham Register, 6 January 1870 (Thursday), p. 3, c. 3.

EIDSON: See entry for HOBBS.

EIDSON: See entry for STUART.

EIDSON: See entry for WILSON.

EILER: On the 22nd inst., by Rev. D.C. Irwin, Mr. Jas. R. EILER and Miss Amanda, daughter of George NICHOLAS, Esq., all of Rockingham.
Rockingham Register and Advertiser, 30 November 1860 (Friday), p. 3, c. 1.

ELBOM: See entry for ORNDORFF.

ELBURN: Near Strasburg, on the 12th inst., by Rev. G.H. Martin, Joseph L. ELBURN and Miss Lydia C. BRUBUCK, all of Shenandoah.
Rockingham Register and Advertiser, 26 December 1867 (Thursday), p. 2, c. 6.

ELICK: See entry for MORRISON.

ELLIOTT: On the 7th inst., at the residence of Dr. S.P.H. Miller, by Rev. Thomas M. Beckham, Frank W. ELLIOTT, of Rockingham, and Miss Annie A. HARRISON, of Indiana.
Rockingham Register and Advertiser, 21 June 1866 (Thursday), p. 2, c. 4.

ELLIS: See entry for FOX.

ELLIS: On the 8th of January, 1865, by Rev. J. Stirewalt, Mr. John A. ELLIS and Miss Hannah R. FOX, all of Page county.
Rockingham Register and Advertiser, 20 January 1865 (Friday), p. 2, c. 4.

ELLIS: On the 4th of April, near Valleysburg, Page county, by Rev. J.S. Bennick, Mr. Jos. H. ELLIS and Miss Sarah C. SOUR.
Rockingham Register and Advertiser, 4 May 1866 (Friday), p. 3, c. 2.

EMICK: See entry for HANCOCK.

EMICK: See entry for THOMEN.

EMPSWILER: See entry for RHINEHART.

EMSWILER: In Turleytown, on Sunday afternoon, the 26th inst., at the residence of the bridegroom, by Rev. Timothy Funk, Samuel G. EMSWILER and Miss Sophia, daughter of David CORRELL, all of Rockingham county.
Rockingham Register and Advertiser, 30

132

August 1866 (Thursday), p. 2, c. 4.

EMSWILER: Near Sherando, on the 3rd inst., by Rev. W.R. Stringer, Wesley EMSWILER and Miss Louisa M. BUTLER, all of Augusta county.

Rockingham Register and Advertiser, 14 November 1867 (Thursday), p. 2, c. 6.

EMSWILLER: See entry for HOTTLE.

ENGLE: See entry for McCAULEY.

ENGLE: On the 7th inst., by Rev. J.S.R. Clarke, Mr. Benj. ENGLE, of Jefferson county, and Miss Virginia C., daughter of Mr. Samuel ROYER, dec'd, of Rockingham.

Rockingham Register and Advertiser, 16 June 1865 (Friday), p. 1, c. 3.

ENGLEMAN: See entry for HARNSBERGER.

ENGLEMAN: On the 16th ult., by Rev. A.A. Bushong, D.B. ENGLEMAN and Miss Mary B. COINER, all of Augusta.

Rockingham Register, 6 January 1870 (Thursday), p. 3, c. 3.

ENGLEMAN: On the 21st inst., at the residence of Jacob Bowman, Esq., near Arbor Hill, By Rev. J.W. Karacofe, J.H. ENGLEMAN and Miss Sarah J. AREHEART, both of Augusta.

Rockingham Register and Advertiser, 28 March 1867 (Thursday), p. 2, c. 6.

ENGLISH: See entry for EYSTER.

ENSOR: On the evening of the 14th ult., at the residence of the bride's father, near Mint Spring, Augusta county, by the Rev. J.C. Dice, Mr. Geo. B. ENSOR, of Davisville, Baltimore county, Md., and Miss Jennie H., daughter of J. BEARD, Esq.

Rockingham Register & Advertiser, 6 October 1865 (Friday), p. 2, c. 2.

ENTLEMAN: See entry for FRENGER.

EPARD: See entry for HAM.

EPARD: See entry for SULLIVAN.

EPARD: See entry for WYANT.

EPARD: At the residence of Jefferson Prope, Rockingham county, Va., on the 11th inst., by Rev. Jno. P. Hyde, Mr. Thomas EPARD and Miss Mary J. MONGER, all of this county.

Rockingham Register & Advertiser, 22
September 1865 (Friday), p. 3, c. 3.

EPERD: See entry for NASELROD.

EPPARD: See entry for BAKER.

EPPARD: See entry for MORRIS.

EPPARD: See entry for STANLEY.

EPPARD: On the 28th ult., by Rev. I. Conder,
G.H. EPPARD, of Page county, and Miss
Sagoubna, daughter of Isaac SHIFTLETT, of
Rockingham county.
Rockingham Register, 3 June 1870
(Thursday), p. 3, c. 3.

ERGENBRIGHT: On Tuesday, November 28th, by
Rev. J.C. Hensell, Mr. Geo. R.
ERGENBRIGHT and Miss Margaret J., eldest
daughter of Robert BURKE, all of
Rockingham.
Rockingham Register & Advertiser, 8
December 1865 (Friday), p. 2, c. 4.

ERVIN: See entry for LOCKRIDGE.

ERVINE: On the 25th of December, 1862, at the
residence of Henry Jones, Esq., by Rev.
Wm. T. Price, Mr. Augustus ERVINE and
Miss Louisa WILSON, of Highland county.
The Rockingham Register, 13 February 1863
(Friday), p. 2, c. 4.

ERVINE: On Monday, the 18th of May, in
Rockbridge, by Rev. Jas. Greer, Mr. John
H. ERVINE, of Rockingham county, and Miss
Ellen J., daughter of Mr. John WEIR, of
Rockbridge county.
Rockingham Register and Advertiser, 12
June 1857 (Friday), p. 3, c. 2.

ERWIN: See entry for McALLISTER.

ERWIN: On the 24th ult., by the Rev. D.W.
Arnold, at the residence of the bride's
father, at Mossy Creek, Augusta county,
Va., Maj. Jared D. ERWIN, of Highland
county, and Miss Mary J. ODER.
The Rockingham Register, 9 October 1863
(Friday), p. 2, c. 4.

ESKRIDGE: See entry for NEWTON.

ESKRIDGE: On the 29th ult., on Cedar Creek,
Mr. Hector ESKRIDGE and Miss Ellen V.
STROSNIDER, all of Shenandoah county.
Rockingham Register and Advertiser, 13

December 1866 (Thursday), p. 2, c. 5.

ESTEP: See entry for BOWMAN.

ESTEP: See entry for BRENNER.

ESTEP: See entry for HUPP.

ESTEP: See entry for MOORE.

ESTEP: See entry for WENGER.

ESTEP: See entry for ZIRKLE (2).

ESTEP: On the 8th ult., [4th inst.], by Rev. Jacob Wine, Mr. John J. ESTEP and Miss Hannah A. LLOYD, all of Shenandoah county.
Rockingham Register and Advertiser, 19 January 1866 (Friday), p. 3, c. 2. Repeated, 2 February 1866 (Friday), p. 3, c. 2. The latter is cited above.

ESTEP: On the 9th inst., by Rev. A.R. Rude, Joseph ESTEP and Miss Martha Jane, daughter of E. WOODS.
Rockingham Register and Advertiser, 18 November 1859 (Friday), p. 2, c. 4.

ETTINGER: See entry for LEE.

ETTINGER: On Thursday, 17th inst., by Rev. H. Wetzel, Mr. John ETTINGER and Miss Sarah KRICKENBARGER, both of Rockingham county.
Rockingham Register and Advertiser, 25 December 1857 (Friday), p. 3, c. 3.

EUBANK: At the residence of the bride's father, in Augusta county, on the 11th inst., by the Rev. John Pinkerton, Mr. R.P. EUBANK, Dep. Sheriff of Augusta county, and Miss Diana M., daughter of Mr. David M. KYLE.
Rockingham Register and Advertiser, 19 July 1861 (Friday), p. 3, c. 3.

EUBANK: On the 8th inst., by Rev. A.A.P. Neel, Thos. W. EUBANK and Miss Annie E. PROFFETT, both of Augusta.
Rockingham Register, 22 October 1868 (Thursday), p. 3, c. 3.

EUTZLER: See entry for MILLER.

EUTZLER: On the 13th of June, by Rev. Frederick Miller, John H. EUTZLER and Miss Ella Jane BATEMAN, all of Rockingham county.
Rockingham Register and Advertiser, 27 June 1867 (Thursday), p. 2, c. 6.

135

EVANS: On Thursday morning, the 12th inst., by Rev. John L. Clark, Edward J. EVANS, of Winchester, and Miss Addie M. LUSHBAUGH, of Staunton.
Rockingham Register and Advertiser, 19 December 1867 (Thursday), p. 2, c. 6.

EVANS: On the 8th ult., by Elder H. Jennings, H.H. EVANS and Miss Rebecca DOWNEY, all of Shenandoah county.
Rockingham Register and Advertiser, 3 January 1867 (Thursday), p. 3, c. 3.

EVANS: On the 23rd ult., by Elder H. Jennings, near Edinburg, Wm. H. EVANS and Miss Virginia C. DOWNEY, both of Shenandoah county.
Rockingham Register, 13 January 1870 (Thursday), p. 3, c. 4.

EVE: In Staunton, on the 1st of March, by Rev. Dr. Sparrow, Dr. Robert C. EVE, of Augusta, Ga., and Miss Willie, daughter of Col. M.G. HARMAN, of Staunton, Va.
Rockingham Register and Advertiser, 7 April 1865 (Friday), p. 2, c. 5. Repeated, 14 April 1865 (Friday), p. 2, c. 5.

EVERLY: See entry for BAKER.

EVERLY: See entry for SHOBE.

EVERLY: Near Wardensville, on the 30th ult., by Rev. C.L. Torreyson, Lewis C. EVERLY and Miss Anna L. SMOOTZ, all of Hardy county.
Rockingham Register, 20 January 1870 (Thursday), p. 2, c. 5.

EVEY: On the 13th of May, by the Rev. Levi Keller, Mr. John EVEY and Mrs. Eliza FADELY, all of Shenandoah.
Rockingham Register, 3 June 1869 (Thursday), p. 3, c. 2.

EVY: See entry for WISE.

EWING: See entry for SITLINGTON.

EWING: On the 25th inst., by Rev. D.C. Irwin, Dr. Wm. D. EWING and Miss Margaret A. SELLERS, both of Augusta county.
Rockingham Register and Advertiser, 28 October 1859 (Friday), p. 2, c. 6.

EYE: On Thursday, the 12th inst., by Rev.

Isaac Soule, Mr. John L. EYE and Miss
Magdalene, daughter of David BLOSSER, all
of Rockingham county.
Rockingham Register and Advertiser, 27
April 1866 (Friday), p. 2, c. 2.
EYSTER: On the 2nd inst., by Rev. Dr. Haynes,
of Middleburg, Loudoun county, Va., at
the residence of the bride's father, in
Staunton, Dr. G.H. EYSTER and Miss Inez
Josephine, daughter of Rev. J.A. ENGLISH.
Rockingham Register, 4 November 1869
(Thursday), p. 2, c. 4.

- F -

FADEL: On the 13th inst., by Rev. John W.
Wolff, Mr. Moses FADEL and Miss Caroline
SHADWELL, all of Shenandoah.
Rockingham Register and Advertiser, 21
December 1860 (Friday), p. 2, c. 6.
FADELEY: See entry for MOONEY.
FADELY: See entry for BELLER.
FADELY: See entry for EVEY.
FADELY: On Thursday the 4th of December,
1862, by Rev. J.P. Cline, near Wunder's
Store, David S. FADELY and Miss Hannah
KERLIN, all of Shenandoah county.
The Rockingham Register, 19 December 1862
(Friday), p. 2, c. 4.
FADELY: On the 26th ult., by Rev. Jacob Wine,
Mr. Michael FADELY and Miss Mary J.
GRANDSTAFF, both of Shenandoah.
Rockingham Register and Advertiser, 14
December 1860 (Friday), p. 2, c. 6.
FAIRBURN: See entry for PENCE.
FAIRBURN: On the 24th of February, by Rev.
Daniel Thomas, Mr. David E. FAIRBURN and
Miss Martha Susan, daughter of John C.
COAKLEY, dec'd, all of Rockingham county.
Rockingham Register and Advertiser, 7
March 1867 (Thursday), p. 3, c. 3.
FAKLE: See entry for SPITLER.
FALL: See entry for MASINCUP.
FALLS: See entry for WHITEZELL.
FALLS: At Mr. Daniel Shaw's, near Sherando,
on the 24th ult., by Rev. W.R. Stringer,

Jeremiah FALLS and Miss Elizabeth LUNSFORD.
Rockingham Register and Advertiser, 3 January 1867 (Thursday), p. 3, c. 3.

FALLY: See entry for GOOD.

FANCIER: On the 24th of December, near New Market, by Rev. S. Henkel, David C. FANCIER and Miss Sarah E. FLEMMINGS, all of Shenandoah county.
Rockingham Register, 14 January 1869 (Thursday), p. 3, c. 3.

FANSELOR: At the house of Mr. Joseph Zehring, on the 13th inst., by the Rev. Henry St. John Rinker, Mr. George FANSELOR and Miss Sarah NEESE, all of Shenandoah county.
Rockingham Register and Advertiser, 28 January 1859 (Friday), p. 2, c. 6.

FANSLER: See entry for KIPPS.

FANSLER: See entry for PENCE.

FANSLER: Near Woodstock, on the 4th inst., by Rev. G.H. Martin, J.W. FANSLER and Miss Mary E., daughter of Col. Isaac HOTTEL, both of Shenandoah county.
Rockingham Register and Advertiser, 23 March 1866 (Friday), p. 3, c. 3.

FANT: On the 7th of October, by the Rev. R.C. Cave, at the residence of the bride's father, Enoch W. FANT and Miss Mary E. RHODES, all of Shenandoah county.
Rockingham Register, 28 October 1869 (Thursday), p. 2, c. 3.

FARIS: On Thursday last, by the Rev. B.N. Brown, Mr. Thomas FARIS to Miss Margaret TAYLOR, all of Staunton, Va.
Rockingham Register and Valley Advertiser, 3 November 1849 (Saturday), p. 2, c. 7.

FARRA: See entry for MYERS.

FARRAR: See entry for HOFFMAN.

FATELY: See entry for FISHER.

FAUBER: See entry for BROOKS.

FAUBER: See entry for FISHER.

FAUBER: See entry for FURR.

FAUBER: See entry for JORDAN.

FAUBUSH: See entry for MESSERLY.

FAUGET: See entry for COLE.

FAUGHT: On the 13th inst., by Rev. T.D. Bell, Mr. John N. FAUGHT and Anna E., daughter of Mr. Daniel BOWMAN, all of this county. Rockingham Register and Virginia Advertiser, 21 December 1855 (Friday), p. 2, c. 8.

FAUNTLEROY: On the evening of the 26th ult., at Winchester, Va., by Rev. J.R. Graham, Dr. A.M. FAUNTLEROY, of Staunton, and Miss Sallie H., daughter of Hon. R.Y. CONRAD, of Frederick county. Rockingham Register and Advertiser, 11 May 1866 (Friday), p. 2, c. 4.

FAUVER: On the 23rd inst., by the Rev. J.H. Crawford, Mr. John B. FAUVER and Miss Louisa B. THOMAS, all of Augusta. Rockingham Register and Advertiser, 4 February 1859 (Friday), p. 2, c. 5.

FAUVER: On the 10th inst., at the residence of the bride's father, by the Rev. J.H. Crawford, Mr. Wm. P. FAUVER and Miss Mary A. ANDERSON, all of Augusta county. Rockingham Register and Advertiser, 25 March 1859 (Friday), p. 3, c. 2.

FAWLEY: See entry for SHOEMAKER.

FAWSET: On the 6th inst., by Elder J. Jennings, Mr. George FAWSET and Miss E. Catharine MARTZ, all of Rockingham. Rockingham Register and Advertiser, 14 September 1860 (Friday), p. 2, c. 5.

FAY: See entry for LEWIS.

FECKER: See entry for PENCE.

FELL: On the 21st ult., at the residence of the bride's father, by Rev. A. Weller, John D. FELL and Miss Virginia SKAGGS, all of Greenbrier county. Rockingham Register and Advertiser, 5 July 1866 (Thursday), p. 3, c. 5.

FELLER: See entry for MELHORN.

FELLER: On the 12th inst., by the Rev. Thomas Miller, Mr. John H. FELLER and Miss Amanda C. COCHENOUR, all of Shenandoah county. Rockingham Register and Advertiser, 27 April 1866 (Friday), p. 2, c. 2.

FETZER: See entry for SPIKER (2).

FETZER: On Thursday the 7th inst., in Pittsburg [sic], Pa., by Rev. Wm. M. Paxton, Mr. James FETZER, formerly of Woodstock, and now Merchant in Wheeling, to Miss Mary Jane, daughter of J. CUTHBERT, Esq., of the former city.
The Rockingham Register and Valley Advertiser, 26 June 1852 (Saturday), p. 2, c. 5.

FIELDING: See entry for HALL.

FIELDING: See entry for MCALLISTER.

FIELDING: On the 1st of May, by Rev. Isaac Long, Eppa FIELDING and Miss Melissa Frances, daughter of Lewis GARRISON, all of Rockingham county.
Rockingham Register and Advertiser, 11 May 1866 (Friday), p. 2, c. 4.

FIFER: On the 1st inst., at the residence of the bride's father, by Rev. Daniel Thomas, Geo. W. FIFER, of Augusta, and Miss Margaret M. CUPP, of Rockingham.
Rockingham Register and Advertiser, 9 March 1866 (Friday), p. 2, c. 3.

FIFER: On the 29th of December, by Rev. John Kline, Mr. Harvey FIFER and Miss Nancy Catharine SUMMERS, all of this county.
Rockingham Register and Advertiser, 17 February 1860 (Friday), p. 2, c. 4.

FIFER: On the 23rd ult., by Rev. Daniel Thomas, Mr. Jeremiah FIFER and Miss Catharine HOLLAND, all of Rockingham.
Rockingham Register and Advertiser, 18 January 1861 (Friday), p. 3, c. 2.

FIFER: On the 4th inst., by the Rev. Jacob Thomas, S.P. FIFER and Miss Lydia SHICKEL, all of Rockingham.
Rockingham Register, 15 December 1870 (Thursday), p. 3, c. 5.

FILCOMB: See entry for HAMMON.

FILLER: See entry for ROLLER.

FILSMOYER: See entry for WOLF.

FILTZMOYER: See entry for WOLF.

FINK: On the 18th ult., by Rev. H. Wetzel, John FINK and Miss Barbara Frances DOVE, both of Rockingham.
Rockingham Register, 8 September 1870

(Thursday), p. 3, c. 3.

FINKS: See entry for KENNEY.

FINKS: On the 20th inst., by Rev. H. Shaull, on Stony Creek, Charles F. FINKS and Miss Carrie B. TRIPLETT, all of Shenandoah county.
Rockingham Register, 31 March 1870 (Thursday), p. 3, c. 3.

FINLEY: See entry for GRATTAN.

FIPER: On the 24th inst., in Staunton, by the Rev. W.E. Baker, Mr. B.F. FIPER and Miss Caroline S. BECKLE.
Rockingham Register and Advertiser, 31 January 1867 (Thursday), p. 3, c. 2.

FIREBAUGH: See entry for BEAR.

FIREBAUGH: At the residence of the bride's father, near New Hope, by Rev. J.J. Engle, Mr. John FIREBAUGH and Miss Mary Jane SHUEY, all of Augusta.
Rockingham Register and Advertiser, 9 January 1868 (Thursday), p. 2, c. 4.

FIREBAUGH: On Monday morning, the 10th inst., by Rev. T.D. Bell, Mr. Samuel A. FIREBAUGH, of Mt. Clinton, and Miss Lizzie L., daughter of Mr. Michael WHITMORE, all of Rockingham county.
Rockingham Register and Advertiser, 13 December 1866 (Thursday), p. 2, c. 5.

FIRTH: See entry for HELMS.

FIRTH: See entry for RHODES.

FISHBACK: On Sunday, the 26th ult., at the residence of Dr. Newman, by Rev. D.C. Irwin, Mr. Wm. McK. FISHBACK, of Bridgewater, and Miss Bettie E. BARAX, both of this county.
The Rockingham Register, 1 May 1863 (Friday), p. 2, c. 5.

FISHBURNE: See entry for KIBLER.

FISHBURNE: On the 10th inst., by Rev. C.S.M. See, E.G. FISHBURNE and Miss Ella L. VAN LEAR, all of Augusta.
Rockingham Register and Advertiser, 24 October 1867 (Thursday), p. 2, c. 7.

FISHEL: On the 5th of January, by Rev. P. Miller, Mr. Jacob FISHEL, of Hampshire, and Miss Mary A. ORNDORFF, of Frederick

county.

Rockingham _Register_ and _Advertiser_, 10
February 1865 (Friday), p. 2, c. 2.

FISHER: See entry for BROBECK.

FISHER: See entry for HOUCK.

FISHER: See entry for JONES.

FISHER: See entry for LICHLITER.

FISHER: See entry for RUSSELL.

FISHER: On the 26th ult., in the Evangelical
Lutheran Church, Winchester, Va., by Rev.
T.W.   Dosh,   Lt.   A.B.   FISHER,   of
Harrisonburg, and Miss Elvina, daughter
of Enoch DINKEL, of Frederick county.

Rockingham _Register_ and _Advertiser_, 11
May 1866 (Friday), p. 2, c. 4.

FISHER: On the 22nd of February, by Rev. C.
Beard, Charles F. FISHER, of Augusta
county, and Miss Samanthia E. HARRIS, of
Nelson county.

Rockingham _Register_, 10 March 1870
(Thursday), p. 2, c. 4.

FISHER: At the residence of the bride's
mother, near Gordonsville, Orange county,
Va., on the 19th of June, by Rev. R.L.
Coleman, D.A. FISHER, Jr., and Miss
Josephine C., daughter of Philip COLE,
dec'd, all formerly of Rockingham county.

Rockingham _Register_ and _Advertiser_, 5
July 1866 (Thursday), p. 3, c. 5.

FISHER: In Staunton, on the 21st inst., by
Rev. W.E. Baker, Mr. Ed. F. FISHER and
Miss Emma FATELY.

Rockingham _Register_, 30 April 1868
(Thursday), p. 2, c. 6.

FISHER: On Thursday the 25th ult., by the
Rev. J. Killian, Mr. Henry FISHER, of
Hampshire county, Va., to Miss Elizabeth
FAUBER, of Augusta.

Rockingham _Register_ and _Valley
Advertiser_, 10 April 1847 (Saturday), p.
3, c. 1.

FISHER: On the 2nd inst., at the residence of
the bride's father, by Rev. John Johnson,
Jesse FISHER, of Hardy county, W.Va., and
Miss Jane E., daughter of Cyrus WELTON,
Esq., of Grant county, W.Va.

142

Rockingham Register, 24 March 1870 (Thursday), p. 3, c. 2.

FITCH: See entry for RAMEY.

FITCH: On the 19th inst., in Greenville, by Rev. Mr. Gaver, Mr. George FITCH, of the 5th Va. Infantry, and Miss Hester A. McGILVRAY.
The Rockingham Register, 25 March 1864 (Friday), p. 2, c. 7.

FITSMOYERS: On the 23rd ult., near Timberville, Rockingham county, Va., by Rev. S. Henkel, Mr. Michael FITSMOYERS and Miss Sarah, daughter of John AREHART.
Rockingham Register & Advertiser, 8 December 1865 (Friday), p. 2, c. 4.

FITZGERALD: See entry for SCHMITT.

FITZSIMMONS: See entry for LONG.

FITZSIMMONS: On the 10th inst., by Elder John Pirkey, J.M. FITZSIMMONS and Miss Kate O'NEIL, all of Shenandoah.
Rockingham Register, 25 November 1869 (Thursday), p. 2, c. 3.

FITZSIMMONS: On Sabbath afternoon, January 20th, by Rev. Jacob Miller, John F. FITZSIMMONS and Miss Susanah, daughter of Christley SIMMERS, all of Rockingham county.
Rockingham Register and Advertiser, 24 January 1867 (Thursday), p. 2, c. 4.

FITZWATERS: At the residence of the bride's father, on the 12th inst., by Rev. John Cline, Mr. James FITZWATERS and Miss Catharine SHOWALTER, all of Rockingham.
Rockingham Register and Advertiser, 24 May 1861 (Friday), p. 3, c. 2.

FIX: See entry for RUSMISELL.

FIX: On the 13th inst., by Rev. J.M. Shreckhise, James FIX and Miss Mary C. ZIMBRO, all of Augusta county.
Rockingham Register 20 August 1868 (Thursday), p. 3, c. 3.

FLAHERTY: In Powell's Fort, on the 13th inst., by Elder Joshua Jennings, Mr. Daniel FLAHERTY to Miss Mary CULLERS, all of Shenandoah county.
The Rockingham Register and Valley

<u>Advertiser</u>, 26 June 1852 (Saturday), p. 2, c. 5.

FLANNAGAN: At Hope Mills, Page county, Va., on the 4th inst., by Rev. J.W. Watson, at the residence of the bride's father, Mr. R.H. FLANNAGAN, of Charlottesville, and Miss Libbia S., daughter of Maj. Lawrence PITMAN, of Page county, Va.
The <u>Rockingham</u> <u>Register</u>, 27 November 1863 (Friday), p. 2, c. 5.

FLEISHER: See entry for CAMPBELL.

FLEISHER: On the 11th inst., by the Rev. L.D. Nixon, Col. H.H. FLEISHER and Miss Lizzie, daughter of Mr. Lewis DAVIS, all of Highland county.
<u>Rockingham</u> <u>Register</u> <u>and</u> <u>Advertiser</u>, 19 August 1859 (Friday), p. 2, c. 5.

FLEMING: See entry for BROWN.

FLEMING: See entry for CAVE.

FLEMING: See entry for MOORE.

FLEMING: See entry for PROCTOR.

FLEMING: See entry for WOODELL.

FLEMING: On the 4th inst., by Rev. Jacob Miller, Mr. John FLEMING and Miss Frances, daughter of Mr. Jacob SWARTZ, all of this county.
<u>Rockingham</u> <u>Register</u> <u>and</u> <u>Advertiser</u>, 14 January 1859 (Friday), p. 3, c. 3.

FLEMINGS: See entry for SMALTS.

FLEMINGS: Near New Market, on the 20th ult., by Rev. S. Henkel, Mr. Abraham FLEMINGS and Miss E.C. PHILIPS.
<u>Rockingham</u> <u>Register</u> <u>and</u> <u>Advertiser</u>, 25 January 1861 (Friday), p. 3, c. 1.

FLEMMING: At Orleans, Va., on Wednesday evening, February 23rd, by Rev. H.E. Johnson, Benton S. FLEMMING, of Page county, and Miss Eugenia M., daughter of Dr. Amos PAYNE, of Orleans.
<u>Rockingham</u> <u>Register</u>, 7 April 1870 (Thursday), p. 2, c. 5.

FLEMMINGS: See entry for FANCIER.

FLETCHER: In Harrisonburg, on Wednesday evening, the 27th ult., at the residence of the bride's father, by Rev. T.D. Bell, A.K. FLETCHER and Miss Virginia C., daughter of Isaac PAUL, Esq., all of this place.

Rockingham Register and Advertiser, 4 April 1867 (Thursday), p. 3, c. 4.

FLETCHER: By Rev. P. Miller, on the 10th of February, 1864, Mr. Jas. H. FLETCHER and Miss Sarah J. OATS, all of Hampshire county.

The Rockingham Register, 26 February 1864 (Friday), p. 2, c. 4.

FLETCHER: On Thursday night last, by Rev. Patterson Fletcher, Mr. Richard P. FLETCHER, Jr., of this county, and Miss Annie MAYHEW, of Maine.

Rockingham Register and Advertiser, 26 December 1856 (Friday), p. 2, c. 7.

FLETCHER: By the Rev. J. Rice Bowman, on the 20th inst., Robert R. FLETCHER and Miss Alice G. HOUCK, both of Harrisonburg.

Rockingham Register, 22 December 1870 (Thursday), p. 2, c. 4.

FLICK: See entry for FRAZIER.

FLICK: On the 4th inst., at the residence of the husband, by Rev. Joseph Holcombe, Silas FLICK and Miss Annie HENSON, all of Rockingham county.

Rockingham Register, 11 February 1869 (Thursday), p. 3, c. 3.

FLICK: Near Mount Clinton, on the 3rd inst., by Rev. Wm. T. Price, Silas FLICK and Miss Hettie E., daughter of Archibald BERRY, all of Rockingham.

Rockingham Register, 10 March 1870 (Thursday), p. 2, c. 4.

FLORY: See entry for SALYARDS.

FLORY: On the 20th ult., by Rev. M. Garber, Mr. J.F. FLORY and Miss E.E. GROVE, all of Augusta.

Rockingham Register and Advertiser, 18 January 1861 (Friday), p. 3, c. 2.

FLORY: On Tuesday, the 3rd inst., near Mt. Solon, Augusta county, by the Rev. Mr. Pinkerton, Mr. Jacob S. FLORY, late of Iowa, and formerly of Virginia, and Miss Elizabeth, eldest daughter of Jacob SANGER, Esq.

Rockingham _Register_ and _Advertiser_, 13
February 1857 (Friday), p. 2, c. 5.

FLORY: On Thursday, the 22nd ult., by Rev.
Daniel Thomas, John G. FLORY, of Iowa,
and Miss Sarah V., daughter of Wm.
WRIGHT, dec'd, of Augusta county.
Rockingham _Register_ and _Advertiser_, 2
March 1866 (Friday), p. 3, c. 3.

FLORY: In Holton, Kansas Territory, on the
5th inst., by George Smith, Esq., Mr.
M.M. FLORY, formerly of Rockingham
county, Va., and Miss Mary J. PHERSON, of
Holton, Kansas Territory.
Rockingham _Register_ and _Advertiser_, 22
October 1858 (Friday), p. 3, c. 2.

FLOYD: In Mt. Solon, on the 21st ult., by the
Rev. Mr. Jefferson, Mr. Edward FLOYD and
Miss Fannie MESSERSMITH.
Rockingham _Register_ and _Advertiser_, 12
January 1866 (Friday), p. 1, c. 3.

FLOYD: On the 19th of February, by Rev. John
E. Massey, Mr. Jos. F. FLOYD to Miss
Sarah Ann, daughter of Lawrence MEEKS,
all of Nelson county.
Rockingham _Register_ and _Virginia_
Advertiser, 14 March 1856 (Friday), p. 3,
c. 1.

FOGEL: See entry for FOGEL.

FOGEL: On the 5th inst., by Elder H.
Jennings, Harvey FOGEL and Mrs. Martha
FOGEL, both of Woodstock.
Rockingham _Register_ and _Advertiser_, 19
March 1868 (Thursday), p. 2, c. 4.

FOGLE: Near New Market, Shenandoah county,
Va., January 19, 1865, by Rev. S. Henkel,
Mr. Jacob FOGLE, of Rockingham, and Miss
Catherine McNEIL, of Shenandoah.
Rockingham _Register_ and _Advertiser_, 3
February 1865 (Friday), p. 1, c. 2.

FOLEY: See entry for GRIGGS.

FOLEY: In Mt. Crawford, on Monday the 26th
inst., by Rev. W.S. Perry, James M. FOLEY
and Miss Sallie M. SHOWALTER, all of
Rockingham county.
Rockingham _Register_, 29 October 1868
(Thursday), p. 3, c. 3.

146

FOLTS: At Jacob Offenbacker's, in Page county, Va., by Rev. J.E. Wasson, W.H. FOLTS and Miss L.A. OFFENBACKER.
Rockingham Register, 10 February 1870 (Thursday), p. 2, c. 5.

FOLTZ: See entry for CHICK.

FOLTZ: See entry for LOUDERBACK.

FOLTZ: See entry for LUTZ.

FOLTZ: On the 25th of March, by Rev. S. Whitmire, J. FOLTZ, of Shenandoah, and Miss Sarah M., daughter of the late Joseph MILLER, of Hardy county, W.Va.
Rockingham Register, 15 April 1869 (Thursday), p. 2, c. 4.

FOLTZ: On the 11th inst., by Rev. Socrates Henkel, Mr. John FOLTZ and Miss Peachy WALTERS, all of Shenandoah county.
Rockingham Register and Virginia Advertiser, 27 May 1854 (Saturday), p. 2, c. 7.

FOLTZ: At Plains' Mill, on the 12th of November, by Rev. John S. Bennick, John P. FOLTZ and Miss Rebecca D., daughter of Siram P. HENKEL, Esq., all of Rockingham county.
Rockingham Register, 19 November 1868 (Thursday), p. 2, c. 5.

FOLTZ: On the 21st ult., by Rev. T. Brashear, Mr. William FOLTZ and Miss Amanda KERLIN, all of Shenandoah county.
Rockingham Register and Advertiser, 5 April 1861 (Friday), p. 2, c. 5.

FONTAINE: See entry for BEOUN.

FORBES: At Millwood, Buckingham county, by the Rev. J. Rice Bowman, on the 14th of February, Col. W.W. FORBES and Mrs. Mary M. KYLE, daughter of Washington SWOOPE, Esq., of Augusta county.
Rockingham Register and Advertiser, 9 March 1866 (Friday), p. 2, c. 3.

FORD: On the 16th ult., by Rev. J.H. Morrison, D.D., Reuben FORD, of Goochland county, and Mary Stuart, daughter of W.H. GRANT, Esq., of Richmond.
Rockingham Register, 1 April 1869 (Thursday), p. 3, c. 3.

FORRER: On the 27th ult., by Rev. Daniel
    Thomas, Martin V. FORRER, of Rockingham,
    and Miss Elizabeth A. HILL, of Augusta
    county.
    Rockingham Register and Advertiser, 10
    January 1867 (Thursday), p. 3, c. 2.
FORRER: Near Salem, Va., on the 18th ult., by
    Rev. Dabney Ball, Samuel FORRER, of
    Augusta, and Miss Sallie E., daughter of
    Joseph DEYERLE, of Roanoke county.
    Rockingham Register, 17 December 1868
    (Thursday), p. 3, c. 2.
FORSYTH: See entry for MARTIN.
FOSTER: See entry for KIBLER.
FOSTER: In Staunton, on the 28th ult., by
    Rev. James A. Latane, James J. FOSTER, of
    Richmond, and Miss Rebecca Porterfield,
    daughter of Edwin M. TAYLOR, Esq.
    Rockingham Register and Advertiser, 5
    December 1867 (Thursday), p. 2, c. 5.
FOSTER: On Thursday evening last, by the Rev.
    J.A. Latane, R.H. FOSTER, Esq., of
    Richmond, and Miss Fannie, daughter of
    Dr. F.T. STRIBLING, of Staunton.
    Rockingham Register and Advertiser, 17
    February 1860 (Friday), p. 2, c. 4.
FOUKE: See entry for HEDRICK.
FOUNTAIN: On the evening of the 23rd inst.,
    by Rev. Mr. Clyner, Mr. N. FOUNTAIN,
    Esq., and Miss Kate, daughter of Chas.
    WELSH, Esq., all of Woodstock.   Mr.
    Fountain is one of the Muhlenburg Rifles.
    He came to Woodstock on the cars, was
    married in the evening, and left for the
    post of military duty next morning ....
    Rockingham Register and Advertiser, 26
    April 1861 (Friday), p. 2, c. 7.
FOUT: See entry for GRAVE.
FOX: See entry for ELLIS.
FOX: See entry for FOX.
FOX: See entry for REXROAD.
FOX: On the 17th inst., at the residence of
    the bride's father, by Rev. J.S. Bennick,
    Ambrose FOX and Miss Mary A. ELLIS, both
    of Page county.
    Rockingham Register, 31 March 1870

(Thursday), p. 3, c. 3.

FOX: On the 2nd inst., by Rev. S. Henkel, Isaac FOX and Miss Julia A. SOURS, all of Page county.

Rockingham Register and Advertiser, 16 January 1868 (Thursday), p. 2, c. 5.

FOX: Near Luray, Page county, on the 3rd inst., by Rev. J.S. Bennick, Noah FOX and Miss Bettie FOX, both of Page county.

Rockingham Register, 17 February 1870 (Thursday), p. 3, c. 2.

FRAINUM: On Tuesday the 24th ult., by the Rev. J. McKendree Reiley, Mr. David FRAINUM, late of Scott's division U.S. Army in Mexico, to Miss Sophronia, daughter of Mr. Jacob BEAR, of Augusta county.

Rockingham Register and Valley Advertiser, 4 November 1848 (Saturday), p. 3, c. 2.

FRANCISCO: See entry for COCHRAN.

FRANCISCO: See entry for RYAN.

FRANCISCO: In Marshall, Saline county, Mo., on the 21st of April, Mr. Geo. M. FRANCISCO to Miss M.Z. HEREFORD.

Rockingham Register, 7 May 1868 (Thursday), p. 2, c. 4.

FRANK: See entry for MINNICK.

FRANK: See entry for NAIR.

FRANK: See entry for SUMMERS.

FRANK: See entry for THOMPSON.

FRANK: On Sunday morning, the 30th of August, by Rev. Jacob Miller, Lemuel FRANK and Miss Elizabeth, daughter of Wm. SIMMERS, all of Rockingham county.

Rockingham Register, 3 September 1868 (Thursday), p. 2, c. 4.

FRANK: At the house of Mr. Wm. Cook, near Plains' Mills, on Thursday, the 17th inst., by Rev. J.P. Cline, William H. FRANK and Nancy Jane CUMMINS.

Rockingham Register and Virginia Advertiser, 1 August 1862 (Friday), p. 2, c. 4.

FRANKUM: On the 14th of March, by Rev. Isaac Soule, John FRANKUM and Miss R.J. ADREW,

all of Rockingham county.
Rockingham Register and Advertiser, 24
March 1865 (Friday), p. 2, c. 3.
FRAVEL: See entry for BARGELT.
FRAVEL: See entry for BISHOP.
FRAVEL: See entry for BOWMAN.
FRAVEL: See entry for GOCHENOUR.
FRAVEL: See entry for HAMMAN.
FRAVEL: See entry for HISEY.
FRAVEL: See entry for RITTENOUR.
FRAVEL: See entry for SHUTTERS.
FRAVEL: On the 2nd of October, by Rev. Jacob
    Spitzer, Mr. Daniel H. FRAVEL and Miss
    Mary E., daughter of Mr. David SPITZER,
    all of Rockingham county.
    The Rockingham Register, 17 October 1862
    (Friday), p. 2, c. 7.
FRAVEL: On the 11th inst., by the Rev. Daniel
    Feete, Mr. David FRAVEL and Miss Louisa
    SUPINGER, all of Woodstock.
    Rockingham Register and Advertiser, 27
    January 1860 (Friday), p. 2, c. 6.
FRAVEL: On the 21st of May, by the Rev. G.B.
    Martin, Mr. George R. FRAVEL and Miss Eva
    C. ORNDORF, all of Shenandoah county.
    Rockingham Register, 18 June 1868
    (Thursday), p. 3, c. 5.
FRAVEL: On the 18th inst., at Luray, Henry C.
    FRAVEL, formerly of Woodstock, and Miss
    Alice WEAVER, of Luray.
    Rockingham Register, 27 January 1870
    (Thursday), p. 2, c. 3.
FRAVEL: On the 22nd ult., by Rev. Mr. Nixon,
    of Hardy county, John W. FRAVEL, of
    Woodstock, and Miss Maggie N. BAKER, of
    Hardy county, West Va.
    Rockingham Register, 13 January 1870
    (Thursday), p. 3, c. 4.
FRAZIER: On Sunday last, by Rev. Benj.
    Bowman, Mr. Henry FRAZIER and Miss
    Barbara FLICK, all of this county.
    Rockingham Register and Virginia
    Advertiser, 30 December 1859 (Friday), p.
    2, c. 5.
FRAZIER: At Warwick, Bath county, Va., on the
    1st inst., by the Rev. W.W. Houston, J.A.

FRAZIER, Esq., of Rockbridge, and Miss
Lilla G. WARWICK.
Rockingham Register, 16 December 1869
(Thursday), p. 2, c. 5.
FREDERICK: See entry for DARFLINGER.
FREED: On the 7th inst., by Rev. J.R.
Wheeler, Mr. G.W. FREED and Mrs. Margaret
H. BARGER, all of Augusta county.
Rockingham Register and Advertiser, 29
June 1860 (Friday), p. 3, c. 2.
FREEMAN: See entry for HOULTZ.
FREEMAN: See entry for MARSH.
FREEMAN: On March 19th, at the Methodist
Church, by Rev. Mr. Harris, Joseph W.
FREEMAN and Miss Fannie, daughter of John
H. NEWCOMB, Esq., all of Staunton.
Rockingham Register, 16 April 1868
(Thursday), p. 2, c. 5.
FREEZE: See entry for FREEZE.
FREEZE: On Thursday, the 26th of January, by
Rev. Jacob Miller, Mr. James Harvey
FREEZE and Miss Josephine C., daughter of
David PALSER, dec'd, all of Rockingham.
Rockingham Register and Advertiser, 17
February 1860 (Friday), p. 2, c. 4.
FREEZE: On Thursday evening, July 26, by Rev.
Joseph Funkhouser, Mr. Jefferson FREEZE,
of Page, and Miss Catharine, daughter of
Dr. Joseph FREEZE, of Rockingham county.
Rockingham Register and Advertiser, 3
August 1860 (Friday), p. 2, c. 5.
FRENCH: See entry for HOGE.
FRENGER: On the 10th of May, at the residence
of the bride, by Rev. J.D. Shirey, Peter
FRENGER and Mrs. Elizabeth ENTLEMAN, all
of Augusta county.
Rockingham Register and Advertiser, 31
May 1866 (Thursday), p. 3, c. 5.
FREY: On the 25th inst., at the residence of
the bride's father, by Rev. D.F. Bittle,
D.D., Rev. Prof. John G. FREY, of Roanoke
College, and Miss Fannie J., youngest
daughter of Wm. PERSINGER, Esq., of
Roanoke county, Va.
Rockingham Register and Virginia
Advertiser, 30 December 1859 (Friday), p.

2, c. 5.

FRIDLEY: See entry for BRYAN.

FRIEL: On July 2nd, 1862, by the Rev. Wm. T. Price, Mr. John FRIEL to Miss Katy GWINN, all of Highland county, Va.
The Rockingham Register, 19 December 1862 (Friday), p. 2, c. 4.

FRIPPE: On Thursday last, by Rev. A. Poe Boude, Rev. E.T.R. FRIPPE, of the Baltimore Annual Conference, M.E. Church, South, and Miss Maggie E., daughter of Michael SELLERS, of Rockingham county.
Rockingham Register, 4 March 1869 (Thursday), p. 2, c. 4.

FRISTOE: See entry for MAUCK.

FRISTOE: On the 11th inst., by Rev. J.W. Watson, Mr. Scott FRISTOE and Miss Mary C. PRESGRAVES, all of Page county.
Rockingham Register & Advertiser, 29 September 1865 (Friday), p. 3, c. 3.

FRITZ: See entry for GRAVES.

FRY: See entry for BARER.
FRY: See entry for BEATTY.
FRY: See entry for COFFMAN.
FRY: See entry for DIXON.
FRY: See entry for DODSON.
FRY: See entry for KIBLER.
FRY: See entry for NEWMAN.
FRY: See entry for RUPERT.
FRY: See entry for VIA.
FRY: See entry for WHITTLINGTON.

FRY: On the 5th inst., Mr. Ephraim FRY and Miss Margaret HUNCHBERGER, all of Shenandoah county.
Rockingham Register and Advertiser, 19 January 1866 (Friday), p. 3, c. 2.

FRY: On the 18th inst., by Rev. Wm. Brown, Mr. Frederick FRY and Miss Elizabeth J., daughter of David KERR, Esq., all of Augusta county.
Rockingham Register and Virginia Advertiser, 21 December 1855 (Friday), p. 2, c. 8.

FRY: On the 19th inst., by the Rev. Joseph Funkhouser, Mr. Jacob S. FRY and Miss Amanda A., daughter of Mr. Elias

MICHAELS, all of Rockingham.
Rockingham Register and Advertiser, 27
January 1860 (Friday), p. 2, c. 6.

FRY: On Sunday, the 22nd inst., near
Bridgewater, at the residence of George
W. Bright, by the Rev. Martin Miller, Mr.
Jesse FRY and Miss Julia A. BRIGHT, all
of this county.
Rockingham Register and Advertiser, 27
May 1859 (Friday), p. 2, c. 6.

FRY: On the 24th ult., by Elder H. Jennings,
Philip FRY and Miss Catharine LITTEN, all
of Shenandoah county.
Rockingham Register and Advertiser, 7
June 1866 (Thursday), p. 3, c. 3.

FRY: On the 17th ult., by Rev. Jacob
Stirewalt, Wm. FRY and Nancy SMITH, all
of Shenandoah.
Rockingham Register and Advertiser, 2
December 1859 (Friday), p. 2, c. 5.

FRY: On the 14th ult., by Rev. H. Wetzel, Wm.
A. FRY and Miss Sarah E. SHIPE, all of
Shenandoah county.
Rockingham Register, 4 June 1868
(Thursday), p. 2, c. 3.

FRYE: See entry for EARLY.

FRYE: See entry for KELLY.

FRYE: On the 7th inst., by Rev. P. Miller,
A.W. FRYE and Miss E. LONGACRE, all of
Hardy county.
Rockingham Register, 28 April 1870
(Thursday), p. 3, c. 3.

FRYE: On the 5th of October, by Rev. P.
Miller, Mr. George W. FRYE and Miss Mary
Ann MICHAEL, all of Hampshire county.
The Rockingham Register, 18 November 1864
(Friday), p. 2, c. 2.

FRYE: By Rev. P. Miller, June 23rd, Mr. H.L.
FRYE and Mrs. Eliza J. WILSON, all of
Hampshire county.
The Rockingham Register, 23 September
1864 (Friday), p. 2, c. 5.

FUDLEY: See entry for HOGSHEAD.

FULK: See entry for BIXLER.

FULK: See entry for CARRIER.

FULK: In Brock's Gap, on the 13th inst., by

Rev. John Kline, Mr. Christopher FULK and Miss Catharine, daughter of Mr. Philip RITCHIE, all of Rockingham.

Rockingham Register and Advertiser, 21 January 1859 (Friday), p. 3, c. 5.

FULK: On the 20th of September, in Cumberland, Maryland, by Rev. P.S. Warren, Harvey FULK and Miss Amanda E. PETERSON, both of Rockingham county, Va.

Rockingham Register, 14 October 1869 (Thursday), p. 2, c. 2.

FULK: On Sunday morning, the 9th of August, by Rev. Jacob Miller, Philip H. FULK and Miss Martha S., daughter of Capt. Addison HARPER, all of Rockingham county.

Rockingham Register, 13 August 1868 (Thursday), p. 2, c. 5.

FULK: At the residence of the bride's father, in Brock's Gap, on the evening of the 14th of February, by Elder Christian Kiser, Wm. FULK and Miss Laura F., daughter of Wm. PETERSON, all of Rockingham county.

Rockingham Register and Advertiser, 27 February 1868 (Thursday), p. 3, c. 3.

FULLER: See entry for PRICE.

FULLER: On the 6th inst., by Rev. Joseph R. Wheeler, John H. FULLER and Mrs. Sarah A. BROOKS, all of Staunton.

Rockingham Register and Advertiser, 14 February 1862 (Friday), p. 2, c. 6.

FULMER: At the residence of the bride's father, in New Market, by Rev. John H. Hunton, on the 9th inst., Mr. William FULMER, of Stuartsville, N.J., and Miss Ellen H., daughter of Dr. Godfrey HENKEL.

Rockingham Register and Advertiser, 18 February 1859 (Friday), p. 2, c. 6.

FULTON: See entry for DICE.

FULTZ: See entry for FULTZ.

FULTZ: See entry for HART.

FULTZ: See entry for WOODS.

FULTZ: In Staunton, on the 28th ult., at the Presbyterian Church, by Rev. Wm. E. Baker, Fred. L. FULTZ and Miss Amanda, daughter of Judge FULTZ.

Rockingham Register, 6 January 1870 (Thursday), p. 3, c. 3.

FUNK: See entry for FUNK.

FUNK: See entry for GONGWER.

FUNK: See entry for KEITH.

FUNK: See entry for WAMPLER.

FUNK: See entry for WHISSEN.

FUNK: On the 1st of April, by Rev. Jacob Miller, Addison J. FUNK and Miss Filoma KITE, all of Rockingham county.

Rockingham Register and Advertiser, 20 April 1866 (Friday), p. 2, c. 3.

FUNK: On the 24th ult., by Rev. Samuel A. Shaver, Mr. Ananias FUNK and Miss Ann Ragina FUNK, all of Shenandoah county.

Rockingham Register and Advertiser, 5 July 1866 (Thursday), p. 3, c. 5.

FUNK: On Wednesday, the 3rd inst., by Rev. H.A. Bovey, Erasmus FUNK, of Singer's Glen, Rockingham county, and Miss Maggie E. JORDAN, of Augusta county.

Rockingham Register, 18 February 1869 (Thursday), p. 2, c. 5.

FUNK: On the 19th of December, by Rev. Geo. Wine, Samuel C. FUNK and Miss Ann E., daughter of John ADAMS, all of Rockingham county.

Rockingham Register and Advertiser, 26 December 1867 (Thursday), p. 2, c. 6.

FUNK: On the 12th inst., by Rev. Levi Keller, Silas M. FUNK and Miss Louisa E. CRABILL, all of Shenandoah.

Rockingham Register and Advertiser, 26 December 1867 (Thursday), p. 2, c. 6.

FUNKHOUSER: See entry for BEELER.

FUNKHOUSER: See entry for GLAZE.

FUNKHOUSER: See entry for MUMAW.

FUNKHOUSER: See entry for NEWLAND.

FUNKHOUSER: See entry for STRICKLER.

FUNKHOUSER: See entry for WALTERS.

FUNKHOUSER: On the 14th inst., in the evening, by Rev. A. Poe Boude, David N. FUNKHOUSER and Miss Georgia V.S., daughter of Wm. ROUDABUSH, all of Rockingham county.

Rockingham Register and Advertiser, 28

February 1867 (Thursday), p. 2, c. 6.

FUNKHOUSER: On the 12th inst., near Cabin Hill, by Rev. J.P. Hyde, George W. FUNKHOUSER and Mrs. Elizabeth C. KIBLER, all of Shenandoah county.
Rockingham Register and Advertiser, 23 January 1868 (Thursday), p. 2, c. 4.

FUNKHOUSER: On   the   6th   inst.,   near Churchville, by Rev. P. Fletcher, J.A.J. FUNKHOUSER, of Rockingham, and Miss Alice HANGER, of Augusta county.
Rockingham Register and Advertiser, 21 November 1867 (Thursday), p. 2, c. 5.

FUNKHOUSER: On the 20th ult., by Rev. Peter Miller, Mr. J.H. FUNKHOUSER and Miss A.J. BEAN, of Hampshire.
Rockingham Register and Advertiser, 11 January 1861 (Friday), p. 3, c. 4.

FUNKHOUSER: On the 20th ult., by Rev. Mr. Haney, James W. FUNKHOUSER and Miss Fannie M. SNAPP, all of Shenandoah.
Rockingham Register and Advertiser, 5 December 1867 (Thursday), p. 2, c. 5.

FUNKHOUSER: On Wednesday afternoon, the 26th ult., by Rev. J.B. Davis, Mr. Milton P. FUNKHOUSER, of Staunton, to Miss Mary J. SCOTT, of this county.
Rockingham Register and Advertiser, 4 November 1859 (Friday), p. 2, c. 6.

FUNKHOUSER: On the 3rd inst., by Rev. Jacob Wine, Mr. Nathaniel N. FUNKHOUSER, of Rockingham, and Miss Sarah C. NEFF, of Shenandoah.
Rockingham Register and Advertiser, 12 October 1860 (Friday), p. 2, c. 4.

FUNKHOUSER: On the 26th of December, 1864, by Elder   H.   Jennings,   Mr.   Samuel   H. FUNKHOUSER to Miss Amanda ROSENBERGER, of Mt. Jackson.
Rockingham Register and Advertiser, 24 February 1865 (Friday), p. 2, c. 5.

FURR: See entry for BOX.

FURR: See entry for MITCHELL.

FURR: See entry for RIDDLE.

FURR: On the 23rd ult., in Staunton, by Rev. George B. Taylor, Mr. Geo. H. FURR and

Miss Keturah FAUBER.
Rockingham Register and Advertiser, 13
May 1859 (Friday), p. 3, c. 4.
FURRELL: See entry for MORRIS.
FURRY: See entry for SPENCE.
FUTT: In Philippi, Barbour county, Va., on
Thursday the 23rd ult., by the Rev.
Francis H. Reed, Mr. Edwin E. FUTT and
Miss Elizabeth Ann, daughter of Mr.
Martin MYERS, formerly of New Market.
Rockingham Register and Valley
Advertiser, 8 June 1850 (Saturday), p. 2,
c. 7.

- G -

GAINES: See entry for BEAR.
GAINES: See entry for BURKHOLDER.
GAINES: See entry for KARICOFE.
GAINES: See entry for NELSON.
GAINS: See entry for KARACOFE.
GAIREY: See entry for GOOD.
GAITHER: See entry for BRYANT.
GAITHER: See entry for DEAN.
GAITHER: See entry for TAYLOR.
GAITHER: See entry for WEST.
GAITHER: On the 8th inst., near Keezeltown,
by Rev. Frederick Miller, Geo. W. GAITHER
and Miss Mary ORNDORFF, all of Rockingham
county.
Rockingham Register, 12 May 1870
(Thursday), p. 3, c. 3.
GAITHER: Near Mt. Sterling, Madison county,
Ohio, on Sunday morning, the 9th of
September, by S. Timmons, Esq., Mr. Jacob
H. GAITHER, late of Rockingham county,
Va., and Miss Jane TAMMADGE, of Madison
county, Ohio.
Rockingham Register and Advertiser, 19
October 1860 (Friday), p. 2, c. 4.
GAITHER: On the 11th ult., by Rev. A.J.
KIBLER, John W. GAITHER and Miss Delila
LEE, all of Rockingham county.
Rockingham Register and Advertiser, 2
March 1866 (Friday), p. 3, c. 3.
GALBRAITH: See entry for HARNSBERGER.

GALLAGHER: In Winchester, on the 18th of April, by the Rev. Norval WILSON, W.W.B. GALLAGHER, Junior Editor of the Virginia Free Press, of Charlestown, and Miss Belle WILSON, daughter of the officiating clergyman.
Rockingham Register and Advertiser, 2 May 1867 (Thursday), p. 2, c. 6.

GAMBRILL: See entry for ZEA.

GANDER: See entry for BRUBAKER.

GANES: On the 11th inst., by Rev. Jacob Thomas, C. GANES, of Barbour county, Va., and Miss Mary J., daughter of David ADAMS, of Augusta county, Va.
Rockingham Register and Advertiser, 16 March 1866 (Friday), p. 3, c. 4.

GARBER: See entry for BALDWIN.

GARBER: See entry for DAVIS.

GARBER: See entry for GREGORY.

GARBER: On Tuesday, the 5th inst., by Rev. Solomon Garber, Rev. Abraham GARBER and Mrs. Sophia HASE, daughter of William BIRD, all of Augusta.
Rockingham Register, 14 October 1869 (Thursday), p. 2, c. 2.

GARBER: On Tuesday, the 19th inst. [sic, ult.], by the Rev. Robert Walker, Mr. Christian C. GARBER, son of Rev. Solomon GARBER, of Rockingham, and Miss Etta B. CONNER, of Augusta ....
Rockingham Register and Advertiser, 1 March 1861 (Friday), p. 3, c. 3.

GARBER: On the 14th of February, by the Rev. Solomon Garber, Serg't Daniel GARBER, Jr., of Co. H, 12th Va. Cavalry, and Miss Fannie COFFMAN, all of Rockingham.
Rockingham Register and Advertiser, 24 February 1865 (Friday), p. 2, c. 5.

GARBER: On the 11th inst., by Rev. Jacob Miller, Isaac M. GARBER and Miss Mollie C., daughter of David DRIVER, all of Rockingham county.
Rockingham Register and Advertiser, 18 April 1867 (Thursday), p. 2, c. 6.

GARBER: Near Timberville, on Thursday, the 23rd of December, by Rev. Jacob Miller,

Jacob GARBER and Miss Rebecca, daughter of Jonas EARLY, all of Rockingham county. Rockingham Register, 6 January 1870 (Thursday), p. 3, c. 3.

GARBER: On Tuesday the 29th of January, by Rev. Geo. B. Taylor, John GARBER and Miss Melinda RISWICK, all of Staunton. Rockingham Register and Advertiser, 14 February 1867 (Thursday), p. 2, c. 6.

GARBER: On the 20th inst., by Rev. Jas. H. Wolff, Mr. Martin K. GARBER, of Augusta, and Miss Elizabeth R. MILLER, of Bath. Rockingham Register and Advertiser, 28 September 1860 (Friday), p. 2, c. 4.

GARBER: On the 14th ult., by the Rev. J.C. Hensell, Mr. Solomon GARBER and Miss Bettie S., eldest daughter of Reuben HUFFMAN, Esq., all of Rockingham. Rockingham Register and Advertiser, 2 March 1860 (Friday), p. 3, c. 2.

GARDNER: See entry for QUITMAN.

GARDNER: On the 16th of July, by Rev. Frederick Miller, at the bride's father's, Brightberry B. GARDNER, of Albemarle county, and Mrs. Eliza Ann COFFMAN, daughter of John HAUGH, of Rockingham county. Rockingham Register and Advertiser, 19 July 1866 (Thursday), p. 3, c. 3.

GARLAND: See entry for MEEM.

GARNEET: On the morning of the 10th inst., at Sycamore Church, by Elder Dr. Hopson, Muscoe GARNEET, of the House of Delegates from Essex, and Miss Mary E., eldest daughter of Mr. John TYLER, of Richmond. Rockingham Register and Advertiser, 18 April 1867 (Thursday), p. 2, c. 6.

GARRISON: See entry for DENNETT.

GARRISON: See entry for FIELDING.

GASSMAN: In Cumberland, Md., Thursday, August 25, 1870, by Rev. J.D. Fitzgerald, Geo. W. GASSMAN, of Harrisonburg, Va., formerly of Cumberland, and Miss Lizzie C., daughter of John YOUNG, dec'd, of Cumberland. Rockingham Register, 1 September 1870

(Thursday), p. 2, c. 3.

GATEWOOD: See entry for ALLEN.

GATEWOOD: See entry for HUDDLESON.

GATEWOOD: At Warwick, Bath county, Va., on
the 1st inst., by the Rev. W.W. Houston,
A.C.L. GATEWOOD, Esq., and Miss Mary F.
WARWICK, all of Bath county.
Rockingham Register, 16 December 1869
(Thursday), p. 2, c. 5.

GAW: On the 22nd ult., at the residence of
Job Turner, Esq., Staunton, by the Rev.
Geo. B. Taylor, Mr. Robert P. GAW, of
Woodstock, to Miss Margaret E. BEAN, of
Staunton, both bride and bridegroom being
Deaf Mutes.
Rockingham Register & Advertiser, 6
October 1865 (Friday), p. 2, c. 2.

GAY: See entry for MOORE.

GAY: At the residence of the bride's father,
in McGaheysville, on Thursday, the 4th
inst., by Rev. Mr. Garver, Gustavus GAY,
of Harrisonburg, and Miss Mary Jane,
daughter of James O'BRIEN, Esq., of
McGaheysville.
Rockingham Register and Advertiser, 18
October 1866 (Thursday), p. 2, c. 4.

GEARHART: See entry for LOVEGROVE.

GEARHEART: See entry for GREAVER.

GELTMACHER: See entry for HORN.

GELTMACHER: See entry for WHITE.

GENTRY: See entry for COATS.

GENTRY: See entry for SIMMERS.

GENTRY: On Saturday the 5th of June, by Rev.
Abraham Knupp, Mr. James GENTRY and Mrs.
Mary Elizabeth RAINS, all of Rockingham
county.
Rockingham Register and Advertiser, 18
June 1858 (Friday), p. 3, c. 4.

GENTRY: At the residence of the bride's
father, in Chester, Va., on the 8th of
December, 1863, by Rev. Alex G. Brown,
Mr. Joseph B. GENTRY and Miss Mollie L.,
eldest daughter of J.M. and Sarah CONRAD.
The Rockingham Register, 8 January 1864
(Friday), p. 2, c. 5.

GEORGE: On the 28th ult., near Williamsport,

Grant county, West Virginia, by Rev. L.W. Haslup, D. Worth GEORGE and Miss Laura F. MARKWOOD.

Rockingham Register, 28 April 1870 (Thursday), p. 3, c. 3.

GERE: See entry for SHIPLEY.

GETE: On the 11th inst., by Rev. Socrates Henkel, Mr. John GETE and Leanah BOWERS, all of Rockingham.

Rockingham Register and Advertiser, 26 December 1856 (Friday), p. 2, c. 7.

GETTS: On the 20th inst., by Rev. Jos. Funkhouser, Levi GETTS, of Shenandoah county, and Miss Sarah Jane DORMAN, of Rockingham county.

Rockingham Register and Advertiser, 27 September 1866 (Thursday), p. 3, c. 3.

GETZ: See entry for WOLF.

GIBBONS: See entry for IRICK.

GIBBS: See entry for LEMON.

GIBSON: On the 16th inst., by the Rev. Isaac Gibson, at the residence of the bride's father, Dr. J. St. Pierre GIBSON and Miss Mary Smith, daughter of Joel S. WALLACE, both of Waynesboro.

Rockingham Register and Advertiser, 30 May 1867 (Thursday), p. 3, c. 3.

GIBSON: On the 29th ult., by Rev. J.S. Pullen, Mr. Jno. L. GIBSON and Miss Alice LIGHTNER, all of Highland county.

Rockingham Register and Advertiser, 15 February 1861 (Friday), p. 2, c. 7.

GIFFIN: On the 17th of November, 1863, by Rev. P. Miller, Mr. John GIFFIN and Miss Mary BROWN, all of Frederick county.

The Rockingham Register, 26 February 1864 (Friday), p. 2, c. 4.

GILBERT: On the 13th inst., by Rev. G.W. Rexrode, Rev. John W. GILBERT, of the United Brethren Church, to Miss Ellen, daughter of Absalom and Emily CLARKE, both of Augusta county.

Rockingham Register and Advertiser, 12 October 1860 (Friday), p. 2, c. 4.

GILES: See entry for CHRISMAN.

GILES: On the 8th inst., at the residence of

the bride's father, by Rev. Wm. Baker, Samuel N. GILES, of Staunton, and Miss Mary Carrol, daughter of Wm. R. DUNLAP, Esq., of Augusta.

Rockingham Register, 16 April 1868 (Thursday), p. 2, c. 5.

GILKELOA: In Greenville, on the 23rd ult., by Rev. Jas. Murray, Dr. I.W. GILKELOA and Miss Kitty, daughter of the late Dr. P. GILLUM.

Rockingham Register, 6 January 1870 (Thursday), p. 3, c. 3.

GILKERSON: See entry for PLECKER.

GILKESON: See entry for BERKELEY.

GILKESON: On the 11th inst., by Rev. Dr. Weed, Andrew Todd GILKESON, of Augusta county, and Miss Emma S. HEISKELL, of Wheeling.

Rockingham Register and Virginia Advertiser, 2 November 1855 (Friday), p. 3, c. 1.

GILKESON: On the 20th ult., at Greenville, by Rev. James Murray, John W. GILKESON and Miss Letitia M. TATE, all of Augusta.

Rockingham Register, 5 November 1868 (Thursday), p. 3, c. 3.

GILKESON: On the 11th inst., near Parnassus, by Rev. J.J. Engle, Thomas E. GILKESON and Miss Sallie J. ALTAFFER, all of Augusta county.

Rockingham Register, 20 January 1870 (Thursday), p. 2, c. 5.

GILKISON: On Thursday, the 4th inst., by Rev. J.C. Hensell, Jas. H. GILKISON and Miss Elizabeth ECHERD, all of Augusta county.

Rockingham Register and Advertiser, 18 October 1866 (Thursday), p. 2, c. 4.

GILL: On the 23rd ult., by Rev. John Clymer, John R. GILL and Miss Mary J. STIDLEY, both of Shenandoah county.

Rockingham Register, 13 January 1870 (Thursday), p. 3. c. 4.

GILLASPY: On the 26th ult., by Rev. John Hutchens, Mr. Geo. W. GILLASPY and Miss Ellen McCLURE, both of Augusta county.

Rockingham Register and Advertiser, 10

January 1862 (Friday), p. 3, c. 2.

GILLOCK: See entry for ALBERT.

GILLUM: See entry for GILKELOA.

GILMER: See entry for BIRD.

GILMER: See entry for GLADWELL.

GILMER: See entry for MINNICK.

GILMER: On Tuesday evening last, by Rev. A. Poe Boude, Rob't H. GILMER and Miss Rebecca S., daughter of Levi CROMER, all of Harrisonburg.
Rockingham Register and Advertiser, 18 April 1867 (Thursday), p. 2, c. 6.

GILMER: In Blacksburg, Montgomery county, on the 12th inst., by the Rev. John W. [torn], Samuel A.B. GILMER, Esq., Editor of the Lewisburg Chronicle, to Miss Sallie E., daughter of the late Col. Elisha CALLISON, Esq., of Greenbrier county.
Rockingham Register and Virginia Advertiser, 21 December 1855 (Friday), p. 2, c. 8.

GILMORE: In New York, on Thursday, the 15th of November, by the Rev. Mr. Scott, of Pensacola, Florida, Col. Harry GILMORE, of the late Confederate States Army, and Mentorian, daughter of the late Col. Jasper STRONG, formerly of the United States Army.
Rockingham Register and Advertiser, 3 January 1867 (Thursday), p. 3, c. 3.

GILMORE: On the 2nd inst., at the residence of the bride's father, by the Rev. W.F. Junkin, Mr. Thomas R. GILMORE and Miss Mary E., daughter of Dr. James L. WATSON, all of Rockbridge county, Va.
Rockingham Register and Advertiser, 16 June 1865 (Friday), p. 1, c. 3.

GILMORE: At the residence of E.J. Williams, in Greene county, Va., on the 20th of December, 1865, by the Rev. Mr. Coleman, Z.D. GILMORE, Esq.,of McGaheysville, Rockingham county, and Miss Phoebe, daughter of John NEWMAN, formerly of Shenandoah county.
Rockingham Register and Advertiser, 12

January 1866 (Friday), p. 1, c. 3.

GINEVAN: On the 25th of May, at the residence of the bride's mother, by the Rev. J.T. Pinkerton, Capt. Matthias GINEVAN, C.S.A., and Miss Lavinia HANSBERGER, of Rockingham county, Va.

Rockingham Register and Advertiser, 16 June 1865 (Friday), p. 1, c. 3.

GISH: See entry for LONG.

GISH: See entry for SHAVER.

GISH: On the 24th of September, by Rev. R.C. Walker, John W. GISH and Miss Mattie J., daughter of James WHEELER, all of Augusta county.

Rockingham Register, 29 October 1868 (Thursday), p. 3, c. 3.

GISINER: November 11th, 1858, by Rev. D. Winters, T.S.W. GISINER, V.D.M., formerly of Brownsburg, Va., and Miss Mary M. SNYPP, of Bath Township, Green county, Ohio.

Rockingham Register and Advertiser, 11 February 1859 (Friday), p. 3, c. 2.

GIVEN: On the 20th inst., by the Rev. Leonidas Butt, J.C. GIVEN, of Woodstock, McHenry county, Ill., and Miss Mary A. RIDER, of Highland county, Va.

Rockingham Register and Advertiser, 30 August 1866 (Thursday), p. 2, c. 4.

GIVENS: See entry for PENCE.

GLADVILLE: See entry for RAY.

GLADVILLE: On the 27th, by the Rev. Mr. Shickell, Mr. Washington GLADVILLE to Miss Mary LONG, all of this county.

Rockingham Register and Valley Advertiser, 30 December 1843 (Saturday), p. 4. c. 1.

GLADWELL: See entry for RANFORD.

GLADWELL: On the 26th inst., by Rev. Wm. E. Baker, Mr. Harvey G. GLADWELL to Mrs. Mary S. TRAWEEK.

Rockingham Register and Advertiser, 30 January 1868 (Thursday), p. 2, c. 4.

GLADWELL: On the 13th of January, by Rev. Jacob Thomas, at his residence, James A. GLADWELL and Miss Lydia M., daughter of

Samuel WHEELBARGER, all of Rockingham county.

Rockingham Register, 20 January 1870 (Thursday), p. 2, c. 5.

GLADWELL: November 27th, 1862, by the Rev. Wm. T. Price, Private John W. GLADWELL, of the Bath cavalry, to Miss Estaline, daughter of Mr. Jacob STEWART, of Highland county, Va.

The Rockingham Register, 19 December 1862 (Friday), p. 2, c. 4.

GLADWELL: On the 11th inst., by Rev. Jas. F. Gilmer, Solomon GLADWELL and Miss Mary E. GILMER, all of Rockingham county.

Rockingham Register, 20 August 1868 (Thursday), p. 3, c. 3.

GLASS: See entry for BISHOP.

GLASS: See entry for SMILEY.

GLASS: On the 6th inst., by Rev. J.D. Shirey, Mr. Jas. W. GLASS and Miss Eliza J. RANSBOTTOM, all of Augusta.

Rockingham Register and Advertiser, 14 December 1860 (Friday), p. 2, c. 6.

GLASS: In Fayetteville, N.C., September 17th, 1863, by the Rev. Joseph C. Huske, Rob't H. GLASS, Esq., of Lynchburg, Va., and Miss Meta, daughter of John W. SANFORD, of the former city.

The Rockingham Register, 25 September 1863 (Friday), p. 2, c. 4.

GLAZE: On the 15th ult., by Rev. J.W. Hott, Zedekiah GLAZE and Miss Rachel A. FUNKHOUSER, all of Shenandoah.

Rockingham Register and Advertiser, 7 February 1867 (Thursday), p. 3, c. 3.

GLEE: On the 9th inst., by Rev. John Harshberger, Mr. James GLEE and Miss Julia Ann, daughter of Michael EARMAN, all of Rockingham.

Rockingham Register and Advertiser, 14 September 1860 (Friday), p. 2, c. 5.

GLEN: On Thursday, 13th inst., by the Rev. Wm. P. Twyman, Mr. Hiram GLEN and Miss Sarah BAUGHER, all of this county.

Rockingham Register and Advertiser, 28 May 1858 (Friday), p. 3, c. 2.

GLENDY: See entry for KELSO.

GLOSSBRENNER: See entry for TURNER.

GLOVER: See entry for HIGH.

GLOVER: On the 13th inst., by Rev. T. Brashear, Mr. Geo. GLOVER and Miss Margaret C., daughter of John PRICE, all of Augusta county.
Rockingham Register and Advertiser, 28 October 1859 (Friday), p. 2, c. 6.

GLOVER: On the 4th inst., near Middlebrook, Augusta county, by Rev. E.H. Jones, Mr. W.P. GLOVER, of Monroe county, W.Va., and Miss Mary J. SKELTON, of Augusta.
Rockingham Register and Advertiser, 26 January 1866 (Friday), p. 3, c. 3.

GLOVIER: See entry for BRIGHT.

GLOVIER: See entry for TAYLOR.

GLOVIER: At Orchard Grove, near Keezeltown, on Thursday, the 11th of February, by Rev. Jos. Funkhouser, Mr. Jno. W. GLOVIER and Miss Melissa H.C., daughter of Riley ARMENTROUT, all of Rockingham county.
The Rockingham Register, 19 February 1864 (Friday), p. 2, c. 6.

GOCHENOUR: See entry for COPP.

GOCHENOUR: See entry for HANSBERGER.

GOCHENOUR: See entry for SCRAGHAN.

GOCHENOUR: On the 28th ult., by Rev. A.R. Rude, Mr. David GOCHENOUR and Barbara Ann KAGY, all of Shenandoah county.
Rockingham Register and Advertiser, 28 January 1859 (Friday), p. 2, c. 6.

GOCHENOUR: Near Woodstock, on the 10th inst., by Rev. G.H. Martin, David H. GOCHENOUR and Miss Barbara Ann, daughter of Wm. FRAVEL, Esq., all of Shenandoah county.
Rockingham Register and Advertiser, 24 May 1866 (Thursday), p. 3, c. 4.

GOCHENOUR: On the 25th ult., by Rev. Martin Garber, Geo. W. GOCHENOUR and Miss Mary M. HAWKINS, all of Augusta county.
Rockingham Register and Advertiser, 9 January 1868 (Thursday), p. 2, c. 4.

GOCHENOUR: On the 31st ult., by Rev. H. St. J. Rinker, Mr. John T. GOCHENOUR and Miss Mary PENCE, all of Shenandoah county.

Rockingham Register and Advertiser, 7
April 1865 (Friday), p. 2, c. 5.
Repeated, 14 April 1865 (Friday), p. 2,
c. 5.

GOCHENOUR: On Thursday, 9th inst., by Rev.
R.P. Kennedy, Martin J. GOCHENOUR, of
Augusta, and Miss Virginia C. ROADCAP, of
Rockingham county.
Rockingham Register and Advertiser, 23
January 1868 (Thursday), p. 2, c. 4.

GOEN: On Tuesday the 11th of March, by the
Rev. Peter Shickle, Mr. Daniel GOEN and
Miss Francis C., daughter of Mr. Samuel
WEITZEL, all of Augusta county.
Rockingham Register and Valley
Advertiser, 19 April 1845 (Saturday), p.
3, c. 1.

GOLDEN: See entry for COFFMAN.

GOLLADAY: See entry for BLACK.

GOLLADAY: See entry for DRUMHELLER.

GOLLADAY: See entry for LICHLITER.

GOLLADAY: See entry for SILVIUS.

GOLLADAY: On the 10th inst., by Rev. H.
Wetzel, David GOLLADAY and Miss Mary S.
SHEETZ, both of Shenandoah county.
Rockingham Register, 24 March 1870
(Thursday), p. 3, c. 2.

GOLLADAY: On the 11th inst., by Elder John
Pirkey, G.W. GOLLADAY and Miss Lucy
SONNER, all of Shenandoah county.
Rockingham Register and Advertiser, 25
April 1867 (Thursday), p. 2, c. 7.

GOLLADAY: On the 14th inst., by Rev. J.R.
Wheeler, Mr. George GOLLADAY and Miss
Martha A.A. WILLIAMS, of Augusta county.
Rockingham Register and Advertiser, 29
June 1860 (Friday), p. 3, c. 2.

GOLLADAY: On the 5th inst., Maj. J.B.
GOLLADAY and Miss Kate LONAS, all of
Shenandoah county.
Rockingham Register, 7 January 1869
(Thursday), p. 3, c. 3.

GOLLADAY: On the 14th inst., by Rev. Samuel
A. Shaver, James GOLLADAY and Miss Atilla
J. MUNCH, all of Shenandoah county.
Rockingham Register and Advertiser, 28

March 1867 (Thursday), p. 2, c. 6.

GOLLIDAY: On the 12th of January, 1865, by Elder H. Jennings, Mr. Samuel C. GOLLIDAY to Miss Lydia C. McINTURFF, all of Shenandoah county.
Rockingham Register and Advertiser, 24 February 1865 (Friday), p. 2, c. 5.

GONGWER: See entry for MINNICK.

GONGWER: On the 10th inst., by Rev. V.F. Bolton, Mr. John B. GONGWER and Miss Mary C.H., daughter of Mr. Jonathan FUNK, all of this county.
Rockingham Register and Advertiser, 17 October 1856 (Friday), p. 2, c. 5.

GOOD: See entry for CLINE.

GOOD: See entry for HIDEN (2).

GOOD: See entry for LITTEN.

GOOD: See entry for LONG.

GOOD: See entry for McCOY.

GOOD: See entry for MARSTEN.

GOOD: See entry for MYERS.

GOOD: See entry for PETERSON.

GOOD: See entry for WEBB.

GOOD: In Newcastle, Henry county, Indiana, February 14th, 1870, Elias GOOD, formerly of New Market, Va., and Miss Jullia A., daughter of Philip D. RINKER, formerly of Hampshire county, W.Va.
Rockingham Register, 17 March 1870 (Thursday), p. 2, c. 4.

GOOD: On the 21st of April, by Rev. Isaac Long, Mr. Franklin J.H. GOOD and Miss Frances C., daughter of Peter SHOWALTER, all of Rockingham county.
The Rockingham Register, 29 April 1864 (Friday), p. 2, c. 5.

GOOD: On the 9th inst., near Alma, by Rev. J.S. Bennick, Jas. M. GOOD and Miss Lydia JUDY, both of Page county.
Rockingham Register, 23 April 1868 (Thursday), p. 2, c. 6.

GOOD: On the 30th ult., by Rev. J.W. Watson, Mr. John GOOD and Miss Barbara, daughter of Henry COMER.
Rockingham Register and Advertiser, 9 November 1860 (Friday), p. 2, c. 6.

GOOD: On Sunday the 14th of August, by Rev. Jacob Miller, John C. GOOD and Miss Rachel A., daughter of Michael J. ZIRKEL, all of Rockingham county.
Rockingham Register, 18 August 1870 (Thursday), p. 3, c. 3.

GOOD: On the 14th inst., by [Rev.] John J. Harshbarger, Mr. Peter GOOD and Miss Sarah Jane FALLY, both of Rockingham county.
Rockingham Register and Advertiser, 25 March 1859 (Friday), p. 3, c. 2.

GOOD: On the 28th of January, at Mt. Jackson, by Rev. W.H. Cone, Mr. Peter GOOD and Miss Abigail SHAFFER, both of Shenandoah county.
The Rockingham Register, 5 February 1864 (Friday), p. 2, c. 6.

GOOD: On the 10th inst., by Rev. A.J. Kibler, Samuel H. GOOD, of Rockingham, and Mrs. L.A. YATES, of Lewinsville, Warren county, Va.
Rockingham Register, 25 August 1870 (Thursday), p. 2, c. 4.

GOOD: On the 21st of April, by Rev. Isaac Long, Silas R. GOOD and Miss Susan, daughter of Jno. GAIREY, all of Rockingham county.
Rockingham Register, 30 April 1868 (Thursday), p. 2, c. 6.

GOOD: At Taylor's Springs, on Thursday the 28th of March, by Rev. Joseph Funkhouser, Mr. Wm. GOOD and Miss Mary Sallie, daughter of Mr. Wm. KELLER, all of Rockingham.
Rockingham Register and Advertiser, 12 April 1861 (Friday), p. 2, c. 4.

GOOD: At the residence of the bride's father, near Turleytown, on Tuesday, the 29th ult., by Rev. Benj. Bowman, Mr. William H. GOOD, of Shenandoah, and Miss Parmelia F., daughter of Col. J. HORN, of this county.
Rockingham Register and Advertiser, 8 June 1860 (Friday), p. 2, c. 5.

GOOD: On Thursday, the 28th of December, by

Rev. Isaac Long, Wm. S. GOOD and Miss
Mary A., daughter of George BERRY, all of
Rockingham county.
Rockingham Register and Advertiser, 19
January 1866 (Friday), p. 3, c. 2.

GOODRIDGE: On the 27th ult., at the Fourth
Presbyterian Church, Baltimore, by the
Rev. John Squires, Geo. K. GOODRIDGE,
Esq., of Norfolk, Va., and Miss Ella S.,
daughter of Dr. John MURPHY, late of
Virginia.
Rockingham Register and Advertiser, 12
December 1867 (Thursday), p. 3, c. 2.

GORDON: See entry for BYRD.

GORDON: See entry for COLEMAN.

GORDON: See entry for LAMB.

GORDON: See entry for POINTS.

GORDON: See entry for SEAL.

GORDON: On the 24th ult., at the Parsonage of
the German Reformed Church, in Woodstock,
by Rev. G.H. Martin, Alexander GORDON and
Miss Mary Ann JENKINS, all of Shenandoah
county.
Rockingham Register and Advertiser, 3
October 1867 (Thursday), p. 2, c. 6.

GORDON: On Thursday, the 18th inst., by Rev.
J. Wine, John GORDON and Miss Magdalene,
daughter of John JONES, dec'd, all of
Rockingham county.
Rockingham Register, 25 November 1869
(Thursday), p. 2, c. 3.

GORDON: On the 11th ult., near Deerfield,
Augusta county, by Rev. J.W. Ryland,
Mitchell GORDON, of Bath county, and Miss
Ellen HULTZ, of Augusta.
Rockingham Register, 2 December 1869
(Thursday), p. 2, c. 3.

GORDON: On the 12th inst., by Rev. Horatio
Thompson, D.D., Mr. Nathaniel T. GORDON,
formerly of Harrisonburg, to Miss Nannie
E., daughter of F.J. CLEMER, Esq., of
Fairfield.
Rockingham Register and Advertiser, 27
January 1860 (Friday), p. 2, c. 6.

GORDON: On the 18th ult., at the residence of
the bride's father, O.L. WILLIAMS, Esq.,

by the Rev. M.B. Edmundson, Samuel D. GORDON, editor of the Wirt County Democrat, and Miss Bettie F. WILLIAMS, all of Wirt county.
Rockingham Register, 9 December 1869 (Thursday), p. 3, c. 2.

GORDON: On Sunday morning last, by Rev. Thos. D. Bell, Capt. T.W. GORDON and Miss Catharine, daughter of Mr. Andrew BEAR, of Harrisonburg.
Rockingham Register and Virginia Advertiser, 18 May 1855 (Friday), p. 3, c. 4.

GOUL: See entry for HINEGARDNER.

GOUL: On the 1st of January, 1863, by the Rev. John W. Howe, Mr. William T. GOUL and Sarah E. WALTER, all of this county.
The Rockingham Register, 9 January 1863 (Friday), p. 2, c. 5.

GOULD: At the residence of the bride's father, near Edinburg, on the 23rd inst., by Rev. Mr. Clymer, Mr. _____ GOULD, of Winchester, and Miss Viola L., daughter of Philip PITMAN, Esq., of Shenandoah county.
Rockingham Register, 30 April 1868 (Thursday), p. 2, c. 6.

GOWEL: At the residence of the bride's father, near New Erection Church, in this county, on Thursday, the 19th inst., by the Rev. P.M. Custer, Mr. Daniel GOWEL and Miss Lizzie, daughter of Jacob LINEWEAVER, Sr., all of Rockingham county.
Rockingham Register and Advertiser, 27 April 1866 (Friday), p. 2, c. 2.

GRABE: See entry for IMMEL.

GRABILL: On the 7th of June, by Rev. Levi Keller, David M. GRAVILL and Disa E. EBERT, both of Shenandoah county.
Rockingham Register, 16 June 1870 (Thursday), p. 3, c. 3.

GRABILL: On Sunday morning last, by Rev. A.P. Boude, George W. GRABILL and Miss Esther G., daughter of Strother SHEETS, all of Rockingham county.

Rockingham Register and Advertiser, 27 April 1866 (Friday), p. 2, c. 2.

GRABILL: On the 2nd inst., by Rev. J.I. Miller, Rev. J.M. GRABILL, of Harrisonburg, Va., and Miss Annie PRATHER, of Clear Spring, Md.

Rockingham Register and Advertiser, 26 November 1858 (Friday), p. 3, c. 2.

GRABILL: On the 19th ult., in the E.M. Church, in Woodstock, by the Rev. J.P. Hyde, John H. GRABILL and Miss Mollie L., daughter of I.N. HOLLINGSWORTH, all of Shenandoah county.

Rockingham Register and Advertiser, 3 January 1867 (Thursday), p. 3, c. 3.

GRADWOHL: On Frederick street, Baltimore, on Wednesday the 3rd of April, by Rabbi Hochheimer, Samuel GRADWOHL and Miss Josephine WISE, both of Harrisonburg.

Rockingham Register and Advertiser, 11 April 1867 (Thursday), p. 3, c. 4.

GRADY: See entry for COAKLEY.

GRADY: See entry for RIMEL.

GRAHAM: See entry for LAMBETH.

GRAHAM: See entry for LAREW.

GRAHAM: On the 18th ult., by the Rev. John Pinkerton, at the residence of the bride's father, near Mt. Solon, Wingfield S. GRAHAM and Miss Dorothy, daughter of Mr. John STOUTAMOYER.

Rockingham Register, 2 December 1869 (Thursday), p. 2, c. 3.

GRANDEL: See entry for SPRINKEL.

GRANDELL: See entry for MILLER.

GRANDLE: See entry for SHOEMAKER.

GRANDSTAFF: See entry for FADELY.

GRANDSTAFF: See entry for LUDWIG.

GRANDSTAFF: See entry for MOORE.

GRANDSTAFF: See entry for REID.

GRANDSTAFF: In Forestville, on Sunday last, by Rev. J.P. Cline, Mr. Jacob F. GRANDSTAFF and Miss Elizabeth BOWMAN, all of Shenandoah.

Rockingham Register and Advertiser, 12 April 1861 (Friday), p. 2, c. 4.

GRANDSTAFF: On the 20th of January, ... Mr.

Joseph GRANDSTAFF and Miss Louisa D. WILLIAMS, all of Hardy county.
Rockingham Register and Advertiser, 10 February 1865 (Friday), p. 2, c. 2.

GRANDSTAFF: At the Lutheran Parsonage, in Woodstock, on the 28th ult., by Rev. Levi Keller, Noah J. GRANDSTAFF and Miss Mary E. RAU, all of Shenandoah.
Rockingham Register, 11 February 1869 (Thursday), p. 3, c. 3.

GRANDSTAFF: On the 19th inst., by Elder Henry Jennings, Mr. Wm. L. GRANDSTAFF and Miss Sarah F. BUCK, all of Shenandoah county.
Rockingham Register, 14 May 1868 (Thursday), p. 2, c. 5.

GRANSTAFF: On the 21st ult., by Elder John H. Menifee, Geo. W. GRANSTAFF and Miss Clarinda JUDD, all of Page county.
Rockingham Register, 2 December 1869 (Thursday), p. 2, c. 3.

GRANT: See entry for FORD.

GRASTY: See entry for GRASTY.

GRASTY: On the 6th ult., at the residence of the bride's father, by Elder R.C. Cave, J.T. GRASTY and Miss ____ GRASTY, all of Orange county.
Rockingham Register, 26 November 1868 (Thursday), p. 2, c. 5.

GRATTAN: See entry for CHRISMAN.

GRATTAN: See entry for DOYLE.

GRATTAN: On the 6th inst., by Rev. F.H. Bowman, at River Side, Capt. Charles GRATTAN, of Rockingham, and Miss Lizzie Crawford, daughter of Samuel F. FINLEY, Esq., of Augusta.
The Rockingham Register, 22 January 1864 (Friday), p. 2, c. 5.

GRATTAN: On the 18th inst., by Rev. J. Rice Bowman, Capt. George G. GRATTAN and Miss M. Ella, daughter of A.E. HENEBERGER, Esq., all of Harrisonburg.
Rockingham Register, 20 October 1870 (Thursday), p. 3, c. 5.

GRAVE: At the residence of the bride's mother, near Frederick city, Md., on the 5th inst., by Rev. Geo. Deihl, Mr.

William P. GRAVE, of the H.L.M. & M. Co.,
of this place, and Miss Julia FOUT, of
the former place.
Rockingham Register, 14 May 1868
(Thursday), p. 2, c. 5.

GRAVES: See entry for KOONTZ.

GRAVES: See entry for LAMB.

GRAVES: On the 23rd inst., by Rev. J.W.
Watson, at the residence of Mr. G.W.
Reedy, Mr. James GRAVES and Miss C.E.
FRITZ, of Lancaster, Pa.
Rockingham Register and Advertiser, 6 May
1859 (Friday), p. 3, c. 2.

GRAY: See entry for DANGERFIELD.

GRAY: See entry for TOWLES.

GRAY: On the 28th ult., by Rev. John Rice
Bowman, James H. GRAY and Miss Lizzie
McLAUGHLIN, all of this place.
Rockingham Register and Advertiser, 3
October 1867 (Thursday), p. 2, c. 6.

GRAY: On Thursday evening last, by the Rev.
Wm. H. Wilson, Mr. John R. GRAY to Miss
Elizabeth JETT, all of this town.
Rockingham Register and Valley
Advertiser, 5 September 1846 (Saturday),
p. 2, c. 7.

GRAY: On the 19th of January, ... Mr. Philip
GRAY and Miss Rebecca HANES, all of
Hampshire county.
Rockingham Register and Advertiser, 10
February 1865 (Friday), p. 2, c. 2.

GRAY: On the 20th ult., by Rev. Wm. D.
Rippetoe, Mr. Samuel GRAY and Miss Mary
S. DECKER, all of Page county.
Rockingham Register and Advertiser, 22
June 1860 (Friday), p. 2, c. 6.
Repeated, 6 July 1860 (Friday), p. 2, c.
6.

GRAY: On the 8th of December, by Rev. P.
Miller, Mr. William GRAY, of Hampshire
county, and Miss Barbara E. WISE, of
Hardy county.
Rockingham Register and Advertiser, 10
February 1865 (Friday), p. 2, c. 2.

GRAYSON: On the 20th inst., by Elder F.M.
Perry, Benjamin F. GRAYSON, Jr., and Miss

174

Martha A., daughter of John GROVE, all of Page county.
Rockingham Register, 29 October 1868 (Thursday), p. 3, c. 3.

GRAYSON: On the 18th ult., by Elder John Clark, Capt. David C. GRAYSON and Miss Mary R., daughter of Elder Wm. C. LAUCK, all of Page county.
Rockingham Register and Advertiser, 9 March 1866 (Friday), p. 2, c. 3.

GREAVER: On Thursday the 7th inst., by Rev. A.J. Bushong, Geo. W. GREAVER and Miss Eliza J. MIZER, all of Augusta county.
Rockingham Register, 28 May 1868 (Thursday), p. 2, c. 6.

GREAVER: By Rev. T.L. Preston, on the 4th inst., Jas. H. GREAVER and Miss Margaret GEARHEART, of Augusta.
Rockingham Register and Advertiser, 11 April 1867 (Thursday), p. 3, c. 4.

GREEN: See entry for BROOKS.

GREEN: See entry for MERRITT.

GREEN: At the Baptist Church in Berryville, on the 27th of October, by Rev. T.B. Shepherd, John A. GREEN and Miss Bettie S. HARDESTY, all of Clarke county.
Rockingham Register, 12 November 1868 (Thursday), p. 3, c. 3.

GREEN: On the evening of the 6th inst., by the Rev. Mr. Slaughter, of Georgetown, D.C., William GREEN, attorney at law, and Daniel S. GREEN, M.D., of the U.S. Navy - the former to Columbia, and the latter to Virginia, daughters of Samuel SLAUGHTER, Esq., of Western View, Culpeper county, Va.
Rockingham Register, 22 April 1837 (Saturday), p. 3, c. 3.

GREGORY: See entry for ROHR.

GREGORY: On the 7th inst., by Rev. J. Armstrong, at the residence of the bride, Chas. E. GREGORY and Miss Margaret R. GARBER, all of Staunton.
Rockingham Register and Advertiser, 14 June 1866 (Thursday), p. 3, c. 4.

GREGORY: On the 28th ult., by Rev. J.R.

Wheeler, Nicholas GREGORY to Miss Sarah GROVE, of Staunton.

Rockingham Register and Advertiser, 15 March 1861 (Friday), p. 2, c. 4.

GREINER: On Tuesday evening last, by the Rev. J.D. Coulling, Mr. Patterson GREINER and Miss Caroline V., daughter of Mr. Benjamin VAN PELT, all of this place.

Rockingham Register and Advertiser, 11 November 1859 (Friday), p. 3, c. 1.

GREINER: At the residence of the bride's father, near Harrisonburg, on New Year's day, by Rev. T.D. Bell, Patterson H. GREINER and Mrs. Margaret BILLHIMER, all of this vicinity.

Rockingham Register and Advertiser, 3 January 1867 (Thursday), p. 3, c. 3.

GRIFFITH: See entry for WETHERHOLTZ.

GRIFFITH: On the 15th inst., by Rev. J.W. Watson, Benjamin F. GRIFFITH and Miss Catharine ALTHER, all of Page county.

Rockingham Register and Advertiser, 26 December 1867 (Thursday), p. 2, c. 6.

GRIGGS: In Barbour county, Ala., on the 9th inst., by Rev. Mr. Gordon, Geo. R. GRIGGS and Miss Mollie A. FOLEY, of Loudoun county, Va.

Rockingham Register, 30 April 1868 (Thursday), p. 2, c. 6.

GRIGSBY: In Washington, D.C., on Tuesday, the 5th of November, by Right Rev. Dr. Ames, Capt. B.M. GRIGSBY, of Va., and Miss Lucie, daughter of Judge W.F. PURCELL, of Washington city.

Rockingham Register, 12 November 1868 (Thursday), p. 3, c. 3.

GRIM: See entry for LOGAN.

GRIM: See entry for THEIS.

GRIM: See entry for WISE.

GRIM: See entry for YOUTSLER.

GRIM: On Thursday morning, the 31st ult., at the Parsonage of the M.E. Church South, in Charlestown, by Rev. Robert Smith, Mr. W.H. GRIM, formerly of Shenandoah county, and Miss Rebecca J. ROWLAND, of Clarke county.

GRIM: On the 20th ult., at the National Hotel, Woodstock, by Rev. W.F. Speak, Mr. Wm. GRIM and Miss Barbara SMOOTS, all of this county.

Rockingham Register and Advertiser, 12 July 1861 (Friday), p. 3, c. 4.

GRIMES: On the 28th ult., by Elder G.W. Wood, John GRIMES and Miss Catharine SHOMO, all of Page county.

Rockingham Register and Advertiser, 26 December 1867 (Thursday), p. 2, c. 6.

GRIMSLEY: See entry for BYERLEY.

GROAH: See entry for McCORMICK.

GROVE: See entry for BUTTERLY.

GROVE: See entry for CLEM.

GROVE: See entry for DIVELBISS.

GROVE: See entry for DOVEL.

GROVE: See entry for FLORY.

GROVE: See entry for GRAYSON.

GROVE: See entry for GREGORY.

GROVE: See entry for MAGSON.

GROVE: See entry for SHRUM.

GROVE: See entry for WAMPLER.

GROVE: On the 23rd of November, at the residence of the bride's father, in Page county, John W. GROVE and Miss Eliza J., daughter of Isaac KOONTZ, Jr.

Rockingham Register, 9 December 1869 (Thursday), p. 3, c. 2.

GROVE: On Thursday morning the 10th inst., in Harrisonburg, by Rev. G.W. Holland, Martin B. GROVE, of Augusta county, and Miss Sallie A., daughter of Joseph MILLER, dec'd, of Rockingham county.

Rockingham Register, 17 February 1870 (Thursday), p. 3, c. 2.

GROVE: At Kanawha, Salines, W.Va., September 29th, by Rev. T.F. Holt, Miles Mc. GROVE, formerly of Harrisonburg, Va., and Miss Mollie V. KNISLY, of Kanawha Valley, W.Va.

Rockingham Register, 18 November 1869 (Thursday), p. 3, c. 2.

GROVE: At the First Congregational Church,

San Francisco, Wednesday evening, 12th ult., by Rev. T. Dwight Hunt, Sam'l C. GROVE and Miss Fannie A. ALLEN.
Rockingham Register and Virginia Advertiser, 27 May 1854 (Saturday), p. 2, c. 7.

GROVE: On the 13th ult., at the residence of Jonathan Seymour, in Hardy county, by Rev. J. Johnston, Dr. Thos. J. GROVE, of Petersburg, Hardy county, and Miss Lizzie NEILL, of Jefferson county.
Rockingham Register and Advertiser, 20 December 1861 (Friday), p. 3, c. 3.

GROVENSTINE: At New Market, on the 4th inst., by Rev. Jacob Stirewalt, William GROVENSTINE and Margaret BOWMAN, all of Shenandoah county.
The Rockingham Register, 9 October 1863 (Friday), p. 2, c. 4.

GRUBB: See entry for WISE.

GULLEY: On the 19th ult., at the Virginia Hotel, in Staunton, G.A. GULLEY and Miss Lucy KEPLINGER, both of Charlottesville, Va.
Rockingham Register and Advertiser, 2 August 1866 (Thursday), p. 2, c. 5.

GUM: See entry for JACK.

GUMM: See entry for HAMILTON.

GUMM: On the 13th ult., at the residence of Jacob Sibert, by Rev. George Huffman, Amos GUMM and Miss Elizabeth PROPST, all of Highland county.
Rockingham Register and Advertiser, 18 October 1866 (Thursday), p. 2, c. 4.

GUMM: On the 13th ult., on Back Creek, by Rev. J.W. Canter, Wills W. GUMM and Miss Nancy C. WADE, all of Highland county.
Rockingham Register and Advertiser, 18 October 1866 (Thursday), p. 2, c. 4.

GUTHRIE: See entry for COPELAND.

GUY: See entry for CARRIER.

GUYEL: See entry for MINNICK.

GWINN: See entry for FRIEL.

GWINN: See entry for TRIMBLE.

GWINN: On the 1st inst., by Rev. J.W. Watson, T.T. GWINN, of Alexandria, Va., and Miss

Maggie R. MOHLER, of Page county. Rockingham Register and Advertiser, 16 January 1868 (Thursday), p. 2, c. 5.

- H -

HAAS: See entry for HILL.

HAAS: See entry for LOGAN.

HAAS: In the M.E. Church, in Woodstock, on Wednesday evening, the 28th of November, by Rev. Jno. P. Hyde, Erasmus C. HAAS and Miss Bettie E., daughter of Benjamin IRVIN, all of Shenandoah county. Rockingham Register and Advertiser, 6 December 1866 (Thursday), p. 3, c. 2.

HAAS: On Thursday of last week, at the residence of the bride's father, in Woodstock, by Rev. J.W. Wolff, Maj. Isaac HAAS, P.M., and Miss Mary C. REED. Rockingham Register and Advertiser, 30 September 1859 (Friday), p. 2, c. 4.

HACKLEY: On the 18th of November, at Hamburg, Page county, by Elder Wm. C. Lauck, Thomas HACKLEY and Miss Pamelia A. KIBLER. Rockingham Register, 9 December 1869 (Thursday), p. 3, c. 2.

HAGA: See entry for ROSENBERGER.

HAGUE: See entry for EARMAN.

HAHN: See entry for HAWKINS.

HAHN: See entry for SHERMAN.

HAHN: See entry for SWISHER.

HAHN: See entry for WHITMORE.

HAILMAN: See entry for MOYERS.

HAINES: On the 2nd inst., by Rev. James A. Latane, Charles E. HAINES, formerly of Winchester, Va., and Miss Rosalie, youngest daughter of Mr. G.A. ARMENTROUT, of Staunton. Rockingham Register, 10 December 1868 (Thursday), p. 3, c. 3.

HAINES: On the 15th ult., by Rev. Mr. Summers, Ellis A. HAINES and Miss Sidney CLOWSER, all of Shenandoah county. Rockingham Register and Advertiser, 6 December 1866 (Thursday), p. 3, c. 2.

HALDERMAN: See entry for HOUFF.

HALE: See entry for LUTZ.

HALL: See entry for COCHRAN.

HALL: See entry for HARRIS.

HALL: See entry for KYLE.

HALL: See entry for POWEL.

HALL: In Christ Church, Baltimore, on December 8th, by Rev. T.U. Dudley, Alexander HALL, formerly of Staunton, and Miss Sophia, daughter of the late Benj. M. DUCKETT, of Prince George county, Md.
Rockingham Register, 13 January 1870 (Thursday), p. 3, c. 4.

HALL: At Wheatland, on the 23rd of September, by Rev. Thomas N. Johnson, Major Houston HALL, of Augusta, and Miss Emmie E., daughter of the late Dr. Wm. P. MOSLEY, of Buckingham county.
Rockingham Register, 8 October 1868 (Thursday), p. 3, c. 3.

HALL: On the 26th ult., by Rev. B.H. Smith, Mr. J.M.C. HALL and Miss M.L. BAKER, both of Augusta.
Rockingham Register and Advertiser, 18 January 1861 (Friday), p. 3, c. 2.

HALL: In Mt. Solon, on the 24th ult., by Rev. J.M. Fallansbee, Jeremiah W. HALL and Miss Elizabeth H. BLAKEMORE, both of Augusta.
Rockingham Register, 10 March 1870 (Thursday), p. 2, c. 4.

HALL: On the 10th of November, by Rev. J.W. Tongue, Jno. W. HALL and Miss Alwilda F. BOWMAN, all of Woodstock, Va.
Rockingham Register, 24 November 1870 (Thursday), p. 2, c. 4.

HALL: On the 4th inst., by Elder Wm. C. Lauck, Theodore H. HALL, of Memphis, Tenn., and Miss Bettie B. CARTER, of Warren county, Va.
Rockingham Register, 20 August 1868 (Thursday), p. 3, c. 3.

HALL: On Sunday morning, the 29th of July, by Rev. John J. Harshbarger, Mr. Wilford J.W. HALL and Miss Mary Ann FIELDING, all of Rockingham.

Rockingham _Register_ and _Advertiser_, 24
August 1860 (Friday), p. 2, c. 5.
HALTERMAN: On the 4th of September, by Rev.
Jacob A. Bovey, Mr. Milton HALTERMAN, of
Hardy, and Miss Elizabeth CARRIER, of
Shenandoah county.
Rockingham _Register_ and _Advertiser_, 16
September 1859 (Friday), p. 2, c. 4.
Repeated, 23 September 1859 (Friday), p.
2, c. 4.
HAM: October 25th, by Rev. John R. Bowman,
John S. HAM and Miss Sarah C. EPARD, all
of Rockingham.
Rockingham _Register_, 18 November 1869
(Thursday), p. 3, c. 2.
HAMILTON: See entry for ALLEN.
HAMILTON: See entry for WILFONG.
HAMILTON: Near McDowell, on the 15th inst.,
by Rev. Wm. T. Price, Chas. A. HAMILTON
and Mrs. Martha A. HINER, all of Highland
county.
Rockingham _Register_ and _Advertiser_, 27
November 1866 (Thursday), p. 2, c. 5.
HAMILTON: On the 13th ult., by Rev. J.W.
Canter, Charles B. HAMILTON, of Bath
county, and Miss E.H. GUMM, of Highland
county.
Rockingham _Register_ and _Advertiser_, 18
October 1866 (Thursday), p. 2, c. 4.
HAMILTON: On the 3rd ult., by Rev. J.W.
Canter, J.G. HAMILTON and Miss Mary C.
TOWNSEND, all of Highland county.
Rockingham _Register_ and _Advertiser_, 18
October 1866 (Thursday), p. 2, c. 4.
HAMILTON: On the 25th ult., by Rev. C.S.M.
See, Mr. John E. HAMILTON and Miss
Theodosia A., daughter of Elisha HUDSON,
all of Augusta.
Rockingham _Register_ and _Advertiser_, 2
November 1860 (Friday), p. 2, c. 5.
HAMMAN: See entry for STICKLEY.
HAMMAN: On the 26th ult., Geo. C. HAMMAN and
Miss Kate FRAVEL, both of Woodstock, Va.
Rockingham _Register_, 8 July 1869
(Thursday), p. 2, c. 5.
HAMMAN: On the 23rd ult., by Rev. Hy. Wetzel,

John HAMMAN and Miss Mary J. MILLER, all of Shenandoah.

Rockingham Register and Advertiser, 6 February 1868 (Thursday), p. 2, c. 4.

HAMMAND: See entry for BORDEN.

HAMMER: See entry for HARRIS.

HAMMER: See entry for WISE.

HAMMER: In Rockingham county, on the 22nd of October, at the residence of the bride's father, by the Rev. Geo. C. Vanderslice, Mr. Wm. H. HAMMER and Miss Sarah HENSLEY. The Rockingham Register, 6 November 1863 (Friday), p. 2, c. 6.

HAMMON: See entry for MILLER.

HAMMON: On Thursday, the 27th ult., by Rev. Wm. J. Miller, Jos. C. HAMMON and Miss Elizabeth FILCOMB, all of Rockingham county.

Rockingham Register, 17 September 1868 (Thursday), p. 2, c. 5.

HAMMON: On the 14th inst., by Rev. Henry St. John Rinker, Mr. Reuben E. HAMMON, of Co. K, 12th Va. Cavalry, and Miss Virginia Ellen, daughter of the late Capt. Israel P. RINKER, all of Shenandoah county, Va. The Rockingham Register, 22 January 1864 (Friday), p. 2, c. 5.

HAMMOND: See entry for MILLER.

HAMMOND: On the 17th inst., at the residence of the bride's father, by Rev. J.F. Liggett, Joseph A. HAMMOND, and Miss Dorah, daughter of Asher ARGEBRIGHT, Esq., all of Rockingham.

Rockingham Register, 24 September 1868 (Thursday), p. 3, c. 4.

HAMRICK: See entry for WHITMORE.

HAMRICK: In Woodstock, on the 29th ult., by Rev. J.P. Hyde, Mr. William H. HAMRICK, of Rockingham county, and Miss Mollie E. MELHORN, of Woodstock.

Rockingham Register and Advertiser, 6 February 1868 (Thursday), p. 2, c. 4.

HANCOCK: At the residence of Reuben Emick, January 16th, 1859, by Rev. Henry King, Mr. James B. HANCOCK, of Licking county, Ohio, to Miss Hannah EMICK, of Walnut

Township, Fairfield county, Ohio.
Rockingham Register and Advertiser, 28
January 1859 (Friday), p. 2, c. 6.

HAND: See entry for O'FERRALL.

HANDLEY: See entry for BENNETT.

HANDY: On the 22nd inst., by Rev. Henry A.
Wise, at the residence of the bride's
father, Dr. Wm. MILLER, of Harrisonburg,
Miss Mary Emma MILLER and Mr. S. K. HANDY
of New Orleans.
Rockingham Register and Advertiser, 25
October 1866 (Thursday), p. 3, c. 3.

HANES: See entry for GRAY.

HANES: See entry for JOHNSON.

HANEY: On the 31st of October, at "Edgemont,"
Page county, the residence of the bride's
parents, by Rev. A. Poe Boude, James D.
HANEY, formerly of Orange county, Va.,
and Miss Annie E., daughter of R.T.
KINGREE, Esq., of Page.
Rockingham Register, 18 November 1869
(Thursday), p. 3, c. 2.

HANEY: On Sunday morning, December 24th, by
Rev. Jacob Thomas, Mr. John HANEY, of
Rockingham, and Miss Hannah, daughter of
Geo. WICLE, of Augusta county.
Rockingham Register and Advertiser, 12
January 1866 (Friday), p. 1, c. 3.

HANEY: On the 25th of November, by Rev.
Samuel Brown, Junius R. HANEY, of
Botetourt, and Miss Nancy, daughter of
Wm. CHAPLAIN, of Rockbridge.
Rockingham Register, 10 December 1868
(Thursday), p. 3, c. 3.

HANGER: See entry for FUNKHOUSER.

HANGER: See entry for HANGER.

HANGER: See entry for SMITH.

HANGER: See entry for WILSON.

HANGER: See entry for YOUNG.

HANGER: On the 30th ult., by the Rev. C.
Beard, Geo. Robertson HANGER and Miss
Elizabeth Virginia HANGER, all of Augusta
county.
Rockingham Register and Advertiser, 13
February 1868 (Thursday), p. 2, c. 5.

HANGER: On the 26th ult., by Rev. W.T.

Richardson, Mr. J.M. HANGER and Miss J.F. WEADE.
Rockingham Register and Advertiser, 24 February 1860 (Friday), p. 2, c. 4.

HANGER: On the evening of the 16th inst., in Middlebrook, by Rev. P.P. Flournoy, John HANGER and Miss Mary MORGAN, all of Augusta.
Rockingham Register and Advertiser, 30 May 1867 (Thursday), p. 3, c. 3.

HANGER: On the 28th of January, 1866, by the Rev. Samuel Kennerly, sen., Mr. W.A. HANGER and Miss Barbara COYNER, all of Augusta county.
Rockingham Register and Advertiser, 9 February 1866 (Friday), p. 3, c. 3. Reprinted, 16 February 1866 (Friday), p. 3, c. 3.

HANLY: See entry for DASHIELL.

HANNON: At the residence of the bride's father, in Woodstock, Va., on the evening of the 4th inst., by Rev. Mr. Armstrong, Mr. Henry W. HANNON, of Charles county, Md., and Miss Hattie C. HOLLINGSWORTH, of Frederick county, Va.
Rockingham Register and Advertiser, 20 January 1865 (Friday), p. 2, c. 4.

HANSAN: Near Newport, Page county, Va., on the 5th inst., by Rev. S. Henkel, James B. HANSAN and Miss Caroline E., daughter of R.M. WALTON, Esq., all of Page county.
Rockingham Register, 19 November 1868 (Thursday), p. 2, c. 5.

HANSBERGER: See entry for CONRAD.

HANSBERGER: See entry for GINEVAN.

HANSBERGER: See entry for HESTER.

HANSBERGER: On Thursday, the 10th inst., in Sangersville, Augusta county, at the residence of the bride's father, by Rev. J.W. Howe, Mr. Geo. W. HANSBERGER, of Rockingham, and Miss Mollie J., daughter of Wm. BEARD, of Mint Spring, Augusta county, Va.
Rockingham Register & Advertiser, 18 August 1865 (Friday), p. 3, c. 3.

HANSBERGER: On the 21st ult., by Elder George

Shaver, James H. HANSBERGER and Miss
Levinia F. GOCHENOUR, all of Shenandoah
county.
Rockingham Register, 1 April 1869
(Thursday), p. 3, c. 3.

HARBAUGH: On the 23rd ult., by Rev. T.
Miller, Mr. Isaac HARBAUGH and Miss Mary
PEER, all of Shenandoah county.
Rockingham Register, 6 May 1869
(Thursday), p. 2, c. 3.

HARDESTY: See entry for GREEN.

HARDESTY: See entry for HARRIS.

HARDIE: In Mt. Jackson, on Wednesday morning,
the 8th inst., at the residence of the
bride's father, by Rev. Silas Billings,
Rev. Henry HARDIE, of Raleigh, N.C., and
Miss Annie A., daughter of Dr. L.
TRIPLETT, of Shenandoah county, Va.
Rockingham Register and Advertiser, 17
August 1860 (Friday), p. 2, c. 5.

HARDIN: See entry for TORNEY.

HARDON: On the 13th inst., Comfort HARDON, of
Martinsburg, to Mrs. Rebecca DYER, of
Pendleton county, Va.
Rockingham Register and Advertiser, 7
October 1859 (Friday), p. 2, c. 4.

HARDY: See entry for BROWN.

HARDY: On the 20th inst., by Rev. George G.
Brooke, Mr. John M. HARDY and Miss Mary
V. BOWLS, all of Staunton.
Rockingham Register and Advertiser, 28
January 1859 (Friday), p. 2, c. 6.

HARLAN: On the 4th inst., by Rev. J.E.
Armstrong, Sam'l HARLAN and Miss Eliza J.
SMITH, all of Augusta county.
Rockingham Register and Advertiser, 13
September 1866 (Thursday), p. 2, c. 5.

HARLER: See entry for LEE.

HARLOW: At Falling Spring, in Greenbrier
county, W.Va., on the 28th ult., by Rev.
James H. Leps, B.F. HARLOW, Esq., editor
of the Greenbrier Independent, and Miss
Nettie C., daughter of B.F. RENICK, Esq.,
all of Greenbrier county.
Rockingham Register and Advertiser, 14
March 1867 (Thursday), p. 3, c. 5.

Repeated, 28 March 1867 (Thursday), p. 2, c. 6. The above is a composite of the two.

HARLOW: On the 11th inst., C.M. HARLOW and Miss N. STRICKLER, both of Page county.
Rockingham Register, 25 November 1869 (Thursday), p. 2, c. 3.

HARLOW: On the 25th ult., at Lebanon, White Sulphur Springs, by Rev. J.R. Van Horn, Franklin HARLOW, of Staunton, and Miss Mary C. CROSS, of Augusta.
Rockingham Register, 2 December 1869 (Thursday), p. 2, c. 3.

HARLOW: By Rev. Henry St. John Rinker, on the 28th ult., near Columbia Furnace, Mr. Joseph HARLOW, of Augusta, and Miss Henrietta LARKINS, of Shenandoah county.
Rockingham Register and Advertiser, 7 January 1859 (Friday), p. 3, c. 1.

HARLOW: On the 17th inst., by Rev. Robert J. Taylor, Thomas HARLOW and Miss Sallie E. PAXTON, all of Rockbridge.
Rockingham Register and Advertiser, 31 January 1867 (Thursday), p. 3, c. 2.

HARMAN: See entry for EVE.

HARMAN: See entry for OPIE.

HARMAN: On the 21st inst., at the residence of the bride's father, by Rev. J. Crickenberger, Jesse HARMAN and Miss Lizzie S. WHISSEN, all of Rockingham.
Rockingham Register and Advertiser, 28 November 1867 (Thursday), p. 2, c. 6.

HARMAN: On the 13th inst., in Christ's Church, in Winchester, by Rev. W.C. Meredith, Capt. Lewis HARMAN, of Staunton, and Miss Ellen, daughter of C.W. PRICE, of Winchester.
Rockingham Register & Advertiser, 22 December 1865 (Friday), p. 3, c. 2.

HARMAN: On Thursday, the 27th ult., by the Rev. T.T. Castleman, Mr. Michael G. HARMAN to Miss Caroline Virginia, daughter of L.L. STEVENSON, Esq., all of Staunton.
Rockingham Register and Valley Advertiser, 8 March 1845 (Saturday), p.

3, c. 3.

HARMON: See entry for McFALL.

HARMON: See entry for OPIE.

HARMON: Near McGaheysville, on the 21st of October, by the Rev. Isaac Long, Henry HARMON and Miss Verinda BEASLEY, all of Rockingham.
Rockingham Register and Advertiser, 22 November 1866 (Thursday), p. 3, c. 3.

HARMON: Near Franklin, Pendleton county, Va., by Rev. S.H. Griffith, Mr. John HARMON, of Rockingham, and Miss Sarah C. DICE, of Pendleton.
Rockingham Register and Advertiser, 24 May 1861 (Friday), p. 3, c. 2.

HARNER: See entry for HARNER.

HARNER: See entry for SHOCKEY.

HARNER: On the 15th of March, by Rev. Isaac Long, John R. HARNER and Miss Frances HARNER, all of this county.
Rockingham Register and Advertiser, 30 March 1866 (Friday), p. 2, c. 3.

HARNSBERGER: See entry for COFFMAN.

HARNSBERGER: In Saline county, Mo., October 26th, by the Rev. Wm. J. Brown, Mr. H.H. HARNSBERGER, of Pettis county, Mo., formerly of this county, to Miss Nannie, daughter of Mr. Hugh GALBRAITH.
Rockingham Register and Advertiser, 18 November 1859 (Friday), p. 2, c. 4.

HARNSBERGER: On the 17th inst., by Rev. H.A. Gaver, at the residence of the bride, Henry HARNSBERGER and Mrs. C. TALIAFERRO, all of Rockingham county.
Rockingham Register and Advertiser, 24 January 1867 (Thursday), p. 2, c. 4.

HARNSBERGER: On the 15th inst., by Rev. C. Beard, Mr. Jacob A. HARNSBERGER, of Rockingham county, and Miss Rebecca V. ENGLEMAN, of Augusta county.
The Rockingham Register, 23 January 1863 (Friday), p. 2, c. 2.

HARNSBERGER: On the 21st of December, by Rev. D.C. Irwin, Mr. Robert HARNSBERGER and Miss Mary E. YOUNG, all of Rockingham county.

Rockingham Register and Advertiser, 12
January 1866 (Friday), p. 1, c. 3.
HARPER: See entry for BREEN.
HARPER: See entry for FULK.
HARPER: See entry for HICKS.
HARPER: See entry for PATTIE.
HARPER: See entry for RANKEN.
HARPER: See entry for SMITH.
HARPER: On the 19th ult., by Rev. W.E. Baker,
    Geo. K. HARPER and Miss Millie S. BRUCE,
    both of Staunton.
Rockingham Register and Advertiser, 2
August 1866 (Thursday), p. 2, c. 5.
HARPER: On Sunday the 11th inst., by the Rev.
    T.H. Busey, Mr. John HARPER to Miss Sarah
    J.   TROUT,   all   of   Port   Republic,
    Rockingham county.
Rockingham   Register   and   Valley
Advertiser, 17 October 1846 (Saturday),
p. 3, c. 1.
HARPER: On Thursday the 29th of July, Mr. Wm.
    HARPER and Miss L. JORDAN, both of
    Pendleton county.
The   Rockingham   Register   and   Valley
Advertiser, 7 August 1852 (Saturday), p.
2, c. 6.
HARPER: On the 23rd ult., on South Branch, by
    Rev. Leonidas Butt, William HARPER,
    Editor of the South Branch Intelligencer,
    and Miss Sallie Lee, daughter of the late
    Dr. Levi KANE, of Hampshire county.
Rockingham Register and Advertiser, 7
November 1867 (Thursday), p. 2, c. 5.
HARRELL: See entry for ALTAFFER.
HARRELL: See entry for WHITMORE.
HARRELL: On the 11th of March, at Mossy
    Creek, by the Rev. T.E. Carson, William
    A. HARRELL and Miss Nancy E. ODER, both
    of Augusta.
Rockingham   Register,   1   April   1869
(Thursday), p. 3, c. 3.
HARRIS: See entry for FISHER.
HARRIS: On the 19th of January, by Rev. W.G.
    Eggleston, Rev. David HARRIS, of the
    Baltimore Conference, and Miss Bernice S.
    DANNER, of Frederick county, Va.

The Rockingham Register, 8 April 1864 (Friday), p. 2, c. 6.

HARRIS: On the 27th of December, at McGaheysville, by Rev. Joseph Funkhouser, Frederick HARRIS and Miss Fannie YAGER, all of Rockingham.

Rockingham Register and Advertiser, 3 January 1867 (Thursday), p. 3, c. 3.

HARRIS: On the 26th of January, at the residence of Mr. ____ Reaton, in Port Republic, by Rev. Jno. P. Hyde, Mr. George W. HARRIS and Miss Nannie J. HALL, both of Rockingham county.

The Rockingham Register, 5 February 1864 (Friday), p. 2, c. 6.

HARRIS: At Dyer's Hotel, Washington city, on the 27th of May, by Rev. A.H. Ames, Henry G. HARRIS and Miss Susan E., daughter of John HAMMER, both of Rockingham county.

Rockingham Register and Advertiser, 29 August 1867 (Thursday), p. 2, c. 5.

HARRIS: On the 30th of January, in Lewisburg, W.Va., by the Rev. J.C. Barr, J.W. HARRIS, Editor and Proprietor of the Scottsville Register, and Miss R. Addie, second daughter of Col. Joel McPHERSON, of that place.

Rockingham Register and Advertiser, 16 February 1866 (Friday), p. 3, c. 3.

HARRIS: On the 7th inst., at the Virginia Hotel, Staunton, by Rev. James Murray, James F. HARRIS and Miss Ozalla F. CRIST.

Rockingham Register, 14 January 1869 (Thursday), p. 3, c. 3.

HARRIS: On the 28th ult., by Rev. John W. Wolff, Mr. James H. HARRIS and Miss Eliza Jane, daughter of Paul ROSENBERGER, all of Augusta county.

Rockingham Register and Advertiser, 12 June 1857 (Friday), p. 3, c. 2.

HARRIS: At the residence of her grandfather, Isaac HARDESTY, Esq., in Harrisonburg, on Wednesday morning last, by Rev. T.D. Bell, Dr. James H. HARRIS, of Mt. Meridian, Augusta county, and Miss Lizzie A., daughter of John E. HARDESTY, dec'd.

The Rockingham Register, 13 March 1863
(Friday), p. 2, c. 5.
HARRIS: On Wednesday, the 26th inst. [sic,
ult.], by the Rev. James Garnett, Mr.
James O. HARRIS, of Rockbridge, to Miss
Bettie A., daughter of Daniel BROWN,
dec'd, of Culpeper.
Rockingham Register and Valley
Advertiser, 5 September 1846 (Saturday),
p. 2, c. 7.
HARRIS: On December 19th, at the residence of
the bride's father, by Rev. John Brower,
John A. HARRIS and Miss Annie E., second
daughter of Mr. Martin YOUNT, of Augusta
county.
Rockingham Register and Advertiser, 6
February 1868 (Thursday), p. 2, c. 4.
HARRISON: See entry for ELLIOTT.
HARRISON: See entry for HINER.
HARRISON: See entry for MARTZ.
HARRISON: In Cumberland, on Tuesday morning
last, by Rev. Mr. Wilson, Mr. Isaac S.
HARRISON and Miss Emma, daughter of Mr.
George T. MARTIN, of Fairmount, Va.
Rockingham Register and Virginia
Advertiser, 13 June 1856 (Friday),p. 2,
c. 2.
HARRISON: On the 6th inst., by Rev. Jos.
Funkhouser, James N. HARRISON and Miss
Mary C. CARRIER, all of Rockingham
county.
Rockingham Register and Advertiser, 13
September 1866 (Thursday), p. 2, c. 5.
HARRISON: On the 16th inst., near Staunton,
by Rev. J.A. Latane, T.B. HARRISON and
Mary Boykin, daughter of David R.
WILLIAMS, formerly of South Carolina.
Rockingham Register, 25 November 1869
(Thursday), p. 2, c. 3.
HARRISON: On the 9th inst., by Rev. S.
Kepler, William C. HARRISON, of this
vicinity, late of Texas, and Miss Minnie
WILLIAMS, of Rockingham county.
Rockingham Register and Advertiser, 16
January 1868 (Thursday), p. 2, c. 5.
HARSHA: At Parnassus, on the 5th inst., by

Rev. A.A.P. Neal, Mr. J. Seymour HARSHA, of Grant county, W.Va., and Miss Jennie E.M. McFALL, of Augusta county, Va.
Rockingham Register and Advertiser, 9 January 1868 (Thursday), p. 2, c. 4.

HARSHBER: See entry for LIGHTFOOT.

HARSHBARGER: On the evening of the 6th inst., by the Rev. H. Wetzel, the Rev. Isaac M. HARSHBARGER, to Miss Catherine LEE, all of Augusta county.
Rockingham Register and Virginia Advertiser, 18 May 1855 (Friday), p. 3, c. 4.

HARSHBERGER: See entry for CULLEN.

HARSHBERGER: On Thursday last, Mr. Shem HARSHBERGER, of this county, and Miss Mary Ann JORDON, of Shenandoah.
Rockingham Register and Virginia Advertiser, 14 March 1856 (Friday), p. 3, c. 1.

HART: On the 27th ult., in the Lutheran church, Winchester, by the Revs. T.W. Dosh and W.E. Krebs, Major C.S. HART, of New Orleans, and Miss Joanna B., daughter of Mr. I. KREBS, of Winchester.
Rockingham Register & Advertiser, 6 October 1865 (Friday), p. 2, c. 2.

HART: December 10, by Rev. Wm. J. Miller, Wm. HART, formerly of Concord Parish, Louisiana, and Miss Nancy FULTZ, of McGaheysville.
Rockingham Register, 17 December 1868 (Thursday), p. 3, c. 2.

HARTIGAL: See entry for McFARLAND.

HARTLEY: See entry for RHODES.

HARTMAN: On the 12th of September, by Rev. Isaac Long, Abraham HARTMAN and Miss Susan, daughter of Philip BAKER, all of Rockingham county.
Rockingham Register and Advertiser, 27 September 1866 (Thursday), p. 2, c. 5.

HARTSHORN: On the 3rd inst., by Rev. J. Rusmisell, Wm. L. HARTSHORN, of Leesburg, and Miss Sarah M. BALTHIS, of Strasburg, Va.
Rockingham Register, 11 February 1869

(Thursday), p. 3, c. 3.

HARTSOCK: On the morning of the 14th ult., in the Funkstown M.E. Church, by Rev. W. Downs, the Rev. Samuel M. HARTSOCK, of the East Baltimore Conference, M.E. Church, to Miss Mollie E., daughter of Simon KNODE, of Funkstown, Washington county. Md.
Rockingham Register and Advertiser, 1 March 1861 (Friday), p. 3, c. 3.

HASE: See entry for GARBER.

HASLER: See entry for DEELS.

HASLER: On the 28th ult., by Rev. I. Conder, George F. HASLER and the widow Amanda E. KEPLINGER, all of Rockingham county.
Rockingham Register and Advertiser, 5 December 1867 (Thursday), p. 2, c. 5.

HASLER: On the 17th inst., by Rev. S. Henkel, John P. HASLER and Miss Sarah A., daughter of John ARMENTROUT, all of Rockingham county.
Rockingham Register and Advertiser, 31 January 1867 (Thursday), p. 3, c. 2.

HATCHER: At Clover, Halifax county, Va., on the 13th inst., by Rev. W.A. Tyree, J. Eppes HATCHER, of Manchester, Va., to Mrs. Sarah BAILEY, of Halifax county, Va.
Rockingham Register, 23 September 1869 (Thursday), p. 2, c. 3.

HATFIELD: See entry for THOMAS.

HAUGH: See entry for PENCE.

HAUGHEY: On the 28th of March, at the residence of W.C.M. Baker, Esq., by Rev. T.M. Findley, Mr. James N. HAUGHEY and Mrs. Mary Elizabeth BASEL, of Xenia, Greene county, Ohio.
Rockingham Register and Advertiser, 4 May 1866 (Friday), p. 3, c. 2.

HAUN: See entry for ALLEN.

HAUPE: October 30th, by Rev. H.H. Hawes, James T. HAUPE, of Augusta, and Miss Amanda J. BOONE, of Rockingham.
Rockingham Register, 18 November 1869 (Thursday), p. 3, c. 2.

HAUS: See entry for BRICKER.

HAUSEFLUCK: See entry for SHIREMAN.

HAUSENFLUCK: On Thursday last, by Rev. Geo.
     Shaver, Mr. Samuel HAUSENFLUCK to Miss
     Harriet MILLER, all of Shenandoah county.
     Rockingham   Register   and   Valley
     Advertiser, 3 November 1849 (Saturday),
     p. 2, c. 7.
HAWES: On the 8th of September, by Rev. Jacob
     Miller, Geo. W. HAWES, Esq., and Miss
     Frances, daughter of Daniel LAYMAN, all
     of Linvill's Creek, Rockingham county.
     Rockingham Register, 15 September 1870
     (Thursday), p. 3, c. 3.
HAWKINS: See entry for GOCHENOUR.
HAWKINS: On Tuesday evening last, by Rev. Mr.
     Carson, at the residence of the bride's
     father, Prof. B.A. HAWKINS, formerly of
     Farmville, Va., and Miss Sallie E.,
     daughter of H. HAHN, all of Rockingham
     county.
     Rockingham Register, 23 April 1868
     (Thursday), p. 2, c. 5.
HAWKINS: On the 4th inst., at the residence
     of Jacob Moyers, by Rev. Jacob Miller,
     David HAWKINS, of Augusta, and Miss
     Margaret M. BOYERS, of Rockingham.
     Rockingham Register, 17 March 1870
     (Thursday), p. 2, c. 4.
HAWKINS: December 19th, at the residence of
     Mr. Richard Hawkins, by the Rev. Wm. H.
     Williams, Mr. James P. HAWKINS, of
     Danville, Va., and Miss Philippina Behn
     McDOWELL, formerly of Charleston, S.C.
     Rockingham Register, 22 December 1870
     (Thursday), p. 2, c. 4.
HAWKINS: On the 12th inst., by Rev. Solomon
     Garber, Mr. John HAWKINS and Miss
     Susannah, daughter of David WAMPLER, all
     of Augusta.
     Rockingham Register and Advertiser, 22
     October 1858 (Friday), p. 3, c. 2.
HAWKINS: In McGaheysville, on the 8th inst.,
     by Rev. James F. Liggett, John H.
     HAWKINS, formerly of Greene county, Va.,
     and Miss Elizabeth V. HESTER, formerly of
     Frederick county, Va., at present all of
     Rockingham.

Rockingham Register, 22 October 1868
(Thursday), p. 3, c. 3.

HAWKINS: On the 30th of September, by the
Rev. Wm. H. Perry, Samuel HAWKINS and
Miss Caroline C.C., daughter of Adam
PIFER, all of Rockingham county.
Rockingham Register and Advertiser, 11
October 1866 (Thursday), p. 3, c. 4.

HAWSE: On Thursday, December 21st, by Rev. A.
Poe Boude, Mr. Jasper HAWSE, of Hardy
county, and Miss Mary A., daughter of Mr.
John K. BEERY, all of Rockingham county.
Rockingham Register and Advertiser, 12
January 1866 (Friday), p. 1, c. 3.

HAYES: On Sunday morning last, the 14th
inst., at the residence of the bride's
mother, by Rev. Joseph Early, Mr. William
B. HAYES and Miss Salina, daughter of
Jacob SONSFRANK, dec'd, all of this
county.
Rockingham Register and Advertiser, 19
July 1861 (Friday), p. 3, c. 3.

HAYNES: See entry for ALEXANDER.

HAYNES: See entry for JOHNSON.

HAYNES: See entry for JUDY.

HAYNES: On the 31st of January, by Rev. Isaac
Long, Jonas HAYNES and Miss Mary Z.
KISER, all of Rockingham county.
Rockingham Register and Advertiser, 21
February 1867 (Thursday), p. 3, c. 2.

HAYNES: At the residence of the bride's
father, in this place, on Thursday
evening last, by Rev. D.C. Petry [?], Mr.
Joseph HAYNES, of Co. B, 45th Georgia
Volunteers, Monroe county, Ga., and Miss
Paulina, daughter of Mr. Thomas BASFORD,
of Harrisonburg.
The Rockingham Register, 20 November 1863
(Friday), p. 2, c. 6.

HAYS: On the 9th inst., by the Rev. J.C.
Hensell, Mr. James M. HAYS, of Augusta
county, and Miss Sophia C. BYRD, of
Rockingham county.
Rockingham Register and Advertiser, 16
September 1859 (Friday), p. 2, c. 4.

HAYS: On the 15th inst., by Rev. Francis

McFarland, D.D., John W. HAYS and Miss
Fannie V. WRIGHT, all of Augusta county.
Rockingham Register, 22 October 1868
(Thursday), p. 3, c. 3.

HAYTER: See entry for HUGHES.

HEATWOLE: See entry for COFFMAN (2).

HEATWOLE: See entry for SHOWALTER.

HEATWOLE: On the 27th ult., by Rev. Jacob
Thomas, Henry G. HEATWOLE and Miss Sarah
F. LONG, all of Rockingham county.
Rockingham Register and Advertiser, 18
October 1866 (Thursday), p. 2, c. 4.

HEATWOLE: On the 13th inst., by the Rev. G.W.
Ship, at the residence of the bride's
father, Mr. J.B. HEATWOLE, formerly of
Rockingham county, to Miss Margaret
SMITH, all of Orange county.
Rockingham Register and Advertiser, 16
November 1860 (Friday), p. 2, c. 4.

HEAVEL: On the 17th inst., in the vicinity of
Harrisonburg, by the Rev. T.D. Bell, Mr.
Wm. HEAVEL and Miss Margaret, daughter of
Mr. James ROADCAP.
Rockingham Register and Advertiser, 22
July 1859 (Friday), p. 2, c. 5.

HEAVENER: On the 9th inst., by the Rev. J.
Pulin, Mr. G.W. HEAVENER to Miss Isabel
LIGHTNER, both of Highland county.
Rockingham Register and Advertiser, 26
March 1858 (Friday), p. 3, c. 2.

HEDRICK: See entry for ACREY.

HEDRICK: See entry for THOMPSON.

HEDRICK: On the 9th inst., at the residence
of F. LISKEY, by Rev. L.S. Reed, H.C.
HEDRICK and Miss Salina LISKEY, all of
Rockingham county.
Rockingham Register, 23 June 1870
(Thursday), p. 2, c. 4.

HEDRICK: At the residence of the bride's
father, George J. FOUKE, by the Rev.
David Long, Mr. Jacob HEDRICK, of
Rockingham, and Miss Emma S. FOUKE, near
Hagerstown, Md.
Rockingham Register & Advertiser, 10
November 1865 (Friday), p. 2, c. 4.

HEDRICK: On the 27th ult., near Parnassus, by

195

Rev. A.A.P. Neel, James J. HEDRICK [HEDRICKS], of Jefferson county, W.Va., and Miss Susan A. WHITMER, of Augusta county, Va.
Rockingham Register, 29 October 1868 (Thursday), p. 3, c. 3. Repeated, 5 November 1868 (Thursday), p. 3, c. 3. The latter is cited above.

HEDRICK: In Middleway, on the 20th ult., by Rev. James C. Stewart, Joseph M. HEDRICK and Miss Mary K., eldest daughter of George MURPHY, Esq., all of Jefferson.
Rockingham Register, 5 November 1868 (Thursday), p. 3, c. 3.

HEDRICK: At the residence of the bride's father, near Bridgewater, on the 19th inst., by Rev. Geo. W. Holland, M. Harvey HEDRICK and Miss Mollie J., second daughter of A.S. WILLIAMS, Esq., all of Rockingham county.
Rockingham Register, 28 May 1868 (Thursday), p. 2, c. 6.

HEDRICK: On the 27th ult., at the residence of the bride's father, in Washington county, Md., by Elder E. Adamson, Mr. Sam'l HEDRICK, of Rockingham county, Va., and Miss Virginia A., daughter of Daniel WITMER, Esq., of Beaver Creek.
Rockingham Register and Advertiser, 19 April 1861 (Friday), p. 2, c. 3.

HEDRICK: On the 13th inst., near Parnassas, by Rev. A.A.P. Neil, Wm. C. HEDRICK and Miss N. Jennie WHITMER, all of Augusta county.
Rockingham Register, 28 May 1868 (Thursday), p. 2, c. 6.

HEFNER: See entry for BUTLER.

HEFNER: At Dayton, on the 22nd inst., by Rev. Samuel Kepler, George W.C. HEFNER, of Augusta county, and Mrs. Caroline MOYERHOEFFER, of Rockingham county.
Rockingham Register and Advertiser, 29 August 1867 (Thursday), p. 2, c. 5.

HEIRER: On the 13th inst., by Rev. James H. Wolff, at the residence of the bride's father, Mr. Benjamin F. HEIRER, of

Rockbridge, and Miss Harriet BOON, of
Bath.
Rockingham Register and Advertiser, 28
September 1860 (Friday), p. 2, c. 4.
HEIRONIMOUS: On the 14th of March, at the
residence of the bride's father, by Rev.
J.W. Lupton, J.B. HEIRONIMOUS, of
Hampshire county, W.Va., and Miss Lizzie
YONLEY, of Frederick county, Va.
Rockingham Register and Advertiser, 6
April 1866 (Friday), p. 3, c. 3.
HEISEY: See entry for COFFMAN.
HEISHMAN: See entry for BOWERS.
HEISHMAN: On the 2nd inst., near Columbia
Furnace, by Rev. Henry St. John Rinker,
Mr. Levi HEISHMAN and Miss Matilda
LINDAMOND - all of Shenandoah county.
Rockingham Register and Advertiser, 10
December 1858 (Friday), p. 3, c. 2.
HEISKEL: See entry for TAYLOR.
HEISKELL: See entry for CARPENTER.
HEISKELL: See entry for GILKESON.
HEISKELL: See entry for WATT.
HEISKELL: At Level Green, on the 29th ult.,
by Rev. James Beaty, Mr. Joseph D.
HEISKELL to Miss Vernon, daughter of Dr.
CHAMBERS, dec'd, all of Hardy county.
Rockingham Register, 7 January 1869
(Thursday), p. 3, c. 3.
HEIZER: On the 7th inst., by Rev. X.J.
Richardson, Mr. Edward HEIZER and Miss
Rebecca A. ALMARODE, all of Augusta
county.
Rockingham Register and Advertiser, 22
July 1859 (Friday), p. 2, c. 5.
HEIZER: On the 21st of February, by Rev.
Horatio Thompson, D.D., J. Frank HEIZER
and Miss Phoebe Ann McCORMICK, all of
Augusta county.
Rockingham Register and Advertiser, 7
March 1867 (Thursday), p. 3, c. 3.
HELBERT: On the 20th inst., by Rev. Abraham
Knopp, Berryman HELBERT and Miss Amy Ann
PENCE, all of Rockingham.
Rockingham Register and Advertiser, 24
October 1867 (Thursday), p. 2, c. 7.

HELBERT: On the 10th inst., by Rev. Abraham
     Knopp, Levi HELBERT and Miss Sally PENCE,
     all of Rockingham.
     Rockingham Register and Advertiser, 24
     October 1867 (Thursday), p. 2, c. 7.
HELBERT: At the residence of Mr. A. Click, by
     Rev. Geo. Wine, Wm. HELBERT and Miss
     Sarah McKEY, all of Rockingham. [No date
     is given.]
     Rockingham Register and Advertiser, 12
     March 1868 (Thursday), p. 2, c. 6.
HELE: See entry for WISSLER.
HELLER: See entry for BECK.
HELLER: See entry for HOLT.
HELLER: See entry for PITMAN.
HELLER: See entry for SNYDER.
HELLER: See entry for WITZ.
HELLER: In Charlottesville, Va., on Wednesday
     morning, March 23rd, by Rev. Dr.
     Michelbacher, A.B. HELLER, of the firm of
     Loewenbach, Heller & Bro., Harrisonburg,
     and Miss Fannie A., daughter of Isaac
     LATTERMAN, of Charlottesville.
     Rockingham Register, 31 March 1870
     (Thursday), p. 3, c. 3.
HELLER: On the 7th of September, by Rev. J.
     Clymer, Adolph HELLER and Miss Ella
     LICHLITER, both of Woodstock.
     Rockingham Register, 15 September 1870
     (Thursday), p. 3, c. 3.
HELLER: On the 23rd ult., by Rev. John W.
     Wolfe, at the Parsonage in Woodstock,
     Harvey HELLER and Miss Amanda SIGLER,
     both of Shenandoah county.
     Rockingham Register, 13 January 1870
     (Thursday), p. 3, c. 4.
HELLER: At Moritz Loewenbach's, in Baltimore
     city, on Sunday evening the 3rd of
     January, by Rev. Deutsch, M.B. HELLER, of
     Harrisonburg, Va., and Miss Lina
     LOEWENSTEIN, of Baltimore.
     Rockingham Register, 7 January 1869
     (Thursday), p. 3, c. 3.
HELM: See entry for STICKLEY.
HELMES: See entry for LANDES.
HELMS: See entry for O'CONNER.

HELMS: On the 5th of September, 1861, by Rev. J.H. Crawford, Mr. Robert A. HELMS and Miss Sarah A. FIRTH, all of Middlebrook, Augusta county, Va.
Rockingham Register and Advertiser, 24 January 1862 (Friday), p. 2, c. 7.

HELMS: On the 27th ult., by Rev. X.J. Richardson, Roland R. HELMS to Miss Mary Ann SWARTZLEY, all of Augusta county.
Rockingham Register and Virginia Advertiser, 11 April 1856 (Friday), p. 2, c. 8.

HELPHENSTINE: See entry for SLATER.

HELSLEY: See entry for STONER.

HELSLEY: On the 17th ult., by Rev. H. Wetzel, J.J. HELSLEY and Miss Sarah M. DELLINGER, all of Shenandoah county.
Rockingham Register, 8 December 1870 (Thursday), p. 2, c. 4.

HELTZEL: See entry for LAGAR.

HELTZEL: See entry for PAYNE.

HENDERSON: See entry for EFFINGER.

HENDERSON: See entry for WILLIAMS.

HENDERSON: On the 21st day of April, by the Rev. Casper Allemong, Mr. John E. HENDERSON and Catharine PLUMB, all of Page county.
Rockingham Register and Advertiser, 6 May 1859 (Friday), p. 3, c. 2.

HENDRICKS: See entry for SIPE.

HENEBERGER: See entry for GRATTAN.

HENEBERGER: On the 30th of September, at the residence of Prof. Campbell, Washington College, by Rev. Wm. S. White, D.D., A.E. HENEBERGER, Esq., of Harrisonburg, and Miss Lucy L., youngest daughter of the late Rev. R.W. BAILEY, D.D.
Rockingham Register, 8 October 1868 (Thursday), p. 3, c. 3.

HENKEL: See entry for COYNER.

HENKEL: See entry for FOLTZ.

HENKEL: See entry for FULMER.

HENKEL: See entry for RICE.

HENKEL: See entry for RODAHOEFFER.

HENKEL: On the 16th inst., in Winchester, by Rev. Mr. Dosh, Dr. C.C. HENKEL, of New

Market, and Miss Maggie MILLER, of Winchester.

Rockingham Register and Advertiser, 31 January 1867 (Thursday), p. 3, c. 2.

HENKEL: On the 21st inst., at the residence of Dr. D. Bashaw, by Rev. R.P. Kennedy, David HENKEL and Mrs. Angeline WOODWARD, all of Augusta.

Rockingham Register and Advertiser, 31 October 1867 (Thursday), p. 2, c. 6.

HENKEL: On the 1st of December, at the residence of John Landes, by Rev. C.B. Hammock, Michael J. HENKEL and Miss Bettie M. LANDES, all of Rockingham.

Rockingham Register, 8 December 1870 (Thursday), p. 2, c. 4.

HENNING: See entry for KENNON.

HENNING: See entry for SIXEAS.

HENRIETTA: On the 24th ult., by Rev. J.M. Clymer, T.J. HENRIETTA and Miss Margaret AMBROSE, all of Shenandoah.

Rockingham Register and Advertiser, 21 November 1867 (Thursday), p. 2, c. 5.

HENRY: See entry for COOK.

HENRY: See entry for HENRY.

HENRY: See entry for WALKER.

HENRY: On the 24th inst., by Rev. W. Eggleston, Franklin HENRY, of Winchester, and Miss Fannie, youngest daughter of Mr. Nelson HENRY, of Clarke county.

Rockingham Register and Advertiser, 30 August 1866 (Thursday), p. 2, c. 4.

HENRY: On the 18th inst., at the residence of the bride's father, by Rev. G.W. Eggleston, Geo. R. HENRY, senior Proprietor of the Winchester News, and Miss A. Lawson HUFF, of Frederick county.

Rockingham Register and Advertiser, 27 June 1867 (Thursday), p. 2, c. 6.

HENSEL: On Tuesday last, by Elder J.J. Jackson, Mr. Geo. L. HENSEL to Miss Lucinda, daughter of Mr. John SPEGLE, all of Shenandoah county.

Rockingham Register and Valley Advertiser, 3 November 1849 (Saturday), p. 2, c. 7.

HENSLEY: See entry for DAVIS.

HENSLEY: See entry for HAMMER.

HENSLEY: See entry for MARSHALL.

HENSLEY: On the 1st day of September, by Rev. L.S. Reed, Calvin HENSLEY and Miss Ardena, daughter of Wm. DEANE, all of Rockingham county.
Rockingham Register, 15 September 1870 (Thursday), p. 3, c. 3.

HENSON: See entry for FLICK.

HENSON: On the 2nd of June, 1870, by Elder George Shaver, Charles HENSON and Miss Mannetta MARSHALL, all of Shenandoah county.
Rockingham Register, 16 June 1870 (Thursday), p. 3, c. 3.

HENSON: On the 22nd ult., Mr. John H. HENSON and Miss Isabella RITENOUR, of Frederick county, Va.
Rockingham Register and Advertiser, 23 March 1866 (Friday), p. 3, c. 3.

HENTON: See entry for ARMENTROUT.

HENTON: See entry for CHAMBERS.

HENTON: See entry for HUFFMAN.

HENTON: On the 26th inst., by Rev. William Brown, David B. HENTON, Esq., to Miss Elizabeth L., daughter of Thos. P. WILSON, Esq., of Augusta.
Rockingham Register and Advertiser, 3 February 1860 (Friday), p. 2, c. 5.

HEPNER: See entry for BARB.

HEPNER: See entry for POLK.

HEPNER: See entry for RYMAN.

HEPNER: See entry for WEST.

HEPNER: At Welsh's Hotel, in Woodstock, by Rev. Wm. S. Baird, Mr. Henry HEPNER and Miss Sarah MOSINGS, all of Shenandoah county.
Rockingham Register and Virginia Advertiser, 27 May 1854 (Saturday), p. 2, c. 7.

HEPNER: On the 22nd inst., by Rev. Jacob Stirewalt, J.L. HEPNER and Miss Barbara MILLER, all of Shenandoah county.
Rockingham Register and Advertiser, 31 October 1867 (Thursday), p. 2, c. 6.

HEREFORD: See entry for FRANCISCO.

HERN: See entry for CLARY.

HERN: On the 15th of September, by Rev. J.W. Howe, Jefferson HERN and Miss Jane WOLFE, all of Rockingham county.
Rockingham Register and Advertiser, 24 October 1867 (Thursday), p. 2, c. 7.

HERNDON: See entry for DAVIS.

HERNDON: At the residence of Mrs. Catharine KIRTLEY, the bride's sister, at 7 1/2 o'clock, A.M., on Tuesday the 17th inst., by Elder T.L. Miller, Mr. Henry HERNDON, of Greene, to Miss Caroline M. LOFLAND, of Rockingham.
Rockingham Register and Advertiser, 27 July 1860 (Friday), p. 2, c. 3.

HERRING: See entry for HUFFMAN.

HERRING: See entry for RUCKMAN.

HERRING: On the 7th inst., at Bridgewater, by the Rev. John Pinkerton, John C. HERRING and Miss Camilla, daughter of Mr. John DINKEL, all of Rockingham.
Rockingham Register and Advertiser, 14 February 1867 (Thursday), p. 2, c. 6.

HERRON: On the 11th inst., at Clarksburg M.E. Church, by Rev. Dr. Thomas B. Sargent, Rev. Levin D. HERRON, of the East Baltimore Conference, and Miss Sallie G. BELT, of Montgomery county, Md.
Rockingham Register and Advertiser, 28 January 1859 (Friday), p. 2, c. 6.

HERSH: See entry for DENTON.

HERSHBARGER: On the 15th inst., near Luray, by Rev. S. Henkel, David H. HERSHBARGER and Miss Susan V., only daughter of John A. SHENK, Esq., all of Page county.
Rockingham Register, 27 May 1869 (Thursday), p. 2, c. 3.

HERSHBERGER: See entry for STIREWALT.

HESS: See entry for HOUSER.

HESS: See entry for SHANK.

HESS: See entry for THOMAS.

HESS: On the 12th inst., by the Rev. Joseph Early, Mr. Frederick HESS and Miss Sarah E. SPITZER, all of this county.
Rockingham Register and Advertiser, 20

December 1861 (Friday), p. 3, c. 3.

HESS: On the 6th inst., by Rev. S. Henkel, Mr. Jno. B. HESS and Miss Mary M., daughter of Dl. LOWRY.

Rockingham Register and Virginia Advertiser, 28 March 1856 (Friday), p. 3, c. 1.

HESS: On the 4th inst., in Staunton, by Rev. J.D. Shirey, Mr. Washington HESS and Miss Mary HUTCHENS, all of Augusta.

Rockingham Register and Advertiser, 14 December 1860 (Friday), p. 2, c. 6.

HESTER: See entry for HAWKINS.

HESTER: At the residence of the bride's father, Rockingham county, Va., on the 3rd inst., by Rev. John P. Hyde, Mr. Erasmus W. HESTER, of Shenandoah, and Miss Rebecca HANSBERGER, of Rockingham county.

Rockingham Register & Advertiser, 11 August 1865 (Friday), p. 2, c. 5.

HESTER: On the 24th of March, by Rev. John Brower, John T. HESTER, of Co. I, 12th Georgia Regiment, and Miss Mary C. VEA, of Augusta county, Va.

The Rockingham Register, 1 April 1864 (Friday), p. 2, c. 6.

HETTRICK: See entry for BOWMAN.

HEVENER: See entry for LUNSFORD.

HEVENER: In Highland county, Va., on the 22nd of December, 1859, by Rev. Mr. Stringer, Mr. George W. HEVENER and Miss Mary C. SUMMERS, formerly of New Market, Shenandoah county, Va.

Rockingham Register and Advertiser, 13 January 1860 (Friday), p. 2, c. 6.

HIBERT: See entry for HILL.

HICKMAN: At "Bonnie Brook," near Dayton, on Thursday morning, the 8th inst., by Rev. J.C. Armstrong, Dr. Joseph T. HICKMAN, of Shenandoah county, and Miss Mary Alice, daughter of John K. MOORE, Esq., of the former place.

Rockingham Register, 15 October 1868 (Thursday), p. 2, c. 3.

HICKMAN: On the 27th ult., by Rev. J.E.

203

Wasson, S.W. HICKMAN, of Bath, to Miss
M.A. WILEY, of Highland.
Rockingham Register and Advertiser, 27
January 1860 (Friday), p. 2, c. 6.

HICKS: On the 16th ult., in Darnestown, Md.,
by the Rev. Mr. Henderson, Rob't M.
HICKS, of Waynesboro, Va., and Miss Annie
E., second daughter of Richard HARPER,
Esq.
Rockingham Register, 2 December 1869
(Thursday), p. 2, c. 3.

HIDEB: See entry for LINTHICUM.

HIDEN: See entry for BRADBURN.

HIDEN: On the 20th inst., on the Bridge at
Harper's Ferry, by Rev. Joseph McFaden,
Geo. HIDEN and Miss Josie GOOD, both of
Rockingham county.
Rockingham Register, 23 July 1868
(Thursday), p. 3, c. 4.

HIDEN: On January 15, 1867, by Rev. Christian
Hartman, Reuben HIDEN and Miss Mollie J.,
daughter of Joseph GOOD, all of Cub Run,
Rockingham county.
Rockingham Register and Advertiser, 24
January 1867 (Thursday), p. 2, c. 4.

HIETT: See entry for MONROE.

HIGGINS: See entry for CONNER.

HIGGINS: On the 5th of January, at Mt. Airy,
Shenandoah county, by Elder John Neff,
Mr. Patrick HIGGINS, of New Orleans, and
Miss Elizabeth IRELAND, of that county.
Rockingham Register and Advertiser, 10
February 1865 (Friday), p. 2, c. 2.

HIGGS: See entry for PAINTER.

HIGGS: On the 19th inst., by Elder G.W.
Woods, Levi HIGGS and Miss Phoebe Ann
PHILLIPS, all of Rockingham.
Rockingham Register, 29 September 1870
(Thursday), p. 2, c. 5.

HIGH: See entry for DERROW.

HIGH: On the 28th of February, by Rev. Jacob
Miller, Grafton HIGH and Harriet GLOVER,
all of Rockingham.
Rockingham Register and Advertiser, 14
March 1867 (Thursday), p. 3, c. 5.

HILBERT: On the 11th inst., by Rev. Jacob

Thomas, Daniel C. HILBERT and Elizabeth ROOF, all of Rockingham county.
Rockingham Register and Advertiser, 18 October 1866 (Thursday), p. 2, c. 4.

HILL: See entry for CURRY.

HILL: See entry for FORRER.

HILL: See entry for HUSTON.

HILL: See entry for HUTCHENS.

HILL: See entry for MADDUX.

HILL: See entry for SIMMONS.

HILL: At the residence of the bride's father, on the 27th of February, by Rev. Solomon Garber, John HILL, of Augusta, and Miss Elizabeth HIBERT, of Rockingham.
Rockingham Register and Advertiser, 12 March 1868 (Thursday), p. 2, c. 6.

HILL: On the 3rd inst., at Jennings Gap, by Rev. Thomas Hildebrand, Mr. John L. HILL and Miss Elizabeth KUNKLE, all of Augusta county.
Rockingham Register and Advertiser, 20 April 1866 (Friday), p. 2, c. 3.

HILL: On the 28th ult., in Covington, Va., by Rev. S.B. Dolly, assisted by Rev. James M. Rice, Rev. W.E. HILL, of Richmond, and Miss Jennie K. PITZER, of Covington.
Rockingham Register, 11 November 1869 (Thursday), p. 3, c. 3.

HILL: On the 26th ult., by Rev. J.M. Clymer, Wm. H. HILL, of Nelson county, and Miss Mary H., daughter of Mr. Isaac HAAS, of Woodstock.
Rockingham Register and Advertiser, 11 July 1867 (Thursday), p. 2, c. 6.

HILLIARD: See entry for PRICE.

HILLIARD: On Tuesday, the 22nd inst., by Rev. G. Woods, James D. HILLIARD and Miss Virginia NISWARNER, both of Rockingham.
Rockingham Register, 31 March 1870 (Thursday), p. 3, c. 3.

HINEGARDNER: See entry for AREHART.

HINEGARDNER: See entry for MILLER.

HINEGARDNER: January 8th, 1860, at the residence of the bride's father, Mr. Adam GOUL, by Rev. J.M. Grabill, Mr. Jacob W. HINEGARDNER and Miss Sarah J. GOUL, all of Rockingham county, Va.

Rockingham Register and Advertiser, 13 January 1860 (Friday), p. 2, c. 6.

HINER: See entry for BIRD.

HINER: See entry for BOLTON.

HINER: See entry for CRAWFORD.

HINER: See entry for DINKEL.

HINER: See entry for HAMILTON.

HINER: See entry for PREFEIT.

HINER: On the morning of the 13th inst., at the American Hotel, Staunton, Va., by the Rev. J.C. Dice, Capt. Harman HINER, of Barboursville, Orange county, and Louisa E. HARRISON, of Augusta county.

Rockingham Register & Advertiser, 22 December 1865 (Friday), p. 3, c. 2.

HINES: On the 23rd ult., by Rev. H. Wetzel, Joseph HINES and Miss Louisa J. RACEY, all of Shenandoah county.

Rockingham Register, 13 August 1868 (Thursday), p. 2, c. 5.

HISEY: See entry for RAU.

HISEY: On the 27th inst., by the Rev. G.W. Anderson, Mr. Isaac HISEY, of Edinburg, Shenandoah county, to Miss Lavillia MAGRUDER, of Frederick county.

Rockingham Register and Advertiser, 8 February 1861 (Friday), p. 3, c. 4.

HISEY: On the 11th inst., by Rev. J.W. Wolff, Mr. Samuel HISEY and Miss Eliza M. FRAVEL, all of this county.

Rockingham Register and Advertiser, 26 August 1859 (Friday), p. 2, c. 5.

HISSELL: On the 5th inst., by the Rev. J.P. Cline, Mr. John HISSELL and Miss Mary JENKINS, all of Shenandoah county.

Rockingham Register and Advertiser, 25 January 1861 (Friday), p. 3, c. 1.

HIT: In Page county, on Thursday the 25th of July, by Elder J.T. Robinson, Mr. James S. HIT, of Culpeper, Va., to Miss Elizabeth, daughter of Rev. G. CLINE, of Page county, Va.

Rockingham Register and Valley Advertiser, 10 August 1850 (Saturday), p. 2, c. 6.

HITE: See entry for POOL.
HITE: See entry for RILEY.
HITE: See entry for VINES.
HITE: On the 18th ult., by Elder Henry Jennings, Geo. HITE and Miss Virginia CLINEDINST, all of Shenandoah.
Rockingham Register and Advertiser, 15 November 1866 (Thursday), p. 2, c. 5.
HITE: On the 1st of December, in Bridgewater, by Rev. James M. Follansbee, Thomas S. HITE and Miss Alpha V. RHODES, all of Rockingham.
Rockingham Register, 8 December 1870 (Thursday), p. 2, c. 4.
HITE: On the 24th of June, by Rev. R.C. Walker, Wm. F. HITE and Miss Sue E., daughter of Dr. Jos. E. WILSON, of Churchville, Augusta county, Va.
Rockingham Register, 2 July 1868 (Thursday), p. 2, c. 4.
HITT: See entry for CUNINGHAM.
HITT: On the 11th of February, by Elder Casper Allemong, Mr. William HITT and Miss Nancy E. CUBBAGE, both of Page county.
Rockingham Register and Advertiser, 11 March 1859 (Friday), p. 2, c. 4.
HIZER: See entry for ROOT.
HOAK: On the 5th inst., John HOAK and Miss Bettie, daughter of J.H. JIRKLE, Esq., all of Page county.
Rockingham Register, 22 December 1870 (Thursday), p. 2, c. 4.
HOARD: See entry for BLISS.
HOBBS: At Wood Lawn, in Augusta county, on the 21st of July, by Rev. T.L. Preston, Lieut. Jas. O. HOBBS and Miss Mollie, daughter of Henry EIDSON, Esq.
Rockingham Register and Advertiser, 1 August 1867 (Thursday), p. 2, c. 6.
HOCKMAN: See entry for BUCHER.
HOCKMAN: See entry for KELLER.
HOCKMAN: See entry for MILLER.
HOCKMAN: See entry for STRICKLER.
HOCKMAN: On the 4th inst., by Rev. G.H. Martin, Mr. John HOCKMAN and Miss

Christina BAKER, all of Shenandoah county.

Rockingham Register and Advertiser, 13 December 1866 (Thursday), p. 2, c. 5.

HOCKMAN: On the 17th ult., John W. HOCKMAN and Mintia A. COPENHAVER, both of Shenandoah county.

Rockingham Register, 8 December 1870 (Thursday), p. 2, c. 4.

HOCKMAN: On the 13th inst., by Rev. W. Rusmisel, Mr. Michael HOCKMAN, of Augusta county, and Miss Mary Ann LONG, of Frederick county.

Rockingham Register and Advertiser, 24 June 1859 (Friday), p. 2, c. 4.

HOCKMAN: On the 10th inst., by Elder Z.J. Compton, Samuel HOCKMAN and Miss C., daughter of J.R. CULLARS, of Warren county.

Rockingham Register, 28 April 1870 (Thursday), p. 3, c. 3.

HODGE: See entry for KIRKPATRICK.

HODGE: See entry for THOMAS.

HODGES: On the 26th of March, by the Rev. John Perkey, Mr. John HODGES and Miss Jermima S. MILLER, formerly of Shenandoah.

Rockingham Register and Advertiser, 20 April 1866 (Friday), p. 2, c. 3.

HOFFMAN: See entry for LIPOP.

HOFFMAN: See entry for ROSS.

HOFFMAN: See entry for THARP.

HOFFMAN: On Tuesday morning, the 4th inst., at Mt. Jackson, Shenandoah, by Elder T. Taylor, E.H.B. HOFFMAN, Esq., of Rockingham, and Miss Mary E. FARRAR, of Shenandoah county.

Rockingham Register and Advertiser, 14 October 1859 (Friday), p. 2, c. 3.

HOFFMAN: On Thursday, the 28th ult., by Elder Henry Jennings, N.M. HOFFMAN, Esq., and Miss Lydia A. CLINEDINST, all of Shenandoah county.

The Rockingham Register, 26 February 1864 (Friday), p. 2, c. 4.

HOGAN: See entry for BRUNK.

HOGE: See entry for McPHERSON.

HOGE: In Abingdon, on the 15th inst., by Rev. Jas. McChain, C.E. HOGE, Esq., of Staunton, and Miss A.B. FRENCH, of Abingdon, Va.
Rockingham Register, 22 October 1868 (Thursday), p. 3, c. 3.

HOGSHEAD: On the 19th of December, by Rev. C.B. Hammock, Mr. Geo. HOGSHEAD and Miss Lydia O. FUDLEY, all of Augusta.
Rockingham Register, 7 January 1869 (Thursday), p. 3, c. 3.

HOLLAND: See entry for FIFER.

HOLLAND: On the 21st inst., by Rev. D.F. Bittle, D.D., Rev. G.W. HOLLAND and Miss R. Pauline BITTLE, all of Salem, Roanoke county, Va.
Rockingham Register and Advertiser, 29 August 1867 (Thursday), p. 2, c. 5.

HOLLAR: See entry for RACEY.

HOLLAR: See entry for ROBINSON.

HOLLAR: See entry for SHIP.

HOLLAR: See entry for THOMPSON.

HOLLEN: See entry for LONG.

HOLLEN: On the 25th of December, by Rev. Solomon Garber, Adam R. HOLLEN and Miss Nancy S., daughter of Abraham MILLER, all of Rockingham.
Rockingham Register and Advertiser, 9 January 1868 (Thursday), p. 2, c. 4.

HOLLEN: On the 19th of July, by the Rev. Jacob Thomas, Mr. Jeremiah HOLLEN and Miss Sarah McDORMAN, all of this county.
Rockingham Register and Advertiser, 27 July 1860 (Friday), p. 2, c. 3.

HOLLEN: Near Rushville, on Thursday evening the 14th inst., by Rev. A. Poe Boude, Peter M. HOLLEN and Miss Emma V., daughter of Barnett R. SPECK, all of Rockingham.
Rockingham Register and Advertiser, 21 November 1867 (Thursday), p. 2, c. 5.

HOLLER: See entry for LANDES.

HOLLER: See entry for LINDAMOOD.

HOLLER: On the 5th inst., by Rev. Levi Keller, Samuel HOLLER and Miss Elizabeth

A. WISMAN, all of Shenandoah county.
Rockingham Register, 21 May 1868
(Thursday), p. 2, c. 5.
HOLLIDAY: On the 9th inst., by Rev. T.F.
Martin,   Col.   F.W.M.   HOLLIDAY,   of
Frederick   county,   and   Miss   Hannah,
daughter of Thomas McCORMICK, Esq., of
Clarke county.
Rockingham Register and Advertiser, 30
January 1868 (Thursday), p. 2, c. 4.
HOLLINGSWORTH: See entry for GRABILL.
HOLLINGSWORTH: See entry for HANNON.
HOLMES: See entry for BOWMAN.
HOLMES: See entry for WATKINS.
HOLSINGER: See entry for HOLSINGER.
HOLSINGER: See entry for STROOP.
HOLSINGER: On Tuesday, the 16th of January,
by   Rev.   Benjamin   Bowman,   Peter   P.
HOLSINGER and Miss Mary Ann KESLER, all
of Rockingham county.
Rockingham Register and Advertiser, 19
January 1866 (Friday), p. 3, c. 2.
HOLSINGER: On the 10th inst., by Rev. Samuel
Wampler, Mr. Philip HOLSINGER and Miss
Delana   HOLSINGER,   both   of   Rockingham
county.
Rockingham Register and Advertiser, 21
February 1862 (Friday), p. 3, c. 2.
HOLT: On   the   29th   ult.,   by Rev. Jos. A.
Snyder, Chas. A. HOLT, Esq., and Miss M.
Lizzie HELLER, all of Shenandoah county.
Rockingham Register and Advertiser, 6
December 1866 (Thursday), p. 3, c. 2.
HOLTZMAN: See entry for COFFMAN.
HOLTZMAN: See entry for DOVEL.
HOLTZMAN: On the 28th ult., by Rev. H. St. J.
Rinker, Mr. B.S. HOLTZMAN and Miss Mary
A. MAPHIS, all of Shenandoah.
Rockingham Register and Advertiser, 14
March 1867 (Thursday), p. 3, c. 5.
HOMAN: See entry for KERR.
HOMAN: See entry for RIDDLE.
HOOK: See entry for BATEMAN.
HOOKE: See entry for SLUSSER.
HOOKE: On Tuesday, the 12th inst., by Rev.
John Brubaker, Mr. Lewis J. HOOKE, of

Roanoke county, Va., formerly of Rockingham, and Miss Lucy A., daughter of Mr. Joseph MOOMAW, of Botetourt county. *Rockingham Register and Advertiser*, 28 June 1866 (Thursday), p. 2, c. 5.

HOOKS: See entry for HUPMON.

HOOVER: See entry for BAYLOR.

HOOVER: See entry for DELLINGER.

HOOVER: See entry for KIBLER.

HOOVER: See entry for KRATZER.

HOOVER: See entry for LAMBERT.

HOOVER: See entry for RHODES.

HOOVER: See entry for RITCHIE.

HOOVER: See entry for SHEETS.

HOOVER: See entry for SMITH.

HOOVER: See entry for STONEBURNER.

HOOVER: On the 25th of September, at the residence of the bride's parents, in Brock's Gap, by Rev. Jacob Miller, Hiram HOOVER, aged 18 years, and Miss Eva, daughter of Philip RITCHIE, aged 15 years. *Rockingham Register*, 6 October 1870 (Thursday), p. 2, c. 4.

HOOVER: On the 24th ult., by Rev. Daniel Thomas, Mr. Jacob HOOVER and Miss Susan E., daughter of Mr. James MAULEY, all of Rockingham county. *Rockingham Register and Advertiser*, 8 January 1858 (Friday), p. 3, c. 1.

HOOVER: On the 22nd inst., by the Rev. H. Tallhelm, Mr. Jacob HOOVER and Miss Sarah Ann, daughter of Mr. Michael RITCHIE, all of Rockingham county. *Rockingham Register and Advertiser*, 30 March 1860 (Friday), p. 2, c. 4.

HOOVER: On the 13th ult., by Rev. H. Wetzel, James HOOVER and Miss Jennie M. COFFELT, all of Shenandoah county. *Rockingham Register and Advertiser*, 4 October 1866 (Thursday), p. 2, c. 5.

HOPEWELL: See entry for RYAN.

HOPEWELL: See entry for SISER.

HOPKINS: See entry for ARGENBRIGHT.

HOPKINS: See entry for BRADSHAW.

HOPKINS: See entry for DAUGHERTY.

211

HOPKINS: See entry for MILLER.

HOPKINS: See entry for PATTERSON.

HOPKINS: See entry for WARREN.

HOPKINS: On the 21st inst., by Rev. T.D. Bell, Mr. Archibald F. HOPKINS, of Company H, 10th Reg't Va. Vols., and Miss Sallie A., daughter of Mr. B. Fielding RALSTON, all of Rockingham county. Rockingham Register, 31 July 1863 (Friday), p. 3, c. 3.

HOPKINS: On the 8th inst., by the Rev. T.D. Bell, Dr. Benjamin F. HOPKINS and Mrs. Fannie A. SMITH, both of Sangerville, Augusta county, Va. Rockingham Register and Advertiser, 16 March 1860 (Friday), p. 2, c. 5.

HOPKINS: In Washington, D.C., on the 14th of December, by Rev. Oliver Cox, Geo. W. HOPKINS, Esq., and Mrs. L. Freddie MOORE, formerly of Virginia. Rockingham Register and Advertiser, 30 January 1868 (Thursday), p. 2, c. 4.

HOPKINS: October 25th, by Rev. T.D. Bell, Mr. Lewis C. HOPKINS and Miss Cornelia D., daughter of Mr. Michael WHITMORE, all of Rockingham county. Rockingham Register & Advertiser, 3 November 1865 (Friday), p. 2, c. 2.

HOPKINS: On the 3rd inst., by Rev. J.W. Howe, Peachy H. HOPKINS and Miss Kate LONG, all of Rockingham. Rockingham Register and Advertiser, 24 October 1867 (Thursday), p. 2, c. 7.

HORDE: On Sunday evening the 24th inst., at the residence of the bride's mother, in Dayton, by Rev. Jacob Thomas, Hiram HORDE and Miss Sarah C. BROWN, all of Rockingham county. Rockingham Register, 28 April 1870 (Thursday), p. 3, c. 3.

HORN: See entry for BAZZEL.

HORN: See entry for GOOD.

HORN: See entry for SWANK.

HORN: At the residence of the bride's father, Jacob GELTMACHER, Niles, Michigan, on Tuesday, the 14th of August, 1866, by the

Rev. Wm. H. Moffet, of the Episcopal Church, Major O.P. HORN, C.S.A., of Virginia, and Miss Hettie M. GELTMACHER ....

Rockingham Register and Advertiser, 23 August 1866 (Thursday), p. 2, c. 7.

HORTON: On Tuesday evening, the 6th of September, by Rev. H. Tallhelm, Mr. Harrison P. HORTON, of Culpeper county, and Miss Sarah BERRY, of Shenandoah county.

The Rockingham Register, 16 September 1864 (Friday), p. 2, c. 5.

HOSHOUR: On the 3rd inst., by Rev. J.R. Wheeler, S.A. HOSHOUR, Esq., and Miss Sarah C. LAMB, both of Staunton.

The Rockingham Register, 19 December 1862 (Friday), p. 2, c. 4.

HOSLER: By Rev. D.C. Irwin, October 25th, Mr. Wm. F. HOSLER and Miss Margaret E.F. ARMENTROUT, both of this county.

Rockingham Register and Advertiser, 2 November 1860 (Friday), p. 2, c. 5.

HOTTEL: See entry for CHRISMAN.

HOTTEL: See entry for DELLINGER.

HOTTEL: See entry for FANSLER.

HOTTEL: See entry for SNARR.

HOTTEL: On the 27th ult., by Rev. Levi Keller, Mr. Geo. W. HOTTEL and Miss Mary Catharine SWISHER, all of Shenandoah.

Rockingham Register and Advertiser, 18 November 1859 (Friday), p. 2, c. 4.

HOTTEL: On the 27th ult., Elder J. Pirkey, James C. HOTTEL and Miss Martha J. BAUSERMAN, all of Shenandoah county.

Rockingham Register and Advertiser, 15 March 1861 (Friday), p. 2, c. 4.

HOTTEL: On the 12th inst., by the Rev. Jacob Miller, Mr. James H. HOTTEL, of Shenandoah, and Miss Nancy, daughter of George RADER, of Rockingham.

Rockingham Register and Advertiser, 20 January 1860 (Friday), p. 2, c. 6.

HOTTEL: On the 22nd ult., at Newtown, by Rev. Mr. Jefferson, Nathan HOTTEL, of New Market, and Miss Mary E. DEWER, of

Frederick.

Rockingham Register, 5 November 1868
(Thursday), p. 3, c. 3.

HOTTINGER: See entry for CARR.

HOTTINGER: On Sunday morning, the 23rd inst.,
by Rev. Jacob Miller, Mr. Harvey
HOTTINGER and Miss Mary Jane, daughter of
Mr. James MAUCK, all of Rockingham
county.

Rockingham Register and Advertiser, 28
September 1860 (Friday), p. 2, c. 4.

HOTTINGER: On the 10th of February, by Rev.
Jacob Wine, Isaac HOTTINGER and Abbie
WILL, all of Rockingham.

Rockingham Register and Advertiser, 24
February 1865 (Friday), p. 2, c. 5.

HOTTINGER: On the 1st of December, near
Mountain Valley Church, by Rev. Joseph
Funkhouser, John HOTTINGER and Miss Jane
B. SMITH, all of Rockingham.

Rockingham Register, 8 December 1870
(Thursday), p. 2, c. 4.

HOTTLE: See entry for COFFMAN.

HOTTLE: See entry for SHEETZ.

HOTTLE: On the 22nd ult., by Rev. Thomas
Miller, Isaac T. HOTTLE and Miss Frances
Jane V., eldest daughter of Rev. H.
WETZEL, all of Shenandoah county.

Rockingham Register and Advertiser, 9
March 1866 (Friday), p. 2, c. 3.

HOTTLE: On the 14th inst., by Rev. G.H.
Martin, Col. Jacob A. HOTTLE and Mrs.
Sarah A. EMSWILLER, all of Shenandoah
county.

Rockingham Register, 23 April 1868
(Thursday), p. 2, c. 6.

HOUCK: See entry for FLETCHER.

HOUCK: In Strasburg, on Sunday evening, the
17th of December, by Elder John Pirkey,
Mr. James HOUCK and Mrs. FISHER, all of
that place.

Rockingham Register and Advertiser, 12
January 1866 (Friday), p. 1, c. 3.

HOUFF: See entry for SHEETS.

HOUFF: On the 27th ult., by Rev. C. Beard,
Mr. Benjamin F. HOUFF and Miss Mary S.

HALDERMAN.

The Rockingham Register, 12 December 1862 (Friday), p. 2, c. 5.

HOUFF: On the 4th inst., at the residence of Mr. Lewis Bailey, by Rev. S. Filler, Mr. Daniel HOUFF, of Augusta county, and Miss Mary Ellen BAILY, of Rockingham county.

Rockingham Register and Advertiser, 12 June 1857 (Friday), p. 3, c. 2.

HOUFF: On the 30th ult., near Spring Hill, by Rev. J.W. Karicofe, John F. HOUFF and Miss Mary V. NEFF, all of Augusta county.

Rockingham Register and Advertiser, 13 June 1867 (Thursday), p. 2, c. 6.

HOUFFE: On Thursday the 10th inst., by the Rev. Peter Shickle, Mr. Peter E. HOUFFE and Miss Rebecca M., eldest daughter of William LINK, Esq., all of Augusta county.

Rockingham Register and Valley Advertiser, 19 April 1845 (Saturday), p. 3, c. 1.

HOULTZ: In Staunton, on the 23rd inst., by Rev. Geo. B. Taylor, Mr. David HOULTZ and Miss Margaret FREEMAN, all of Augusta county.

Rockingham Register and Advertiser, 31 January 1862 (Friday), p. 2, c. 7.

HOUNSHELL: At the residence of the bride's father, near Lewisburg, Va., on the 30th of December, 1861, by Rev. J. Calvin Barr, Maj. D.S. HOUNSHELL, of the 51st Reg't Va. Vols., and Miss Lucie, daughter of John RODGERS, Esq., of Greenbrier county, Va.

Rockingham Register and Advertiser, 17 January 1862 (Friday), p. 3, c. 1.

HOUSAFLUCK: In Newtown, Frederick county, Va., on the 10th inst., by Rev. Mr. Rusmizel, Mr. Calvin HOUSAFLUCK and Miss Rachel A. SHIREMAN, all of Shenandoah county.

Rockingham Register and Advertiser, 28 July 1865 (Friday), p. 2, c. 6.

HOUSEMAN: By Rev. C.B. HAMMACK, on Saturday, the 30th of March, at the residence of

Mr. John Moyers, Mr. Jacob HOUSEMAN and Mrs. Mary TEAFORD, all of Augusta.
Rockingham Register and Advertiser, 12 April 1861 (Friday), p. 2, c. 4.

HOUSEMAN: On the 16th inst., by Rev. G.W. Statton, Mr. Jas. W. HOUSEMAN and Miss Catharine Virginia, daughter of Rev. Jacob BARE, dec'd, all of Augusta county, Va.
Rockingham Register and Advertiser, 24 June 1859 (Friday), p. 2, c. 4.

HOUSER: On the 26th of November, by Rev. Timothy Funk, Geo. HOUSER and Miss Sallie E. PAULSEL, all of Rockingham.
Rockingham Register and Advertiser, 6 December 1866 (Thursday), p. 3, c. 2.

HOUSER: On the 29th ult., near Midway, Augusta county, by the Rev. C. Dameron, S.F. HOUSER and Miss Hattie G., eldest daughter of Wm. HESS, Esq.
Rockingham Register, 13 May 1869 (Thursday), p. 3, c. 3.

HOUSEWORTH: October 26, at McMullan's Mill, Greene county, Va., by the Rev. Mr. Moss, Henry HOUSEWORTH and Miss Mattie McMULLAN, formerly of Brownsville, Union county, Indiana.
Rockingham Register & Advertiser, 8 December 1865 (Friday), p. 2, c. 4.

HOUSMAN: At the Healing Springs, on Wednesday morning, June 6th, by Rev. Lorenzo D. Nixon, Mr. Simon P. HOUSMAN, of Botetourt, and Miss Julia F.H. PITZER, of Bath county, Va.
Rockingham Register and Advertiser, 22 June 1860 (Friday), p. 2, c. 6 .

HOUSTON: See entry for MORROW.

HOUSTON: See entry for PAUL.

HOUSTON: See entry for SCOTT.

HOUSTON: On Thursday evening the 23rd ult., by the Rev. James Paine, Mr. W. HOUSTON and Miss Annette S., daughter of Thomas WILSON, Esq., near Fairfield, and of Rockbridge county.
Rockingham Register and Valley Advertiser, 8 June 1850 (Saturday), p. 2,

216

c. 7.

HOUSTON: On the 14th of November, by Rev. S.R. HOUSTON, his son, Rev. R.R. HOUSTON, of Monroe, and Miss Maggie STEEL, of Greenbrier county, Va.
The Rockingham Register, 12 December 1862 (Friday), p. 2, c. 5.

HOWARD: See entry for McGUFFEY.

HOWARD: See entry for RAY.

HOWDERSUELL: On the 27th ult., at the residence of the bride's father, near Staunton, by the Rev. G. Kramer, Rufus A. HOWDERSUELL, of Fauquier, and Miss Martha E., daughter of Maurice PARKER, Esq.
Rockingham Register, 4 November 1869 (Thursday), p. 2, c. 4.

HOWE: On the 2nd inst., by Rev. D. Feete, Mr. Edward HOWE and Miss Elizabeth C., daughter of Philip MILLER, of Woodstock.
Rockingham Register and Advertiser, 11 January 1861 (Friday), p. 3, c. 4.

HOWELL: See entry for EAST.

HOWVER: On Sunday, July 5th, near Hopkins' Schoolhouse, by Rev. J.W. Howe, Mr. Joseph HOWVER and Miss Lucretia J., daughter of Mr. Wm. RALSTON, all of Rockingham county.
The Rockingham Register, 10 July 1863 (Friday), p. 2, c. 5.

HOY: See entry for VINES.

HUCKSTEP: See entry for ROUDABUSH.

HUDDLE: See entry for SWITZER.

HUDDLESON: At the residence of the bride's parents, in Harrisonburg, on Wednesday evening the 16th inst., by Rev. Jas. S. Gardner, Wm. Henry HUDDLESON, of the vicinity of Woodstock, Va., and Miss Mary F., daughter of John GATEWOOD, Esq., Editor of the Old Commonwealth, of Harrisonburg.
Rockingham Register, 24 February 1870 (Thursday), p. 2, c. 5.

HUDGENS: On December 24th, by Rev. Solomon Garber, Franklin HUDGENS and Miss Mary W. SMALS, all of Bridgewater, Rockingham

county.
Rockingham Register, 7 January 1869 (Thursday), p. 3, c. 3.

HUDLOWE: See entry for KYGER.

HUDLOWE: See entry for PRICE.

HUDSON: See entry for HAMILTON.

HUFF: See entry for CAUFMAN.

HUFF: See entry for CLINE.

HUFF: See entry for HENRY.

HUFF: See entry for SHEPHERD.

HUFF: On Sunday, the 24th inst., by the Rev. J.W. Howe, Mr. Ephraim P. HUFF to Miss Amanda, daughter of Thomas CUMMONS, all of Rockingham.
Rockingham Register and Advertiser, 29 November 1861 (Friday), p. 3, c. 1.

HUFFER: See entry for POOL.

HUFFMAN: See entry for BOWMAN.

HUFFMAN: See entry for BRUBECKER.

HUFFMAN: See entry for CALVERT.

HUFFMAN: See entry for DOLLY.

HUFFMAN: See entry for GARBER.

HUFFMAN: See entry for HUFFMAN.

HUFFMAN: See entry for JETT.

HUFFMAN: See entry for KEYSER.

HUFFMAN: See entry for LOUGH.

HUFFMAN: See entry for LUCAS.

HUFFMAN: See entry for MONGER.

HUFFMAN: See entry for RITCHIE.

HUFFMAN: See entry for SAUFLEY.

HUFFMAN: See entry for SHIPMAN.

HUFFMAN: See entry for SHOWALTER.

HUFFMAN: See entry for SIBERT.

HUFFMAN: See entry for TUTWILER.

HUFFMAN: See entry for WHEELBERGER.

HUFFMAN: June 21st, 1870, by Rev. J. Follinsbee, Capt. D.W. HUFFMAN and Miss Berta B., youngest daughter of Dr. Wm. HERRING, dec'd, all of Bridgewater.
Rockingham Register, 30 June 1870 (Thursday), p. 2. c. 5.

HUFFMAN: At the residence of Mr. David Snyder, near Augusta Springs, on November 29th, by Rev. J.W. Grimm, Rev. Geo. HUFFMAN, of Virginia Annual Conference, United Brethren in Christ, and Miss

Catharine SNYDER, all of Augusta county. *Rockingham Register and Advertiser*, 20 December 1866 (Thursday), p. 2, c. 5.

HUFFMAN: On the 25th ult., near Mt. Crawford, by Rev. G. Stevenson, Hiram HUFFMAN and Miss Maggie A., daughter of Jacob LAGO, all of Rockingham. *Rockingham Register and Advertiser*, 5 December 1867 (Thursday), p. 2, c. 5.

HUFFMAN: On the 18th inst., by Rev. J. Markwood, Mr. J.H. HUFFMAN and Miss Ellen M., daughter of J.B. SNAPP, of Edenburg [sic, Edinburg]. *Rockingham Register and Virginia Advertiser*, 28 March 1856 (Friday), p. 3, c. 1.

HUFFMAN: On the 8th of March, by Rev. A.P. Boude, Mr. James HUFFMAN and Miss Mary E. HENTON, all of Rockingham county. *Rockingham Register and Advertiser*, 27 April 1866 (Friday), p. 2, c. 2.

HUFFMAN: By Rev. Harvey Gilmore, October the 19th, James S. HUFFMAN and Miss Sarah F., daughter of Jacob LUDWICK, of Rockbridge. *Rockingham Register*, 28 October 1869 (Thursday), p. 2, c. 3.

HUFFMAN: On the 23rd of December, 1869, at Burke's Mill, by the Rev. Christian Hartman, Jas. S. HUFFMAN and Mary A. SPITLER, both of Augusta. *Rockingham Register*, 6 January 1870 (Thursday), p. 3, c. 3.

HUFFMAN: At Lebanon, White Sulphur Springs, by Rev. H.A. Bovey, Jasper M. HUFFMAN, of Barbour county, and Miss Mary A.E. RHYAN, of Augusta county. *Rockingham Register and Advertiser*, 1 November 1866 (Thursday), p. 3, c. 4.

HUFFMAN: On the 26th of November, by Elder C. Allemong, Mr. John P. HUFFMAN, of Rockingham county, and Mary SECRIST, of Page county. *The Rockingham Register*, 11 December 1863 (Friday), p. 2, c. 6.

HUFFMAN: On the 9th inst., at the residence of the bride's father, near Staunton, by

Rev. R.C. Walker, Lewis V. HUFFMAN and
Miss Mary E., daughter of Capt. Alex.
ANDERSON, of Augusta.
Rockingham Register, 16 April 1868
(Thursday), p. 2, c. 5.

HUFFMAN: On Sunday, the 18th of February, by
Rev. Jacob Miller, Mr. Madison HUFFMAN
and Miss Margaret Jane, daughter of
Reuben TERRELL, all of Rockingham county.
Rockingham Register and Advertiser, 23
February 1866 (Friday), p. 2, c. 4.

HUFFMAN: On the 27th ult., by Rev. Levi
Keller, Robert A. HUFFMAN and Miss Roanna
HUFFMAN, both of Madison county, Va.
Rockingham Register and Advertiser, 23
March 1866 (Friday), p. 3, c. 3.

HUFFMAN: On Tuesday evening, the 25th ult.,
by Rev. J.C. Hensell, Wm. D. HUFFMAN, of
Augusta, and Miss Elizabeth S., eldest
daughter of Wm. RUEBUSH, of Rockingham.
Rockingham Register and Advertiser, 4
July 1867 (Thursday), p. 2, c. 6.

HUFFMAN: In the Baptist Church, near Mt.
Crawford, by Rev. W.A. Whitescarver, on
the 16th inst., Wm. D. HUFFMAN and Miss
Sarah C. WISE, all of Rockingham.
Rockingham Register, 23 December 1869
(Thursday), p. 3, c. 2.

HUGHART: On May 18th, by Rev. Harvey Gilmore,
Jas. P. HUGHART, of Bath county, to Miss
Mary E. McCUTCHEN, of Augusta.
Rockingham Register, 27 May 1869
(Thursday), p. 2, c. 3.

HUGHES: See entry for VADEN.

HUGHES: In the vicinity of Bristol, Tenn., on
Tuesday morning, May 6th, 1862, by Rev.
W.W. Neal, Mr. Edward G.F. HUGHES, of
Sullivan county, Tenn., formerly of
Rockingham county, Va., and Miss Dorcas
M. HAYTER, of Washington county, Va.
Rockingham Register and Virginia
Advertiser, 1 August 1862 (Friday), p. 2,
c. 4.

HUGHES: On the 27th of January, in Rushville,
by Rev. Daniel Thomas, Franklin HUGHES
and Miss Frances, daughter of Wm.

MESSERSMITH, all of Rockingham county. *Rockingham Register and Advertiser*, 21 February 1867 (Thursday), p. 3, c. 2.

HULL: See entry for CROSSLEY.

HULL: See entry for WALLACE.

HULL: On the 27th ult., at the residence of the bride's father, by Rev. Jos. Crickenberger, Andrew A. HULL, of Highland county, and Miss Mary J., daughter of James A. CAMPBELL, of Rockingham. *Rockingham Register and Advertiser*, 5 December 1867 (Thursday), p. 2, c. 5.

HULLS: See entry for MILLEE.

HULTZ: See entry for GORDON.

HULVA: On the 21st ult., by Elder J. Jennings, Mr. David C. HULVA and Miss Sarah RIDDLE, all of Rockingham. *Rockingham Register and Advertiser*, 14 September 1860 (Friday), p. 2, c. 5.

HULVEY: See entry for SHEETS.

HUME: See entry for RICE.

HUMPHREY: See entry for SAMPSON.

HUMPHREYS: See entry for BAGBY.

HUMPHREYS: See entry for TAYLOR.

HUMPHREYS: See entry for TIMBERLAKE.

HUMPHREYS: See entry for WILSON.

HUMPHREYS: On the 4th inst., by Rev. R.W. Watts, at "Chestnut Avenue," Mr. John B. HUMPHREYS, of Augusta, to Miss Laura J. MUNDAY, of Albemarle. *Rockingham Register*, 18 June 1868 (Thursday), p. 3, c. 5.

HUMPHREYS: In Staunton, on the 10th inst., by the Rev. S.D. Stuart, Mr. Wm. W. HUMPHREYS and Miss Mary E. LAYNE. *Rockingham Register*, 14 August 1863 (Friday), p. 3, c. 1.

HUNCHBERGER: See entry for FRY.

HUNSICKER: On the 17th ult., by Rev. J.W. Watson, Daniel J. HUNSICKER and Mrs. Ursula A. WATSON, all of Page county. *Rockingham Register and Advertiser*, 7 November 1867 (Thursday), p. 2, c. 5.

HUNTER: See entry for PECK.

HUNTER: See entry for RIMEL.

HUNTER: See entry for SPITLER.

HUNTER: On Wednesday, June 10, in the Disciple's Church, at Louisa Courthouse, Va., by Rev. L.A. Cutler, C.W. HUNTER, of Staunton, Va., to Miss Lute M., daughter of Maj. F. Wm. JONES, of Louisa Courthouse.
Rockingham Register, 18 June 1868 (Thursday), p. 3, c. 5.

HUNTER: On Thursday, November 23rd, at Cedar Grove, King George county, Va., by Rev. Mr. Friend, Major Robert W. HUNTER, of Winchester, and Miss Margaretta, daughter of Dr. R.H. STUART.
Rockingham Register & Advertiser, 22 December 1865 (Friday), p. 3, c. 2.

HUNTER: On Tuesday morning last, by the Rev. T.T. Castleman, Wm. J. HUNTER and Miss Hannah, daughter of Sam'l WOODWARD, of Augusta county.
Rockingham Register and Virginia Advertiser, 21 December 1855 (Friday), p. 2, c. 8.

HUNTON: On the 14th ult., in Frieden's Church, in Shenandoah county, by Rev. S. Henkel, Rev. John H. HUNTON and Miss Lavenia P., daughter of Wm. BAKER, Esq.
Rockingham Register and Advertiser, 13 January 1860 (Friday), p. 2, c. 6.

HUPHMAN: On the 11th of October, at the residence of the bride, by the Rev. W.T. Price, James HUPHMAN and Mrs. Hetty KINCAID, all of Highland county.
Rockingham Register and Advertiser, 8 November 1866 (Thursday), p. 3, c. 4.

HUPMON: On the morning of the 4th inst., by Rev. Wm. T. Price, Jas. S. HUPMON, Esq., and Miss Margaret J. HOOKS, all of Highland county, Va.
Rockingham Register and Advertiser, 15 July 1859 (Friday), p. 3, c. 2.

HUPP: See entry for BURKETT.

HUPP: See entry for OLLINGER.

HUPP: See entry for SHAVER.

HUPP: On the 27th of February, by Rev. Isaac Soule, J.W. HUPP and Miss Elizabeth

222

WHITMER, all of Rockingham.
Rockingham Register and Advertiser, 12
March 1868 (Thursday), p. 2, c. 6.

HUPP: On the 20th of December, by Rev. Jacob
Wine, Matthias HUPP and Miss Amanda
ESTEP, all of Rockingham.
Rockingham Register and Advertiser, 7
February 1867 (Thursday), p. 3, c. 3.

HURD: By Rev. P. Miller, on the 31st of
December, 1863, Mr. Chas. HURD, formerly
of Ohio, but late of the Confederate
Army, and Miss Sarah A. MAPHIS, of
Hampshire county.
The Rockingham Register, 26 February 1864
(Friday), p. 2, c. 4.

HURLEY: See entry for SHEENEN.

HURST: See entry for WALLACE.

HUSER: On the 15th inst., by Elder John
Clark, Jos. E. HUSER and Miss Virginia
McINTOSH, all of Page county.
Rockingham Register and Advertiser, 30
January 1868 (Thursday), p. 2, c. 4.

HUSSEY: On the 23rd of February, by Rev. Dl.
Thomas, Sergeant James R. HUSSEY, of
Alexandria, Va., and member of Co. L,
62nd Va. Regiment Cavalry, to Miss Sarah
J., daughter of David and Sarah H.
VANFOSSEN, of Rockingham county.
Rockingham Register and Advertiser, 24
March 1865 (Friday), p. 2, c. 3.

HUSTON: See entry for LUPTON.

HUSTON: See entry for WALKER.

HUSTON: On Thursday, the 18th [of] November,
by the same [Rev. Jacob Miller], Mr.
Nathan HUSTON and Miss Mary, daughter of
Jacob HILL, dec'd, - all of this county.
Rockingham Register and Advertiser, 26
November 1858 (Friday), p. 3, c. 2.

HUTCHENS: See entry for CARWELL.

HUTCHENS: See entry for HESS.

HUTCHENS: On the 27th ult., by Rev. J.M.
Shreckhise, Anderson HUTCHENS and Miss
Rebecca S. HILL, all of Augusta.
Rockingham Register, 5 November 1868
(Thursday), p. 3, c. 3.

HUTCHESON: See entry for CAMPBELL.

HUTCHINS: See entry for TERRELL.

HUTCHINSON: On Thursday evening the 27th ult., by Rev. James S. Gardner, at the residence of the bride's father, James A. HUTCHINSON and Miss Mary Virginia, daughter of S.P. REAMER, of Harrisonburg. Rockingham Register, 3 February 1870 (Thursday), p. 3, c. 4.

HUTCHINSON: On the 28th ult., by Rev. Thos. Ward White, Jesse T. HUTCHINSON, Esq., and Miss Emily S., daughter of A. LINK, Esq., of Augusta. Rockingham Register and Advertiser, 7 December 1860 (Friday), p. 2, c. 6.

HUTCHINSON: On the 17th ult., at Mt. Jackson, by Rev. John W. Wolfe, John S. HUTCHINSON and Miss Alice A., daughter of Richard MILLER, Esq., all of Edinburg. Rockingham Register, 1 April 1869 (Thursday), p. 3, c. 3.

HUTTER: See entry for CRITES.

HYDE: On Wednesday the 7th inst., by Rev. Joshua Jennings, Mr. D.B. HYDE, of Augusta, and Miss Sue E., daughter of Mr. Peter NEFF, of Rockingham county. Rockingham Register and Advertiser, 10 January 1862 (Friday), p. 3, c. 2.

HYDE: In Brucetown, Va., February 23rd, 1864, at the residence of the bride's father, by Rev. W.G. Eggleston, Rev. John P. HYDE, of the Baltimore Annual Conference, and Miss Mollie, youngest daughter of James TANQUARY, Esq. The Rockingham Register, 4 March 1864 (Friday), p. 2, c. 6.

HYDE: In this place, on the 8th inst., by Rev. John Thrush, Mr. Joseph P. HYDE, formerly of Shenandoah county, and Miss Margaret L., daughter of Mr. F.[?] S. RAGAN, all of Harrisonburg. Rockingham Register and Virginia Advertiser, 11 April 1856 (Friday), p. 2, c. 8.

HYDECKER: On the 12th of November, by Elder G.W. Woods, John C. HYDECKER and Miss Emily C. MARTZ, all of Rockingham county.

Rockingham Register, 19 November 1868
(Thursday), p. 2, c. 5.
HYDER: See entry for CORDER.

- I -

IMBODEN: On Thursday, the 12th inst., by the
Rev. George W. McPhail, D.D., at Mulberry
Hill, the residence of the bride's
father, in Charlotte county, Va., John D.
IMBODEN, Esq., of Staunton, Va., and Miss
Mary W., eldest daughter of John B.
McPHAIL.
Rockingham Register and Advertiser, 27
May 1859 (Friday), p. 2, c. 6.
IMMEL: In New Market, on the 17th inst., by
Rev. S. Henkel, Henry IMMEL and Elizabeth
GRABE, both from Germany.
Rockingham Register and Advertiser, 29
June 1860 (Friday), p. 3, c. 2.
IRELAND: See entry for HIGGINS.
IRICK: See entry for DILLARD.
IRICK: See entry for DOLD.
IRICK: See entry for STERLING.
IRICK: On the 23rd of April, in Georgia, by
the Rev. B. Arbogast, A.B. IRICK, Esq.,
and Virginia M., daughter of John
GIBBONS, of Rockingham county, Va.
The Rockingham Register, 1 May 1863
(Friday), p. 2, c. 5.
IRICK: On Wednesday evening last, at the
residence of the bride's father, in
Harrisonburg, by Rev. J. Rice Bowman,
Samuel IRICK and Miss Ida F., daughter of
Thomas STERLING, all of this place.
Rockingham Register, 22 October 1868
(Thursday), p. 3, c. 3.
IRVIN: See entry for HAAS.
IRVINE: See entry for MORRISON.
IRWIN: See entry for ARTHUR.

- J -

JACK: On the 13th ult., by the Rev. Stephen
Smith, Martin M. JACK and Miss Sarah V.
GUM, all of Highland county.

Rockingham _Register_ and _Advertiser_, 18
July 1867 (Thursday), p. 2, c. 6.

JACKSON: See entry for SPITZER.

JACKSON: On the 14th of May, 1860, by Rev.
Abraham Knupp, Mr. Andrew JACKSON and
Miss Susanna PERRY, all of Rockingham
county.

Rockingham _Register_ and _Advertiser_, 22
June 1860 (Friday), p. 2, c. 6.

JACKSON: On the 5th inst., by Rev. James
Beaty, Henry C. JACKSON, of Shenandoah,
and Miss Mary C. DAVIS, of Romney, W.Va.

Rockingham _Register_ and _Advertiser_, 16
January 1868 (Thursday), p. 2, c. 5.

JACKSON: On the 24th of November, by Rev.
Robert J. Taylor, Jesse M. JACKSON, of
Bath county, and Miss Parmelia J.
TINSLEY; also, at the same time and
place, and by the same, John A. KEZER, of
Alleghany, and Miss Virginia C. TINSLEY.

Rockingham _Register_, 10 December 1868
(Thursday), p. 3, c. 3.

JACKSON: On the 7th of April, at the
residence of the bride's father, by Rev.
T.W. Lewis, Serg't William A. JACKSON, of
Co. C, 4th Va. Cavalry, and Miss Emily,
daughter of Erasmus SPRINKEL, all of
Madison county.

The _Rockingham_ _Register_, 29 April 1864
(Friday), p. 2, c. 5.

JAMES: See entry for BALTZEL.

JAMES: See entry for O'CONNELL.

JAMES: On the 3rd day of July, by P.B.
Allison, Esq., Mr. Wm. JAMES, of Easton,
Missouri, and Miss Ann SMITH, of the town
of Lafayette, K.T.

Rockingham _Register_ and _Advertiser_, 26
August 1859 (Friday), p. 2, c. 5.

JAMES: On the 5th inst., at Bakersville
Church, Washington county, Md., by Rev.
H.M. Fare, W.W. JAMES, Mail Agent O., A.
& R.R.R., and Miss Sue U. LEFEVRE.

Rockingham _Register_, 20 January 1870
(Thursday), p. 2, c. 5.

JAMES: Near Edom, on Sunday afternoon, the
22nd of December, by Rev. Jacob Miller,

Mr. Wm. M. JAMES and Miss Verinda, daughter of Mr. Joseph LONGLEY, all of Rockingham county.
Rockingham Register and Virginia Advertiser, 3 January 1862 (Friday), p. 1, c. 4.

JAMISON: See entry for ANDERSON.

JARMAN: See entry for RODES.

JARROLS: See entry for DETAMORE.

JAVINS: On the 23rd of February, by Rev. Dl. Thomas, Edward S. JAVINS, of Alexandria, Va., member of Co. L, 62nd Va. Regiment, and Miss Juliet A., daughter of Wm. CURRY, of Rockingham county.
Rockingham Register and Advertiser, 24 March 1865 (Friday), p. 2, c. 3.

JEFFERSON: See entry for RINKER.

JEFFERSON: On the 15th inst., by Rev. D.W. Arnold, at the residence of the bride's father, near Parnassus, Rev. Geo. R. JEFFERSON and Sarah M. WHITMORE.
The Rockingham Register, 30 October 1863 (Friday), p. 2, c. 7.

JENKINS: See entry for GORDON.

JENKINS: See entry for HISSELL.

JENKINS: See entry for KITE.

JENKINS: See entry for ODEN.

JENKINS: See entry for PLAUGAR.

JENKINS: See entry for VANCE.

JENKINS: At Welsh's Hotel, in Woodstock, on the 21st ult., by Rev. Wm. Warden, Mr. Gabriel JENKINS and Miss Rebecca F. DRUMMOND, all of Shenandoah.
Rockingham Register and Advertiser, 1 July 1859 (Friday), p. 2, c. 4.

JENKINS: On the 3rd inst., by Rev. Daniel Feete, Mr. Oliver P. JENKINS and Miss Elizabeth RUDY, all of Shenandoah county.
Rockingham Register and Advertiser, 18 November 1859 (Friday), p. 2, c. 4.

JENNINGS: See entry for ROHR.

JERRELL: See entry for DUVALL.

JETT: See entry for GRAY.

JETT: On the 11th inst., by Elder F.M. Perry, Wm. D. JETT and Miss L.E. HUFFMAN, all of Page county.

Rockingham Register, 25 November 1869
(Thursday), p. 2, c. 3.
JEWEL: On Thursday last, by the Rev. Henry
Brown, Mr. Samuel JEWEL to Miss Nancy
RAUSEY, all of this county.
Rockingham Register and Valley
Advertiser, 5 September 1846 (Saturday),
p. 2, c. 7.
JIRKLE: See entry for HOAK.
JISLOR: See entry for WILKIN.
JOHNS: See entry for MASSINCUT.
JOHNS: On Thursday, the 26th of April, by
Rev. Geo. A. Shuey, Mr. Geo. W. JOHNS and
Miss Eliza J. MITCHELL, all of Augusta
county.
Rockingham Register and Advertiser, 4 May
1860 (Friday), p. 2, c. 4.
JOHNS: On the 21st inst., by Rev. T.
Brashear, Wm. JOHNS to Miss Margaret J.
PETERS, all of Augusta county.
Rockingham Register and Advertiser, 31
August 1860 (Friday), p. 2, c. 4.
JOHNSON: See entry for BEARD.
JOHNSON: See entry for CEASE.
JOHNSON: See entry for LEAP.
JOHNSON: See entry for PALMER.
JOHNSON: See entry for PIRKEY.
JOHNSON: On the 22nd inst., at the residence
of the bride's father, by Rev. John R.
Effinger, of Washington city, Mr. A.H.
JOHNSON, of Alexandria, and Miss Annie
M., daughter of John S. EFFINGER, Esq.,
of Harrisonburg.
Rockingham Register and Advertiser, 30
November 1860 (Friday), p. 3, c. 1.
JOHNSON: In Augusta county, Va., December
10th, by Rev. Samuel KENNERLY, Rev. B.H.
JOHNSON, of the Virginia Conference, and
Miss Susan Arabella, daughter of the
officiating minister.
Rockingham Register and Advertiser, 10
January 1862 (Friday), p. 3, c. 2.
JOHNSON: On the 9th inst., by Rev. John
Pinkerton, at the residence of Mr. Thos.
Fulton, Mr. Eliphalet JOHNSON, of
Spottsylvania county, and Miss Mary E.

BRIGHTWELL, of Rockingham.
Rockingham Register and Advertiser, 17
May 1861 (Friday), p. 3, c. 3.

JOHNSON: On the 5th ult., by Rev. J.L.
Clarke, G.C. JOHNSON, of Lynchburg, and
Miss Mary E.V. POINTER, of Rockbridge.
Rockingham Register and Advertiser, 2
August 1866 (Thursday), p. 2, c. 5.

JOHNSON: On the 21st of November, George H.
JOHNSON and Miss Susan V. RODGERS, all of
Augusta county.
Rockingham Register and Advertiser, 13
December 1866 (Thursday), p. 2, c. 5.

JOHNSON: On the 19th of January, by Elder P.
McInturff, Mr. Henry JOHNSON and Miss
Emily HANES, both of Page county, Va.
Rockingham Register and Advertiser, 3
February 1865 (Friday), p. 1, c. 2.

JOHNSON: On the 27th of February, by Rev.
Isaac Long, at residence of officiating
minister, Henry JOHNSON and Miss Susan,
daughter of Peter HAYNES, all of
Rockingham county.
Rockingham Register and Advertiser, 23
March 1866 (Friday), p. 3, c. 3.

JOHNSON: In Fayette county, Va., September
20th, by the Rev. John Thomas, Mr. Hiram
JOHNSON, of Fayette county, and Miss Mary
Lydia, daughter of Mr. Jacob SENGER,
formerly of Augusta county ....
Rockingham Register and Advertiser, 5
October 1860 (Friday), p. 2, c. 3.

JOHNSON: At Mt. Solon, on the 9th inst., by
the Rev. John Pinkerton, Prof. Howard H.
JOHNSON, of Moorefield, Hardy county,
W.Va., to Miss Susan B., daughter of
Gabriel BARBEE, Esq., of Lynchburg.
Rockingham Register, 16 July 1868
(Thursday), p. 2, c. 6.

JOHNSON: On the 18th inst. [sic, ult.], at
the M.E. Parsonage, in Staunton, by the
Rev. G.G. Brooke, Mr. Isaac N. JOHNSON to
Miss Cynthia Ann PALMER, of Augusta
county.
Rockingham Register and Advertiser, 2
September 1859 (Friday), p. 2, c. 5.

JOHNSON: On Wednesday, the 8th inst., by Rev. Jno. Johnston, Col. Jacob JOHNSON, of Pendleton county, and Miss Clarissa G.B., youngest daughter of Tyre MAUPIN, dec'd.
Rockingham Register and Advertiser, 17 June 1859 (Friday), p. 3, c. 3.

JOHNSON: On Sunday, the 24th inst., by Rev. Jos. Funkhouser, Joseph F. JOHNSON and Miss Elizabeth V. LONG, all of Rockingham county.
The Rockingham Register, 29 April 1864 (Friday), p. 2, c. 5.

JOHNSON: On the 22nd of February, by Rev. B.H. Johnson, Mr. Julien A. JOHNSON and Miss Lucy Ella, daughter of Rev. Samuel KENNERLY, all of Augusta county.
Rockingham Register and Advertiser, 16 March 1866 (Friday), p. 3, c. 4.

JOHNSON: On the 21st of December, by Elder Paul Yates, Mr. Middleton M. JOHNSON, of Rappahannock, and Miss Eliza M. COMPTON, of Page county.
Rockingham Register and Advertiser, 19 January 1866 (Friday), p. 3, c. 2.

JOHNSON: On the 29th of October, by Rev. J.M. Shreckhise, Thomas JOHNSON and Miss Delila ALLEN, all of Augusta county.
Rockingham Register, 12 November 1868 (Thursday), p. 3, c. 3.

JOHNSON: On the 3rd of March, 1867, by Rev. Joseph Funkhouser, at Orchard Grove, in their saddles, Wellington JOHNSON, of Page, and Miss Sallie M. WHITE, of Rockingham.
Rockingham Register and Advertiser, 14 March 1867 (Thursday), p. 3, c. 5.

JOHNSON: On Thursday the 31st ult., by Rev. John Harshbarger, Mr. Wm. Benjamin JOHNSON and Miss Mary, daughter of Mr. John MANNING, all of this county.
Rockingham Register and Advertiser, 8 April 1859 (Friday), p. 3, c. 1.

JOHNSON: On the 22nd of February, by Rev. Jos. Funkhouser, at the residence of the bride's parents, near Peale's Cross-Roads, Rockingham county, Wm. M. JOHNSON,

of Page county, and Miss Malissa M. OFFENBERGER, of Rockingham.
Rockingham Register, 10 March 1870 (Thursday), p. 2, c. 4.

JOHNSTON: On the 15th inst., by Rev. W.E. Baker, Mr. J.M. JOHNSTON and Miss Sue R. McCUTCHEN, all of Augusta.
Rockingham Register and Advertiser, 22 November 1866 (Thursday), p. 3, c. 3.

JOHNSTON: At the Warm Springs, on the 22nd inst., by Rev. L.D. Nixon, Mr. J.S. JOHNSTON, of Lewisburg, to Miss Mary E., second daughter of Col. Wm. W. SHIELDS, of Bath.
Rockingham Register and Advertiser, 31 August 1860 (Friday), p. 2, c. 4.

JOHNSTON: On the 14th ult., at the residence of the bride's father, by the Rev. Geo. W. White, Major John W. JOHNSTON, of Botetourt county, Va., to Miss Bettie Dixon, daughter of S.H. ALEXANDER, Esq., of Moorefield, Hardy county, W.Va.
Rockingham Register, 6 January 1870 (Thursday), p. 3, c. 3.

JONEE: See entry for ZEHRING.
JONES: See entry for ANDERSON.
JONES: See entry for BILLHIMER.
JONES: See entry for BOWMAN.
JONES: See entry for CARDEN.
JONES: See entry for EFFINGER (2).
JONES: See entry for GORDON.
JONES: See entry for HUNTER.
JONES: See entry for LUDWIG.
JONES: See entry for McGINTY.
JONES: See entry for PAUL.
JONES: See entry for RISQUE.
JONES: See entry for SHACKLETT.
JONES: See entry for STERLING.

JONES: At Abingdon, Va., on the 20th of September, Major David A. JONES, late of Harrisonburg, and Miss Nannie MONTGOMERY, of Abingdon.
Rockingham Register, 15 October 1868 (Thursday), p. 2, c. 3.

JONES: On Thursday the 1st inst., by Rev. A.P. Boude, Rev. E.H. JONES, of the

Baltimore Annual Conference of the M.E.
Church, and Miss Mary E. RUSMISEL, of
Middlebrook, Augusta county, Virginia.
Rockingham Register and Advertiser, 23
June 1865 (Friday), p. 1, c. 4.

JONES: On the 28th ult., by Rev. Levi Keller,
Even JONES, of Rockingham, and Miss
Catharine WOLFE, of Shenandoah.
Rockingham Register and Advertiser, 12
December 1867 (Thursday), p. 3, c. 2.

JONES: On the 12th ult., by Rev. S.F. Butts,
Dr. H.H. JONES and Miss Jemima J. EAGLE,
all of Highland county.
Rockingham Register and Advertiser, 3
October 1867 (Thursday), p. 2, c. 6.

JONES: On the 18th ult., by Rev. J.
Stirewalt, Israel JONES and Sarah BOWERS,
all of Rockingham.
Rockingham Register and Advertiser, 2
November 1860 (Friday), p. 2, c. 5.

JONES: On the 4th of April, at Woodboro, by
Rev. M. Butt, J. Marshall JONES and Miss
Ledora, youngest daughter of Rev. J.S.
PULLEN, all of Highland.
Rockingham Register and Advertiser, 18
April 1867 (Thursday), p. 2, c. 6.

JONES: Near Staunton, on the 30th ult., by
Rev. J.I. Miller, John H. JONES and Miss
Harriet E. PRICE, all of Augusta county.
Rockingham Register and Advertiser, 6
February 1868 (Thursday), p. 2, c. 4.

JONES: On the 18th of October, by the Rev.
W.T. Price, in Monterey, Jos. JONES and
Miss Sarah FISHER, all of Highland
county.
Rockingham Register and Advertiser, 8
November 1866 (Thursday), p. 3, c. 4.

JONES: On the 20th ult., by Rev. J. Wine,
Tho's JONES and Miss Lenah RYMAN, all of
Shenandoah county.
Rockingham Register and Advertiser, 26
December 1856 (Friday), p. 2, c. 6.

JORDAN: See entry for ALEXANDER.
JORDAN: See entry for DUNNIVANT.
JORDAN: See entry for FUNK.
JORDAN: See entry for HARPER.

JORDAN: See entry for RUST.

JORDAN: See entry for STOVER.

JORDAN: See entry for TAYLOR.

JORDAN: On the 8th inst., by Rev. Jacob
    Thomas, Andrew J. JORDAN, of Highland
    county, Va., and Miss Catharine, daughter
    of George WINE, of this county.
    Rockingham Register and Advertiser, 16
    March 1866 (Friday), p. 3, c. 4.

JORDAN: On the 26th of January, at Mt.
    Jackson, by Elder R.C. Cave, Capt. DeWitt
    C. JORDAN and Miss Lelia P. SIGLER, all
    of Shenandoah.
    Rockingham Register, 4 March 1869
    (Thursday), p. 2, c. 4.

JORDAN: On the 2nd inst., by Rev. J.
    Stirewalt, Mr. Hiram A. JORDAN and Susan
    SHUTTER, all of Forestville.
    Rockingham Register and Advertiser, 21
    September 1860 (Friday), p. 2, c. 4.

JORDAN: On the 27th, by the Rev. Mr.
    Shickell,   Mr.   Isaac   JORDAN,   of
    Rockingham, to Miss Sally A. FAUBER, of
    Augusta.
    Rockingham Register and Advertiser, 30
    December 1843 (Saturday), p. 4, c. 1.

JORDAN: On the 20th ult., by Rev. L. Keller,
    John H.A. JORDAN and Miss Sarah G. REEDY,
    all of Shenandoah county.
    Rockingham Register and Advertiser, 26
    December 1856 (Friday), p. 2, c. 7.

JORDON: See entry for HARSHBERGER.

JOSEPH: See entry for TETER.

JOSEPH: See entry for YAGO.

JUDD: See entry for BASH.

JUDD: See entry for GRANSTAFF.

JUDD: On the 11th ult., by Rev. J.W. Watson,
    Mr. J.B. JUDD and Miss Elizabeth A.,
    daughter of David BLOSSER.
    Rockingham Register and Advertiser, 9
    November 1860 (Friday), p. 2, c. 6.

JUDD: On Tuesday, the 15th inst. [sic, ult.],
    at Springfield, by Rev. A. Poe Boude, Mr.
    Lorenzo W. JUDD and Miss Mollie C.
    KIBLER, all of Page county.
    The Rockingham Register, 2 October 1863

(Friday), p. 2, c. 5.

JUDD: Week before last, in Luray, by Elder F.M. Perry, Samuel JUDD and Miss Virginia DUNKAN, all of Luray.
Rockingham Register, 3 June 1870 (Thursday), p. 3, c. 3.

JUDY: See entry for GOOD.

JUDY: See entry for KITE.

JUDY: October 25th, by Rev. I. Conder, David JUDY and Miss Catharine HAYNES, all of Rockingham.
Rockingham Register, 18 November 1869 (Thursday), p. 3, c. 2.

JUNKIN: On the 5th of November, by Rev. Wm. F. Junkin, Lieut. George. G. JUNKIN and Miss Bettie S., daughter of R.D. MONTAGUE, Esq., of Christiansburg, Va.
The Rockingham Register, 12 December 1862 (Friday), p. 2, c. 5.

- K -

KAGEY: See entry for ZIRKLE.

KAGY: See entry for GOCHENOUR.

KAIN: On the 24th ult., on the Island, at the residence of the officiating clergyman, Rev. Jno. C. Dice, near Moorefield, Joshua P. KAIN and Miss Alice, daughter of Jacob COOK, all of Hardy county.
Rockingham Register, 20 January 1870 (Thursday), p. 2, c. 5.

KANE: See entry for HARPER.

KARACOFE: By the same [Rev. Daniel Thomas], on the 11th inst., Mr. Benjamin A. KARACOFE to Miss Elizabeth C., daughter of John DRIVER, all of Augusta.
Rockingham Register and Advertiser, 19 March 1858 (Friday), p. 3, c. 3.

KARACOFE: On the 12th of April, at the residence of the bride's mother, by Rev. J.A. Kibler, Mr. Wm. H.H. KARACOFE, of Augusta, and Miss Lucinda GAINS, of Rockingham.
Rockingham Register and Advertiser, 4 May 1866 (Friday), p. 3, c. 2.

KARICOFE: See entry for BAILEY.

KARICOFE: See entry for SANDY.

KARICOFE: On the 12th inst., by Rev. A.J. Kibler, Wm. H.H. KARICOFE and Miss Lucinda, daughter of Rebecca GAINES, of Dry River, in this county.
Rockingham Register and Advertiser, 20 April 1866 (Friday), p. 2, c. 3.

KARRICKOFE: On the 2nd inst., by Rev. Jacob Thomas, Mr. Silas KARRICKOFE and Miss Mary E. KERLING, both of Augusta county.
Rockingham Register and Advertiser, 28 December 1860 (Friday), p. 1, c. 5.

KARRICOFE: Near Mt. Solon, on the 16th ult., by the Rev. John Pinkerton, John V. KARRICOFE to Catharine A., youngest daughter of John H. KERLIN.
Rockingham Register, 6 January 1870 (Thursday), p. 3, c. 3.

KAUFMAN: See entry for ROTHGER.

KEADLE: On the 5th inst., by Rev. J.W. Bennett, Andrew J. KEADLE and Miss Caroline, daughter of Rob't COALTER, all of Monroe county, W.Va.
Rockingham Register and Advertiser, 28 June 1866 (Thursday), p. 2, c. 5.

KEAGY: At the residence of the bride's father, near Harrisonburg, on the 21st of December, by Rev. B.N. Pool, Mr. John KEAGY and Miss Mollie C., daughter of Mr. Levi SHAVER, all of Rockingham county.
Rockingham Register and Advertiser, 12 January 1866 (Friday), p. 1, c. 3.

KEATON: See entry for CASSADAY.

KEAVALL: On the 8th inst., near Buckton, by Elder John Clarke, Presley KEAVALL and Miss Isabella V. BENNETT.
Rockingham Register, 23 April 1868 (Thursday), p. 2, c. 6.

KEE: On January 29th, in Mt. Crawford, by Rev. J.C. Hensell, Pinkney KEE and Miss Jane A. BASKIN, all of Rockingham.
Rockingham Register and Advertiser, 7 February 1867 (Thursday), p. 3, c. 3.

KEENAN: See entry for CLARY.

KEERAN: On Thursday, the 6th inst., at Hill's Hotel, in this place, by Rev. Jas. N.

Davis, Mr. Thomas J. KEERAN and Miss Mary
KLINE, all of Rockingham county.
Rockingham Register and Advertiser, 21
October 1859 (Friday), p. 2, c. 5.

KEEWRIGHT: On the 27th ult., at
McGaheysville, by Rev. I. Conder, Wm.
KEEWRIGHT and Miss Sarah E., daughter of
B.B. CAVE.
Rockingham Register, 10 November 1870
(Thursday), p. 2, c. 5.

KEFFER: See entry for RICHARDS.

KEIFFER: See entry for SHANK.

KEIFFER: At the residence of the bride's
father, near Singer's Glen, Rockingham
county, by Rev. Jacob Miller, L. Rolland
KEIFFER and Miss S. Virginia STINESPRING,
all of Rockingham.
Rockingham Register, 17 March 1870
(Thursday), p. 2, c. 4.

KEISER: On the 27th ult., by Rev. C. Beard,
Mr. Andrew G. KEISER and Miss Elizabeth
C. SWISHER, all of Augusta county.
Rockingham Register and Advertiser, 7
October 1859 (Friday), p. 2, c. 4.

KEISER: On September 24th, by Rev. C.S.M.
See, Mr. Geo. F. KEISER and Miss Susan J.
CROBARGER, all of Augusta.
Rockingham Register and Advertiser, 2
November 1860 (Friday), p. 2, c. 5.

KEISER: On the 20th ult., by the Rev. C.
Beard, Wm. A. KEISER and Miss Frances A.
SHUMAKER, all of Augusta county.
Rockingham Register, 3 September 1868
(Thursday), p. 2, c. 4.

KEISTER: See entry for ABBOTT.

KEISTER: On Tuesday evening, the 13th inst.,
at the residence of the bride's father,
by Rev. W.G. Coe, Cyrus KEISTER, of
Strasburg, Va., and Miss Fannie E.,
daughter of Joseph S. SPENGLER, Esq., of
Warren county.
Rockingham Register and Advertiser, 22
November 1866 (Thursday), p. 3, c. 3.

KEISTER: On the 25th of February, by Rev.
Jacob Thomas, in the Clerk's Office in
Harrisonburg, Isaac KEISTER and Mrs. Mary

E. BYERS, all of Rockingham county.
Rockingham Register, 4 March 1869 (Thursday), p. 2, c. 4.

KEITH: On the 30th ult., by the Rev. Thomas D. Bell, Mr. James M. KEITH, of Lewis county, Va., and Miss Sarah F.J., daughter of Mr. Jonathan FUNK, of Rockingham county.
Rockingham Register and Advertiser, 8 July 1859 (Friday), p. 2, c. 5.

KELLER: See entry for GOOD.

KELLER: See entry for MAUZY.

KELLER: See entry for OGDEN.

KELLER: See entry for SANDY.

KELLER: See entry for SHOWALTER.

KELLER: On the 12th inst., near Frieden's Church, by Rev. G.H. Martin, Amos KELLER and Miss Elizabeth A. SNARE, all of Shenandoah county.
Rockingham Register and Advertiser, 23 May 1867 (Thursday), p. 2, c. 6.

KELLER: On the 15th ult., near Hebron Church, by Rev. Geo. H. Martin, Ananias KELLER and Miss Mary Francis, daughter of Noah HOCKMAN, all of Shenandoah county.
Rockingham Register, 1 October 1868 (Thursday), p. 3, c. 3.

KELLER: On the 5th inst., by Rev. H. Tallhelm, Mr. Isaac N. KELLER and Miss Maria, daughter of Mr. Elijah DUDLEY, all of this county.
Rockingham Register and Advertiser, 10 February 1860 (Friday), p. 2, c. 5.

KELLER: On Thursday the 20th inst., by Rev. Levi Keller, Mr. John KELLER, of Augusta county, and Miss Margaret SHAVER, of Rockingham county.
Rockingham Register and Valley Advertiser, 29 May 1852 (Saturday), p. 2, c. 6.

KELLER: On Thursday the 30th of December, by Rev. John J. Harshberger, Mr. John N. KELLER and Miss Mary Ann, daughter of Mr. Jacob KOONTS, all of this county.
Rockingham Register and Advertiser, 7 January 1859 (Friday), p. 3, c. 1.

KELLER: On Tuesday morning last, by Rev. Robert Gray, Mr. Lawrence KELLER and Miss Mary E., daughter of Mr. Jacob OTT, of Woodstock, Va.
Rockingham Register and Advertiser, 3 June 1859 (Friday), p. 3, c. 2.

KELLER: On February 17th, by Rev. P. Fletcher, at the residence of the bride's mother, near Churchville, T.F.R. KELLER and Francis Jane LIVICK, all of Augusta.
Rockingham Register, 3 March 1870 (Thursday), p. 2, c. 5.

KELLER: On Thursday evening, the 5th inst., by Rev. G.A. Shuey, Mr. Wm. KELLER and Miss Frances BROWN, all of Augusta.
Rockingham Register and Advertiser, 13 May 1859 (Friday), p. 3, c. 4.

KELLER: On the 30th ult., by the same [Rev. Daniel Feete], Mr. William J. KELLER and Miss Lydia, daughter of Augustine BORDEN - all of Shenandoah county.
Rockingham Register and Advertiser, 10 December 1858 (Friday), p. 3, c. 2.

KELLEY: On the 14th ult., by the Rev. Geo. A. Shuey, Mr. James W. KELLEY and Miss Sevilla A. KOONTZ, both of Augusta.
Rockingham Register and Advertiser, 12 January 1866 (Friday), p. 1, c. 3.

KELLEY: Near Timberville, by Rev. S. Henkel, Mr. Thomas KELLEY and Miss Elizabeth WISE, the former of Boston, Massachusetts, and the latter of Rockingham, Va.
Rockingham Register and Advertiser, 5 October 1860 (Friday), p. 2, c. 3.

KELLY: See entry for KINNIREY.

KELLY: On the 10th of December, by Rev. Jacob Wine, Bryan KELLY and Susanna FRYE.
The Rockingham Register, 15 January 1864 (Friday), p. 2, c. 6.

KELLY: At the Presbyterian Parsonage, in this place, on Thursday evening last, the 7th inst., by Rev. J. Rice Bowman, Joseph H. KELLY and Miss Mary Margaret, daughter of the late Wm. D. PAYNE, dec'd, all of Harrisonburg.

Rockingham Register, 14 May 1868 (Thursday), p. 2, c. 5.

KELLY: At the Presbyterian Parsonage, in this place, on the 19th inst., by Rev. J. Rice Bowman, Lucien S. KELLY, of Harrisonburg, and Miss Sallie, daughter of R.W. BRYAN, of Bridgewater, Va.
Rockingham Register and Advertiser, 21 November 1867 (Thursday), p. 2, c. 5.

KELSO: BY the Rev. W.G. Campbell, on the 25th ult., Hugh KELSO and Miss Mary M. GLENDY, of Rockbridge.
Rockingham Register and Advertiser, 4 January 1861 (Friday), p. 3, c. 4.

KELSO: On the 21st of April, by Rev. R. Lewis McCune, Mr. John M. KELSO, A.M., Principal of the Danville Institute, Pa., to Miss Drucilla G., daughter of W. RAMSEY, Esq., of Augusta county, Virginia.
Rockingham Register and Advertiser, 29 April 1859 (Friday), p. 3, c. 2.

KEMP: See entry for MARSHALL.

KEMP: See entry for RAMEY.

KEMP: On the 20th ult., by Rev. J.W. Watson, Mr. Fayette KEMP and Miss Bettie TOBIN, all of Hamburg, Page county.
Rockingham Register and Advertiser, 22 June 1860 (Friday), p. 2, c. 6. Repeated, 6 July 1860 (Friday), p. 2, c. 6.

KEMPER: See entry for STRAYER.

KEMPER: See entry for YOUNG.

KENDRICK: See entry for CRAWFORD.

KENDRICK: See entry for NEFF.

KENDRICK: On the evening of the 15th, by the Rev. Silas Billings, Mr. William KENDRICK to Miss Melvina V., daughter of Mr. Reuben BIRD, of Strasburg.
Rockingham Register and Valley Advertiser, 19 April 1845 (Saturday), p. 3, c. 1.

KENEEDY: On the 16th inst., by Rev. H. Wetzel, Mr. Geo. KENEEDY, of Augusta county, and Miss Eliza BROWN, of Rockingham county, Va.

Rockingham Register and Advertiser, 19
March 1858 (Friday), p. 3, c. 3.

KENNEDY: See entry for McCLURE.

KENNEDY: On the 30th of April, by Rev. J.C.
Hensell, J.M.C. KENNEDY, of Rockbridge
county, and Miss Elizabeth C., youngest
daughter of Emmanuel WISE, of Rockingham
county.

Rockingham Register, 7 May 1868
(Thursday), p. 2, c. 4.

KENNEDY: On Monday evening last, in
Harrisonburg, by Rev. Thos. H.
Hildebrand, Corporal Wm. S. KENNEDY,
C.S.A., of Odweta [sic, possibly Odum]
county, Georgia, and Miss Mary E.,
daughter of Col. A.J. VAN PELT, of this
place.

The Rockingham Register, 3 April 1863
(Friday), p. 2, c. 6.

KENNERLY: See entry for JOHNSON (2).

KENNEY: On the 16th ult., at the residence of
the bride's father, in Howard county,
Mo., by the Rev. Noah Flood, James
KENNEY, Esq., of Harrisonburg, Va., and
Miss Annie, daughter of J.F. FINKS, Esq.

Rockingham Register and Advertiser, 1
July 1859 (Friday), p. 2, c. 4.

KENNON: In Stanardsville, Greene county, Va.,
on the 15th inst., by Rev. Philip S.
Carpenter, Mr. Wm. R. KENNON, of Franklin
county, Mo., and Miss Letitia Susan,
daughter of Mr. James B. HENNING, of the
former place.

Rockingham Register and Advertiser, 26
October 1860 (Friday), p. 2, c. 6.

KENT: See entry for BELL.

KENT: At the residence of Col. John B.
Baldwin, on Saturday morning, September
11th, Jos. F. KENT, of Wythe county, to
Miss Virginia F. PEYTON, of Staunton.

Rockingham Register, 23 September 1869
(Thursday), p. 2, c. 3.

KEPLINGER: See entry for GULLEY.

KEPLINGER: See entry for HASLER.

KERAN: See entry for NICHOLAS.

KERBY: See entry for CRICKENBERGER.

KERCZEWSKY: On Wednesday, the 11th inst., by Rev. Joseph R. Wheeler, Mr. Joseph KERCZEWSKY, of Poland, and Miss Mary KEY, of Staunton.
The Rockingham Register, 20 February 1863 (Friday), p. 2, c. 3.

KERLIN: See entry for BAKER.

KERLIN: See entry for FADELY.

KERLIN: See entry for FOLTZ.

KERLIN: See entry for KARRICOFE.

KERLIN: On the 4th inst., by Rev. John W. Wolf, Thomas J. KERLIN, Esq., and Miss Sallie C., daughter of the late James RUDDLE, all of Shenandoah county.
Rockingham Register and Advertiser, 22 June 1860 (Friday), p. 2, c. 6. Repeated, 6 July 1860 (Friday), p. 2, c. 6.

KERLING: See entry for KARRICKOFE.

KERN: See entry for STICKLEY.

KERN: See entry for SWEENY.

KERR: See entry for COMPTON.

KERR: See entry for DUNLAP.

KERR: See entry for FRY.

KERR: See entry for STEPHENSON.

KERR: On the 6th inst., by Rev. W.R. Stringer, in Middlebrook, Mr. _____ KERR and Miss Fannie MORGAN, all of Augusta county.
Rockingham Register and Advertiser, 27 September 1866 (Thursday), p. 3, c. 3.

KERR: On Thursday, the 22nd inst., by Elder J. Jennings, Mr. Alexander KERR, of Augusta county, and Miss Frances V., daughter of Mr. John R. HOMAN, of Rockingham county.
Rockingham Register and Virginia Advertiser, 30 December 1859 (Friday), p. 2, c. 5.

KERR: On Tuesday, the 28th ult., on Thorny Creek, by Rev. James Wanless, George KERR, Esq., and Miss Patsy Ann, eldest daughter of John McELWEE, of Bath county, all of Pocahontas county.
Rockingham Register and Advertiser, 15 July 1859 (Friday), p. 3, c. 2.

KERR: On the 24th of April, by the Rev. Mr.
Carrington, William KERR, Esq., of
Augusta county, and Miss Nannie, daughter
of Daniel WILLIAMSON, Esq., of Charlotte
county.
Rockingham Register and Advertiser, 30
May 1867 (Thursday), p. 3, c. 3.
KERRICOFE: See entry for LINAWEAVER.
KERSHNER: See entry for VINT.
KESLER: See entry for DEPOY.
KESLER: See entry for HOLSINGER.
KEY: See entry for KERCZEWSKY.
KEYSER: See entry for BUMGARNER.
KEYSER: See entry for BURNER.
KEYSER: See entry for KEYSER.
KEYSER: See entry for LENZ.
KEYSER: See entry for MILTON.
KEYSER: See entry for NALLE.
KEYSER: See entry for STEP.
KEYSER: On the 23rd ult., by Rev. Wm. C.
Lauck, Jos. W. KEYSER and Miss Sallie V.
KEYSER, all of Page county.
Rockingham Register and Advertiser, 7
November 1867 (Thursday), p. 2, c. 5.
KEYSER: On the 21st inst., by Elder A.C.
Booton, at Valley Rest, Page county, Va.,
Dr. M.H. KEYSER, late of Hardy, and Miss
Nannie C. KITE, of Page.
Rockingham Register and Advertiser, 31
May 1861 (Friday), p. 3, c. 1.
KEYSER: On the 18th ult., by Rev. O.
Grimsley, Capt. N.H. KEYSER, of Page, and
Miss Annie, daughter of B.F. MILLER, of
Rappahannock.
Rockingham Register and Advertiser, 16
January 1868 (Thursday), p. 2, c. 5.
KEYSER: On the 17th of January, by Elder P.
McInturff, Mr. William H. KEYSER and Miss
Sarah HUFFMAN, all of Page county, Va.
Rockingham Register and Advertiser, 3
February 1865 (Friday), p. 1, c. 2.
KEYTON: At David Wright's, near Dayton, on
the 6th inst., by Rev. George Wine, Jas.
W. KEYTON and Miss Elizabeth F. SNELL,
all of Rockingham.
Rockingham Register, 20 October 1870

242

(Thursday), p. 3, c. 5.

KEZER: On the 24th of November, by Rev. Robert J. Taylor, Jesse M. JACKSON, of Bath county, and Miss Parmelia J. TINSLEY; also, at the same time and place, and by the same, John A. KEZER, of Alleghany, and Miss Virginia C. TINSLEY. Rockingham Register, 10 December 1868 (Thursday), p. 3, c. 3.

KIBBLINGER: On the 10th of November, by Rev. Isaac Long, William C. KIBBLINGER and Miss Louisa E., daughter of Robert E. COOK, all of Rockingham. Rockingham Register and Advertiser, 22 November 1866 (Thursday), p. 3, c. 3.

KIBLER: See entry for BARR.

KIBLER: See entry for CHADDUCK.

KIBLER: See entry for FUNKHOUSER.

KIBLER: See entry for HACKLEY.

KIBLER: See entry for JUDD.

KIBLER: See entry for LINEWEAVER.

KIBLER: See entry for RICHARD.

KIBLER: On the 16th ult., by Rev. Daniel Feete, Mr. George KIBLER and Miss Mary FRY, all of Shenandoah. Rockingham Register and Advertiser, 2 March 1860 (Friday), p. 3, c. 2.

KIBLER: Near Spring Hill, on the 24th ult., by Rev. C.B. Hammack, Green M. KIBLER and Miss Almira E., daughter of Mr. Daniel FISHBURNE, all of Augusta county. Rockingham Register, 6 January 1870 (Thursday), p. 3, c. 3.

KIBLER: On the 12th of December, by Elder C. Allemong, Mr. Hiram KIBLER and Miss Mary C. STRICKLER, both of Page county. Rockingham Register and Advertiser, 12 January 1866 (Friday), p. 2, c. 3.

KIBLER: On the 7th of September, 1862, by Rev. J.W. Howe, Mr. Isaac T. KIBLER, of Page county, and Miss Ann Eliza KOONTZ, of Rockingham. Rockingham Register and Virginia Advertiser, 12 September 1862 (Friday), p. 2, c. 2.

KIBLER: By Rev. G.H. Martin, on the 22nd of

243

November, near Woodstock, Mr. James A. KIBLER and Miss Amanda L.F. HOOVER, all of Shenandoah county.
Rockingham Register and Advertiser, 13 December 1866 (Thursday), p. 2, c. 5.

KIBLER: At the Lutheran Parsonage, in Woodstock, on the 28th ult., by Rev. Levi Keller, Jeremiah KIBLER and Miss Amanda C. FOSTER, all of Shenandoah.
Rockingham Register, 11 February 1869 (Thursday), p. 3, c. 3.

KIBLER: On the 25th of November, at Edenburg [sic, Edinburg], Shenandoah county, by Elder Wm. C. Lauck, John W. KIBLER and Miss Maria J. COMER.
Rockingham Register, 9 December 1869 (Thursday), p. 3, c. 2.

KIBLINGER: On the 9th inst., by Elder W.C. Lauck, F.M. KIBLINGER and Miss S.E. WOLFENBERGER, all of Page county.
Rockingham Register, 25 November 1869 (Thursday), p. 2, c. 3.

KIBLINGER: December 18th, at the residence of the bride's father, by Rev. R. Smith, William C. KIBLINGER and Miss Elizabeth M. BLOSE, all of Rockingham county.
Rockingham Register and Advertiser, 23 December 1859 (Friday), p. 2, c. 5.

KICE: On the 4th inst., by the Rev. T.T. Castleman, Mr. John KICE, of Missouri, to Miss Margaret BOWLES, of Staunton.
Rockingham Register and Valley Advertiser, 13 September 1851 (Saturday), p. 2, c. 7.

KIEFFER: See entry for RUEBUSH.

KIGER: See entry for ALMOND.

KIGER: See entry for SMITH.

KILBY: See entry for O'BRIEN.

KILLION: On the 18th inst., by Rev. T.D. Bell, Cyrus W. KILLION, of Augusta county, and Miss Fannie F., daughter of Mr. Jeshua PENCE, of Rockingham.
Rockingham Register and Advertiser, 25 October 1866 (Thursday), p. 3, c. 3.

KILMER: On the 11th inst., by Rev. J. Pinkterton, at the residence of the bride's mother, in Rockingham county, Mr. B.J. KILMER, of Co. B, 1st Va. Cavalry, of Berkeley county, and Miss Lizzie C., daughter of Mr. Hugh DEVER, dec'd.

The Rockingham Register, 19 February 1864 (Friday), p. 2, c. 6.

KINCAID: See entry for HUPHMAN.

KINCAID: On Wednesday, October 15, 1862, by the Rev. Wm. T. Price, Major Floyd KINCAID, of Bath county, to Miss Lizzie, youngest daughter of Wm. R. STUART, Esq., of Highland, Va.

The Rockingham Register, 19 December 1862 (Friday), p. 2, c. 4.

KING: See entry for BERRY.

KING: See entry for BOYD.

KING: See entry for CHEWNING.

KING: See entry for SILLINGS.

KING: See entry for WELCH.

KING: In Staunton, on the 26th inst., at the residence of Geo. Harlan, by Rev. G.C. Cramer, A.C. KING, of Augusta, and Mrs. Martha F. BROWN, of Albemarle.

Rockingham Register, 30 September 1869 (Thursday), p. 2, c. 4.

KING: On the 8th ult., at "Long Meadows," the residence of the bride's parents, by Rev. Geo. A. Long, Augustus KING and Miss Nannie R., daughter of Col. G.W.S. BOWMAN, all of Warren county, Va.

Rockingham Register, 27 January 1870 (Thursday), p. 2, c. 3.

KINGREE: See entry for HANEY.

KINNEY: At Trinity Church, Staunton, on the 9th of July, Mr. John M. KINNEY, of Beaufort, South Carolina, and Miss Mary F. BEIRNE, of Staunton, Va.

Rockingham Register and Advertiser, 23 August 1861 (Friday), p. 3, c. 4.

KINNIREY: On the 13th ult., by Rev. J.H. Walters, Thos. KINNIREY and Miss Mary KELLY, both of Alleghany.

Rockingham Register and Advertiser, 9 March 1866 (Friday), p. 2, c. 3.

KIPPS: See entry for BOWMAN.

KIPPS: See entry for RIFE.

KIPPS: On the 18th ult., by Rev. S. Henkel,
    Adam KIPPS and Miss Barbara A. FANSLER,
    all of Shenandoah county.
    Rockingham Register and Advertiser, 2 May
    1867 (Thursday), p. 2, c. 6.
KIRACOFE: On the 11th inst., by Rev. James
    Beaty, Mr. George M. KIRACOFE, formerly
    of Augusta county, and Miss Margaret A.,
    youngest daughter of Jarret ARMSTRONG,
    Esq., of Highland county.
    Rockingham Register and Advertiser, 23
    September 1859 (Friday), p. 2, c. 4.
KIRACOFE: Near Dayton, in this county, on the
    30th of August, by Rev. Geo. V. Leech,
    Capt. N.B. KIRACOFE, of Augusta county,
    and Miss Caroline Virginia, daughter of
    Austin COAKLEY, dec'd, of Rockingham
    county.
    Rockingham Register and Advertiser, 5
    October 1860 (Friday), p. 2, c. 3.
KIRBY: On the 19th of March, by Rev. John
    Wine, Mr. George W. KIRBY, of Fauquier
    county, Va., and Miss Elenora MYERS, of
    Shenandoah county.
    The Rockingham Register, 27 March 1863
    (Friday), p. 2, c. 6.
KIRBY: On the 4th inst., by Rev. J.W. Hott,
    Joseph H. KIRBY and Miss Frances KIRLIN,
    all of Shenandoah county.
    Rockingham Register and Advertiser, 25
    April 1867 (Thursday), p. 2, c. 7.
KIRKER: On the evening of the 20th inst., in
    New Market, by Rev. J.P. Cline, Maj. W.H.
    KIRKER and Miss Kate A. CALVERT.
    The Rockingham Register, 29 May 1863
    (Friday), p. 2, c. 6.
KIRKPATRICK: On the 14th inst., near Salem
    Church, by Rev. Jacob Miller, Benj. F.
    KIRKPATRICK and Virginia C., daughter of
    John SWANK, all of Rockingham county.
    Rockingham Register, 21 May 1868
    (Thursday), p. 2, c. 5.
KIRKPATRICK: On the 11th ult., by Rev. Wm. S.
    McClanahan, Capt. Robt. D. KIRKPATRICK
    and Miss Maggie E. TEAFORD, both of
    Rockbridge.

Rockingham Register and Advertiser, 2 November 1860 (Friday), p. 2, c. 5.
KIRKPATRICK: On the 14th inst., by the Rev. Wm. G. Coe, Mr. Wm. R.W. KIRKPATRICK, of Spruce Hill, to Mrs. Fanny HODGE, all of Bath county, Va.
Rockingham Register and Advertiser, 26 December 1856 (Friday), p. 2, c. 7.
KIRLIN: See entry for KIRBY.
KIRTZ: See entry for ORNDORFF.
KISER: See entry for COINER.
KISER: See entry for HAYNES.
KISER: In the evening, on the 14th inst., by Rev. J.C. Hensel, Pleasant A. KISER to Miss Mollie J., second daughter of John F. CRAUN, all of Rockingham.
Rockingham Register and Advertiser, 23 May 1867 (Thursday), p. 2, c. 6.
KISLING: On the 10th ult., at the residence of the late Michael Miller, near Salem, Roanoke county, by the Rev. Dr. Bittle, Mr. Geo. J. KISLING, of Rockingham, and Miss Sallie A. MILLER, of Roanoke.
Rockingham Register and Advertiser, 9 January 1868 (Thursday), p. 2, c. 4.
KITE: See entry for BROWN.
KITE: See entry for CLINEDINST.
KITE: See entry for CLORE.
KITE: See entry for FUNK.
KITE: See entry for KEYSER.
KITE: See entry for KITE.
KITE: See entry for KOONTZ.
KITE: See entry for LILLARD.
KITE: See entry for NAUMAN.
KITE: See entry for SHULER.
KITE: See entry for STRASBURG.
KITE: See entry for STRICKLER.
KITE: On the 11th inst., by Elder Paul Yates, A.M. KITE and Miss M.E. BRUBAKER, all of Page county.
Rockingham Register, 25 November 1869 (Thursday), p. 2, c. 3.
KITE: At Strole's Mill, in Page county, on the 23rd ult., by Rev. J.P. Cline, Benjamin KITE and Elizabeth A., youngest daughter of John STROLE, Esq.

The Rockingham Register, 1 May 1863 (Friday), p. 2, c. 5.

KITE: On the 20th ult., by Rev. Jacob Stirewalt, David KITE and Mary JUDY, both of Page.

Rockingham Register and Advertiser, 2 December 1859 (Friday), p. 2, c. 5.

KITE: Near Criglersville, Madison county, on the 1st inst., by Rev. Mr. Baily, David KITE, of Page, and Mrs. Ellen B. THOMAS, of Madison county.

Rockingham Register, 15 April 1869 (Thursday), p. 2, c. 4.

KITE: On the 3rd inst., by Rev. J. Watson, Mr. Francis D. KITE and Miss Julia A., daughter of Jacob STROLE, Esq., all of Page county.

Rockingham Register and Advertiser, 15 July 1859 (Friday), p. 3, c. 2.

KITE: On the 11th of January, by Rev. Casper Allemong, Mr. Hardin KITE, of Page county, and Miss Eliza JENKINS, of the county of Rockingham.

Rockingham Register and Advertiser, 24 January 1862 (Friday), p. 2, c. 7.

KITE: On the 31st ult., at the residence of the bride's parents, by Rev. Aaron Boon, Mr. Jacob KITE and Miss Mary C. LUCAS, both of Page county.

Rockingham Register and Advertiser, 29 June 1860 (Friday), p. 2, c. 5.

KITE: On the 4th inst., by Rev. J. Watson, Mr. Martin V. KITE and Miss Virginia A., daughter of David KITE, all of Page county.

Rockingham Register and Advertiser, 15 July 1859 (Friday), p. 3, c. 2.

KITT: On the 24th of January, by Elder C. Allemong, Andrew J. KITT and Miss Rebecca MORRIS, all of Page county.

Rockingham Register and Advertiser, 4 April 1867 (Thursday), p. 3, c. 4.

KITZMILLER: See entry for RHODES.

KIZER: On Sunday morning, the 24th of June, by Rev. Wm. H. Hale, at the residence of the bride's father, Elder J. WISEMAN, of

248

Sumner county, Tennessee, Wm. E. KIZER, of Salem, Roanoke county, Va., and Miss Minerva C. WISEMAN.
Rockingham Register and Advertiser, 6 July 1860 (Friday), p. 2, c. 6.

KLINE: See entry for ARION.

KLINE: See entry for KEERAN.

KLINE: See entry for KLINE.

KLINE: See entry for SCHMUCKER.

KLINE: See entry for WAMPLER.

KLINE: On the 9th inst., by Rev. John Allemong, Mr. Charles O. KLINE, of Port Republic, Rockingham county, and Miss Mary C. YEAKLE, of N.T. Stephensburg, Frederick county.
Rockingham Register and Advertiser, 26 April 1861 (Friday), p. 2, c. 7.

KLINE: On Thursday the 10th of May, by Rev. John Kline, Mr. Frederick KLINE & Miss Mary, daughter of Mr. Samuel KLINE, all of Rockingham county.
Rockingham Register and Virginia Advertiser, 18 May 1855 (Friday), p. 3, c. 4.

KLINE: On the 12th of March, by Rev. Jacob Miller, Mr. Isaac B. KLINE and Miss Rebecca J., daughter of Samuel MYERS, dec'd, all of Rockingham.
Rockingham Register and Advertiser, 24 March 1865 (Friday), p. 2, c. 3.

KLINE: On the 13th ult., by the Rev. Jacob Miller, John G. KLINE and Miss Martha Jane, daughter of Christian MOYERS, all of Rockingham county.
Rockingham Register and Advertiser, 3 January 1867 (Thursday), p. 3, c. 3.

KNEFF: On the 8th inst., by Rev. Jacob Wine, Michael KNEFF, of Shenandoah, and Miss Barbara DELAUGHTER, of Rockingham.
Rockingham Register, 24 February 1870 (Thursday), p. 2, c. 5.

KNICELY: See entry for ARGABRIGHT.

KNIPPLE: See entry for SAVAGE.

KNIPPLE: In Dayton, January 3rd, by Rev. J.M. Grabill, Mr. Addison W. KNIPPLE, of Augusta county, and Miss Mary Ann L.,

249

daughter of Joseph and Elizabeth MILLER, of Rockingham county.
Rockingham Register and Advertiser, 13 January 1860 (Friday), p. 2, c. 6.

KNIPPLE: Near Cross Keys, on the 22nd inst., by Rev. H.A. Gaven, E.B. KNIPPLE and Miss F.N. COFFMAN, all of Rockingham county.
Rockingham Register and Advertiser, 27 November 1866 (Thursday), p. 2, c. 5.

KNISLY: See entry for GROVE.

KNODE: See entry for HARTSOCK.

KNOPP: See entry for DOVEL.

KNOWLES: See entry for RUPERT.

KOINER: See entry for KOINER.

KOINER: See entry for PATTERSON.

KOINER: See entry for SENEKER.

KOINER: On the 25th ult., near Waynesboro, Cornelius KOINER and Miss Mary Susan KOINER, all of Augusta.
Rockingham Register, 2 December 1869 (Thursday), p. 2, c. 3.

KOOGLAR: On the 7th inst., by Rev. J.M. Shreckhise, Mr. James A. KOOGLAR and Miss Elizabeth C. CALE, all of Augusta.
Rockingham Register, 23 June 1870 (Thursday), p. 2, c. 4.

KOOGLER: See entry for CUNNINGHAM.

KOOGLER: On Thursday, March 8th, by Rev. G.W. Statton, Mr. James W. KOOGLER and Miss Mary F. CURRY, all of Augusta.
Rockingham Register and Advertiser, 16 March 1860 (Friday), p. 2, c. 5.

KOONS: On the 24th ult., by Rev. D.C. Irwin, John George KOONS and Miss Nancy AMBROSE, all of Rockingham county.
The Rockingham Register, 4 December 1863 (Friday), p. 2, c. 5.

KOONTS: See entry for KELLER.

KOONTZ: See entry for CLEM.

KOONTZ: See entry for CROSBY.

KOONTZ: See entry for ECHARD.

KOONTZ: See entry for GROVE.

KOONTZ: See entry for KELLEY.

KOONTZ: See entry for KIBLER.

KOONTZ: See entry for LARKINS.

KOONTZ: See entry for LINCOLN.

KOONTZ: See entry for McCANN.
KOONTZ: See entry for McINTURFF.
KOONTZ: See entry for PROPES.
KOONTZ: See entry for WINE.
KOONTZ: On Thursday evening, the 18th inst.,
     by Rev. A. Poe Boude, Adam KOONTZ and
     Miss Margaret E. ECHARD, all of
     Rockingham.
     Rockingham Register and Advertiser, 25
     October 1866 (Thursday), p. 3, c. 3.
KOONTZ: At the residence of the bride's
     father, on Thursday afternoon, the 25th
     of July, by Rev. S. Kepler, Edward KOONTZ
     and Miss Sarah E., daughter of Franklin
     LISKEY, all of this vicinity.
     Rockingham Register and Advertiser, 1
     August 1867 (Thursday), p. 2, c. 6.
KOONTZ: On the 14th ult., by Rev. J.W.
     Watson, Mr. J.W. KOONTZ and Miss Eliza
     J., daughter of Paschal GRAVES, dec'd.
     Rockingham Register and Advertiser, 9
     November 1860 (Friday), p. 2, c. 6.
KOONTZ: At Keezeltown, on the 5th of
     November, by Rev. Jos. Funkhouser, Mr.
     Peter KOONTZ and Miss Harriet DAVIS, all
     of Rockingham county.
     Rockingham Register and Advertiser, 20
     December 1861 (Friday), p. 3, c. 3.
KOONTZ: On Thursday, the 15th of February, by
     Rev. Jos. Funkhouser, Mr. Peter A. KOONTZ
     and Miss Henrietta, daughter of Mr.
     Joseph ARMENTROUT, all of Rockingham
     county.
     Rockingham Register and Advertiser, 23
     February 1866 (Friday), p. 2, c. 4.
KOONTZ: On the 23rd of October, by Rev. John
     J. Harshberger, Mr. Peter W. KOONTZ and
     Miss Elizabeth A. CROMER, all of
     Rockingham county.
     The Rockingham Register, 14 November 1862
     (Friday), p. 2, c. 6.
KOONTZ: On Thursday the 1st inst., near
     Taylor's Spring, by Rev. A. Poe Boude,
     Mr. Robert KOONTZ and Miss Margaret A.,
     daughter of Robert COX, all of Rockingham
     county.

Rockingham <u>Register</u> and <u>Advertiser</u>, 9
February 1866 (Friday), p. 3, c. 3.

KOONTZ: On the 30th ult., by Rev. ____, Thos. J. KOONTZ, of Page county, and Miss Hellen V. MARTZ, of Rockingham county.
Rockingham <u>Register</u> and <u>Advertiser</u>, 13
February 1868 (Thursday), p. 2, c. 5.

KOONTZ: On the 17th inst., [<u>sic</u>, ult.], by Rev. J.W. Wattson, Mr. William KOONTZ and Miss Adaline, daughter of Mr. Jas. KITE, all of Page county.
Rockingham <u>Register</u> and <u>Advertiser</u>, 2
September 1859 (Friday), p. 2, c. 5.

KOONTZ: On the 30th ult., by Rev. J.W. Howe, Wm. F. KOONTZ and Miss Maria F., daughter of Richard CLATTERBUCK, all of Rockingham county.
Rockingham <u>Register</u> and <u>Advertiser</u>, 10
January 1867 (Thursday), p. 3, c. 2.

KRAMER: See entry for RADER.

KRATZER: On Sunday evening, the 30th of April, by Rev. Jacob Miller, Mr. Christian KRATZER and Miss Mary Catharine, daughter of John HOOVER, all of Rockingham county.
Rockingham <u>Register</u> and <u>Advertiser</u>, 5 May
1865 (Friday), p. 2, c. 5.

KRAUSE: On the 3rd inst., by Rev. Levi Keller, Mr. John A. KRAUSE and Miss Ann E. BORROW, both of Woodstock.
Rockingham <u>Register</u> and <u>Advertiser</u>, 26
August 1859 (Friday), p. 2, c. 5.

KREBS: See entry for HART.

KREBS: Near Harrisonburg, on Tuesday evening last, by Rev. D.C. Irwin, Mr. H. Clay KREBS, of Winchester, Va., and Miss M. Lizzie, daughter of Wm. BEARD, of Rockingham.
Rockingham <u>Register</u> & <u>Advertiser</u>, 3
November 1865 (Friday), p. 2, c. 2.

KRICKENBARGER: See entry for ETTINGER.

KRICKENBERGER: See entry for ADAMS.

KRONK: See entry for LIGGETT.

KRONK: At Forestville, on the 16th inst., by Rev. J.P. Cline, Mr. James W. KRONK and Miss Diana WHISTLER, all of Shenandoah

county.

Rockingham Register and Virginia Advertiser, 27 May 1854 (Saturday), p. 2, c. 7.

KUNKLE: See entry for HILL.

KURTZ: On the 1st inst., by Rev. Robt. J. Taylor, John KURTZ and Miss Alice NORTH, both of Rockbridge.

Rockingham Register, 20 January 1870 (Thursday), p. 2, c. 5.

KURTZ: On Tuesday, 23rd ult., by the Rev. Dr. Finley, Peter L. KURTZ and Miss Mary A. STEELE, both of Winchester.

Rockingham Register, 2 December 1869 (Thursday), p. 2, c. 3.

KUSER: See entry for ODER.

KUYKENDALL: See entry for SIMMONS.

KYGER: See entry for MILLER.

KYGER: See entry for MOYERHOEFFER.

KYGER: See entry for PIRKEY.

KYGER: On the 29th of January, by Rev. Isaac Long, Jacob KYGER and Miss Virginia F., daughter of Wm. SAUFLEY, all of Rockingham county.

Rockingham Register and Advertiser, 21 February 1867 (Thursday), p. 3, c. 2.

KYGER: On Thursday, the 2nd inst., by Rev. Isaac Long, Mr. John St. C. KYGER and Miss Amanda, daughter of Elie HUDLOWE, all of Rockingham.

The Rockingham Register, 10 October 1862 (Friday), p. 2, c. 7.

KYLE: See entry for EUBANK.

KYLE: See entry for FORBES.

KYLE: See entry for REID.

KYLE: In this place, on Wednesday morning last, by Rev. Wm. H. Wheelwright, Mr. Robert M. KYLE, Jr., of Rockingham, and Miss Margaret M., daughter of Mr. Robert HALL, of Madison county, Va.

Rockingham Register and Valley Advertiser, 29 May 1852 (Saturday), p. 2, c. 6.

KYLE: On Tuesday last, by the Rev. J.H. Brown, William KYLE, Esq., to Miss Felicia G. POINTS, all of Staunton.

Rockingham Register and Valley Advertiser, 17 October 1846 (Saturday), p. 3, c. 1.

- L -

LACKEY: At Variety Springs, on the 11th inst., by the Rev. Geo. B. Taylor, Mr. George W. LACKEY and Miss Willie M. BURRUSS.
Rockingham Register and Advertiser, 9 January 1868 (Thursday), p. 2, c. 4.

LACKIE: On Thursday, the 8th inst., by the Rev. J.C. Hensell, Mr. Robert J. LACKIE, of Augusta, to Miss Sarah Margaret, daughter of George CARPENTER, of Rockingham.
Rockingham Register and Advertiser, 23 December 1859 (Friday), p. 2, c. 5.

LAFFERTY: On Sunday morning, the 14th inst., at Orchard Grove, near Keezeltown, by Rev. Joseph Funkhouser, Mr. Addison LAFFERTY and Miss Eliza BREEDEN, both of Rockingham county.
The Rockingham Register, 19 August 1864 (Friday), p. 2, c. 3.

LAFFERTY: At Licking, Albemarle county, Va., on Wednesday, the 28th inst., by the Rev. R.N. Sledd, the Rev. Jno. J. LAFFERTY, of the Virginia Annual Conference, and Miss Mattie A., daughter of Capt. Bezaleel BROWN.
Rockingham Register and Advertiser, 27 April 1860 (Friday), p. 2, c. 4.

LAFOLLETTE: On the 20th ult., by Rev. Peter Miller, Mr. Silas LAFOLLETTE and Miss Ann M. McILWEE, of Hampshire.
Rockingham Register and Advertiser, 11 January 1861 (Friday), p. 3, c. 4.

LAGAR: October 12th, by the Rev. P. Miller, Amos LAGAR and Mrs. Delila HELTZEL, all of Hardy county, W.Va.
Rockingham Register, 18 November 1869 (Thursday), p. 3, c. 2.

LAGO: See entry for HUFFMAN.
LAGO: See entry for WISE.

LAHMAN: See entry for WEAVER.

LAM: On the 19th of July, by Rev. Isaac Long, Reuben F. LAM, a gallant soldier of the Peaked Mountain Tigers, 10th Va. Regiment, C.S.A., and Miss Nancy C., daughter of Samuel CLINE, all of Rockingham.
Rockingham Register, 30 July 1868 (Thursday), p. 3, c. 3.

LAM: On the 18th of January, by Elder C. Allemong, William LAM, of Rockingham, and Miss Sarah J. LONG, of Page county.
Rockingham Register and Advertiser, 17 February 1865 (Friday), p. 2, c. 4.

LAMB: See entry for CARPENTER.

LAMB: See entry for HOSHOUR.

LAMB: See entry for PALMER.

LAMB: See entry for POWELL.

LAMB: See entry for SHOEMAKER.

LAMB: On Thursday morning the 28th ult., by the Rev. Peter Shickle, Mr. Andrew LAMB and Miss Malinda GORDON, all of Augusta county.
Rockingham Register and Valley Advertiser, 19 April 1845 (Saturday), p. 3, c. 1.

LAMB: On the 6th of December, by Rev. Isaac Long, Mr. Andrew F. LAMB and Miss Matilda Catharine, daughter of James GRAVES, all of Rockingham county.
Rockingham Register & Advertiser, 22 December 1865 (Friday), p. 3, c. 2.

LAMB: On the 26th inst., near McGaheysville, by the Rev. John P. Hyde, Mr. John LAMB and Miss Mary E. WARBLE, both of Rockingham.
Rockingham Register and Advertiser, 12 January 1866 (Friday), p. 2, c. 3.

LAMB: On Monday morning, July 31st, by Rev. L.S. Reed, Levi LAMB and Miss Catharine BREEDEN, all of Rockingham county.
Rockingham Register, 4 August 1870 (Thursday), p. 3, c. 2.

LAMB: On the 12th inst., by Rev. J.W. Howe, Mr. Newton H. LAMB and Miss Nancy BERRY, all of this county.

Rockingham Register and Advertiser, 27
December 1861 (Friday), p. 2, c. 7.

LAMB: On Sunday, the 23rd of June, by Rev. Joseph Early, Mr. Wm. H. LAMB and Miss Elizabeth, daughter of Wm. SANDEY, all of Rockingham county.

Rockingham Register and Advertiser, 5
July 1861 (Friday), p. 3, c. 3.

LAMBERT: See entry for SHAY.

LAMBERT: On the 17th inst., in Staunton, by Rev. Wm. E. Baker, Charles P. LAMBERT and Miss Sallie B. BURDETT, of Staunton.

Rockingham Register, 26 November 1868
(Thursday), p. 2, c. 5.

LAMBERT: On the 5th of June, by the Rev. Mr. Fox, Captain E.L. LAMBERT, formerly of Alexandria, and Miss Bettie A. PARTLOW, of Rappahannock, Va.

Rockingham Register and Virginia
Advertiser, 27 June 1862 (Friday), p. 2,
c. 5.

LAMBERT: On the 7th of February, by Rev. M. Shreckhise, Mr. Peter LAMBERT, Jr., and Miss Dianna CURRY.

Rockingham Register and Advertiser, 18
February 1859 (Friday), p. 2, c. 6.

LAMBERT: On the 21st inst. [sic, ult.], by Rev. G.W. Statton, Mr. Samuel LAMBERT to Miss Sarah C. CARACOFE, all of Augusta county.

Rockingham Register and Advertiser, 2
September 1859 (Friday), p. 2, c. 5.

LAMBERT: On the 26th ult., near Woodstock, by Rev. G.H. Martin, Mr. William LAMBERT and Miss Margaret A. HOOVER, both of Shenandoah county.

Rockingham Register and Advertiser, 11
May 1866 (Friday), p. 2, c. 4.

LAMBETH: On Tuesday evening, the 17th inst., by Rev. James R. Waggener, Rev. Samuel S. LAMBETH, of the Virginia Annual Conference, M.E. Church South, and Miss Alice H., daughter of the late B.F. GRAHAM, Esq., of Greenville, Augusta county, Virginia.

Rockingham Register and Advertiser, 27

May 1859 (Friday), p. 2, c. 6.

LAMMA: On the 27th ult., by the Rev. S. Henkel, Franklin LAMMA and Miss Mary J. SOUTHARD.
Rockingham Register and Advertiser, 10 January 1867 (Thursday), p. 3, c. 2.

LANCASTER: See entry for SPEARS.

LANDACRE: See entry for DYER.

LANDACRE: See entry for ROBISON.

LANDES: See entry for HENKEL.

LANDES: See entry for LANDES.

LANDES: See entry for SHIFFLETT.

LANDES: On the 24th of December, by Rev. Joseph Early, Mr. Abraham LANDES and Miss Mary Ann HOLLER, both of Augusta county.
Rockingham Register and Advertiser, 10 January 1862 (Friday), p. 3, c. 2.

LANDES: On Sunday morning, the 13th of March, at Shem Bowman's, in Rockingham county, by Rev. Christian Hartman, David LANDES and Miss Sallie, daughter of Rob't CHANDLER, all of Rockingham. These are the parties referred to in the Register a fortnight since as having gone to Harper's Ferry to be wedded, but failed to consummate their wishes and returned to Rockingham without having been married. They are now legally joined together, and pursuing life's journey in happiness and peace.
Rockingham Register, 17 March 1870 (Thursday), p. 2, c. 4.

LANDES: On the 24th of October, by Rev. Christian Beard, David N. LANDES and Miss Sarah M.S. SHANK, all of Rockingham county.
Rockingham Register and Advertiser, 7 November 1867 (Thursday), p. 2, c. 5.

LANDES: On the 1st inst., at Mt. Crawford, by Rev. J.E. Chambliss, George W. LANDES and Miss Martha J. HELMES, all of Rockingham county.
Rockingham Register, 8 October 1868 (Thursday), p. 3, c. 3.

LANDES: In Mt. Crawford, on the 21st inst., by the Rev. J.C. Hensell, Geo. W. LANDES and Miss Martha S. LANDES, all of Rockingham county.

Rockingham Register, 28 July 1870 (Thursday), p. 3, c. 3.

LANDES: On Sunday the 23rd inst., at Pleasant Run, by Rev. I. Long, J.W. LANDES and Miss Lucy Ann Elizabeth, daughter of Solomon MESSERLY, dec'd, all of Rockingham.

Rockingham Register and Advertiser, 27 February 1868 (Thursday), p. 3, c. 3.

LANDES: On Thursday, the 8th inst., by Rev. J.C. Hensel, Mr. Noah LANDES and Miss Salinda E. SHELTON, all of Rockingham.

Rockingham Register and Advertiser, 16 March 1860 (Friday), p. 2, c. 5.

LANDES: On the 28th ult., by Rev. H. Wetzel, Mr. W.A. LANDES to Miss Delila E., daughter of Mr. David ALEXANDER, all of Augusta county.

Rockingham Register and Advertiser, 15 March 1861 (Friday), p. 2, c. 4.

LANDIS: See entry for STOVER.

LANDIS: On the 31st of December, by Rev. Jacob Thomas, George H. LANDIS and Miss Lydia C. BUMPHRY, all of Augusta.

Rockingham Register, 7 January 1869 (Thursday), p. 3, c. 3.

LANDSMAN: See entry for MILLER.

LANE: On Monday, the 3rd of March, 1862, by the Rev. William Reed, at Paynetown, Washington county, Tenn., Mr. Francis W. LANE to Miss Phebe DESHLER, late of Rockingham county, Va.

Rockingham Register and Virginia Advertiser, 30 May 1862 (Friday), p. 2, c. 6.

LANGDON: On the 16th ult., by Rev. J.W. Watson, James R. LANGDON, of Baltimore, and Miss Mary L. BAER, of Luray, Page county.

Rockingham Register and Advertiser, 17 January 1867 (Thursday), p. 3, c. 3.

LANGE: At the Virginia Hotel, in Staunton, on the 7th of June, by Rev. W.E. Baker, Mr. W.D. LANGE and Miss Louisa MARPLE.

Rockingham Register and Advertiser, 29 June 1860 (Friday), p. 3, c. 2.

LANKFORD: See entry for CHARLTON.

LANTZ: See entry for NISWANDER.

LANTZ: See entry for PAINTER.

LANTZ: See entry for WRIGHT.

LAPORTE: On the 16th inst., near Deerfield, in Augusta county, by Rev. George A. Shuey, Alex. LAPORTE and Miss Rachel Ann ROBERTS.
Rockingham Register and Advertiser, 27 June 1867 (Thursday), p. 2, c. 6.

LAREW: See entry for WADDY.

LAREW: In Greenville, on the 2nd inst., by Rev. S.S. Lambeth, Wm. J. LAREW and Miss E.P. GRAHAM, both of Augusta.
Rockingham Register, 11 November 1869 (Thursday), p. 3, c. 3.

LARKINS: See entry for HARLOW.

LARKINS: See entry for VEACH.

LARKINS: On Thursday, the 15th inst., Mr. Samuel M. LARKINS and Miss Mary Jane, daughter of James T. KOONTZ, all of Page county.
Rockingham Register and Virginia Advertiser, 30 December 1859 (Friday), p. 2, c. 5.

LARKINS: On the 28th ult., at the M.E. Parsonage, in Woodstock, by Rev. John P. Hyde, Mr. Wm. A. LARKINS and Miss Hellen C. ALLEN, all of Shenandoah county.
Rockingham Register and Advertiser, 7 June 1866 (Thursday), p. 3, c. 3.

LATTERMAN: See entry for HELLER.

LAUCK: See entry for DONELEY.

LAUCK: See entry for GRAYSON.

LAUCKE: See entry for WILKINS.

LAUGHLIN: See entry for WRIGHT.

LAUGHLIN: In Woodstock, on Wednesday, the 27th of October, by Rev. J.W. Wolfe, Wm. LAUGHLIN, of Strasburg, and Miss Mary E. COFFELT, all of Shenandoah county.
Rockingham Register, 4 November 1869 (Thursday), p. 2, c. 4.

LAWRENCE: See entry for THOMPSON.

LAWRENCE: In New Market, on the 31st of May,

by Rev. S. Henkel, Mr. Robert H. LAWRENCE
and Miss Elizabeth A., eldest daughter of
Mrs. Caroline ROBERTS.
Rockingham Register and Advertiser, 15
June 1860 (Friday), p. 2, c. 5.

LAWSON: On Thursday, 6th January, by Rev.
Gasper [sic] Allemong, Mr. John LAWSON,
of Greene county, and Miss Matilda A.,
daughter of Chapman COLLIER, of this
county.
Rockingham Register and Advertiser, 14
January 1859 (Friday), p. 3, c. 3.

LAYMAN: See entry for ARTZ.
LAYMAN: See entry for COPP.
LAYMAN: See entry for HAWES.
LAYMAN: See entry for OTT.
LAYMAN: See entry for TAYLOR.
LAYMAN: See entry for WHITMORE.
LAYMAN: On the 17th inst., by the Rev. J.A.
Bovey, Mr. Henry LAYMAN and Miss Mary J.,
daughter of Mr. John STRICKLER, all of
Rockingham.
Rockingham Register and Advertiser, 25
February 1859 (Friday), p. 2, c. 5.

LAYNE: See entry for ARMENTROUT.
LAYNE: See entry for HUMPHREYS.
LAYTON: See entry for BARTLEY.
LEAP: See entry for EATON.
LEAP: See entry for YAGER.
LEAP: On the 18th inst., by Rev. L.S. Reed,
Jos. S. LEAP and Miss Onnielarker B.,
daughter of A.J. JOHNSON, all of
Rockingham county.
Rockingham Register, 22 September 1870
(Thursday), p. 2, c. 5.

LEE: See entry for GAITHER.
LEE: See entry for HARSHBARGER.
LEE: See entry for PAINTER.
LEE: See entry for RIMEL.
LEE: On the 9th inst., by Rev. W. Rusmisel,
Geo. W. LEE and Miss Carrie V. COPP, all
of Shenandoah county.
Rockingham Register and Advertiser, 24
May 1866 (Thursday), p. 3, c. 4.

LEE: On the 18th inst., near Burke's Mill, by
the Rev. T. Brashear, Mr. James LEE, of

Rockingham, and Miss Cynthia HARLER, all
of Augusta county.
Rockingham Register and Advertiser, 26
September 1856 (Friday), p. 2, c. 6.

LEE: On the 23rd of April, at Harper's Ferry,
by Rev. G.G. Baker, Vandiver H. LEE and
Miss Amanda C. ETTINGER, both of
Rockingham county.
Rockingham Register, 2 July 1868
(Thursday), p. 2, c. 4.

LEE: On the 27th of December, 1864, by Rev.
J.W. Howe, Mr. Warfield LEE and Miss
Elizabeth F. CHAPMAN, all of Rockingham
county.
Rockingham Register and Advertiser, 24
February 1865 (Friday), p. 2, c. 5.

LEEDY: See entry for COOL.

LEEDY: On Tuesday, the 14th inst., by Rev.
Thos. Hildebrand, Mr. William LEEDY and
Miss Frances CARREL, all of Rockingham.
Rockingham Register and Advertiser, 16
November 1860 (Friday), p. 2, c. 4.

LEFEVRE: See entry for JAMES.

LEHEW: On the morning of the 24th of
November, at the residence of the bride's
mother, near Buckton Station, by Rev.
Jas. S. Petty, C. Edwin LEHEW and Miss
Annis S. BUCK, all of Warren county.
Rockingham Register, 8 December 1870
(Thursday), p. 2, c. 4.

LEMING: On the 18th ult., by Rev. J.W.
Watson, Mr. Noah F. LEMING and Miss
Elizabeth, daughter of David STRICKLER,
dec'd.
Rockingham Register and Advertiser, 9
November 1860 (Friday), p. 2, c. 6.

LEMLEY: At the residence of the bride's
father, in this place, on Thursday last,
by Rev. A. Poe Boude, W.E. LEMLEY,
formerly of Frederick county, Va., and
Miss Lucy A., daughter of Daniel P.
RAGAN, of Harrisonburg.
Rockingham Register, 2 July 1868
(Thursday), p. 2, c. 4.

LEMON: See entry for McCLUNG.

LEMON: Near Salt Petre Cave, Botetourt

county, Va., by the Rev. ____, Mr. ____ LEMON and Mrs. Melissa Kate GIBBS, all of Botetourt county.

Rockingham Register and Advertiser, 28 March 1867 (Thursday), p. 2, c. 6.

LEMON: On the 13th inst., at Edinburg, by Elder H. Jennings, Mr. David H. LEMON, formerly of Maryland, and Miss Isabella ORNDORF, of Shenandoah.

Rockingham Register and Advertiser, 28 June 1866 (Thursday), p. 2, c. 5.

LENTZ: On the 6th inst., by the Rev. H. Tallhelm, Mr. George LENTZ and Miss Mary Ann, youngest daughter of Mr. Lewis CAPLINGER, all of Rockingham.

Rockingham Register and Advertiser, 11 May 1860 (Friday), p. 2, c. 6.

LENTZ: On the 3rd inst., near Cross Roads, by Rev. A.A.P. Neel, Jacob LENTZ, of Ohio, and Miss Mary A. COFFMAN, of Shenandoah county.

Rockingham Register and Advertiser, 17 January 1867 (Thursday), p. 3, c. 3.

LENTZE: See entry for MAY.

LENZ: On Thursday morning, August 24th, by the Rev. Geo. G. Brooke, Rev. Leopold LENZ, of the Baltimore Conference, to Miss Sarah C., daughter of the late Fleming KEYSER, Esq., of Alleghany county.

Rockingham Register & Advertiser, 6 October 1865 (Friday), p. 2, c. 2.

LEONARD: On the 22nd inst., at the residence of the bride's father, by Rev. C. Beard, Mr. J.H. LEONARD and Miss Nannie YOUNT, both of Augusta county.

Rockingham Register and Advertiser, 31 January 1867 (Thursday), p. 3, c. 2.

LEPLINE: On the 5th inst., by Rev. L. Keller, in Woodstock, Peter LEPLINE and Miss Catherine E. SPENGLER, both of Shenandoah county.

Rockingham Register and Advertiser, 19 March 1868 (Thursday), p. 2, c. 4.

LEUTZ: See entry for CAPLINGER.

LEVEL: On Tuesday the 28th of December, by

Rev. B.F. Creel, Mr. Thomas F. LEVEL, of Rockingham county, and Miss Ella A., daughter of John R. MUNDAY, of Stanardsville, Va.
Rockingham Register and Advertiser, 7 January 1859 (Friday), p. 3, c. 1.

LEWEN: See entry for WALKER.

LEWIS: See entry for ANDERSON.

LEWIS: See entry for BEALL.

LEWIS: See entry for BOTTS.

LEWIS: See entry for EDWARDT.

LEWIS: See entry for WALTON.

LEWIS: In Washington city, on the 3rd of July, by the Rev. Dr. Pinkney, Daniel Sheffey LEWIS, Esq., of Rockingham county, Va., and Miss Isabella M., daughter of John Minor BOTTS, of Auburn, Culpeper county, Va.
Rockingham Register, 30 July 1868 (Thursday), p. 3, c. 3.

LEWIS: On the 2nd inst., at Sigler's Saw Mill, by Rev. H. St. J. Rinker, Jacob LEWIS and Miss Eliza A. FAY, all of Shenandoah county.
Rockingham Register and Advertiser, 30 January 1868 (Thursday), p. 2, c. 4.

LEWIS: On the 26th of October, at Port Republic, by the Rev. Geo. V. Leech, James Allen LEWIS and Mary Louisa, daughter of R.W. PALMER, dec'd, of that place.
The Rockingham Register, 7 November 1862 (Friday), p. 2, c. 6.

LEWIS: On the 27th of September, at the residence of the bride's parents, by Rev. Isaac Long, St. Clair K. LEWIS, formerly of Saline county, Missouri, and Miss Martha Jane, daughter of Jacob BYERLY, Esq., of Pleasant Run, Rockingham county.
Rockingham Register and Advertiser, 4 October 1866 (Thursday), p. 2, c. 5.

LEWIS: On Wednesday, the 22nd of February, at Rev. Mr. Irwin's Church, in Harrisonburg, by Rev. Mr. Taylor, Surgeon T.M. LEWIS, C.S.A., and the accomplished Miss M.I., daughter of Capt. Alex'r BAKER, Post

Quartermaster at Harrisonburg.

Rockingham Register and Advertiser, 24 February 1865 (Friday), p. 2, c. 5.

LICHLITER: See entry for HELLER.

LICHLITER: See entry for LICHLITER.

LICHLITER: On the 20th inst., in Powell's Fort, by Rev. Samuel Shaver, Andrew J. LICHLITER and Miss R.V., daughter of Henry LICHLITER, all of Shenandoah.

Rockingham Register, 5 May 1870 (Thursday), p. 3, c. 2.

LICHLITER: In Greenville, Green county, Tenn., by the Rev. Mr. Stradley, Mr. D.H. LICHLITER, of Woodstock, Va., and Miss Sally E. FISHER, formerly of this place.

Rockingham Register and Advertiser, 23 March 1860 (Friday), p. 2, c. 6.

LICHLITER: On the 28th of September, by Rev. Samuel Shaver, Mr. Wm. LICHLITER and Mrs. Margaret CONNER, all of Shenandoah county.

Rockingham Register & Advertiser, 27 October 1865 (Friday), p. 2, c. 3.

LICHLITER: On the morning of the 2nd inst., by Rev. H. Wetzel, William B. LICHLITER and Miss Matilda GOLLADAY, both of Shenandoah county.

Rockingham Register, 13 January 1870 (Thursday), p. 3, c. 4.

LIFE: See entry for DEVERS.

LIFE: On the 4th inst., by Rev. John Pinkerton, Mr. Henry LIFE, M.D., of Highland, and Miss Fanny CRAWFORD, of Augusta county.

Rockingham Register and Advertiser, 21 October 1859 (Friday), p. 2, c. 5.

LIGGETT: See entry for MAUZY.

LIGGETT: See entry for SNYDER.

LIGGETT: By Rev. T. Brashear, on the 22nd ult., Mr. Samuel LIGGETT and Miss Mary A. KRONK, all of Shenandoah county.

Rockingham Register and Advertiser, 5 April 1861 (Friday), p. 2, c. 5.

LIGHT: See entry for AREY.

LIGHTFOOT: On the 6th of November, by Rev. J.P. Cline, Lewis B. LIGHTFOOT, of

Georgia infantry, and Miss Sarah
HARSHBER, of Shenandoah county.
The Rockingham Register, 19 December 1862
(Friday), p. 2, c. 4.
LIGHTNER: See entry for CLEEK.
LIGHTNER: See entry for GIBSON.
LIGHTNER: See entry for HEAVENER.
LIGHTNER: See entry for LIGHTNER.
LIGHTNER: On the 17th ult., by Rev. J.W.
Canter, William T. LIGHTNER, of Augusta,
and Miss Dora M., daughter of Wm.
LIGHTNER, Esq., of Highland county.
Rockingham Register, 8 October 1868
(Thursday), p. 3, c. 3.
LIGON: On the 29th ult., by Rev. B.M. Wailes,
Dr. John LIGON and Miss Sallie G.
WARWICK, all of Nelson.
Rockingham Register and Advertiser, 14
December 1860 (Friday), p. 2, c. 6.
LILLARD: In Washington, D.C., on the 21st of
December, by Rev. E.H. Gray, Howard M.
LILLARD and Miss Elizabeth C., daughter
of Geo. L. KITE, of Page county.
Rockingham Register, 14 January 1869
(Thursday), p. 3, c. 3.
LINAWEAVER: On the 22nd of October, by Rev.
Jacob Miller, Charles B. LINAWEAVER and
Miss Rebecca C., daughter of Eli ANDES,
all of Rockingham county.
Rockingham Register, 12 November 1868
(Thursday), p. 3, c. 3.
LINAWEAVER: On the 30th of October, by Rev.
Wm. Pinkerton, Jas. A. LINAWEAVER, of
Rockingham, and Miss Rebecca KERRICOFE,
of Augusta.
Rockingham Register and Advertiser, 14
November 1856 (Friday), p. 2, c. 6.
LINCOLN: See entry for BROCK.
LINCOLN: See entry for TAYLOR.
LINCOLN: See entry for WOOD.
LINCOLN: On Tuesday evening, the 23rd of
April, by Rev. A.P. Boude, at the
residence of the bride's mother, Capt.
A.C. LINCOLN, late of the Confederate
States Army, and Miss Mary E., daughter
of P.P. KOONTZ, dec'd, all of Rockingham

county.

Rockingham Register and Advertiser, 2 May 1867 (Thursday), p. 2, c. 6.

LINDABERG: On the 24th of March, by Elder J. Pirkey, Wm. M. LINDABERG, of Hampshire county, W.Va., and Miss E.A. STICKLEY, of Shenandoah.

Rockingham Register, 23 April 1868 (Thursday), p. 2, c. 5.

LINDAMOOD: See entry for BREDEN.

LINDAMOOD: See entry for HEISHMAN.

LINDAMOOD: See entry for MILLER.

LINDAMOOD: On the Bridge at Harper's Ferry, on the 4th inst., by Rev. J.A. McFaden, _____ LINDAMOOD and Miss Sarah E. HOLLER, both of Shenandoah county.

Rockingham Register, 17 February 1870 (Thursday), p. 3, c. 2.

LINDAMOOD: On Thursday, the 20th of February, by Rev. W.J. Miller, Enos LINDAMOOD and Miss Sarah M. BERRY, all of McGaheysville, Rockingham county.

Rockingham Register and Advertiser, 5 March 1868 (Thursday), p. 2, c. 4.

LINDAMOOD: On the 29th of December, by Rev. Jacob Wine, Sylvanus LINDAMOOD and Sarah BOWMAN.

The Rockingham Register, 15 January 1864 (Friday), p. 2, c. 6.

LINDAMOOD: October 30th, by Rev. Wm. J. Miller, Whitfield LINDAMOOD and Miss Diana C. CRAWFORD, all of Rockingham.

Rockingham Register, 18 November 1869 (Thursday), p. 3, c. 2.

LINDIN: On the 4th inst., by Rev. Mr. Hensell, Mr. Michael LINDIN and Miss Virginia F. BARE, all of Rockingham.

Rockingham Register and Advertiser, 7 June 1861 (Friday), p. 3, c. 2.

LINEAWEAVER: On the 17th of November, at the residence of Mrs. Salome RALSTON, the bride's mother, by Rev. W.T. Price, James M. LINEAWEAVER and Miss Sarah C., daughter of Benjamin RALSTON, dec'd, all of this county.

Rockingham Register, 24 November 1870

(Thursday), p. 2, c. 4.

LINEBAUGH: See entry for RIMEL.

LINEWEAVER: See entry for GOWEL.

LINEWEAVER: See entry for McINTURFF.

LINEWEAVER: See entry for ROADES.

LINEWEAVER: At the Lutheran Parsonage, in Strasburg, on the 30th ult., by Rev. Levi Keller, Mr. Jacob LINEWEAVER and Miss Maria KIBLER, all of Shenandoah county. Rockingham Register and Advertiser, 7 January 1859 (Friday), p. 3, c. 1.

LINK: See entry for BOONE.

LINK: See entry for HOUFFE.

LINK: See entry for HUTCHINSON.

LINK: See entry for YANCEY.

LINN: On the 15th inst., by the Rev. John Perkey, Mr. George LINN, of Frederick, and Miss Catherine BLY, of Shenandoah county. Rockingham Register and Advertiser, 20 April 1866 (Friday), p. 2, c. 3.

LINNEWEAVER: At the residence of the bride's parents, on the 12th inst., by Rev. Jacob Miller, Wm. T. LINNEWEAVER and Miss Lydia F., daughter of Henry WENGER, all of Rockingham county. Rockingham Register, 26 May 1870 (Thursday), p. 2, c. 6.

LINTHICUM: On the 31st ult., by Rev. Thos. Hildebrand, Morgan LINTHICUM and Miss Bettie HIDEB, all of Hardy county, W.Va. Rockingham Register and Advertiser, 16 January 1868 (Thursday), p. 2, c. 5.

LINTHICUM: On the 19th ult., by Elder George Loy, Mr. William K. LINTHICUM, of Pendleton county, and Miss Susan BOWMAN, of Hampshire county. Rockingham Register and Advertiser, 31 August 1860 (Friday), p. 2, c. 4.

LIONBERGER: On the 16th of April, in Boonville, Missouri, by the Rev. F.R. Haleman, J.H. LIONBERGER, Luray, Va., and Miss Laura Y. MEGUIER. Rockingham Register and Advertiser, 9 May 1867 (Thursday), p. 2, c. 5.

LIPOP: On Thursday, the 3rd inst., at

Independence, Va., by Rev. Lee C. Brown, Mr. Joseph W. LIPOP, of Charlottesville, Va., to Mrs. Susan E. HOFFMAN, daughter of Col. John DICKENSON, of Grayson county, Va.
Rockingham Register and Advertiser, 18 May 1866 (Friday), p. 2, c. 4.

LIPSCOMB: See entry for SHELTON.
LISKEY: See entry for BROWN.
LISKEY: See entry for HEDRICK.
LISKEY: See entry for KOONTZ.
LISKEY: See entry for LONG.
LISKEY: See entry for SNYDER.
LITTELL: In the Church at McGaheysville, on Sunday morning last, by Rev. T.A. Morgan, Mr. Joseph J. LITTELL and Miss Isaphfne B., eldest daughter of Mr. Tobias McGahey, dec'd, all of Rockingham county.
Rockingham Register and Valley Advertiser, 3 November 1849, (Saturday), p. 2, c. 7.

LITTEN: See entry for FRY.
LITTEN: On the 30th ult., by Rev. H. Wetzel, Benjamin LITTEN and Miss Mary C. CHILCOTT, all of Shenandoah county.
Rockingham Register, 13 August 1868 (Thursday), p. 2, c. 5.

LITTEN: On the 31st of December, near New Market, by Rev. S. Henkel, John W. LITTEN and Miss Pamelia Ann GOOD, all of Shenandoah county.
Rockingham Register, 14 January 1869 (Thursday), p. 3, c. 3.

LITTLE: See entry for PENCE.
LITTLE: See entry for PHILLIPS.
LITTLE: On the 13th inst., by Rev. A.B. Woodfin, Mr. J.T. LITTLE, of Alabama, and Miss Mary M. PARRISH, of Augusta county.
Rockingham Register and Advertiser, 22 November 1866 (Thursday), p. 3, c. 3.

LITTON: In Sangersville, on the 1st inst., by the Rev. John Pinkerton, Mr. Osbert L. LITTON to Miss Adaline E. BLAKEMORE, all of Augusta county.
Rockingham Register and Advertiser, 9 August 1861 (Friday), p. 3, c. 4.

LIVICK: See entry for DULL.

LIVICK: See entry for KELLER.

LIVICK: Near Goshen, Rockbridge county, on the 23rd ult., by Rev. J.I. Miller, A.J. LIVICK, of Augusta, and Miss Ginnie ROBINSON, of Rockbridge county.
Rockingham Register, 6 January 1870 (Thursday), p. 3, c. 3.

LLOYD: See entry for ESTEP.

LLOYD: See entry for ZIRKLE.

LOCKE: At Blackoak, the residence of the bride's father, by Elder F.M. Perry, Dr. Theo. H. LOCKE and Miss Sudie F., daughter of Jos. W. ALMOND, Esq., all of Page county.
Rockingham Register, 24 September 1868 (Thursday), p. 3, c. 4.

LOCKMILLER: On the 16th ult., by Rev. John Clymer, John H. LOCKMILLER and Miss Caroline ORNDORFF, all of Shenandoah county.
Rockingham Register, 6 January 1870 (Thursday), p. 3, c. 3.

LOCKRIDGE: See entry for BICKLE.

LOCKRIDGE: On the 15th of May, at the residence of the bride's father, near Greenbank, Pocahontas county, by Rev. C.A. Joyce, Stephen A. LOCKRIDGE, of Highland county, and Miss Laura A. ERVIN.
Rockingham Register and Advertiser, 28 June 1866 (Thursday), p. 2, c. 5.

LOCKRIDGE: In Nevada, Iowa, on the 19th ult., by Rev. R. Swearingen, Mr. Wm. LOCKRIDGE, formerly of Va., and Miss L.A. STETSON, late of Kenton, Ohio, all of Nevada, Story county, Iowa.
Rockingham Register and Advertiser, 10 February 1860 (Friday), p. 2, c. 5.

LOEWENSTEIN: See entry for HELLER.

LOEWENSTEIN: See entry for LOZWENBACH.

LOFLAND: See entry for HERNDON.

LOFTUS: On Thursday, the 18th of September, by Rev. Jacob Miller, Mr.Archibald LOFTUS and Mrs. Mary E. BLACK, all of Rockingham county.
Rockingham Register and Virginia

<u>Advertiser</u>, 26 September 1862 (Friday), p. 2, c. 2.

LOGAN: See entry for ARNOLD.

LOGAN: See entry for STERLING.

LOGAN: See entry for WYANT.

LOGAN: On the 2nd inst., by the Rev. J.N. Davis, Mr. Benjamin E. LONG and Miss Elizabeth, daughter of Mr. William REHERD - all of this county.
<u>Rockingham</u> <u>Register</u> <u>and</u> <u>Advertiser</u>, 10 December 1858 (Friday), p. 3, c. 2.

LOGAN: On Tuesday morning last, at 8 o'clock, at the residence of the bride's father, in Woodstock, by the Rev. J.D. Coulling, Joseph T. LOGAN, Esq., the junior editor of the <u>Register</u>, and Miss M. Addie Hamilton, only daughter of Maj. John HAAS, of Woodstock.
<u>Rockingham</u> <u>Register</u> <u>and</u> <u>Advertiser</u>, 11 November 1859 (Friday), p. 3, c. 1.

LOGAN: On the 22nd ult., by Rev. C. Hartman, Thomas G. LOGAN and Miss Sarah C. GRIM, all of this county.
<u>Rockingham</u> <u>Register</u>, 24 March 1870 (Thursday), p. 3, c. 2.

LOGAN: On the 5th inst., by Rev. J.L. Clark, W.T. LOGAN, one of the editors and proprietors of the <u>New Era</u>, and Miss Margaret A. SHOWERS, all of Martinsburg, W.Va.
<u>Rockingham</u> <u>Register</u>, 19 August 1869 (Thursday), p. 3, c. 2.

LOHR: On the 24th of March, by Rev. Samuel Wampler, Mr. Michael LOHR and Miss Elizabeth, daughter of Philip SPITZER, all of Rockingham county.
<u>The</u> <u>Rockingham</u> <u>Register</u>, 8 April 1864 (Friday), p. 2, c. 6.

LOHR: On the 2nd inst., by the Rev. J.B. Davis, Mr. Wm. K. LOHR and Miss Sarah POWERS, both of Augusta county.
<u>Rockingham</u> <u>Register</u> <u>and</u> <u>Advertiser</u>, 25 March 1859 (Friday), p. 3, c. 2.

LOKER: On the 26th day of May, by Rev. Joseph Funkhouser, Mr. David LOKER and Miss Sarah C., daughter of Mr. George LONG, all of the neighborhood of Fellowship, Rockingham county.

Rockingham Register and Advertiser, 3 June 1859 (Friday), p. 3, c. 2.

LONAS: See entry for GOLLADAY.

LONAS: See entry for SAGER.

LONAS: On the 15th inst., by Rev. Levi Keller, Jacob LONAS and Miss Chrisnina WALTER, all of Shenandoah.

Rockingham Register and Advertiser, 31 October 1867 (Thursday), p. 2, c. 6.

LONDON: On Tuesday evening, 9th inst., by Rev. Mr. Reed, Dr. H. LONDON, Esq., and Miss Mary E., daughter of James CASKIE, Esq., all of Richmond, Va.

Rockingham Register and Virginia Advertiser, 27 May 1854 (Saturday), p. 2, c. 7.

LONG: See entry for BRUBAKER.

LONG: See entry for GLADVILLE.

LONG: See entry for HEATWOLE.

LONG: See entry for HOCKMAN.

LONG: See entry for HOPKINS.

LONG: See entry for JOHNSON.

LONG: See entry for LAM.

LONG: See entry for LOKER.

LONG: See entry for LONG (2).

LONG: See entry for McFARLAND.

LONG: See entry for MILLER.

LONG: See entry for NISWANDER.

LONG: See entry for REUBUSH.

LONG: See entry for SHICKLE.

LONG: See entry for SHIFFLET.

LONG: See entry for SHRUM.

LONG: See entry for SPITZER.

LONG: See entry for SWARTS.

LONG: See entry for WEBB.

LONG: See entry for WILLICE.

LONG: See entry for WILSON.

LONG: On December 22nd, near Mt. Clinton, by Rev. T.D. Bell, Andrew H. LONG and Miss Mary Susan, daughter of Michael WHITMORE, all of Rockingham.

Rockingham Register, 7 January 1869 (Thursday), p. 3, c. 3.

LONG: On Monday last, by Rev. Geo. V. Leech,

Conrad LONG and Miss Fanny BAKER, both of Rockingham.

Rockingham Register and Advertiser, 25 January 1861 (Friday), p. 3, c. 1.

LONG: On January 10th, by Rev. Daniel Thomas, Emanuel LONG and Miss Elizabeth J., daughter of Samuel MILLER, all of Rockingham county.

Rockingham Register and Advertiser, 31 January 1867 (Thursday), p. 3, c. 2.

LONG: On the 22nd ult., at Edmund Rosenberger's, in Rockingham county, by Rev. S. Henkel, Erasmus LONG and Miss S.C. ROSENBERGER, both of Rockingham county.

Rockingham Register, 3 March 1870 (Thursday), p. 2, c. 5.

LONG: On the 3rd of October, by Rev. Solomon Garber, George H. LONG and Miss Josephine, daughter of David SWARTZ, all of Rockingham county.

Rockingham Register, 27 October 1870 (Thursday), p. 2, c. 4.

LONG: On the 19th ult., by Rev. Mr. Beattie, Isaac LONG and Miss Bessie MOHLER, of Page county.

Rockingham Register and Advertiser, 26 December 1856 (Friday), p. 2, c. 7.

LONG: On the 18th inst., by Rev. T.D. Bell, Mr. John M. LONG and Miss Eliza A. BORTON, all of Rockingham county.

The Rockingham Register, 23 September 1864 (Friday), p. 2, c. 5.

LONG: On the 29th ult., by Rev. Wm. Brown, Mr. John T. LONG, of Rockingham, to Miss Rebecca J., daughter of Sam'l M. LONG, Esq., of Augusta county.

Rockingham Register and Advertiser, 13 February 1857 (Friday), p. 2, c. 5.

LONG: On Christmas day, at the residence of the bride's mother, near Fellowship Church, by Rev. A. Poe Boude, Marion LONG and Miss Martha Ann GISH, all of Rockingham county.

Rockingham Register and Advertiser, 3 January 1867 (Thursday), p. 3, c. 3.

LONG: On the 11th inst., by Elder W.C. Lauck, P.J. LONG and Miss M.C. LONG, all of Page county.
Rockingham Register, 25 November 1869 (Thursday), p. 2, c. 3.

LONG: On the 17th of April, by Rev. Isaac Long, Patrick H. LONG and Miss Frances, daughter of Joseph GOOD, all of Rockingham county.
Rockingham Register and Advertiser, 11 May 1866 (Friday), p. 2, c. 4.

LONG: On the 25th of November, by Rev. John Pirkey, Mr. Robert L. LONG and Miss Mary E. FITZSIMMONS, all of Shenandoah county.
Rockingham Register and Advertiser, 13 December 1866 (Thursday), p. 2, c. 5.

LONG: On the 14th inst., by Rev. Jacob Thomas, Simeon LONG and Miss Margaret E., daughter of Elias HOLLEN, all of Rockingham county.
Rockingham Register, 22 December 1870 (Thursday), p. 2, c. 4.

LONG: On the 3rd inst., at the residence of the bride's parents, by Rev. Solomon Garber, Wm. LONG and Miss Mary Ann, daughter of David SHANK, all of Rockingham county.
Rockingham Register, 17 February 1870 (Thursday), p. 3, c. 2.

LONG: On the 8th inst., by Rev. Joseph Funkhouser, Wm. C. LONG and Miss Mary J., daughter of Franklin LISKEY, all of Rockingham county.
Rockingham Register and Advertiser, 16 March 1866 (Friday), p. 3, c. 4.

LONG: On Sunday, the 25th inst., in the Chesnut Ridge, by Rev. Joseph Funkhouser, Mr. William Henry LONG and Miss Eliza Elizabeth RANKIN, all of Rockingham county.
The Rockingham Register, 30 October 1863 (Friday), p. 2, c. 7.

LONGACRE: See entry for FRYE.

LONGAKER: On Sabbath morning last, by Rev. T. Hildebrand, Mr. Andrew J. LONGAKER and Mrs. Susan Jane BROWN, all of

Harrisonburg.

Rockingham Register and Advertiser, 24
May 1861 (Friday), p. 3, c. 2.

LONGLEY: See entry for JAMES.

LOOKER: See entry for BRUNK.

LORENTZ: See entry for BEARD.

LORING: See entry for PAINTER.

LOTTS: See entry for BALLEW.

LOUDERBACK: At New Port, Page county, October
31st, by Rev. S. Henkel, Jacob LOUDERBACK
and Miss Sarah A. WALTON, all of Page
county.

Rockingham Register and Advertiser, 14
November 1867 (Thursday), p. 2, c. 6.

LOUDERBACK: In Harrisonburg, March 24th, by
Rev. Geo. W. Holland, Martin V.
LOUDERBACK and Sarah E. FOLTZ, of Page
county.

Rockingham Register, 1 April 1869
(Thursday), p. 3, c. 3.

LOUGH: See entry for CALHOON.

LOUGH: On the 17th inst., a cheval, in
Bridgewater, by Rev. Thos. E. Carson,
John W. LOUGH, of Pendleton, and Miss
Martha C.R. HUFFMAN, of Rockingham
county.

Rockingham Register, 26 November 1868
(Thursday), p. 2, c. 5.

LOVEGROVE: On the 22nd inst., by the Rev.
J.W. Kiracofe, William LOVEGROVE and Miss
Sarah E. GEARHART, both of Augusta
county.

Rockingham Register and Advertiser, 29
August 1867 (Thursday), p. 2, c. 5.

LOVERIDGE: See entry for CLARKE.

LOVING: At Mt. Moriah Church, in Albemarle
county, on the 31st of August, by Rev.
Nelson, Mr. Seaton H. LOVING, Clerk of
Nelson county, and Miss Martha J.E.
THOMPKINS, of Albemarle.

Rockingham Register and Advertiser, 9
September 1859 (Friday), p. 2, c. 4.

LOWERY: See entry for WISEMAN.

LOWMAN: In Dayton, on Sunday last, by the
Rev. H. Hoffman, Mr. Reuben P. LOWMAN and

Miss Elizabeth C., daughter of Abram WILLIAMS, all of Rockingham county.
Rockingham Register and Virginia Advertiser, 8 August 1862 (Friday), p. 2, c. 4.

LOWMAN: On the 9th ult., by the Rev. Samuel Brown, Mr. W.C. LOWMAN to Miss Sarah SWINK, all of Rockbridge.
Rockingham Register and Advertiser, 6 September 1866 (Thursday), p. 2, c. 5.

LOWNER: See entry for WISE.

LOWREY: On the 25th of November, by Rev. Christopher Kyger, Jos. LOWREY and Miss Catherine WETZEL.
Rockingham Register and Advertiser, 3 January 1867 (Thursday), p. 3, c. 3.

LOWRY: See entry for BOWYER.

LOWRY: See entry for HESS.

LOWRY: On the 21st ult., by Rev. S. Henkel, Isaac LOWRY and Miss Hannah SAYLAW, all of Rockingham.
Rockingham Register and Advertiser, 5 December 1867 (Thursday), p. 2, c. 5.

LOZWENBACH: In Milwaukee, Wisconsin, on Sunday the 14th inst., Mr. Moritz LOZWENBACH, merchant, formerly of Harrisonburg, Va., and Miss Bettie LOEWENSTEIN, of Milwaukee.
Rockingham Register and Advertiser, 26 January 1866 (Friday), p. 3, c. 3.

LUCAS: See entry for KITE.

LUCAS: See entry for SMILEY.

LUCAS: On the 14th inst., by Rev. J.W. Watson, Mr. Henry LUCAS and Miss Sallie, daughter of John RUFFNER, dec'd, all of Page county.
Rockingham Register & Advertiser, 29 September 1865 (Friday), p. 3, c. 3.

LUCAS: On Thursday evening, the 25th of August, by Elder P. McInturf, Mr. Nathan LUCAS and Miss Alpley HUFFMAN, all of Page county.
The Rockingham Register, 9 September 1864 (Friday), p. 2, c. 3.

LUCKETT: On the 17th inst., near Walatoola Springs, by Rev. F. Beal, of Covington,

Captain Joseph LUCKETT and Miss Duck, eldest daughter of Mrs. Lucy MINOR, all of Bath county, Va.
Rockingham Register, 24 February 1870 (Thursday), p. 2, c. 5.

LUDWICK: See entry for HUFFMAN.

LUDWIG: See entry for MOHLER.

LUDWIG: On the 9th inst., by Rev. J. Pirkey, Amos B. LUDWIG, of Shenandoah, and Jaquelina M. JONES, of Frederick county.
Rockingham Register and Advertiser, 31 January 1862 (Friday), p. 2, c. 7.

LUDWIG: In Edinburg, on the 17th ult., by Rev. H. Shaul, John M. LUDWIG and Miss Sarah E. GRANDSTAFF, all of Shenandoah county.
Rockingham Register, 3 September 1868 (Thursday), p. 2, c. 4.

LUNSFORD: See entry for FALLS.

LUNSFORD: On the 15th inst., at the residence of the bride's mother, by the Rev. Jas. L. Snyder, Joshua LUNSFORD and Miss Lavinia E. HEVENER, all of Highland county.
Rockingham Register, 23 June 1870 (Thursday), p. 2, c. 4.

LUNSFORD: On the 16th ult., by the Rev. Samuel Brown, Mr. Thomas B. LUNSFORD, of Stafford county, to Miss Bettie B. CALHOUN, of Rockbridge.
Rockingham Register and Advertiser, 6 September 1866 (Thursday), p. 2, c. 5.

LUPTON: On the 20th inst., at Newcastle, Craig county, Va., by the Rev. Mr. Mauzy, I.B. LUPTON, of Harrisonburg, and Miss M.J., daughter of David W. HUSTON, dec'd, formerly of Rockingham county, Va.
Rockingham Register, 27 October 1870 (Thursday), p. 2, c. 4.

LURTY: On the 22nd inst., at the residence of the bride's father, by Rev. D.C. Irwin, Capt. Warren S. LURTY and Miss Minnie C., daughter of Dr. A.M. NEWMAN, all of Harrisonburg.
Rockingham Register and Advertiser, 24 May 1866 (Thursday), p. 3, c. 4.

LUSHBAUGH: See entry for EVANS.

LUTHOLTZ: See entry for ARMENTROUT.

LUTZ: See entry for DELLINGER.

LUTZ: See entry for McNEAL.

LUTZ: See entry for SHANK.

LUTZ: On the 19th ult., by the Rev. J.C. Hensell, Mr. B. LUTZ and Miss L. Maggie SLUSSER, all of Rockingham county.
Rockingham Register and Advertiser, 5 April 1861 (Friday), p. 2, c. 5.

LUTZ: On the 7th inst., near Mt. Sidney, Augusta county, by Rev. Frederick Miller, David F. LUTZ, of Rockingham, and Miss Susan M., daughter of Sam'l HALE, of Augusta.
Rockingham Register and Advertiser, 21 February 1867 (Thursday), p. 3, c. 2.

LUTZ: On the 19th inst., by Rev. V.F. Bolton, Mr. Geo. LUTZ, of this county, and Mrs. Rebecca WALKER, of Augusta county.
Rockingham Register and Advertiser, 26 September 1856 (Friday), p. 2, c. 6.

LUTZ: On the 25th of September, by the Rev. Peter Shickel, Mr. George R. LUTZ and Miss Mary PIFER, all of Rockingham county.
Rockingham Register and Valley Advertiser, 11 October 1845 (Saturday), p. 2, c. 6.

LUTZ: On the 11th inst., by Rev. J.C. Hensell, Henry R. LUTZ, of East Tennessee, and Miss Mollie J. PLECKER, of Rockingham county.
Rockingham Register and Advertiser, 18 October 1866 (Thursday), p. 2, c. 4.

LUTZ: On the 21st of October, near Mt. Clifton, Shenandoah county, by Rev. H. Shaull, Isaac LUTZ and Miss Mary C., daughter of Aaron FOLTZ, Esq.
Rockingham Register, 3 February 1870 (Thursday), p. 3, c. 4.

LYNCH: On the 6th of September, by the Rev. Solomon Garber, Mr. John LYNCH, of Upshur county, Va., and Miss Maria WHORLEY, of Rockingham.
The Rockingham Register, 25 September

1863 (Friday), p. 2, c. 4.
LYNE: See entry for COOTES.

- Mc -

McAFFERTY: See entry for WENGER.

McALISTER: On the 5th inst., in this place, by Rev. J.N. Davis, Mr. W.C. McALISTER and Miss Margaret C. ROYER.
Rockingham Register and Advertiser, 14 January 1859 (Friday), p. 3, c. 3.

McALLESTER: On the 31st of July, 1866, by Rev. E.C. Alamong, Wm. McALLESTER and Harriet SHIFTLEY, both of Greene county, Va.
Rockingham Register and Advertiser, 30 August 1866 (Thursday), p. 2, c. 4.

McALLISTER: On the 12th ult., by Rev. J.J. Engle, Mr. Richard McALLISTER and Miss Martha J. FIELDING, all of Augusta county.
Rockingham Register and Advertiser, 9 January 1868 (Thursday), p. 2, c. 4.

McALLISTER: At Walnut Grove, Bath county, Va., on the 27th of October, at 9 o'clock, A.M., by Rev. James M. Rice, of Covington, Wm. M. McALLISTER, of Warm Springs, and Miss Maggie A., daughter of James R. ERWIN.
Rockingham Register, 2 December 1869 (Thursday), p. 2, c. 3.

McCALL: See entry for ANDREW.

McCALL: See entry for DRIVER.

McCALLISTER: On the 21st of March, by Elder C. Allemong, William McCALLISTER and Miss Rebecca S. COMER, all of Page county.
Rockingham Register and Advertiser, 4 April 1867 (Thursday), p. 3, c. 4.

McCANN: On the 24th ult., by Rev. J.W. Wolff, N.F. McCANN, of Norfolk, formerly of Shenandoah county, and Miss Nellie F. KOONTZ, of Edingburg [sic, Edinburg].
Rockingham Register, 8 July 1869 (Thursday), p. 2, c. 5.

McCAULEY: See entry for SISLER.

McCAULEY: On the 20th inst., at Mr. Jacob

Lineweaver's, by Rev. T.D. Bell, Mr. Benjamin F. McCAULEY and Miss Mary Jane ENGLE, both of Hampshire county.
The Rockingham Register, 25 September 1863 (Friday), p. 2, c. 4.

McCAULEY: On the 21st of October, by the Rev. Christian Hartman, Daniel McCAULEY and Miss Elizabeth, daughter of John BURK, all of Rockingham.
Rockingham Register and Advertiser, 22 November 1866 (Thursday), p. 3, c. 3.

McCAULEY: On the 22nd December, by Rev. John Miller, Mr. John McCAULEY and Miss Martha CRAWFORD, all of Augusta county.
Rockingham Register and Advertiser, 10 January 1862 (Friday), p. 3, c. 2.

McCAUSLAND: See entry for NEAL.

McCELLAS: On the 25th of December last, by Rev. John S. Blain, at Wilderfield, Bath county, Va., Harvey McCELLAS, Esq., and Miss Lizzie, eldest daughter of Mr. L. WALKER, of said county.
Rockingham Register and Advertiser, 17 January 1862 (Friday), p. 3, c. 1.

McCHESNEY: See entry for CRAIG.

McCHESNEY: See entry for DUNLAP.

McCLANNAHAN: On the 8th of December 1864, by Elder H. Jennings, of Edinburg, Mr. Geo. W. McCLANNAHAN to Miss Rebecca Frances, daughter of Hiram BOWMAN, of Powell's Fort, Shenandoah county.
Rockingham Register and Advertiser, 24 February 1865 (Friday), p. 2, c. 5.

McCLEARY: See entry for McNUTT.

McCLELLAN: In Versailles, Morgan county, Mo., on the 2nd inst., by the Rev. A. Eastis, Dr. J.J. McCLELLAN to Miss Mary C., daughter of Wm. CAMERON, Esq., formerly of Augusta county, Va.
Rockingham Register and Advertiser, 26 March 1858 (Friday), p. 3, c. 2.

McCLINTIC: On Tuesday, the 14th ult., at Mill Point, by Rev. M.D. Dunlap, Wm. McCLINTIC, of Bath county, and Miss Mary Ann, only daughter of Sampson L. MATTHEWS, dec'd, of Pocahontas county.

Rockingham Register and Advertiser, 15 July 1859 (Friday), p. 3, c. 2.

McCLOUD: On the 24th of September, at Harper's Ferry, by Rev. G.G. Brooke, Mr. N. McCLOUD and Miss R.J. TOMLINSON, all of Highland county.

Rockingham Register and Advertiser, 5 October 1860 (Friday), p. 2, c. 3.

McCLUNG: On the 29th ult., by Rev. Jacob Winter, Andrew A. McCLUNG, of Augusta, to Estiline M., daughter of Samuel WILSON, Esq., of Rockbridge.

Rockingham Register and Virginia Advertiser, 13 June 1856 (Friday), p. 2, c. 2.

McCLUNG: On the 16th inst., by Rev. H.H. Hawes, at the residence of Mr. George C. PATTERSON, father of the brides, Dr. Wm. J. BELL and Miss Mary A., and J.F. McCLUNG and Miss Maria Virginia, all of Augusta.

Rockingham Register and Advertiser, 24 October 1867 (Thursday), p. 2, c. 7.

McCLUNG: On Tuesday, the 14th inst., near McDowell, by Rev. W.T. Price, Mr. Silas McCLUNG, of Highland, and Miss Nannie J. LEMON, of Botetourt county, Va.

Rockingham Register, 30 April 1868 (Thursday), p. 2, c. 6.

McCLURE: See entry for COX.

McCLURE: See entry for GILLASPY.

McCLURE: See entry for OVERALT.

McCLURE: On the 22nd of September, by Rev. C. Beard, Mr. James McCLURE and Miss Eliza G. KENNEDY, all of Augusta county.

Rockingham Register and Advertiser, 7 October 1859 (Friday), p. 2, c. 4.

McCOLLY: On the 7th inst., by Rev. J.J. Harshberger, Mr. Larkin McCOLLY and Miss Catharine, daughter of Mr. Thomas BEX, all of Rockingham.

Rockingham Register and Advertiser, 23 March 1860 (Friday), p. 2, c. 6.

McCORMICK: See entry for HEIZER.

McCORMICK: See entry for HOLLIDAY.

McCORMICK: On Thursday, the 22nd ult., by

Rev. James Beatty, Mr. Joseph J. McCORMICK, of Rockbridge, to Miss Elizabeth S. GROAH, of Augusta county. *Rockingham Register and Advertiser*, 6 August 1858 (Friday), p. 3, c. 2.

McCOWAN: On the 9th inst., by Rev. X.J. Richardson, Mr. Andrew J. McCOWAN, of Rockbridge, to Miss Sophia M. SPITLER, daughter of John SPITLER, Esq., of Augusta county. *Rockingham Register and Virginia Advertiser*, 18 May 1855 (Friday), p. 3, c. 4.

McCOY: See entry for BOGGS.

McCOY: See entry for PULLEN.

McCOY: See entry for WILSON.

McCOY: On the 17th of September, by the Rev. Daniel Thomas, Mr. Andrew Jackson McCOY, of Highland, to Miss Sarah A. GOOD, of Augusta. *Rockingham Register and Advertiser*, 3 October 1856 (Friday), p. 2, c. 6.

McCUE: See entry for BELL.

McCUE: See entry for CRAIG.

McCUE: See entry for THRIFT.

McCUE: On the 2nd inst., at Lebanon Church, ALbemarle county, by [Rev.] H.H. Geary, John W. McCUE, of Nelson, and Miss Mary A. SHEPHERD, of Albemarle. *Rockingham Register*, 11 November 1869 (Thursday), p. 3, c. 3.

McCULLOCK: On Thursday, the 9th, by the Rev. Samuel Kennerly, Dr. George W. McCULLOCK, of New Hope, to Miss Nancy, daughter of Henry MILLER, Esq., of Rockingham. *Rockingham Register*, 18 April 1835 (Saturday), p. 3, c. 3.

McCUNE: On the 28th ult., near Waynesboro, by Rev. C. Beard, Col. Sam'l McCUNE and Miss Mary E. RAMSEY, both of Augusta county. *Rockingham Register*, 11 November 1869 (Thursday), p. 3, c. 3.

McCUTCHAN: See entry for BROWN.

McCUTCHEN: See entry for DIZARD.

McCUTCHEN: See entry for HUGHART.

McCUTCHEN: See entry for JOHNSTON.

McCUTCHEN: See entry for WETZEL.

McCUTCHEN: On the 5th inst., at the residence of Mr. Wm. Swink, by Rev. C.S.M. See, Mr. Jas. McCUTCHEN and Miss Sallie CHRIST, all of Augusta.
Rockingham Register and Advertiser, 20 April 1866 (Friday), p. 2, c. 3.

McCUTCHEN: On the 24th of June, near Summerdean, by Rev. Harvey Gilmore, Jas. R. McCUTCHEN and Miss L.E., daughter of Mr. David BAYLOR, all of Augusta county.
Rockingham Register, 15 July 1869 (Thursday), p. 3, c. 3.

McDANIEL: See entry for WEAVER.

McDANIEL: On the 23rd of December, by Rev. Wm. J. Miller, Calvin McDANIEL, of Page county, and Miss Nancy E. SMITH, of Rockingham county.
Rockingham Register, 7 January 1869 (Thursday), p. 3, c. 3.

McDANIEL: On the 24th of February, by Elder C. Allemong, James McDANIEL, of Rockingham, and Miss Sarah A. SHIFFLETT, of Greene.
Rockingham Register and Advertiser, 4 April 1867 (Thursday), p. 3, c. 4.

McDANNA: On the 6th inst., by Rev. George A. Shuey, Samuel McDANNA and Miss Sarah C. STANTON, all of Augusta county.
Rockingham Register and Advertiser, 13 December 1866 (Thursday), p. 2, c. 5.

McDANNALD: On the 15th of May, by Rev. Samuel Brown, at the house of Mr. Andrew Bratton, Mr. George W. McDANNALD to Miss Rebecca A. BRATTON, all of Bath county.
Rockingham Register and Virginia Advertiser, 13 June 1856 (Friday), p. 2, c. 2.

McDONALD: On the 10th inst., at St. Paul's Church, Richmond, Va., by the Rev. William H. Kinckle, Mr. Jas. McDONALD, former editor of the Lynchburg Virginian, and at present associate editor of the Richmond Whig, and Mrs. Carrie M. SAUNDERS, daughter of the late Lewis LUDLAM, of Richmond.

Rockingham *Register* and *Advertiser*, 25
November 1859 (Friday), p. 2, c. 4.

McDORMAN: See entry for HOLLEN.

McDORMAN: See entry for SHERFEY.

McDORMAN: On Thursday, the 18th of September,
by Rev. Jacob Miller, Mr. Samuel McDORMAN
and Miss Nancy Catharine SMITH, all of
Rockingham.
Rockingham *Register* and *Virginia*
Advertiser, 26 September 1862 (Friday),
p. 2, c. 2.

McDOWELL: See entry for HAWKINS.

McDOWELL: See entry for MILLER.

McDOWELL: See entry for Ross.

McELWEE: See entry for ARBOGAST.

McELWEE: See entry for KERR.

McFALL: See entry for HARSHA.

McFALL: On the 23rd of January, by Rev. J.M.
Fallansbee, J.A. McFALL and Miss Radie M.
HARMON, both of Augusta county.
Rockingham *Register*, 10 February 1870
(Thursday), p. 2, c. 5.

McFARLAND: See entry for WALTON.

McFARLAND: On the 14th inst., at the
residence of the bride's father, Jas. W.
LONG, near Burke's Mill, Augusta county,
by Rev. G.W. Stevenson, Eli N. McFARLAND,
of Independence, Missouri, and Miss
Maggie M. LONG, of Augusta county.
Rockingham *Register* and *Advertiser*, 16
May 1867 (Thursday), p. 2, c. 5.

McFARLAND: Near Strasburg, on the 10th inst.,
by Rev. W. Rusmisell, James McFARLAND and
Miss Barbara BLY, all of Shenandoah
county.
Rockingham *Register* and *Advertiser*, 31
October 1867 (Thursday), p. 2, c. 6.

McFARLAND: On the 3rd of August, by Rev. J.P.
Cline, Mr. W.L. McFARLAND and Mrs. Anna
E. HARTIGAL, all of Shenandoah county.
Rockingham *Register* & *Advertiser*, 6
October 1865 (Friday), p. 2, c. 2.

McGAHEY: See entry for LITTELL.

McGEE: See entry for NEWHAM.

McGEE: On the 26th inst., at the residence of
the bride's father, by Rev. Thos. U.

Dudley, Wm. G. McGEE, of Bedford county, and Miss Annie M., daughter of Nelson SPRINKEL, Esq., of Harrisonburg.
Rockingham Register and Advertiser, 28 November 1867 (Thursday), p. 2, c. 6.

McGILVARAY: See entry for ROBINSON.

McGILVRAY: See entry for BUMGARDNER.

McGILVRAY: See entry for FITCH.

McGINTY: On the 18th of June, by Rev. R.C. Walker, Robert A. McGINTY and Miss M. Jennie JONES, all of Augusta county.
Rockingham Register, 2 July 1868 (Thursday), p. 2, c. 4.

McGLAUCHLIN: See entry for STERLING.

McGLAUGHLIN: On the 13th of May, at Marlin Bottom, by Rev. Mr. Sixeas, Andrew McGLAUGHLIN and Miss Mary PRICE, all of Pocahontas county, W.Va.
Rockingham Register and Advertiser, 11 July 1867 (Thursday), p. 2, c. 6.

McGUFFEY: At the University of Virginia, on Tuesday, the 2nd inst., by the Rev. R.K. Meade, Rev. Wm. H. McGUFFEY, Professor of Moral Philosophy in the University, to Laura P., daughter of Professor Henry HOWARD.
Rockingham Register and Valley Advertiser, 13 September 1851 (Saturday), p. 2, c. 7.

McGUFFIN: See entry for TRIBBET.

McGUFFIN: October 12th, by Rev. Harvey Gilmore, A.G. McGUFFIN, of Warm Springs, and Miss V.C., daughter of David CLEMMER, of Augusta county.
Rockingham Register, 28 October 1869 (Thursday), p. 2, c. 3.

McGUFFIN: On Tuesday morning, the 18th inst., by the Rev. J.R. Wilson, Mr. David C. McGUFFIN and Miss Susan M. WILSON, all of Staunton.
Rockingham Register and Virginia Advertiser, 21 December 1855 (Friday), p. 2, c. 8.

McGUIRE: On the 19th ult., by the Rev. Jas. A. Latane, J. McGUIRE, of Washington city, and Miss Anna, daughter of Alfred

CHAPMAN, Esq., of Staunton.

Rockingham Register and Advertiser, 3 January 1867 (Thursday), p. 3, c. 3.

McILWEE: See entry for LAFOLLETTE.

McINTOSH: See entry for HUSER.

McINTURFF: See entry for GOLLIDAY.

McINTURFF: On the 29th of November, by Rev. G.H. Martin, Mr. Henry C. McINTURFF and Mrs. Maria LINEWEAVER, all of Shenandoah county.

Rockingham Register and Advertiser, 13 December 1866 (Thursday), p. 2, c. 5.

McINTURFF: On the 17th inst., by Rev. J.M. CLYMER, Joseph B. McINTURFF and Miss Ellen O. KOONTZ, all of Shenandoah.

Rockingham Register and Advertiser, 31 October 1867 (Thursday), p. 2, c. 6.

McINTYRE: At the residence of Mr. A.H. Campbell, in Smythe county, on Thursday night last, by the Rev. Miles Foy, Mr. John W. McINTYRE and Miss Cavie SLATER, formerly of Harrisonburg, Va.

Rockingham Register and Advertiser, 14 October 1859 (Friday), p. 2, c. 3.

McKAY: See entry for TRIPLETT.

McKEEVER: See entry for DINGES.

McKELVEY: See entry for BROOKS.

McKEY: See entry for HELBERT.

McKIM: On Thursday, the 25th of February, at Trinity Church, by Rev. F.H. PHILIPS, assisted by Rev. Mr. Latane, Lt. Randolph H. McKIM, of Baltimore, and Miss Agnes Gray, daughter of Rev. F.H. PHILIPS, of Staunton, Va.

The Rockingham Register, 6 March 1863 (Friday), p. 2, c. 4.

McKUSICK: See entry for CONRAD.

McLAUGHLIN: See entry for AYERS.

McLAUGHLIN: See entry for GRAY.

McLAUGHLIN: On the 25th October, by Rev. Jacob Thomas, Joseph E. McLAUGHLIN and Miss Lydia M.S., daughter of Jacob SIMMERS, all of Rockingham.

Rockingham Register and Advertiser, 8 November 1866 (Thursday), p. 3, c. 4.

McLEOD: See entry for BYRD.

285

McLEOD: See entry for MEDBURY.

McLEOD: See entry for SMITH.

McLEOD: On the 10th inst., near Parnassus, Augusta county, Va., by Rev. R.C. Walker, James P. McLEOD, of Rockingham, and Miss M. Ella, daughter of the late Enos SILLING, of Augusta county.
Rockingham Register, 17 September 1868 (Thursday), p. 2, c. 5.

McLOUD: See entry for McMULLIN.

McLOUD: On Sunday, the 31st of July, by Rev. Jacob Miller, Mr. John McLOUD and Miss Frances, daughter of Jesse T. CROPPER, all of Rockingham county.
Rockingham Register and Advertiser, 19 August 1859 (Friday), p. 2, c. 5.

McMAHON: See entry for CLEARY.

McMAHON: See entry for WALL.

McMULLAN: See entry for HOUSEWORTH.

McMULLAN: See entry for MALONE.

McMULLEN: See entry for ROGERS.

McMULLEN: See entry for WHETSEL.

McMULLEN: See entry for ZIRKLE.

McMULLIN: See entry for BEERY.

McMULLIN: On Tuesday, the 4th of October, by Rev. Benj. Bowman, Mr. John H. McMULLIN and Miss Mattie J., daughter of John McLOUD, dec'd, all of Rockingham county.
Rockingham Register and Advertiser, 14 October 1859 (Friday), p. 2, c. 3.

MacMURDO: See entry for RIVES.

McNEAL: On the 20th ult., by Rev. Henry St. J. Rinker, Mr. James McNEAL and Miss Caroline LUTZ, all of Shenandoah county.
Rockingham Register and Advertiser, 5 October 1860 (Friday), p. 2, c. 3.

McNEAL: On the 9th inst., by Rev. J.P. Cline, James McNEAL and Catharine ZIRKLE.
Rockingham Register and Advertiser, 17 February 1865 (Friday), p. 2, c. 4.

McNEIL: See entry for FOGLE.

McNEILL: On Monday evening, September 14th, in Alleghany county, Md., by Rev. Mr. Wilson, Capt. Jesse C. McNEILL, C.S.A., and Miss Sarah Elizabeth, daughter of R.B. SHERRARD, Esq., all of Hardy county

. . . .
Rockingham <u>Register</u> & <u>Advertiser</u>, 10
November 1865 (Friday), p. 2, c. 4.

McNETT: See entry for NICHOLAS.

McNETT: On Sunday, the 22nd of January, by
Rev. Jacob Miller, Mr. Joseph M. McNETT
and Miss Elizabeth Susan, daughter of Mr.
John BERRY, all of Rockingham.
Rockingham <u>Register</u> and <u>Advertiser</u>, 27
January 1860 (Friday), p. 2, c. 6.

McNUTT: On the 4th inst., at St. Francis
Church, by Rev. Father Weed, John A.
McNUTT and Miss Maria M. McCLEARY, all of
Staunton.
Rockingham <u>Register</u>, 13 May 1869
(Thursday), p. 3, c. 3.

McPHAIL: See entry for IMBODEN.

McPHEETERS: February 5th, at the residence of
the bride's father, by Rev. T.L. Preston,
Robert P. McPHEETERS to Miss Mary M.P.
SPECK, all of Augusta.
Rockingham <u>Register</u> and <u>Advertiser</u>, 13
February 1868 (Thursday), p. 2, c. 5.

McPHERSON: See entry for HARRIS.

McPHERSON: On the 12th inst., by Rev. P.C.
HOGE, Dr. John H. McPHERSON, of
Lewisburg, son of Col. Joel McPHERSON,
Clerk of Greenbrier county, to Miss Mary
Jane, daughter of the officiating
clergyman.
Rockingham <u>Register</u> and <u>Advertiser</u>, 21
June 1861 (Friday), p. 3, c. 3.

McQUAIDE: See entry for WALL.

McWAY: On the 2nd inst., by Rev. H. St. J.
Rinker, Mr. A.J. McWAY and Miss Delilah
ANDRICK, all of Shenandoah county.
The Rockingham <u>Register</u>, 13 May 1864
(Friday), p. 2, c. 5.

- M -

MACKEY: See entry for CRAWFORD.

MADDOX: See entry for SIMPSON.

MADDUX: At the Yarborough House, in Raleigh,
on Saturday morning, the 29th inst., by
Rev. J.A.M. Atkinson, Dr. T. Clay MADDUX

to Miss Bettie F. HILL, both of Virginia.
The Rockingham Register, 11 September
1863 (Friday), p. 2, c. 3.

MADISON: On the 26th ult., by Rev. W.T.
Richardson, Mr. Wm. MADISON and Miss
Elizabeth MOONEY.
Rockingham Register and Advertiser, 24
February 1860 (Friday), p. 2, c. 4.

MAGANN: On the 18th of January, near
Waynesboro, by Rev. C. Beard, W.H. MAGANN
and Miss Mollie E. BLACKWELL, both of
Augusta.
Rockingham Register, 10 February 1870
(Thursday), p. 2, c. 5.

MAGGARD: See entry for WOOD.

MAGRUDER: See entry for HISEY.

MAGRUDER: See entry for WARREN.

MAGRUDER: On the 9th inst., by Rev. Dr. Boyd,
Dr. Geo. W. MAGRUDER, of Woodstock, and
Miss Kate B., daughter of the late
Humphrey B. POWELL, of Loudoun county.
Rockingham Register and Advertiser, 31
January 1862 (Friday), p. 2, c. 7.

MAGRUDER: On the 10th inst., by Rev. J.E.
Armstrong, John William MAGRUDER and Miss
Mary Lou, daughter of Wm. DONALDSON,
Esq., all of Woodstock, Va.
Rockingham Register, 17 December 1868
(Thursday), p. 3, c. 2.

MAGSON: On Thursday, the 3rd inst., at
Neffstown, near Winchester, by Rev. W.G.
Eggleston, John M. MAGSON and Miss Hannah
Ellen GROVE, all of Frederick county.
Rockingham Register & Advertiser, 25
August 1865 (Friday), p. 3, c. 3.

MAHON: On the 3rd of May, in Staunton, by
Rev. Father Weed, J.J. MAHON and Miss
Julia F., youngest daughter of Mathias
SCHMITT, all of Staunton.
Rockingham Register, 19 May 1870
(Thursday), p. 3, c. 4.

MAHONE: On the 21st inst., near Linville, by
Rev. A. Poe Boude, Silfon J. MAHONE and
Miss Mary BRYANT, all of Rockingham
county.
Rockingham Register and Advertiser, 28

November 1867 (Thursday), p. 2, c. 6.

MAHONEY: At the residence of James C. Riley, on the 10th inst., by Rev. J.L. Clark, John T. MAHONEY and Miss Sarah M. RILEY, all of Augusta county.
Rockingham Register and Advertiser, 17 October 1867 (Thursday), p. 3, c. 3.

MAIDEN: See entry for WEAVER.

MALLOW: On the 6th inst., on South River, in Pendleton county, by Rev. J.H. Temple, at the residence of the bride's mother, Mrs. Jane DYER, Mr. George M. MALLOW and Miss Sarah M. DYER.
Rockingham Register and Advertiser, 21 February 1862 (Friday), p. 3, c. 2.

MALONE: October 26, at the residence of the bride's father, at McMullan's Mill, Greene county, Va., by the Rev. Mr. Moss, John W. MALONE and Miss Caroline, daughter of Neal McMULLAN.
Rockingham Register & Advertiser, 8 December 1865 (Friday), p. 2, c. 4.

MANLEY: See entry for WEST.

MANN: On the 24th ult., by Rev. Samuel Brown, Mr. Wm. A. MANN, proprietor of the Rockbridge Baths, and Miss M.A., daughter of Capt. Jno. P. PORTER, of Bath.
Rockingham Register and Advertiser, 2 November 1860 (Friday), p. 2, c. 5.

MANNING: See entry for JOHNSON.

MANNING: At Belmont Hall, the residence of the bride's father, on Wednesday evening, the 4th inst., by Rev. Dr. Sparrow, Miss Minnie E., second daughter of J.N. COWAN, of Rockingham county, to Private Charles J. MANNING, Co. B, 12th Va. Cavalry, of Jefferson county, Va.
The Rockingham Register, 13 May 1864 (Friday), p. 2, c. 5.

MANNING: At Belmont, the residence of the bride's father, on the morning of the 15th inst., by Rev. T.U. Dudley, Frank L. MANNING, of Jefferson county, West Virginia, and Miss Laura Antoinette, daughter of J.N. COWAN, Esq., of Rockingham county.

<u>Rockingham</u> <u>Register</u> <u>and</u> <u>Advertiser</u>, 23
January 1868 (Thursday), p. 2, c. 4.

MANUEL: See entry for MILLER.

MANUEL: On the 16th ult., at New Town
Stephensburg, by Rev. John W. Wolfe, J.W.
MANUEL and Mrs. Anna S. BUCHER, both of
Frederick county, Va.

<u>Rockingham</u> <u>Register</u>, 13 January 1870
(Thursday), p. 3, c. 4.

MAPHIS: See entry for HOLTZMAN.

MAPHIS: See entry for HURD.

MAPHIS: See entry for NEWLAND.

MAPHIS: See entry for RICKARD.

MAPHIS: See entry for RUBY.

MAPHIS: See entry for SAUM.

MAPHIS: See entry for SHADWELL.

MAPHIS: See entry for WILSON.

MAPHIS: See entry for WISEMAN.

MAPHIS: On Monday last, by Rev. Solomon
Garber, John MAPHIS, of Shenandoah
county, and Mrs. Mary COFFMAN, of
Rockingham county.

<u>Rockingham</u> <u>Register</u>, 21 April 1870
(Thursday), p. 3, c. 3.

MAPHIS: On the 13th ult., by Elder John
Pirkey, P.W. MAPHIS and Miss L.C.,
daughter of Jas. RHODES, Esq., of
Saumsville, Shenandoah county, Va.

<u>Rockingham</u> <u>Register</u>, 12 November 1868
(Thursday), p. 3, c. 3.

MAPHIS: On the 4th inst., at the residence of
the bride's father, near Dayton, by Rev.
Thos. Hildebrand, Mr. Reuben MAPHIS, of
Shenandoah county, and Miss Phoebe Ann,
daughter of Mr. Nevil ROGERS, of
Rockingham.

<u>Rockingham</u> <u>Register</u> <u>and</u> <u>Advertiser</u>, 14
March 1862 (Friday), p. 3, c. 2.

MARION: See entry for CHILDRESS.

MARKWOOD: See entry for GEORGE.

MARKWOOD: On Tuesday evening, the 7th inst.,
by Rev. G.G. Brooke, Mr. Ben. F. MARKWOOD
and Miss Mary WILLIAMS, both of Staunton.

<u>Rockingham</u> <u>Register</u> <u>and</u> <u>Advertiser</u>, 17
February 1860 (Friday), p. 2, c. 4.

MARPLE: See entry for LANGE.

MARSH: Near Barterbrook, on the 3rd inst., by Rev. C.S.M. See, James W. MARSH and Miss Willie A. FREEMAN, all of Augusta county. Rockingham Register, 12 November 1868 (Thursday), p. 3, c. 3.

MARSHALL: See entry for HENSON.

MARSHALL: See entry for TAYLOR.

MARSHALL: In Berryville, on Tuesday morning, 16th inst., by Rev. Mr. Whittle, Edward C. MARSHALL, Jr., of Markham, Fauquier county, and Miss Virginia E., daughter of Dr. Sam'l TAYLOR, of the former place. Rockingham Register and Advertiser, 26 December 1856 (Friday), p. 2, c. 7.

MARSHALL: On the 1st day of March, by Elder Casper Allemong, William A. MARSHALL and Miss Frances C. HENSLEY, both of Rockingham county. The Rockingham Register, 11 March 1864 (Friday), p. 2, c. 6.

MARSHALL: On the 24th inst., at New Market, by Rev. L. Lenz, Mr. Wm. H. MARSHALL, of Shenandoah county, and Miss Sallie C. KEMP, of New Market. The Rockingham Register, 29 May 1863 (Friday), p. 2, c. 6.

MARSTEN: On the 16th of May, by the Rev. Levi Keller, Mr. Joseph MARSTEN and Miss Catharine GOOD, all of Shenandoah. Rockingham Register, 3 June 1869 (Thursday), p. 3, c. 2.

MARTIN: See entry for ARMSTRONG.

MARTIN: See entry for HARRISON.

MARTIN: See entry for PERRY.

MARTIN: In Honeyville, Page county, on the 14th inst., by Rev. S. Henkel, J.D. MARTIN and Miss Mary C. NAUMAN. Rockingham Register, 28 April 1870 (Thursday), p. 3, c. 3.

MARTIN: On Wednesday the 28th ult., by the Rev. A.A. Eskridge, the Rev. J.S. MARTIN, of the Baltimore Conference, to Miss Susan P., daughter of John RUFF, Esq., of Lexington. Rockingham Register, 10 March 1838 (Saturday), p. 3, c. 4.

MARTIN: On the 28th ult., by Rev. Mr. Petty, Jno. T. MARTIN and Miss A.A. FORSYTH, all of Warren county.
Rockingham Register and Advertiser, 12 December 1867 (Thursday), p. 3, c. 2.

MARTIN: At Barter Brook, Augusta county, March 28th, by the Rev. Wm. Richardson, Wm. MARTIN, Esq., Ass't Clerk, Va. House of Delegates, to Lizzie N., eldest daughter of Dr. T.W. SHELTON, o f Barter Brook.
Rockingham Register and Advertiser, 5 May 1865 (Friday), p. 2, c. 5.

MARTZ: See entry for ARMENTROUT.

MARTZ: See entry for FAWSET.

MARTZ: See entry for HYDECKER.

MARTZ: See entry for KOONTZ.

MARTZ: On Wednesday morning last, at the residence of the bride's father, by Rev. J.D. Coulling, Mr. D.H. Lee MARTZ, of Harrisonburg, and Miss Mary N., daughter of Robert CARTER, Esq., of Nelson county, Va.
Rockingham Register and Advertiser, 16 November 1860 (Friday), p. 2, c. 4.

MARTZ: On the 3rd of April, by Rev. Benjamin Bowman, Mr. Daniel G. MARTZ and Miss Lydia Ann SELLERS, all of Rockingham county.
Rockingham Register and Advertiser, 6 April 1860 (Friday), p. 2, c. 6.

MARTZ: On the 22nd ult., by Rev. G.W. Woods, Isaac P. MARTZ and Miss Amanda V. STRICKLER, all of Rockingham county.
Rockingham Register, 8 July 1869 (Thursday), p. 2, c. 5.

MARTZ: On the 12th of November, by Rev. Thomas Bryley, Micahel J. MARTZ and Miss Barbara C. HARRISON, all of Rockingham county.
Rockingham Register, 10 December 1868 (Thursday), p. 3, c. 3.

MASINCUP: Near Churchville, on the 14th inst., by Rev. A.A.P. Neel, David V. MASINCUP and Miss Mary M. FALL, all of Augusta county.

Rockingham <u>Register</u> and <u>Advertiser</u>, 21 November 1867 (Thursday), p. 2, c. 5.

MASON: At Christ's Church, Warm Springs, Va., by W.N. Pendleton, D.D., of Lexington, Rev. Richard H. MASON to Miss Isabella H. DANGERFIELD, both of Bath county, Va.

Rockingham <u>Register</u>, 7 May 1868 (Thursday), p. 2, c. 4.

MASSIE: At Fruit Hill, the residence of the bride's father, in Rockbridge county, on Tuesday morning, the 23rd ult., by Rev. Wm. F. Jenkin, Mr. Hope MASSIE, of Nelson county, and Miss Liora W., daughter of Mr. Madison H. EFFINGER.

The <u>Rockingham Register</u>, 4 March 1864 (Friday), p. 2, c. 6.

MASSIE: On the 3rd inst., by the Rev. Mr. Willis, Lieut. J.W. MASSIE, of Augusta county, to Miss Sarah UMBLES, of Lexington.

Rockingham <u>Register</u> and <u>Valley Advertiser</u>, 13 October 1849 (Saturday), p. 2, c. 5.

MASSIE: On the 17th inst., by Rev. H. Tallhelm, Thomas W. MASSIE, of Frederick, and Miss Jennie F. WHISSEN, of Shenandoah county.

Rockingham <u>Register</u> and <u>Advertiser</u>, 31 May 1866 (Thursday), p. 3, c. 5.

MASSINCUT: On the 31st ult., by Rev. Geo. A. Shuey, Mr. Wm. L. MASSINCUT to Miss Frances JOHNS, all of Augusta county.

Rockingham <u>Register</u> and <u>Advertiser</u>, 19 June 1857 (Friday), p. 3, c. 2.

MASTERS: See entry for MATHENEY.

MATHENEY: On December 9th, at Wintergreen, near Sherando, by Rev. J.N. Lockridge, Capt. Lafayette D. MATHENEY and Miss Martha C.D. MASTERS, all of Augusta.

Rockingham <u>Register</u>, 16 December 1869 (Thursday), p. 2, c. 5.

MATHENY: See entry for RAINES.

MATHIAS: Near Lost River, on the 10th inst., by Rev. S. Whitmer, Mr. Joseph MATHIAS and Miss Susan, daughter of Nathan MONGOLD, all of Hardy county, Va.

Rockingham Register and Virginia Advertiser, 18 July 1856 (Friday), p. 2, c. 8.

MATTHEWS: See entry for McCLINTIC.

MATTHIAS: On the 13th inst., by Rev. H. Wetzel, on Lost River, in Hardy county, West Virginia, John T. MATTHIAS and Miss Mary A. BOWMAN, both of Hardy county.
Rockingham Register, 24 March 1870 (Thursday), p. 3, c. 2.

MAUCK: See entry for ASHENFELTER.

MAUCK: See entry for HOTTINGER.

MAUCK: See entry for MILLER.

MAUCK: See entry for MYERS.

MAUCK: On Sunday morning, the 23rd of December, 1860, Mr. Daniel W. MAUCK and Miss Ann Rebecca, daughter of Mr. Jacob MAY, all of Rockingham county.
Rockingham Register and Advertiser, 28 December 1860 (Friday), p. 1, c. 5.

MAUCK: On the 4th inst., by Elder L.J. Compton, J.B. MAUCK and Miss Isabella FRISTOE, all of Warren county.
Rockingham Register, 25 November 1869 (Thursday), p. 2, c. 3.

MAUCK: On the 16th inst., by Rev. T.D. Bell, Lieut. Joseph W. MAUCK, of Co. H, 10th Regt., and Miss Fannie E., daughter of the late Benj. H. RALSTON, all of Rockingham.
The Rockingham Register, 21 August 1863 (Friday), p. 2, c. 3.

MAUCK: On Thursday evening, September 15, 1870, in this place, by Rev. J.S. Gardner, Samuel H. MAUCK and Miss Mattie E., daughter of John MESSERLEY, Esq., all of Harrisonburg.
Rockingham Register, 29 September 1870 (Thursday), p. 2, c. 5.

MAULEY: See entry for HOOVER.

MAUPIN: See entry for JOHNSON.

MAUPIN: See entry for PENNYBACKER.

MAUPIN: On the 23rd ult., by the Rev. J.N. Davis, Mr. J.S. MAUPIN and Miss Kate S., daughter of Waller ODER, Esq., all of Augusta county, Va.

Rockingham <u>Register</u> <u>and</u> <u>Advertiser</u>, 1
July 1859 (Friday), p. 2, c. 4.
MAUZY: See entry for BURTON.

MAUZY: See entry for YANCEY.

MAUZY: On Tuesday morning the 24th ult., by
Rev. J.C. Hensell, at the residence of
Capt. Ed. S. Yancey, Mr. Jos. J.N. MAUZY
and Miss Maggie J. YANCEY, all of
Rockingham county.
Rockingham <u>Register</u> & <u>Advertiser</u>, 3
November 1865 (Friday), p. 2, c. 2.
MAUZY: In Frederick City, Md., on the 6th
inst., by the Rev. D. Zachariah, Mr.
Joseph L. MAUZY, of Harper's-Ferry, Va.,
to Miss Catharine E. KELLER, of Frederick
county, Md.
Rockingham   <u>Register</u>   <u>and</u>   <u>Valley</u>
<u>Advertiser</u>, 17 October 1846 (Saturday),
p. 3, c. 1.
MAUZY: On Wednesday morning, the 27th ult.,
at the residence of the bride's parents,
near Harrisonburg, by Rev. John Cosby,
Thomas G. MAUZY and Miss Annabel,
daughter of Philip LIGGETT, all of
Rockingham county.
Rockingham <u>Register</u>, 11 November 1869
(Thursday), p. 3, c. 3.
MAUZY: On the 14th inst., by the Rev. John J.
Lafferty, Mr. W.G. MAUZY and Miss Fannie
R. RUSH, both of Rockingham.
Rockingham <u>Register</u> <u>and</u> <u>Advertiser</u>, 17
February 1860 (Friday), p. 2, c. 4.
MAY: See entry for BEARD.

MAY: See entry for CARTER.

MAY: See entry for CLARKE.

MAY: See entry for DOOLEY.

MAY: See entry for MAUCK.

MAY: See entry for PAULSEL.

MAY: See entry for ROBERTSON.

MAY: Near Cross Keys, on Thursday evening,
the 9th inst., by Rev. A.M. Evers, Mr.
Erasmus H. MAY and Miss Sarah C.,
daughter of Rev. G.W. REXRODE, all of
Rockingham county.
Rockingham <u>Register</u> & <u>Advertiser</u>, 15
November 1865 (Friday), p. 2, c. 4.

MAY: On the 4th inst., by the Rev. Jacob B. Houck, Mr. George MAY to Miss Priscilla LENTZE, both of this county.
Rockingham Register, 10 March 1838 (Saturday), p. 3, c. 4.

MAY: On the 21st ult., at the residence of the bride's father, in Staunton, by the Rev. Wm. E. Baker, Geo. W. MAY and Miss Kitty Lomax, daughter of Dr. Alex. WADDELL.
Rockingham Register, 6 January 1870 (Thursday), p. 3, c. 3.

MAY: On the 15th ult., by Rev. V.T. Settle, Mr. Harrison MAY and Miss Dorothy E. VANTER, all of Rockingham.
Rockingham Register and Advertiser, 2 March 1860 (Friday), p. 3, c. 2.

MAY: On the 31st of January, 1860, by the Rev. J.W. Howe, Rev. Moses MAY, of the Baltimore Conference, and Miss Margaret COLLEY, of Bath county.
Rockingham Register and Advertiser, 17 February 1860 (Friday), p. 2, c. 4.

MAYES: On the 20th ult., by Rev. J.W. Watson, Henry M. MAYES and Miss Sarah C., daughter of Abraham DOVAL, of Page.
Rockingham Register and Advertiser, 18 November 1859 (Friday), p. 2, c. 4.

MAYHEW: See entry for FLETCHER.

MAYSO: See entry for VAN LEAR.

MEADOWS: See entry for BREEDEN.

MEAN: On the 5th inst., by Rev. L. Keller, Nathan T. MEAN, of Rockingham, and Miss Susan M. SINE, of Shenandoah.
Rockingham Register and Advertiser, 19 March 1868 (Thursday), p. 2, c. 4.

MEDBURY: On the 28th of February, in Winchester, by Rev. Wm. F. Ward, John A. MEDBURY, of Keekonk, Mass., and Miss Clara J., daughter of Angus McLEOD, formerly of Liverpool, Nova Scotia.
Rockingham Register and Advertiser, 28 March 1867 (Thursday), p. 2, c. 6.

MEEK: See entry for CARSON.

MEEKS: See entry for FLOYD.

MEEM: See entry for PEACHY.

MEEM: In Lynchburg, on Monday evening, the
5th inst., by the Rev. Wm. H. Kincle,
Gen. Gilbert S. MEEM, of Shenandoah
county, and Nannie R., daughter of Hugh
A.   GARLAND,   dec'd,   formerly   of
Petersburg.
The Rockingham Register, 16 October 1863
(Friday), p. 2, c. 5.
MEGUIER: See entry for LIONBERGER.
MELHORN: See entry for HAMRICK.
MELHORN: See entry for SPINKS.
MELHORN: See entry for STEARNS.
MELHORN: On Tuesday last, by the Rev. T.
Hildebrand, Mr. John W. MELHORN and Miss
Fannie C., daughter of Mr. Jacob AMMON,
all of this county.
Rockingham Register and Advertiser, 15
February 1861 (Friday), p. 2, c. 7.
MELHORN: On the 24th of December, by Rev.
Levi Keller, Joseph B. MELHORN and Miss
Emma FELLER, all of Shenandoah county.
Rockingham Register, 14 January 1869
(Thursday), p. 3, c. 3.
MELLONEE: On the 23rd ult., by Rev. Wm. A.
Whitescarver, Geo. W. MELLONEE, of
Grafton, W.Va., and Miss C. Annie E.
CREEL, of Pruntytown, W.Va.
Rockingham Register, 7 April 1870
(Thursday), p. 2, c. 5.
MERICA: See entry for TURNER.
MERRITT: On Thursday evening, November 4th,
at the residence of the bride's father,
the Hon. James S. GREEN, by Rev. Bishop
E.M. Marvin, John W. MERRITT, of
Staunton, Va., and Miss Sue E. GREEN, of
St. Louis, Mo.
Rockingham Register, 2 December 1869
(Thursday), p. 2, c. 3.
MESMER: See entry for NOTT.
MESSERLEY: See entry for MAUCK.
MESSERLY: See entry for LANDES.
MESSERLY: By Rev. Joseph Early, on the 26th
of May, Mr. Wm. MESSERLY and Miss Lucy
Margaret, daughter of Jacob DINKLE, all
of Mt. Crawford.
Rockingham Register and Advertiser, 5

July 1861 (Friday), p. 3, c. 3.
MESSERLY: On the 28th ult., at Hill's Hotel,
Harrisonburg, Va., by Rev. T.D. Bell, Mr.
William S. MESSERLY and Miss Elizabeth
FAUBUSH, both of Mt. Crawford.
Rockingham Register and Advertiser, 12
January 1866 (Friday), p. 1, c. 3.
MESSERSMITH: See entry for COMPTON.
MESSERSMITH: See entry for CRAWFORD.
MESSERSMITH: See entry for FLOYD.
MESSERSMITH: See entry for HUGHES.
MESSICK: See entry for COFFMAN.
MESSICK: On Thursday of last week, the 11th
inst., by the Rev. Mr. Boyd, Mr. Gessner
MESSICK and Miss Margaret, daughter of
Mr. William RODGERS, all of this county.
Rockingham Register, 20 February
(Saturday), p. 3, c. 2.
MEYERHOEFFER: See entry for BEGONE.
MEYERHOEFFER: See engry for BEGOON.
MICHAEL: See entry for EARLY.
MICHAEL: See entry for FRYE.
MICHAEL: See entry for MICHAEL.
MICHAEL: See entry for SAMPSON.
MICHAEL: See entry for SOWERS.
MICHAEL: On Thursday, the 25th of June, in
McGaheysville, by Rev. J.C. Hensel,
Richard D. MICHAEL and Miss Martha J.,
daughter of Abraham MICHAEL, all of
Rockingham county.
Rockingham Register, 2 July 1868
(Thursday), p. 2, c. 4.
MICHAEL: On the 1st day of March, by Rev.
Isaac Long, Wm. F. MICHAEL and Miss
Frances C., daughter of Geo. BERRY, all
of Rockingham county.
Rockingham Register and Advertiser, 23
March 1866 (Friday), p. 3, c. 3.
MICHAELS: See entry for FRY.
MICHAELS: On Thursday, the 20th ult., by Rev.
J.C. Hensel, Wm. H. MICHAELS and Miss
Mary F. PENCE, all of Rockingham county.
Rockingham Register and Advertiser, 4
October 1866 (Thursday), p. 2, c. 5.
MICHIE: See entry for MICHIE.
MICHIE: On the 3rd inst., at Rockland,

Loudoun county, Va., by Rev. E.T.
Perkins, Henry B. MICHIE, of Staunton,
and Miss Virginia, only daughter of the
late Henry BEDINGER.
Rockingham Register and Advertiser, 18
October 1866 (Thursday), p. 2, c. 4.

MICHIE: At Belle Air, on the 24th ult., by
the Rev. Mr. Slack, Mr. Octavius G.
MICHIE to Miss Sarah A.M., daughter of
Capt. James MICHIE, all of Albemarle.
Rockingham Register and Valley
Advertiser, 4 November 1848 (Saturday),
p. 3, c. 2.

MILBUN: On the 28th ult., Wm. H. MILBUN and
Miss M. BARROW, of Frederick county, Va.
Rockingham Register and Advertiser, 23
March 1866 (Friday), p. 3, c. 3.

MILEER: On the 9th inst., by Rev. Jacob
Stirewalt, Noah MILEER and Miss Elizabeth
Ann MILLER, all of Shenandoah.
Rockingham Register and Advertiser, 20
September 1866 (Thursday), p. 3, c. 4.

MILEY: See entry for RIDDLEBERGER.

MILEY: See entry for SWAN.

MILLEE: On the 2nd inst., in Baltimore,
Maryland, by Rev. Dr. McCron, Rev. J.J.
MILLEE, pastor-elect of Shepherdstown,
Va., and Miss Lida HULLS, of Baltimore.
Rockingham Register and Advertiser, 12
October 1860 (Friday), p. 2, c. 4.

MILLER: See entry for ARMENTROUT.

MILLER: See entry for BRUBAKER.

MILLER: See entry for CARPENTER.

MILLER: See entry for CHANDLER.

MILLER: See entry for CLINE (2).

MILLER: See entry for COAKLEY.

MILLER: See entry for CRAWFORD (2).

MILLER: See entry for DINGLEDINE (2).

MILLER: See entry for FOLTZ.

MILLER: See entry for GARBER.

MILLER: See entry for GROVE.

MILLER: See entry for HAMMAN.

MILLER: See entry for HANDY.

MILLER: See entry for HAUSENFLUCK.

MILLER: See entry for HENKEL.

MILLER: See entry for HEPNER.

MILLER: See entry for HODGES.
MILLER: See entry for HOLLEN.
MILLER: See entry for HOWE.
MILLER: See entry for HUTCHINSON.
MILLER: See entry for KEYSER.
MILLER: See entry for KISLING.
MILLER: See entry for KNIPPLE.
MILLER: See entry for LONG.
MILLER: See entry for McCULLOCK.
MILLER: See entry for MILEER.
MILLER: See entry for MILLER.
MILLER: See entry for NISWANDER.
MILLER: See entry for OREBAUGH.
MILLER: See entry for PENCE.
MILLER: See entry for PENNYWITT.
MILLER: See entry for PHILLIPS.
MILLER: See entry for RHODES.
MILLER: See entry for RIMEL.
MILLER: See entry for RIPPETOE.
MILLER: See entry for RITENOUR.
MILLER: See entry for ROYSTON.
MILLER: See entry for RYMAN.
MILLER: See entry for SAUM.
MILLER: See entry for SHICKEL.
MILLER: See entry for SHOEMAKER.
MILLER: See entry for SNELL.
MILLER: See entry for STRICKLER.
MILLER: See entry for VARNER.
MILLER: See entry for WAMPLER.
MILLER: See entry for WILL.
MILLER: See entry for WILLS.
MILLER: See entry for WRIGHT.
MILLER: On the 23rd of October, by Rev. Solomon Garber, Andrew Davidson MILLER, of Augusta, and Mrs. Elizabeth BROWN, of Rockingham county.
Rockingham Register, 27 October 1870 (Thursday), p. 2, c. 4.
MILLER: On the 25th ult., by Rev. J.W. Watson, Mr. Andrew J. MILLER and Miss Susan C., daughter of Samuel COMER.
Rockingham Register and Advertiser, 9 November 1860 (Friday), p. 2, c. 6.
MILLER: On the 9th of August, by the Rev. W.W. Trimble, Mr. Benj. MILLER and Mary Susan, daughter of David SENSEBAUGH, all

300

of Rockbridge county.

Rockingham Register and Advertiser, 25 October 1866 (Thursday), p. 3, c. 3.

MILLER: At the residence of Sam'l S. Miller, near Bridgewater, on Sunday, the 19th inst., by Rev. Solomon Garber, Benjamin F. MILLER and Miss Susan F., daughter of Wm. R. LONG, all of Rockingham county.

Rockingham Register, 23 July 1868 (Thursday), p. 3, c. 4.

MILLER: On the 30th of December, by Rev. J.A. Bovey, at the residence of the bride's mother, Mr. Brown MILLER and Miss Sarah A. BILLHIMER, all of Rockingham.

Rockingham Register and Advertiser, 7 January 1859 (Friday), p. 3, c. 1.

MILLER: On the 15th inst., by Rev. Gleason, Corporal Charles B. MILLER, of Company G, 10th Va. Infantry, and Miss Sallie E. PURVIES, of Nelson county, Va.

The Rockingham Register, 26 February 1864 (Friday), p. 2, c. 4.

MILLER: On Monday last, April 8, 1861, by Rev. S.S. Lambeth, Mr. Chas. L. MILLER and Miss Emma L. SLATER, all of Harrisonburg.

Rockingham Register and Advertiser, 12 April 1861 (Friday), p. 2, c. 4.

MILLER: On the 24th of November, at the residence of Mrs. Elizabeth SNYDER, the bride's mother, near Ottobine, by Rev. George Wine, Christian C. MILLER and Miss Fannie F. SNYDER, all of Rockingham.

Rockingham Register, 1 December 1870 (Thursday), p. 2, c. 4. Repeated, 8 December 1870 (Thursday), p. 2, c. 4.

MILLER: On Sunday morning, October 18th, in Brock's Gap, by Rev. Jacob Miller, Daniel MILLER and Miss Doreatha ROADCAP, all of Rockingham.

Rockingham Register, 22 October 1868 (Thursday), p. 3, c. 3. Repeated, 5 November 1868 (Thursday), p. 3. c. 3.

MILLER: On Sunday, the 7th of June, by Rev. Joseph Early, Mr. David MILLER and Miss Amanda, daughter of Mr. Henry

HINEGARDNER, all of Rockingham county. The Rockingham Register, 12 June 1863 (Friday), p. 2, c. 6.

MILLER: On Wednesday, September 25th, at Port Republic, by Rev. A. Poe Boude, David F. MILLER and Miss Salina H., daughter of Geo. W. EUTZLER, all of Rockingham. Rockingham Register and Advertiser, 3 October 1867 (Thursday), p. 2, c. 6.

MILLER: October 23rd, by Rev. D.A. Long, David R. MILLER and Miss Sarah M. HOPKINS, all of Rockingham. Rockingham Register, 18 November 1869 (Thursday), p. 3, c. 2.

MILLER: On the 31st ult., by Rev. H. St. J. Rinker, Capt. Ed. T. MILLER and Miss Hattie HAMMOND, all of Orkney Springs, Shenandoah county. Rockingham Register and Advertiser, 7 April 1865 (Friday), p. 2, c. 5. Repeated, 14 April 1865 (Friday), p. 2, c. 5. [See MILLER-HAMMON entry, Rockingham Register and Advertiser, 21 April 1865 (Friday), p. 2, c. 5.]

MILLER: At Sunny Side, Shenandoah county, Va., the residence of Capt. William Miller, on the 30th of March, by Rev. H. St. John Rinker, Miss Hattie M. HAMMON, of Delaware, and Lt. Edward T. MILLER, formerly of Alexandria, Va. Rockingham Register and Advertiser, 21 April 1865 (Friday), p. 2, c. 5.

MILLER: On Thursday, the 19th inst., by Rev. Isaac Long, George MILLER and Miss Sallie A. WHITMER, all of Rockingham. Rockingham Register and Advertiser, 27 April 1866 (Friday), p. 2, c. 2.

MILLER: On the 6th inst., by Rev. T.D. Bell, Mr. Geo. H. MILLER and Miss Catharine C., daughter of Mr. Tandy DOVEL, all of Rockingham county. Rockingham Register and Advertiser, 14 October 1859 (Friday), p. 2, c. 3.

MILLER: On the 9th inst., by Rev. Daniel Thomas, Mr. Henry MILLER and Miss Hannah J., daughter of Mr. Martin SNYDER, all of

Rockingham county.

Rockingham Register and Advertiser, 21 October 1859 (Friday), p. 2, c. 5.

MILLER: On Thursday, the 27th of September, by Rev. Daniel Thomas, Mr. Henry MILLER and Miss Sarah, daughter of Robt. WRIGHT, all of Rockingham.

Rockingham Register and Advertiser, 19 October 1860 (Friday), p. 2, c. 4.

MILLER: On the 13th inst., by the Rev. Isaac Long, Isaac N. MILLER and Miss Mary Margaret, daughter of Alexander KYGER, all of Rockingham.

Rockingham Register and Advertiser, 20 February 1868 (Thursday), p. 2, c. 6.

MILLER: On the 28th of May, at the residence of the bride's father, by Rev. J.W. Watson, J.G.H. MILLER, of East Rockingham, and Miss Sallie P., daughter of Jacob BRUBAKER, of Page county, Va.

Rockingham Register, 18 June 1868 (Thursday), p. 3, c. 5.

MILLER: On the 23rd ult., by Rev. Jacob Wine, Jacob MILLER and Miss Mary SPITLER, all of Shenandoah county.

Rockingham Register, 7 July 1870 (Thursday), p. 3, c. 3.

MILLER: On the 2nd inst., by Rev. H. Shaull, Jeremiah MILLER and Miss Nancy Ann MINNICK, all of Shenandoah.

Rockingham Register and Advertiser, 16 January 1868 (Thursday), p. 2, c. 5.

MILLER: At Col Alto, near Lexington, by the Rev. Wm. S. White, D.D., on the 3rd inst., Rev. John MILLER, of Philadelphia, to Mrs. Sallie C.P. McDOWELL.

Rockingham Register and Advertiser, 14 November 1856 (Friday), p. 2, c. 6.

MILLER: On the 11th inst., by Elder Geo. Shaver, Mr. Jno. MILLER, of Strasburg, and Miss Lucy SPIKER, of Maurertown, Shenandoah county.

Rockingham Register and Advertiser, 28 July 1865 (Friday), p. 2, c. 6.

MILLER: On the 4th inst., by Rev. Jacob Thomas, John M. MILLER and Miss Anna

COFFMAN, all of Rockingham county.
Rockingham Register and Advertiser, 18 October 1866 (Thursday), p. 2, c. 4.

MILLER: On the 23rd ult., by Rev. I. Condor, John M. MILLER and Miss Eliza C. MANUEL.
Rockingham Register, 7 April 1870 (Thursday), p. 2, c. 5.

MILLER: On the 15th inst., by Rev. P.H. Whisner, John P. MILLER and Miss Mary A. BAGGS, all of Rockbridge.
Rockingham Register and Advertiser, 31 October 1867 (Thursday), p. 2, c. 6.

MILLER: On the 23rd of May, by Rev. J.W. Howe, Mr. John W. MILLER and Miss Amanda J. LANDSMAN, all of Rockingham.
Rockingham Register and Advertiser, 14 June 1861 (Friday), p. 3, c. 3.

MILLER: On the 6th inst., by Rev. J.E. Armstrong, John W. MILLER and Miss S. Virginia, daughter of Capt. R.C. MAUCK, dec'd, of Harrisonburg.
Rockingham Register and Advertiser, 13 September 1866 (Thursday), p. 2, c. 5.

MILLER: On Tuesday evening last, at Rawley Springs, by Rev. P.F. August, Joseph MILLER and Miss Louisa, daughter of John SITES, dec'd, all of Rockingham.
Rockingham Register and Advertiser, 8 November 1866 (Thursday), p. 3, c. 4.

MILLER: On the 24th ult., by Rev. J.A. Snyder, Lewis M. MILLER, of Winchester, and Miss Mary Ellen, daughter of Rev. J.P. CLINE, of Shenandoah county.
Rockingham Register and Advertiser, 7 June 1866 (Thursday), p. 3, c. 3.

MILLER: In Trinity Church, Staunton, on Thursday evening, December the 15th, by Rev. J.A. Latane, M. Erskine MILLER, of Huntsville, Alabama, and Miss Harriette, daughter of General John ECHOLS, of Staunton.
Rockingham Register, 22 December 1870 (Thursday), p. 2, c. 4.

MILLER: On Tuesday last, by the Rev. James W. Phillips, Mr. Matthew MILLER, of Mount Crawford, to Miss Jennetta, daughter of

Mr. Daniel RAGAN, of this place.
Rockingham Register, 10 March 1838 (Saturday), p. 3, c. 4.

MILLER: On the 18th ult., by Rev. J.S. Bennick, Paul MILLER and Miss Delilah SOURS, all of Page county.
Rockingham Register and Advertiser, 2 May 1867 (Thursday), p. 2, c. 6.

MILLER: On the 17th of December, by Rev. Joseph Holcomb, in front of his residence, on horseback, Peachy MILLER and Miss Lydia GRANDELL, all of Rockingham.
Rockingham Register, 7 January 1869 (Thursday), p. 3, c. 3.

MILLER: On the 26th of December, 1867, by Rev. Jacob Miller, Peter A. MILLER and Miss Nancy, daughter of John TAYLOR, all of Rockingham county.
Rockingham Register and Advertiser, 9 January 1868 (Thursday), p. 2, c. 4.

MILLER: On Thursday, the 6th inst., by the Rev. Daniel Garber, Mr. Samuel MILLER to Miss Catharine, daughter of Mr. Abraham CLICK, all of Rockingham county.
Rockingham Register, 22 April 1837 (Saturday), p. 3, c. 3.

MILLER: On Thursday, the 21st of December, by Rev. Daniel Thomas, at the residence of the bride's father, Mr. Samuel MILLER and Miss Catharine, daughter of Mr. Michael WINE, all of Briery Branch, Rockingham county.
Rockingham Register and Advertiser, 12 January 1866 (Friday), p. 1, c. 3.

MILLER: On the 2nd inst., by Elder George Shaver, Mr. Samuel F. MILLER, of Augusta, and Miss Catharine HOCKMAN, of Shenandoah county.
Rockingham Register and Advertiser, 17 June 1859 (Friday), p. 3, c. 3.

MILLER: Near Fellowship, on Thursday, the 7th inst., by Rev. A. Poe Boude, Samuel S. MILLER and Miss Annie M. LONG, all of this county.
Rockingham Register and Advertiser, 14

June 1866 (Thursday), p. 3, c. 4.

MILLER: On the 7th inst., by Rev. Jacob Miller, Sam'l S. MILLER and Miss Catharine MYERS, all of Rockingham county.

Rockingham Register and Advertiser, 20 September 1866 (Thursday), p. 3, c. 4.

MILLER: On the 30th of November, in Harrisonburg, by Rev. B.F. Moomaw, Mr. Simon MILLER, aged 67 years, and Miss Hannah BAXTER, aged 60, all of Rockingham.

Rockingham Register & Advertiser, 8 December 1865 (Friday), p. 2, c. 4.

MILLER: On the 24th of December, by Rev. Jacob Miller, Thompson MILLER and Miss Sarah MILLER, all of Rockingham county.

Rockingham Register, 7 January 1869 (Thursday), p. 3, c. 3.

MILLER: On the 25th ult., at the residence of the bride's father, by Rev. A.P. Boude, V.H. MILLER and Miss Lizzie E., daughter of Geo. WHITESELL, Esq., all of Rockingham.

Rockingham Register, 3 February 1870 (Thursday), p. 3, c. 4.

MILLER: On the 20th inst., by Rev. J.M. Shreckhise, William MILLER and Miss Sarah E. COOK, all of Augusta county.

Rockingham Register and Advertiser, 27 September 1866 (Thursday), p. 3, c. 3.

MILLER: On September 2nd, by Rev. J.M. Schreckhise, William A. MILLER to Miss Rebecca A. SENSEBAUGH, all of Rockbridge.

Rockingham Register, 16 September 1869 (Thursday), p. 3, c. 3.

MILLER: On Thursday, April 4th, at the residence of the bride's father, Alex. BROWNLEE, by Rev. Mr. Pinkerton, Wm. C. MILLER and Miss Mary S. BROWNLEE, all of Augusta.

Rockingham Register and Advertiser, 25 April 1867 (Thursday), p. 2, c. 7.

MILLER: On the 1st inst., by Elder John Pirkey, Mr. William F. MILLER and Miss Eveline SPIKER, both of Shenandoah

county.

Rockingham Register and Advertiser, 17 June 1859 (Friday), p. 3, c. 3.

MILLER: On the 13th inst., by Rev. Jos. Funkhouser, Mr. Wm. H. MILLER to Miss Martha E. ARTZ, all of Shenandoah county. The Rockingham Register and Valley Advertiser, 22 November 1851 (Saturday), p. 3, c. 1.

MILLER: On the 4th ult., by Rev. Henry St. John Rinker, Wm. H. MILLER and Miss Mary F. LINDAMOOD, all of Shenandoah county. Rockingham Register and Advertiser, 2 May 1867 (Thursday), p. 2, c. 6.

MILLS: See entry for ATWOOD.

MILLS: See entry for BELL.

MILLS: On the 3rd inst., by Rev. John D. Miller, John D. MILLS and Miss L. Catharine, daughter of William MINNICK, all of Broadway, Rockingham county. Rockingham Register, 17 November 1870 (Thursday), p. 2, c. 3.

MILTON: Near Grove Hill, Page county, by Elder C. Allemong, on Thursday, the 27th day of February, 1862, Mr. John M. MILTON, a volunteer in Capt. Young's Company in the 10th Regiment of Va. Vols., and Miss Sarah A. KEYSER, of the county of Page. Rockingham Register and Advertiser, 14 March 1862 (Friday), p. 3, c. 2.

MINICH: See entry for STANELY.

MINNICH: On the 18th ult., by Rev. Wm. M. Dunlap, at the residence of Elizabeth Price, in this county, Mr. John M. MINNICH, aged 23, and Miss Mary PRICE, aged 34. Rockingham Register and Virginia Advertiser, 18 May 1855 (Friday), p. 3, c. 4.

MINNICK: See entry for BELL.

MINNICK: See entry for MILLER.

MINNICK: See entry for MILLS.

MINNICK: See entry for STANLEY.

MINNICK: On the 8th inst., by Rev. Isaac Soule, Edward H. MINNICK and Miss

Elizabeth J. GONGWER, all of this county.
Rockingham Register, 24 March 1870
(Thursday), p. 3, c. 2.
MINNICK: On the 4th of August, by Rev. Daniel
Thomas, Mr. Elisha MINNICK and Miss Mary,
daughter of John CLADEBUCK, all of
Rockingham county.
Rockingham Register and Advertiser, 2
September 1859 (Friday), p. 2, c. 5.
MINNICK: Near Plains' Mills, on Thursday the
4th of December, 1862, by Rev. J.P.
Cline, Samuel MINNICK and Miss Catharine
FRANK, all of Rockingham county.
The Rockingham Register, 19 December 1862
(Friday), p. 2, c. 4.
MINNICK: On the 27th of November, by Rev.
Christopher Kyger, Wm. MINNICK and Miss
_____ GUYEL.
Rockingham Register and Advertiser, 3
January 1867 (Thursday), p. 3, c. 3.
MINNICK: On Thursday the 29th of October, by
Rev. Isaac Soule, Wm. MINNICK and Miss
Margaret Ellen, daughter of Wm. GILMER,
all of Rockingham county.
Rockingham Register, 19 November 1868
(Thursday), p. 2, c. 5.
MINOR: See entry for LUCKETT.
MINOR: See entry for WORKMAN.
MINOR: On the 25th ult., by Rev. Wm. Brown,
Dr. J.G. MINOR, of Bridgewater, and Miss
Martha J., daughter of Maj. James
CRAWFORD, of Augusta.
Rockingham Register and Advertiser, 2
November 1860 (Friday), p. 2, c. 5.
MISH: See entry for DUNLAP.
MISNER: See entry for MISNER.
MISNER: At Staunton, in the Clerk's Office,
on the 16th inst., by Rev. Wm. A. Harris,
Robert F. MISNER and Mrs. Sarah MISNER,
all of Augusta county.
Rockingham Register, 23 July 1868
(Thursday), p. 3, c. 4.
MITCHELL: See entry for AVIS.
MITCHELL: See entry for JOHNS.
MITCHELL: See entry for PARROW.
MITCHELL: See entry for SUPPLE.

MITCHELL: On the 21st ult., at the Haskil House, Galesburg, Illinois, by A.J. Wiley, Esq., Dr. J.B. MITCHELL, formerly of this county, and Miss D.S., daughter of Dr. Geo. PRICE, of Abingdon, Illinois. Rockingham Register and Advertiser, 15 May 1857 (Friday), p. 3, c. 2.

MITCHELL: On the 4th inst., by Rev. J. Witherson, J.T. MITCHELL, Jr., of Augusta, and Bettie W. YOUNG, of Nelson. Rockingham Register, 11 November 1869 (Thursday), p. 3, c. 3.

MITCHELL: At Cherry Grove, in this county, on the 12th ult., by Rev. Jacob Miller, Dr. Jacob A. MITCHELL and Miss Emma C., daughter of Henry FURR, all of Rockingham. Rockingham Register, 5 May 1870 (Thursday), p. 3, c. 2.

MIZER: See entry for GREAVER.

MOFFETT: See entry for BLACK.

MOFFETT: See entry for THOMPSON.

MOFFETT: See entry for ZIRKLE.

MOFFETT: At the Virginia House, Richmond, on Monday, the 24th ult., by the Rev. Dr. Empie, Col. Anderson MOFFETT, of Rockingham county, Va., and Miss Margaret, youngest daughter of Capt. James DAVIS, of that city. Rockingham Register and Valley Advertiser, 8 March 1845 (Saturday), p. 3, c. 3.

MOFFETT: On the 10th inst., at Jacob Price's, Shenandoah county, by Elder J.M. Urner, Miss Sallie E. PENDERGAST, formerly of Page county, and George MOFFETT, of Rockingham county. Rockingham Register, 24 March 1870 (Thursday), p. 3, c. 2.

MOFFETT: At Dunmore, the residence of the bride's father, in Pocahontas county, W.Va., on the 14th of September, by Rev. Mr. Butts, George H. MOFFETT, of Huntersville, to Miss Marietta, daughter of Isaac MOORE, Esq. Rockingham Register, 14 October 1869

(Thursday), p. 2, c. 2.

MOHLER: See entry for GWINN.

MOHLER: See entry for LONG.

MOHLER: See entry for PROFIT.

MOHLER: On the 1st March, by Rev. H. St. J.
Rinker, Lt. Jacob W. MOHLER and Miss
Martha H. LUDWIG, all of Shenandoah.
Rockingham Register and Advertiser, 7
April 1865 (Friday), p. 2, c. 5.
Repeated, 14 April 1865 (Friday), p. 2,
c. 5.

MONDAY: On the 21st of January, by the Rev.
Isaac Long, Henry MONDAY, formerly of
Albemarle county, and Miss Elizabeth,
daughter of Peachy ROADCAP, of Rockingham
county.
Rockingham Register, 18 February 1869
(Thursday), p. 2, c. 5.

MONEYMAKER: See entry for PATTERSON.

MONGER: See entry for EPARD.

MONGER: At the Steam Saw-Mill of Dr. S.
Miller, in this county, on the 5th inst.,
by Rev. Wm. J. Miller, G.W. MONGER and
Miss Mollie E. DEARING, all of
Rockingham.
Rockingham Register and Advertiser, 19
March 1868 (Thursday), p. 2, c. 4.

MONGER: On the 26th ult., at the residence of
the bride's father, by Rev. Geo. R.
Jefferson, John B. MONGER and Miss
Elizabeth HUFFMAN, all of Page county.
Rockingham Register and Advertiser, 21
November 1867 (Thursday), p. 2, c. 5.

MONGOLD: See entry for MATHIAS.

MONROE: On the 8th ult., by the Rev. John
Arnold, Mr. Thomas MONROE to Miss Lucy,
daughter of Mr. John HIETT, of Hampshire
county.
Rockingham Register and Valley
Advertiser, 24 March 1849 (Saturday), p.
2, c. 7.

MONTAGUE: See entry for JUNKIN.

MONTGOMERY: See entry for JONES.

MONTGOMERY: On the 9th inst., at the
residence of the bride's father, by Rev.
R. Smith, Thomas A. MONTGOMERY and Miss

310

Elizabeth BEARD, all of Augusta county.
Rockingham Register and Advertiser, 24
January 1862 (Friday), p. 2, c. 7.

MOOHENY: On the 22nd ult., by Rev. Daniel
Thomas, Mr. Joseph MOOHENY and Miss Susan
CLATTERBUCK, all of Rockingham.
Rockingham Register and Advertiser, 21
December 1860 (Friday), p. 2, c. 6.

MOOMAW: See entry for HOOKE.

MOOMAW: On Tuesday, the 12th of October, by
the Rev. Solomon Garber, Ananias J.
MOOMAW, of Botetourt, and Miss Rebecca
BOWMAN, of this county.
Rockingham Register, 14 October 1869
(Thursday), p. 2, c. 2.

MOONEY: See entry for MADISON.

MOONEY: On the 26th ult., by the Rev. H. St.
John Rinker, Mr. Samuel MOONEY and Miss
Leannah FADELEY, all of Shenandoah.
Rockingham Register and Advertiser, 3
February 1860 (Friday), p. 2, c. 5.

MOORE: See entry for ALLEN.

MOORE: See entry for BATEMAN.

MOORE: See entry for BURKHOLDER.

MOORE: See entry for CARPENTER.

MOORE: See entry for COWELL.

MOORE: See entry for HICKMAN.

MOORE: See entry for HOPKINS.

MOORE: See entry for MOFFETT.

MOORE: See entry for MOYERS.

MOORE: See entry for OTT.

MOORE: See entry for POLLARD.

MOORE: See entry for SHELTON.

MOORE: On the 7th inst., by Elder John Clark,
Edward MOORE, Editor of the *Virginia
Valley Gazette*, and Miss Mary C. BOLEN,
of Warren county, Va.
Rockingham Register and Advertiser, 15
April 1859 (Friday), p. 3, c. 1.

MOORE: On Thursday, the 20th of January, by
Rev. Jacob Miller, Mr. George MOORE and
Miss Leannah, daughter of Jacob REEDY,
all of Rockingham county.
Rockingham Register and Advertiser, 4
February 1859 (Friday), p. 2, c. 5.

MOORE: On Wednesday, September 25th, at Port

Republic, Geo. E. MOORE and Amanda J. SHEETS, all of Rockingham.

Rockingham Register and Advertiser, 3 October 1867 (Thursday), p. 2, c. 6.

MOORE: On Thursday the 14th inst., by Rev. Jos. Funkhouser, at that gentleman's residence, George W. MOORE and Mrs. Barbara Ann FLEMING, both formerly of the Poor House of Rockingham.

Rockingham Register, 21 May 1868 (Thursday), p. 2, c. 5.

MOORE: On Back Creek, on the 20th inst., by Rev. Wm. T. Price, Hamilton MOORE and Miss Sally DEVIER, all of Highland county.

Rockingham Register and Advertiser, 27 November 1866 (Thursday), p. 2, c. 5.

MOORE: Near Brandy Station, Culpeper county, on the 29th ult., by Rev. A.D. Pollack, J.S. MOORE, of Lynchburg, and Miss Nellie H. WISE, of that county.

Rockingham Register, 6 January 1870 (Thursday), p. 3, c. 3.

MOORE: At the residence of the bride's father, near Timberville, on Thursday, August 31st, by Rev. J. Stirewalt, Mr. James H. MOORE, of Tucker county, and Miss Catharine BOWMAN, of Rockingham county.

Rockingham Register & Advertiser, 15 September 1865 (Friday), p. 3, c. 3.

MOORE: On the 15th inst., by the Rev. Daniel Thomas, Mr. John H. MOORE and Miss Roda Ellen SWARTZ, both of Rockingham.

Rockingham Register and Advertiser, 23 March 1860 (Friday), p. 2, c. 6.

MOORE: On the 3rd inst., at Edinburg, by Rev. D.G. BRAGONIER, Col. L.T. MOORE, of Winchester, and Miss Mary F., daughter of the officiating minister.

Rockingham Register and Advertiser, 18 October 1866 (Thursday), p. 2, c. 4.

MOORE: On the 28th ult., at her father's residence, on Smith's Creek, Rockingham county, Miss Sallie A., daughter of Reuben Zirkel, Esq., and Oatis F. MOORE, all of Rockingham.

Rockingham Register and Advertiser, 6 February 1868 (Thursday), p. 2, c. 4.

MOORE: On Tuesday evening, May 1st, at Melrose, by Rev. A.P. Boude, Mr. Reuben W. MOORE and Miss Fannie E. CHRISMAN, all of Rockingham county.

Rockingham Register and Advertiser, 4 May 1866 (Friday), p. 3, c. 2.

MOORE: On the evening of the 6th ult., by the Rev. H. Tallhelm, Capt. S.K. MOORE and Miss R.E.S., daughter of John GRANDSTAFF, all of Shenandoah county.

Rockingham Register and Advertiser, 3 January 1867 (Thursday), p. 3, c. 3.

MOORE: In Forestville, on Sunday last, by Rev. J.P. Cline, Mr. Wm. MOORE and Miss Malinda ESTEP, all of that place.

Rockingham Register and Advertiser, 12 April 1861 (Friday), p. 2, c. 4.

MOORE: At Mr. John M. Garber's, near Forestville, Shenandoah county, Va., on the 9th of May, 1870, by Rev. J.S. Bennick, Wm. P. MOORE and Miss Hannah SHEFFER, both of Shenandoah.

Rockingham Register, 26 May 1870 (Thursday), p. 2, c. 6.

MOORE: On Tuesday, the 19th inst., on Stony Creek, by Rev. Joshua Buckley, Mr. Wm. R. MOORE and Miss Ruth, second daughter of Robert T. GAY, Esq., all of Pocahontas county.

Rockingham Register and Advertiser, 29 June 1860 (Friday), p. 2, c. 5.

MOORMAN: On Thursday, the 25th ult., by the Rev. Samuel Houston, Dr. John J. MOORMAN, of Harrisonburg, to Miss Martha, daughter of Capt. Thomas NEWELL, of Botetourt county.

Rockingham Weekly Register, 12 May 1827 (Saturday), p. 3, c. 3.

MORGAN: See entry for CALE.

MORGAN: See entry for HANGER.

MORGAN: See entry for KERR.

MORRIS: See entry for KITT.

MORRIS: On the 10th of June, by Rev. Jacob

Miller, Alfred MORRIS and Miss Louisa, daughter of Peter ACKER, all of Rockingham county.

Rockingham Register and Advertiser, 13 June 1867 (Thursday), p. 2, c. 6.

MORRIS: On the 27th of January, at Mr. Z. Gilmore's, in McGaheysville, by Rev. J.C. Hensell, Derritt MORRIS and Miss Sarah C. CRAWFORD, all of Rockingham county.

Rockingham Register and Advertiser, 7 February 1867 (Thursday), p. 3, c. 3.

MORRIS: On the 31st of December, by Elder C. Allemong, Henry MORRIS, of Rockingham, and Miss Sarah FURRELL, of Page county.

Rockingham Register and Advertiser, 12 January 1866 (Friday), p. 2, c. 3.

MORRIS: At Peale's Cross-Roads, on Sunday the 26th inst., by Rev. Jos. Funkhouser, Jos. W. MORRIS and Miss Mary F. BROCK, all of Rockingham county.

Rockingham Register and Advertiser, 30 May 1867 (Thursday), p. 3, c. 3.

MORRIS: On the 27th ult., at No. 2 Furnace, by Rev. A.P. Boude, Thos. MORRIS and Miss _____ EPPARD, all of Rockingham.

Rockingham Register, 3 February 1870 (Thursday), p. 3, c. 4.

MORRISON: See entry for CORNELL.

MORRISON: See entry for RODEFER.

MORRISON: See entry for YANCEY.

MORRISON: On the 16th ult., by the Rev. Samuel Brown, Mr. Henry A. MORRISON, of Sheffield, England, to Miss Margaret A. IRVINE, of Rockbridge.

Rockingham Register and Advertiser, 6 September 1866 (Thursday), p. 2, c. 5.

MORRISON: On the 26th ult., by Rev. J.A. Snyder, Mr. Hugh MORRISON, of Harrisonburg, and Miss Susan A. ELICK, of Woodstock.

Rockingham Register and Advertiser, 11 May 1866 (Friday), p. 2, c. 4.

MORROW: At Independence, Texas, August 2, by Rev. Wm. Carey Crane, D.D., Joseph C. Styles MORROW, Esq., of Georgetown, Texas, to Miss Nannie E., eldest daughter

of General Sam. HOUSTON, dec'd.
Rockingham Register and Advertiser, 6
September 1866 (Thursday), p. 2, c. 5.

MORT: See entry for BUSHONG.

MORTON: See entry for BOTKIN.

MOSINGO: On the 13th inst., by Rev. A.R.
Rude, Mr. Benjamin MOSINGO and Miss
Rebecca CAMPBELL.
Rockingham Register and Advertiser, 28
January 1859 (Friday), p. 2, c. 6.

MOSINGS: See entry for HEPNER.

MOSLEY: See entry for HALL.

MOSS: Near Harrisonburg, on Thursday, the
23rd of December, by Rev. Jacob Miller,
Elberton MOSS and Miss Louisa, daughter
of R.A. VIAR, all of Rockingham county.
Rockingham Register, 6 January 1870
(Thursday), p. 3, c. 3.

MOWBRAY: On the 10th of November, by Rev.
J.W. Howe, Mr. Benjamin W. MOWBRAY and
Miss Lydia Catharine, daughter of Mr. Wm.
THACKER, all of North Mountain,
Rockingham county.
The Rockingham Register, 27 November 1863
(Friday), p. 2, c. 5.

MOWRY: See entry for COINER.

MOWRY: See entry for WATSON.

MOWRY: On the 3rd inst., by Elder John
Pirkey, Mr. Robert A. MOWRY and Miss
Elizabeth SPIKER, all of Shenandoah
county.
Rockingham Register and Advertiser, 24
May 1866 (Thursday), p. 3, c. 4.

MOYERHEFFER: See entry for O'NEAL.

MOYERHOEFFER: See entry for HEFNER.

MOYERHOEFFER: See entry for SAUFLEY.

MOYERHOEFFER: On the 16th of May, by Rev.
Frederick Miller, John W. MOYERHOEFFER
and Miss Elizabeth C., daughter of Wm.
KYGER, all of Rockingham county.
Rockingham Register, 20 May 1869
(Thursday), p. 2, c. 3.

MOYERS: See entry for BOWMAN.

MOYERS: See entry for HAWKINS.

MOYERS: See entry for KLINE.

MOYERS: See entry for RADER.

MOYERS: On Thursday the 8th inst., at candlelight, by the Rev. T.H. Busey, Mr. Abner MOYERS to Miss Virinda M., daughter of Mr. George BAUGHER, all of Rockingham county.
Rockingham Register and Valley Advertiser, 27 October 1846 (Saturday), p. 3, c. 1.

MOYERS: On Sunday morning last, by the Rev. Jacob Miller, Mr. Charles W. MOYERS and Miss Mary J. SWARTZ, all of this county.
Rockingham Register and Advertiser, 29 March 1861 (Friday), p. 3, c. 1.

MOYERS: On the 17th ult., at Cherry Grove, by Rev. J.D. Shirey, Garvis F. MOYERS, of N.T. Stephensburg, and Miss Augusta E. HAILMAN, of Augusta.
Rockingham Register and Advertiser, 3 October 1867 (Thursday), p. 2, c. 6.

MOYERS: At North Mountain, on the morning of the 2nd inst., by the Rev. Jacob Miller, Michael G. MOYERS and Mrs. Lean MOORE, all of Rockingham county.
Rockingham Register, 6 January 1870 (Thursday), p. 3, c. 3.

MUDDEMAN: On the 13th inst., by Rev. Samuel Wampler, David MUDDEMAN and Miss Lydia ALEXANDER, both of Rockingham county.
Rockingham Register and Advertiser, 21 February 1862 (Friday), p. 3, c. 2.

MULLEN: On the 22nd of March, by Rev. Jacob Miller, Mr. Stephen M. MULLEN and Mary Ann, daughter of Samuel DAUGHERTY, dec'd, all of Rockingham county.
Rockingham Register and Advertiser, 6 April 1860 (Friday), p. 2, c. 6.

MULLIN: On Sunday, the 25th of September, in Bridgewater, by the Rev. J.M. Grabill, Mr. John E. MULLIN, of Augusta county, and Miss Rosannah, daughter of Mr. Isaac NISWANDER, of Rockingham.
Rockingham Register and Advertiser, 30 September 1859 (Friday), p. 2, c. 4.

MUMAW: See entry for ANDRICK.
MUMAW: See entry for SHIFFLET.
MUMAW: See entry for SHILLENBURG.

MUMAW: On the 19th of January, by Rev. Jacob Wine, George MUMAW and Julia Ann BARB. *Rockingham Register and Advertiser*, 27 January 1865 (Friday), p. 1, c. 3.

MUMAW: On the 14th ult., by Rev. H. Wetzel, Jacob MUMAW and Miss Emeline FUNKHOUSER, both of Shenandoah. *Rockingham Register*, 8 September 1870 (Thursday), p. 3, c. 3.

MUMAW: On the 3rd, by Rev. John G. Wolff, Mr. Philip MUMAW to Miss Elizabeth VEACH, all of Shenandoah county. *The Rockingham Register and Valley Advertiser*, 26 June 1852 (Saturday), p. 2, c. 5.

MUMAW: At Woodstock, on the 12th inst., by Rev. A.R. Rude, Mr. Simon MUMAW, of Rockingham, and Miss Catharine TUSING, of Shenandoah county. *Rockingham Register and Advertiser*, 23 September 1859 (Friday), p. 2, c. 4.

MUMAW: On the 22nd of November, by Rev. Solomon Garber, Wm. H. MUMAW, of Shenandoah county, and Miss Martha M., daughter of Wm. ADAMS, dec'd, of Rockingham. *Rockingham Register and Advertiser*, 6 December 1866 (Thursday), p. 3, c. 2.

MUNCH: See entry for GOLLADAY.

MUNCH: On the 13th ult., by Elder Thornton H. Taylor, Mr. Addison MUNCH and Miss Mary A. SHIPE, all of Shenandoah county. *Rockingham Register and Advertiser*, 5 October 1860 (Friday), p. 2, c. 3.

MUNDAY: See entry for HUMPHREYS.

MUNDAY: See entry for LEVEL.

MURPHY: See entry for GOODRIDGE.

MURPHY: See entry for HEDRICK.

MURPHY: See entry for NEWMAN.

MURPHY: See entry for SUGHURN.

MURRAY: See entry for BEERY.

MURRAY: See entry for SHENK.

MURRAY: See entry for TUTWEILER.

MURRAY: See entry for WITMIRE.

MURRAY: On the 10th inst., at the residence of the bride's mother, by the Rev. J.

West Johnson, John MURRAY, of Baltimore
city, and Miss Sally Virginia NASSAU, of
Shenandoah county, Va.
The Rockingham Register, 16 January 1863
(Friday), p. 2, c. 6.
MUSE: See entry for EGGLESTON.
MUSE: See entry for TRONE.
MYERS: See entry for CLEEK.
MYERS: See entry for FUTT.
MYERS: See entry for KIRBY.
MYERS: See entry for KLINE.
MYERS: See entry for MILLER.
MYERS: See entry for MYERS.
MYERS: See entry for NEFF.
MYERS: See entry for REED.
MYERS: See entry for RIELY.
MYERS: See entry for TRUEHART.
MYERS: See entry for WHITE.
MYERS: On Thursday evening, the 19th ult., at
    Berwick, Columbia county, Pa., by Rev.
    Mr. Hotterstein, A.J. MYERS, of Pa., and
    Miss Annie E., only daughter of Ab'm
    MYERS, of Shenandoah county.
    Rockingham Register and Advertiser, 2
    August 1866 (Thursday), p. 2, c. 5.
MYERS: On Thursday, the 28th of December, by
    Rev. Solomon Garber, Abraham P. MYERS, of
    Linvill's Creek, and Miss Christina V.,
    daughter of John P. and Anna GOOD, all of
    Rockingham county.
    Rockingham Register and Advertiser, 19
    January 1866 (Friday), p. 3, c. 2.
MYERS: In this place, on Monday evening last,
    by the Rev. J.S.R. Clarke, Lt. C.C. MYERS
    and Miss Sallie N., daughter of the late
    Capt. R.C. MAUCK, of Harrisonburg.
    Rockingham Register & Advertiser, 8
    September 1865 (Friday), p. 3, c. 2.
MYERS: On the 29th ult., by Elder John
    Pirkey, Derostus F.W. MYERS and Miss Mary
    L. FARRA, all of Shenandoah.
    Rockingham Register and Advertiser, 7
    June 1866 (Thursday), p. 3, c. 3.
MYERS: On the 30th ult., on Smith's Creek, at
    the residence of the bride's father, by
    Rev. Jacob Miller, Mr. Erasmus P. MYERS

and Miss Molly E. SELLERS, all of
Rockingham.
Rockingham Register, 3 June 1869
(Thursday), p. 3, c. 2.

MYERS: On the 9th inst., by Rev. Benjamin
Bowman, Mr. Isaac C. MYERS and Miss
Hannah E. RALSTON.
Rockingham Register and Advertiser, 21
September 1860 (Friday), p. 2, c. 4.

MYERS: By the Rev. Daniel Thomas, on the 14th
inst., Mr. Isaac S. MYERS and Miss Lydia
E., daughter of Rev. John WINE, of this
county.
Rockingham Register and Virginia
Advertiser, 22 February 1856 (Friday), p.
2, c. 8.

MYERS: On Thursday, the 1st inst., by Rev.
H.A. Garver, Dr. J.L. MYERS, of
Waynesboro, Augusta county, and Miss
Maggie J. PALMER, of Port Republic, Va.
Rockingham Register and Advertiser, 9
March 1866 (Friday), p. 2, c. 3.

MYERS: On the evening of the 14th inst., by
Rev. Jacob Miller, at Green Mount, John
J. MYERS and Miss Hester P., daughter of
Z.S. ROUDABUSH, all of Rockingham.
Rockingham Register, 21 May 1868
(Thursday), p. 2, c. 5.

MYERS: On the 22nd inst., in Hebron Church,
by Rev. T.L. Preston, Mr. John K. MYERS,
of Rockbridge, to Miss Mary E. VAN PELT,
of Augusta.
Rockingham Register and Advertiser, 30
January 1868 (Thursday), p. 2, c. 4.

MYERS: On Tuesday evening, the 2nd inst., by
Rev. O.P. Wirgman, Mr. Levi MYERS to Miss
Angeline M. BATIS - all of Augusta
county.
Rockingham Register and Advertiser, 10
December 1858 (Friday), p. 3, c. 2.

MYERS: On the 21st of December, by Rev. Jacob
Thomas, Mr. Peter H. MYERS and Miss
Elizabeth, daughter of Abram BURKEHOLDER,
all of Rockingham county.
Rockingham Register and Advertiser, 12
January 1866 (Friday), p. 1, c. 3.

MYERS: On the 26th of December, 1867, by Rev. Jacob Miller, Raphael MYERS and Miss Sallie F., daughter of Samuel ZIGLER, all of Rockingham county.
Rockingham Register and Advertiser, 9 January 1868 (Thursday), p. 2, c. 4.

MYERS: On the 28th ult., by Rev. Wm. R. Harris, Samuel D. MYERS and Miss Maggie J. RUNNELS, all of Staunton.
Rockingham Register and Advertiser, 4 April 1867 (Thursday), p. 3, c. 4.

MYERS: In Staunton, at 1 o'clock, on Monday evening last, by Rev. Geo. G. Brooke, Mr. Samuel D. MYERS, professor of "the art preservation of arts," of Harrisonburg, and Miss Ella A., daughter of Mr. Horace SEELY, of Staunton, Va.
Rockingham Register and Advertiser, 2 March 1860 (Friday), p. 3, c. 2.

MYERS: At the parsonage of Dr. Huston, in Baltimore, by Rev. Dr. Huston, on the 17th of November, Wm. H. MYERS and Miss E.C. VAN PELT, all of Augusta.
Rockingham Register, 17 December 1868 (Thursday), p. 3, c. 2.

- N -

NAIR: See entry for SHIRFEY.

NAIR: On the 16th of March, by Rev. Daniel Thomas, Mr. Hugh M. NAIR and Mrs. Mary Ann, widow of Joseph FRANK, dec'd, all of Rockingham county.
Rockingham Register and Advertiser, 31 March 1865 (Friday), p. 2, c. 3.

NALLE: On the 22nd of February, at the residence of the bride's father, in Page county, by the Rev. Mr. Locke, Joseph NALLE, of Atlanta, Ga., and Miss Sally J., daughter of Col. Andrew KEYSER.
Rockingham Register and Advertiser, 23 March 1866 (Friday), p. 3, c. 3. Reprinted, 30 March 1866 (Friday), p. 2, c. 3. As the latter is more complete, it is cited above.

NASELROD: On the 12th of January, by Rev.

Jacob Wine, Job NASELROD and Mary Ettie EPERD.

Rockingham Register and Advertiser, 27 January 1865 (Friday), p. 1, c. 3.

NASSAU: See entry for MURRAY.

NAUGLE: See entry for DELLINGER.

NAUMAN: See entry for MARTIN.

NAUMAN: In New Market, on the 8th inst., by Rev. S. Hinkle, Hiram C. NAUMAN and Miss Elenora C. KITE, both of Page county.

Rockingham Register, 17 February 1870 (Thursday), p. 3, c. 2.

NEAL: In Lafayette county, Missouri, on the 7th of November, at the residence of the bride's father, by Rev. E.S. Dulin, Mr. Lewis NEAL and Miss Jennie S., daughter of Wm. McCAUSLAND, Esq.

Rockingham Register and Advertiser, 22 November 1866 (Thursday), p. 3, c. 3.

NEASE: See entry for CLEM.

NEBB: On the 21st ult., near Woodstock, by Rev. John P. Hyde, Philip NEBB, of Shenandoah, and Miss Mary A. WILSON, of Hardy county.

Rockingham Register and Advertiser, 5 July 1866 (Thursday), p. 3, c. 5.

NEESE: See entry for FANSELOR.

NEFF: See entry for BEERY.

NEFF: See entry for CLINE.

NEFF: See entry for COOTES.

NEFF: See entry for COX.

NEFF: See entry for CRAWN.

NEFF: See entry for FUNKHOUSER.

NEFF: See entry for HOUFF.

NEFF: See entry for HYDE.

NEFF: See entry for SHEETS.

NEFF: See entry for WHITMORE.

NEFF: On the 19th of January, by Rev. Jacob Wine, at the residence of the bride's father, Abraham C. NEFF and Miss Louisa, daughter of Jacob MYERS, all of Shenandoah county.

Rockingham Register and Advertiser, 27 January 1865 (Friday), p. 1, c. 3.

NEFF: On the 17th of December, by Rev. J.B. Snyder, Capt. Jacob NEFF and Miss Cora B.

KENDRICK, of Mt. Jackson, Va.
Rockingham Register and Advertiser, 9
January 1868 (Thursday), p. 2, c. 4.

NEFF: On the 21st of October, by Rev. J.P.
Cline, John M. NEFF and Miss Louisa
RINKER, all of Shenandoah county.
The Rockingham Register, 19 December 1862
(Friday), p. 2, c. 4.

NEFF: On Wednesday evening last, by the Rev.
Jacob B. Houck, Mr. Josiah NEFF to Miss
Caroline TAYLOR, all of this county.
Rockingham Register, 11 March 1837
(Saturday), p. 3, c. 5.

NEFF: On the 12th inst., at the residence of
the bride's mother, by Rev. Timothy Funk,
Michael NEFF and Miss Leanna O'ROARK, all
of Rockingham.
Rockingham Register, 23 December 1869
(Thursday), p. 3, c. 2.

NEFF: On the 4th ult., Mr. Mortimer NEFF, of
Hardy, and Miss Harriet RHINEHEART, of
Ritchie county.
Rockingham Register and Advertiser, 11
January 1861 (Friday), p. 3, c. 4.

NEHER: See entry for ARION.

NEILL: See entry for GROVE.

NELSON: See entry for CARSON.

NELSON: On Monday evening, the 26th inst., by
Rev. D.C. Irwin, James T. NELSON, of
Henry county, Missouri, and Miss Harriet
K. GAINES, of Rockingham county, Va.
Rockingham Register and Advertiser, 30
March 1866 (Friday), p. 2, c. 3.

NELSON: In Staunton, on Thursday of last
week, by the Rev. T.T. Castleman, Rev.
Robert NELSON, of Lexington, Va., to Miss
Rosa E., daughter of James POINTS, Esq.,
of Staunton.
*Rockingham Register and Valley
Advertiser*, 4 November 1848 (Saturday),
p. 3, c. 2.

NESSELRODT: On the 24th ult., by Rev. H. St.
J. Rinker, Mr. Andrew J. NESSELRODT and
Miss Anna BARB, all of Shenandoah county.
The Rockingham Register, 13 May 1864
(Friday), p. 2, c. 5.

NEWCOMB: See entry for FREEMAN.

NEWELL: See entry for MOORMAN.

NEWHAM: On Tuesday the 14th of November, by
Rev. Benjamin Bowman, Capt. Samuel K.
NEWHAM and Miss Fannie, daughter of Mr.
David SHIRKEY, all of Rockingham.
Rockingham Register & Advertiser, 1
December 1865 (Friday), p. 2, c. 4.

NEWHAM: In Kansas City, Mo., on Tuesday
morning, October 5th, at the residence of
Mrs. Nellie McGee, Will W. NEWHAM,
formerly of Rockingham county, Va., and
Miss Annie, of Kansas City, youngest
daughter of the late F.P. McGEE, dec'd.
Rockingham Register, 4 November 1869
(Thursday), p. 2, c. 4.

NEWLAND: On the 16th ult., at the Parsonage
of the German Reformed Church, by Rev.
Daniel Feete, Mr. Isaac NEWLAND and Miss
Sallie FUNKHOUSER, all of Shenandoah.
Rockingham Register and Advertiser, 2
March 1860 (Friday), p. 3, c. 2.

NEWLAND: On the 19th ult., by Rev. D. Feete,
Mr. Jesse NEWLAND, of Woodstock, and Miss
Frances, daughter of Mr. Geo. SHEETZ, of
Shenandoah.
Rockingham Register and Advertiser, 11
January 1861 (Friday), p. 3, c. 4.

NEWLAND: At Hawkinstown, on the 8th inst., by
Rev. J.D. Freed, Joseph W. NEWLAND and
Miss Lucy J., daughter of Jacob MAPHIS,
all of Shenandoah.
Rockingham Register, 15 April 1869
(Thursday), p. 2, c. 4.

NEWMAN: See entry for CRIST.

NEWMAN: See entry for GILMORE.

NEWMAN: See entry for LURTY.

NEWMAN: See entry for YANCEY.

NEWMAN: On Tuesday evening last, by the Rev.
A.W. Kilpatrick, Dr. Anderson M. NEWMAN,
of this place, to Miss Rebecca, daughter
of Zebulon DYER, Esq., of Franklin,
Pendleton county.
Rockingham Register, 18 April 1835
(Saturday), p. 3, c. 3.

NEWMAN: At the residence of the bride's

parents, on Tuesday the 4th inst., by Rev. T.D. Bell, Lieut. Anderson M. NEWMAN, Jr., C.S.A., and Miss Haddie A., daughter of Henry OTT, all of Harrisonburg.

Rockingham Register and Advertiser, 14 April 1865 (Friday), p. 2, c. 5.

NEWMAN: On the 16th ult., by Rev. Henry St. John Rinker, John NEWMAN and Miss Rebecca FRY, all of Shenandoah county.

Rockingham Register and Advertiser, 2 May 1867 (Thursday), p. 2, c. 6.

NEWMAN: At the residence of George W. Murphy, Esq., in New Market, on the 26th ult., by Rev. W.R. Stringer, John W. NEWMAN, Esq., of New Market, and Miss Lizzie, daughter of Mr. George MURPHY, of Jefferson county, West Virginia.

Rockingham Register, 4 November 1869 (Thursday), p. 2, c. 4.

NEWMAN: In Staunton, on the 9th inst., by Rev. Wm. E. Baker, Mr. Wm. NEWMAN and Miss Rebecca TRAYER, both of that place.

Rockingham Register and Advertiser, 16 September 1859 (Friday), p. 2, c. 4.

NEWTON: See entry for COOTES.

NEWTON: On the 29th of April, in Port Lavaca, Texas, by Rev. F.A. McShaw, Frank McC. NEWTON, of San Antonio, Texas, and Miss Clarinda M. SIBERT, of Shenandoah county, Va.

Rockingham Register and Advertiser, 25 May 1860 (Friday), p. 2, c. 5.

NEWTON: In Lewiston, Miffin [sic] county, Pa., on the 12th inst. [sic, ult.], by Rev. A.A. ESKRIDGE, Capt. J.W. NEWTON, of Augusta county, Va., and Miss M.W., daughter of the officiating minister.

Rockingham Register and Advertiser, 1 March 1861 (Friday), p. 3, c. 3.

NICELY: See entry for TAYLOR.

NICELY: On the 13th of January, by Rev. Jacob Thomas, Louis B. NICELY and Miss Mary F., daughter of Daniel COAKLEY, all of Rockingham county.

Rockingham Register, 20 January 1870

(Thursday), p. 2, c. 5.

NICEWANDER: On Thursday, the 21st ult., by
    Rev. G.H. Ray, Mr. Abraham NICEWANDER and
    Miss Catharine BICKEL, all of this town.
    Rockingham Register and Advertiser, 2
    March 1860 (Friday), p. 3, c. 2.

NICHAL: See entry for SLUSSER.

NICHOL: See entry for SMELSER.

NICHOLAS: See entry for CARRIER.

NICHOLAS: See entry for EILER.

NICHOLAS: On the 18th inst., by Rev. I.
    Conder, at the residence of the
    bridegroom, A.P. NICHOLAS and Miss Hanna
    McNETT, all of Rockingham county.
    Rockingham Register, 25 November 1869
    (Thursday), p. 2, c. 3.

NICHOLAS: On the 30th ult., by Rev. John
    Clymer, J.H. NICHOLAS and Miss Martha
    WALKER, both of Shenandoah county.
    Rockingham Register, 13 January 1870
    (Thursday), p. 3, c. 4.

NICHOLAS: On the 24th of May, by Rev. John D.
    Freed, Mr. Joshua NICHOLAS to Miss Susan
    SIMMONS, all of Pendleton county.
    Rockingham Register and Advertiser, 19
    June 1857 (Friday), p. 3, c. 2.

NICHOLAS: On Tuesday, the 3rd inst., at the
    residence of the bride's father, by Rev.
    R. Smith, Wm. P. NICHOLAS and Rebecca J.
    KERAN, all of Rockingham.
    Rockingham Register and Advertiser, 13
    May 1859 (Friday), p. 3, c. 4.

NIESWANDER: See entry for BRENNEMAN.

NIGHTEN: See entry for STOVER.

NISEWANDER: See entry for PETERSON.

NISEWANDER: On the 17th of June, by Rev.
    Abraham Knupp, Mr. Erasmus NISEWANDER and
    Miss Mary E. SIMMERS, all of Rockingham
    county.
    Rockingham Register and Advertiser, 22
    June 1860 (Friday), p. 2, c. 6.

NISEWANDER: On Sunday, the 24th inst., by
    Rev. Daniel Thomas, Mr. Henry C.
    NISEWANDER and Miss Elizabeth G.,
    daughter of Mr. James A. CAMPBELL, all of
    Rockingham county.

The <u>Rockingham</u> <u>Register</u>, 29 January 1864
(Friday), p. 2, c. 6.

NISEWANDER: On Wednesday, the 7th of March,
near Melrose, by Rev. Jacob Miller, John
W. NISEWANDER and Miss Lydia, daughter of
Sam'l R. SPRINKEL, all of Rockingham
county.

<u>Rockingham</u> <u>Register</u> <u>and</u> <u>Advertiser</u>, 30
March 1866 (Friday), p. 2, c. 3.

NISWANDER: See entry for MULLIN.

NISWANDER: On Thursday, the 9th of February,
1865, by Rev. Daniel Thomas, Mr. Abram
NISWANDER and Miss Charlotte LANTZ, all
of Bridgewater.

<u>Rockingham</u> <u>Register</u> <u>and</u> <u>Advertiser</u>, 17
February 1865 (Friday), p. 2, c. 4.

NISWANDER: On Sunday, December 25th, 1859, at
the residence of the bride's father, near
South English, Keokuk county, Iowa, by
Rev. David Brower, Mr. Daniel NISWANDER,
formerly of Rockingham county, Va., and
Miss Sarah Ann, daughter of David
COFFMAN, Esq., formerly of Augusta
county, Va.

<u>Rockingham</u> <u>Register</u> <u>and</u> <u>Advertiser</u>, 13
January 1860 (Friday), p. 2, c. 6.

NISWANDER: On Thursday, the 7th of November,
at Rev. Solomon Garber's, Geo. W.
NISWANDER and Miss Fannie C. LONG, all of
Bridgewater, Rockingham county.

<u>Rockingham</u> <u>Register</u> <u>and</u> <u>Advertiser</u>, 14
November 1867 (Thursday), p. 2, c. 6.

NISWANDER: On the 8th inst., by the Rev. John
Thrush, at the residence of Mr. James
Baker, Mr. Isaac N. NISWANDER to Miss
Mary Elizabeth BAKER, all of this county.

<u>Rockingham</u> <u>Register</u> <u>and</u> <u>Advertiser</u>, 13
February 1857 (Friday), p. 2, c. 5.

NISWANDER: On Thursday, the 17th of
September, by Rev. Jacob Miller, Jacob B.
NISWANDER and Miss Catharine D., daughter
of Jno. J. MILLER, all of Rockingham
county.

<u>Rockingham</u> <u>Register</u>, 24 September 1868
(Thursday), p. 3, c. 4.

NISWANDER: On the 2nd of March, by Rev. Jacob

Miller, Joseph E. NISWANDER and Miss Mary
E., daughter of Michael SHOWALTER, all of
Rockingham.
Rockingham Register and Advertiser, 24
March 1865 (Friday), p. 2, c. 3.

NISWARNER: See entry for HILLIARD.

NISWARNER: See entry for PICKERING.

NOEL: See entry for BEARD.

NORRIS: On the 4th inst., by Rev. Jas. E.
Armstrong, Mr. Joseph E. NORRIS, of
Hagerstown, Md., and Miss Mary C. TROUT,
of Woodstock, Va.
Rockingham Register and Advertiser, 19
January 1866 (Friday), p. 3, c. 2.

NORTH: See entry for KURTZ.

NOTT: On Monday evening, the 8th inst., by
Rev. C.P. Krauth, Mr. Casper NOTT to Miss
Mary Ann, eldest daughter of Mr. Jacob
MESMER, all of Winchester.
*Rockingham Register and Valley
Advertiser*, 13 October 1849 (Saturday),
p. 2, c. 5.

NOTTINGHAM: See entry for BELL.

NUCKALLS: See entry for DABNEY.

NUCKOLS: On Thursday, September 15th, by Rev.
P.B. Smith, Mr. John NUCKOLS, formerly of
Indiana, and Miss Sarah F., daughter of
Mr. Henry SHELTON, of Back Creek, Bath
county.
Rockingham Register and Advertiser, 7
October 1859 (Friday), p. 2, c. 4.

NULL: See entry for SAFLEY.

NULL: On the 15th ult., by Rev. J.W. Howe,
Leonard NULL and Miss Laura V. CRABILL,
all of Rockingham.
Rockingham Register and Advertiser, 19
December 1867 (Thursday), p. 2, c. 6.

- O -

OAKS: On the 4th inst., by the Rev. A.W.
Kilpatrick, Mr. Thomas OAKS to Miss
Malinda BLAIN, both of this county.
Rockingham Register, 15 April 1837
(Saturday), p. 3, c. 3.

OATES: See entry for STRAUGHAN.

OATS: See entry for FLETCHER.

OATS: See entry for WALKER.

O'BRIEN: See entry for GAY.

O'BRIEN: In Woodstock, on the 26th ult., by Rev. J.W. Wolff, Mr. Hugh B. O'BRIEN, of Rockingham, and Miss Mary J. KILBY, of Culpeper.
Rockingham Register and Advertiser, 11 January 1861 (Friday), p. 3, c. 4.

O'BRIEN: In Port Republic, by Rev. Jno. P. Hyde, Mr. James O'BRIEN and Mrs. Mary COONTZ, both of Rockingham county.
The Rockingham Register, 15 January 1864 (Friday), p. 2, c. 6.

OCHELTREE: On the 13th inst., by Rev. C. Beard, Mr. John P. OCHELTREE and Miss Eliza SWITZER, all of Augusta county.
Rockingham Register and Advertiser, 28 October 1859 (Friday), p. 2, c. 6.

O'CONNELL: At Rev. A.P. Boude's residence, by that clergyman, on the 8th inst., Michael O'CONNELL, of Augusta county, and Miss Drusilla JAMES, of Rockingham.
Rockingham Register and Advertiser, 16 January 1868 (Thursday), p. 2, c. 5.

O'CONNER: At the Catholic Chapel, in Staunton, on the 7th of May last, by Rev. Father Bixio, Thomas O'CONNER, formerly of Harrisonburg, and Miss Anna Maria HELMS, formerly of Mt. Crawford, Rockingham county.
Rockingham Register and Advertiser, 13 September 1866 (Thursday), p. 2, c. 5.

ODEN: On the 19th ult., by Rev. R.K. Rude, Mr. Bushrod F. ODEN and Miss Ellen C. JENKINS, all of Shenandoah.
Rockingham Register and Advertiser, 18 May 1860 (Friday), p. 3, c. 4.

ODER: See entry for CRAUN.

ODER: See entry for ERWIN.

ODER: See entry for HARRELL.

ODER: See entry for MAUPIN.

ODER: At Happy Creek Station, M.G.R.R., on Wednesday, February 20th, 1867, by Rev. Wm. Gwynn Coe, J. Benson ODER and Miss Adele R., daughter of Jacob KUSER, Esq., all of Warren county, Va.

Rockingham Register and Advertiser, 14 March 1867 (Thursday), p. 3, c. 5.

O'FERRALL: At the residence of Capt. Thomas Wolverton, at Enterprise, Miss., on the 8th February, by Rev. E.H. Rutherford, Lt. Col. Charles T. O'FERRALL, of Va., and Mrs. Anna E. HAND, daughter of Col. Robert McLAIN, of Miss.

Rockingham Register and Advertiser, 7 April 1865 (Friday), p. 2, c. 5. Repeated, 14 April 1865 (Friday), p. 2, c. 5.

OFFENBACKER: See entry for FOLTS.

OFFENBERGER: See entry for JOHNSON.

OGDEN: On the 23rd ult., by Elder John Pirkey, Mr. John T. OGDEN, of Frederick, and Miss Mary A. KELLER, of Shenandoah county.

Rockingham Register and Advertiser, 29 July 1859 (Friday), p. 3, c. 2.

OLINGER: See entry for STARK.

OLLINGER: On the 6th inst., by Rev. J.A. Snyder, Wm. H. OLLINGER and Miss Mary A. HUPP, all of Shenandoah.

Rockingham Register, 17 November 1870 (Thursday), p. 2, c. 3.

O'NEAL: See entry for VAN PELT.

O'NEAL: See entry for WOODWARD.

O'NEAL: On the 25th ult., by Rev. Levi Keller, Dennis O'NEAL and Miss Elizabeth Frances BURNER, both of Shenandoah.

Rockingham Register, 8 September 1870 (Thursday), p. 3, c. 3.

O'NEAL: On the 16th of February, by Rev. Solomon Garber, Timothy O'NEAL, of Cork county, Ireland, and Mrs. Caroline MOYERHEFFER, widow of Jno. [sic, Andrew Jackson] MOYERHEFFER, dec'd, of Dayton.

Rockingham Register and Advertiser, 24 February 1865 (Friday), p. 2, c. 5.

O'NEALE: See entry for CARTER.

O'NEIL: See entry for FITZSIMMONS.

OPIE: At the residence of the bride, in the city of Wheeling, on Tuesday evening, the 24th ult., by Rev. Dr. H.R. Weed, Mr.

H.L. OPIE, Jr., of Staunton, and Miss Julia C. PAULL, of that city.
Rockingham Register and Advertiser, 11 May 1860 (Friday), p. 2, c. 6.

OPIE: At Bardstown, Kentucky, on the 31st of March, by Rev. J.V. Cosby, H.L. OPIE, of Staunton, and Miss Sue W. SIMMONS, of the former place.
Rockingham Register, 16 April 1868 (Thursday), p. 2, c. 5.

OPIE: On the 17th inst., at Trinity Church, Staunton, by Rev. J.A. Latane, Capt. John N. OPIE and Miss Belle, second daughter of Col. M.G. HARMAN, both of Staunton.
Rockingham Register and Advertiser, 25 October 1866 (Thursday), p. 3, c. 3.

OPIE: On the 13th inst., at Trinity Church, in Staunton, by Rev. Mr. Latane, Dr. Thomas OPIE, of Baltimore, and Miss Sallie, daughter of Col. M.G. HARMON.
Rockingham Register and Advertiser, 21 November 1867 (Thursday), p. 2, c. 5.

OREBACK: See entry for WOLF.

OREBAUGH: See entry for OREBAUGH.

OREBAUGH: On the 22nd ult., by Rev. X.J. Richardson, Mr. Henry A. OREBAUGH, of Green county, to Miss Frances E., daughter of Mr. David ARGENBRIGHT, of this county.
Rockingham Register and Advertiser, 6 April 1860 (Friday), p. 2, c. 6.

OREBAUGH: On Tuesday the 23rd ult., by the Rev. H. Wetzel, Mr. John W. OREBAUGH and Miss Elizabeth E. MILLER, both of Augusta county.
Rockingham Register and Virginia Advertiser, 2 November 1855 (Friday), p. 3, c. 1.

OREBAUGH: Near Timberville, Rockingham county, Va., on the 24th of December, by Rev. S. Henkel, William OREBAUGH and Miss Amanda OREBAUGH, both of Rockingham.
Rockingham Register, 13 January 1870 (Thursday), p. 3, c. 4.

OREPAUGH: On the 20th day of February, 1845, by the Rev. J.A. Van Lear, Mr. George A.

OREPAUGH to Miss Elizabeth STANDAMIRE, all of Augusta county.
Rockingham Register and Valley Advertiser, 8 March 1845 (Saturday), p. 3, c. 3.

ORNDOFF: See entry for DYER.
ORNDORF: See entry for BOLLINGER.
ORNDORF: See entry for FRAVEL.
ORNDORF: See entry for LEMON.
ORNDORF: See entry for SNYDER.
ORNDORFF: See entry for FISHEL.
ORNDORFF: See entry for GAITHER.
ORNDORFF: See entry for LOCKMILLER.
ORNDORFF: See entry for ORNDORFF.
ORNDORFF: See entry for ROGERS.
ORNDORFF: On the 29th ult., Mr. Ira H. ORNDORFF and Mrs. M.E. ELBOM, all of Cedar Creek, Shenandoah county.
Rockingham Register and Advertiser, 13 December 1866 (Thursday), p. 2, c. 5.
ORNDORFF: In Shepherdstown, on the 5th inst., by Rev. W.G. Coe, John ORNDORFF, of Shenandoah county, and Elizabeth PEAR, of Jefferson county, W.Va.
Rockingham Register and Advertiser, 13 February 1868 (Thursday), p. 2, c. 5.
ORNDORFF: On the 4th inst., by Rev. J. Summers, Mason D. ORNDORFF and Miss Mary C. ORNDORFF, all of Shenandoah county.
Rockingham Register and Advertiser, 18 October 1866 (Thursday), p. 2, c. 4.
ORNDORFF: On the 7th of August, by the Rev. Thos. Miller, Mr. Samuel ORNDORFF and Miss Mary KIRTZ, all of Shenandoah county.
Rockingham Register & Advertiser, 27 October 1865 (Friday), p. 2, c. 3.
O'ROARK: See entry for ARMENTROUT.
O'ROARK: See entry for CHAPMAN.
O'ROARK: See entry for NEFF.
O'ROARK: On the 5th inst., at the residence of the bride's father, by the Rev. H. Tallhelm, Mr. Timothy O'ROARK and Miss Catharine PICKERING, both of this county.
Rockingham Register and Advertiser, 13 January 1860 (Friday), p. 2, c. 6.

OSBORN: On the 15th inst., near Columbia
     Furnace, by Rev. St. John Rinker, Dr.
     OSBORN, of Mt. Clifton, and Miss CLARK,
     of Columbia Furnace.
     Rockingham Register, 22 December 1870
     (Thursday), p. 2, c. 4.
OTT: See entry for DOLD.
OTT: See entry for KELLER.
OTT: See entry for NEWMAN.
OTT: See entry for OTT.
OTT: April 28th, 1870, at Fairfield, Va., by
     Rev. Harvey Gilmore, D.A. OTT, of Augusta
     county, and Miss Sue G. MOORE, of
     Fairfield.
     Rockingham Register, 26 May 1870
     (Thursday), p. 2, c. 6.
OTT: On the 27th ult., by Rev. C. Beard, Mr.
     Frederick C. OTT and Miss Harrietta C.
     LAYMAN.
     The Rockingham Register, 12 December 1862
     (Friday), p. 2, c. 5.
OTT: On Thursday afternoon, the 8th inst., at
     the M.E. Church Parsonage in
     Harrisonburg, by Rev. Thos. Hildebrand,
     Mr. Theophilas OTT and Miss Mary,
     daughter of Mr. Henry OTT, all of this
     place.
     Rockingham Register and Advertiser, 16
     November 1860 (Friday), p. 2, c. 4.
OVERALT: Near Mill Point, on the 30th ult.,
     by Rev. Joshua Buckley, George OVERALT,
     formerly of Rockingham, and Miss Mary
     McCLURE, of Pocahontas.
     Rockingham Register and Advertiser, 21
     January 1859 (Friday), p. 3, c. 5.
OVERHOLT: See entry for PATTERSON.
OVERHOLTZ: On the 14th inst., in Mount
     Jackson, by Elder Henry Jennings, Samuel
     P. OVERHOLTZ and Miss Cornelia
     ROSENBERGER, all of Shenandoah county.
     Rockingham Register and Advertiser, 28
     February 1867 (Thursday), p. 2, c. 6.

- P -

PACE: On the 25th ult., at Cedar Hill, in

Augusta county, by Rev. Mr. Hensel, Theodore A. PACE, of Richmond, and Miss Ella R. WATTS, of Augusta.
Rockingham Register and Advertiser, 2 May 1867 (Thursday), p. 2, c. 6.

PAGE: See entry for COOKE.

PAGE: See entry for PENDLETON.

PAINTER: See entry for SHEETZ.

PAINTER: At the Clerk's office of Page county, on the 20th ult., by J.W. Watson, Issac N. PAINTER to Barbara A. SHARK, all of Page county.
Rockingham Register, 7 October 1869 (Thursday), p. 2, c. 3.

PAINTER: On the 7th inst., by Rev. George W. Bailey, Joseph PAINTER and Mrs. Polly A. HIGGS, all of Page county.
Rockingham Register and Advertiser, 21 November 1867 (Thursday), p. 2, c. 5.

PAINTER: On the 17th of July last, at Somerset, Wabash county, Indiana, Mr. Rhesa A. PAINTER, formerly of Shenandoah county, and Miss Martha Jane LORING, of Grant county, Indiana.
Rockingham Register and Advertiser, 2 September 1859 (Friday), p. 2, c. 5.

PAINTER: On the 20th inst., by Rev. W.S. Perry, Romanus PAINTER, of Shenandoah, and Miss Bettie Chapman LEE, of Rockingham.
Rockingham Register and Advertiser, 27 November 1866 (Thursday), p. 2, c. 5.

PAINTER: On the 18th of August, by the Rev. Thos. Miller, Mr. Samuel PAINTER and Miss Martha LANTZ, all of Shenandoah county.
Rockingham Register & Advertiser, 27 October 1865 (Friday), p. 2, c. 3.

PALMER: See entry for JOHNSON.

PALMER: See entry for LEWIS.

PALMER: See entry for MYERS.

PALMER: See entry for WEAVER.

PALMER: On the 7th inst., near Waynesboro, Augusta county, by Rev. W.R. Stringer, M.V. PALMER and Miss Hattie E. PATTERSON.
Rockingham Register and Advertiser, 14 February 1867 (Thursday), p. 2, c. 6.

PALMER: On the 2nd inst., by the Rev. Wm. Brown, D.D., Capt. P.O. PALMER and Mrs. Eliza A. LAMB, all of Augusta county. Rockingham Register and Advertiser, 10 February 1860 (Friday), p. 2, c. 5.

PALMER: On the 23rd ult., by Rev. G.G. Brooke, Mr. Samuel C. PALMER and Miss Elizabeth G. JOHNSON. Rockingham Register and Advertiser, 14 January 1859 (Friday), p. 3, c. 3.

PALSER: See entry for FREEZE.

PANNEL: See entry for SPEEK.

PANNILL: On Thursday, the 26th inst., at the residence of Benjamin Walker, Esq., Orange county, by the Rev. Benjamin L. Hume, Baldwin PANNILL, Esq., to Miss Mary S. DUNN, all of Orange. Rockingham Register and Advertiser, 28 December 1860 (Friday), p. 1, c. 5.

PARK: On the 13th inst., by Rev. P. Miller, Mr. William PARK and Miss Susan A. BRILL, all of Hampshire county. The Rockingham Register, 23 September 1864 (Friday), p. 2, c. 5.

PARKER: See entry for BICKLE.

PARKER: See entry for HOWDERSUELL.

PARKER: On the 15th inst., by Rev. Samuel Brown, Horatio T. PARKER and Miss Jennie C. BAIN, all of Rockbridge. Rockingham Register and Advertiser, 31 January 1867 (Thursday), p. 3, c. 2.

PARKS: On the 16th inst., by Rev. P.H. Whisner, James C. PARKS and Miss Virginia AGNOR, all of Lexington. Rockingham Register and Advertiser, 31 October 1867 (Thursday), p. 2, c. 6.

PARR: See entry for BRADY.

PARRILL: Near Wardensville, November 12th, by the Rev. P. Miller, Mr. Jacob PARRILL, of Hampshire county, and Miss Clarinda R.A. REYNOLDS, of Hardy county. The Rockingham Register, 27 November 1863 (Friday), p. 2, c. 5.

PARRISH: See entry for LITTLE.

PARROTT: See entry for BLOSSER.

PARROTT: See entry for SHOWALTER.

334

PARROW: On the 29th ult., by Rev. J.A.
    Latane, Dr. Chas. H. PARROW, of Nelson,
    to Miss Fannie A. MITCHELL, of Augusta
    county.
    Rockingham Register, 6 May 1869
    (Thursday), p. 2, c. 3.
PARSONS: See entry for VANMETER.
PARTLOW: See entry for LAMBERT.
PATERSON: See entry for SMILEY.
PATTERSON: See entry for ALLEN.
PATTERSON: See entry for BELL.
PATTERSON: See entry for McCLUNG.
PATTERSON: See entry for PALMER.
PATTERSON: On the 21st ult., on South River,
    by the Rev. J. Killian, Capt. Benjamin G.
    PATTERSON, of Harrisonburg, to Miss
    Fannie, daughter of Martin KOINER, of
    Augusta county.
    Rockingham Register & Advertiser, 6
    October 1865 (Friday), p. 2, c. 2.
PATTERSON: On Thursday, the 9th inst., by the
    Rev. Thos. D. Bell, Mr. Charles Stuart
    PATTERSON, of Augusta, and Miss Margaret
    Jane, daughter of Maj. David R. HOPKINS,
    of Rockingham.
    Rockingham Register and Advertiser, 17
    June 1859 (Friday), p. 3, c. 3.
PATTERSON: On the 5th inst., by Rev. J.W.F.
    Graham, Mr. J.H. PATTERSON, of Highland,
    and Miss Maggie E. SLAVEN, of Pocahontas
    county, Va.
    Rockingham Register and Advertiser, 15
    February 1861 (Friday), p. 2, c. 7.
PATTERSON: On the 4th day of September, 1870,
    near Waynesboro, by Rev. J.E. Seneker,
    J.L. PATTERSON and Miss Emma A. OVERHOLT,
    all of Augusta county.
    Rockingham Register, 15 September 1870
    (Thursday), p. 3, c. 3.
PATTERSON: On the 22nd ult., at the Lutheran
    Parsonage, near Waynesboro, by Rev. C.
    Beard, James A. PATTERSON, Jr., and Miss
    Nannie E. SMITH, both of Augusta.
    Rockingham Register and Advertiser, 6
    December 1866 (Thursday), p. 3, c. 2.
PATTERSON: On the 6th inst., near

335

Schutterly's Mill, by the Rev. R.C. Walker, John W. PATTERSON and Miss Sarah E. MONEYMAKER, all of Augusta.
Rockingham Register and Advertiser, 27 June 1867 (Thursday), p. 2, c. 6.

PATTERSON: At Maple Lawn, Highland county, July 5th, by Rev. R.S. Kennedy, Dr. Pryne PATTERSON, of Pocahontas, and Miss Lizzie, daughter of B.B. CAMPBELL, Esq.
Rockingham Register and Advertiser, 2 August 1866 (Thursday), p. 2, c. 5.

PATTERSON: On the 5th inst., by Rev. T.D. Bell, Mr. Samuel W. PATTERSON, of Augusta county, and Miss Hetty Jane, daughter of Mr. David BEAR, of Rockingham county.
The Rockingham Register, 13 November 1863 (Friday), p. 2, c. 6.

PATTIE: On the 3rd inst., at the residence of the bride's father, by Rev. W.H. Foote, D.D., Champ. W. PATTIE and Miss Nannie McClintock, second daughter of Wm. HARPER, Esq., editor of the South Branch Intelligencer, all of Romney, W.Va.
Rockingham Register, 11 November 1869 (Thursday), p. 3, c. 3.

PATTON: On the 28th of April, by the Rev. Wm. S. White, D.D., at Stone Cottage, near Lexington, Jas. T. PATTON, Esq., Editor of the Parkersburg Gazette, and Miss Agnes M., daughter of Col. A. BARCLAY, dec'd.
Rockingham Register and Advertiser, 13 May 1859 (Friday), p. 3, c. 4.

PAUL: See entry for FLETCHER.

PAUL: On the 18th inst., by Rev. Daniel Thomas, Mr. Isaac PAUL to Miss Rebecca Catharine, daughter of Christian WEEAN, all of Rockingham.
Rockingham Register and Advertiser, 26 March 1858 (Friday), p. 3, c. 2.

PAUL: At "Collicello," the residence of the bride's father, on Monday evening, the 12th inst., by Rev. Thos. U. Dudley, Mr. Robert C. PAUL and Miss Ettie C., youngest daughter of Capt. David S. JONES, all of Harrisonburg.

336

Rockingham Register, 15 October 1868 (Thursday), p. 2, c. 3.

PAUL: On Tuesday evening last, near Harrisonburg, by Rev. J.S.R. Clarke, Mr. Wm. I. PAUL, 7th Va. Cavalry, Rosser's Brigade, and Miss Julia HOUSTON, all of this vicinity.

Rockingham Register and Advertiser, 24 February 1865 (Friday), p. 2, c. 5.

PAULEY: See entry for COARSEY.

PAULL: See entry for OPIE.

PAULSEL: See entry for HOUSER.

PAULSEL: On Thursday, the 3rd inst., by Rev. Jacob Miller, Mr. John PAULSEL and Miss Rebecca Jane, youngest daughter of Levi MAY, dec'd, all of this county.

Rockingham Register and Advertiser, 11 May 1860 (Friday), p. 2, c. 6.

PAULSEL: Near Noblesville, Hamilton county, Indiana, on Tuesday, the 11th of August, by the Rev. Thomas M. Bernah, Mr. Peter PAULSEL, formerly of Rockingham county, and Eliza Clark, eldest daughter of Roswell BURROUGH, of Hamilton county, Ind.

Rockingham Register and Advertiser, 26 August 1859 (Friday), p. 2, c. 5.

PAXTON: See entry for HARLOW.

PAYNE: See entry for BOX.

PAYNE: See entry for CORBIN.

PAYNE: See entry for FLEMMING.

PAYNE: See entry for KELLY.

PAYNE: See entry for SIBERT.

PAYNE: On the 10th inst., by Rev. Daniel Thomas, Henry H. PAYNE and Miss Susannah, daughter of Jas. C. HELTZEL, Esq., all of Rockingham county.

Rockingham Register and Advertiser, 21 November 1867 (Thursday), p. 2, c. 5.

PAYNE: At Orange C.H., on Tuesday evening, the 3rd inst., by the Rev. D.B. Erving, Mr. John S. PAYNE, Editor of the Southern Chronicle, and Miss Mary Virginia THRIFT, both of Orange.

Rockingham Register and Advertiser, 18 February 1859 (Friday), p. 2, c. 6.

PAYTON: On the 27th September, by the Rev.
T.A. Morgan, Mr. John W. PAYTON and Miss
Elizabeth BAILEY, all of Rockingham
county.
Rockingham Register and Valley
Advertiser, 13 October 1849 (Saturday),
p. 2, c. 5.

PEACHY: On Wednesday evening, the 15th inst.,
W.D. PEACHY, of Alexandria, Va., and Miss
Lelia R., daughter of Dr. A. Russell
MEEM, dec'd, of Shenandoah county.
Rockingham Register, 23 December 1869
(Thursday), p. 3, c. 2.

PEACO: See entry for PEACO.

PEACO: See entry for WRIGHT.

PEACO: On the 20th inst., near Waynesboro,
Augusta county, by Rev. W.R. Stringer,
Alexander S. PEACO and Miss Elizabeth M.
PEACO.
Rockingham Register and Advertiser, 27
June 1867 (Thursday), p. 2, c. 6.

PEALE: On the 28th of April, by Rev. T.W.
Toby, Mr. A.N. PEALE, of Rockingham
county, Va., and Miss Sallie Jane,
daughter of Henry BUSHNELL, Esq., of
Caswell county, N.C.
Rockingham Register and Advertiser, 12
June 1857 (Friday), p. 3, c. 2.

PEAR: See entry for ORNDORFF.

PEARL: On the 14th of July, by Rev. Isaac
Long, Joseph PEARL, formerly of Botetourt
county, and Miss Maggie, daughter of
Jacob SIPE, all of Rockingham county, Va.
Rockingham Register, 21 July 1870
(Thursday), p. 3, c. 3.

PEARL: On the 18th inst., by Elder H.
Jennings, Otto PEARL and Miss Amanda
RHINEHART, all of Shenandoah county.
Rockingham Register and Advertiser, 28
March 1867 (Thursday), p. 2, c. 6.

PEARSON: See entry for PHILIPS.

PECK: See entry for WEBB.

PECK: On the 9th inst., by Rev. W.C. McCarty,
Captain H.H. PECK and Miss Christiana
HUNTER.
Rockingham Register and Advertiser, 26

October 1860 (Friday), p. 2, c. 6.

PEEL: See entry for DENTON.

PEER: See entry for HARBAUGH.

PEER: See entry for SNIDER.

PELTER: On Wednesday, the 15th ult., at the residence of Samuel Paul, by Rev. Wm. Pinkerton, Geo. W. PELTER and Miss Effie G., daughter of J. Hamilton BROWN, dec'd, both of Augusta county.
Rockingham Register and Advertiser, 13 June 1867 (Thursday), p. 2, c. 6.

PEMBERTON: See entry for WILEY.

PENCE: See entry for BURKE.

PENCE: See entry for GOCHENOUR.

PENCE: See entry for HELBERT (2).

PENCE: See entry for KILLION.

PENCE: See entry for MICHAELS.

PENCE: Near Forestville, on the 2nd inst., by Rev. Jacob Stirewalt, Mr. Adam PENCE and Miss Sarah, daughter of Capt. John PETERS, all of Shenandoah.
Rockingham Register & Advertiser, 17 November 1865 (Friday), p. 2, c. 4.

PENCE: On the 8th of September, at Pleasant Run, by the Rev. Isaac Long, Calvin W. PENCE and Miss Fannie B., daughter of John RHODES, dec'd, all of Rockingham.
Rockingham Register, 15 September 1870 (Thursday), p. 3, c. 3.

PENCE: On Thursday, the 5th inst., by the Rev. Mr. Eskridge, Mr. Cyrus PENCE to Miss Eliza, daughter of Mr. Joseph LITTLE, all of New Market.
Rockingham Register, 14 February 1835 (Saturday), p. 3, c. 3.

PENCE: On the 26th of May, by Rev. J. Stirewalt, Mr. Ephraim PENCE, ofRockingham, and Miss Ann E. FAIRBURN, of Shenandoah.
Rockingham Register and Advertiser, 1 July 1859 (Friday), p. 2, c. 4.

PENCE: On the 11th inst., by Rev. Jacob Miller, Franklin PENCE and Miss Elizabeth F., daughter of Levi BAXTER, all of Rockingham county.
Rockingham Register and Advertiser, 18

October 1866 (Thursday), p. 2, c. 4.

PENCE: On the 28th ult., by Rev. John W. Wolff, Mr. George PENCE and Miss Frances J.C., daughter of Mr. John HAUGH, all of this county.

Rockingham Register and Advertiser, 12 June 1857 (Friday), p. 3, c. 2.

PENCE: On the 30th of September, by the Rev. Jacob Miller, Mr. Hugh B. PENCE and Miss Sarah C. ASHENFELTER, all of Rockingham county.

Rockingham Register and Advertiser, 11 October 1866 (Thursday), p. 3, c. 4.

PENCE: In the Baptist Meeting-house, near Mt. Crawford, by Rev. Wm. S. Perry, on the 24th of December, John W. PENCE and Miss Julia Ann WHISMAN, all of Mt. Crawford, Va.

Rockingham Register, 14 January 1869 (Thursday), p. 3, c. 3.

PENCE: On Tuesday last, the 13th inst., by Rev. Jos. Funkhouser, Mr. Joshua PENCE and Miss Elizabeth, daughter of Mr. Abraham BOWMAN, all of Rockingham county.

Rockingham Register and Advertiser, 16 December 1859 (Friday), p. 3, c. 1.

PENCE: On the 19th of January last, by Rev. Abram Knopp, Sen., Mr. Lemuel A. PENCE and Miss Harriet, daughter of Reuben DERROW, all of Rockingham.

Rockingham Register and Advertiser, 3 February 1860 (Friday), p. 2, c. 5.

PENCE: On the 2nd inst., Mr. Moses PENCE and Miss Barbara FANSLER, all of Shenandoah county.

Rockingham Register and Advertiser, 13 December 1866 (Thursday), p. 2, c. 5.

PENCE: On the 8th inst., by Rev. J.J. Harshberger, Mr. Peter PENCE and Miss Margaret, daughter of Mr. Daniel MILLER, all of Rockingham.

Rockingham Register and Advertiser, 23 March 1860 (Friday), p. 2, c. 6.

PENCE: On Thursday, the 19th of January, by Rev. Jacob Miller, Mr. Samuel PENCE and Miss Rebecca A., daughter of Mr. Alex. A.

BLAKELEY, all of Rockingham.
Rockingham Register and Advertiser, 27
January 1860 (Friday), p. 2, c. 6.

PENCE: In Waverly, Missouri, on the 16th
inst., at the residence of R.B. Cauthorn,
by Rev. J.W. Clark, Mr. Wm. PENCE, of
Rockingham county, Va., and Miss Cynthia
J. GIVENS, of Cooper county, Mo.
Rockingham Register and Advertiser, 5
October 1860 (Friday), p. 2, c. 3.

PENCE: On the 18th ult., by Rev. Henry St.
John Rinker, Wm. PENCE and Miss Ann R.
FECKER, all of Shenandoah county.
Rockingham Register, 3 September 1868
(Thursday), p. 2, c. 4.

PENCE: On the 20th ult., at Wunder's Store,
by the Rev. S. Henkel, Wm. A. PENCE and
Miss Mary H., daughter of Chas. S.
WUNDER, all of Shenandoah.
Rockingham Register and Advertiser, 10
January 1867 (Thursday), p. 3, c. 2.

PENDERGAST: See entry for MOFFETT.

PENDLETON: On Monday morning last, at the
residence of the bride's mother, by Rev.
D.C. Irwin, Mr. David E. PENDLETON,
C.S.A., of Baltimore, Md., and Miss Laura
C. SLATER, of Harrisonburg, Va.
The Rockingham Register, 18 March 1864
(Friday), p. 2, c. 7.

PENDLETON: On the 11th inst., at Mansfield,
Clarke county, by Rev. F.M. Whittle,
Gurdon H. PENDLETON and Miss Jane Byrd,
daughter of Mann R. PAGE.
Rockingham Register and Virginia
Advertiser, 27 May 1854 (Saturday), p. 2,
c. 7.

PENN: See entry for BURKHOLDER.

PENNYBACKER: See entry for BROCK.

PENNYBACKER: See entry for DEVIER.

PENNYBACKER: See entry for PENNYBACKER.

PENNYBACKER: On Thursday morning, the 5th of
April, at the residence of the bride's
father, by Rev. Timothy Funk, Derrick
PENNYBACKER and Miss Lizzie, daughter of
Jno. J. BOWMAN, all of Linvill's Creek,
Rockingham county.

341

Rockingham Register and Advertiser, 13 April 1866 (Friday), p. 3, c. 2.

PENNYBACKER: On Wednesday, the 4th inst., by Rev. Mr. Keighburne, Frank S. PENNYBACKER, of Mt. Jackson, and Miss Lue E. WHITE, of Loudoun county.

Rockingham Register and Advertiser, 12 December 1867 (Thursday), p. 3, c. 2.

PENNYBACKER: On Monday evening, August 28th, at the bride's residence, on Linvill's Creek, in this county, by Rev.Patterson Fletcher, John D. PENNYBACKER, Esq., of this place, and Mrs. Mary E. MAUPIN, of this county.

Rockingham Register & Advertiser, 8 September 1865 (Friday), p. 3, c. 2.

PENNYBACKER: On the 19th inst., by Rev. T.D. Bell, Mr. Joseph S. PENNYBACKER and Mrs. Sarah A. PENNYBACKER, widow of the late Judge PENNYBACKER.

Rockingham Register and Advertiser, 27 December 1861 (Friday), p. 2, c. 7.

PENNYWITT: See entry for WALTERS.

PENNYWITT: On the 16th inst., by Rev. J. Stirewalt, Mr. John D. PENNYWITT and Miss Sarah Catherine MILLER, all of Shenandoah county, Va.

Rockingham Register and Advertiser, 26 April 1861 (Friday), p. 2, c. 7.

PERCIVAL: See entry for RITTENOUR.

PERKEY: On the 1st of April, by Rev. Isaac Long, Henry PERKEY and Miss Elizabeth, daughter of Zachariah RAINES, all of Rockingham county.

Rockingham Register, 20 May 1869 (Thursday), p. 2, c. 3.

PERKINS: See entry for CARR.

PERKINS: See entry for WILLIAMS.

PERKINS: On the 26th ult., near Bridgewater, by Rev. George W. Stevenson, Adam PERKINS, of Augusta, and Miss S.S. BARRACK, of Rockingham county.

Rockingham Register and Advertiser, 3 October 1867 (Thursday), p. 2, c. 6.

PERKINS: On the 24th of November, in Montgomery county, Md., by Rev. Father

Mackey, Wm. PERKINS and Mrs. Margaret
TOOMAY, widow of Jeremiah TOOMAY, dec'd,
formerly of Harrisonburg, Va.
Rockingham Register, 1 December 1870
(Thursday), p. 2, c. 4.

PERRY: See entry for JACKSON.

PERRY: At Shenstone, Shenandoah county, Va.,
the residence of the bride's father, on
the morning of the 16th inst., by the
Rev. A.R. Rude, Joseph H. PERRY, of
Alexandria, and Miss Ada L., daughter of
Wm. SIGLER, Esq.
Rockingham Register and Advertiser, 26
April 1861 (Friday), p. 2, c. 7.

PERRY: On the 21st ult., at the Charles
Street Church, Baltimore, by Rev. John B.
MARTIN, Rev. Wm. J. PERRY, of the
Baltimore Conference, and Miss Hattie R.,
daughter of the officiating minister.
Rockingham Register and Advertiser, 8
March 1861 (Friday), p. 3, c. 1.

PERRY: On the 6th inst., by Rev. Benton
Shepherd, of Charlestown, Rev. Wm. S.
PERRY, of Rockingham county, and Miss
Emma Virginia, daughter of Dr. BONHAM, of
Clarke county, Va.
Rockingham Register and Advertiser, 15
November 1866 (Thursday), p. 2, c. 5.

PERSINGER: See entry for FREY.

PETERFISH: See entry for DOVAL.

PETERS: See entry for JOHNS.

PETERS: See entry for PENCE.

PETERS: On the 15th inst., by Rev. Samuel
Shaver, R.A. PETERS and Miss Mary C.
SHEETS, all of Shenandoah county.
Rockingham Register, 3 February 1870
(Thursday), p. 3, c. 4.

PETERSON: See entry for FULK (2).

PETERSON: On the 3rd inst., at the residence
of Mr. Areheart, near Sangersville, by
the Rev. J.T. Eakin, Mr. Chas. W.
PETERSON to Miss Mary GOOD, of Augusta
county.
Rockingham Register and Virginia
Advertiser, 14 December 1855 (Friday), p.
2, c. 8.

PETERSON: On the 30th of December, by Rev. P.A. Peterson, Rev. E.M. PETERSON, of the Va. Conference, M.E. Church, South, and Miss Mary F., daughter of Samuel RUTH, Esq., of Richmond, Va.
Rockingham Register, 7 January 1869 (Thursday), p. 3, c. 3.

PETERSON: At the residence of the bride's father, in Dayton, Rockingham county, Va., on the evening of the 17th inst., by Rev. George W. Holland, Wm. Henry PETERSON, of Rockingham county, Va., and Miss Mary Amanda, youngest daughter of Daniel M. NISEWANDER, formerly of Washington county, Maryland.
Rockingham Register and Advertiser, 26 December 1867 (Thursday), p. 2, c. 6.

PETRIE: On Tuesday, the 13th of March, by the Rev. John Heck, Mr. John S. PETRIE, of Rockingham county, Va., and Miss Elizabeth G., daughter of Capt. Henry CLAPPER, of Washington county, Md.
Rockingham Register and Advertiser, 6 April 1860 (Friday), p. 2, c. 6.

PETTUS: See entry for STEVENS.

PEYTON: See entry for BROWN.

PEYTON: See entry for COCHRANE.

PEYTON: See entry for KENT.

PEYTON: On the 21st inst., at the residence of Mr. Isaac W. Garth, Albemarle county, by Rev. Wm. P. Farish, Col. Chas. S. PEYTON, of Staunton, and Miss Sallie E., youngest daughter of Nimrod BRAMHAM, Esq.
Rockingham Register and Advertiser, 28 November 1867 (Thursday), p. 2, c. 6.

PEYTON: On the 24th ult., at Willow Spout, by the Rev. J.C. Wheat, E.G. PEYTON and Miss Kate N. WOODWARD, both of Augusta.
Rockingham Register, 2 December 1869 (Thursday), p. 2, c. 3.

PHARES: On Thursday, the 11th inst., by Rev. S.F. Butts, at the residence of Capt. John Waybright, Robert PHARES, of Pendleton county, W.Va., and Miss Phoebe Jane WAYBRIGHT, of Highland county.
Rockingham Register and Advertiser, 25

April 1867 (Thursday), p. 2, c. 7.

PHELPS: On the 16th inst., at the residence of Wm. L. Herr, in Staunton,by N.J.B. Morgan, D.D., Rev. E.P. PHELPS, of the Va. Conference, M.E. Church, and Mrs. J.W. CARRINGTON, of Texas.
Rockingham Register, 25 November 1869 (Thursday), p. 2, c. 3.

PHERSON: See entry for FLORY.

PHILINS: On the 15th inst., by Rev. H. Wetzel, Wm. PHILLINS and Miss Lydia SWARTZ, both of Shenandoah county.
Rockingham Register, 24 March 1870 (Thursday), p. 3, c. 2.

PHILIPS: See entry for DEVER.

PHILIPS: See entry for FLEMINGS.

PHILIPS: See entry for McKIM.

PHILIPS: See entry for SHEETZ.

PHILIPS: On the 28th of January, by Rev. W.H. Cone, Mr. George W. PHILIPS and Miss Nancy E. PEARSON, both of Shenandoah county.
The Rockingham Register, 5 February 1864 (Friday), p. 2, c. 6.

PHILLIPS: See entry for DAVIES.

PHILLIPS: See entry for HIGGS.

PHILLIPS: See entry for WANLESS.

PHILLIPS: On the 24th of December, by Rev. H. Shaull, James R. PHILLIPS and Miss Emily S. LITTLE, all of Shenandoah county.
Rockingham Register, 14 January 1869 (Thursday), p. 3, c. 3.

PHILLIPS: On the 21st inst., in Staunton, by the Rev. R.H. Phillips, assisted by the Rev. J.S. Latane, Reuben T. PHILLIPS and Miss Fannie S., daughter of W.H. TAMS, Esq.
Rockingham Register and Advertiser, 30 May 1867 (Thursday), p. 3, c. 3.

PHILLIPS: On the 4th inst., by Rev. Isaac Long, Wm. Hiram PHILLIPS and Miss Margaret, daughter of James MILLER, all of Rockingham county.
Rockingham Register and Advertiser, 18 October 1866 (Thursday), p. 2, c. 4.

PICKERING: See entry for BAZZLE.

PICKERING: See entry for BRILL.

PICKERING: See entry for O'ROARK.

PICKERING: On the 17th inst., by the Rev. J.A. Bovey, Mr. Abraham PICKERING and Miss Lydia, daughter of Mr. Tobias BEAM, all of this county.
Rockingham Register and Advertiser, 25 February 1859 (Friday), p. 2, c. 5.

PICKERING: On Tuesday, the 22nd inst., by Rev. G. Woods, Jacob PICKERING and Miss Lucy NISWARNER, both of Rockingham.
Rockingham Register, 31 March 1870 (Thursday), p. 3, c. 3.

PIERCE: See entry for BUSH.

PIFER: See entry for DINKLE.

PIFER: See entry for HAWKINS.

PIFER: See entry for LUTZ.

PIFER: See entry for SNAPP.

PIFER: See entry for WHITE.

PIPER: On the 25th of February, by Rev. Jacob Miller, Mr. Morgan D. PIPER and Miss Catharine C. SPRINKEL, all of Rockingham.
The Rockingham Register, 18 March 1864 (Friday), p. 2, c. 7.

PIRKEY: Near Port Republic, on the 24th of December, by Rev. Isaac Long, ALbert Hamilton PIRKEY and Mrs. Amanda KYGER, daughter of Elias HUDLOWE, all of Rockingham county.
Rockingham Register and Advertiser, 23 January 1868 (Thursday), p. 2, c. 4.

PIRKEY: December 20th, at the house of the bride's father, by Rev. R. Smith, Oscar F.A. PIRKEY, Esq., and Miss Sarah E. JOHNSON, all of Rockingham.
Rockingham Register and Advertiser, 28 December 1860 (Friday), p. 1, c. 5.

PIRKEY: On Thursday evening, 3rd inst., at the residence of the bride's father, by Elder C.W. Sewell, Prof. Oval PIRKEY, of Strasburg, Va., and Miss Maggie E., daughter of O.D. WILLIAMS, Esq., of Alexandria, Tennessee.
Rockingham Register and Advertiser, 18 November 1859 (Friday), p. 2, c. 4.

PITMAN: See entry for BORDEN.

PITMAN: See entry for FLANNAGAN.
PITMAN: See entry for GOULD.
PITMAN: See entry for POWERS.
PITMAN: On the 20th ult., at "Red Banks," by Rev. J.W. Wolff, Mr. John L. PITMAN and Miss Mary Jane, daughter of Mr. William RIPLEY, all of Shenandoah county. Rockingham Register and Advertiser, 5 October 1860 (Friday), p. 2, c. 3.
PITMAN: On the 16th inst., by Rev. T.W.L. Dosh, Philip PITMAN, of Winchester, and Miss Mattie C. HELLER, of Woodstock, Va. Rockingham Register, 23 April 1868 (Thursday), p. 2, c. 5.
PITTINGTON: See entry for TAYLOR.
PITZER: See entry for HILL.
PITZER: See entry for HOUSMAN.
PLANT: At St. Francis' Church, Staunton, September 8th, by Rev. Father J. Ambler Weed, Benj. PLANT and Mrs. Mary BECK, all of Staunton. Rockingham Register, 17 September 1868 (Thursday), p. 2, c. 5.
PLAUGAR: On the 12th ult., by Rev. J.W. Watson, Mr. Wm. H. PLAUGAR and Mrs. Sarah E. JENKINS. Rockingham Register and Advertiser, 9 November 1860 (Friday), p. 2, c. 6.
PLAUGER: At the Lutheran Parsonage, in Woodstock, on the 20th ult., by Rev. Levi Keller, John PLAUGER and Miss Sarah E. WILLIAMS, all of Shenandoah county. Rockingham Register and Advertiser, 11 July 1867 (Thursday), p. 2, c. 6.
PLECKER: See entry for CROUSEHORN.
PLECKER: See entry for LUTZ.
PLECKER: See entry for WHITMORE.
PLECKER: See entry for WISE.
PLECKER: On the 22nd ult., in the Methodist Episcopal Church, in Fincastle, by Rev. J.L. Gilbert, A.H. PLECKER, of Augusta county, and Miss Maggie Bell BACKENSTO, of Fincastle, Va. Rockingham Register, 12 November 1868 (Thursday), p. 3, c. 3.
PLECKER: On Thursday, the 19th ult., by Rev.

J.C. Hensell, Mr. Daniel PLECKER and Miss Mary S., only daughter of Mr. Harrison TEAFORD, of Augusta county.
Rockingham Register & Advertiser, 3 November 1865 (Friday), p. 2, c. 2.

PLECKER: At Prairie City, Illinois, on New Year's Day, 1867, by Rev. Mr. Warner, J.H. PLECKER, formerly of Rockingham county, and M.E., daughter of L.I. WASHBURNE.
Rockingham Register and Advertiser, 24 January 1867 (Thursday), p. 2, c. 4.

PLECKER: On Thursday, the 13th inst., by the Rev. John C. Lyon, Mr. John PLECKER to Miss Sarah GILKERSON, both of Mt. Crawford.
Rockingham Register, 22 April 1837 (Saturday), p. 3, c. 3.

PLECKER: On the 3rd inst., by Rev. J.C. Hensell, John S. PLECKER and Miss Martha J., eldest daughter of John W. WISE, all of this county.
Rockingham Register, 24 March 1870 (Thursday), p. 3, c. 2.

PLUMB: See entry for HENDERSON.

PLUMB: On the 5th of January, 1860, by Rev. W.T. Richardson, Mr. Alfred PLUMB and Miss M.E. RIDDLE.
Rockingham Register and Advertiser, 24 February 1860 (Friday), p. 2, c. 4.

PLUNKETT: See entry for BOUDE.

POAGE: On the 15th inst., near New Hope, by Rev. B.M. Smith, Mr. George POAGE to Miss _____ SIMS.
The Rockingham Register and Valley Advertiser, 26 June 1852 (Saturday), p. 2, c. 5.

POE: By Rev. J.A. McFaden, on the Bridge at Harper's Ferry, July 26th, Winterton D. POE and Miss Sarah V. BEATLY, both of Rockingham county, Va.
Rockingham Register, 18 August 1870 (Thursday), p. 3, c. 3.

POINDEXTER: On the 5th of May, by the Rev. James A. Latane, H.W.R. POINDEXTER and Mrs. Fannie E. BAKER, eldest daughter of

Geo. A. ARMENTROUT, of Staunton.

Rockingham Register, 19 May 1870 (Thursday), p. 3, c. 4.

POINTER: See entry for JOHNSON.

POINTS: See entry for KYLE.

POINTS: See entry for NELSON.

POINTS: At the Wesleyan Female Institute, in Staunton, on the 4th inst., by Rev. J.L. Clark, Prof. Leonidas POINTS and Miss Belle, daughter of Col. T.A. GORDON, of Madison county.

Rockingham Register and Advertiser, 11 July 1867 (Thursday), p. 2, c. 6.

POINTS: In Albemarle county, on the 4th inst., by the Rev. Jno. A. Broadus, Dr. W.J. POINTS, of White Hall, to Miss Cornelia V., daughter of Capt. Bezaleel BROWN.

Rockingham Register and Virginia Advertiser, 14 December 1855 (Friday), p. 2, c. 8.

POLK: On the 30th of March, by Rev. Jacob Wine, Mr. James POLK and Sarah Elizabeth HEPNER, all of Shenandoah county, Va.

The Rockingham Register, 1 April 1864 (Friday), p. 2, c. 6.

POLK: On the 26th ult., by Rev. Hy. Wetzel, Mr. John M. POLK and Miss Barbara Ellen WETHERHULTZ, all of Shenandoah.

Rockingham Register and Advertiser, 6 February 1868 (Thursday), p. 2, c. 4.

POLLACK: At the residence of the bride's father, in Harrisonburg, on Wednesday evening last, by the Rev. A.P. Boude, Mr. Samuel W. POLLACK and Miss Mollie Lupton, daughter of Daniel P. RAGAN, all of Harrisonburg.

Rockingham Register & Advertiser, 1 December 1865 (Friday), p. 2, c. 4.

POLLARD: See entry for CALDWELL.

POLLARD: See entry for QUINLAN.

POLLARD: In Dayton, on Tuesday the 20th inst., by Rev. J.M. Grabill, Mr. Wm. POLLARD and Miss Elizabeth M. MOORE, all of Dayton, Rockingham county.

Rockingham Register and Advertiser, 30

March 1860 (Friday), p. 2, c. 4.
POLMER: See entry for ROSEE.
POOL: See entry for BUTCHER.
POOL: See entry for CALDWELL.
POOL: On the 9th ult., by Rev. G.W. Stevenson, David S. POOL and Miss Margaret, daughter of Fred. K. SPECK, Esq., all of Bridgewater.
Rockingham Register and Advertiser, 18 October 1866 (Thursday), p. 2, c. 4.
POOL: On the 14th inst., [sic, ult.], at the residence of the bride's father, by the Rev. D.W. Arnold, Mr. Richard N. POOL, of Rockingham, and Miss Josie M. HITE, of Augusta.
Rockingham Register and Advertiser, 1 March 1861 (Friday), p. 3, c. 3.
POOL: On the 30th ult., by Rev. J.W. Hott, Robert POOL and Miss Eliza HUFFER, all of Augusta county.
Rockingham Register, 6 January 1870 (Thursday), p. 3, c. 3.
PORTER: See entry for MANN.
POTTER: See entry for CREWS.
POWEL: See entry for COMER.
POWEL: See entry for POWEL.
POWEL: On the 18th of September, by the Rev. A.J. Coffman, Mr. Hiram POWEL and Miss Julia Ann POWEL, all of Rockingham.
Rockingham Register and Advertiser, 3 October 1856 (Friday), p. 2, c. 6.
POWEL: On the 26th ult., by Elder C. Allemong, Mr. Jeremiah POWEL and Miss Malinda HALL, both of Rockingham.
Rockingham Register and Advertiser, 9 November 1860 (Friday), p. 2, c. 6.
POWELL: See entry for BATEMAN.
POWELL: See entry for MAGRUDER.
POWELL: See entry for POWELL.
POWELL: See entry for SPINDLE.
POWELL: On Wednesday morning, the 5th inst., in Staunton, by the Rev. J.A. Latane, Hugh L. POWELL, of New York city, late of Va., and Miss Ella, daughter of Dr. F.T. STRIBLING, of Staunton.
Rockingham Register and Advertiser, 13

350

June 1867 (Thursday), p. 2, c. 6.

POWELL: On the 9th inst., by the Rev. Joseph Funkhouser, Mr. Jared A. POWELL and Miss Sarah Jane LAMB, all of this county.
Rockingham Register and Advertiser, 17 August 1860 (Friday), p. 2, c. 5.

POWELL: On the 4th of September, by the Rev. A.J. Coffman, Mr. Lafayette POWELL and Miss Mary POWELL, all of Rockingham county.
Rockingham Register and Advertiser, 3 October 1856 (Friday), p. 2, c. 6.

POWELL: On the 1st inst., by Elder C. Allemong, Moses POWELL and Miss Rebecca Jane SHIFLETT, all of Rockingham county.
Rockingham Register and Advertiser, 16 February 1866 (Friday), p. 3, c. 3.

POWERS: See entry for LOHR.

POWERS: See entry for SYMINGTON.

POWERS: On the 21st ult., by Rev. John W. Watson, Henry M. POWERS, of Staunton, and Miss Rebecca D., daughter of Lawrence PITMAN, Esq., of Page county.
Rockingham Register, 13 August 1868 (Thursday), p. 2, c. 5.

POWERS: On the 9th inst., by Rev. Joseph R. Wheeler, Mr. Wm. F. POWERS and Miss Ellen C. BENNETT, all of Augusta.
Rockingham Register and Advertiser, 19 April 1861 (Friday), p. 2, c. 3.

PRATHER: See entry for GRABILL.

PRATT: On the 3rd inst., by the Rev. T. Edwin Brown, assisted by Dr. G.W. Samson, Lieut. G. Julian PRATT, of Charlottesville, Va., and Miss Mary E., eldest daughter of Eleazer and Margaret BROWN, of Washington city.
Rockingham Register & Advertiser, 27 October 1865 (Friday), p. 2, c. 3.

PREFEIT: In Bridgewater, the 15th inst., by Rev. G.W. Statton, Mr. Philip PREFEIT, of Frederick county, Va., and Miss Frances M. HINER, of Rockingham.
Rockingham Register and Advertiser, 23 March 1860 (Friday), p. 2, c. 6.

PRESGRAVES: See entry for FRISTOE.

PRICE: See entry for ARMENTROUT (2).
PRICE: See entry for ARMSTRONG.
PRICE: See entry for DUNCAN.
PRICE: See entry for GLOVER.
PRICE: See entry for HARMAN.
PRICE: See entry for JONES.
PRICE: See entry for McGLAUGHLIN.
PRICE: See entry for MINNICH.
PRICE: See entry for MITCHELL.
PRICE: See entry for TAYLOR.
PRICE: On the 12th inst., by Rev. J.W. Watson, Mr. Benjamin Q. PRICE, of Rockingham, and Miss Elizabeth N., daughter of Jacob BRUBAKER, of Page county.
Rockingham Register & Advertiser, 29 September 1865 (Friday), p. 3, c. 3.
PRICE: On the 24th of March, by Rev. Wm. S. Baird, Mr. David W. PRICE, of Washington county, and Miss Ann E. FULLER, of Augusta county, Va.
The Rockingham Register, 1 April 1864 (Friday), p. 2, c. 6.
PRICE: On the 4th inst., at the Forge near Port Republic, early in the morning, by Rev. A.J. Coffman, Mr. George W. PRICE, of Scotland county, Mo., to Miss Elizabeth, daughter of John and Elizabeth BREWER, of Rockingham county, Va.
Rockingham Register and Virginia Advertiser, 14 March 1856 (Friday), p. 3, c. 1.
PRICE: On the 17th of June, by Rev. Daniel Thomas, Mr. Isaac PRICE and Miss Margaret, daughter of Mr. Jno. DETAMORE, all of Rockingham county.
Rockingham Register and Advertiser, 6 July 1860 (Friday), p. 2, c. 6.
PRICE: On the 1st of September, by Rev. Christain Hartman, Samuel PRICE and Miss Emma Jane, daughter of Mr. Henry HUDLOWE, all of Rockingham county.
Rockingham Register, 16 September 1869 (Thursday), p. 3, c. 3.
PRICE: In Boonsboro, Maryland, on the 6th of May, by the Rev. M.L. Shuford, Mr. Samuel

J. PRICE, Editor of the Page Valley [Va.]
Courier, late of this town, and Miss
Sophia Louisa HILLIARD, of Hagerstown,
Washington county, Maryland.
Rockingham Register and Advertiser, 16
May 1867 (Thursday), p. 2, c. 5.
PRIEST: See entry for CARRECOFE.
PRIEST: On the 24th of December, by Rev. Wm.
H. Dinkle, at the residence of James
Devier, on Spring Creek, James A. PRIEST,
of Pendleton county, W.Va., and Miss
Maggie E. DINKEL, of Rockingham county.
Rockingham Register, 14 January 1869
(Thursday), p. 3, c. 3.
PRINTZ: See entry for PRINTZ (3).
PRINTZ: See entry for WARREN.
PRINTZ: On the 14th inst., at Stony Man, Page
county, Va., by Rev. I.S. Bennick, Mr. A.
PRINTZ, son of Reuben PRINTZ, Esq., and
Miss Sallie A., daughter of Aaron PRINTZ,
Esq., both of Page county, Va.
Rockingham Register, 28 October 1869
(Thursday), p. 2, c. 3.
PRINTZ: Near Stony Man, Page county, on the
17th inst., by Rev. S. Henkel, Jacob
PRINTZ and Miss Caroline PRINTZ, all of
Page county.
Rockingham Register and Advertiser, 31
October 1867 (Thursday), p. 2, c. 6.
PRINTZ: On the 9th inst., by Rev. J.
Stirewalt, John D. PRINTZ and Miss
Lavinia PRINTZ, both of Page county.
Rockingham Register, 23 April 1868
(Thursday), p. 2, c. 6.
PRITCHARD: See entry for BOTT.
PROCTOR: See entry for STODDARD.
PROCTOR: On the 3rd inst., by Rev. A. Rude,
Mr. Noah H. PROCTOR and Miss Anna
FLEMING, both of Shenandoah county.
Rockingham Register and Advertiser, 25
May 1860 (Friday), p. 2, c. 5.
PROCTOR: By Elder H. Jennings, on the 9th of
December, Ralph P. PROCTOR and Miss Mary
Ellen COOPER.
Rockingham Register, 6 January 1870
(Thursday), p. 3, c. 3.

PROFFETT: See entry for EUBANK.

PROFIT: On the 21st of March, by Rev. Henry St. John Rinker, Jacob PROFIT and Miss Mary MOHLER, all of Shenandoah county. Rockingham Register and Advertiser, 11 April 1867 (Thursday), p. 3, c. 4.

PROPES: On the 1st inst., by Elder A.C. Booton, Mr. Henry PROPES and Miss Bettie KOONTZ, all of Page county. Rockingham Register and Advertiser, 18 May 1860 (Friday), p. 3, c. 4.

PROPS: On the 23rd ult., by the Rev. R.C. Walker, S.H. PROPS and Miss Lydia C. SILLING, both of Augusta. Rockingham Register, 6 January 1870 (Thursday), p. 3, c. 3.

PROPST: See entry for GUMM.

PROPST: On the 9th of December, by Rev. Sam'l B. Dolly, Mr. Joel G.A. PROPST, of South Fork, Pendleton county, and Miss Christianna WILFONG, of the top peak of the Alleghany mountain. Rockingham Register and Advertiser, 28 December 1860 (Friday), p. 1, c. 5.

PUGH: Near Broadway, on Thursday morning, the 23rd of December, by Rev. Thos. D. Bell, P.W. PUGH and Miss Mollie E., daughter of Geo. BRANNER, Esq., dec'd, all of Rockingham county. Rockingham Register, 6 January 1870 (Thursday), p. 3, c. 3.

PULLEN: See entry for JONES.

PULLEN: See entry for REED.

PULLEN: On the 12th of July, near Doe Hill, by Rev. W.T. Price, Capt. H. Brown PULLEN and Miss Lydia Virginia; also, at the same time and place, Hezekiah WILSON and Miss Matilda Ann, daughters of Mrs. Mary McCOY, all of Highland county. Rockingham Register and Advertiser, 2 August 1866 (Thursday), p. 2, c. 5.

PULLENS: See entry for BARE.

PULLIN: On the 5th of July, by the Rev. J.V.T. Graham, Mr. Asbury PULLIN and Miss Rachel BIRD, all of Highland county, Va. Rockingham Register and Advertiser, 3

August 1860 (Friday), p. 2, c. 5.

PULLIN: On the 22nd ult., by Rev. John Pinkerton, Mr. Balser H. PULLIN, of Highland, and Miss Martha DEVER, of Rockingham.
Rockingham Register and Advertiser, 2 March 1860 (Friday), p. 3, c. 2.

PUMPHREY: See entry for CUPP.

PURCELL: See entry for GRIGSBY.

PURVIES: See entry for MILLER.

- Q -

QUAINTANCE: See entry for TIDLER.

QUAINTANCE: See entry for WINDLE.

QUAINTANCE: On the 24th ult., by Rev. O. Grimsley, Taylor QUAINTANCE and Miss Mittie RIVERCOMB, all of Madison county.
Rockingham Register and Advertiser, 16 January 1868 (Thursday), p. 2, c. 5.

QUIESENBERRY: See entry for SHELLY.

QUINLAN: On the 17th of October, 1861, by Rev. Solomon Garber, Mr. Timothy QUINLAN, of Ireland, and Miss Margaret J., daughter of Charles POLLARD, dec'd, of Rockingham county.
Rockingham Register and Virginia Advertiser, 8 November 1861 (Friday), p. 2, c. 2.

QUITMAN: Near Selma, Alabama, on the 20th of April last, F. Henry QUITMAN, son of Gen. QUITMAN of Mississippi, and Miss Mary, only daughter of Col. Virgil T. GARDNER, of Dallas county, Alabama.
Rockingham Register and Virginia Advertiser, 27 May 1854 (Saturday), p. 2, c. 7.

- R -

RACEY: See entry for HINES.

RACEY: On the 17th ult., by Rev. H. Wetzel, Christopher C. RACEY and Miss Sarah E. HOLLAR, all of Shenandoah county.
Rockingham Register, 1 October 1868 (Thursday), p. 3, c. 3.

355

RADENER: See entry for SHEETS.

RADER: See entry for HOTTEL.

RADER: On the 24th of November, A.J. RADER, formerly of Rockingham county, Va., and Mrs. E.R. WRIGHT, both of Pettis county, Missouri.
Rockingham Register, 10 December 1868 (Thursday), p. 3, c. 3.

RADER: On the 20th of December, 1860, ... Mr. Derrick RADER and Miss Hattie, daughter of Mr. Jacob MOYERS, all of Rockingham.
Rockingham Register and Advertiser, 28 December 1860 (Friday), p. 1, c. 5.

RADER: On the 20th ult., at the residence of Dr. J.Q. Winfield, Broadway, by the Rev. Thos. D. Bell, Peter RADER and Miss Lizzie KRAMER, all of Rockingham county.
Rockingham Register and Advertiser, 3 January 1867 (Thursday), p. 3, c. 3.

RAGAN: See entry for HYDE.

RAGAN: See entry for LEMLEY.

RAGAN: See entry for MILLER.

RAGAN: See entry for POLLACK.

RAINES: See entry for PERKEY.

RAINES: See entry for SHIFLETT.

RAINES: On January 1, 1867, by Rev. Christian Hartman, Noah RAINES and Miss Cornelia F., daughter of Fielding MATHENY, all of Rockingham county.
Rockingham Register and Advertiser, 24 January 1867 (Thursday), p. 2, c. 4.

RAINS: See entry for GENTRY.

RALSTON: See entry for BEAR.

RALSTON: See entry for CROMER.

RALSTON: See entry for DOVE.

RALSTON: See entry for HOPKINS.

RALSTON: See entry for HOWVER.

RALSTON: See entry for LINEAWEAVER.

RALSTON: See entry for MAUCK.

RALSTON: See entry for MYERS.

RALSTON: See entry for STEELE.

RALSTON: See entry for ZIRKLE.

RALSTON: On Friday morning the 19th inst., by the same [Rev. F.A. Merser], John H. RALSTON, Esq., and Miss Mary Francis, daughter of Mr. David BARE, - all of

North Mountain, Rockingham county.
Rockingham Register and Advertiser, 26 November 1858 (Friday), p. 3, c. 2.

RALSTON: On the 20th ult., near McDowell, by Rev. W.T. Price, Samuel RALSTON and Miss Maggie WAGGY, all of Highland county.
Rockingham Register and Advertiser, 5 December 1867 (Thursday), p. 2, c. 5.

RAMEY: On the 23rd of March, near Rockland Mills, by Rev. R. Smith, Mr. Michael RAMEY, of Co. A, 12th Va. Cavalry, Rosser's Brigade, and Miss Lucy F. FITCH, of Augusta county, Va.
The Rockingham Register, 1 April 1864 (Friday), p. 2, c. 6.

RAMEY: On the 16th ult., by Rev. John W. Watson, Philip RAMEY, of Woodstock, and Mrs. Mary C. KEMP, of Luray, Va.
Rockingham Register and Advertiser, 7 February 1867 (Thursday), p. 3, c. 3.

RAMSEY: See entry for KELSO.

RAMSEY: See entry for McCUNE.

RAMSEY: See entry for TAYLOR.

RAMSEY: See entry for WHEELBARGER.

RAMSEY: On the 7th inst., at the Virginia Hotel, Staunton, by Rev. James Murray, Jacob RAMSEY and Miss Mary A.R. BARTLEY.
Rockingham Register, 14 January 1869 (Thursday), p. 3, c. 3.

RANDAL: On the 2nd of January, by Rev. Isaac Long, George RANDAL and Miss Columbia F., daughter of Jacob SIPE, all of Rockingham county.
Rockingham Register and Advertiser, 23 January 1868 (Thursday), p. 2, c. 4.

RANDOLPH: On the 20th ult., on Beaver Creek, by Rev. Daniel Thomas, Benj. H. RANDOLPH, of Augusta county, and Miss Mary E. RULEMAN, of Rockingham.
Rockingham Register and Advertiser, 10 January 1867 (Thursday), p. 3, c. 2.

RANDULIFFE: See entry for CURRY.

RANFORD: On the 21st ult., by the Rev. T.W. Kiracofe, Mr. William J. RANFORD to Miss Sarah GLADWELL, all of Augusta county.
Rockingham Register & Advertiser, 6

October 1865 (Friday), p. 2, c. 2.

RANKEN: On the 21st inst., by Rev. Daniel Thomas, Mr. Abraham RANKEN, of Rockingham, and Miss Phebe HARPER, of Knapp's Creek, Pocahontas county.
Rockingham Register and Advertiser, 30 September 1859 (Friday), p. 2, c. 4.

RANKIN: See entry for CURRY.

RANKIN: See entry for LONG.

RANKIN: See entry for THOMAS.

RANKIN: See entry for VAN PELT.

RANSBOTTOM: See entry for GLASS.

RAU: See entry for GRANDSTAFF.

RAU: On the 7th, by Rev. Mr. Winton, Mr. David RAU and Miss Lydia BEOHM, all of Edinburg.
Rockingham Register and Advertiser, 1 July 1859 (Friday), p. 2, c. 4.

RAU: On the 27th ult., by Rev. H. Tallhelm, Mr. Jas. W. RAU and Miss Amanda A. HISEY, all of Shenandoah.
Rockingham Register and Advertiser, 14 March 1867 (Thursday), p. 3, c. 5.

RAUSEY: See entry for JEWEL.

RAY: On the 14th inst., by the Rev. Mr. Shickell, Mr. David RAY to Miss Jane GLADVILLE, all of Rockingham.
Rockingham Register and Valley Advertiser, 30 December 1843 (Saturday), p. 4, c. 1.

RAY: On the 3rd inst., at the residence of John C. Heiskell, in Romney, by Rev. Wm. H. Foote, D.D., Justian RAY, of Sigourney, Keokuk county, and Miss Lucy A. HOWARD, formerly of Romney.
Rockingham Register and Advertiser, 18 November 1859 (Friday), p. 2, c. 4.

READ: On the 19th ult., at the residence of the bride's mother, by Rev. T.W. Lewis, Jno. H. READ, of New Market, and Miss Vic S. CARPENTER, of Madison C.H.
Rockingham Register and Advertiser, 10 January 1867 (Thursday), p. 3, c. 2.

READ: On the 18th inst., by the Rev. C.S.M. See, Mr. Thomas G. READ and Miss Martha S., daughter of Robert M. WHITE, Esq., of

Augusta.
Rockingham Register and Advertiser, 2
November 1860 (Friday), p. 2, c. 5.

REAGAN: On the 8th inst., at the Lexington
Hotel, by the Rev. P.H. Whisner, Mr. Hugh
L. REAGAN, of Staunton, Va., to Miss
Mollie A. SANDFORD, of Rockbridge.
Rockingham Register and Advertiser, 22
November 1866 (Thursday), p. 3, c. 3.

REAMER: See entry for EICHELBERGER.

REAMER: See entry for HUTCHINSON.

REATON: See entry for BYRD.

REDIFER: See entry for WILCHER.

REED: See entry for HAAS.

REED: On the 23rd ult., by Rev. G.W. Woods,
A.S. REED and Miss Mary E. SHOMO, all of
Rockingham county.
Rockingham Register, 8 July 1869
(Thursday), p. 2, c. 5.

REED: On the 8th inst., by Rev. C. Beard, Mr.
John W. REED, of Frederick county, to
Miss Tabitha G. MYERS, of Augusta county.
Rockingham Register and Advertiser, 22
November 1866 (Thursday), p. 3, c. 3.

REED: On the 12th ult., by Rev. John S.
Pullen, Thomas REED, of Harrison county,
W.Va., and Mrs. Susan E. PULLEN, all of
Highland county.
Rockingham Register and Advertiser, 18
October 1866 (Thursday), p. 2, c. 4.

REEDY: See entry for JORDAN.

REEDY: See entry for MOORE.

REEDY: On Sunday last, by the Rev. H.
Hoffman, Mr. Thomas REEDY, of
Harrisonburg, and Miss Catharine ACUFF,
of Dayton.
Rockingham Register & Advertiser, 8
September 1865 (Friday), p. 3, c. 2.

REEVES: At the American Hotel, in Staunton,
on the 2nd inst., by Rev. John Pinkerton,
Mr. Thos. REEVES and Miss Mary CARROL,
both of Augusta.
Rockingham Register and Advertiser, 17
May 1861 (Friday), p. 3, c. 3.

REHERD: See entry for LONG.

REHERD: On Thursday, the 28th of May, on

Smith's Creek, Rockingham county, by Rev.
J.H. Moore, Mr. George W. REHERD and Miss
C., daughter of Mr. Cyrus RHODES, all of
Rockingham.
The Rockingham Register, 5 June 1863
(Friday), p. 2, c. 6.

REHERD: On Sunday morning, the 16th of April,
by the Rev. A.P. Boude, at the residence
of the bride's father, Lewis REHERD, of
Harrisonburg, and Miss Maggie E.,
daughter of Levi SHAVER, of this
vicinity.
Rockingham Register and Advertiser, 20
April 1866 (Friday), p. 2, c. 3.

REID: See entry for BRAGONIER.

REID: See entry for COINER.

REID: See entry for WALKER.

REID: On Thursday, March 31st, by Rev. A. Poe
Boude, Mr. John K. REID, of Shenandoah,
and Miss Judy Ann GRANDSTAFF, of
Rockingham.
The Rockingham Register, 8 April 1864
(Friday), p. 2, c. 6.

REID: At the residence of the bride, in this
place, on Tuesday afternoon last, by Rev.
C.V. Bingley, Rev. L.S. REID, P.E.
Charlottesville District, Va. Conference,
E.M. Church, and Mrs. Mary C. KYLE, of
Harrisonburg.
Rockingham Register and Advertiser, 13
December 1866 (Thursday), p. 2, c. 5.

REID: Near Grove Hill, Page county, on
Thursday, the 21st of January, 1864, at
the residence of the bride's father, by
Elder C. Allemong, Lt. Peter C. REID, of
Co. D, 7th Va. Cavalry, and Miss Susan
E., daughter of Geo. and Susan SUMMERS,
all of Page county.
The Rockingham Register, 29 January 1864
(Friday), p. 2, c. 6.

RENICK: See entry for HARLOW.

RETSEL: On the 25th ult., in Harrisonburg, by
Rev. T.D. Bell, Mr. Joseph RETSEL and
Miss Mansilla E. DEEHL, all of this
county.
Rockingham Register and Advertiser, 5

July 1861 (Friday), p. 3, c. 3.

REUBUSH: On the 3rd inst., by Rev. Timothy Funk, Wm. H. REUBUSH, formerly of Augusta county, and Miss Nancy A., daughter of Albert LONG, all of Rockingham county.
Rockingham Register and Advertiser, 17 October 1867 (Thursday), p. 3, c. 3.

REVERCOMB: See entry for WITTS.

REXROAD: On the 11th ult., by the Rev. Stephen Smith, Samuel C. REXROAD, of Pendleton county, W.Va., and Miss Martha J. FOX, of Highland county.
Rockingham Register and Advertiser, 18 July 1867 (Thursday), p. 2, c. 6.

REXRODE: See entry for MAY.

REYNOLDS: See entry for PARRILL.

REYNOLDS: Near Lexington, on the 26th of August, by Rev. J.C. Richardson, Mr. O.B. REYNOLDS and Miss Mary J., daughter of Mr. Eli COX, all of Rockbridge county.
Rockingham Register and Advertiser, 26 September 1856 (Friday), p. 2, c. 6.

RHEA: See entry for AYERS.

RHINEHART: See entry for PEARL.

RHINEHART: On the 12th inst., at the residence of Mrs. Susan Rhinehart, by Rev. D.A. Long, Dewitt C. RHINEHART and Miss Mary C. EMPSWILER, all of Rockingham county.
Rockingham Register, 27 October 1870 (Thursday), p. 2, c. 4.

RHINEHEART: See entry for NEFF.

RHODES: See entry for COOLEY.

RHODES: See entry for FANT.

RHODES: See entry for HITE.

RHODES: See entry for MAPHIS.

RHODES: See entry for PENCE.

RHODES: See entry for REHERD.

RHODES: See entry for SHANK.

RHODES: See entry for SIBERT.

RHODES: See entry for WENGER.

RHODES: On the 13th of April, by Rev. D.D. Swaney, Mr. Asbury F. RHODES, formerly of Rockingham county, Va., and Miss Rose Ann CASEBEERE, of Shelby county, Illinois.
Rockingham Register and Advertiser, 29

April 1859 (Friday), p. 3, c. 2.

RHODES: November 10, by Rev. J.M. Follansbee, C.E. RHODES and Miss Maggie E. THOMPSON, all of Rockingham county.
Rockingham Register, 24 November 1870 (Thursday), p. 2, c. 4.

RHODES: On Saturday, the 15th inst., by the Rev. Jacob B. Houck, Mr. Castle RHODES to Miss Mary, daughter of Mr. Henry CARRIER, all of Smith's Creek, Rockingham county.
Rockingham Register, 29 October 1836 (Saturday), p. 3, c. 4.

RHODES: On the 23rd ult., by the Rev. Mr. Gibbons, Mr. E.P. RHODES, of Lexington, Va., and Miss Martha E. SENSENEY, of Middleton, Va.
Rockingham Register and Advertiser, 9 November 1860 (Friday), p. 2, c. 6.

RHODES: By the Rev. Daniel Feete, on the 6th inst., Mr. Frederick S. RHODES to Miss Elizabeth, daughter of Mr. John WHITMORE, all of Rockingham.
Rockingham Register and Advertiser, 14 November 1856 (Friday), p. 2, c. 6.

RHODES: On the 11th inst., by Rev. Jacob Thomas, Frederick S. RHODES and Miss Catharine SWARTS, all of Rockingham county.
Rockingham Register and Advertiser, 18 October 1866 (Thursday), p. 2, c. 4.

RHODES: In Asheville, N.C., on the 4th inst., by Rev. Mr. Wood, at the residence of the bride's father, Capt. George A. RHODES, of Staunton, Va., and Miss Emily S., eldest daughter of A.M. KITZMILLER, Esq., of Jefferson county, Va.
The Rockingham Register, 29 January 1864 (Friday), p. 2, c. 6.

RHODES: On Sunday, the 4th inst., at the residence of Cyrus Rhodes, Esq., on Smith's Creek, by Rev. Jos. Funkhouser, Jacob M. RHODES and Miss Mary M., only daughter of Michael ALDER, dec'd, all of Rockingham county.
Rockingham Register and Advertiser, 8 November 1866 (Thursday), p. 3, c. 4.

RHODES: On Sunday morning, the 21st of August, at Orchard Grove, near Keezeltown, by Rev. Joseph Funkhouser, James M. RHODES and Miss Jane Ann, daughter of James THOMPSON, all of Rockingham county.
Rockingham Register, 25 August 1870 (Thursday), p. 2, c. 4.

RHODES: On the 28th ult., by Rev. Wm. H. Dinkel, near New Market, John RHODES and Miss Mary E., daughter of B. HOOVER, Esq., all of Rockingham.
Rockingham Register and Advertiser, 6 December 1866 (Thursday), p. 3, c. 2.

RHODES: On January 24, by Rev. D.C. Irwin, at his front gate, in Harrisonburg, at an early hour in the morning, John RHODES and Miss Ann Eliza, daughter of John MILLER, dec'd, all of Rockingham county ....
Rockingham Register and Advertiser, 31 January 1867 (Thursday), p. 3, c. 2.

RHODES: On the 24th ult., by Rev. Solomon Garber, John RHODES and Miss Amanda WHITSEL, all of Rockingham county.
Rockingham Register, 8 October 1868 (Thursday), p. 3, c. 3.

RHODES: On the 6th inst., on Dry River, by Rev. J.N. Davis, Mr. John H. RHODES and Miss Josephine Virginia SPECK, all of this county.
Rockingham Register and Advertiser, 9 December 1859 (Friday), p. 2, c. 5.

RHODES: On Tuesday the 20th inst., by the Rev. John A. Collins, Mr. John W. RHODES, of Oskaloosa, Iowa, to Miss Mary W., daughter of Samuel HARTLEY, Esq., of Winchester, Va.
Rockingham Register and Valley Advertiser, 24 March 1849 (Saturday), p. 2, c. 7.

RHODES: On the 22nd inst., by Rev. Timothy Funk, Joseph W. RHODES and Miss Maria J., daughter of Harvey WHITMORE, all of Rockingham county.
Rockingham Register and Advertiser, 27

September 1866 (Thursday), p. 3, c. 3.

RHODES: On the 2nd inst., in Lexington, Va., by the Rev. Mr. Willis, Lieut. R. RHODES, assistant professor of Tactics in the Virginia Military Institute, to Miss Jane F. BAXTER, all of that place.
Rockingham Register and Valley Advertiser, 13 October 1849 (Saturday), p. 2, c. 5.

RHODES: At the bride's residence in Middlebrook, on Tuesday, 15th ult., by Rev. J. Lantz, Samuel L. RHODES to Miss Maggie C., the youngest daughter of Capt. Robert FIRTH.
Rockingham Register, 14 October 1869 (Thursday), p. 2, c. 2.

RHYAN: See entry for HUFFMAN.

RIBBLE: In this place, on Thursday afternoon last, by Rev. R.H. Walton, Dr. Geo. W. RIBBLE, of Salem, Roanoke county, Va., and Miss Virginia C., daughter of Mr. Geo. CONRAD, dec'd, of Harrisonburg.
Rockingham Register and Virginia Advertiser, 3 January 1862 (Friday), p. 1, c. 4.

RICE: See entry for CRABILL.

RICE: See entry for SNAPP.

RICE: See entry for SOULE.

RICE: On the 19th of July, by Rev. Daniel Thomas, Mr. Benjamin RICE and Miss Elizabeth, daughter of Mr. John HUME, all of Rockingham county.
Rockingham Register and Advertiser, 2 September 1859 (Friday), p. 2, c. 5.

RICE: On the 15th of September, at New Market, by Rev. S. Henkel, Mr. Jacob W. RICE and Miss Anna Maria, daughter of S.D. HENKEL, all of New Market.
The Rockingham Register, 2 October 1863 (Friday), p. 2, c. 5.

RICE: On the 4th of January, 1870, near Point Pleasant, Mason county, W.Va., by Rev. B.B. Blair, James L. RICE, formerly of Rockingham county, Va., and Miss Mattie BALL, of Mason county, W.Va.
Rockingham Register, 3 February 1870

(Thursday), p. 3, c. 4.

RICE: At the residence of the bride's father, on Linvill's Creek, on Thursday evening of last week, August 24th, by Rev. A.J. Kibler, Mr. Joseph S. RICE and Miss Octavia M., daughter of Mr. Jesse BURKHOLDER, all of this county.
Rockingham Register & Advertiser, 1 September 1865 (Friday), p. 2, c. 4.

RICE: On the 27th of January, 1863, by the Rev. Jacob Stirewalt, Mr. William H. RICE and Miss Mary F. CLINEDINST, all of New Market, Va.
The Rockingham Register, 6 February 1863 (Friday), p. 2, c. 5.

RICE: In Bastrop, Texas, on the 14th of April, by Rev. J.H. Sheppard, Mr. William P. RICE, late of Virginia, and Miss Margaret A. BARKER, of Bastrop.
Rockingham Register and Advertiser, 27 May 1859 (Friday), p. 2, c. 6.

RICHARD: On the 16th inst., [sic, ult], by Rev. J.W. Watson, Mr. John S. RICHARD and Miss Susan E., daughter of David KIBLER, of Page county.
Rockingham Register and Advertiser, 1 July 1859 (Friday), p. 2, c. 4.

RICHARDS: See entry for BYERLY.

RICHARDS: On the 18th ult., on South River, by Rev. W.R. Stringer, John E. RICHARDS and Miss Mary E. TRUSLER, all of Augusta county.
Rockingham Register and Advertiser, 3 January 1867 (Thursday), p. 3, c. 3.

RICHARDS: At Pembroke Springs, Frederick county, Va., at the residence of the bride's father, on Tuesday, the 18th of September, Mr. Wm. H. RICHARDS and Miss Mary E., daughter of Mr. John KEFFER, formerly of Woodstock, Va.
The Rockingham Register, 6 November 1863 (Friday), p. 2, c. 6.

RICHARDSON: See entry for CLARY.

RICHARDSON: On the 12th inst., at the Eutaw House, in Baltimore, by Rev. Dr. Bullock, C.A. RICHARDSON and Miss Josie BROOKS, both of Staunton.

Rockingham Register, 20 January 1870 (Thursday), p. 2, c. 5.

RICHARDSON: On the 21st inst., by Rev. Wm. E. Baker, in Staunton, Capt. John RICHARDSON, of Richmond, and Miss Sallie, second daughter of Samuel B. BROWN, Esq., formerly of Staunton, but now of Georgia.
Rockingham Register and Advertiser, 30 January 1868 (Thursday), p. 2, c. 4.

RICHMOND: See entry for CALDWELL.

RICHMOND: On the morning of the 7th ult., by the Rev. Thomas Owen, Mr. James S.W. CALDWELL to Miss Edmonia Virginia, only child of Major Edmund RICHMOND; and, on the evening of the same day, the parents of this young and interesting couple, Maj. Edmund RICHMOND and Mrs. Lydia E. CALDWELL, sister of the late ex-President James K. POLK, were joined in marriage by the Rev. Arthur Davis, all of Haywood county, Tennessee.
Rockingham Register and Valley Advertiser, 13 October 1849 (Saturday), p. 2, c. 5.

RICKARD: On the 3rd inst., by Elder George Shaver, at the residence of the bride's father, Mr. Asher W. RICKARD and Miss Rebecca Jane MAPHIS, all of Shenandoah.
Rockingham Register and Advertiser, 18 May 1860 (Friday), p. 3, c. 4.

RIDDLE: See entry for ARMENTROUT.

RIDDLE: See entry for HULVA.

RIDDLE: See entry for PLUMB.

RIDDLE: See entry for SHAVER.

RIDDLE: See entry for SLUSSER.

RIDDLE: See entry for STOMBOCK.

RIDDLE: On the 15th inst., by Rev. Solomon Garber, Mr. Andrew J. RIDDLE and Miss Elizabeth FURR, of Augusta county.
Rockingham Register and Advertiser, 19 March 1858 (Friday), p. 3, c. 3.

RIDDLE: On the 28th of June, near Broadway, by Rev. Jacob Miller, James H. RIDDLE, formerly of Pendleton county, W.Va., and Miss Caroline P., daughter of John R.

HOMAN, dec'd, of Linvill's Creek, Rockingham county.

Rockingham Register, 2 July 1868 (Thursday), p. 2, c. 4.

RIDDLE: On the 27th of January, by Rev. A.A.J. Bushong, T.L. RIDDLE and Miss M.J. ALLEN, both of Augusta.

Rockingham Register, 10 February 1870 (Thursday), p. 2, c. 5.

RIDDLEBERGER: On the 14th of October, by the Rev. R.C. Cave, at the residence of the bride's father, Wm. Ira RIDDLEBERGER and Miss Arabel R. MILEY, all of Edinburg.

Rockingham Register, 28 October 1869 (Thursday), p. 2, c. 3.

RIDENOUR: See entry for ZIMMER.

RIDENOUR: On the 26th of June, 1870, by Rev. J. Nicholas, M.A. RIDENOUR and Miss Macey ROADCAP, both of Baltimore.

Rockingham Register, 21 July 1870 (Thursday), p. 3, c. 3.

RIDER: See entry for GIVEN.

RIELY: On the 18th of September, in Winchester, by Rev. J.R. Graham, J. Chap RIELY and Miss Bettie B., daughter of Henry MYERS, dec'd, all of that place.

Rockingham Register and Advertiser, 10 October 1867 (Thursday), p. 3, c. 3.

RIFE: See entry for DRIVER.

RIFE: On the 25th ult., near Timberville, by Rev. J. Stirewalt, Henry A. RIFE and Miss Emma E. KIPPS, both of Rockingham.

Rockingham Register and Advertiser, 2 February 1866 (Friday), p. 3, c. 2.

RILEY: See entry for BROWN.

RILEY: See entry for MAHONEY.

RILEY: In Staunton, on the Thursday the 6th inst., by Rev. John L. Clarke, Mr. Berry L. RILEY and Miss Lizzie A. BROWN, all of Staunton.

Rockingham Register and Advertiser, 13 February 1868 (Thursday), p. 2, c. 5.

RILEY: At "Miller Hotel," Baltimore, Md., on Thursday, December 7th, by Rev. Benj. Hengst, Capt. J.G. RILEY, of West Va., and Miss Ella A. HITE, of Augusta county.

<u>Rockingham</u> <u>Register</u> & <u>Advertiser</u> , 22
December 1865 (Friday), p. 3, c. 2.
RILLER: On the 20th of August, by Rev. Jacob
Wine, Mr. Moses RILLER and Miss Mary Jane
TUSSING, all of Rockingham county.
<u>The</u> <u>Rockingham</u> <u>Register</u>, 16 September
1864 (Friday), p. 2, c. 5.
RIMEL: On the 28th of July, by Rev. Jacob
Miller, Jacob F. RIMEL and Miss Mary
Virginia, daughter of Jacob LEE, all of
Rockingham county.
<u>Rockingham</u> <u>Register</u>, 4 August 1870
(Thursday), p. 3, c. 2.
RIMEL: On Thursday the 31st ult., by Rev.
John Harshbarger, Mr. Jacob H. RIMEL and
Miss Rebecca SWANY, all of this county.
<u>Rockingham</u> <u>Register</u> <u>and</u> <u>Advertiser</u>, 8
April 1859 (Friday), p. 3, c. 1.
RIMEL: On the 13th inst., by Rev. J.C.
Hensell, Mr. John M. RIMEL and Miss
Elizabeth S. HUNTER, both of Augusta.
<u>Rockingham</u> <u>Register</u> <u>and</u> <u>Advertiser</u>, 21
December 1860 (Friday), p. 2, c. 6.
RIMEL: On Thursday, the 2nd inst., by Rev.
Joseph Funkhouser, Mr. John T. RIMEL and
Miss Martha LINEBAUGH, all of Rockingham
county.
<u>Rockingham</u> <u>Register</u> <u>and</u> <u>Advertiser</u>, 10
February 1860 (Friday), p. 2, c. 5.
RIMEL: Near Keezletown, on the 8th inst., by
Rev. T. Brashear, Mr. Philip F. RIMEL and
Miss Ruthy Ann MILLER, all of Rockingham
county.
<u>Rockingham</u> <u>Register</u> <u>and</u> <u>Advertiser</u>, 17
October 1856 (Friday), p. 2, c. 5.
RIMEL: On the 3rd inst., by Rev. J.H.T.
Lower, Mr. William RIMEL and Miss Hannah
Ann GRADY, all of Rockingham county.
<u>The</u> <u>Rockingham</u> <u>Register</u>, 22 January 1864
(Friday), p. 2, c. 5.
RINEHART: On the 14th of October, by the Rev.
Jacob Miller, at the residence of the
bride's mother, A.R. RINEHART and Miss
Maggie M., daughter of Mrs. Catharine
BAXTER, all of Linvill's Creek,
Rockingham county.

Rockingham Register, 21 October 1869 (Thursday), p. 2, c. 3.

RINKER: See entry for GOOD.

RINKER: See entry for HAMMON.

RINKER: See entry for NEFF.

RINKER: On the 27th of November, by Rev. John Pirkey, Mr. Fenton T. RINKER and Miss Rebecca Ellen SWISHER, all of Shenandoah county.

Rockingham Register and Advertiser, 13 December 1866 (Thursday), p. 2, c. 5.

RINKER: On the 28th ult., at the residence of Dr. J.W. Best, by Rev. W.G. Eggleston, Jacob Z. RINKER, of Shenandoah, and Miss Sophia L. JEFFERSON, of Frederick county.

Rockingham Register, 17 December 1868 (Thursday), p. 3, c. 2.

RINKER: In New Market, on the 17th of November, by Rev. J.P. Cline, Mr. Lemuel P. RINKER and Miss Mary Ellen ZIRKLE, all of Shenandoah county.

The Rockingham Register and Advertiser, 16 December 1864 (Friday), p. 2, c. 1.

RIPLEY: See entry for PITMAN.

RIPPETOE: See entry for BOWCOCK.

RIPPETOE: On the 27th of February, by Rev. J.A. McCauly, Rev. Wm. D. RIPPETOE, of the Baltimore Conference, and Miss Mary MILLER, of Warren county, Va.

Rockingham Register and Advertiser, 9 March 1860 (Friday), p. 3, c. 2.

RISER: On the 23rd ult., by Rev. C. Beard, Mr. Jacob W. RISER and Miss Elizabeth M. CULLEN.

Rockingham Register and Advertiser, 2 November 1860 (Friday), p. 2, c. 5.

RISQUE: On the 22nd ult., in the Centenary Church at Lynchburg, by Rev. Geo. Langhorn, J. Willie RISQUE, formerly of Staunton, and Miss Nelia A. JONES, of Lynchburg.

Rockingham Register, 6 January 1870 (Thursday), p. 3, c. 3.

RISWICK: See entry for GARBER.

RITCHEY: See entry for CRIST.

RITCHIE: See entry for BOWERS.

RITCHIE: See entry for FULK.

RITCHIE: See entry for HOOVER (2).

RITCHIE: See entry for RITCHIE.

RITCHIE: On Sunday, the 7th of August, by Rev. Jacob Miller, Mr. Abram RITCHIE and Miss Sarah, daughter of Mr. Daniel HOOVER, all of Rockingham county.
Rockingham Register and Advertiser, 19 August 1859 (Friday), p. 2, c. 5.

RITCHIE: On the 16th of February, at the residence of the bride's father, in the vicinity of Bloomington, McLean county, Illinois, by Rev. W. Crandall, Addison RITCHIE, of Rockingham county, Va., and Miss Isabella BOZARTH.
Rockingham Register and Advertiser, 9 March 1860 (Friday), p. 3, c. 2.

RITCHIE: On the 15th inst., by Rev. Michael B.E. Kline, Frederick RITCHIE and Miss Virginia, daughter of Oliver TRUMBO, all of Rockingham county.
Rockingham Register, 22 September 1870 (Thursday), p. 2, c. 5.

RITCHIE: On the 25th of November, by Rev. Christopher Kyger, Isaac RITCHIE, aged 65 years, and Mary RITCHIE, aged 45 years.
Rockingham Register and Advertiser, 3 January 1867 (Thursday), p. 3, c. 3.

RITCHIE: On the 21st inst., by Rev. A. Kibler, Mr. Isaac F. RITCHIE and Miss Josephine, daughter of Joseph CROMER, all of Rockingham county.
Rockingham Register & Advertiser, 29 September 1865 (Friday), p. 3, c. 3.

RITCHIE: On Thursday the 2nd of October, by the Rev. Benjamin Bowman, Mr. James RITCHIE and Miss Magdalene, daughter of Peter BRENEMAN, all of Rockingham county.
Rockingham Register and Advertiser, 17 October 1856 (Friday), p. 2, c. 5.

RITCHIE: On the 11th inst., by Rev. J. Hensel, Jas. K.P. RITCHIE and Miss Dolly J. HUFFMAN, all of Rockingham county.
Rockingham Register, 25 November 1869 (Thursday), p. 2, c. 3.

RITENOUR: See entry for HENSON.

RITENOUR: See entry for RITENOUR.

RITENOUR: On the 21st ult., by Rev. Jonas W. Wakeman, Granson RITENOUR and Miss Susan RITENOUR, all of Shenandoah county.
Rockingham Register and Advertiser, 2 May 1867 (Thursday), p. 2, c. 6.

RITENOUR: On the 27th ult., by Rev. James D. Tabler, Hampson RITENOUR and Miss Martha E. MILLER, all of Shenandoah county.
Rockingham Register and Advertiser, 18 October 1866 (Thursday), p. 2, c. 4.

RITENOUR: On Monday, the 28th inst., by the Rev. J.C. Hensell, Mr. Isaac RITENOUR and Miss Mary C. BOWERS, all of Rockingham county.
The Rockingham Register, 2 December 1864 (Friday), p. 1, c. 4.

RITTENOUR: On the 6th inst., by Rev. G.R. Martin, Mr. Calvert L. RITTENOUR and Miss Sarah Catharine FRAVEL, all of Shenandoah county.
Rockingham Register and Advertiser, 19 January 1866 (Friday), p. 3, c. 2.

RITTENOUR: In Woodstock, Va., on Friday evening, the 25th of July, by Rev. Mr. Clymer, Wm. Henry RITTENOUR, of Harrisonburg, and Miss Annie Amelia PERCIVAL, of Winchester, Virginia ....
Rockingham Register and Virginia Advertiser, 15 August 1862 (Friday), p. 2, c. 4.

RIVERCOMB: See entry for DICE.

RIVERCOMB: See entry for QUAINTANCE.

RIVERCOMB: In Mt. Solon, April 7, by the Rev. James M. Follansbee, George RIVERCOMB, lately of Fresnel [sic] county, California, and formerly of Augusta county, and Miss Mary Jane BLAKEMORE, of Augusta.
Rockingham Register, 21 April 1870 (Thursday), p. 3, c. 3.

RIVERCOMB: Near Jackson's River, Bath county, on the 25th of October, by Rev. Wm. W. Houston, Henry H. RIVERCOMB and Miss Harriet CLEEK.
Rockingham Register and Advertiser, 8

November 1866 (Thursday), p. 3, c. 4.

RIVES: See entry for DeVERE.

RIVES: See entry for SIGOURNEY.

RIVES: On Tuesday evening, at St. Paul's Church, Richmond, by the Rev. Dr. Minnegerode, Alfred, son of the Hon. Wm. C. RIVES, and Saide C., only daughter of James B. MacMURDO, and granddaughter of the late Bishop MOORE.
Rockingham Register and Advertiser, 18 February 1859 (Friday), p. 2, c. 6.

ROACH: On the 24th of June, by Elder C. Allemong, Wm. ROACH, of Rockingham county, and Miss Sarah BEASLEY, of Greene county.
Rockingham Register and Advertiser, 26 July 1866 (Thursday), p. 3, c. 2.

ROADCAP: See entry for GOCHENOUR.

ROADCAP: See entry for HEAVEL.

ROADCAP: See entry for MILLER.

RAODCAP: See entry for MONDAY.

ROADCAP: See entry for RIDENOUR.

ROADCAP: See entry for STICKLAND.

ROADCAP: See entry for WELCH.

ROADES: On the 28th of February, by Rev. T.D. Bell, Mr. David E. ROADES and Miss Fannie, daughter of Jacob LINEWEAVER, Sr., all of Rockingham county.
Rockingham Register and Advertiser, 7 March 1867 (Thursday), p. 3, c. 3.

ROBERTS: See entry for LAPORTE.

ROBERTS: See entry for LAWRENCE.

ROBERTS: See entry for SHIFFLETT.

ROBERTS: See entry for WEAST.

ROBERTS: See entry for WOOD.

ROBERTS: On the 6th inst., by Rev. John Pinkerton, Robert L. ROBERTS, of Jefferson county, W.Va., and Miss Margaret E., daughter of Jacob SCHRECKHISE.
Rockingham Register, 15 April 1869 (Thursday), p. 2, c. 4.

ROBERTS: On the 6th day of November, 1862, by the Rev. Isaac Long, Thomas ROBERTS and Rebecca BLOCE.
The Rockingham Register, 28 November 1862

(Friday), p. 2, c. 5.

ROBERTSON: On Thursday evening, the 3rd inst., by Rev. J.C. Hensell, Mr. Henry CARTER and Miss Mary E.; and, Mr. George W. ROBERTSON and Miss Eliza J., both daughters of Daniel MAY, of Mt. Crawford. The Rockingham Register, 11 March 1864 (Friday), p. 2, c. 6.

ROBINSON: See entry for DETRICK.

ROBINSON: See entry for LIVICK.

ROBINSON: On the 7th inst., by Elder John Pirkey, Jacob ROBINSON and Miss Elizabeth C. BAKER, all of Warren county. Rockingham Register, 21 May 1868 (Thursday), p. 2, c. 5.

ROBINSON: At the residence of the bride's father, on the 11th inst., by Rev. Jacob Spitzer, James W. ROBINSON, of Prince Edward county, Va., and Miss Hannah E., daughter of David HOLLAR, of Rockingham county. The Rockingham Register and Advertiser, 16 December 1864 (Friday), p. 2, c. 1.

ROBINSON: On the 15th ult., by Rev. C. Dameron, Sam'l ROBINSON and Althea A. McGILVARAY, both of Augusta. Rockingham Register, 6 May 1869 (Thursday), p. 2, c. 3.

ROBISON: By the Rev. Peter Miller, December 12th, Mr. Jacob ROBISON, of Augusta county, Va., and Miss Hannah LANDACRE, of Hardy County, W.Va. Rockingham Register and Advertiser, 9 February 1866 (Friday), p. 3, c. 3.

ROCKAFELLER: See entry for WILLIAMS.

RODAHEFFER: On the 12th of February, by Rev. Jno. J. Harshbarger, Mr. John RODAHEFFER and Miss Columbia E. SLATER, all of Rockingham county. Rockingham Register and Advertiser, 22 February 1861 (Friday), p. 2, c. 6.

RODAHOEFFER: On the 18th inst., by the Rev. S. Filler, Mr. Geo. RODAHOEFFER and Miss Mary, daughter of Mr. Samuel HENKEL, - all of Rockingham county. Rockingham Register and Advertiser, 26

November 1858 (Friday), p. 3, c. 2.

RODEFER: On Thursday evening, the 19th inst., in Woodstock, by Rev. J.P. Hyde, Mr. Jas. H. RODEFER and Miss Jennie MORRISON.
Rockingham Register and Advertiser, 28 June 1866 (Thursday), p. 2, c. 5.

RODEFFER: See entry for WALTER.

RODEFFER: On the 27th ult., by Rev. Mr. Whisler, at the residence of the bride's father, M.M.G. RODEFFER, of Shenandoah county, and Miss Mary K. SOUDER, of Loudoun.
Rockingham Register and Advertiser, 23 March 1866 (Friday), p. 3, c. 3.

RODES: On the 5th inst., in Albemarle county, by Rev. R.N. Sledd, Mr. John W. RODES and Miss Clotilda A., daughter of M.B. JARMAN, Esq.
Rockingham Register and Advertiser, 21 December 1860 (Friday), p. 2, c. 6.

RODGERS: See entry for CARPENTER.
RODGERS: See entry for CROSBY.
RODGERS: See entry for DAVIS.
RODGERS: See entry for DEVERICKE.
RODGERS: See entry for HOUNSHELL.
RODGERS: See entry for JOHNSON.
RODGERS: See entry for MESSICK.
RODGERS: See entry for WILLIAMS.

RODGERS: On the 27th ult., by Rev. Mr. Long, John RODGERS, of Kansas, and Miss Kate YOST, of Strasburg, Va.
Rockingham Register, 17 November 1870 (Thursday), p. 2, c. 3.

RODGERS: Near Winchester, on the 4th inst., by the Rev. Norval Wilson, William RODGERS, of the State of North Carolina, and Miss Annie CATON, of Strasburg, Va.
Rockingham Register & Advertiser, 25 August 1865 (Friday), p. 3, c. 3.

ROGERS: See entry for ARMENTROUT.
ROGERS: See entry for CAMPBELL.
ROGERS: See entry for MAPHIS.

ROGERS: On the 18th of January, ... Mr. Geo. M. ROGERS and Miss Mollie A. ORNDORFF, all of Hardy county.
Rockingham Register and Advertiser, 10

February 1865 (Friday), p. 2, c. 2.

ROGERS: At the residence of the bride's mother, on Wednesday, the 11th inst., by Rev. G.W. Holland, Granville ROGERS and Miss Jennie, daughter of John ALLEBAUGH, dec'd, all of Bridgewater.
Rockingham Register and Advertiser, 19 March 1868 (Thursday), p. 2, c. 4.

ROGERS: On the 14th last, at Hill's Hotel, Harrisonburg, by Rev. Geo. W. Hollard, Mr. James ROGERS and Miss Julia SHEPLER, all of Rockingham county.
Rockingham Register and Advertiser, 22 February 1861 (Friday), p. 2, c. 6.

ROGERS: On Tuesday morning last, near Barboursville, Va., by Rev. Z.E. Harrison, Mr. James G. ROGERS, of Rockingham county, and Miss Margaret B. DOUGLAS, of Orange county, Va.
The Rockingham Register, 17 October 1862 (Friday), p. 2, c. 7.

ROGERS: On the 21st inst., near Fort Lewis, by Rev. T.W. Walker, R.M. ROGERS, of Calhoun county, Va., and Miss Sallie E. McMULLEN, of Bath county, Va.
Rockingham Register and Advertiser, 30 August 1866 (Thursday), p. 2, c. 4.

ROHR: See entry for CRIGLER.

ROHR: On Wednesday morning last, by the Rev. B.H. Johnson, Mr. Alfred C. ROHR, of Harrisonburg, and Miss Ann S., daughter of Mr. Wm. C. JENNINGS, of Rockingham county.
Rockingham Register and Valley Advertiser, 10 August 1850 (Saturday), p. 2, c. 6.

ROHR: On Thursday morning last, by Rev. Wm. H. Wheelwright, Mr. Alfred C. ROHR, of Harrisonburg, and Miss Sarah Cornelia, daughter of James GREGORY, Esq., of Staunton, Va.
The Rockingham Register and Valley Advertiser, 26 June 1852 (Saturday), p. 2, c. 5.

ROHR: On Thursday morning, 23rd December, 1869, at the residence of the bride's

mother, by Rev. Dr. Arnold, W.S. ROHR, of
Harrisonburg, and Miss Ella T., daughter
of the late John COLEMAN, Esq., of
Richmond, Va.
Rockingham Register, 6 January 1870
(Thursday), p. 3, c. 3.

ROHR: In Harrisonburg, on Monday evening, the
13th inst., by Rev. J.W. Moore, Mr. Wm.
A.S. ROHR, of Dayton, Rockingham county,
and Miss Annie E. SLATER, ... of
Harrisonburg.
Rockingham Register, 17 July 1863
(Friday), p. 3, c. 1.

ROLER: On the 11th ult., by the Rev. P.M.
Custer, C.A. ROLER and Miss Emma V.,
daughter of Col. Samuel D. CRAWFORD, all
of Augusta.
Rockingham Register and Advertiser, 3
January 1867 (Thursday), p. 3, c. 3.

ROLER: On the 21st, by the Rev. Mr. Shickell,
Mr. Peter S. ROLER to Miss Frances S.
ALLEBAUGH, all of this county.
Rockingham Register and Valley
Advertiser, 30 December 1843 (Saturday),
p. 4. c. 1.

ROLFE: On the 17th inst., at the residence of
the bride's father, Judge BEANE, of
Elkhart county, Indiana, by Rev. H. Bair,
Mr. Addison B. ROLFE, of Augusta county,
Va., and Miss Libbie R. BEANE.
Rockingham Register and Advertiser, 31
May 1866 (Thursday), p. 3, c. 5.

ROLLER: See entry for BOWMAN.

ROLLER: See entry for SWITZER.

ROLLER: On the 24th of November, by Rev. J.C.
Hensel, Mr. Albert H. ROLLER, of Augusta,
and Miss Annie E., daughter of Mr. Geo.
CARPENTER, of Rockingham county.
The Rockingham Register, 4 December 1863
(Friday), p. 2, c. 5.

ROLLER: On the 9th inst., at the residence of
the bride's father, near Mt. Crawford, by
Rev. Geo. W. Holland, Emanuel ROLLER,
Jr., and Miss Elizabeth E., second
daughter of Abram SHANK, all of
Rockingham.

Rockingham Register, 16 April 1868 (Thursday), p. 2, c. 5.

ROLLER: On Thursday, the 8th of February, by Rev. J.C. Hensell, Mr. Henry W. ROLLER and Miss Mary Ann, eldest daughter of George SAUFLEY, Esq., all of Rockingham county.

Rockingham Register and Advertiser, 23 February 1866 (Friday), p. 2, c. 4.

ROLLER: On the 15th inst., by Rev. Daniel Feete, Mr. Jacob ROLLER and Miss Mary E. DELLINGER, all of Shenandoah county.

Rockingham Register and Advertiser, 30 September 1859 (Friday), p. 2, c. 4.

ROLLER: On the 3rd of September, by Rev. J.J. Engle, Jacob C. ROLLER and Mrs. Henrietta A. WHITE, all of Augusta.

Rockingham Register and Advertiser, 17 October 1867 (Thursday), p. 3, c. 3.

ROLLER: On Sunday morning, 15th inst., at the residence of the bride's mother, by Rev. Geo. W. Holland, John H. ROLLER, of Augusta, and Miss Lizzie C., daughter of Rev. Samuel FILLER, dec'd, of Rockingham.

Rockingham Register, 19 November 1868 (Thursday), p. 2, c. 5.

ROLLER: On the 7th inst., at the residence of Wm. Waddy, Esq., in Louisa county, by the Rev. Dr. M. Pendleton, Josiah S. ROLLER, Esq., of Rockingham, to Miss Jennie E., daughter of John S. WHITESCARVER, Esq., of Harrison county, Va.

The Rockingham Register, 11 September 1863 (Friday), p. 2, c. 3.

ROOF: See entry for HILBERT.

ROOMBURG: On the 18th ult., Mr. _____ ROOMBURG and Mrs. Lydia DRUMMOND, both of Shenandoah county.

Rockingham Register, 2 July 1868 (Thursday), p. 2, c. 4.

ROOT: On the 27th of January, by Rev. S. Henkel, Mr. Wm. ROOT, of Lynchburg, Va., and Miss Elizabeth BUSH, of New Market.

The Rockingham Register, 6 February 1863 (Friday), p. 2, c. 5.

ROOT: On the 22nd of September, by Rev. C.

Beard, William ROOT and Miss Margaret F. HIZER, all of Augusta county.

Rockingham Register and Advertiser, 10 October 1867 (Thursday), p. 3, c. 3.

ROOTS: On the 19th inst., by Rev. J.R. Wheeler, Mr. John A. ROOTS and Evaline F. BURKETT, all of Augusta county.

Rockingham Register and Advertiser, 27 September 1861 (Friday), p. 3, c. 3.

ROPER: See entry for CLARK.

ROSACRANS: See entry for WHISTLER.

ROSEBROUGH: See entry for CONRAD.

ROSEE: On the 12th inst., at the residence of the bride's father, by the Rev. J.H. Crawford, Mr. John H. ROSEE and Miss Minerva F. POLMER, all of Augusta.

Rockingham Register and Advertiser, 20 May 1859 (Friday), p. 2, c. 6.

ROSEN: See entry for SWARTZEL.

ROSENBERGER: See entry for BEIDLER.

ROSENBERGER: See entry for BOWMAN.

ROSENBERGER: See entry for FUNKHOUSER.

ROSENBERGER: See entry for HARRIS.

ROSENBERGER: See entry for LONG.

ROSENBERGER: See entry for OVERHOLTZ.

ROSENBERGER: In Mountain Valley, on the 26th ult., by Rev. J.C. Grimm, Andrew J. ROSENBERGER and Miss Eliza Ann HAGA, both of Rockingham county.

Rockingham Register, 3 June 1870 (Thursday), p. 3, c. 3.

ROSENBERGER: On the 15th ult., by Rev. J.W. Hott, David ROSENBERGER and Miss Seatta BEYDLER, all of Shenandoah.

Rockingham Register and Advertiser, 7 February 1867 (Thursday), p. 3, c. 3.

ROSENBERGER: On the 10th inst., by Rev. L. Keller, Elijah ROSENBERGER and Miss Margaret, youngest daughter of Mr. David CRABILL, all of Shenandoah county.

Rockingham Register and Advertiser, 24 October 1867 (Thursday), p. 2, c. 7.

ROSENBERGER: On the 14th of December, by Rev. S. Henkel, at the residence of the bride's father, Mr. Harvey J. ROSENBERGER and Miss Martha E., daughter of Reuben

ZIRKLE, Esq., all of Rockingham county. *Rockingham Register and Advertiser*, 12 January 1866 (Friday), p. 1, c. 3.

ROSS: See entry for CLINE.

ROSS: See entry for SHUMAKE.

ROSS: On the 2nd inst., by the Rev. G.W. Statton, Mr. David ROSS and Miss Julian, youngest daughter of Mr. Jacob WHITZEL, all of Rockingham. *Rockingham Register and Advertiser*, 10 June 1859 (Friday), p. 3, c. 2.

ROSS: By Rev. G.W. Statton, on Tuesday, May 10th, Mr. J. Newman ROSS and Miss Perthena M. HOFFMAN, all of Rockingham county. *Rockingham Register and Advertiser*, 20 May 1859 (Friday), p. 2, c. 6.

ROSS: At Colo Alto, near Lexington, Va., on the 8th inst., by Rev. W.S. White, D.D., Rev. John B. ROSS, Pastor of Roanoke church, Charlotte, Va., to Miss Mary Breckenridge, daughter of the late Gov. James McDOWELL. *Rockingham Register and Virginia Advertiser*, 18 May 1855 (Friday), p. 3, c. 4.

ROSSER: See entry for BROILS.

ROSSON: See entry for SUTTON.

ROTHGEB: See entry for BRUCE.

ROTHGER: On the 24th of March, at the residence of Col. Mann Spitler, by Rev. Wm. C. Lauck, Mr. A.B. ROTHGER, of Page county, and Miss Sue E., daughter of M.R. KAUFMAN, Esq., of Frederick county, Va. *The Rockingham Register*, 1 April 1864 (Friday), p. 2, c. 6.

ROTHWELL: See entry for BOYD.

ROUDABUSH: See entry for ASHBY.

ROUDABUSH: See entry for BATEMAN.

ROUDABUSH: See entry for FUNKHOUSER.

ROUDABUSH: See entry for MYERS.

ROUDABUSH: December 1, by Rev. Wm. J. Miller, Rev. George I. ROUDABUSH and Miss Martha C. HUCKSTEP, all of Greene county. *Rockingham Register*, 17 December 1868 (Thursday), p. 3, c. 2.

ROWAN: See entry for BERRY.

ROWELL: On Monday, December 13th, at the residence of the bride's mother, in Dry Grove, Ill., Milo ROWELL, of Burlingame, Kansas, and Miss Lou COYNER.
Rockingham Register, 13 January 1870 (Thursday), p. 3, c. 4.

ROWEN: On the 6th of December, by Rev. Isaac Long, Mr. Jacob N. ROWEN, formerly of Lewis county, Va., and Miss Caroline, daughter of Mr. Allison BREEDEN, of Rockingham county.
Rockingham Register & Advertiser, 22 December 1865 (Friday), p. 3, c. 2.

ROWLAND: See entry for DUDLEY.

ROWLAND: See entry for GRIM.

ROYER: See entry for ENGLE.

ROYER: See entry for McALISTER.

ROYER: See entry for RUSH.

ROYSTON: On Wednesday evening, January 24th, by Rev. S. Henkel, Matthew T. ROYSTON, of Clarke county, and Miss Viana MILLER, of New Market.
Rockingham Register and Advertiser, 2 February 1866 (Friday), p. 3, c. 2.

RUBUSH: See entry for SWINK.

RUBY: At the residence of Capt. James N. Swann, on Thursday evening, the 21st inst., by Rev. W.R. Stringer, Mr. Homer RUBY and Miss Mollie C. MAPHIS, all of Shenandoah county.
Rockingham Register, 5 May 1870 (Thursday), p. 3, c. 2.

RUCKMAN: At Oakland, on Thursday, December 8th, by the Rev. Mr. Pinkerton, Mr. D.V. RUCKMAN, of Highland, and Miss Anna S., youngest daughter of Bethuvel HERRING, Esq., of Augusta county.
Rockingham Register and Advertiser, 14 January 1859 (Friday), p. 3, c. 3.

RUDD: See entry for SHINN.

RUDDLE: See entry for KERLIN.

RUDOLPH: On the 3rd of October, by Rev. P. Miller, Mr. Jacob RUDOLPH and Miss Cora BOWERS, all of Hampshire county, Va.
The Rockingham Register, 18 November 1864

(Friday), p. 2, c. 2.

RUDY: See entry for JENKINS.

RUEBUSH: See entry for HUFFMAN.

RUEBUSH: On the 28th ult., by Rev. Benjamin Funk, Mr. Ephraim RUEBUSH and Miss Lucilla V. KIEFFER, all of Singer's Glen, Rockingham county.
Rockingham Register and Advertiser, 5 April 1861 (Friday), p. 2, c. 5.

RUFF: See entry for CLARKE.

RUFF: See entry for MARTIN.

RUFF: See entry for SHANK.

RUFFNER: See entry for LUCAS.

RUFFNER: See entry for STOVER.

RUFFNER: On the 13th inst., by the Rev. J. Funkhouser, Mr. Robert H. RUFFNER, of Page, and Miss Elvira, daughter of Mr. John STEPHENS, dec'd, of Rockingham.
Rockingham Register and Advertiser, 21 January 1859 (Friday), p. 3, c. 5.

RULEMAN: See entry for RANDOLPH.

RUMBAUGH: See entry for CLINEDINST.

RUNCLE: See entry for THOMAS.

RUNCLE: In McGaheysville, on the 28th of February, by Rev. J.F. Liggett, Jacob RUNCLE and Miss Ann Eliza, daughter of Aaron DENNETT, Esq., Postmaster of that town.
Rockingham Register, 4 March 1869 (Thursday), p. 2, c. 4.

RUNCLE: On the 29th of January, by Rev. Isaac Long, William J. RUNCLE and Miss Rebecca, daughter of Henry BEAZLEY, all of Rockingham county.
Rockingham Register and Advertiser, 21 February 1867 (Thursday), p. 3, c. 2.

RUNKLE: On Thursday last, by Rev. Joseph Funkhouser, Mr. John O. RUNKLE and Miss Elizabeth, daughter of Mr. John WILLIAMS, all of this county.
Rockingham Register and Advertiser, 13 May 1859 (Friday), p. 3, c. 4.

RUNNELS: See entry for MYERS.

RUPERT: In Pekin, Ill., on the 7th inst., by Rev. E.M. Whitney, Gideon H. RUPERT, Esq., of Pekin, and Mrs. Elizabeth

KNOWLES, of Peoria, Ill.
Rockingham Register, 30 April 1868 (Thursday), p. 2, c. 6.

RUPERT: On the 9th ult., by Rev. J. Stirewalt, Mr. Jacob C. RUPERT and Miss Abigail COFFMAN, all of Shenandoah.
Rockingham Register and Advertiser, 2 March 1860 (Friday), p. 3, c. 2.

RUPERT: At the residence of the bride's father, near the Cross Roads, on the 12th of March, 1868, by Rev. Jacob Stirewalt, S. RUPERT and Miss Lavina FRY, all of Shenandoah county.
Rockingham Register, 26 March 1868 (Thursday), p. 2, c. 4.

RUSH: See entry for CRIZEE.

RUSH: See entry for MAUZY.

RUSH: On Thursday, the 14th inst., by Rev. J.C. Hensell, Charles R. RUSH, Esq., and Miss Phoeba Catharine, daughter of David SCOTT, all of Rockingham county.
The Rockingham Register, 22 January 1864 (Friday), p. 2, c. 5.

RUSH: On the 30th ult., by Rev. Isaac Long, Jacob H.F. RUSH and Miss Lurena [sic, Luemma], daughter of Samuel ROYER, all of Rockingham county.
Rockingham Register and Advertiser, 13 September 1866 (Thursday), p. 2, c. 5.

RUSMISEL: See entry for JONES.

RUSMISEL: Near Deerfield, in this county, on the 1st inst., by Rev. J.S. Blain, Mr. George RUSMISEL and Mattie D., daughter of the late Thomas CLAYTON, dec'd.
Rockingham Register, 22 December 1870 (Thursday), p. 2, c. 4.

RUSMISELL: See entry for BRUBECK.

RUSMISELL: On Thursday, January 30th, at the house of the bride's brother, Joseph L. FIX, by the Rev. H. Getzendanner, Mr. David RUSMISELL to Miss Isabella FIX, all of Augusta.
Rockingham Register and Advertiser, 13 February 1868 (Thursday), p. 2, c. 5.

RUSSELL: On the 6th of March, by Rev. Jacob Miller, Mr. George RUSSELL, C.S.A., of

Alexandria county, and Miss Mary C. TAYLOR, of Rockingham county.
The Rockingham Register, 18 March 1864 (Friday), p. 2, c. 7.

RUSSELL: On the 13th ult., by Rev. Wm. A. McDonald, James P. RUSSELL and Miss Sarah C. FISHER, all of Rockbridge.
Rockingham Register and Advertiser, 4 October 1866 (Thursday), p. 2, c. 5.

RUST: On the 3rd inst., by Rev. Kenloch Nelson, Nimrod Ashby RUST, of Fauquier county, and Miss Mary Blanche, daughter of F.H. JORDAN, Esq., of Page county.
Rockingham Register, 12 November 1868 (Thursday), p. 3, c. 3.

RUTH: See entry for PETERSON.

RUTHERFORD: See entry for WILLIAMS.

RUTHERFORD: See entry for YOST.

RUTHERFORD: On the 3rd inst., by Rev. John Clymer, John RUTHERFORD and Miss Lila SHEFFER, of Shenandoah.
Rockingham Register, 17 November 1870 (Thursday), p. 2, c. 3.

RUTLEDGE: See entry for BAILEY.

RYAN: See entry for BYERLY.

RYAN: On Thursday, February 7th, on "Blennerhassett's Island," near Bridgewater, by Rev. R.N. Pool, Isaac RYAN, of Shenandoah county, and Miss Emily R., daughter of Thos. A. HOPEWELL, of Rockingham county.
Rockingham Register and Advertiser, 14 Febraury 1867 (Thursday), p. 2, c. 6.

RYAN: On the 14th inst., by Rev. W.E. Baker, at the residence of C.C. Francisco, Esq., Lt. Joseph N. RYAN amd Miss Mattie E. FRANCISCO, all of Augusta.
Rockingham Register and Advertiser, 23 May 1867 (Thursday), p. 2, c. 6.

RYAN: On the 20th inst., in Mt. Jackson, Shenandoah county, by Rev. W.H. Cone, Thomas W. RYAN, of Port Republic, Va., and Mrs. Christina ALLEN, of Mt. Jackson.
The Rockingham Register, 23 January 1863 (Friday), p. 2, c. 2.

RYMAL: On the 15th of December, by Rev.

Christopher Kyger, Sam. A. RYMAL and Miss Eldnora WILL.

Rockingham Register and Advertiser, 3 January 1867 (Thursday), p. 3, c. 3.

RYMAN: See entry for BUSHONG.

RYMAN: See entry for JONES.

RYMAN: On the 10th of January, 1865, by Rev. Jacob Wine, David RYMAN and Catharine CARRIER, all of Shenandoah county.

Rockingham Register and Advertiser, 27 January 1865 (Friday), p. 1, c. 3.

RYMAN: On the 2nd inst., Mr. John RYMAN and Miss Rosanah MILLER, all of Shenandoah county.

Rockingham Register and Advertiser, 19 January 1866 (Friday), p. 3, c. 2.

RYMAN: On the 17th ult., by Rev. J.S. Bennick, Samuel RYMAN and Miss Sarah HEPNER, all of Shenandoah.

Rockingham Register, 8 December 1870 (Thursday), p. 2, c. 4.

- S -

SAFFELL: See entry for VENABLE.

SAFLEY: See entry for SCOTT.

SAFLEY: On the 3rd inst., at the residence of the bride's father, by Rev. H. Tallhelm, Isaac N.B. SAFLEY, son of Wm. SAFLEY, Esq., and Miss J.V. NULL, all of this county.

Rockingham Register, 5 November 1868 (Thursday), p. 3, c. 3.

SAGER: On the 8th ult., by Rev. A.R. Rude, Mr. John H. SAGER and Miss Leah LONAS.

Rockingham Register and Advertiser, 14 December 1860 (Friday), p. 2, c. 6.

SALTZGIVER: On Friday, April 19th, in the Lutheran Church, Frederick city, Md., by Rev. Geo. Deal, Mr. Geo. E. SALTZGIVER, of Charlottesville, Va., and Miss M.M., daughter of the late Rev. Dr. WATCHER, of Frederick city, Md.

Rockingham Register and Advertiser, 13 May 1859 (Friday), p. 3, c. 4.

SALYARDS: On the 5th inst., by Rev. J.

Stirewalt, Mr. G. Webster SALYARDS to
Miss Rebecca SHOMO, all of New Market,
Va.
The *Rockingham* *Register* *and* *Valley*
Advertiser, 22 November 1851 (Saturday),
p. 3, c. 1.
SALYARDS: At the N.S. Presbyterian parsonage,
in Harrisonburg, on Sunday morning last,
by Rev. T. Bell, Professor Joseph
SALYARDS, of Pleasant Grove Academy. and
Miss Elizabeth FLORY, of the neighborhood
of Frieden's Church.
Rockingham *Register* *and* *Advertiser*, 15
March 1861 (Friday), p. 2, c. 4.
SAMPSON: See entry for AMMON.
SAMPSON: On the 10th of January, 1865, by
Rev. Isaac Long, Mr. Henry SAMPSON and
Miss Sarah E. MICHAEL, all of Rockingham
county.
Rockingham *Register* *and* *Advertiser*, 20
January 1865 (Friday), p. 2, c. 4.
SAMPSON: On the 29th ult., by Rev. Martin
Garber, Mr. Layton M. SAMPSON and Miss
Susan E. HUMPHREY, all of Augusta county.
Rockingham *Register* *and* *Advertiser*, 9
January 1868 (Thursday), p. 2, c. 4.
SAMUELS: See entry for DAVIS.
SAMUELS: On Thursday evening, the 13th inst.,
by Rev. M. Lohr, Mr. Joseph SAMUELS, of
Augusta, and Miss Fannie J., daughter of
Mr. Jesse BURKHOLDER, of Rockingham
county.
Rockingham *Register* *and* *Advertiser*, 21
September 1860 (Friday), p. 2, c. 4.
SANDERSON: See entry for WILSON.
SANDEY: See entry for LAMB.
SANFORD: See entry for GLASS.
SANDFORD: See entry for REAGAN.
SANDY: See entry for TUTWILER.
SANDY: On the 15th of November, by Rev.
Solomon Garber, John H. SANDY and Miss
Mary F., daughter of George KARICOFE, all
of Rockingham county.
Rockingham *Register* *and* *Advertiser*, 6
December 1866 (Thursday), p. 3, c. 2.
SANDY: On the 2nd inst., by Rev. Fred.

Miller, Wm. J. SANDY and Miss Susan R. KELLER, all of Rockingham county.

Rockingham Register and Advertiser, 16 January 1868 (Thursday), p. 2, c. 5.

SANGER: See entry for CRUMPACKER.

SANGER: See entry for FLORY.

SANGER: See entry for TURNER.

SANGER: On the 16th inst., by Rev. Jos. Funkhouser, at Lacy Springs, John F. SANGER and Miss S.A.C. WOOD.

Rockingham Register, 25 November 1869 (Thursday), p. 2, c. 3.

SAUFLEY: See entry for KYGER.

SAUFLEY: See entry for ROLLER.

SAUFLEY: On Thursday, the 17th of December, by Rev. J.C. Hensell, Joseph F. SAUFLEY and Miss Louisa M., third daughter of Reuben HUFFMAN, all of Rockingham county.

Rockingham Register, 7 January 1869 (Thursday), p. 3, c. 3.

SAUFLEY: On the 27th ult., by Rev. J.C. Hensell, William McK. SAUFLEY and Miss Josephine A. L., daughter of Michael and Barbara MOYERHOEFFER, all of Rockingham county.

Rockingham Register and Advertiser, 6 April 1866 (Friday), p. 3, c. 3.

SAUFLY: On Thursday, the 13th inst., by Rev. J.C. Hensell, Mr. George H. SAUFLY and Miss Susan C., daughter of Mr. Benjamin BYERLY, of Augusta county.

Rockingham Register and Advertiser, 28 February 1862 (Friday), p. 3, c. 3.

SAUM: On the 23rd ult., at the residence of Dr. E. Cathrill, Norfolk, Va., by Rev. I.G. Jones, D.D., J.F. SAUM, of Edinburg, Shenandoah county, Va., and Miss Bettie S., only daughter of Dr. W.W. CLEMENTS, of North Hampton county, N.C.

Rockingham Register, 13 January 1870 (Thursday), p. 3, c. 4.

SAUM: On the 28th ult., by Elder R.C. Cave, J.W. SAUM and Miss Sallie E. MAPHIS, all of Shenandoah county.

Rockingham Register, 3 February 1870 (Thursday), p. 3, c. 4.

SAUM: On the 25th ult., by Elder J. Pirkey,
Mr. Marlen G. SAUM and Miss Angeline
MILLER, all of Shenandoah.
Rockingham Register and Advertiser, 2
November 1860 (Friday), p. 2, c. 5.

SAUNDERS: See entry for CONTRI.

SAUNDERS: See entry for CROSS.

SAUNDERS: See entry for McDONALD.

SAUPE: On the 7th of January, 1863, at the
residence of the bride, in Staunton, by
Rev. Jos. R. Wheeler, Charles H. SAUPE
and Mrs. Frances STRAUGMAN, all of
Staunton, Va.
The Rockingham Register, 16 January 1863
(Friday), p. 2, c. 6.

SAVAGE: In Mt. Meridian, on the 4th inst., by
the Rev. G.W. Statton, Mr. George SAVAGE
to Miss M. J. KNIPPLE, of Augusta.
Rockingham Register and Advertiser, 23
December 1859 (Friday), p. 2, c. 5.

SAYLAW: See entry for LOWRY.

SCALES: See entry for WAY.

SCHANK: On the 15th inst., by Rev. Thomas
Hildebrand, Mr. Martin L. SCHANK, of
Shenandoah county, and Miss Elizabeth J.,
daughter of Mr. Albert J. WILHITE, of
Bridgewater, Rockingham county.
The Rockingham Register, 30 January 1863
(Friday), p. 2, c. 4.

SCHERER: At St. Francis' Church, Staunton,
September 8th, by Rev. Father J. Ambler
Weed, John B. SCHERER, Jr., and Miss
Johanna SULLIVAN, all of Staunton.
Rockingham Register, 17 September 1868
(Thursday), p. 2, c. 5.

SCHMITT: See entry for MAHON.

SCHMITT: In Washington, D.C., on the 9th
inst., by Rev. Father McCarty, P.F.
SCHMITT, of Staunton, to Miss Maggie S.
FITZGERALD, of Washington.
Rockingham Register, 26 May 1870
(Thursday), p. 2, c. 6.

SCHMUCKER: See entry for BOWMAN.

SCHMUCKER: On the 1st inst., in Strasburg, by
Rev. W. Rusmisell, Morgan F. SCHMUCKER
and Miss Ann E. BAUSERMAN, all of

Shenandoah county.

Rockingham Register, 22 October 1868 (Thursday), p. 3, c. 3.

SCHMUCKER: By Rev. Jacob Miller, on the 7th of March, Samuel C. SCHMUCKER, of Shenandoah, and Salome D., daughter of David KLINE, of Rockingham.

Rockingham Register and Advertiser, 14 March 1867 (Thursday), p. 3, c. 5.

SCHRECKHISE: See entry for ROBERTS.

SCOTT: See entry for DAVIS.

SCOTT: See entry for FUNKHOUSER.

SCOTT: See entry for RUSH.

SCOTT: See entry for TERELL.

SCOTT: See entry for WILLIAMS.

SCOTT: In Salem, Roanoke county, Va., on Thursday, the 28th of April, by Rev. D.F. Bittle, D.D., Dr. E.H. SCOTT, of Harrisonburg, and Miss Ella HOUSTON, adopted daughter of Professor J. J. MOORMAN, of Washington Medical College, Baltimore, Md.

Rockingham Register, 5 May 1870 (Thursday), p. 3, c. 2.

SCOTT: On the 24th of December, by Rev. James F. Liggett, John D. SCOTT and Miss Margaret S., daughter of Aaron DENNETT, all of McGaheysville, Rockingham county.

Rockingham Register, 7 January 1869 (Thursday), p. 3, c. 3.

SCOTT: On Thursday the 12th of September, by the Rev. Isaac Long, Mr. Reuben SCOTT to Miss Mary, daughter of Wm. and Margaret SAFLEY, all of Rockingham county.

Rockingham Register and Advertiser, 4 October 1861 (Friday), p. 3, c. 3.

SCOTT: On the 4th of April, at the United States Legation in Rio de Janeiro, by the Rev. Mr. Colby, Robert G. SCOTT, Jr., Esq., U.S. Consul, of Richmond, Va., and Miss Anna Kittridge, daughter of Wm. THOMPSON, Esq., of West Trenton, Maine.

Rockingham Register and Advertiser, 27 May 1859 (Friday), p. 2, c. 6.

SCRAGHAN: On the 20th of February, by Rev. Martin Garber, Jacob S. SCRAGHAN and

Elizabeth S. GOCHENOUR, all of Augusta
county.
Rockingham Register, 3 March 1870
(Thursday), p. 2, c. 5.
SEAL: In Page county, on the 9th of April, by
Rev. John P. Hyde, Mr. James B. SEAL and
Mrs. Mary E. GORDON.
Rockingham Register and Advertiser, 21
April 1865 (Friday), p. 2, c. 5.
SEAWRIGHT: At Mt. Crawford, on Thursday,
December 28th, by Rev. E.P. Veitch, Mr.
John SEAWRIGHT, of Augusta county, and
Miss Fannie J. CUPP, of Rockingham
county.
Rockingham Register and Advertiser, 12
January 1866 (Friday), p. 2, c. 3.
SECRIST: See entry for HUFFMAN.
SECRIST: On Thursday evening, August 31st, at
the residence of the bride's father, on
Pleasant Run, Mr. M. Harvey SECRIST and
Miss Margaret Ann, eldest daughter of Dr.
John DILLER, all of this county.
Rockingham Register & Advertiser, 8
September 1865 (Friday), p. 3, c. 2.
SEELY: See entry for MYERS.
SEIVER: See entry for SUDDARTH.
SEIVER: At the residence of the bride's
father, on the 11th ult., by Rev. J.A.
Snyder, Geo. W. SEIVER and Miss Elizabeth
C., daughter of Thomas CORBIN, all of
Shenandoah.
Rockingham Register and Advertiser, 15
November 1866 (Thursday), p. 2, c. 5.
SELLERS: See entry for ARMENTROUT.
SELLERS: See entry for EWING.
SELLERS: See entry for FRIPPE.
SELLERS: See entry for MARTZ.
SELLERS: See entry for MYERS.
SELLERS: On Thursday, the 1st inst., by the
Rev. J.C. Hensell, Mr. John W. SELLERS,
of Rockingham county, and Miss Martha E.
WOOD, of Albemarle county.
Rockingham Register and Advertiser, 16
September 1859 (Friday), p. 2, c. 4.
SENCINDIVER: See entry for BORUM.
SENEKER: On the 12th inst., by Rev. J.

Killian, Rev. Jas. SENEKER and Miss Sallie, daughter of Martin KOINER, of Augusta county.

Rockingham Register and Advertiser, 27 September 1866 (Thursday), p. 3, c. 3.

SENGER: See entry for JOHNSON.

SENGER: By Rev. P. Miller, on the 30th ult., Jacob SENGER, Jr., and Miss Semantha A. BAUGHMAN, all of Hardy county.

Rockingham Register, 20 January 1870 (Thursday), p. 2, c. 5.

SENSEBAUGH: See entry for MILLER (2).

SENSENEY: See entry for RHODES.

SETTLE: At Mt. Crawford, on the 30th of April, by Rev. George B. Taylor, Rev. Vincent T. SETTLE, pastor of the Baptist church at Mt. Crawford, and Miss Carrie L. TURLEY.

Rockingham Register and Advertiser, 13 May 1859 (Friday), p. 3, c. 4.

SEVIER: On the 24th ult., at New Hampden, by Rev. W.T. Price, James W. SEVIER, Jr., and Miss Mattie E. SNYDER, all of Highland.

Rockingham Register, 4 March 1869 (Thursday), p. 2, c. 4.

SHACKLETT: At the residence of the bride's father, "Quaker Valley," Pittsburg [sic], Pa., on Thursday the 18th of June, by Rev. J.B. Bittenger, D.D., Wm. SHACKLETT and Miss Mary Atwood, daughter of Wm. P. JONES, Esq.

Rockingham Register, 9 July 1868 (Thursday), p. 2, c. 5.

SHADWELL: See entry for FADEL.

SHADWELL: In Edinburg, on the 21st ult., by Rev. H. Shaull, Samuel SHADWELL and Miss Catherine MAPHIS, all of Shenandoah county.

Rockingham Register, 7 May 1868 (Thursday), p. 2, c. 4.

SHAFER: See entry for SHUMATE.

SHAFER: On the 8th of March, by Rev. Jacob Miller, Mr. John SHAFER and Miss Mary E., daughter of Geo. ARMENTROUT, all of Rockingham county.

Rockingham *Register* and *Advertiser*, 6 April 1860 (Friday), p. 2, c. 6.

SHAFFER: See entry for GOOD.

SHAFFER: Near Pine Forge, in Shenandoah county, Virginia, on the 7th inst., by Elder Geo. W. Woods, Mr. John R. SHAFFER and Miss Sallie BAILEY.

Rockingham *Register* & *Advertiser*, 17 November 1865 (Friday), p. 2, c. 4.

SHANDS: See entry for BOWER.

SHANHOLTZ: See entry for EDWARDS.

SHANK: See entry for BODKIN.

SHANK: See entry for BRENEMAN.

SHANK: See entry for BURKHOLDER.

SHANK: See entry for LANDES.

SHANK: See entry for LONG.

SHANK: See entry for ROLLER.

SHANK: See entry for SHANK.

SHANK: See entry for SWOPE.

SHANK: On the 26th of August, by Rev. Benj. Funk, Mr. C.F. SHANK and Miss Lizzie BEERY, all of Rockingham.

Rockingham *Register* and *Advertiser*, 19 October 1860 (Friday), p. 2, c. 4.

SHANK: On Sunday the 1st of June, by Rev. Joseph Early, Mr. Daniel SHANK and Miss Elizabeth, daughter of Frederick HESS, all of Rockingham county.

Rockingham *Register* and *Virginia Advertiser*, 25 July 1862 (Friday), p. 2, c. 4.

SHANK: On the 3rd inst., at the residence of the bride's father, by Rev. Thomas E. Carson, Daniel P. SHANK, of Rockingham, and Miss Mary C. RUFF, of Augusta county.

Rockingham *Register*, 10 December 1868 (Thursday), p. 3, c. 3.

SHANK: On Thursday, the 7th of October, by the Rev. Solomon Garber, David SHANK, Jr., and Miss S. BOWMAN, all of Rockingham.

Rockingham *Register*, 14 October 1869 (Thursday), p. 2, c. 2.

SHANK: On the 5th inst., by Rev. T.D. Bell, Gabriel SHANK, Color-Sergeant of the 10th Regiment, and Miss Ann Amelia KEIFFER, all of Rockingham.

The Rockingham Register, 10 October 1862 (Friday), p. 2, c. 7.

SHANK: On the 23rd of December, by the Rev. Peter SHICKEL, Mr. Henry SHANK and Miss Mary LUTZ, all of this county.

Rockingham Register, 15 January 1842 (Saturday), p. 3, c. 1.

SHANK: Near New Market, on the 6th inst., by Rev. S. Henkle, J.A. SHANK, of Page county, and Miss Nancy T. STRICKLER, of Shenandoah county.

Rockingham Register, 17 February 1870 (Thursday), p. 3, c. 2.

SHANK: At the Presbyterian Parsonage, in this place, on Sunday morning, November 22nd, by Rev. J. Rice Bowman, Jacob SHANK and Mrs. Anna RHODES, widow of Peter RHODES, all of Rockingham county.

Rockingham Register, 10 December 1868 (Thursday), p. 3, c. 3.

SHANK: On the 20th ult., near Green Valley, at the residence of the bride's father, by Rev. Leopold Lenz, Mr. L.D. SHANK and Miss Martha A., daughter of Peter BRIGHT, all of Bath county.

Rockingham Register and Advertiser, 14 March 1862 (Friday), p. 3, c. 2.

SHANK: On Thursday, the 11th inst., by Rev. Levi Keller, Mr. Noah SHANK and Mrs. Henry SHANK, all of Page county.

The Rockingham Register, 26 June 1863 (Friday), p. 2, c. 5.

SHANK: On the 22nd ult., by Rev. Jacob Stirewalt, Mr. Wm. J. SHANK and Miss Nancy, daughter of John BEAVER, of Page county.

Rockingham Register and Virginia Advertiser, 13 June 1856 (Friday), p. 2, c. 2.

SHANNON: See entry for HARRY.

SHARK: See entry for PAINTER.

SHARP: See entry for SOUTHALL.

SHARP: On the 5th inst., near Buchannon [sic], Upshur county, W.Va., by the Rev. Dr. Young, Alexander A. SHARP, of

Jefferson county, Tenn.,and Miss L.,
daughter of the widow Dorcas B. THOMPSON,
formerly of Augusta county.
Rockingham Register, 26 May 1870
(Thursday), p. 2, c. 6.
SHAVER: See entry for KEAGY.
SHAVER: See entry for KELLER.
SHAVER: See entry for REHERD.
SHAVER: See entry for TATE.
SHAVER: See entry for VANFOSSEN.
SHAVER: On the 14th inst., at the residence
of the bride's parents, by Rev. J.S.
Gardner, E.M. SHAVER and Miss Eliza M.,
daughter of Martin CROMER, all of
Rockingham county.
Rockingham Register, 26 May 1870
(Thursday), p. 2, c. 6.
SHAVER: On the 9th inst., by Rev. Jas. F.
Liggett, Hugh B. SHAVER, of Texas,
formerly of Rockingham county, Va., and
Miss Siddie E., daughter of Dr. A. WOLFE,
dec'd, of East Rockingham.
Rockingham Register, 20 August 1868
(Thursday), p. 3, c. 3.
SHAVER: On the 24th of February, by Rev. C.
Beard, Jacob H. SHAVER, of Rockbridge,
and Miss Annie E. COINER, of Augusta.
Rockingham Register, 10 March 1870
(Thursday), p. 2, c. 4.
SHAVER: On the 30th of August, by Rev. Jacob
Miller, Mr. Jno. E. SHAVER and Mrs. Sarah
RIDDLE, all of Rockingham county.
The Rockingham Register, 18 September
1863 (Friday), p. 2, c. 5.
SHAVER: On Thursday the 15th inst., by Rev.
Geo. W. Holland, at the residence of the
bride's father, Joseph E. SHAVER and Miss
Mary E., daughter of Samuel SLUSSER, all
of Rockingham county.
Rockingham Register, 22 October 1868
(Thursday), p. 3, c. 3.
SHAVER: On the 12th inst., by Rev. J.P.
Cline, Mr. Moses SHAVER and Miss
Elizabeth, daughter of Mr. Samuel HUPP,
of Shenandoah county.
Rockingham Register and Advertiser, 27

April 1860 (Friday), p. 2, c. 4.

SHAVER: Near Fincastle, Va., on Tuesday, the 27th of November, by Rev. Peter Nininger, Samuel L. SHAVER, of Rockingham county, and Miss Mollie C., daughter of Jacob GISH, dec'd, of Botetourt county.
Rockingham Register and Advertiser, 20 December 1866 (Thursday), p. 2, c. 5.

SHAW: See entry for BAILEY.

SHAY: On the 23rd March, by Rev. D.C. Irwin, Mr. Patrick SHAY and Miss Sallie Ann LAMBERT, both of Rockingham.
Rockingham Register and Advertiser, 1 April 1859 (Friday), p. 3, c. 2.

SHEA: On the 14th of September, 1869, by the Rev. E.T.R. Trippe, John SHEA to Miss Rebecca Jane COINER, all of Augusta.
Rockingham Register, 23 September 1869 (Thursday), p. 2, c. 3.

SHEARER: See entry for SHIPLER.

SHEENEN: On New Year's day, near Harrisonburg, by Rev. Father Bixio, Serg't Wm. SHEENEN, C.S.A., and Miss Susan, daughter of Daniel HURLEY, all of Rockingham.
Rockingham Register and Advertiser, 13 January 1865 (Friday), p. 2, c. 1.

SHEETS: See entry for BOWERS.

SHEETS: See entry for BOYD.

SHEETS: See entry for BRICKER.

SHEETS: See entry for BURGESS.

SHEETS: See entry for EARMON.

SHEETS: See entry for GRABILL.

SHEETS: See entry for MOORE.

SHEETS: See entry for PETERS.

SHEETS: See entry for STICKLEY.

SHEETS: On the 6th inst., at the M.E. Parsonage, Gospel Hill, by Rev. Geo. G. Brooke, Albert R. SHEETS and Elizabeth Jane HULVEY, of Augusta county.
Rockingham Register and Advertiser, 14 October 1859 (Friday), p. 2, c. 3.

SHEETS: On the 19th of August, by Rev. R.N. Pool, Christian SHEETS, of Bridgewater, and Miss Barbara HOOVER, all of Rockingham county.

394

Rockingham Register and Advertiser, 13 September 1866 (Thursday), p. 2, c. 5.

SHEETS: On Thursday, the 19th ult., by Rev. J.C. Hensell, Mr. John D. SHEETS and Miss Frances D. RADENER, both of Augusta county, Va.

Rockingham Register & Advertiser, 3 November 1865 (Friday), p. 2, c. 2.

SHEETS: On the 24th ult., by Rev. Joseph R. Wheeler, Mr. John R. SHEETS and Miss Mary D. SNYDER, all of Augusta county.

Rockingham Register and Advertiser, 7 March 1862 (Friday), p. 3, c. 2.

SHEETS: On the 14th ult., by the Rev. Jacob B. Houck, Mr. Joseph H. SHEETS and Miss Catharine A. NEFF, all of Rockingham county.

Rockingham Register and Valley Advertiser, 8 June 1850 (Saturday), p. 2, c. 7.

SHEETS: On the 8th inst., by Rev. Jos. Funkhouser, Joseph H. SHEETS and Miss Hettie M. BROWN, all of Rockingham.

Rockingham Register and Advertiser, 15 November 1866 (Thursday), p. 2, c. 5.

SHEETS: On Thursday evening of last week, by the Rev. A.W. Kil[pat]rick, Mr. Samuel SHEETS to Miss Mary HOUFF, all of this county.

Rockingham Register, 2 July 1836 (Saturday), p. 3, c. 3.

SHEETZ: See entry for GOLLADAY.

SHEETZ: See entry for NEWLAND.

SHEETZ: On the 7th inst., Mr. Daniel H. SHEETZ and Miss Lydia PHILIPS, all of Shenandoah county.

Rockingham Register and Advertiser, 19 January 1866 (Friday), p. 3, c. 2.

SHEETZ: On the 22nd of December, by Rev. John M. Clymer, Mr. Isaac B. SHEETZ and Miss Sarah C. PAINTER, all of Shenandoah county.

Rockingham Register and Advertiser, 12 January 1866 (Friday), p. 2, c. 3.

SHEETZ: On the 30th ult., by Rev. D. Feete, Mr. William SHEETZ and Miss Mary E.

BEOHM, all of Shenandoah county.
Rockingham Register and Advertiser, 4
February 1859 (Friday), p. 2, c. 5.
SHEETZ: On the 28th ult., by Rev. D. Feete,
Mr. Wm. W. SHEETZ and Miss Christina F.,
daughter of Mr. Thomas HOTTLE, all of
Shenandoah.
Rockingham Register and Advertiser, 12
April 1861 (Friday), p. 2, c. 4.
SHEFFER: See entry for MOORE.
SHEFFER: See entry for RUTHERFORD.
SHEIRY: In Harrisonburg, on Monday evening,
the 13th inst., by Rev. J.W. Moore, Mr.
Gideon SHEIRY, of Washington county, Md.,
Foreman in the Register office, and Miss
Ella Marceline, daughter of John SLATER,
dec'd, of this place.
Rockingham Register, 17 July 1863
(Friday), p. 3, c. 1.
SHELLY: In Staunton, Va., by Rev. J.I.
Miller, Mr. John H.M. SHELLY and Miss
Marinda A. QUIESENBERRY, both of Augusta
county.
Rockingham Register, 1 December 1870
(Thursday), p. 2, c. 4.
SHELTMAN: See entry for AGNER.
SHELTMAN: See entry for VAN PELT.
SHELTON: See entry for BOLTON.
SHELTON: See entry for LANDES.
SHELTON: See entry for MARTIN.
SHELTON: See entry for NUCKOLS.
SHELTON: On the 10th inst., at Kirk's Tavern,
by Rev. D. Parmer, Mr. Thomas M. SHELTON
and Miss Margaret T., daughter of Preston
MOORE, late of Bath county, Va.
Rockingham Register and Advertiser, 20
April 1860 (Friday), p. 2, c. 5.
SHELTON: On the 31st of July, at Mountain
Top, Augusta county, by Rev. Geo. B.
Taylor, Dr. Thomas W. SHELTON and Miss
Sarah F. LIPSCOMB.
Rockingham Register and Advertiser, 23
August 1861 (Friday), p. 3, c. 4.
SHENK: See entry for HERSHBARGER.
SHENK: See entry for WANGER.
SHENK: On the 20th inst., [by] Rev. John W.

Watson, H.C. SHENK and Miss Mary Ellen MURRAY, all of Page county.
Rockingham Register and Advertiser, 29 August 1867 (Thursday), p. 2, c. 5.

SHENK: On the 20th inst., by Elder F.M. Perry, Harrison S. SHENK and Mrs. Sarah C. BEECH, all of Page county.
Rockingham Register and Advertiser, 29 August 1867 (Thursday), p. 2, c. 5.

SHEPERD: See entry for VANCE.

SHEPHERD: See entry for BERRY.

SHEPHERD: See entry for CASTLEMAN.

SHEPHERD: See entry for McCUE.

SHEPHERD: On the 26th ult., by Rev. B.H. Smith, Mr. N.H. SHEPHERD, of Henrico, and Miss Caroline M. HUFF, of Augusta.
Rockingham Register and Advertiser, 18 January 1861 (Friday), p. 3, c. 2.

SHEPLER: See entry for ROGERS.

SHEPP: On Thursday, the 25th of January, by Rev. Wm. J. Miller, Charles N. SHEPP and Miss Mollie J. COFFMAN, all near East Point, Rockingham county.
Rockingham Register and Advertiser, 6 February 1868 (Thursday), p. 2, c. 4.

SHERFEY: See entry for SHOWALTER.

SHERFEY: On the 26th of April, by Rev. Isaac Soule, Mr. Benjamin F. SHERFEY and Miss Sarah F., daughter of Henry McDORMAN, all of Dry River, Rockingham county.
Rockingham Register and Advertiser, 11 May 1866 (Friday), p. 2, c. 4.

SHERMAN: On the 6th inst., on Linvill's Creek, by Rev. Jos. Holcombe, Daniel W. SHERMAN, of Alexandria, and Miss Elizabeth M., daughter of Morgan CHAPMAN, of Rockingham county.
Rockingham Register and Advertiser, 21 June 1866 (Thursday), p. 2, c. 4.

SHERMAN: On Thursday, the 15th inst., by Rev. J.C. Hensell, Mr. George F. SHERMAN and Miss Eliza M. HAHN, all of Rockingham county.
The Rockingham Register, 23 September 1864 (Friday), p. 2, c. 5.

SHERRARD: See entry for McNEILL.

SHERRARD: On Thursday, October 26th, near Lexington, Va., by the Rev. Mr. White, Mr. Joseph H. SHERRARD, of Winchester, and Miss Rose CAMERON, of Rockbridge county, Va.
Rockingham Register & Advertiser, 10 November 1865 (Friday), p. 2, c. 4.

SHICKEL: See entry for FIFER.

SHICKEL: On Thursday, the 22nd ult., by Rev. Daniel Thomas, Jos. SHICKEL and Miss Nancy E., daughter of John MILLER, all of Rockingham.
Rockingham Register and Advertiser, 2 March 1866 (Friday), p. 3, c. 3.

SHICKLE: On the 5th inst., by Rev. Jacob Thomas, Daniel SHICKLE and Miss Catharine, daughter of Samuel E. LONG, all of Rockingham county.
Rockingham Register, 12 November 1868 (Thursday), p. 3, c. 3.

SHIELDS: See entry for COLLINS.

SHIELDS: See entry for JOHNSTON.

SHIFFLET: April 3rd, by Rev. A.J. Kibler, Bennet SHIFFLET and Miss Mary LONG, all of Rockingham county.
Rockingham Register, 21 April 1870 (Thursday), p. 3, c. 3.

SHIFFLET: On the 6th inst., by Rev. G.H. Martin, Mr. Edward SHIFFLET and Miss Harriett J. MUMAW, all of Rockingham county.
Rockingham Register and Advertiser, 13 December 1866 (Thursday), p. 2, c. 5.

SHIFFLETT: See entry for McDANIEL.

SHIFFLETT: See entry for SHIFFLETT.

SHIFFLETT: On the 8th of July, at Mt. Pleasant Church, by Rev. Frederick Miller, George SHIFFLETT and Miss Lydia Jane, daughter of David LANDES, all of Rockingham county.
Rockingham Register and Advertiser, 19 July 1866 (Thursday), p. 3, c. 3.

SHIFFLETT: On the 7th inst., by Rev. Isaac Long, Henry SHIFFLETT and Miss Agnes SHIFFLETT, all of Rockingham county.
Rockingham Register, 21 May 1868

(Thursday), p. 2, c. 5.

SHIFFLETT: On the 16th inst., at the residence of the bride's father, in Bridgewater, by Rev. G.W. Stevenson, Robert H. SHIFFLETT, of Augusta county, and Miss Dorinda J. WISE, of Rockingham. Rockingham Register and Advertiser, 23 May 1867 (Thursday), p. 2, c. 6.

SHIFFLETT: On the 27th ult., by Rev. Geo. B. Taylor, Sam'l SHIFFLETT, of Greene county, and Miss Sarah M. ROBERTS. Rockingham Register, 6 May 1869 (Thursday), p. 2, c. 3.

SHIFLET: On the 16th ult., by Rev. Isaac Long, Cornelius Turner SHIFLET and Miss Maria J., daughter of Benson BERRY, all of Rockingham county. Rockingham Register and Advertiser, 13 September 1866 (Thursday), p. 2, c. 5.

SHIFLETT: See entry for POWELL.

SHIFLETT: See entry for SHIFLETT.

SHIFLETT: See entry for SMITH.

SHIFLETT: See entry for SWAN.

SHIFLETT: On the 24th of December, by Rev. Joseph Funkhouser, Mr. Brazel SHIFLETT and Miss Mary C. WHITSEL, all of Rockingham county. The Rockingham Register, 8 January 1864 (Friday), p. 2, c. 5.

SHIFLETT: On Thursday the 17th of October, by Rev. Jos. Funkhouser, Mr. John T. SHIFLETT and Miss Harriet SHIFLETT, all of Rockingham county. Rockingham Register and Virginia Advertiser, 18 [sic, 25] October 1861 (Friday), p. , c. 7.

SHIFLETT: On Thursday, the 28th of December, by Rev. Isaac Long, Robert T. SHIFLETT and Miss Elizabeth, daughter of Henry RAINES, all of Rockingham county. Rockingham Register and Advertiser, 19 January 1866 (Friday), p. 3, c. 2.

SHIFTLETT: See entry for EPPARD.

SHIFTLEY: See entry for McALLESTER.

SHILLENBURG: On the 27th ult., by Rev. Henry St. J. Rinker, Mr. Lewis D. SHILLENBURG and Miss Lydia A. MUMAW, all of Shenandoah county.

Rockingham Register and Advertiser, 5 October 1860 (Friday), p. 2, c. 3.

SHILLINGBURG: On the 5th inst., near Frieden's Church, A. SHILLINGBURG and Caroline VARTS, both of Shenandoah.

Rockingham Register, 26 November 1868 (Thursday), p. 2, c. 5.

SHINN: On the 26th ult., by Rev. James T. Johnson, James W. SHINN and Miss Maggie RUDD, all of Alexandria.

Rockingham Register and Advertiser, 3 January 1867 (Thursday), p. 3, c. 3.

SHIP: See entry for BRUMBACH.

SHIP: On the 7th, by Rev. H. St. John Rinker, Mr. John SHIP and Miss Elizabeth HOLLAR, of Shenandoah county.

Rockingham Register and Advertiser, 29 April 1859 (Friday), p. 3, c. 2.

SHIPE: See entry for MUNCH.

SHIPLER: At Slate Creek, Idaho county, Idaho Territory, February 1st, Mr. Frank SHIPLER and Miss Bettie, youngest daughter of Hon. F.A. SHEARER, formerly of Winchester, Va.

Rockingham Register and Advertiser, 20 April 1866 (Friday), p. 2, c. 3.

SHIPLET: On the 3rd inst., by Rev. Jacob Thomas, Martin S. SHIPLET and Miss Catharine E., daughter of the late Wm. WRIGHT, near Moscow, Augusta county.

Rockingham Register, 17 September 1868 (Thursday), p. 2, c. 5.

SHIPLEY: In Baltimore, on the 26th of October, by the Rev. Jno. A. GERE, D.D., Rev. J. Lester SHIPLEY, of the Virginia Annual Conference, and Miss E. Gussie, fourth daughter of the officiating minister.

Rockingham Register & Advertiser, 10 November 1865 (Friday), p. 2, c. 4.

SHIPMAN: On the morning of the 5th inst., by Rev. H. St. J. Rinker, Mr. Francis SHIPMAN, of Rockingham county, and Mrs. Ellen HUFFMAN, of Shenandoah county.

The Rockingham Register, 13 May 1864 (Friday), p. 2, c. 5.

SHIPP: On the 9th inst., by Rev. J.W. Wolf, F. SHIPP and Miss A. K. DAY, all of Shenandoah county.

Rockingham Register, 25 November 1869 (Thursday), p. 2, c. 3.

SHIREMAN: See entry for COOK.

SHIREMAN: See entry for HOUSAFLUCK.

SHIREMAN: On the 26th ult., by the Rev. H. St. John Rinker, Mr. Reuben SHIREMAN and Miss Margaret HAUSEFLUCK, all of Shenandoah.

Rockingham Register and Advertiser, 3 February 1860 (Friday), p. 2, c. 5.

SHIRFEY: On Thursday, the 5th inst., by the Rev. Wright Burgess, Mr. Reuben SHIRFEY, of Rockingham, to Miss Susan, daughter of Mr. William NAIR, of Augusta county.

Rockingham Register, 21 February 1835 (Saturday), p. 3, c. 3.

SHIRKEY: See entry for NEWHAM.

SHIRKEY: See entry for SHOUP.

SHIRKEY: On the 23rd of August, at New Town, Rockingham county, by Rev. Abraham Knopp, Sen., Gideon SHIRKEY (son of Andrew) and Miss Catharine, daughter of John TOPPEN, all of Rockingham county.

Rockingham Register, 27 August 1868 (Thursday), p. 3, c. 3.

SHIRKEY: On Tuesday the 14th of November, by Rev. Benjamin Bowman, Mr. Samuel SHIRKEY and Miss Kate, daughter of John ZIGLER, Esq., all of Rockingham.

Rockingham Register & Advertiser, 1 December 1865 (Friday), p. 2, c. 4.

SHIRLEY: On Sunday the 10th inst., at the residence of J.D. Irwin, by the Rev. W.T. Price, Mr. Jonathan SHIRLEY, of Indiana, and Miss Maggie E. SWOOPE, of Highland.

Rockingham Register and Advertiser, 28 March 1867 (Thursday), p. 2, c. 6.

SHMITT: See entry for CLOWER.

SHOBE: In Cumberland, Md., on the 10th of November, 1869, A.W. SHOBE, of Grant county, and Miss Sallie M. STICKLET, of

Hampshire county.

Rockingham Register, 20 January 1870 (Thursday), p. 2, c. 5.

SHOBE: On the 10th ult., by Rev. John Johnson, at the residence of John Taylor, Esq., M.W. SHOBE and Miss Hannah EVERLY, all of Grant county, W.Va.

Rockingham Register, 24 March 1870 (Thursday), p. 3, c. 2.

SHOCKEY: On the 22nd of November, at East Point, Rockingham county, by Rev. Isaac Long, G.W. SHOCKEY, of Morgan county, W.Va., and Miss Annie E., daughter of Joseph HARNER, of Rockingham county.

Rockingham Register and Advertiser, 20 December 1866 (Thursday), p. 2, c. 5.

SHOEMAKER: See entry for WHISLER.

SHOEMAKER: See entry for WOOD.

SHOEMAKER: On Sunday, the 26th inst., by Rev. Jacob Miller, Christian C. SHOEMAKER and Miss Rebecca, daughter of Anthony SHOWALTER, all of Rockingham county.

Rockingham Register and Advertiser, 30 August 1866 (Thursday), p. 2, c. 4.

SHOEMAKER: On Thursday, the 11th inst., by Rev. John Kline, Mr. George SHOEMAKER and Miss Lydia, daughter of Mr. Andrew LAMB, all of Brock's Gap, Rockingham county.

Rockingham Register and Virginia Advertiser, 21 December 1855 (Friday), p. 2, c. 8.

SHOEMAKER: On the 19th inst., by Rev. J.N. Davis, Mr. Jno. F. SHOEMAKER and Miss Phebe, daughter of Elijah GRANDLE, all of this county.

Rockingham Register and Advertiser, 27 May 1859 (Friday), p. 2, c. 6.

SHOEMAKER: On the 10th inst., by J.W. Howe, Wesley H. SHOEMAKER and Miss Margaret, daughter of Philip MILLER, all of Rockingham county.

Rockingham Register and Advertiser, 24 January 1867 (Thursday), p. 2, c. 4.

SHOEMAKER: On the 28th of January, by Rev. Jacob Miller, Wm. H. SHOEMAKER and Miss Mary S., daughter of Geo. W. FAWLEY, all

of Brock's Gap, Rockingham county.
Rockingham Register, 11 February 1869 (Thursday), p. 3, c. 3.

SHOKEY: On the 27th ult., by Elder H. Jennings, Mr. Jacob SHOKEY, of Morgan county, and Miss Ann E., daughter of Jacob COPP, of Shenandoah.
Rockingham Register and Advertiser, 11 January 1861 (Friday), p. 3, c. 4.

SHOMO: See entry for BREEDLOVE.

SHOMO: See entry for GRIMES.

SHOMO: See entry for REED.

SHOMO: See entry for SALYARDS.

SHORT: See entry for CUBBAGE.

SHOTTS: See entry for ALBERT.

SHOUP: See entry for ACKER.

SHOUP: On the 19th of August, by Rev. Jacob Miller, Capt. Jno. C. SHOUP and Miss Sarah V., daughter of David SHIRKEY, all of Linvill's Creek, Rockingham county.
The Rockingham Register, 18 September 1863 (Friday), p. 2, c. 5.

SHOUPE: On Monday morning last, at the residence of the bride's brother, at Broadway, by the Rev. J.S.R. Clarke, Mr. Henry L. SHOUPE and Miss Emma, daughter of Dr. Richard WINFIELD, dec'd, all of Linvill's Creek, Rockingham county.
Rockingham Register & Advertiser, 29 September 1865 (Friday), p. 3, c. 3.

SHOWALTER: See entry for ATKINS.

SHOWALTER: See entry for BEATTY.

SHOWALTER: See entry for BRYAN.

SHOWALTER: See entry for CRIST.

SHOWALTER: See entry for DAVIS.

SHOWALTER: See entry for FITZWATERS.

SHOWALTER: See entry for FOLEY.

SHOWALTER: See entry for GOOD.

SHOWALTER: See entry for NISWANDER.

SHOWALTER: See entry for SHOEMAKER.

SHOWALTER: See entry for SWARTZ.

SHOWALTER: See entry for SHOWALTER.

SHOWALTER: See entry for SNITEMAN.

SHOWALTER: See entry for VARNER.

SHOWALTER: See entry for WINE.

SHOWALTER: On the 18th inst., by Rev. Jacob

Thomas, at the residence of the bride's
father, A. SHOWALTER and Miss Mary Ann,
daughter of Hugh SWOPE, all of Rockingham
county.
Rockingham Register and Advertiser, 25
October 1866 (Thursday), p. 3, c. 3.

SHOWALTER: On the 18th inst., by Rev. Jacob
Thomas, at the residence of Hugh SWOPE,
David B. SHOWALTER and Miss Susan C.,
daughter of Reuben SWOPE, all of
Rockingham county.
Rockingham Register and Advertiser, 25
October 1866 (Thursday), p. 3, c. 3.

SHOWALTER: On Tuesday, the 16th of January,
by Rev. Jacob Miller, Mr. Henry H.
SHOWALTER and Miss Hannah Catharine,
daughter of James BROWN, all of
Rockingham county.
Rockingham Register and Advertiser, 19
January 1866 (Friday), p. 3, c. 2.

SHOWALTER: On the 27th ult., by Rev. G.W.
Statton, Mr. James E. SHOWALTER and Miss
Louisa, youngest daughter of Col. R.M.
SHERFEY, all of Rockingham county.
Rockingham Register and Advertiser, 7
October 1859 (Friday), p. 2, c. 4.

SHOWALTER: On the 10th inst., by Rev. Jacob
Miller, Michael A. SHOWALTER and Miss
Emily J. WHISLER, all of Rockingham.
Rockingham Register and Advertiser, 24
January 1867 (Thursday), p. 2, c. 4.

SHOWALTER: On Sunday morning, at the
parsonage in Mt. Crawford, by the Rev.
J.C. Hensell, Nimrod S. SHOWALTER and
Mrs. Catharine HUFFMAN.
Rockingham Register, 1 September 1870
(Thursday), p. 2, c. 3.

SHOWALTER: On the 29th of December, by Rev.
Christian Hartman, Peter H. SHOWALTER and
Miss Magdalene F., daughter of David G.
HEATWOLE, all of Rockingham county.
Rockingham Register, 14 January 1869
(Thursday), p. 3, c. 3.

SHOWALTER: On the 23rd ult., by Rev. John W.
Wolff, Mr. Robinson SHOWALTER and Miss
Sarah SHOWALTER, all of this county.

Rockingham Register and Advertiser, 7
January 1859 (Friday), p. 3, c. 1.
SHOWALTER: On Tuesday last, by the Rev. Wm.
H. Wilson, Mr. Wm. SHOWALTER to Miss Mary
Ann E., daughter of Mr Philip PARROTT,
all of this county.
Rockingham Register and Valley
Advertiser, 5 September 1846 (Saturday),
p. 2, c. 7.
SHOWALTER: At the residence of the bride's
mother, in Fairfield county, Ohio, on the
23rd of August, by the Rev. Mr. Reed, Wm.
B. SHOWALTER, formerly of Rockingham
county, Va., and Miss Dorah, daughter of
Joseph KELLER, dec'd, of Fairfield
county, Ohio.
Rockingham Register, 8 September 1870
(Thursday), p. 3, c. 3.
SHOWERS: See entry for ALBURTIS.
SHOWERS: See entry for LOGAN.
SHRUM: On the 19th inst., in this place, by
Rev. J.N. Davis, Mr. Alfred SHRUM and
Miss M.J. LONG.
Rockingham Register and Advertiser, 23
December 1859 (Friday), p. 2, c. 5.
SHRUM: At the residence of Jacob ROHR, Sen'r,
in this place, on Wednesday morning last,
by Rev. Thos. Hildebrand, Mr. Martin L.
SHRUM, of Shenandoah county, Printer and
Volunteer in the Confederate Army, and
Miss Malinda J., daughter of Mrs. John
GROVE, of this county.
The Rockingham Register, 20 February 1863
(Friday), p. 2, c. 3.
SHUE: See entry for BEARD.
SHUE: See entry for COOK.
SHUE: At the residence of the bride's
parents, in the vicinity of Harrisonburg,
on Wednesday morning last, by Rev. A.W.
Weddell, Edwin R. SHUE and Miss Emma V.,
daughter of Geo. W. EFFINGER, Esq., all
of this vicinity.
Rockingham Register, 6 October 1870
(Thursday), p. 2, c. 4.
SHUE: On the 18th ult., by the Rev. Mr.
Conry, Mr. Robert G. SHUE, formerly of

this place, to Miss Mary Ellen TIFFANY, of Oxford, Ohio.

Rockingham Register and Valley Advertiser, 5 September 1846 (Saturday), p. 2, c. 7.

SHUEY: See entry for FIREBAUGH.

SHUEY: On the 29th ult., at Traveller's Repose, Pocahontas county, W.Va., by Rev. Mr. Joyce, A.H. SHUEY, of Augusta, and Miss Eliza J. ARBOGAST, of Pocahontas.

Rockingham Register, 15 October 1868 (Thursday), p. 2, c. 3.

SHUEY: On New Year's day, by Rev. Mr. Bowerson, Mr. C.B. SHUEY, of Shueyville, and Miss Clarinda V. BROWN, all of Johnson county, Iowa, and formerly of Augusta county.

Rockingham Register and Advertiser, 18 January 1861 (Friday), p. 3, c. 2.

SHUFF: See entry for BURNER.

SHULER: See entry for STROLE.

SHULER: On the 18th of July, at the residence of the bride, by Rev. Aaron Boon, Mr. Geo. SHULER and Mrs. Eve KITE, both of Page county.

Rockingham Register and Advertiser, 20 July 1860 (Friday), p. 2, c. 3.

SHULL: See entry for BOWMAN.

SHULTZ: See entry for BERRY.

SHULTZ: See entry for BOGGS.

SHUMAKE: At Mt. Sidney, June 4th, by Rev. J.J. Engle, Wm. SHUMAKE and Miss Martha A. ROSS, all of Augusta county.

Rockingham Register, 11 June 1868 (Thursday), p. 2, c. 5.

SHUMAKER: See entry for KEISER.

SHUMATE: See entry for SHUMATE.

SHUMATE: On the 30th ult., at the residence of the bride's mother, by the Rev. Mr. Pratt, Thomas SHUMATE, of Staunton, to Miss Jennie M., daughter of David SHAFER, dec'd, of Rockbridge.

Rockingham Register, 8 December 1870 (Thursday), p. 2, c. 4.

SHUMATE: On the 2nd inst., at the residence of the bride's father, Wm. J. SHUMATE,

Esq., near Staunton, Va., by Rev. John J. Lafferty, Maj. Thomas SHUMATE and Miss Carrie M. SHUMATE, both of Augusta county.

Rockingham Register and Advertiser, 4 October 1866 (Thursday), p. 2, c. 5.

SHUTTER: See entry for JORDAN.

SHUTTERS: On the 19th inst., by the Rev. W.H. Cone, Mr. Christopher SHUTTERS and Miss Elizabeth FRAVEL, all of Shenandoah.

Rockingham Register and Advertiser, 3 June 1859 (Friday), p. 3, c. 2.

SIBERT: See entry for CEASE.

SIBERT: See entry for NEWTON.

SIBERT: See entry for SIBERT.

SIBERT: See entry for STONESEFFER.

SIBERT: See entry for WEITZEL.

SIBERT: On the 10th inst., by Rev. G. Stevenson, D.F. SIBERT, of Bridgewater, and Miss Kennie B., daughter of L. SIBERT, Esq., of Mt. Solon, Augusta county.

Rockingham Register and Advertiser, 19 December 1867 (Thursday), p. 2, c. 6.

SIBERT: On the 21st inst., by Elder F.M. Perry, J.B. SIBERT, of Berkeley county, and Miss Alice M. BURACKER, of Luray, Va.

Rockingham Register and Advertiser, 30 January 1868 (Thursday), p. 2, c. 4.

SIBERT: On the morning of the 17th inst., by Rev. Thos. L. Hoyle, Col. James Harrison SIBERT, of Shenandoah county, and Mrs. Elizabeth J. PAYNE, of Madison county.

Rockingham Register and Advertiser, 3 February 1860 (Friday), p. 2, c. 5.

SIBERT: On Monday last, by Rev. Geo. V. Leech, at Bridgewater, Mr. John SIBERT and Mrs. Kate A.E. RHODES.

Rockingham Register and Advertiser, 25 January 1861 (Friday), p. 3, c. 1.

SIBERT: In Bridgewater, on the morning of the 19th inst., by Rev. G. Statton, Mr. John H. SIBERT and Miss Rachel J. HUFFMAN, all of this county.

Rockingham Register and Advertiser, 27 May 1859 (Friday), p. 2, c. 6.

SIBERT: On the 25th ult., by Rev. Levi Keller, Mr. Philip W. SIBERT and Miss Isabella V. WALKER, all of Shenandoah county.
Rockingham Register, 6 May 1869 (Thursday), p. 2, c. 3.

SIBLE: On the 16th inst., by the Rev. Geo. Shumaker, Mr. Josiah SIBLE and Miss Deborah K., only daughter of Wm. D. WAGGONER, all of Pendleton county.
Rockingham Register and Advertiser, 24 January 1862 (Friday), p. 2, c. 7.

SIBOLE: On the 15th inst., in Strasburg, by Rev. W. Rusmisell, Lemuel SIBOLE and Miss Elizabeth DAVIDSON, both of Strasburg.
Rockingham Register and Advertiser, 29 August 1867 (Thursday), p. 2, c. 5.

SIGLER: See entry for DOVEL.

SIGLER: See entry for HELLER.

SIGLER: See entry for JORDAN.

SIGLER: See entry for PERRY.

SIGLER: On the 2nd day of May, by Rev. Isaac Long, A.J. SIGLER and Miss Malinda SMITH, all of Rockingham county.
Rockingham Register, 11 June 1868 (Thursday), p. 2, c. 5.

SIGOURNEY: At Castle Hill, on the 10th inst., by Rev. E. Boyden, Henry SIGOURNEY, Esq., of Boston, and Miss Amelie Louise, daughter of Hon. Wm. C. RIVES.
Rockingham Register and Virginia Advertiser, 27 May 1854 (Saturday), p. 2, c. 7.

SILBER: On the 26th of December, by Rev. T.D. Bell, Mr. Joseph R. SILBER, of Harrisburg, Pa., and Miss Nancy, daughter of the late William SWARTZ, of Rockingham.
Rockingham Register and Advertiser, 9 January 1868 (Thursday), p. 2, c. 4.

SILLING: See entry for McLEOD.

SILLING: See entry for PROPS.

SILLING: On the 16th inst., by Rev. R.C. Walker, John A. SILLING and Miss Mary C. STOVER.
Rockingham Register, 23 December 1869

(Thursday), p. 3, c. 2.

SILLINGS: On the 6th ult., by Rev. G.G. Brooke, Mr. Armstrong R. SILLINGS and Miss Charity A. KING, all of Augusta county.
Rockingham Register and Advertiser, 6 May 1859 (Friday), p. 3, c. 2.

SILVEY: See entry for ALEXANDER.

SILVIUS: On the 10th inst., by Rev. Jacob Wine, J. SILVIUS, of Rockingham county, and Miss Susan GOLLADAY, of Shenandoah county.
Rockingham Register, 24 March 1870 (Thursday), p. 3, c. 2.

SIMMERS: See entry for BAZZLE.

SIMMERS: See entry for FITZSIMMONS.

SIMMERS: See entry for FRANK.

SIMMERS: See entry for McLAUGHLIN.

SIMMERS: See entry for NISEWANDER.

SIMMERS: On the 29th of November, by Rev. Timothy Funk, Jacob SIMMERS and Miss Malinda C. GENTRY, all of Rockingham county.
Rockingham Register and Advertiser, 6 December 1866 (Thursday), p. 3, c. 2.

SIMMONS: See entry for NICHOLAS.

SIMMONS: See entry for OPIE.

SIMMONS: See entry for SNYDER.

SIMMONS: On Thursday the 14th inst., at the residence of Wm. S. Miller, Esq., in Rockingham county, by Rev. Edward Pritchett, Dr. H.A. SIMMONS, of Greene county, Va., and Miss Pamelia W. YAGER, of Orange county, Va.
Rockingham Register and Advertiser, 21 February 1867 (Thursday), p. 3, c. 2.

SIMMONS: On the 21st of September, by Rev. A. Beaty, Mr. Jeremiah SIMMONS and Miss Valeria A. HILL, all of Pendleton county.
Rockingham Register and Advertiser, 30 September 1859 (Friday), p. 2, c. 4.

SIMMONS: Mr. Wm. SIMMONS and Annie SIMMS, of Bath county, were married in Washington by the Rev. Peyton Browne last week.
Rockingham Register, 13 January 1870 (Thursday), p. 3, c. 4.

SIMMONS: At the bride's residence, in Moorefield, on the 13th inst., by the Rev. J.C. Dice, Wm. M. SIMMONS, of Washington Territory, and Mrs. Ann KUYKENDALL.
Rockingham Register, 27 August 1868 (Thursday), p. 3, c. 3.

SIMMS: See entry for SIMMONS.

SIMPSON: See entry for BEATTY.

SIMPSON: See entry for CARROLL.

SIMPSON: On the 18th inst., in the M.E. Church, Unionville, Jefferson county, by Rev. Mr. Kreglo, Lieut. Frank A. SIMPSON and Miss Mary F., daughter of Mr. Lo. MADDOX.
Rockingham Register and Advertiser, 4 October 1866 (Thursday), p. 2, c. 5.

SIMPSON: At Burke's Mill, on the 13th ult., by Rev. J.W. Howe, Robert A. SIMPSON and Miss Mary E. CHAPLIN, all of Augusta county.
Rockingham Register and Advertiser, 4 October 1866 (Thursday), p. 2, c. 5.

SIMS: See entry for POAGE.

SINCLAIR: See entry for BROADDUS.

SINDSON: In Bath county, on the 16th of October, by Rev. W.W. Houston, Geo. W. SINDSON and Miss Mary A CLEEK.
Rockingham Register and Advertiser, 1 November 1866 (Thursday), p. 3, c. 4.

SINE: See entry for COLLINS.

SINE: See entry for MEAN.

SINE: On the 25th ult., by Rev. David Feete, Mr. Eli SINE and Miss Rachael Ann STULTZ - all of Shenandoah county.
Rockingham Register and Advertiser, 10 December 1858 (Friday), p. 3, c. 2.

SINE: On the 14th of March, by Rev. Henry St. John Rinker, Lemuel SINE and Miss Virginia BETTS, all of Shenandoah county.
Rockingham Register and Advertiser, 11 April 1867 (Thursday), p. 3, c. 4.

SIPE: See entry for PEARL.

SIPE: See entry for RANDAL.

SIPE: On the 11th inst., by Rev. Isaac Long, Archibald SIPE and Miss Annie C., daughter of John HENDRICKS, all of Shenandoah county.

Rockingham Register and Advertiser, 18 April 1867 (Thursday), p. 2, c. 6.

SIPE: On the 18th of September, by Rev. Isaac Long, Robert A. SIPE and Miss Jennie Ann WHITE, all of Rockingham county.

Rockingham Register and Advertiser, 4 October 1866 (Thursday), p. 2, c. 5.

SISER: On Thursday, the 2nd inst., Joseph SISER and Miss Lydia HOPEWELL, all of Shenandoah county.

Rockingham Register and Advertiser, 15 November 1866 (Thursday), p. 2, c. 5.

SISLER: On the 9th of July, by Rev. Isaac Long, Henry SISLER and Miss Virginia, daughter of Holland McCAULEY, all of Rockingham.

Rockingham Register, 30 July 1868 (Thursday), p. 3, c. 3.

SITE: See entry for EARMAN.

SITES: See entry for BOWMAN.

SITES: See entry for MILLER.

SITES: On the 28th ult., near New Market, by Rev. Wm. H. Dinkel, William SITES, of Rockingham, and Miss Kate N., daughter of Rev. J.P. Cline, dec'd, of Rockingham.

Rockingham Register and Advertiser, 6 December 1866 (Thursday), p. 3, c. 2.

SITLINGTON: See entry for DICKENSON.

SITLINGTON: On Wednesday evening last, by the Rev. Henry Brown, Mr. Robert SITLINGTON, of Pendleton county, to Miss Henrietta, daughter of Mr. Wm. EWING, of Rockingham county.

Rockingham Register, 16 January 1841 (Saturday), p. 3, c. 3.

SITLINGTON: On the 9th ult., at Mt. Pleasant, Rockbridge, by Rev. A.D. Hepburn, Mr. Wm. A. SITLINGTON, of Bath, to Miss Jane Ann, daughter of Joseph WALKER, Esq.

Rockingham Register and Advertiser, 2 December 1859 (Friday), p. 2, c. 5.

SIXEAS: On the 11th inst., in Frankford, by Rev. J.P. Etchison, Rev. P.S.E. SIXEAS, of the Baltimore Conference, and Miss

Virginia P., daughter of Thos. A.
HENNING, of Greenbrier.
Rockingham Register and Advertiser, 28
January 1859 (Friday), p. 2, c. 6.
SKAGGS: See entry for FELL.
SKELTON: See entry for GLOVER.
SLATER: See entry for McINTYRE.
SLATER: See entry for MILLER.
SLATER: See entry for PENDLETON.
SLATER: See entry for RODAHEFFER.
SLATER: See entry for ROHR.
SLATER: See entry for SHEIRY.
SLATER: In Winchester, on Monday the 21st
inst., by Rev. Dr. Finley, Wm. K. SLATER
and Miss Sallie E., daughter of O.P.
HELPHENSTINE, both of Harrisonburg.
Rockingham Register, 24 September 1868
(Thursday), p. 3, c. 4.
SLAUGHTER: See entry for DRAKE.
SLAUGHTER: See entry for GREEN.
SLAVEN: See entry for ARBOGAST.
SLAVEN: See entry for PATTERSON.
SLOAT: See entry for WELLMAN.
SLUSSER: See entry for LUTZ.
SLUSSER: See entry for SHAVER.
SLUSSER: On the 2nd inst., by Rev. H.
Tallhelm, Mr. Jacob S. SLUSSER and Miss
Adaline N. NICHAL, all of this county.
Rockingham Register and Advertiser, 9
January 1868 (Thursday), p. 2, c. 4.
SLUSSER: On the 6th of May, by Rev. Frederick
Miller, Stephen S. SLUSSER and Miss
Cornelia A., daughter of Harrison RIDDLE,
all of Rockingham county.
Rockingham Register, 20 May 1869
(Thursday), p. 2, c. 3.
SLUSSER: On the 23rd ult., by Rev. J.C.
Hensell, Mr. Wm. Stewart SLUSSER and Miss
Mary Elizabeth, daughter of Col. William
W. HOOKE, all of this county.
Rockingham Register and Advertiser, 14
February 1862 (Friday), p. 2, c. 6.
SMALS: See entry for HUDGENS.
SMALS: On Monday, the 10th inst., by the Rev.
John C. Lyon, Mr. John R. SMALS to Miss
Susan, daughter of Mr. Jacob DINKLE, all

of this county.

Rockingham Register, 15 September 1838 (Saturday), p. 3, c. 2.

SMALS: On Tuesday, the 5th of November, on the banks of the Potomac, in Berkeley county, W.Va., by Rev. M.L. Cullar, N.M. SMALS, of Rockingham, and Miss Kate S., daughter of Nicholas F. BAKER, of Berkeley county, W.Va.

Rockingham Register and Advertiser, 14 November 1867 (Thursday), p. 2, c. 6.

SMALTS: On Thursday, the 26th of February, in Bridgewater, Rockingham county, by Rev. Thos. Hildebrand, Capt. Adam H. SMALTS, C.S.A., and Miss Hettie J., daughter of Mr. John FLEMINGS, all of Bridgewater.

The Rockingham Register, 6 March 1863 (Friday), p. 2, c. 4.

SMELSER: On the 14th inst., by Rev. J.W. Watson, Mr. John SMELSER and Miss Elizabeth NICHOL, of Page county.

Rockingham Register & Advertiser, 29 September 1865 (Friday), p. 3, c. 3.

SMELTZ: See entry for DOWNEY.

SMILEY: See entry for WISEMAN.

SMILEY: At the Clerk's office, in Harrisonburg, Thursday, September 2, by Rev. Geo. W. Holland, Hugh H. SMILEY and Miss Mary A. GLASS, all of Rockingham.

Rockingham Register, 9 September 1869 (Thursday), p. 3, c. 2.

SMILEY: On the 19th inst., at the house of the bride's father in Rockbridge county, by the Rev. J.A. Crawford, Mr. Jas. R. SMILEY to Miss Susan J. PATERSON, both of Rockbridge.

Rockingham Register and Advertiser, 25 November 1859 (Friday), p. 2, c. 4.

SMILEY: On the 20th of May, by Rev. J.M. Shreckhise, William SMILEY and Miss Hannah A. LUCAS, all of Augusta.

Rockingham Register, 3 June 1869 (Thursday), p. 3, c. 2.

SMITH: See entry for BLAIR.

SMITH: See entry for BUCHANAN.

SMITH: See entry for CAVE.

SMITH: See entry for CLOUDAS.
SMITH: See entry for COLLINS.
SMITH: See entry for CORBIN.
SMITH: See entry for DANNER.
SMITH: See entry for DECKER.
SMITH: See entry for FRY.
SMITH: See entry for HARLAN.
SMITH: See entry for HEATWOLE.
SMITH: See entry for HOPKINS.
SMITH: See entry for HOTTINGER.
SMITH: See entry for JAMES.
SMITH: See entry for McDANIEL.
SMITH: See entry for McDORMAN.
SMITH: See entry for PATTERSON.
SMITH: See entry for SIGLER.
SMITH: See entry for STRAYER.
SMITH: See entry for SUMMERS.
SMITH: See entry for TRAINUM.
SMITH: See entry for TUSING.
SMITH: See entry for WINE.
SMITH: See entry for YANCY.

SMITH: On the 15th inst., by Rev. Thomas Miller, Mr. Amalphus SMITH and Miss Diana BORDEN, all of Shenandoah.
Rockingham Register and Advertiser, 23 March 1860 (Friday), p. 2, c. 6.

SMITH: At Keezeltown, on the 15th inst., by Rev. Jos. Funkhouser, Charles Henry SMITH and Miss Roxey Ann KIGER, all of Rockingham county.
Rockingham Register, 29 October 1868 (Thursday), p. 3, c. 3.

SMITH: On Tuesday evening last, by the Rev. Henry Brown, Mr. Charles P. SMITH and Miss Virginia BUTLER, all of Harrisonburg.
Rockingham Register and Valley Advertiser, 10 August 1850 (Saturday), p. 2, c. 6.

SMITH: On Monday the 23rd ult., in Washington city, D.C., by the Rev. Mr. Ballantyne, E. Jaquelin SMITH, Esq., of Winchester, to Miss Ella Alice, daughter of the late Richard B. BUCKNER, of Fauquier county, Va.
Rockingham Register and Valley

Advertiser, 4 November 1848 (Saturday), p. 3, c. 2.
SMITH: On the 21st ult., by Rev. G.W. Statton, Mr. Geo. F. SMITH and Miss Martha Jane, eldest daughter of Capt. Jacob HOOVER, all of Augusta.
Rockingham Register and Advertiser, 6 May 1859 (Friday), p. 3, c. 2.
SMITH: At the residence of the bride's father, on the 14th inst., by the Rev. Thos. Hilderbrand, Isaac D. SMITH, of Grant county, to Miss Mary HARPER, of Pendleton county.
Rockingham Register, 6 January 1870 (Thursday), p. 3, c. 3.
SMITH: On the Bridge at Harper's Ferry, on Tuesday evening, 8 1/2 o'clock, May 18th, by Rev. William E. Hammond, Mr. J.K. SMITH, of this place, and Miss Abbie, daughter of Joseph BEZANSON, of Rockingham county, formerly of Liverpool, Nova Scotia.
Rockingham Register and Advertiser, 28 May 1858 (Friday), p. 3, c. 2.
SMITH: On the 21st inst., by Rev. W.F. Broaddus, in Charlottesville, J. Massie SMITH and Miss Nellie TIMBERLAKE.
Rockingham Register and Advertiser, 30 May 1867 (Thursday), p. 3, c. 3.
SMITH: At Oak Flat, Pendleton county, W.Va., at the residence of the bride's mother, Mrs. Elizabeth TEMPLE, November 27th, by Rev. J.H. Temple, John F. SMITH, Esq., of Washington county, East Tennessee, and Miss Adeline T., daughter of H.T. TEMPLE, Esq., dec'd.
Rockingham Register, 1 December 1870 (Thursday), p. 2, c.4.
SMITH: On Wednesday morning, in the Presbyterian Church of Charlottesville, by the Rev. J. Henry Smith, Mr. Josiah H. SMITH, of Powhatan, formerly of Staunton, and Miss Fannie E. SHIFLETT, of Charlottesville.
Rockingham Register and Advertiser, 11 February 1859 (Friday), p. 3, c. 2.

SMITH: On the 11th inst., by the Rev. Geo. B. Taylor, at the residence of the bride's father, in Staunton, ... Mr. N.C. SMITH, of Rockingham county, to Miss Cecilia B. McLEOD, formerly of Liverpool, Nova Scotia.
Rockingham Register and Advertiser, 16 August 1861 (Friday), p. 3, c. 3.

SMITH: On the 18th inst., by Rev. G.G. Brooke, Mr. R.P. SMITH and Miss Mary Jane, eldest daughter of Mr. Robinson HANGER, of Augusta county.
Rockingham Register and Advertiser, 30 September 1859 (Friday), p. 2, c. 4.

SMITH: On the 31st of December, by Rev. Isaac Long, William F. SMITH and Miss Nancy C., daughter of Wm. H. VAN PELT, all of Rockingham county.
Rockingham Register, 7 January 1869 (Thursday), p. 3, c. 3.

SMITH: On Thursday, the 13th of January, by Rev. Jacob Miller, Mr. Wm. S. SMITH and Miss Rebecca BUSH, all of Rockingham county.
Rockingham Register and Advertiser, 4 February 1859 (Friday), p. 2, c. 5.

SMOOT: On the 29th ult., at the Central Hotel, in Mt. Jackson, by Rev. J.M. Clymer, Daniel SMOOT and Miss Annie A., daughter of L. WALTERS, Esq.
Rockingham Register, 7 January 1869 (Thursday), p. 3, c. 3.

SMOOT: On the 8th inst., by Elder John Pirkey, James SMOOT, Esq., and Miss Mary M., daughter of the late Philip STICKLEY, all of Shenandoah county.
Rockingham Register and Advertiser, 23 September 1859 (Friday), p. 2, c. 4.

SMOOTS: See entry for GRIM.

SMOOTZ: See entry for CRABILL.

SMOOTZ: See entry for DOLL.

SMOOTZ: See entry for EVERLY.

SMOOTZ: Near Forestville, in Shenandoah county, on Sunday, the 26th ult., by Rev. J.P. Cline, Henry M. SMOOTZ and Cynthiana CUMMINGS.

The <u>Rockingham</u> <u>Register</u>, 1 May 1863 (Friday), p. 2, c. 5.

SMOOTZ: On the 11th inst., at the Lutheran Parsonage in Strasburg, by Rev. L. Keller, Mr. Jacob SMOOTZ and Martha E. COPP, both of Shenandoah county.

<u>Rockingham</u> <u>Register</u> <u>and</u> <u>Advertiser</u>, 28 May 1858 (Friday), p. 3, c. 2.

SNAPP: See entry for FUNKHOUSER.

SNAPP: See entry for HUFFMAN.

SNAPP: See entry for SWITZER.

SNAPP: On the 18th inst., by Elder John Pirkey, Mr. Bennett SNAPP, of Frederick, and Miss Lydia A. PIFER, of Shenandoah county.

<u>Rockingham</u> <u>Register</u> <u>and</u> <u>Advertiser</u>, 29 July 1859 (Friday), p. 3, c. 2.

SNAPP: On the 14th ult., by Rev. J.A. Snyder, Peter H. SNAPP and Miss Louisa RICE, all of Shenandoah county.

<u>Rockingham</u> <u>Register</u>, 6 January 1870 (Thursday), p. 3, c. 3.

SNAPP: On the 3rd inst., by Rev. Benjamin Bowman, Mr. William H. SNAPP, of Frederick county, Va., and Miss Sallie, daughter of Mr. James WILLIAMS, of Edom, Rockingham county, Va.

The <u>Rockingham</u> <u>Register</u>, 15 January 1864 (Friday), p. 2, c. 6.

SNARE: See entry for KELLER.

SNARR: See entry for WISMAN.

SNARR: On the 3rd inst., by Rev. H. Wetsel, Mr. Calvin W. SNARR and Miss Lydia M. COFFMAN, all of Shenandoah.

<u>Rockingham</u> <u>Register</u>, 17 June 1869 (Thursday), p. 2, c. 6.

SNARR: On the 24th ult., in Woodstock, by Rev. Levi Keller, George H. SNARR and Mrs. Rebecca A. HOTTEL, all of Shenandoah county.

<u>Rockingham</u> <u>Register</u> <u>and</u> <u>Advertiser</u>, 11 July 1867 (Thursday), p. 2, c. 6.

SNELL: See entry for KEYTON.

SNELL: See entry for SWARTS.

SNELL: On the 16th inst., near Dayton, by Rev. Solomon Garber, Mr. Jacob SNELL and

Miss Lydia MILLER, all of this county.
Rockingham Register and Advertiser, 21
June 1861 (Friday), p. 3, c. 3.
SNIDER: See entry for CLEMMER.
SNIDER: On the 13th inst., by Rev. Geo. G.
    Brooke, Mr. John B. SNIDER, formerly of
    Chambersburg, Pa., to Miss Emma A. PEER,
    of Staunton.
    Rockingham Register and Advertiser, 23
    December 1859 (Friday), p. 2, c. 5.
SNIDER: On the 6th inst., at the Virginia
    Hotel, in Staunton, by Rev. Geo. Kramer,
    Samuel G. SNIDER and Miss Polina A.
    STINNETT, all of Augusta county.
    Rockingham Register,   13   May   1869
    (Thursday), p. 3, c. 3.
SNITEMAN: Near Waynesboro, on the 2nd inst.,
    by Rev. Martin Garber, Joseph SNITEMAN
    and Hester M. SHOWALTER, both of Augusta.
    Rockingham Register and Advertiser, 23
    January 1868 (Thursday), p. 2, c. 4.
SNOWDEN: On Tuesday, the 5th inst., by Rev.
    C.B. Dana, Edgar SNOWDEN, Jr., and
    Clarence Powell, daughter of John H.
    BRENT, Esq., all of Alexandria.
    Rockingham Register and Advertiser, 15
    May 1857 (Friday), p. 3, c. 2.
SNYDER: See entry for BLANTON.
SNYDER: See entry for CAMPBELL.
SNYDER: See entry for HUFFMAN.
SNYDER: See entry for MILLER (2).
SNYDER: See entry for SEVIER.
SNYDER: See entry for SHEETS.
SNYDER: See entry for WIMER.
SNYDER: On the 23rd ult., in Crab Bottom, by
    Rev. W.T. Price, Calvin C. SNYDER and
    Miss Louisa SIMMONS, all of Highland.
    Rockingham Register,   4   March   1869
    (Thursday), p. 2, c. 4.
SNYDER: By Rev. P. Miller, November 25th, at
    Mountain Falls in Virginia, George W.
    SNYDER, Jr., of Hardy county, W.Va., and
    Miss E.C. LIGGETT, of Shenandoah county,
    Va.
    Rockingham Register, 9 December 1869
    (Thursday), p. 3, c. 2.

SNYDER: On the 27th ult., by Rev. T.W. Dosh, Rev. Joseph A. SNYDER and Miss Virginia ALLEN, all of Shenandoah county.
Rockingham Register and Advertiser, 6 December 1866 (Thursday), p. 3, c. 2.

SNYDER: On the 17th of February, by the Rev. Mr. Gilbert, Rev. Jos. E. SNYDER, formerly of Staunton, and Miss Theresa E. HELLER, of Woodstock.
Rockingham Register and Advertiser, 7 March 1862 (Friday), p. 3, c. 2.

SNYDER: On the 4th ult., by Rev. J.W. Watson, Joseph W. SNYDER and Miss Jane, daughter of John DOFFENMOYER, all of Page.
Rockingham Register and Advertiser, 2 November 1860 (Friday), p. 2, c. 5.

SNYDER: By the Rev. Peter Miller, January 18th, Mr. Martin V. SNYDER and Miss Mahala ORNDORF, all of Hardy county.
Rockingham Register and Advertiser, 9 February 1866 (Friday), p. 3, c. 3.

SNYDER: On Tuesday, the 11th of February, in Frederick city, Md., by Rev. Dr. Zacharias, Mr. Robert H. SNYDER and Miss Elizabeth A., daughter of Mr. George LISKEY, all of the vicinity of Harrisonburg.
Rockingham Register and Advertiser, 20 February 1868 (Thursday), p. 2, c. 6.

SNYDER: On the 21st ult., by Rev. W.E. Baker, Stanley F. SNYDER and Miss Lucilla A. CALVERT, all of Staunton.
Rockingham Register and Advertiser, 3 October 1867 (Thursday), p. 2, c. 6.

SNYDER: On the 11th ult., in Crab Bottom, by Rev. S.H. Butts, Washington SNYDER and Miss Mary C. BRANTNER, all of Highland county.
Rockingham Register and Advertiser, 18 October 1866 (Thursday), p. 2, c. 4.

SNYPP: See entry for GISINER.

SOMERS: See entry for ZIRKLE.

SOMMERS: By Elder H. Jennings, on the 12th of December, James SOMMERS and Miss Catharine CLINEDIST, all of Shenandoah county.

> Rockingham Register, 6 January 1870 (Thursday), p. 3, c. 3.

SONNER: See entry for GOLLADAY.

SONSFRANK: See entry for HAYES.

SOUDER: See entry for RODEFFER.

SOULE: On the evening of the 18th of April, by Rev. G.W. Stevenson, Mr. John F. SOULE and Miss Molly E. RICE, all of Rockingham county.

> Rockingham Register and Advertiser, 16 May 1867 (Thursday), p. 2, c. 5.

SOUR: See entry for ELLIS.

SOURS: See entry for BEHM.

SOURS: See entry for FOX.

SOURS: See entry for MILLER.

SOUTH: See entry for CLINEDINST.

SOUTHALL: In Norfolk, on the 10th inst., James C. SOUTHALL, editor of the Richmond Enquirer, to Miss Eliza, daughter of Wm. W. SHARP.

> Rockingham Register, 18 November 1869 (Thursday), p. 3, c. 2.

SOUTHARD: See entry for LAMMA.

SOWERS: On Thursday, the 25th of June, in McGaheysville, by Rev. J.C. Hensel, Joseph SOWERS and Miss Annie H., daughter of Abraham MICHAEL, all of Rockingham county.

> Rockingham Register, 2 July 1868 (Thursday), p. 2, c. 4.

SOWERS: On the 6th inst., by Rev. Benton Shepherd, of Charlestown, Wm. B.C. SOWERS, of Clarke county, and Miss Kate K. TURLEY, of Mt. Crawford, Rockingham county, Va.

> Rockingham Register and Advertiser, 15 November 1866 (Thursday), p. 2, c. 5.

SPEARS: On the evening of the 22nd inst., by Rev. J.E. Armstrong, William Henry SPEARS and Miss Mary E., daughter of Geo. D. LANCASTER, dec'd, all of Staunton.

> Rockingham Register and Advertiser, 30 March 1866 (Friday), p. 2, c. 3.

SPECK: See entry for HOLLEN.

SPECK: See entry for McPHEETERS.

SPECK: See entry for POOL.

SPECK: See entry for RHODES.

SPEEK: On the 31st of August, 1859, near Waynesboro, by Rev. Mr. Wirgman, Mr. Sansford H. SPEEK and Miss Frances, daughter of Mr. John PANNEL, all of Augusta.
Rockingham Register and Advertiser, 9 September 1859 (Friday), p. 2, c. 4.

SPEGLE: See entry for HENSEL.

SPENCE: On Thursday, the 4th inst., in Bridgewater, by Rev. A. Poe Boude, Jos. H. SPENCE, of Maryland, and Miss Anna Eliza FURRY, of the former place.
Rockingham Register and Advertiser, 11 October 1866 (Thursday), p. 3, c. 4.

SPENCER: See entry for STERLING.

SPENGLER: See entry for KEISTER.

SPENGLER: See entry for LEPLINE.

SPENGLER: Near Mt. Jackson, Shenandoah county, Va., on the 2nd inst., by Rev. D.G. Bragonier, Lieutenant Joseph H. SPENGLER and Miss Mary C., eldest daughter of Israel ALLEN.
The Rockingham Register, 10 April 1863 (Friday), p. 2, c. 5.

SPIGGLE: See entry for BILLHIMER.

SPIGLE: On the 13th inst., near Lantz's Mill, by Rev. H. Shaull, Samuel SPIGLE and Miss Delilah BOWMAN, all of Shenandoah county.
Rockingham Register, 24 September 1868 (Thursday), p. 3, c. 4.

SPIKER: See entry for MILLER (2).

SPIKER: See entry for MOWRY.

SPIKER: On Thursday the 14th inst., by Rev. Jos. Funkhouser, Mr. Harrison SPIKER and Miss Jemima FETZER, all of Shenandoah county.
Rockingham Register and Valley Advertiser, 29 May 1852 (Saturday), p. 2, c. 6.

SPIKER: On Thursday, the 24th of December, by Rev. Joseph Funkhouser, Mr. John SPIKER and Miss _____, daughter of Mr. David FETZER, both of Shenandoah county.
Rockingham Register and Advertiser, 8 January 1858 (Friday), p. 3, c. 1.

SPINDLE: On the 14th of November, at the residence of the bride's father, by Rev. Mr. Barker, Robert H. SPINDLE, Esq., of Waverly, Rockingham county, and Miss Maggie, daughter of Rev. James L. POWELL, of Spottsylvania county, Va.
Rockingham Register and Advertiser, 24 January 1862 (Friday), p. 2, c. 7.

SPINKS: In Woodstock, Va., on the 23rd inst., by Rev. Wm. F. Speake, Mr. Thomas SPINKS, formerly of Alexandria, and Miss Sue E., daughter of Mr. Michael MELHORN, of Woodstock.
Rockingham Register and Advertiser, 31 January 1862 (Friday), p. 2, c. 7.

SPITLER: See entry for HUFFMAN.

SPITLER: See entry for MILLER.

SPITLER: See entry for McCOWAN.

SPITLER: On the evening of the 15th inst., by Rev. H. Wetzel, Mr. Jacob F. SPITLER and Miss Elizabeth R., daughter of Mr. John EARHART, near Mt. Solon, all of Augusta county.
Rockingham Register and Advertiser, 23 March 1860 (Friday), p. 2, c. 6.

SPITLER: On the 6th inst., by Rev. W.C. McCarty, Mr. Jacob W. SPITLER to Miss Mary J. HUNTER, all of Augusta county, Va.
Rockingham Register and Advertiser, 14 October 1859 (Friday), p. 2, c. 3.

SPITLER: At the residence of the bride's parents, near Mt. Sidney, March 25th, by Rev. J.J. Engle, Jared W. SPITLER and Miss Sallie F. FAKLE, all of Augusta.
Rockingham Register, 15 April 1869 (Thursday), p. 2, c. 4.

SPITLER: On the 20th inst., by Rev. Mr. Brashier, Mr. Samuel SPITLER and Miss Elizabeth A. STRASBURG, both of Augusta county.
Rockingham Register and Advertiser, 25 May 1860 (Friday), p. 2, c. 5.

SPITLER: On Thursday evening, May 17th, by Rev. J.W. Karicofe, Thomas S. SPITLER and Miss Virginia BISHOP, all of Augusta

county.

Rockingham Register and Advertiser, 24 May 1866 (Thursday), p. 3, c. 4.

SPITZER: See entry for DEANERS.

SPITZER: See entry for FRAVEL.

SPITZER: See entry for HESS.

SPITZER: See entry for LOHR.

SPITZER: On the 13th inst., by Rev. Wm. J. Miller, John A. SPITZER and Miss Mary JACKSON, all of Augusta county.

Rockingham Register, 27 May 1869 (Thursday), p. 2, c. 3.

SPITZER: On the 13th inst., by Rev. Jacob Miller, Jos. E. SPITZER and Miss Fannie E., daughter of John LONG, all of Rockingham county.

Rockingham Register, 25 November 1869 (Thursday), p. 2, c. 3.

SPRINKEL: See entry for BOYLAN.

SPRINKEL: See entry for DWYER.

SPRINKEL: See entry for JACKSON.

SPRINKEL: See entry for McGEE.

SPRINKEL: See entry for NISEWANDER.

SPRINKEL: See entry for PIPER.

SPRINKEL: See entry for WAKENIGHT.

SPRINKEL: On the 6th inst., by Rev. H.A. Bovey, Mr. Charles W. SPRINKEL and Miss Nancy E. GRANDEL, all of Rockingham.

Rockingham Register, 17 June 1869 (Thursday), p. 2, c. 6.

SPRINKEL: On the 17th ult., by Rev. J.W. Howe, Jacob SPRINKEL and Miss Drusilla CORNER, all of Rockingham county.

Rockingham Register and Advertiser, 4 October 1866 (Thursday), p. 2, c. 5.

SPRINKLE: See entry for CHAPMAN.

SPRINKLE: On Sunday last, by the Rev. C. Kyser, Mr. John C. SPRINKLE & Miss Mary, daughter of Abraham BRENNEMAN, all of Rockingham county.

Rockingham Register and Virginia Advertiser, 11 May 1855 (Friday), p. 3, c. 3.

SPROUL: On the 11th inst., by Rev. Wm. Pinkerton, Mr. Archibald D. SPROUL and Miss Eugenie E., daughter of James

BUMGARDNER, Esq., all of Augusta county.
Rockingham Register and Advertiser, 21
October 1859 (Friday), p. 2, c. 5.

STABLER: See entry for SWARTZ.

STANDAMIRE: See entry for OREPAUGH.

STANLEY: On the 12th of July, by Elder C.
Allemong, Charles STANLEY, of Page
county, and Miss Mary Jane CROFT, of
Rockingham.
Rockingham Register and Advertiser, 26
July 1866 (Thursday), p. 3, c. 2.

STANLEY: In Sacramento, California, on the
10th of May last, the Hon. Edward
STANLEY, formerly of North Carolina, and
Miss Cornelia BALDWIN, formerly of
Staunton.
Rockingham Register and Advertiser, 17
June 1859 (Friday), p. 3, c. 3.

STANLEY: On the 21st of March, by Elder C.
Allemong, Isaac H. STANLEY and Miss
Sidney Ellen EPPARD, all of Rockingham
county.
Rockingham Register and Advertiser, 4
April 1867 (Thursday), p. 3, c. 4.

STANLEY: At Rev. G.W. Stanley's near Lacey's
Spring, Rockingham county, on Thursday
morning, the 14th inst., by Rev. J.W.
Howe, Mr. John STANLEY, of Page county,
and Miss Eliza, daughter of Mr. Israel
MINNICK, of Rockingham.
Rockingham Register and Advertiser, 15
March 1861 (Friday), p. 2, c. 4.

STANLEY: On the 3rd of May, by Rev. Isaac
Soule, Mr. John STANLEY and Dorcas A.,
daughter of Elijah MINICH, all of
Rockingham county.
Rockingham Register and Advertiser, 11
May 1866 (Friday), p. 2, c. 4.

STANTON: See entry for McDANNA.

STARK: On the 1st of April, by Rev. S.
Henkel, Adam STARK and Miss Artemiss
OLINGER, all of Shenandoah county.
Rockingham Register and Advertiser, 2 May
1867 (Thursday), p. 2, c. 6.

STAUBUS: See entry for CUPP.

STEARNS: On the 16th inst., by Rev. J.E.

Armstrong, Mr. Alvin STEARNS, of New York, and Miss Henrietta MELHORN, of Woodstock, Va.
Rockingham Register & Advertiser, 27 October 1865 (Friday), p. 2, c. 3.

STEARNS: At the American Legation, in Paris, November 10th, by Rev. Dr. Sampson, of New York, Zenus B. STEARNS, eldest son of Franklin STEARNS, Esq., of Richmond, Va., and Miss Cicely, daughter of Prof. John F. COLLINS, of London.
Rockingham Register, 9 December 1869 (Thursday), p. 3, c. 2.

STEED: See entry for BLY.

STEEL: See entry for HOUSTON.

STEELE: See entry for KURTZ.

STEELE: See entry for STEELE.

STEELE: On the 6th inst., by Rev. T.D. Bell, Capt. James STEELE and Miss Susan, daughter of Mr. Jesse RALSTON, all of this county.
Rockingham Register and Virginia Advertiser, 15 November 1861 (Friday), p. 2, c. 2.

STEELE: On Tuesday, the 6th inst., by Rev. J.C. Hensell, Mr. Robert STEELE, son of David STEELE, dec'd, of Rockingham, to Miss Susan STEELE, of Augusta.
Rockingham Register and Advertiser, 16 April 1858 (Friday), p. 3, c. 2.

STEP: On Thursday evening, August 28th, by Rev. Ambrose Booten, David STEP and Miss Catharine KEYSER, all of Page county, Va.
Rockingham Register and Virginia Advertiser, 5 September 1862 (Friday), p. 2, c. 3.

STEPHENS: See entry for RUFFNER.

STEPHENS: On the 15th of January, 1863, by the Rev. J.W. Howe, Mr. William S. STEPHENS and Miss Nancy THOMAS, all of this county.
The Rockingham Register, 23 January 1863 (Friday), p. 2, c. 2.

STEPHENSON: On the 11th ult., by the Rev. Benj. Tallman, Mr. Adam STEPHENSON, Sr., of Highland county, to Miss Elizabeth, daughter of the late Daniel KERR, of Pocahontas county.

Rockingham Register and Valley Advertiser, 4 November 1848 (Saturday), p. 3, c. 2.

STEPHENSON: On the 7th inst., by Rev. Mr. Walker, K.B. STEPHENSON, Esq., of Parkersburg, and Miss Bettie G., daughter of Mark BIRD, Esq., of Woodstock.

Rockingham Register and Advertiser, 23 December 1859 (Friday), p. 2, c. 5.

STERLING: See entry for IRICK.

STERLING: On the 5th inst., by Rev. J. Rice Bowman, Andrew J. STERLING and Miss Sue J. SPENCER, all of Harrisonburg, Va.

Rockingham Register, 12 November 1868 (Thursday), p. 3, c. 3.

STERLING: In Charlottesville, on Thursday morning, the 29th ult., at the residence of the bride's father, by the Rev. Mr. Judkins, Mr. Chas. H. STERLING, formerly of this place, and Miss Sallie W., daughter of Robert S. JONES, Esq., all of Charlottesville, Va.

Rockingham Register and Advertiser, 4 November 1859 (Friday), p. 2, c. 6.

STERLING: At the Washington House, in Hagerstown, Md., on the 19th ult., by the Rev. Mr. Ayrault, Mr. O.C. STERLING, Jr., and Miss Margaret E.J., daughter of Geo. S. LOGAN, dec'd, both of Harrisonburg.

Rockingham Register and Virginia Advertiser, 1 August 1856 (Friday), p. 3, c. 1.

STERLING: On Wednesday morning last, by Rev. T.D. Bell, Mr. Samuel R. STERLING and Miss Estaline, daughter of David IRICK, dec'd, all of Harrisonburg.

Rockingham Register and Advertiser, 19 October 1860 (Friday), p. 2, c. 4.

STERLING: At the residence of the bride's mother, in this place, on Monday evening last, by Rev. A. Poe Boude, Thomas O. STERLING and Miss Martha, daughter of Webster McGLAUCHLIN, dec'd.

Rockingham Register and Advertiser, 6

February 1868 (Thursday), p. 2, c. 4.

STERN: See entry for WILL.

STERN: On Thursday the 3rd inst., by Rev. Christopher Keyser, Mr. Lemuel STERN and Miss Margaret BROCK, all of this county. Rockingham Register and Virginia Advertiser, 11 April 1856 (Friday), p. 2, c. 8.

STETSON: See entry for LOCKRIDGE.

STEVENS: See entry for STRICKLER.

STEVENS: In Chattooga county, Georgia, on the 26th ult., by Rev. T.C. Reynolds, E.H. STEVENS, formerly of Harrisonburg, Va., and Miss Lucie Linton, daughter of Dr. John PETTUS. Rockingham Register, 11 November 1869 (Thursday), p. 3, c. 3.

STEVENS: On Tuesday, January 26th, at the residence of the bride's father, Vienna, La., by Rev. N.A. Cravens, Dr. John H. STEVENS, formerly of Harrisonburg, Va., and Miss Mary C., only daughter of Rev. Sam'l ARMSTRONG. Rockingham Register, 4 March 1869 (Thursday), p. 2, c. 4.

STEVENSON: See entry for HARMAN.

STEWART: See entry for GLADWELL.

STICKLAND: On the 7th ult., by Rev. Isaac Long, Horace STICKLAND and Miss Margaret ROADCAP, all of Rockingham. Rockingham Register, 5 November 1868 (Thursday), p. 3, c. 3.

STICKLET: See entry for SHOBE.

STICKLEY: See entry for LINDABERG.

STICKLEY: See entry for SMOOT.

STICKLEY: On the 17th ult., by Rev. Levi Keller, in Powel's Fort, B.M. STICKLEY and Miss Ora BOWMAN, all of Shenandoah. Rockingham Register, 8 December 1870 (Thursday), p. 2, c. 4.

STICKLEY: On the 17th of May, by Rev. John Landstreet, E.E. STICKLEY, Esq., of Shenandoah county, and Miss Sophie, daughter of Rev. Joseph HELM, of Loudoun county. Rockingham Register, 23 June 1870

(Thursday), p. 2, c. 4.

STICKLEY: On the 24th ult., by Elder J. Pirkey, James STICKLEY and Miss Barbara HAMMAN, both of Shenandoah county.
Rockingham Register and Advertiser, 7 June 1866 (Thursday), p. 3, c. 3.

STICKLEY: On the 3rd inst., by Rev. Henry St. J. Rinker, Mr. Philip STICKLEY and Miss Mary WOLF, all of Shenandoah county.
Rockingham Register and Advertiser, 18 March 1859 (Friday), p. 3, c. 1.

STICKLEY: On the 29th of November, by Rev. John Pirkey, Mr. Philip D. STICKLEY and Miss Mattie Virginia BOYER, all of Shenandoah county.
Rockingham Register and Advertiser, 13 December 1866 (Thursday), p. 2, c. 5.

STICKLEY: On Thursday the 18th inst., by Rev. F.A. Mercer, Mr. Samuel STICKLEY and Miss Sarah A. SHEETS, of Mt. Crawford.
Rockingham Register and Advertiser, 26 November 1858 (Friday), p. 3, c. 2.

STICKLEY: On the 4th inst., Mr. Samuel STICKLEY and Bettie WOLF.
Rockingham Register and Advertiser, 23 March 1866 (Friday), p. 3, c. 3.

STICKLEY: On the 18th ult., by Rev. J.A. Snyder, Mr. Wm. STICKLEY and Miss Susannah KERN, both of Shenandoah.
Rockingham Register and Advertiser, 11 January 1861 (Friday), p. 3, c. 4.

STICKLEY: On the 27th ult., Wm. STICKLEY, of Shenandoah, and Miss ____ BROWNING, of Rappahannock.
Rockingham Register, 17 November 1870 (Thursday), p. 2, c. 3.

STIDLEY: See entry for GILL.

STINEBUCK: See entry for BALDWIN.

STINEHARDT: See entry for ACKERMAN.

STINESPRING: See entry for KEIFFER.

STINNETT: See entry for SNIDER.

STIREWALT: On the 3rd inst., by Rev. J.S. Bennick, Rev. John N. STIREWALT, of Shenandoah, and Miss Emmie A. HERSHBERGER, of Page county, Va.
Rockingham Register, 7 November 1870

(Thursday), p. 2, c. 3.

STOCKDALE: See entry for DULL.

STODDARD: On the 24th of April, by Rev. J.W. Howe, Albert H. STODDARD, of Staunton, and Miss Sallie E. PROCTOR, of Rockingham.

Rockingham Register and Advertiser, 31 May 1866 (Thursday), p. 3, c. 5.

STOGDALE: Near Parnassus, on the 15th inst., by Rev. G.W. Hott, George W. STOGDALE and Miss Margaret J. BROWN, all of Augusta county.

Rockingham Register, 22 December 1870 (Thursday), p. 2, c. 4.

STOMBOCK: On the 11th inst., by the Rev. Daniel Thomas, Mr. Jacob STOMBOCK and Miss Ruth Ellen RIDDLE, both of Augusta.

Rockingham Register and Advertiser, 23 March 1860 (Friday), p. 2, c. 6.

STONE: On the 10th inst., by Rev. Solomon Garber, Abel D. STONE, of Keokuk county, Iowa, and Miss Rebecca, daughter of Joseph BIERLY, dec'd, of Rockingham county.

Rockingham Register and Advertiser, 14 November 1867 (Thursday), p. 2, c. 6.

STONE: Near Hermitage, on the 5th inst., by Rev. Jno. Brower, Isaac H. STONE and Miss Sarah BROWER, all of Augusta county.

Rockingham Register and Advertiser, 10 October 1867 (Thursday), p. 3, c. 3.

STONEBURNER: On the 25th ult., at the residence of the bride's father, near Staunton, by Rev. J.I. Miller, Charles D. STONEBURNER, Foreman of the Vindicator office, and Miss Blanche L. TRENARY.

Rockingham Register and Advertiser, 4 July 1867 (Thursday), p. 2, c. 6.

STONEBURNER: On the 7th inst., by Rev. J.P. Hyde, near Woodstock, Wm. H. STONEBURNER and Miss Margaret HOOVER, all of Shenandoah county.

Rockingham Register and Advertiser, 21 February 1867 (Thursday), p. 3, c. 2.

STONER: On the 25th ult., by Rev. H.S.J. Rinker, Mr. Jno. M. STONER and Miss A.J.

429

HELSLEY, all of Shenandoah.
Rockingham Register and Advertiser, 11
January 1861 (Friday), p. 3, c. 4.

STONESEFFER: In New Market, on Tuesday
morning last, by Rev. David Henkel, Mr.
Franklin Harvey STONESEFFER, formerly of
Rappahannock county, Va., and Miss
Virginia E., daughter of Joseph R.
SIBERT, of New Market.
The Rockingham Register and Valley
Advertiser, 26 June 1852 (Saturday), p.
2, c. 5.

STORY: Married, in Rothbury, Mr. E. STORY, to
Susan, daughter of Mr. W. COXON.
Rockingham Register, 30 May 1833
(Saturday), p. 3, c. 4.

STOUFFER: See entry for VALENTINE.

STOUTAMIORE: On the 24th ult., by Rev. I.
Conder, G.W. STOUTAMIORE and Miss E.M.
VANCE, both of Augusta county.
Rockingham Register, 1 April 1869
(Thursday), p. 3, c. 3.

STOUTAMOYER: See entry for GRAHAM.

STOVER: See entry for SILLING.

STOVER: On the 3rd inst., by Rev. H. St. John
Rinker, Mr. Abraham STOVER and Miss
Barbara JORDAN, all of Shenandoah county.
Rockingham Register and Advertiser, 29
April 1859 (Friday), p. 3, c. 2.

STOVER: On the 20th ult., by Elder Wm. E.
Lauck, John W. STOVER and Miss Mattie T.
RUFFNER, all of Page county.
Rockingham Register, 12 November 1868
(Thursday), p. 3, c. 3.

STOVER: On the 9th ult., by the Rev. C.
Beard, Simon P. STOVER and Miss Diana A.
LANDIS, all of Augusta county.
Rockingham Register, 3 September 1868
(Thursday), p. 2, c. 4.

STOVER: On the 24th of December, by Rev. Wm.
J. Miller, Wm. H. STOVER and Miss Mary
Jane NIGHTEN, all of Rockingham.
Rockingham Register, 7 January 1869
(Thursday), p. 3, c. 3.

STRADERMAN: On the 24th ult., by Rev. H.
Wetzel, Jacob STRADERMAN and Miss Sarah

BRUMBACK, all of Shenandoah.
Rockingham Register, 8 July 1869
(Thursday), p. 2, c. 5.
STRASBURG: See entry for SPITLER.
STRASBURG: At the residence of the bride's
mother, on Thursday morning, the 21st of
October, by Rev. E.F. Busey, David E.
STRASBURG, Esq., Junior Editor of the
Staunton Spectator, and Miss Emma J.,
daughter of Conrad KITE, dec'd, of East
Rockingham.
Rockingham Register, 28 October 1869
(Thursday), p. 2, c. 3.
STRAUGHAN: On the 14th inst., at the United
States Hotel, Washington city, by the
Rev. Byron Sunderland, D.D., Mr. John J.
STRAUGHAN and Miss Sarah M. OATES, both
of Staunton, Va.
Rockingham Register and Advertiser, 25
May 1860 (Friday), p. 2, c. 5.
STRAUGMAN: See entry for SAUPE.
STRAWDERMAN: On the 9th inst., at the
residence of David Funkhouser, Esq., near
Orkney Springs, Jefferson STRAWDERMAN, of
Hardy county, and Miss Barbara DELAUTER,
of Shenandoah county.
Rockingham Register and Advertiser, 20
September 1866 (Thursday), p. 3, c. 4.
STRAYER: On Wednesday the 25th ult., by the
Rev. J.A. Van Lear, Crawford C. STRAYER,
Esq., of Harrisonburg, and Miss Juliet
L., daughter of Mr. Abraham SMITH, of
North River, Rockingham county ....
Rockingham Register and Valley
Advertiser, 4 November 1848 (Saturday),
p. 3, c. 2.
STRAYER: On the 18th inst., by Rev. John W.
Wolfe, Mr. George G. STRAYER, of
Rockingham, to Miss Fannie T., daughter
of B.F. KEMPER, Esq., of Augusta county.
Rockingham Register, 27 October 1870
(Thursday), p. 2, c. 4.
STRIBLING: See entry for FOSTER.
STRIBLING: See entry for POWELL.
STRICKLER: See entry for BRADLEY.
STRICKLER: See entry for CARDER.

STRICKLER: See entry for HARLOW.
STRICKLER: See entry for KIBLER.
STRICKLER: See entry for LAYMAN.
STRICKLER: See entry for LEMING.
STRICKLER: See entry for MARTZ.
STRICKLER: See entry for SHANK.
STRICKLER: See entry for STROLE.
STRICKLER: On the 17th inst., by Rev. J.W.
Hott, at Edinburg, Abraham STRICKLER and
Miss Virginia FUNKHOUSER, all of
Shenandoah.
Rockingham Register and Advertiser, 26
December 1867 (Thursday), p. 2, c. 6.
STRICKLER: On the 20th inst., near Lacy
Springs, at the residence of the bride's
mother, by Rev. H.A. Bovey, Benjamin F.
STRICKLER and Miss Melvina STEVENS, all
of Rockingham county.
Rockingham Register, 27 May 1869
(Thursday), p. 2, c. 3.
STRICKLER: On the 19th ult., by Rev. J.M.
Shreckhise, Daniel STRICKLER and Mrs.
Susan MILLER, all of Rockbridge.
Rockingham Register and Advertiser, 3
October 1867 (Thursday), p. 2, c. 6.
STRICKLER: At the residence of the
officiating minister, Elder J. Pirkey, in
Strasburg, on the 19th ult., Capt. M.
STRICKLER and Mrs. Carrie V. HOCKMAN, all
of Shenandoah.
Rockingham Register, 11 November 1869
(Thursday), p. 3, c. 3.
STRICKLER: On the 5th inst., by John W.
Watson, Mr. Martin STRICKLER and Miss
Margaret, daughter of John KITE, Senr.,
dec'd, all of Page county.
Rockingham Register and Advertiser, 20
July 1860 (Friday), p. 2, c. 3.
STROLE: See entry for CLEM.
STROLE: See entry for KITE (2).
STROLE: On the 22nd ult., by Rev. S. Henkel,
near Liberty, Page county, Va., Alfred E.
STROLE and Miss Sarah F., daughter of
David STRICKLER.
Rockingham Register & Advertiser, 8
December 1865 (Friday), p. 2, c. 4.

STROLE: At the residence of the bride's father, in Page county, on the 13th inst., by Rev. S. Henkel, John STROLE and Miss Emma J., daughter of John SHULER, Esq.
Rockingham Register and Advertiser, 27 June 1967 (Thursday), p. 2, c. 6.

STRONG: See entry for GILMORE.

STRONG: See entry for WOODZEL.

STROOP: On the 1st of December, 1859, by Rev. Abram Knopp, Sen., Mr. Noah STROOP, of Page county, and Miss Sophia, daughter of Mr.   John   HOLSINGER   (cooper),   of Rockingham.
Rockingham Register and Advertiser, 3 February 1860 (Friday), p. 2, c. 5.

STROSNIDER: See entry for ESKRIDGE.

STROSNIDER: November 4th, by the Rev. P. Miller, J.H. STROSNIDER, of Shenandoah county, Va., and Miss Mary E. DYER, of Hardy county, W.Va.
Rockingham Register, 18 November 1869 (Thursday), p. 3, c. 2.

STUART: See entry for BOWEN.

STUART: See entry for HUNTER.

STUART: See entry for KINCAID.

STUART: On the 19th of September, Maj. A.B. STUART and Mrs. Susan EIDSON, of Augusta county.
Rockingham Register and Advertiser, 25 October 1866 (Thursday), p. 3, c. 3.

STUART: In Monterey, on the 8th inst., by Rev. Wm. T. Price, David M. STUART and Mrs. Elizabeth BENNETT, all of Highland county.
Rockingham Register and Advertiser, 27 November 1866 (Thursday), p. 2, c. 5.

STUBBLEFIELD: On Wednesday evening, the 15th inst., at the residence of the bride's father, by Rev. George W. White, James C. STUBBLEFIELD, of Cumberland, Md., to Miss Annie F. WHITING, of Hardy county, W.Va.
Rockingham Register, 23 September 1869 (Thursday), p. 2, c. 3.

STULTZ: See entry for SINE.

SUDDARTH: In New Hampden, on the 18th inst.,

by Rev. S.B. Dolly, B.F. SUDDARTH and Miss Sue F. SEIVER, all of Highland county.

Rockingham Register and Advertiser, 27 June 1867 (Thursday), p. 2, c. 6.

SUGHURN: On Sunday morning, the 23rd of February, by Rev. Father Weed, Michael SUGHURN and Miss Margaret, daughter of Patrick MURPHY, all of Rockingham county.

Rockingham Register and Advertiser, 5 March 1868 (Thursday), p. 2, c. 4.

SULLIVAN: See entry for ALMON.

SULLIVAN: See entry for BAUGHER.

SULLIVAN: See entry for SCHERER.

SULLIVAN: At the residence of Daniel Epard, in Page county, Va., on the 1st of July, 1865, by Rev. Jno. P. Hyde, Mr. Bluford G. SULLIVAN and Miss Sarah F. EPARD.

Rockingham Register and Advertiser, 7 July 1865 (Friday), p. 2, c. 4.

SULLIVAN: On the 25th ult., at the residence of the bride's father, by Rev. J.S. Gardner, W.F. SULLIVAN, of New Liberty, Kentucky, and Miss Ada F., daughter of Levi CROMER, of Rockingham county.

Rockingham Register, 3 June 1870 (Thursday), p. 3, c. 3.

SUMMERS: See entry for DOVEL.

SUMMERS: See entry for FIFER.

SUMMERS: See entry for HEVENER.

SUMMERS: See entry for REID.

SUMMERS: On the 11th inst., at the residence of Capt. John P. Brock, by Rev. Jacob Miller, D.B. SUMMERS and Miss Martha, daughter of John FRANK, dec'd, all of Rockingham county.

Rockingham Register, 22 September 1870 (Thursday), p. 2, c. 5.

SUMMERS: By Elder Henry Jennings, Mr. Samuel SUMMERS and Miss Sarah F. SMITH, all of Shenandoah county. [No date is given.]

Rockingham Register, 14 May 1868 (Thursday), p. 2, c. 5.

SUPINGER: See entry for FRAVEL.

SUPPLE: On Thursday evening, the 25th ult., by the Rev. George G. Brooke, Mr. James

434

SUPPLE and Miss Sarah W. MITCHELL, all of Augusta county.
Rockingham Register and Advertiser, 10 December 1858 (Friday), p. 3, c. 2.

SUTHERLAND: On the 26th of February, by Rev. John E. Massey, Mr. Jos. SUTHERLAND to Miss A. Bettie, daughter of Mr. Prichard ANDERSON, all of Albemarle county, Va.
Rockingham Register and Virginia Advertiser, 14 March 1856 (Friday), p. 3, c. 1.

SUTLER: On the 16th of August, by Rev. G.H. Rexroads, Mr. W.M. SUTLER and Mrs. R.V. CONRAD, of Rockingham county.
The Rockingham Register, 9 October 1863 (Friday), p. 2, c. 4.

SUTTON: On the 17th inst., by Rev. W.C. McCarty, Mr. Joshua SUTTON and Miss Sarah ROSSON.
Rockingham Register and Advertiser, 22 July 1859 (Friday), p. 2, c. 5.

SWADLEY: On the 24th ult., near Monterey, by Rev. S.H. Butts, Lieut. A.F. SWADLEY and Miss Phoebe C. TRIMBLE, all of Highland county.
Rockingham Register and Advertiser, 18 October 1866 (Thursday), p. 2, c. 4.

SWAN: On the 4th of May, by Rev. Isaac Long, Benjamin SWAN and Mrs. Mary SHIFLETT, daughter of Wm. GRUB, all of Rockingham county.
Rockingham Register, 20 May 1869 (Thursday), p. 2, c. 3.

SWAN: On the 11th inst., by Rev. R.C. Cave, W.G. SWAN and Miss Isabel V. MILEY, all of Shenandoah county.
Rockingham Register, 25 November 1869 (Thursday), p. 2, c. 3.

SWANK: See entry for BEERY.

SWANK: See entry for KIRKPATRICK.

SWANK: On the 22nd inst., by Rev. J.W. Howe, Mr. John P. SWANK and Miss Mary Elizabeth, daughter of Col. Jackson HORN, all of Rockingham.
The Rockingham Register, 27 November 1863 (Friday), p. 2, c. 5.

SWANSON: See entry for THOMPSON.
SWANY: See entry for RIMEL.
SWARTS: See entry for RHODES.
SWARTS: On the 11th inst., by Rev. Jacob
Thomas, George W. SWARTS and Miss Rebecca
SNELL, all of Rockingham county.
Rockingham Register and Advertiser, 18
October 1866 (Thursday), p. 2, c. 4.
SWARTS: October 30th, by Rev. Daniel Thomas,
Mr. William SWARTS and Miss Margaret,
daughter of Mr. Samuel LONG, all of
Rockingham.
Rockingham Register and Advertiser, 25
November 1859 (Friday), p. 2, c. 4.
SWARTZ: See entry for BOWLES.
SWARTZ: See entry for FLEMING.
SWARTZ: See entry for LONG.
SWARTZ: See entry for MOORE.
SWARTZ: See entry for MOYERS.
SWARTZ: See entry for PHILINS.
SWARTZ: See entry for SILBER.
SWARTZ: On Sunday the 21st of November, by
the same [Rev. T.D. Bell], Mr. David
SWARTZ and Miss Charity, daughter of Mr.
Christian SHOWALTER, - all of Rockingham
county.
Rockingham Register and Advertiser, 26
November 1858 (Friday), p. 3, c. 2.
SWARTZ: At the Episcopal Methodist Parsonage,
in Woodstock, on the 25th ult., by Rev.
J.P. Hyde, Harrison SWARTZ and Miss
Belinda C. STABLER, all of Shenandoah
county.
Rockingham Register and Advertiser, 5
September 1867 (Thursday), p. 2, c. 6.
SWARTZ: On the 21st ult., by Rev. Levi
Keller, Silas SWARTZ and Miss Katie WEBB,
both of Shenandoah county.
Rockingham Register, 13 January 1870
(Thursday), p. 3, c. 4.
SWARTZ: On the 8th inst., by Rev. J.H.
Hunton, Mr. Wm. SWARTZ and Miss Harriet,
daughter of Mr. Isaac BAKER, all of
Shenandoah county.
Rockingham Register and Advertiser, 23
December 1859 (Friday), p. 2, c. 5.

SWARTZEL: On the 14th inst., by Rev. J.H. Crawford, Mr. Harrison T. SWARTZEL and Miss Elizabeth M. ROSEN, all of Augusta county.
Rockingham Register and Advertiser, 22 October 1858 (Friday), p. 3, c. 2.

SWARTZLEY: See entry for HELMS.

SWATSLEY: On the 2nd ult., Mr. John C. SWATSLEY, of Illinois, and Miss Jennie L. CAMERON, of Missouri, both formerly of Augusta.
Rockingham Register and Advertiser, 9 November 1860 (Friday), p. 2, c. 6.

SWEENY: On the 10th inst., near Fairview, by Rev. George H. Martin, John W. SWEENY and Miss Almada J. KERN, both of Shenandoah county.
Rockingham Register, 24 November 1870 (Thursday), p. 2, c. 4.

SWINK: See entry for CARSON.

SWINK: See entry for CEASE.

SWINK: See entry for LOWMAN.

SWINK: On the 3rd of February, by the Rev. G.W. Statton, Mr. James SWINK and Miss Rebecca B., daughter of Mr. Peter RUBUSH, all of Augusta county.
Rockingham Register and Advertiser, 11 February 1859 (Friday), p. 3, c. 2.

SWISHER: See entry for HOTTEL.

SWISHER: See entry for KEISER.

SWISHER: See entry for RINKER.

SWISHER: In the Bean Settlement, at the residence of the bride's father, on the 30th ult., by Rev. Lorenzo D. Nixon, Philip SWISHER and Miss Sarah M. BEAN, all of Hardy.
Rockingham Register, 20 January 1870 (Thursday), p. 2, c. 5.

SWISHER: On the 1st inst., by Rev. Jacob A. Bovey, Mr. William B. SWISHER, formerly of this county, now of Kentucky, and Miss Frances, daughter of the late Jos. HAHN, of this county.
Rockingham Register and Advertiser, 16 September 1859 (Friday), p. 2, c. 4.

SWITZER: See entry for BRANHAM.

SWITZER: See entry for OCHELTREE.

SWITZER: On the 5th inst., by Rev. Solomon Garber, Benj. SWITZER, of Bond county, Ill., and Miss Susan HUDDLE, of Rockingham county.
Rockingham Register and Advertiser, 16 January 1868 (Thursday), p. 2, c. 5.

SWITZER: On the 14th inst., by Rev. Mr. Hensel, in Hensel's Church [German Reformed], Mt. Crawford, John A. SWITZER and Miss Caroline, daughter of Col. Peter ROLLER, all of Rockingham.
Rockingham Register and Advertiser, 16 May 1867 (Thursday), p. 2, c. 5. Repeated, 23 May 1867 (Thursday), p. 2, c. 6. The above is a composite of the two.

SWITZER: On the 17th of September, at Mt. Crawford, by Rev. T.E. Carson, Mr. Samuel C. SWITZER, of Rockingham, and Miss Mollie M. SNAPP, of Augusta county.
Rockingham Register, 15 October 1868 (Thursday), p. 2, c. 3.

SWOOPE: See entry for SHIRLEY.

SWOPE: See entry for SHOWALTER (2).

SWOPE: On the 11th inst., by Rev. Jacob Miller, John R. SWOPE and Miss Elizabeth SHANK, all of Rockingham county.
Rockingham Register and Advertiser, 20 September 1866 (Thursday), p. 3, c. 4.

SYDENSTRICKER: In Lewisburg, on Thursday evening, the 1st inst., by Rev. G.G. Smith, Mr. O.P. SYDENSTRICKER and Miss Sue C., daughter of Dr. Wm. H. SYME.
Rockingham Register, 15 October 1868 (Thursday), p. 2, c. 3.

SYME: See entry for SYDENSTRICKER.

SYMINGTON: On the 3rd inst., at Trinity Church, Staunton, by Rev. W.H. Meade, Capt. W. Stuart SYMINGTON, of Maryland, and Miss Lilia W., daughter of Pike POWERS, Esq., of Staunton.
Rockingham Register and Advertiser, 11 October 1866 (Thursday), p. 3, c. 4.

- T -

TABLER: See entry for BOWMAN.

TALCOTT: See entry for CLINE.

TALIAFERRO: See entry for HARNSBERGER.

TALLAFERRO: In the M.E. Church, South,
    Fredericksburg, Va., on the morning of
    the 19th ult., by Rev. B.P. Warwick, Mr.
    James M. TALLAFERRO, Esq., State Senator
    of the Stafford district, and Miss Anne
    E. COLEMAN, both of Stafford county, Va.
    Rockingham Register and Advertiser, 20
    January 1860 (Friday), p. 2, c. 6.

TALLEY: See entry for CAMPBELL.

TALLEY: On the 10th inst., at the residence
    of   Mr.   Jacob   Neff,   by   Rev.   John
    Pinkerton, Lewellen A.S. TALLEY, of Clay
    county, Mo., and Miss Louisa A., daughter
    of Jacob COWGER, Esq.
    Rockingham Register, 17 September 1868
    (Thursday), p. 2, c. 5.

TAMMADGE: See entry for GAITHER.

TAMS: See entry for PHILLIPS.

TANNER: On the 15th inst., by Rev. Geo. B.
    Taylor, William TANNER and Miss Mary
    Susan COOK, all of Augusta.
    Rockingham Register, 22 October 1868
    (Thursday), p. 3, c. 3.

TANQUARY: See entry for HYDE.

TARLETON: At the residence of the bride's
    father, in Pocahontas county, on the 13th
    of September, 1860, by the Rev. S.B.
    Dolly,   Dr.   Lovel   C.   TARLETON,   of
    Monongalia county, and Miss Maggie H.
    ARBOGAST, all of Virginia ....
    Rockingham Register and Advertiser, 28
    September 1860 (Friday), p. 2, c. 4.

TARR: On Sunday the 26th ult., at Spring
    Hill, by the Rev. W. Burgess, Mr. Abraham
    TARR to Miss Susan Jane THOMASON, all of
    Augusta county.
    Rockingham   Register   and   Valley
    Advertiser, 8 June 1859 (Saturday), p. 2,
    c. 7.

TATE: See entry for BRANNAN.

TATE: See entry for CREIGH.

TATE: See entry for GILKESON.

TATE: See entry for TATE.

TATE: On the 17th inst., by Rev. L.B. Madison, Jas. T. TATE, of Fauquier, and Miss Margaret S. SHAVER, formerly of Augusta.
Rockingham Register and Advertiser, 24 October 1867 (Thursday), p. 2, c. 7.

TATE: On the 24th ult., by Rev. P.P. Flournoy, John M. TATE, Esq., of Wythe, and Miss Rebecca C., daughter of John A. TATE, dec'd, of Augusta county.
Rockingham Register and Advertiser, 1 August 1867 (Thursday), p. 2, c. 6.

TAYLOR: See entry for ALMARODE.
TAYLOR: See entry for CUNNINGHAM.
TAYLOR: See entry for FARIS.
TAYLOR: See entry for FOSTER.
TAYLOR: See entry for MARSHALL.
TAYLOR: See entry for MILLER.
TAYLOR: See entry for NEFF.
TAYLOR: See entry for RUSSELL.
TAYLOR: See entry for WEBB.
TAYLOR: See entry for WEEKS.

TAYLOR: At Orchard Grove, near Keezeltown, on the 10th of April, by Rev. Jos. Funkhouser, Camilias TAYLOR and Miss Elizabeth J. TERRILL, all of Rockingham county.
The Rockingham Register, 15 April 1864 (Friday), p. 2, c. 4.

TAYLOR: On the 21st ult., by Rev. J.W. Howe, Erasmus TAYLOR and Miss Lydia A. LAYMAN, all of Rockingham.
Rockingham Register and Advertiser, 19 December 1867 (Thursday), p. 2, c. 6.

TAYLOR: Near Newport, on the 2nd inst., by Rev. J.M. Shreckhise, Henry H. TAYLOR, of Rockbridge, and Miss Mary Jane PRICE, of Augusta county.
Rockingham Register and Advertiser, 23 January 1868 (Thursday), p. 2, c. 4.

TAYLOR: On the 18th inst., near Warm Springs, Va., by Rev. S. Rider, J.F. TAYLOR and Miss M.A., daughter of Albert JORDAN.
Rockingham Register, 25 November 1869 (Thursday), p. 2, c. 3.

TAYLOR: In Harrisonburg, by Rev. J.S.

Gardner, on the 15th inst., J. Harvey TAYLOR and Miss Barbara C. GAITHER, all of Rockingham.
Rockingham Register, 23 December 1869 (Thursday), p. 3, c. 2.

TAYLOR: At the Parsonage, on the 16th inst., by the Rev. Geo. G. Brooke, Mr. James E. TAYLOR and Miss Winnie HUMPHREYS, all of Staunton.
Rockingham Register and Advertiser, 24 February 1860 (Friday), p. 2, c. 4.

TAYLOR: Near Dayton, on the 3rd inst., by Rev. Solomon Garber, James W. TAYLOR and Miss Sarah MARSHALL, all of Rockingham.
Rockingham Register and Advertiser, 17 October 1867 (Thursday), p. 3, c. 3.

TAYLOR: On Tuesday, the 18th inst., by Rev. George B. Taylor, Mr. John H. TAYLOR and Miss Sarah Catharine RAMSEY.
Rockingham Register and Advertiser, 28 February 1862 (Friday), p. 3, c. 3.

TAYLOR: On Thursday morning last, at the residence of the bride's father, near Lacy [sic] Spring, by Rev. A. Poe Boude, Prof. Jno. W. TAYLOR, A.M., and Miss Virginia C., daughter of Jacob LINCOLN, all of Rockingham county.
Rockingham Register, 28 May 1868 (Thursday), p. 2, c. 6.

TAYLOR: On the 6th inst., by Rev. Wm. E. Baker, Dr. John W. TAYLOR and Miss Bettie A. CRAWFORD, all of Augusta.
Rockingham Register, 14 January 1869 (Thursday), p. 3, c. 3.

TAYLOR: At the residence of the Rev. George Wine, on Silver Creek, on the 26th of July, Jos. B. TAYLOR and Miss Mary A. NICELY, all of Rockingham.
Rockingham Register, 30 July 1868 (Thursday), p. 3, c. 3.

TAYLOR: On Wednesday, June 1st, by Rev. John F. Baker, Sam'l K. TAYLOR and Miss Sallie R., daughter of Porterfield A. HEISKEL, all of Augusta county.
Rockingham Register and Advertiser, 17 June 1859 (Friday), p. 3, c. 3.

TAYLOR: By Rev. Abraham Knupp, on the 11th day of May, Mr. Wesley TAYLOR and Miss Elizabeth GLOVIER, all of Rockingham. Rockingham Register and Advertiser, 18 June 1858 (Friday), p. 3, c. 4.

TAYLOR: On the 9th inst., by Rev. Joseph Holcomb, Wm. F. TAYLOR and Miss Mary A. PITTINGTON, all of this county. Rockingham Register and Advertiser, 30 May 1867 (Thursday), p. 3, c. 3.

TEABO: On Tuesday morning, 22nd ult., by the Rev. Mr. Williams, Alex. H. TEABO to Miss Sallie V. WORSHAM, both of Staunton. Rockingham Register, 1 December 1870 (Thursday), p. 2, c. 4.

TEAFORD: See entry for EDMONSON.

TEAFORD: See entry for HOUSEMAN.

TEAFORD: See entry for KIRKPATRICK.

TEAFORD: See entry for PLECKER.

TEAFORD: See entry for WILSON.

TEAWALT: On the evening of the 7th inst., at the residence of the bride's father, near Mint Spring, Augusta county, by the Rev. Mr. Dice, Mr. Wm. H. TEAWALT, of Woodstock, Shenandoah county, and Miss Mary Lizzie, daughter of David BEARD, Esq. Rockingham Register & Advertiser, 22 September 1865 (Friday), p. 3, c. 3.

TEECH: In Washington, D.C., on the 7th inst., by Rev. F.S. Cassidy, Rev. George [torn] TEECH [? badly worn], of the Baltimore Annual Conference, to Miss Jennie BEALL, of Prince George county, Md. Rockingham Register and Advertiser, 15 March 1861 (Friday), p. 2, c. 4.

TEMPLE: See entry for CALDWELL.

TEMPLE: See entry for SMITH.

TEMPLETON: See entry for WILSON.

TERELL: On the 16th inst., by Rev. James M. Rice, Wm. H. TERELL, Esq., of Warm Springs, Va., to Mrs. Rachel C. SCOTT, of Covington, Va. Rockingham Register and Advertiser, 2 March 1860 (Friday), p. 3, c. 2.

TERRELL: See entry for HUFFMAN.

TERRELL: In Staunton, at the residence of Mr.
H. Risk, on the 5th inst., by the Rev.
George B. Taylor, Mr. Henry L. TERRELL,
of Augusta county, and Miss Mary F.
HUTCHINS, of Rockbridge.
Rockingham Register and Advertiser, 15
June 1860 (Friday), p. 2, c. 5.

TERRILL: See entry for TAYLOR.

TETER: Near Rawley Springs, on Dry River,
recently, at the residence of G.H. Teter,
by Rev. Wm. M. Dunlap, Mr. George H.
TETER, aged 24 years, and Miss Maria
JOSEPH, aged 22 years, all of Rockingham
county, Va.
Rockingham Register and Virginia
Advertiser, 18 May 1855 (Friday), p. 3,
c. 4.

TEWALT: On the 24th ult., by Elder John
Pirkey, [torn] N. TEWALT and Miss
Elizabeth BOOTH, all of Shenandoah.
Rockingham Register, 10 March 1870
(Thursday), p. 2, c. 4.

THACKER: See entry for MOWBRAY.

THARP: In Powell's Fort, on Tuesday the 11th
inst., by Rev. W. Torry, Mr. Wm. THARP to
Miss Louisa HOFFMAN, all of Shenandoah
county.
The Rockingham Register and Valley
Advertiser, 22 November 1851 (Saturday),
p. 3, c. 1.

THEIS: On the 25th ult., by Rev. J.W.
Stirewalt, Mr. Christian THEIS and Miss
Elenora A., daughter of Samuel GRIM, all
of Shenandoah.
Rockingham Register and Advertiser, 9
November 1860 (Friday), p. 2, c. 6.

THOMAS: See entry for BROCKENBROUGH.

THOMAS: See entry for CLICK.

THOMAS: See entry for CONWAY.

THOMAS: See entry for FAUVER.

THOMAS: See entry for KITE.

THOMAS: See entry for STEPHENS.

THOMAS: On Thursday, the 30th of April, by
Rev. J.C. Hensell, Mr. Benjamin F. THOMAS
and Mrs. Columbia J. RANKIN, all of

Rockingham.

The Rockingham Register, 15 May 1863 (Friday), p. 2, c. 6.

THOMAS: On Thursday evening, the 28th of December, 1865, near East Point, by Rev. Jos. Funkhouser, Esq., Mr. Benjamin T. THOMAS and Miss Ann Virginia, daughter of Joseph RUNCLE, dec'd, all of Rockingham county.

Rockingham Register and Advertiser, 12 January 1866 (Friday), p. 1, c. 3.

THOMAS: On the 31st of December, by Rev. Jacob Thomas, Mr. Jacob J. THOMAS and Miss Regina, daughter of Frederick HESS, all of Rockingham county.

Rockingham Register and Advertiser, 12 January 1866 (Friday), p. 1, c. 3.

THOMAS: On the 7th ult., by Rev. J.S. Blain, at Willow Hill, Mr. James THOMAS, of Richmond, to Miss J. Robertine HODGE, of Augusta.

Rockingham Register and Advertiser, 6 August 1858 (Friday), p. 3, c. 2.

THOMAS: On the 9th inst., by the Rev. John Thrush, Mr. James W. THOMAS to Miss Mary M. HATFIELD, all of Bridgewater.

Rockingham Register and Advertiser, 14 November 1856 (Friday), p. 2, c. 6.

THOMASON: See entry for TARR.

THOMEN: On Thursday, March 31st, at the residence of the bride's father, by the Rev. D. Shrader, Mr. Martin K. THOMEN and Miss Sarah F. EMICK, both of Walnut Township, Fairfield county, Ohio.

Rockingham Register and Advertiser, 22 April 1859 (Friday), p. 3, c. 1.

THOMPSON: See entry for BARTIN.
THOMPSON: See entry for CLEMENTS.
THOMPSON: See entry for RHODES (2).
THOMPSON: See entry for SCOTT.
THOMPSON: See entry for SHARP.
THOMPSON: See entry for WHITMER.
THOMPSON: See entry for WHITMORE.
THOMPSON: See entry for WILLSON.
THOMPSON: On the 9th of September, by Elder L.J. Compton, E.D. THOMPSON and Miss S.E.

LAWRENCE, all of Warren.

Rockingham Register, 25 November 1869 (Thursday), p. 2, c. 3.

THOMPSON: On the 7th, by Rev. H. St. John Rinker, George THOMPSON and Miss Mary Ann HOLLAR.

Rockingham Register and Advertiser, 29 April 1859 (Friday), p. 3, c. 2.

THOMPSON: On the 25th ult., by Rev. Daniel Thomas, Geo. W. THOMPSON and Miss Frances A. FRANK, all of Rockingham.

Rockingham Register and Advertiser, 10 January 1867 (Thursday), p. 3, c. 2.

THOMPSON: In Dayton, on Thursday, the 23rd inst., by Rev. Solomon Garber, John S. THOMPSON and Miss Catharine, daughter of John HEDRICK, all of Rockingham county.

Rockingham Register and Advertiser, 30 August 1866 (Thursday), p. 2, c. 4.

THOMPSON: On the 31st ult., by Rev. J.C. Howe, Joseph THOMPSON, of Montgomery county, Ohio, and Miss Amanda C.V. CARRIER, of Rockingham county, Va.

Rockingham Register and Advertiser, 9 August 1866 (Thursday), p. 3, c. 4.

THOMPSON: At "Milendo," Halifax county, the residence of the bride's mother, on Monday, the 6th inst., by Rev. A. Martin, Judge Lucas P. THOMPSON, of Staunton, to Miss Catharine S. CARRINGTON.

Rockingham Register and Advertiser, 31 August 1860 (Friday), p. 2, c. 4.

THOMPSON: On Wednesday morning last, in Harrisonburg, by the Rev. H. Hoffman, Mr. Thomas THOMPSON, of Maryland, a Confederate soldier, and Miss Harriet, daughter of Joseph SWANSON, of Harrisonburg.

The Rockingham Register, 19 June 1863 (Friday), p. 2, c. 5.

THOMPSON: At Long Meadows, the residence of Mrs. I.S. McCue, in Augusta county, Va., on the 22nd of March, by Rev. W.T. Richardson, Lieut. Col. W.P. THOMPSON, 19th Va. Cavalry, formerly of Wheeling, Va., and Miss M. Lina, daughter of the late Henry MOFFETT, Esq., of Pocahontas county, Va.

The Rockingham Register, 1 April 1864 (Friday), p. 2, c. 6.

THORNHILL: On the 28th of December, 1869, by Elder Z.J. Compton, John A. THORNHILL and Miss Fannie A. ATWOOD, of Warren county.

Rockingham Register, 3 March 1870 (Thursday), p. 2, c. 5.

THORNTON: On the 12th of June, near Front Royal, by Rev. ____, James THORNTON, of Rappahannock county, and Miss ____ TRIPLETT, of Warren county.

Rockingham Register and Advertiser, 27 June 1867 (Thursday), p. 2, c. 6.

THORNTON: On the 25th ult., at Buffalo Gap, Obadiah THORNTON and Miss Hannah M. TRIDLEY, all of Augusta.

Rockingham Register, 2 December 1869 (Thursday), p. 2, c. 3.

THRIFT: See entry for PAYNE.

THRIFT: On the 15th inst., by Rev. F.H. Bowman, George N. THRIFT, of Madison county, and Miss Bettie K., daughter of the late Thomas W. McCUE, of Augusta.

Rockingham Register and Advertiser, 24 October 1867 (Thursday), p. 2, c. 7.

THROOP: See entry for AMISS.

THUMA: See entry for BYERLY.

THUMA: See entry for CRUM.

THUMA: See entry for WHITE.

THURMOND: See entry for BLEDSOE.

TIDLER: On the 28th ult., at the residence of the bride's father, by Rev. O. Grimsley, Geo. W. TIDLER, of New Market, and Miss Fannie QUAINTANCE, of Rappahannock county.

Rockingham Register, 11 June 1868 (Thursday), p. 2, c. 5.

TIFFANY: See entry for SHUE.

TIMBERLAKE: See entry for SMITH.

TIMBERLAKE: At the residence of Mr. S.N. Bagby in Staunton, on the morning of the 15th inst., by Rev. Mr. Williams, J.L. TIMBERLAKE and Miss Mary Ellen HUMPHREYS, both of that place.

Rockingham Register, 24 February 1870 (Thursday), p. 2, c. 5.

TINSLEY: See entry for JACKSON.

TINSLEY: See entry for KEZER.

TIPPING: See entry for BELL.

TISDALE: See entry for DESPER.

TOBIN: See entry for KEMP.

TODD: On Thursday evening, 9th inst., at the residence of the bride's mother, by Rev. J.A. March, John TODD, of Nashville, Tenn., and Miss Mollie Wilson BOYD, of Boydton, Warren county, Va.
Rockingham Register, 16 September 1869 (Thursday), p. 3, c. 3.

TOMLINSON: See entry for McCLOUD.

TOMPKINS: See entry for LOVING.

TOOMAY: See entry for PERKINS.

TOPPEN: See entry for SHIRKEY.

TORNEY: In Monterey, on the 11th of June, by Rev. W.T. Price, Wellington A. TORNEY, of Canada West, and Miss Sue M. HARDIN.
Rockingham Register and Advertiser, 11 July 1867 (Thursday), p. 2, c. 6.

TOWLES: At the residence of the bride's mother, at Madison C.H., on Wednesday morning, the 12th inst., by Rev. John W. George, Mr. Thomas R. TOWLES, of Orange county, and Miss Bettie C. GRAY, of Madison county.
Rockingham Register and Advertiser, 28 September 1860 (Friday), p. 2, c. 4.

TOWNSEND: See entry for HAMILTON.

TRAINUM: On the 24th of March, by Rev. D.B. Ewing, David C. TRAINUM and Miss Frances L. SMITH, both of Augusta.
Rockingham Register, 7 April 1870 (Thursday), p. 2, c. 5.

TRAISTER: On the 1st inst., by Rev. J.W. Watson, John Geary TRAISTER and Miss Virginia, daughter of Wm. VIANDS, of Page county.
Rockingham Register, 12 November 1868 (Thursday), p. 3, c. 3.

TRAWEEK: See entry for GLADWELL.

TRAYER: See entry for NEWMAN.

TRENARY: See entry for STONEBURNER.

TREVEY: See entry for BRIDGE.

TREVY: On the 18th ult., by Rev. John
     Pinkerton, Dr. J.M. TREVY and Miss Mary
     V., daughter of Mr. R.H. DUDLEY, all of
     Augusta county.
     Rockingham Register and Advertiser, 9
     January 1868 (Thursday), p. 2, c. 4.

TRIBBET: On the 8th inst., by Rev. Mr.
     Flournoy,   Mr.   John   TRIBBET,   of
     Rockbridge, to Miss Sue McGUFFIN, of
     Greenville, Augusta county.
     Rockingham Register and Advertiser, 22
     November 1866 (Thursday), p. 3, c. 3.

TRIDLEY: See entry for THORNTON.

TRIMBLE: See entry for SWADLEY.

TRIMBLE: In Monterey, on the 5th of July, by
     Rev. James Snyder, Marion TRIMBLE and
     Miss Catharine GWINN, all of Highland
     county.
     Rockingham Register and Advertiser, 2
     August 1866 (Thursday), p. 2, c. 5.

TRIPLETT: See entry for FINKS.

TRIPLETT: See entry for HARDIE.

TRIPLETT: See entry for THORNTON.

TRIPLETT: Near Front Royal, on the 11th of
     June, by Elder G.W. Woods, W.B. TRIPLETT,
     of Warren county, and Miss E.A. WOODS,
     formerly of Shenandoah.
     Rockingham Register and Advertiser, 27
     June 1867 (Thursday), p. 2, c. 6.

TRIPLETT: In Woodstock, on Thursday the 6th
     inst., by Rev. Mr. Clymer, Dr. Wm. H.
     TRIPLETT and Miss Hattie McKAY, formerly
     of Warren county, Va.
     Rockingham Register and Advertiser, 13
     June 1867 (Thursday), p. 2, c. 6.

TRONE: At Mountain House, Frederick county,
     on the 5th inst., by Rev. W.G. Eggleston,
     Rev. John L. TRONE, of the Baltimore
     Annual Conference, and Miss Mary Ansley,
     second daughter of the late Major E.R.
     MUSE.
     Rockingham Register and Advertiser, 28
     January 1859 (Friday), p. 2, c. 6.

TROTTER: See entry for BELL.

TROUT: See entry for BIERLY.

TROUT: See entry for HARPER.

TROUT: See entry for NORRIS.

TROUT: See entry for WAIPPLE.

TROUT: In Woodstock, on Monday last, by Rev. J.R. Grandin, Capt. James E. TROUT and Miss Sallie E., daughter of Mr. John CLINEDINST, all of Woodstock.
Rockingham Register and Virginia Advertiser, 20 June 1862 (Friday), p. 3, c. 5.

TROUT: On the 13th inst., by Rev. J.C. Hensel, at the residence of the bride's father, Mr. Jas. R. TROUT and Miss Amanda, daughter of George AREY, all of Augusta county.
Rockingham Register and Advertiser, 28 April 1865 (Friday), p. 2, c. 5.

TROUT: On the 15th inst., at St. Paul's Church, Baltimore, by Rev. Dr. M. Mahan, P.H. TROUT, of Staunton, and Miss Olivia, fourth daughter of Judge N.E. BENSON, dec'd, of Montgomery, Alabama.
Rockingham Register and Advertiser, 23 May 1867 (Thursday), p. 2, c. 6.

TROWERS: See entry for CLEVELAND.

TRUEHART: In the Methodist church in Staunton, on the 10th inst., by the Rev. Wm. A. Harris, Prof. W.C. TRUEHART and Miss Sallie C. MYERS, of Jefferson county, W.Va.
Rockingham Register, 18 November 1869 (Thursday), p. 3, c. 2.

TRUEHEART: On the 30th ult., at Glenmoon, the residence of the bride's father, by Rev. Jas. Beatty, Henry M. TRUEHEART, of Galveston, Texas, and Annie V., youngest daughter of Wm. S. CUNNINGHAM, Esq.
Rockingham Register and Advertiser, 8 November 1866 (Thursday), p. 3, c. 4.

TRUMBO: See entry for RITCHIE.

TRUSLER: See entry for BOLTON.

TURNER: On the 26th of January, by Rev. George Wine, Samuel TURNER and Mrs. Sarah SANGER, widow of Joseph SANGER, dec'd, all of Rockingham.
Rockingham Register and Advertiser, 6

February 1868 (Thursday), p. 2, c. 4.

TRUSLER: See entry for RICHARDS.

TRUSSEL: See entry for TRUSSEL.

TRUSSEL: At New Market, on the 20th of March, by Rev. S. Henkel, Charles W. TRUSSEL, of Jefferson, and Miss C.M. TRUSSEL, of Frederick county.
Rockingham Register and Advertiser, 7 April 1865 (Friday), p. 2, c. 5. Repeated, 14 April 1865 (Friday), p. 2, c. 5.

TUMBLINSON: See entry for CLENDENEN.

TURLEY: See entry for DUEY.

TURLEY: See entry for SETTLE.

TURLEY: See entry for SOWERS.

TURNER: See entry for AYERS.

TURNER: See entry for BROWN.

TURNER: See entry for CLICK.

TURNER: On the 28th of January, by Elder C. Allemong, Franklin TURNER and Miss Amanda MERICA, both of Page county.
Rockingham Register and Advertiser, 16 February 1866 (Friday), p. 3, c. 3.

TURNER: On the 23rd inst., by Rev. Prof. Yonce, of Roanoke College, Prof. James H. TURNER, of Harrisonburg Male Academy, and Miss Josie, daughter of Bishop J.J. GLOSSBRENNER, of Augusta county.
Rockingham Register and Advertiser, 31 October 1867 (Thursday), p. 2, c. 6.

TURNER: On the 25th ult., by the Rev. Samuel Brown, Mr. Robert L. TURNER to Miss Margaret BANE, all of Rockbridge.
Rockingham Register and Advertiser, 6 September 1866 (Thursday), p. 2, c. 5.

TUSING: See entry for MUMAW.

TUSING: On the 2nd inst., by Rev. Jacob Stirewalt, Mr. Elijah TUSING and Miss Ann Elizabeth SMITH, both of Rockingham.
Rockingham Register & Advertiser, 17 November 1865 (Friday), p. 2, c. 4.

TUSSING: See entry for RILLER.

TUSSING: See entry for WEANNING.

TUSSING: See entry for ZIRKLE.

TUTWILER: See entry for WELLER.

TUTWEILER: On Thursday, May 12th, by Rev.

G.W. Statton, Mr. Geo. W. TUTWEILER, of this county, and Miss E.F. MURRAY, of Augusta county.
Rockingham Register and Advertiser, 27 May 1859 (Friday), p. 2, c. 6.

TUTWILER: On the 9th inst., by the Rev. V.T. Settle, Mr. Edward TUTWILER and Miss Lucy A. DINKEL, all of Mount Crawford.
Rockingham Register and Advertiser, 28 January 1859 (Friday), p. 2, c. 6.

TUTWILER: On the 11th inst., by Rev. J.C. Hensel, Jos. L. TUTWILER and Miss M.F. HUFFMAN, all of Rockingham.
Rockingham Register, 25 November 1869 (Thursday), p. 2, c. 3.

TUTWILER: On the 13th of August, by Rev. Solomon Garber, Peter C. TUTWILER and Miss Sallie C. SANDY, all of Rockingham county.
Rockingham Register, 3 September 1868 (Thursday), p. 2, c. 4.

TUTWILER: On the 20th ult., by Rev. C. Beard, at the residence of the bride's father, near Naked Creek, R.F. TUTWILER and Miss Susan A. WRIGHT, both of Augusta county.
Rockingham Register and Advertiser, 5 March 1868 (Thursday), p. 2, c. 4.

TUTWILER: In Keezeltown, on the 5th of July, by Rev. J.C. Howe, William H. TUTWILER and Miss Mary B. DUDLEY, all of Rockingham.
Rockingham Register and Advertiser, 26 July 1866 (Thursday), p. 3, c. 2. Repeated, 9 August 1866 (Thursday), p. 3, c. 4.

TWYMAN: At "Spring Hill," Spottsylvania county, Va., the residence of the bride's father, on the morning of the 19th June, by Rev. Thomas A. Ware, of the Fredericksburg district, Rev. William Pleasant TWYMAN, of the Virginia Conference, M.E. Church, South, and Miss Julia D., daughter of Claiborne DUVALL, Esq.
Rockingham Register and Advertiser, 6 July 1860 (Friday), p. 2, c. 6.

Repeated, 31 August 1860 (Friday), p. 2,
c. 4. The above is the latter notice.
TYLER: See entry for BLACK.
TYLER: See entry for GARNEET.

- U -

UMBLES: See entry for MASSIE.
UPDIKE: On the 17th ult., by Rev. W.F.
Junkin, Capt. J.G. UPDIKE, Stonewall
Brigade, and Miss Rebecca AGNER, all of
Rockbridge.
Rockingham Register and Advertiser, 3
October 1867 (Thursday), p. 2, c. 6.
UTZ: See entry for CARPENTER.

- V -

VADEN: On Sunday, August 6, at Rushville,
Rockingham county, by Rev. Isaac Soule,
Mr. Wm. A. VADEN, of South Carolina, and
Miss Sarah F., daughter of Nathaniel
HUGHES, of Rockingham.
Rockingham Register & Advertiser, 11
August 1865 (Friday), p. 2, c. 5.
VALENTINE: Near Greenville, on the 12th
inst., by Rev. W.R. Stringer, Geo. G.
VALENTINE and Miss Lula B. STOUFFER, all
of Augusta county.
Rockingham Register and Advertiser, 27
September 1866 (Thursday), p. 3, c. 3.
VALENTINE: On the 18th ult., near
Charlottesville, by Rev. Mr. Bowman, John
C. VALENTINE, of Augusta, and Miss Sarah
F. BURGESS, of Albemarle.
Rockingham Register, 4 March 1869
(Thursday), p. 2, c. 4.
VANCE: See entry for STOUTAMIORE.
VANCE: On the 2nd ult., by Rev. John L.
Blakemore, Mr. Archibald VANCE to Miss
Catherine J. SHEPERD, all of Augusta
county.
Rockingham Register and Virginia
Advertiser, 11 April 1856 (Friday), p. 2,
c. 8.
VANCE: On the 21st inst., by Rev. S.F. Butts,

William VANCE, Jr., and Miss Helen M.
JENKINS, formerly of Rockingham.
Rockingham Register and Advertiser, 25
April 1867 (Thursday), p. 2, c. 7.

VANFOSSEN: See entry for HUSSEY.

VANFOSSEN: On the 23rd inst., by Rev. Geo. A.
Shuey, Mr. James W. VANFOSSEN to Miss
Elizabeth M., daughter of Jacob SHAVER,
all of Augusta county.
Rockingham Register and Advertiser, 28
May 1858 (Friday), p. 3, c. 2.

VAN LEAR: See entry for ARBUCKEL.

VAN LEAR: See entry for FISHBURNE.

VAN LEAR: On the 24th of April, at the Warm
Springs, by the Rev. Wm. T. Price, D.
Newton VAN LEAR, Esq., and Miss Nannie
R., daughter of George MAYSO, Esq., all
of Augusta.
Rockingham Register and Advertiser, 4 May
1860 (Friday), p. 2, c. 4.

VANMETER: On the 31st ult., by Rev. John C.
Dice, Solomon VANMETER, of Piatte county,
Ill., formerly of Hardy county, and Miss
Ann Jemima, daughter of David C. PARSONS,
dec'd, of Hampshire.
Rockingham Register and Advertiser, 16
January 1868 (Thursday), p. 2, c. 5.

VAN ORY: On the 2nd inst., by Rev. Geo. W.
Woods, Robert VAN ORY and Miss Mary S.
CAVE, all of Page county.
Rockingham Register and Advertiser, 28
November 1867 (Thursday), p. 2, c. 6.

VAN PELT: See entry for BAYLOR.
VAN PELT: See entry for BOYD.
VAN PELT: See entry for CAMPBELL.
VAN PELT: See entry for GREINER.
VAN PELT: See entry for KENNEDY.
VAN PELT: See entry for MYERS (2).
VAN PELT: See entry for SMITH.
VAN PELT: See entry for WRIGHT.

VAN PELT: On Tuesday the 24th ult., by the
Rev. Wesley Rohr, Mr. Andrew J. VAN PELT,
of this place, to Miss Lucinda, daughter
of Mr. John SHELTMAN, dec'd, of
Rockbridge county.
Rockingham Register, 4 January 1840

(Saturday), p. 3, c. 3.

VAN PELT: In Bridgewater, on the 22nd ult., by Rev. R.N. Pool, B.S. VAN PELT, Proprietor "American Hotel," in this place, and Miss Addie, daughter of John R. O'NEAL, Esq., of Orange county, Va. Rockingham Register and Advertiser, 2 March 1866 (Friday), p. 3, c. 3.

VAN PELT: On Thursday, the 13th inst., by the Rev. John C. Lyon, Mr. David VAN PELT to Miss Maria RANKIN, both of Augusta county. Rockingham Register, 15 September 1838 (Saturday), p. 3, c. 2.

VANTER: See entry for MAY.

VARNER: See entry for COLLINS.

VARNER: On the 16th inst., at the residence of the bride, on Lost River, Hardy county, by Elder A.C. Booton, David VARNER, Sen., of Page county, aged 77 years, and Mrs. Mary MILLER, widow of Michael MILLER, dec'd, aged 63 years. Rockingham Register and Advertiser, 25 November 1859 (Friday), p. 2, c. 4.

VARNER: On Thursday, the 25th ult., by Rev. Martin Garber, Mr. Henry H. VARNER and Miss Agnes A. SHOWALTER, all of Augusta county. Rockingham Register, 1 September 1870 (Thursday), p. 2, c. 3.

VARTS: See entry for SHILLINGBURG.

VASS: See entry for WHITE.

VEA: See entry for HESTER.

VEACH: See entry for MUMAW.

VEACH: On the 21st inst., by Rev. S.J. Rinker, near Columbia Furnace, Mr. Joseph VEACH and Miss Ann M. LARKINS, all of Shenandoah county. Rockingham Register and Advertiser, 6 May 1859 (Friday), p. 3, c. 2.

VENABLE: On the 8th last, in Front Royal, at the residence of the bride's father, by Rev. James Petty, James T. VENABLE, of Middletown, Va., and Miss Annie L. SAFFELL. Rockingham Register and Advertiser, 23

March 1866 (Friday), p. 3, c. 3.

VESS: In Bath county, Va., on the 9th of October, by Rev. W.W. Houston, Jacob H. VESS and Miss Margaret C. BETHEL.
Rockingham Register and Advertiser, 1 November 1866 (Thursday), p. 3, c. 4.

VIA: On the 10th inst., at the residence of Z.W. Fry, by the Rev. R.P. Kennedy, C.C. VIA and Miss Mary E. FRY, all of Rockbridge.
Rockingham Register, 17 March 1870 (Thursday), p. 2, c. 4.

VIANDS: See entry for TRAISTER.

VIAR: See entry for MOSS.

VIGER: See entry for CHANDLER.

VINCENT: On the 6th of April, by Rev. Solomon Garber, John N. VINCENT, formerly of Frederick county, Va., and Miss Elizabeth A. BUTCHER, formerly of Rockland county, Illinois.
Rockingham Register and Advertiser, 21 April 1865 (Friday), p. 2, c. 5.

VINES: See entry for BURKHOLDER.

VINES: On the 12th ult., near Greenville, by Rev. W.A. McDonald, Mr. Isaac Newton VINES and Miss Narcissus V. HITE, all of Augusta county.
Rockingham Register and Advertiser, 9 January 1868 (Thursday), p. 2, c. 4.

VINES: On the 28th ult., by Rev. G.G. Brooke, Mr. Wm. F. VINES and Miss Susan HOY, all of Staunton.
Rockingham Register and Advertiser, 6 May 1859 (Friday), p. 3, c. 2.

VINT: On the 1st inst., at the bride's home, near Deerfield, by Rev. A.A.P. Neel, Mr. Esau VINT, of Highland county, and Miss Elizabeth F. KERSHNER, of Augusta county.
Rockingham Register, 15 October 1868 (Thursday), p. 2, c. 3.

- W -

WADDELL: See entry for MAY.

WADDELL: On Thursday, the 28th ult., in Lewisburg, by Rev. John McElhenny, D.D.,

Mr. Wm. H. WADDELL, of Staunton, and Miss Maggie A. BURWELL, of Lewisburg. *Rockingham Register and Advertiser*, 5 August 1859 (Friday), p. 3, c. 2.

WADDY: At the residence of the bride's father, on Tuesday, the 12th inst., by Rev. Frances McFarland, Lt. Joseph W. WADDY, of Louisa county, and Miss Mary Lizzie, daughter of Mr. John J. LAREW, of Augusta county. *Rockingham Register & Advertiser*, 22 December 1865 (Friday), p. 3, c. 2.

WADE: See entry for BRYSON.

WADE: See entry for GUMM.

WAGGONER: See entry for SIBLE.

WAGGY: See entry for RALSTON.

WAIPPLE: At the residence of Mrs. E. Harrison, on the 19th of May, by Elder J.R. Harrison, A.B. WAIPPLE, formerly of Harrisonburg, and Mrs. Priscilla J. TROUT, of Botetourt Springs, Roanoke county, Va. *The Rockingham Register*, 26 June 1863 (Friday), p. 2, c. 5.

WAKENIGHT: On Tuesday evening, the 21st ult., at the residence of the bride's parents, by Rev. J. Rice Bowman, John T. WAKENIGHT, formerly of Washington county, Md., to Miss Wyoming C., daughter of J. Gambill SPRINKEL, of Harrisonburg, Va. *Rockingham Register*, 7 October 1869 (Thursday), p. 2, c. 3.

WALDEN: On the 18th inst., at the residence of the bride's parents, by Rev. A.R. Reede, Miss Kittie, only daughter of Maj. J.D. WILLIAMSON, of Rockingham county, to Captain Austin T. WALDEN, of Rappahannock county. *Rockingham Register and Advertiser*, 21 February 1862 (Friday), p. 3, c. 2.

WALKER: See entry for BREITT.

WALKER: See entry for LUTZ.

WALKER: See entry for McCELLAS.

WALKER: See entry for NICHOLAS.

WALKER: See entry for SIBERT.

WALKER: See entry for SITLINGTON.

WALKER: See entry for ZIRKLE.

WALKER: On the 21st inst., by Rev. John Kline, Arthur G. WALKER, of Shenandoah county, and Miss Catharine WAMPLER, of Rockingham.
The Rockingham Register, 26 December 1862 (Friday), p. 2, c. 4.

WALKER: On Wednesday evening last, at the residence of A.M. Effinger, in this place, by the Rev. D.C. Irwin, Dr. Geo. G. WALKER, of Augusta county, and Miss Margaret M., daughter of Col. A. HUSTON, dec'd, of Rockingham.
Rockingham Register and Advertiser, 13 July 1860 (Friday), p. 2, c. 6.

WALKER: On the 26th of December, by Rev. P. Miller, Mr. Nathaniel WALKER, of Hardy, and Miss Mary E. OATS, of Hampshire county.
Rockingham Register and Advertiser, 10 February 1865 (Friday), p. 2, c. 2.

WALKER: On the 19th of May, 1860, by Rev. Abraham Knupp, Mr. Reuben WALKER and Miss Amanda REID, all of Rockingham county.
Rockingham Register and Advertiser, 22 June 1860 (Friday), p. 2, c. 6.

WALKER: November 9, by Rev. H.H. Hawes, Silas H. WALKER, of Augusta, and Miss Laura BOONE, of Rockingham county.
Rockingham Register, 24 November 1870 (Thursday), p. 2, c. 4.

WALKER: On the 30th of December, 1869, by Elder Z.J. Compton, W. WALKER and Miss Mary E. HENRY, both of Warren county.
Rockingham Register, 3 March 1870 (Thursday), p. 2, c. 5.

WALKER: On the 6th of October, by the Rev. Francis McFarland, D.D., Mr. Wm. H. WALKER, of Louisa county, to Miss Nannie M., daughter of the Rev. John S. BLAIN, of Williamsville, Bath county.
Rockingham Register and Valley Advertiser, 3 November 1849 (Saturday), p. 2, c. 7.

WALKER: On Sunday evening, the 28th of August, by Rev. H. Tallhelm, Mr. Wm. H.

WALKER, of Missouri, and Miss Mary J.
LEWEN, of Shenandoah county, Va.
The Rockingham Register, 16 September
1864 (Friday), p. 2, c. 5.
WALKER: On the 8th ult., by the Rev. C.S.M.
See, Mr. Z.J. WALKER, of Brownsburg, Va.,
to Miss Bettie B., daughter of Mr. John
BROOKS, of Augusta, Va.
Rockingham Register and Advertiser, 2
December 1859 (Friday), p. 2, c. 5.
WALL: At the Catholic Church, in Staunton, on
the 29th of January, by Rev. Father
Walters, A.H. WALL and Miss Margarett
McMAHON, both of Staunton.
Rockingham Register and Advertiser, 14
February 1867 (Thursday), p. 2, c. 6.
WALL: On the 24th inst. [sic, ult.], at the
American Hotel, in Staunton, by the Rev.
J. Telling, D.D., Mr. Andrew J. WALL, of
the Western N.C.R.R., and Miss Annie E.
McQUAIDE, of Harrisonburg.
Rockingham Register and Advertiser, 1
March 1861 (Friday), p. 3, c. 3.
WALLACE: See entry for GIBSON.
WALLACE: October 6th, at the residence of the
bride's mother, by the Rev. ____, C.R.
WALLACE, of Bath county, and Miss Maggie
E. HULL, of Highland county.
Rockingham Register, 18 November 1869
(Thursday), p. 3, c. 2.
WALLACE: On the 20th of February, by Rev. W.
Trimble, Mr. Edwin WALLACE and Miss
Nannie J., daughter of the late Isaac
BRYAN, all of Rockbridge county.
Rockingham Register and Advertiser, 16
March 1866 (Friday), p. 3, c. 4.
WALLACE: On the 27th ult., by Rev. W.H.
McGuffey, L.L.D., Dr. G. Walker WALLACE,
of Norfolk, and Miss Sallie Willie,
daughter of John W. CHEWING, Esq., of
Albemarle.
Rockingham Register, 4 November 1869
(Thursday), p. 2, c. 4.
WALLACE: At Cleek's Mill, Bath county, on the
25th of October, by Rev. Wm. W. Preston,
Thomas B. WALLACE to Miss Nancy G. CLEEK.

Rockingham <u>Register</u> and <u>Advertiser</u>, 8
November 1866 (Thursday), p. 3, c. 4.

WALLACE: On Tuesday evening, 11th inst., by
the Rev. Dr. Dutton, Dr. William WALLACE,
lately of this place, and Miss Jennie A.,
daughter of William HURST, Esq., of
Jefferson county.

Rockingham <u>Register</u> and <u>Advertiser</u>, 21
October 1859 (Friday), p. 2, c. 5.

WALTER: See entry for BAKER.

WALTER: See entry for GOUL.

WALTER: See entry for LONAS.

WALTER: On the 10th inst., at the residence
of Mr. Daniel Ryman, by [Rev.] A.A.P.
Neel, Mr. Andrew J. WALTER and Miss
Amanda WOLFE, all of Shenandoah county.

Rockingham <u>Register</u> and <u>Advertiser</u>, 20
April 1866 (Friday), p. 2, c. 3.

WALTER: On the 18th inst., by Rev. J.P. Hyde,
Dorsey WALTER, of Winchester, and Miss
Annie L. RODEFFER, of Woodstock, Va.

Rockingham <u>Register</u> and <u>Advertiser</u>, 26
December 1867 (Thursday), p. 2, c. 6.

WALTERS: See entry for FOLTZ.

WALTERS: See entry for SMOOT.

WALTERS: On the 13th of September, by Rev.
Jacob Stirewalt, Mr. Frederick C. WALTERS
and Miss Amanda FUNKHOUSER, all of
Shenandoah county.

The <u>Rockingham</u> <u>Register</u>, 9 October 1863
(Friday), p. 2, c. 4.

WALTERS: On the 6th ult., by Rev. J.
Stirewalt, Washington WALTERS and Miss
Elizabeth PENNYWITT, all of Shenandoah
county.

Rockingham <u>Register</u> and <u>Advertiser</u>, 17
January 1867 (Thursday), p. 3, c. 3.

WALTERS: On the 14th inst., by the Rev. J.S.
Blain, Dr. Wm. L. WALTERS and Miss Hannah
E. CALHOUN, all of Augusta county.

Rockingham <u>Register</u> and <u>Advertiser</u>, 22
October 1858 (Friday), p. 3, c. 2.

WALTON: See entry for BYRD.

WALTON: See entry for HANSAN.

WALTON: See entry for LOUDERBACK.

WALTON: See entry for WALTON.

459

WALTON: On the 21st inst., by Rev. David Harris, Col. David H. WALTON, of Woodstock, and Miss Ella L. DANNER, of Middletown, Frederick county.
Rockingham Register and Advertiser, 28 November 1867 (Thursday), p. 2, c. 6.

WALTON: On the 14th ult., by Elder John Neff, Lamar WALTON and Miss Margaret McFARLAND, all of Shenandoah county.
Rockingham Register and Advertiser, 7 April 1865 (Friday), p. 2, c. 5. Repeated, 14 April 1865 (Friday), p. 2, c. 5.

WALTON: In this place, on Wednesday morning last, by Rev. Patterson Fletcher, Rev. R.H. WALTON, of Broadway, Rockingham county, and Miss Annie T., daughter of Thomas LEWIS, Esq., dec'd, of Harrisonburg.
Rockingham Register and Advertiser, 23 March 1860 (Friday), p. 2, c. 6.

WALTON: At the American Hotel, in Staunton, on the 30th ult., by Rev. Jno. L. Clarke, Wm. C. WALTON and Miss Catharine H. WALTON, all of Augusta county.
Rockingham Register and Advertiser, 5 September 1867 (Thursday), p. 2, c. 6.

WAMPLER: See entry for CRIST.

WAMPLER: See entry for HAWKINS.

WAMPLER: See entry for WALKER.

WAMPLER: Near Timberville, on the 6th of February, by Rev. Jacob Wine, Mr. Frederick WAMPLER and Miss Anna, daughter of Mr. Daniel DRIVER, all of Rockingham county.
Rockingham Register and Advertiser, 14 February 1862 (Friday), p. 2, c. 6.

WAMPLER: At the residence of the bride's father, in Augusta county, on Monday, the 22nd of October, by Rev. Frederick Miller, John WAMPLER, of Rockingham, and Miss Catharine A., daughter of Sam'l MILLER, of Augusta.
Rockingham Register, 5 November 1868 (Thursday), p. 3, c. 3.

WAMPLER: On Thursday, the 15th of February,

460

by Rev. Jacob Miller, Mr. Johnathan WAMPLER and Miss Elizabeth, daughter of Johnathan FUNK, all of Rockingham county. Rockingham Register and Advertiser, 23 February 1866 (Friday), p. 2, c. 4.

WAMPLER: On the 7th inst., by Rev. Jacob Miller, Samuel D. WAMPLER and Miss Catharine R. KLINE, all of Rockingham county.
Rockingham Register and Advertiser, 21 February 1867 (Thursday), p. 3, c. 2.

WAMPLER: On the 29th ult., by Rev. Martin Garber, Mr. Samuel L. WAMPLER and Miss Mary F. GROVE, all of Augusta county.
Rockingham Register and Advertiser, 9 January 1868 (Thursday), p. 2, c. 4.

WANGER: On the 2nd inst., by Rev. Joseph Early, Martin H. WANGER, of Augusta, and Miss Barbara SHENK, of Rockingham.
Rockingham Register and Advertiser, 17 January 1862 (Friday), p. 3, c. 1.

WANLESS: On Jackson's River, May 3rd, by Rev. Lorenzo D. Nixon, Mr. Brison H. WANLESS, of Upshur county, and Miss Sarah Ann PHILLIPS, of Bath county, Va.
Rockingham Register and Advertiser, 22 June 1860 (Friday), p. 2, c. 6.

WARBLE: See entry for LAMB.

WARBLE: On the 28th of May, by Rev. Isaac Long, James W. WARBLE and Miss Mary BEASLY, all of Rockingham county.
Rockingham Register, 11 June 1868 (Thursday), p. 2, c. 5.

WARD: See entry for ARGENBRIGHT.

WARNER: See entry for COPP.

WARREN: See entry for BEVER.

WARREN: On Wednesday the 5th inst., by Rev. Danl. Ewing, Maj. E. Tiffin H. WARREN, of this place, and Miss Virginia W. MAGRUDER, of Orange county.
Rockingham Register and Virginia Advertiser, 14 December 1855 (Friday), p. 2, c. 8.

WARREN: At Midway, Bath county, Va., on 27th of October, by Rev. Jas. M. Rice, J.W. WARREN, of Hot Springs, and Miss Jennie

A. HOPKINS.
Rockingham Register, 2 December 1869
(Thursday), p. 2, c. 3.
WARREN: On the 15th inst., at the residence
of the bride's father, L.S. PRINTZ, Esq.,
near Blosserville, Page county, Mr.
Thomas WARREN and Miss Pamila PRINTZ, by
Rev. J.W. Watson, all of Page county.
Rockingham Register, 27 October 1870
(Thursday), p. 2, c. 4.
WARTMANN: On Thursday evening, the 4th inst.,
by the Rev. L.F. Way, Henry T. WARTMANN,
Esq., one of the Editors of the Register,
and Miss Annie R., daughter of Maj. Abram
BYRD, all of Harrisonburg, Va.
Rockingham Register and Advertiser, 12
July 1861 (Friday), p. 3, c. 4.
WARTMANN: At Bethezel, near Greenwood, the
residence of the bride's parents, on
Thursday morning the 25th of February, by
Rev. John L. Clarke, John H. WARTMANN,
Editor of the Rockingham Register, and
Miss Amanda J., daughter of Joseph
DETTOR, Esq., of Albemarle county.
Rockingham Register, 4 March 1869
(Thursday), p. 2, c. 4.
WARWICK: See entry for FRAZIER.
WARWICK: See entry for GATEWOOD.
WARWICK: See entry for LIGON.
WASHBURNE: See entry for PLECKER.
WATCHER: See entry for SALTZGIVER.
WATKINS: On the 16th inst., by Rev. J.W.
Jones, John WATKINS and Miss Jennie L.
HOLMES, all of Rockbridge.
Rockingham Register and Advertiser, 31
January 1867 (Thursday), p. 3, c. 2.
WATKINS: On the 13th inst., by Rev. J.C.
Barr, Wm. L. WATKINS, of Tazewell county,
and Miss Mary A., daughter of the late
David S. CREIGH, of Greenbrier.
Rockingham Register and Advertiser, 27
June 1867 (Thursday), p. 2, c. 6.
WATSON: See entry for GILMORE.
WATSON: See entry for HUNSICKER.
WATSON: See entry for WOODWARD.
WATSON: On the 27th ult., on the Bridge at

Harper's Ferry, by Rev. J.A. McFaden, James WATSON and Mary MOWRY, both of Shenandoah.

Rockingham Register, 10 February 1870 (Thursday), p. 2, c. 5.

WATT: On Thursday, the 14th inst., at the residence of the bride's father, Mr. Wade B. HEISKELL, by Rev. Jas. A. Latane, Dr. J.N. WATT and Miss Julia B. HEISKELL, all of Staunton.

Rockingham Register and Advertiser, 21 June 1866 (Thursday), p. 2, c. 4.

WATTS: See entry for PACE.

WAY: On the 6th of September, by Rev. S.E. Joyner, Rev. F.L. WAY, of the Virginia Annual Conference, and Miss Sallie J. SCALES, of Patrick county, Va.

Rockingham Register and Advertiser, 14 September 1860 (Friday), p. 2, c. 5.

WAYAT: See entry for BLEDSOE.

WAYBRIGHT: See entry for PHARES.

WEADE: See entry for HANGER.

WEAN: See entry for BEAM.

WEAN: On Sunday the 30th of November, by Rev. John Kline, Mr. Noah WEAN and Miss Barbara Ann BOWMAN, all of Rockingham county.

The Rockingham Register, 12 December 1862 (Friday), p. 2, c. 5.

WEANNING: On Thursday, the 4th of June, by Rev. John Kline, Mr. Isaac F. WEANNING and Miss Catharine, daughter of Mr. Abram TUSSING, all of this county.

Rockingham Register and Advertiser, 19 June 1857 (Friday), p. 3, c. 2.

WEAST: On Monday the 12th inst., by the Rev. J. Reubush, Mr. Henry WEAST to Miss Mary ROBERTS, both of South River, near Weyer's Cave.

Rockingham Register and Valley Advertiser, 17 October 1846 (Saturday), p. 3, c. 1.

WEAVER: See entry for FRAVEL.

WEAVER: On the 3rd of March, by Rev. Jacob Wine, Enez WEAVER and Polly A. DELAUGHTER.

Rockingham Register, 17 March 1870 (Thursday), p. 2, c. 4.

WEAVER: On the 27th of September, by Rev. J.F. Liggett, L.H. WEAVER and Miss Mattie C., daughter of Robert PALMER, dec'd, all of Rockingham.

Rockingham Register, 20 October 1870 (Thursday), p. 3, c. 5.

WEAVER: At New Market, on the 23rd ult., by Rev. E.L. Kreglo, Rice W. WEAVER and Miss Mary, daughter of Mr. Jacob McDANIEL.

Rockingham Register and Advertiser, 28 January 1859 (Friday), p. 2, c. 6.

WEAVER: December 10, by Rev. Jacob Thomas, Samuel WEAVER and Miss Mary, daughter of Abraham LAHMAN, all of Rockingham county.

Rockingham Register, 17 December 1868 (Thursday), p. 3, c. 2.

WEAVER: On the 26th of October, by Rev. Isaac Long, Wm. J. WEAVER and Miss Emma Virginia, daughter of Wm. M. MAIDEN, all of Rockingham county.

Rockingham Register, 28 October 1869 (Thursday), p. 2, c. 3.

WEBB: See entry for BURKHOLDER.

WEBB: See entry for SWARTZ.

WEBB: See entry for WILKIN.

WEBB: On the 18th inst., at Taylorsville, by the Rev. John H. Taylor, George S. WEBB to Miss Maggie E. TAYLOR, both of Albemarle.

Rockingham Register, 27 May 1869 (Thursday), p. 2, c. 3.

WEBB: On the 10th of May, at Cabin Hill, Shenandoah county, by Levi Keller, Henry W. WEBB and Miss Mary R. LONG, both of Shenandoah county.

Rockingham Register, 19 May 1870 (Thursday), p. 3, c. 4.

WEBB: On the 22nd ult., near Cross Roads, by Rev. A.A.P. Neel, Jacob WEBB, of Maryland, and Miss Annie M. GOOD, of Shenandoah county.

Rockingham Register and Advertiser, 17 January 1867 (Thursday), p. 3, c. 3.

WEBB: On Wednesday morning, October 1st, by

the Rev. G.W. Israel, Capt. John C. WEBB to Miss Harriet H. PECK, all of Augusta county.

Rockingham Register and Valley Advertiser, 11 October 1845 (Saturday), p. 2, c. 6.

WEBB: At Meadow Dale, on Wednesday, the 2nd February, by Rev. Wm. Brown, Dr. Jos. B. WEBB, of Mt. Crawford, Rockingham county, Va., and Miss Cornelia J., youngest daughter of James CRAIG, Esq., of Augusta county.

Rockingham Register and Advertiser, 25 February 1859 (Friday), p. 2, c. 5.

WEEAN: See entry for PAUL.

WEEKS: On the 26th ult., by Rev. S.H. Cummings, Mr. Elisha WEEKS and Miss Lucy TAYLOR, all of Augusta.

Rockingham Register and Advertiser, 18 November 1859 (Friday), p. 2, c. 4.

WEIR: See entry for ERVINE.

WEITZEL: See entry for GOEN.

WEITZEL: On Tuesday morning, the 16th inst., by Elder Henry Jennings, Mr. Samuel WEITZEL, formerly of Rockingham county, and Miss S.A. SIBERT, of Shenandoah county.

Rockingham Register and Advertiser, 26 April 1861 (Friday), p. 2, c. 7.

WELCH: On the 31st of August, by the Rev. Solomon Garber, Mr. Martin WELCH and Miss Julia ROADCAP, all of this county.

Rockingham Register & Advertiser, 8 September 1865 (Friday), p. 3, c. 2.

WELCH: In the Catholic Church in Staunton, on Sunday evening the 21st of January, by Rev. Father Bixio, Patrick WELCH and Miss Ellen, daughter of Garrett KING, all of this vicinity.

Rockingham Register and Advertiser, 2 February 1866 (Friday), p. 3, c. 2.

WELLER: On Sunday morning last, by Rev. H. Myers, Mr. Lemuel WELLER and Miss Margaret COOK, all of Augusta county.

Rockingham Register and Advertiser, 26 September 1856 (Friday), p. 2, c. 6.

WELLER: On Thursday the 18th day of April, by
Rev. J.C. Hensell, Wm. F. WELLER and Miss
Delilah TUTWILER, all of Rockingham.
Rockingham Register and Advertiser, 9 May
1867 (Thursday), p. 2, c. 5.
WELLMAN: On the 29th of October, by Rev. W.F.
Ward, James H. WELLMAN, of Harrisonburg,
and Miss Laura V. SLOAT, of Winchester,
Va.
Rockingham Register, 12 November 1868
(Thursday), p. 3, c. 3.
WELSH: See entry for FOUNTAIN.
WELSH: On the 6th ult., by Rev. J. Soule, Mr.
Adam WELSH and Miss Rhoda BRIDGES, all of
this county.
Rockingham Register and Advertiser, 14
January 1859 (Friday), p. 3, c. 3.
WELTON: See entry for FISHER.
WENGER: See entry for LINNEWEAVER.
WENGER: On the 26th of February, by Rev. S.
Garber, Benj. WENGER and Miss J.A. ESTEP,
all of Rockingham county.
Rockingham Register and Advertiser, 24
March 1865 (Friday), p. 2, c. 3.
WENGER: On the 24th ult., by Rev. Solomon
Garber, Gideon F. WENGER and Miss
Catharine RHODES, all of Rockingham
county.
Rockingham Register, 8 October 1868
(Thursday), p. 3, c. 3.
WENGER: On the 5th inst., at the residence of
the bride's father, by Rev. D. Brower,
Joseph H. WENGER, formerly of Edom, Va.,
and Miss E.L. McAFFERTY, of South
English, Iowa.
Rockingham Register, 23 April 1868
(Thursday), p. 2, c. 5.
WESCOTT: At Washington city, on Thursday, the
13th ult., by the Rev. Norval Wilson, Mr.
James WESCOTT to Miss Harriet Ann
CALVERT, both of that city.
Rockingham Register and Valley
Advertiser, 8 March 1845 (Saturday), p.
3, c. 4.
WEST: On Thursday evening, the 21st inst., at
Belmont Hall, the residence of the

bride's father, by Rev. J.C. Wheat, Mr. Eugene WEST, of Frederick county, Md., a member of Co. G, 7th Va. Cavalry, and Miss Annie L., eldest daughter of J.N. COWAN, of Rockingham county.
The Rockingham Register, 29 April 1864 (Friday), p. 2, c. 5.

WEST: On the 26th of February, by the Rev. T.D. Bell, Mr. John W. WEST and Miss Eliza A. GAITHER, all of Rockingham.
Rockingham Register and Advertiser, 1 March 1861 (Friday), p. 3, c. 3.

WEST: On the 7th of February, by the Rev. Solomon Garber, Mr. Tolbert WEST, of Randolph county, Va., and Miss Margaret MANLEY, of Rockingham.
Rockingham Register and Advertiser, 24 February 1865 (Friday), p. 2, c. 5.

WEST: On the 15th of November, 1864, by Rev. W.H. Cone, Mr. W.B. WEST, of Baltimore city, and Miss Mary A. HEPNER, of Shenandoah county.
The Rockingham Register, 5 February 1864 (Friday), p. 2, c. 6.

WESTON: At Runnimede, on the 3rd inst., by Rev. Wm. Torrey, Mr. Charles T. WESTON, of Honesdale, Pa., to Miss Mary C. CRAWFORD, of Shenandoah.
The Rockingham Register and Valley Advertiser, 26 June 1852 (Saturday), p. 2, c. 5.

WETHERHOLTZ: On the 29th of December, 1864, by Rev. J. Stirewalt, Mr. Jonathan WETHERHOLTZ and Miss Julia A. GRIFFITH, all of Page county.
Rockingham Register and Advertiser, 20 January 1865 (Friday), p. 2, c. 4.

WETHERHULTZ: See entry for POLK.

WETZEL: See entry for HOTTLE.

WETZEL: See entry for LOWREY.

WETZEL: On the 26th ult., by Rev. M.D. Dunlap, Mr. David S. WETZEL, of Lewisburg, Va., to Miss Christiana J. McCUTCHEN, of Pocahontas county, Va.
Rockingham Register and Advertiser, 12 October 1860 (Friday), p. 2, c. 4.

467

WETZEL: On the 14th inst., by Rev. H. Wetzel, Ezra WETZEL and Miss Emily A. WIREMAN, both of Shenandoah county.
Rockingham Register, 30 September 1869 (Thursday), p. 2, c. 4.

WETZEL: On the 5th inst., by Rev. Levi Keller, Lemuel WETZEL and Miss Mary CLICK, all of Shenandoah.
Rockingham Register and Advertiser, 16 January 1868 (Thursday), p. 2, c. 5.

WHEELBARGER: See entry for GLADWELL.

WHEELBARGER: On the 12th of July, by Rev. G.B. Hammock, Jas. F. WHEELBARGER and Miss Susan A. RAMSEY, all of Rockingham.
Rockingham Register, 30 July 1868 (Thursday), p. 3, c. 3.

WHEELBERGER: On the 14th ult., by the Rev. J.C. HENSELL, Mr. John H. WHEELBERGER and Miss Sarah E., eldest daughter of Mr. Elijah HUFFMAN, of Rockingham.
Rockingham Register & Advertiser, 6 October 1865 (Friday), p. 2, c. 2.

WHEELER: See entry for AREY.

WHEELER: See entry for GISH.

WHEELER: On the 30th of October, by Rev. Solomon Garber, near Bridgewater, Mr. Peter WHEELER and Miss Mary Ann, daughter of Mr. Resin BRYAN, all of Rockingham.
Rockingham Register and Virginia Advertiser, 8 November 1861 (Friday), p. 2, c. 2.

WHEELER: On Thursday, the 9th inst., by Rev. J.C. Hensell, Wm. H.H. WHEELER and Miss Martha Jane, eldest daughter of Peter WISE.
Rockingham Register, 16 December 1869 (Thursday), p. 2, c. 5.

WHETSEL: On the 8th inst., by Rev. Jacob Miller, David WHETSEL, formerly of Page county, and Miss Fannie L., daughter of Isaac McMULLEN, all of Rockingham.
Rockingham Register, 17 June 1869 (Thursday), p. 2, c. 6.

WHISLER: See entry for BLAZER.

WHISLER: See entry for SHOWALTER.

WHISLER: See entry for WRIGHT.

WHISLER: On the 17th inst., by Rev. Jacob Miller, Cambysus R. WHISLER and Miss Martha, daughter of Levi SHOEMAKER, all of Rockingham county.
Rockingham Register and Advertiser, 21 February 1867 (Thursday), p. 3, c. 2.
WHISMAN: See entry for PENCE.
WHISSEN: See entry for COMER.
WHISSEN: See entry for HARMAN.
WHISSEN: See entry for MASSIE.
WHISSEN: On the 28th of March, by Rev. Daniel Thomas, Jacob H. WHISSEN and Miss Susan J., daughter of Christian FUNK, all of Rockingham.
Rockingham Register and Advertiser, 4 April 1867 (Thursday), p. 3, c. 4.
WHISTLER: See entry for KRONK.
WHISTLER: In South English, Keokuk county, Iowa, on the 12th of April, by Rev. Mr. Smock, Leri WHISTLER, formerly of Shenandoah, and Miss Daziah ROSACRANS, of Keokuk.
Rockingham Register and Advertiser, 4 May 1860 (Friday), p. 2, c. 4.
WHITE: See entry for DAY.
WHITE: See entry for DUNN.
WHITE: See entry for JOHNSON.
WHITE: See entry for PENNYBACKER.
WHITE: See entry for READ.
WHITE: See entry for ROLLER.
WHITE: See entry for SIPE.
WHITE: On North River, at the residence of the bride's father, on Sunday evening last, by Rev. J.C. Hensell, Mr. C.C. WHITE, of Harrisonburg, and Miss Margaret, daughter of Mr. John THUMA, of Rockingham county.
Rockingham Register and Advertiser, 25 November 1859 (Friday), p. 2, c. 4.
WHITE: On the 1st of July, 1862, by Rev. J.W. Howe, Mr. Charles T. WHITE, of Greene, and Miss Josephine S., daughter of Mr. Archibald BROOK, of Rockingham county.
Rockingham Register and Virginia Advertiser, 11 July 1862 (Friday), p. 2, c. 6.

WHITE: On the 4th inst., in Mt. Crawford, by
the Rev. Daniel Feete, Mr. George W.
WHITE, of Augusta county, to Miss
Elizabeth PIFER, of Rockingham.
Rockingham Register and Advertiser, 14
November 1856 (Friday), p. 2, c. 6.

WHITE: In the Presbyterian Church in
Lexington, on Wednesday evening of last
week, by the Rev. W.S. White, D.D., Rev.
Henry M. WHITE, of Roanoke, and Miss Mary
Miller, daughter of John H. MYERS, Esq.,
Cashier of the Rockbridge Bank.
Rockingham Register and Advertiser, 14
September 1860 (Friday), p. 2, c. 5.

WHITE: At Niles, Michigan, on the evening of
the 13th of December, ... Miss Lizzie M.,
... daughter of J. GELTMACHER, Esq., a
former citizen of Rockingham county, ...
[to] Mr. R.J. WHITE, of Detroit, Michigan
....
Rockingham Register, 22 December 1870
(Thursday), p. 2, c. 4.

WHITE: In the 2nd Presbyterian Church, in
Richmond, on Thursday, 26th ult., by the
Rev. Edward Martin, Robert WHITE, Esq.,
of Hampshire, and Miss Ellen, daughter of
James C. VASS, Esq., of the vicinity of
Richmond.
Rockingham Register and Advertiser, 17
June 1859 (Friday), p. 3, c. 3.

WHITE: On the 14th inst., by the Rev. Dr. Wm.
S. WHITE, Thomas S. WHITE, of Salem, and
Miss Sallie E., daughter of the late Col.
Andrew W. CAMERON, of Rockbridge.
Rockingham Register and Advertiser, 30
May 1867 (Thursday), p. 3, c. 3.

WHITESCARVER: See entry for ROLLER.

WHITESCARVER: On Tuesday evening, the 22nd
ult., by the Rev. J.C. Hensell, Mr.
Benjamin F. WHITESCARVER and Miss Annie
E., eldest daughter of Mr. Henry H.
WYANT, all of Rockingham county, Va.
Rockingham Register & Advertiser, 22
September 1865 (Friday), p. 3, c. 3.

WHITESELL: See entry for ALMARODE.

WHITESELL: See entry for COYNER.

WHITESELL: See entry for MILLER.

WHITESELL: Near Staunton, on the 1st inst.,
    by the Rev. W.R. Stringer, Daniel P.
    WHITESELL and Mrs. Mary E. DAVIS, all of
    Augusta.
    Rockingham Register, 8 October 1868
    (Thursday), p. 3, c. 3.

WHITEZELL: On the 23rd ult., by Rev. G.W.
    Statton, Mr. Simon C. WHITEZELL and Miss
    Mary C. FALLS, all of Rockingham.
    Rockingham Register and Advertiser, 4
    January 1861 (Friday), p. 3, c. 4.

WHITING: See entry for STUBBLEFIELD.

WHITLOCK: See entry for CARROL.

WHITLOCK: On Monday evening, the 16th inst.,
    by Rev. Joseph Funkhouser, Pleasant
    WHITLOCK and Miss Caroline E. WINEGORD,
    all of Rockingham county.
    Rockingham Register, 19 August 1869
    (Thursday), p. 3, c. 2.

WHITMER: See entry for HEDRICK (2).

WHITMER: See entry for HUPP.

WHITMER: See entry for MILLER.

WHITMER: See entry for WILSON.

WHITMER: On the 21st inst., by Rev. T.
    Brashear, Mr. Andrew J. WHITMER and Miss
    Nancy S., daughter of Wm. ANDERSON, all
    of this county.
    Rockingham Register and Advertiser, 26
    March 1858 (Friday), p. 3, c. 2.

WHITMER: By the Rev. R.C. Walker, on the 13th
    inst., Mr. Daniel WHITMER and Miss Sarah
    CARL, all of Augusta.
    Rockingham Register and Advertiser, 28
    January 1859 (Friday), p. 2, c. 6.

WHITMER: At Dovesville, in this county, on
    the 1st inst., by Rev. Socrates Henkel,
    Mr. Suffary WHITMER, of Hardy county, to
    Miss Catharine WITTIG, of Rockingham
    county.
    Rockingham Register and Advertiser, 16
    April 1858 (Friday), p. 3, c. 2.

WHITMER: On the 5th inst., at the residence
    of the bride's father, in Rockbridge
    county, by Rev. Dr. Junkin, Wm. C.
    WHITMER and Miss Rachel McC., daughter of

Chas. S. THOMPSON, Esq., formerly of Rockingham.

Rockingham Register and Advertiser, 12 December 1867 (Thursday), p. 3. c. 2.

WHITMORE: See entry for BAKER.

WHITMORE: See entry for CARPENTER.

WHITMORE: See entry for FIREBAUGH.

WHITMORE: See entry for HOPKINS.

WHITMORE: See entry for JEFFERSON.

WHITMORE: See entry for LONG.

WHITMORE: See entry for RHODES (2).

WHITMORE: See entry for WINTERMYER.

WHITMORE: On the 5th inst., by Rev. D.W. Arnold, at the residence of the bride's father, Mr. B.F. WHITMORE and Miss Sarah J. HAMRICK, all of Augusta county.

Rockingham Register and Advertiser, 19 April 1861 (Friday), p. 2, c. 3.

WHITMORE: On the 3rd inst., by Rev. Jacob Miller, Benj. WHITMORE and Miss Rutha Jane ARMENTROUT, all of Rockingham.

Rockingham Register and Advertiser, 10 January 1867 (Thursday), p. 3, c. 2.

WHITMORE: On Sunday morning, the 9th inst., by Rev. J.C. Hensell, George D. WHITMORE and Miss Eliza Jane CRAUN, all of Rockingham county.

Rockingham Register, 13 May 1869 (Thursday), p. 3, c. 3.

WHITMORE: On the 23rd of November, near Waynesboro, by Rev. Mr. Walker, Mr. Henry WHITMORE and Miss Nannie E. LAYMAN, all of Augusta.

Rockingham Register and Advertiser, 12 January 1866 (Friday), p. 1, c. 3.

WHITMORE: On the 20th ult., by Rev. J.W. Howe, Isaac N. WHITMORE and Miss Susan V. THOMPSON, all of Rockingham county.

Rockingham Register and Advertiser, 4 October 1866 (Thursday), p. 2, c. 5.

WHITMORE: On the 22nd of February, by Rev. W. Trimble, Mr. John WHITMORE, of Roanoke, and Miss Sallie M., daughter of Wm. A. WILSON, of Rockbridge.

Rockingham Register and Advertiser, 16 March 1866 (Friday), p. 3, c. 4.

WHITMORE: On Wednesday, the 26th ult., by Rev. Isaac Long, Joseph A. WHITMORE, of Augusta county, and Miss Mary A., second daughter of Mr. Hammond HAHN, of Rockingham county.
Rockingham Register and Advertiser, 4 October 1866 (Thursday), p. 2, c. 5.

WHITMORE: On the 22nd ult., by Rev. J.M. Follansbee, Mr. Lewis E. WHITMORE and Miss Alice Ann HARRELL, all of Augusta.
Rockingham Register, 1 December 1870 (Thursday), p. 2, c. 4.

WHITMORE: On the 9th inst., by Rev. J.C. Hensell, Mr. Peter W. WHITMORE and Miss Elizabeth S., daughter of Mr. Peter PLECKER, all of Rockingham.
Rockingham Register and Advertiser, 21 December 1860 (Friday), p. 2, c. 6.

WHITMORE: On the 3rd inst., at the house of Mr. Josiah Neff, by the Rev. John Pinkerton, Mr. Samuel WHITMORE and Miss Sarah A. NEFF, all of Augusta county.
Rockingham Register and Advertiser, 11 November 1859 (Friday), p. 3, c. 1.

WHITMORE: On the 17th inst., at the residence of Mr. Abraham Hockman, by Rev. John Neff, Silastine WHITMORE, of Hardy county, and Miss Sarah, daughter of Washington BASEY, dec'd, of Shenandoah county.
Rockingham Register and Advertiser, 31 May 1866 (Thursday), p. 3, c. 5.

WHITMORE: On the 22nd ult., at Bath, by the Rev. Mr. Jacobs, Wm. WHITMORE, of Va., to Mary N., daughter of the late Col. J.W.M. BENNIEN, of Ga.
Rockingham Register, 7 May 1868 (Thursday), p. 2, c. 4.

WHITSEL: See entry for RHODES.

WHITSEL: See entry for SHIFLETT.

WHITTINGTON: On the 1st March, by Rev. H. St. J. Rinker, John WHITTINGTON and Miss Sophia FRY.
Rockingham Register and Advertiser, 7 April 1865 (Friday), p. 2, c. 5. Repeated, 14 April 1865 (Friday), p. 2,

c. 5.

WHITZEL: See entry for ROSS.

WHOLEY: On the 27th of February, at St. Francis' Church, by the Rev. Father Farran, Wm. WHOLEY, of the Stonewall Brigade, and Miss Hannah COLLINS, of Staunton.

Rockingham Register and Advertiser, 7 March 1867 (Thursday), p. 3, c. 3.

WHORLEY: See entry for LYNCH.

WICLE: See entry for HANEY.

WIESON: See entry for WILSON.

WIGGONTON: On the 9th of January, 1859, at the Strawbridge, by Rev. B.B. Hamlen, Mr. William H. WIGGONTON and Miss Ellen J.V. BARNS, all of Harper's Ferry.

Rockingham Register and Advertiser, 18 February 1859 (Friday), p. 2, c. 6.

WILCHER: On the 18th ult., near Parnassus, by Rev. R.C. Walker, Jos. WILCHER and Miss Casendine E. REDIFER, all of Augusta county.

Rockingham Register and Advertiser, 2 May 1867 (Thursday), p. 2, c. 6.

WILEY: See entry for HICKMAN.

WILEY: In Staunton, on the 14th inst., by Rev. Geo. B. Taylor, Joseph G. WILEY and Miss Amelia W. PEMBERTON, of Staunton.

Rockingham Register, 21 October 1869 (Thursday), p. 2, c. 3.

WILFONG: See entry for PROPST.

WILFONG: On Thursday, October 13th, 1870, on North Fork, near Green Bank, by Rev. H.A.J. Francis, John WILFONG, Esq., of Highland county, Va., and Miss Anna C., daughter of James G. HAMILTON, of Pocahontas county, W.Va.

Rockingham Register, 27 October 1870 (Thursday), p. 2, c. 4.

WILHITE: See entry for BRICKER.

WILHITE: See entry for SCHANK.

WILKIN: On the 4th inst., by Rev. H. Wetzel, Daniel WILKIN and Miss Susan WEBB, all of Shenandoah county.

Rockingham Register, 15 April 1869 (Thursday), p. 2, c. 4.

474

WILKIN: On the 16th inst., by Rev. Geo. Wine, Noah WILKIN, of Hardy county, West Virginia, and Miss Mary E. JISLOR, of Augusta county.
Rockingham Register and Advertiser, 23 January 1868 (Thursday), p. 2, c. 4.

WILKINS: On the morning of the 14th inst., at the residence of the bride's mother, in N.T. Stephensburg, by Rev. J.F. Allemong, A.T. ("Tom") WILKINS, of Rockingham county, and Miss Virginia LAUCKE, of Frederick county.
Rockingham Register and Advertiser, 29 August 1867 (Thursday), p. 2, c. 5.

WILKINS: On the 7th inst., by Rev. H. Wetzel, Jacob WILKINS and Miss Lydia F. DELLINGER, all of Shenandoah county.
Rockingham Register and Advertiser, 31 January 1867 (Thursday), p. 3, c. 2.

WILL: See entry for HOTTINGER.

WILL: See entry for RYMAL.

WILL: On the 4th inst., near Timberville, by Rev. H. St. J. Rinker, Charles B. WILL and Miss Elizabeth E. MILLER, all of Rockingham.
Rockingham Register, 8 July 1869 (Thursday), p. 2, c. 5.

WILL: On the 18th ult., near Timberville, by the Rev. S. Henkel, Ephraim WILL, Esq., and Miss Angeline STERN.
Rockingham Register, 2 December 1869 (Thursday), p. 2, c. 3.

WILLIAMS: See entry for AVERITT.
WILLIAMS: See entry for BEASLEY.
WILLIAMS: See entry for BIERLY.
WILLIAMS: See entry for CRAWFORD.
WILLIAMS: See entry for DEPOY.
WILLIAMS: See entry for GOLLADAY.
WILLIAMS: See entry for GORDON.
WILLIAMS: See entry for GRANDSTAFF.
WILLIAMS: See entry for HARRISON (2).
WILLIAMS: See entry for HEDRICK.
WILLIAMS: See entry for LOWMAN.
WILLIAMS: See entry for MARKWOOD.
WILLIAMS: See entry for PIRKEY.
WILLIAMS: See entry for PLAUGER.

WILLIAMS: See entry for RUNKLE.

WILLIAMS: See entry for SNAPP.

WILLIAMS: On January 4, 1867, by Rev. Christian Hartman, Geo. E. WILLIAMS and Miss Sarah J., daughter of George W. SCOTT, all of Rockingham county.
Rockingham Register and Advertiser, 24 January 1867, (Thursday), p. 2, c. 4.

WILLIAMS: On the 29th of December, by Elder John Clark, James E. WILLIAMS and Miss Eliza Ann RUTHERFORD, all of Rappahannock county.
Rockingham Register, 14 January 1869 (Thursday), p. 3, c. 3.

WILLIAMS: In McGaheysville, on Thursday, the 4th of June, by Rev. Jos. Funkhouser, Mr. John WILLIAMS and Miss Virginia E., daughter of William RODGERS, all of Rockingham county.
The Rockingham Register, 12 June 1863 (Friday), p. 2, c. 6.

WILLIAMS: On the 12th of March, by Rev. Jacob Miller, John C. WILLIAMS and Miss Lydia J., daughter of Rodney ATCHISON, all of Rockingham.
Rockingham Register and Advertiser, 4 April 1867 (Thursday), p. 3, c. 4.

WILLIAMS: In Hagerstown, on Thursday evening, the 27th ult., by the Rev. Joseph E. Johnston, Mr. O.L. WILLIAMS, of Winchester, Va., to Miss Mary E., youngest daughter of the late Gen. Thomas A. PERKINS, of the former place.
Rockingham Register and Valley Advertiser, 8 March 1845 (Saturday), p. 3, c. 3.

WILLIAMS: At the Methodist Parsonage, in Fredericksburg, on the 25th ult., by Rev. E.B. Smith, Thomas WILLIAMS and Miss Susan E. ROCKAFELLER, both of Stafford county.
Rockingham Register, 15 April 1869 (Thursday), p. 2, c. 4.

WILLIAMS: At the residence of the bride, by Rev. J.B. Tullis, Rev. W.G. WILLIAMS, of the East Texas Conference, formerly of

Virginia, and Mrs. R.L.C. HENDERSON, of Anderson county, Texas.

Rockingham Register and Advertiser, 2 March 1860 (Friday), p. 3, c. 2.

WILLIAMSON: See entry for KERR.

WILLIAMSON: See entry for WALDEN.

WILLICE: On the 9th of December, by the Rev. J.W. Howe, Mr. Thomas M. WILLICE and Miss Margaret E. LONG, all of this county.

Rockingham Register and Advertiser, 13 December 1866 (Thursday), p. 2, c. 5.

WILLIS: At the residence of Joseph K. Smith, in Harrisonburg, on Thursday evening last, by Rev. Jas. S. Gardner, George W. WILLIS, of this place, and Miss Mary, daughter of Joseph BEZANSON, of Burke's Mill, Augusta county.

Rockingham Register, 9 December 1869 (Thursday), p. 3, c. 2.

WILLS: See entry for WILLS.

WILLS: On the 3rd ult., Mr. John W. WILLS, of Augusta county, to Miss Sarah A. MILLER, of Highland.

Rockingham Register and Valley Advertiser, 13 September 1851 (Saturday), p. 2, c. 7.

WILLS: On the 7th inst., by Rev. J.W. Bennett, S.C. WILLS, formerly of Augusta county, and Mrs. Mary E. WILLS, of Peterstown, W.Va.

Rockingham Register and Advertiser, 28 June 1866 (Thursday), p. 2, c. 5.

WILLSON: On the 23rd of November, at "Glennesvis," Augusta county, the residence of the bride's father, Charles S. THOMSON [sic], by the Rev. E.D. Junkin, Samuel N. WILLSON, of Rockbridge, and Miss Phebe Jane THOMPSON.

Rockingham Register, 2 December 1869 (Thursday), p. 2, c. 3.

WILMER: On the 25th ult., by Rev. Thos. Miller, Jacob WILMER and Miss Mary BEHM, all of Shenandoah county.

Rockingham Register and Advertiser, 9 August 1866 (Thursday), p. 3, c. 4.

WILSON: See entry for AVIS.

WILSON: See entry for CHESHIRE.
WILSON: See entry for CHRISTIE.
WILSON: See entry for CRIGLER.
WILSON: See entry for ERVINE.
WILSON: See entry for FRYE.
WILSON: See entry for GALLAGHER.
WILSON: See entry for HENTON.
WILSON: See entry for HITE.
WILSON: See entry for HOUSTON.
WILSON: See entry for McCLUNG.
WILSON: See entry for McGUFFIN.
WILSON: See entry for NEBB.
WILSON: See entry for WHITMORE.
WILSON: See entry for WITTIG.
WILSON: In Bridgewater, on the 22nd inst., by
    Rev. Geo. W. Holland, Capt. A.H. WILSON,
    of Harrisonburg, and Miss Josie, youngest
    daughter of John ALLEBAUGH, dec'd.
    Rockingham Register, 24 February 1870
    (Thursday), p. 2, c. 5.
WILSON: On the 26th ult., by Rev. Horatio
    Thompson, D.D., Geo. W. WILSON and Miss
    Ellen Baxter BROWN, all of Augusta
    county.
    Rockingham Register, 10 December 1868
    (Thursday), p. 3, c. 3.
WILSON: On the 12th of July, near Doe Hill,
    by Rev. W.T. Price, Capt. H. Brown PULLEN
    and Miss Lydia Virginia; also, at the
    same time and place, Hezekiah WILSON and
    Miss Matilda Ann, daughters of Mrs. Mary
    McCOY, all of Highland county.
    Rockingham Register and Advertiser, 2
    August 1866 (Thursday), p. 2, c. 5.
WILSON: In Strasburg on the 3rd inst., by
    Rev. L. Keller, Mr. James WILSON & Miss
    Margaret BORUM, all of that place.
    Rockingham Register and Virginia
    Advertiser, 18 May 1855 (Friday), p. 3,
    c. 4.
WILSON: On the 23rd of December, by Rev. J.M.
    Shreckhise, Mr. John B. WILSON and Miss
    Catharine TEAFORD, all of Rockbridge.
    Rockingham Register, 7 January 1869
    (Thursday), p. 3, c. 3.
WILSON: On the 1st inst., by Rev. R.C.

Walker, John H. WILSON and Miss Rachel E. HANGER.

Rockingham Register and Advertiser, 8 November 1866 (Thursday), p. 3, c. 4.

WILSON: In Middlebrook, on Tuesday, the 16th inst., Dr. Joseph WILSON and Miss Ann SANDERSON, all of Augusta county.

Rockingham Register and Virginia Advertiser, 27 May 1854 (Saturday), p. 2, c. 7.

WILSON: On Thursday, April 4th, at the residence of the bride's father, Alex. BROWNLEE, by Rev. Mr. Pinkerton, Joseph WILSON and Mrs. Margaret E. WIESON, all of Augusta.

Rockingham Register and Advertiser, 25 April 1867 (Thursday), p. 2, c. 7.

WILSON: On the 28th ult., at the residence of Mr. Alex. H. McComb, by Rev. Mr. Preston, Jos. A. WILSON and Miss Agnes A. LONG, all of Augusta county.

Rockingham Register and Advertiser, 5 July 1866 (Thursday), p. 3, c. 5.

WILSON: At the residence of the bride's mother, in Bridgewater, Rockingham county, Va., at 8 o'clock, on Wednesday morning, the 16th of September, by Rev. J.R. Bowman, Osborne WILSON, Esq., of Monterey, Highland county, Va., and Miss Lizzie F., daughter of Mrs. Elizabeth WHITMER, of Bridgewater.

Rockingham Register, 17 September 1868 (Thursday), p. 2, c. 5.

WILSON: On the 22nd ult., near Staunton, by Rev. Wm. E. Baker, Capt. Peter E. WILSON and Miss Margaret J.B. EIDSON, of Augusta.

Rockingham Register, 5 November 1868 (Thursday), p. 3, c. 3.

WILSON: On Thursday, the 24th ult., by Rev. C.L. Damron, Rev. Rufus H. WILSON, of the Baltimore Conference, and Miss Mary Lou TEMPLETON, of Fairfield, Rockbridge county, Va.

Rockingham Register, 3 March 1870 (Thursday), p. 2, c. 5.

WILSON: On the 8th inst., by Rev. Mr. Murray, near Greenville, Thomas WILSON, of Indiana, and Miss Lucinda E. HUMPHREYS, of Augusta county.
Rockingham Register, 29 October 1868 (Thursday), p. 3, c. 3.

WILSON: On the 13th inst., by Rev. P. Miller, Mr. Z.L. WILSON and Miss R.A. MAPHIS, all of Hampshire county.
The Rockingham Register, 23 September 1864 (Friday), p. 2, c. 5.

WIMER: See entry for WIMER.

WIMER: On the 29th ult., by Rev. George W. Rexroad, Mr. Jacob WIMER and Miss Margaret, daughter of George WIMER, Esq., both of Pendleton county, Virginia ....
Rockingham Register and Advertiser, 14 October 1859 (Friday), p. 2, c. 3.

WIMER: On the 11th ult., in Monterey, by Rev. W.T. Price, Joseph WIMER and Miss Margaret S. SNYDER, all of Highland.
Rockingham Register, 4 March 1869 (Thursday), p. 2, c. 4.

WINDLE: See entry for ZIRKLE.

WINDLE: On the 28th ult., by Rev. D. Feete, Mr. John WINDLE and Miss Mary M. COPP, all of Shenandoah county.
Rockingham Register and Advertiser, 7 January 1859 (Friday), p. 3, c. 1.

WINDLE: On the 23rd ult., at the bride's residence, in Culpeper county, by Rev. Mr. Grimsley, Mrs. Sevilla F. QUAINTANCE and John P. WINDLE, Esq., of New Market.
Rockingham Register and Advertiser, 8 November 1866 (Thursday), p. 3, c. 4.

WINDLE: At Mt. Jackson, May 25th, by the Rev. A.R. Rude, Mr. Wm. L. WINDLE and Miss Sarah J. BRYAN, both of Mt. Jackson.
Rockingham Register and Advertiser, 10 June 1859 (Friday), p. 3, c. 2.

WINE: See entry for BAKER.

WINE: See entry for JORDAN.

WINE: See entry for MILLER.

WINE: See entry for MYERS.

WINE: On the 9th of May, by Rev. Isaac Long, Daniel WINE and Miss Rutha Ann, daughter

of Adam SHOWALTER, all of Rockingham
county.
Rockingham Register, 20 May 1869
(Thursday), p. 2, c. 3.
WINE: On the morning of the 10th ult., near
Ottobine Church, by Rev. G.W. Stevenson,
Geo. H. WINE and Miss Mary F. DINKLE, all
of Rockingham county.
Rockingham Register and Advertiser, 17
January 1867 (Thursday), p. 3, c. 3.
WINE: On Tuesday, May 9th, by Rev. Jacob
Wine, Mr. Michael WINE and Miss Mary
KOONTZ, all of Shenandoah.
Rockingham Register and Advertiser, 28
July 1865 (Friday), p. 2, c. 6.
WINE: On the 24th of December, by Elder Jacob
Wine, Samuel A. WINE and Miss Sallie J.
COFFMAN, all of Shenandoah county.
Rockingham Register and Advertiser, 9
January 1868 (Thursday), p. 2, c. 4.
WINE: On the 31st of December, by Rev. Isaac
Long, Solomon A. WINE and Miss Sarah F.,
daughter of Harvey F. SMITH, all of
Rockingham county.
Rockingham Register, 7 January 1869
(Thursday), p. 3, c. 3.
WINEGORD: See entry for WHITLOCK.
WINFIELD: See entry for SHOUPE.
WINFIELD: See entry for YOST.
WINGFIELD: See entry for BRIGHTMAN.
WINSBOROUGH: See entry for YANCEY.
WINTERMYER: On the 28th of April, by Rev.
J.W. Howe, William WINTERMYER and Miss
Mary E. WHITMORE, all of Rockingham
county.
Rockingham Register, 21 May 1868
(Thursday), p. 2, c. 5.
WIREMAN: See entry for WETZEL.
WISE: See entry for BENNICK.
WISE: See entry for BYRD.
WISE: See entry for GRADWOHL.
WISE: See entry for GRAY.
WISE: See entry for HUFFMAN.
WISE: See entry for KELLEY.
WISE: See entry for KENNEDY.
WISE: See entry for MOORE.

WISE: See entry for PLECKER.

WISE: See entry for SHIFFLETT.

WISE: See entry for WHEELER.

WISE: In Staunton, on Wednesday evening, the 25th of October, by Rev. M.J. Michelbacher, Mr. Adolph WISE, of Harrisonburg, and Miss Fannie R. BOWERS, of Staunton, Va.
Rockingham Register & Advertiser, 3 November 1865 (Friday), p. 2, c. 2.

WISE: In Baltimore city, on the 2nd inst., by Rev. Dr. Deutsch, Albert A. WISE, of Harrisonburg, and Miss Minnie E. LOWNER, of Augusta county.
Rockingham Register, 13 May 1869 (Thursday), p. 3, c. 3.

WISE: By Rev. Valentine F. Bolton, in Harrisonburg, on the 14th of February, Mr. Cyrus S. WISE and Miss Delilah, daughter of Peter GRUBB, all of this county.
Rockingham Register and Virginia Advertiser, 22 February 1856 (Friday), p. 2, c. 8.

WISE: On Thursday, the 9th inst., by Rev. J.C. Hensell, John C. WISE, of Rockingham, and Miss Sarah E., second daughter of Samuel PLECKER, of Augusta county.
Rockingham Register and Advertiser, 23 January 1868 (Thursday), p. 2, c. 4.

WISE: By Rev. A.D. Pollack, on the 28th ult., Lewis A. WISE, of Culpeper, and Miss Harriet F. COOK, of Augusta county.
Rockingham Register, 6 January 1870 (Thursday), p. 3, c. 3.

WISE: On the 18th inst., at Emmanuel Church, in New Market, by Rev. J.S. Bennick, Peter D. WISE, of Rockingham, and Miss Lucy GRIM, of Shenandoah county.
Rockingham Register, 27 May 1869 (Thursday), p. 2, c. 3.

WISE: On the 17th inst., at Montezuma, by Rev. Wm. H. Dinkel, Capt. Sam'l WISE and Miss Sallie F. HAMMER, all of Rockingham county.

Rockingham Register, 24 September 1868 (Thursday), p. 3, c. 4.

WISE: On the 25th ult., by Rev. Daniel Thomas, Sam'l N. WISE, of Rockingham, and Miss Mary M., daughter of Michael EVY, of Augusta.

Rockingham Register and Advertiser, 2 March 1866 (Friday), p. 3, c. 3.

WISE: On the 14th inst., by Rev. Mr. Hensel, in Hensel's Church [German Reformed], William Henry WISE and Miss Mary E., eldest daughter of Jacob LAGO, all of Rockingham.

Rockingham Register and Advertiser, 16 May 1867 (Thursday), p. 2, c. 5. Repeated, 23 May 1867 (Thursday), p. 2, c. 6. The above is a composite of the two.

WISEMAN: See entry for AKENS.

WISEMAN: See entry for DAUGHERTY.

WISEMAN: See entry for KIZER.

WISEMAN: On the 18th inst., by the Rev. Geo. G. Brooke, Jacob F. WISEMAN and Hannah M. LOWERY.

Rockingham Register and Advertiser, 27 May 1859 (Friday), p. 2, c. 6.

WISEMAN: On the 28th ult., by Rev. A.L. Hogshead, Mr. James M. WISEMAN and Miss Mary C. SMILEY, all of Rockbridge county.

Rockingham Register and Advertiser, 19 January 1866 (Friday), p. 3, c. 2.

WISEMAN: On the 7th inst., near Woodstock, by Rev. J.P. Hyde, John H. WISEMAN and Miss Marinda V. MAPHIS, all of Shenandoah county.

Rockingham Register and Advertiser, 21 February 1867 (Thursday), p. 3, c. 2.

WISMAN: See entry for HOLLER.

WISMAN: On the 28th inst., [sic, ult.], by the Rev. Levi Keller, Mr. Geo. S. WISMAN and Miss Rebecca F. SNARR, all of Shenandoah county.

Rockingham Register and Advertiser, 9 March 1860 (Friday), p. 3, c. 2.

WISSLER: On the 25th of May, at Columbia Furnace, by Rev. J.M. Clymer, Mr. Aaron

WISSLER, of Augusta county, and Miss Emily R. HELE, of Elora, Canada.

Rockingham Register, 3 June 1869 (Thursday), p. 3, c. 2.

WITHERS: See entry for WITHERS.

WITHERS: On the 20th ult., in Lexington, by Rev. Wm. M. McElwee, James WITHERS and Miss Mary E. WITHERS, both of Rockbridge county.

Rockingham Register and Advertiser, 4 October 1866 (Thursday), p. 2, c. 5.

WITHROW: See entry for CALDWELL.

WITMER: See entry for HEDRICK.

WITMIRE: On the 5th inst., near Williamsport, Maryland, by Rev. M.L. Culler, John WITMIRE, of Shenandoah county, Va., and Miss Mary Jane MURRAY, of Washington county, Maryland.

Rockingham Register and Advertiser, 21 November 1867 (Thursday), p. 2, c. 5.

WITTIG: See entry for WHITMER.

WITTIG: On Thursday, September 29th, at the residence of the bride's father, Sweedlin Valley, Pendleton county, Va., by Rev. S. Henkel, Mr. George WITTIG, of Dovesville, Rockingham county, Va., and Miss Rachel B. WILSON.

Rockingham Register and Advertiser, 21 October 1859 (Friday), p. 2, c. 5.

WITTS: On Tuesday evening, March 30th, by the Rev. J.A. Van Lear, Mr. Philip WITTS, of Harrisonburg, to Miss Jemima REVERCOMB, of Augusta county.

Rockingham Register and Valley Advertiser, 10 April 1847 (Saturday), p. 3, c. 1.

WITZ: On the morning of the 2nd inst., in Harrisonburg, by Rev. T.D. Bell, Mr. Isaac WITZ, of Staunton, and Miss Fannie F., eldest daughter of the late Herman HELLER, dec'd, of this place.

Rockingham Register and Advertiser, 4 August 1865 (Friday), p. 3, c. 2.

WOLF: See entry for BOWERS.

WOLF: See entry for STICKLEY (2).

WOLF: Near Mt. Jackson, Shenandoah county, on

the 10th inst., by Rev. J.S. Bennick, Charles WOLF, son of Isaac WOLF, and Miss Sarah M., daughter of John FILTZMOYER, both of Shenandoah county.
Rockingham Register, 24 February 1870 (Thursday), p. 2, c. 5.

WOLF: Near Mt. Jackson, on the 30th ult., by Rev. S. Henkel, Isaac WOLF and Lydia GETZ, both of Shenandoah.
Rockingham Register, 13 January 1870 (Thursday), p. 3, c. 4.

WOLF: On the 23rd inst., by Rev. Henry St. John Rinker, Mr. Noah WOLF, of Shenandoah county, and Miss Sarah Ann OREBACK, of Rockingham.
Rockingham Register and Advertiser, 7 January 1859 (Friday), p. 3, c. 1.

WOLF: On the 8th inst., by Rev. S. Henkel, Mr. William WOLF and Miss Lydia, daughter of John FILSMOYER, Esq., all of Shenandoah county.
Rockingham Register and Advertiser, 23 September 1859 (Friday), p. 2, c. 4.

WOLFE: See entry for HERN.
WOLFE: See entry for JONES.
WOLFE: See entry for SHAVER.
WOLFE: See entry for WALTER.
WOLFENBERGER: See entry for KIBLINGER.
WOLFLY: See entry for DOVEL.
WOOD: See entry for SANGER.
WOOD: See entry for SELLERS.
WOOD: On Tuesday morning, the 23rd of April, at Abraham Lincoln's, at Lacy Aprings, by Rev. A.P. Boude, Lt. John D. WOOD, late of the Confederate States Army, and Miss Fannie E., daughter of Preston LINCOLN, dec'd, all of Rockingham county.
Rockingham Register and Advertiser, 2 May 1867 (Thursday), p. 2, c. 6.

WOOD: On the 28th ult., by the Rev. J.C. Hensell, Mr. John J. WOOD, of Albemarle county, and Miss Elizabeth MAGGARD, of Rockingham.
Rockingham Register & Advertiser, 6 October 1865 (Friday), p. 2, c. 2.

WOOD: On the 5th of November, by Rev. Jacob

Miller, Samuel A. WOOD and Miss Leanah, daughter of Levi SHOEMAKER, all of Rockingham county.
Rockingham Register, 12 November 1868 (Thursday), p. 3, c. 3.

WOOD: On the 27th ult., by Rev. E.L. Kreglo, Mr. Wm. C.C. WOOD and Miss Mollie A. ROBERTS, all of Page county.
Rockingham Register and Advertiser, 13 January 1860 (Friday), p. 2, c. 6.

WOODDELL: On Tuesday, June 7th, at "Frost," by Rev. Marvin L. Hawley, Mr. John B. WOODDELL, of Pocahontas county, and Miss Louisa BUMGARDNER, late of Harrison county.
Rockingham Register and Advertiser, 15 July 1859 (Friday), p. 3, c. 2.

WOODELL: On the 25th ult., by Rev. Daniel Thomas, Wm. E. WOODELL and Miss Frances Ann FLEMING, all of Rockingham.
Rockingham Register and Advertiser, 10 January 1867 (Thursday), p. 3, c. 2.

WOODS: See entry for ESTEP.

WOODS: See entry for TRIPLETT.

WOODS: On the 29th ult., by Rev. P. Fletcher, Jacob H. WOODS and Miss Margaret A. FULTZ, all of Shenandoah county.
Rockingham Register and Advertiser, 21 November 1867 (Thursday), p. 2, c. 5.

WOODWARD: See entry for BURNETT.

WOODWARD: See entry for HENKEL.

WOODWARD: See entry for HUNTER.

WOODWARD: See entry for PEYTON.

WOODWARD: On the 11th inst., at the residence of Dr. J.M. Watson, Barterbrook, Augusta county, by Rev. Jas. A. Latane, Capt. John H. WOODWARD, of Augusta, and Miss Susie A. WATSON, of Albemarle.
Rockingham Register, 19 November 1868 (Thursday), p. 2, c. 5.

WOODWARD: On the 15th inst., in Staunton, by Rev. J.M. Shreckhise, John P. WOODWARD and Miss Lucy R. WRIGHT, of Augusta county.
Rockingham Register, 23 December 1869 (Thursday), p. 3, c. 2.

WOODWARD: On the morning of the 25th ult., by Rev. Wm. E. Baker, at the residence of the bride's father, in Staunton, Sam'l M. WOODWARD, of Staunton, and Miss Virginia, daughter of Jno. T. ARNALL, Esq.
Rockingham Register and Advertiser, 5 March 1868 (Thursday), p. 2, c. 4.

WOODWARD: On the 21st of March, by Elder John Pirkey, William H. WOODWARD and Miss Ella J. O'NEAL, all of Shenandoah county.
Rockingham Register and Advertiser, 4 April 1867 (Thursday), p. 3, c. 4.

WOODZEL: At the Warm Springs, May 15th, by Rev. Lorenzo D. Nixon, Mr. James WOODZEL and Miss Esther A. STRONG, both of Bath county.
Rockingham Register and Advertiser, 22 June 1860 (Friday), p. 2, c. 6.

WORKMAN: On Wednesday, the 18th ult., at Wertland, the residence of Wm. Wertenbaker, Esq., by the Rev. Jacob R. Scott, Chaplain of the University of Virginia, Mr. Wm. H. R. WORKMAN, of S.C., to Miss Maria W., youngest daughter of the late Warner W. MINOR, Esq.
Rockingham Register and Valley Advertiser, 4 November 1848 (Saturday), p. 3, c. 2.

WORSHAM: See entry for TEABO.
WRIGHT: See entry for FLORY.
WRIGHT: See entry for HAYS.
WRIGHT: See entry for MILLER.
WRIGHT: See entry for RADER.
WRIGHT: See entry for SHIPLET.
WRIGHT: See entry for TUTWILER.
WRIGHT: See entry for WOODWARD.
WRIGHT: In Bridgewater, on the 9th inst., by Rev. Wm. H. Dinkle, Daniel B. WRIGHT and Miss Maggie V. LANTZ, all of Rockingham county.
Rockingham Register and Advertiser, 30 January 1868 (Thursday), p. 2, c. 4.

WRIGHT: On the 28th ult., at the residence of Henry Whisler, by Rev. Solomon Garber, Mr. Daniel J. WRIGHT and Miss Barbara WHISLER, all of this county.

487

Rockingham _Register_ & _Advertiser_, 6
October 1865 (Friday), p. 2, c. 2.
WRIGHT: On the 20th inst., by the Rev. Wm. E.
Baker, George W. WRIGHT and Miss Sarah
Mildred COX, of Augusta county.
Rockingham _Register_, 27 January 1870
(Thursday), p. 2, c. 3.
WRIGHT: On the 8th inst., by Rev. H.H. Hawes,
J.F. WRIGHT and Miss Martha J. BUNCH, all
of Augusta.
Rockingham _Register_ _and_ _Advertiser_, 24
October 1867 (Thursday), p. 2, c. 7.
WRIGHT: On Thursday, the 14th inst., by Rev.
Wm. E. Baker, James WRIGHT and Miss
Hannah, daughter of W.W. PEACO.
Rockingham _Register_ _and_ _Advertiser_, 21
June 1866 (Thursday), p. 2, c. 4.
WRIGHT: On the 10th inst., by Rev. Wm. J.
Miller, James F. WRIGHT and Miss Melvina
L. ARGENBRIGHT, all of Rockingham.
Rockingham _Register_, 17 September 1868
(Thursday), p. 2, c. 5.
WRIGHT: On Thursday, the 26th of January, by
Rev. Daniel Thomas, Mr. John T. WRIGHT
and Miss Elizabeth, daughter of Rev.
Martin MILLER, all of Rockingham.
Rockingham _Register_ _and_ _Advertiser_, 3
February 1860 (Friday), p. 2, c. 5.
WRIGHT: On the 28th of December, by Rev.
Jacob Thomas, Mr. John W. WRIGHT and Miss
Mary L., daughter of Wm. H. VAN PELT, all
of Rockingham county.
Rockingham _Register_ _and_ _Advertiser_, 12
January 1866 (Friday), p. 1, c. 3.
WRIGHT: On the 26th ult., at Hebron Church,
by Rev. Thomas L. Preston, Leander WRIGHT
and Miss Mary F. LAUGHLIN.
Rockingham _Register_ _and_ _Advertiser_, 4
April 1867 (Thursday), p. 3, c. 4.
WRIGHT: On the 30th ult., at Parnassus, by
Rev. A.A.P. Neel, Wm. T. WRIGHT and Miss
Sarah F. BURGESS, all of Augusta county.
Rockingham _Register_ _and_ _Advertiser_, 13
June 1867 (Thursday), p. 2, c. 6.
WUNDER: See entry for PENCE.
WUNDER: In Fairfax county, Va., on the 7th

inst., by the Rev. R.M. Brown, Mr. George Ott WUNDER, formerly of Shenandoah county, and Miss Annie M. COCKRELL.
Rockingham Register and Advertiser, 22 October 1858 (Friday), p. 3, c. 2.

WUNDER: On the 15th of December, by Rev. J.A. Snyder, Henry S. WUNDER and Miss Duna B., second daughter of Joseph M. and Mary C. ALLEN, all of Shenandoah county.
Rockingham Register, 14 January 1869 (Thursday), p. 3, c. 3.

WYANT: See entry for BAUGHER.

WYANT: See entry for CULLEN.

WYANT: See entry for WHITESCARVER.

WYANT: On the 15th inst., by Rev. A.J. Coffman, Mr. Augustine WYANT to Miss Amanda LONG, all of this county.
Rockingham Register and Virginia Advertiser, 1 August 1856 (Friday), p. 3, c. 1.

WYANT: At the Shenandoah Iron Works, on Thursday, December 23rd, by Rev. A. Poe Boude, David W. WYANT and Miss E. Matilda EPARD, all of Page county.
Rockingham Register, 6 January 1870 (Thursday), p. 3, c. 3.

WYSMAN: See entry for DELLINGER.

- Y -

YAGER: See entry for HARRIS.

YAGER: See entry for SIMMONS.

YAGER: On the 12th ult., in Fauquier county, by the Rev. Mr. Gardiner, Mr. Frank W. YAGER, of Page county, Va., and Miss Genevieve T., daughter of Col. Robert S. ASHBY, formerly of Alexandria, Va.
Rockingham Register & Advertiser, 17 November 1865 (Friday), p. 2, c. 4.

YAGER: On Thursday, the 14th inst., by Rev. Isaac Long, Lorenzo F. YAGER and Miss Sallie C., daughter of Jacob LEAP, all of McGaheysville, Rockingham county.
Rockingham Register and Advertiser, 21 June 1866 (Thursday), p. 2, c. 4.

YAGO: On the 28th of March, by Rev. C.B.

Hammack, Mr. John YAGO and Miss Mary Y. JOSEPH, all of Augusta.
Rockingham Register and Advertiser, 12 April 1861 (Friday), p. 2, c. 4.

YANCEY: See entry for MAUZY.

YANCEY: On the 24th inst., at the residence of Mr. A.F. Cramer, Cumberland, Maryland, by the Rev. J.K. Cramer, Charles A. YANCEY, Esq., of Harrisonburg, Va., and Miss Julia P., second daughter of the late Daniel B. MORRISON, Esq., of Martinsburg, W.Va.
Rockingham Register and Advertiser, 31 January 1867 (Thursday), p. 3, c. 2.

YANCEY: On Tuesday the 3rd of August, by the Rev. Wm. P. Twyman, Mr. Edward YANCEY and Miss Fannie, daughter of Albert MAUZY, dec'd, all of Rockingham.
Rockingham Register and Advertiser, 6 August 1858 (Friday), p. 3, c. 2.

YANCEY: On Tuesday evening, November 21, in Mt. Crawford, by Rev. J.C. Hensell, Mr. James G. YANCEY and Miss Phoebe C. BLOSE, all of Rockingham county.
Rockingham Register & Advertiser, 8 December 1865 (Friday), p. 2, c. 4.

YANCEY: On the 18th inst., by Rev. Wm. Brown, Joseph A. YANCEY, of Richmond, and Miss Mary H., daughter of A. LINK, of Augusta.
Rockingham Register and Advertiser, 28 January 1859 (Friday), p. 2, c. 6.

YANCEY: At "Rockland" near this place, on Tuesday morning last, by Rev. J.H. Bocock, Thos. L. YANCEY, Esq., and Miss Maggie Louisa, eldest daughter of Dr. A.M. NEWMAN, all of this county.
Rockingham Register and Virginia Advertiser, 7 December 1855 (Friday), p. 3, c. 5.

YANCEY: On the 16th ult., in McGaheysville, by the Rev. J.J. Lafferty, Capt. Wm. B. YANCEY and Miss V.J. WINSBOROUGH, all of Rockingham.
Rockingham Register and Advertiser, 2 March 1860 (Friday), p. 3, c. 2.

YANCY: On Thursday, the 4th inst., by the

Rev. William Hank, Captain William YANCY
to Miss Mary K., daughter of the late Wm.
SMITH, all of this county.
Rockingham Weekly Register, 6 November
1830 (Saturday), p. 3, c. 2.

YATES: See entry for BEAM.

YATES: See entry for GOOD.

YATES: On the 23rd of December, 1862, by the
Rev. J.W. Howe, Mr. Samuel J. YATES and
Miss Rebecca BELVER, all of Rockingham.
The Rockingham Register, 2 January 1863
(Friday), p. 2, c. 3.

YEAKLE: See entry for KLINE.

YEW: On the 20th ult., by Rev. J.H. Hunton,
Mr. J.M. YEW and Miss C.E. DIRTING, all
of Shenandoah.
Rockingham Register and Advertiser, 11
January 1861 (Friday), p. 3, c. 4.

YEWEL: On the 24th inst., by Rev. W.G.
Campbell, at the residence of the bride's
father, Mr. John D. YEWEL, of Rockbridge,
and Miss Frances, only daughter of St.
Clair YOUNG, Esq., of Augusta.
Rockingham Register and Advertiser, 1
June 1860 (Friday), p. 3, c. 4.

YONLEY: See entry for HEIRONIMOUS.

YOST: See entry for BROWN.

YOST: See entry for RODGERS.

YOST: In the vicinity of this place, on
Tuesday evening last, by the Rev. Gerard
Morgan, Mr. John B. YOST to Miss Maria
B., daughter of the late Col. Archibald
RUTHERFORD, all of this place.
Rockingham Register, 9 March 1833
(Saturday), p. 3, c. 4.

YOST: At J.N. Liggett's, Esq., near Dayton,
on Thursday evening the 21st inst., by
Rev. R.H. Walton, Maj. Samuel M. YOST, of
Sante [sic] Fe, N.M., and Miss Kate,
daughter of Dr. R. WINFIELD, dec'd, of
Rockingham county, Va.
Rockingham Register and Advertiser, 29
July 1859 (Friday), p. 3, c. 2.

YOUNG: See entry for GASSMAN.

YOUNG: See entry for HARNSBERGER.

YOUNG: See entry for MITCHELL.

YOUNG: See entry for YEWEL.

YOUNG: See entry for ZIGLER.

YOUNG: On the 13th inst., by Rev. R.C. Walker, at the residence of the bride's father, Lieut. A.B. YOUNG, of Lewis county, W.Va., and Miss E.A. HANGER, of Augusta.
Rockingham Register and Advertiser, 23 May 1867 (Thursday), p. 2, c. 6.

YOUNG: At the residence of Dr. B.M. Atkinson, in Staunton, on the 8th inst., by Rev. J.M. Latane, Lieut. Charles YOUNG, of Staunton, and Miss Agnes, youngest daughter of the late Roger B. ATKINSON, of Lunenburg county, Va.
Rockingham Register and Advertiser, 23 March 1866 (Friday), p. 3, c. 3.

YOUNG: On the 9th inst., by Rev. J.M. Clymer, at Strasburg, G.L. YOUNG and Miss Elizabeth V. BENNER, all of Shenandoah county.
Rockingham Register and Advertiser, 23 January 1868 (Thursday), p. 2, c. 4.

YOUNG: November 3, 1869, at the residence of the bride's parents near Port Republic, by Rev. John Cosby, Mr. Wm. H. YOUNG, of San Antonio, Texas, and Miss Fanny M., daughter of Dr. G.W. KEMPER, of Rockingham.
Rockingham Register, 18 November 1869 (Thursday), p. 3, c. 2.

YOUNT: See entry for HARRIS.

YOUNT: See entry for LEONARD.

YOUNT: In Staunton, on the 17th inst., at the residence of E.M. CUSHING, Esq., by Rev. J.E. Armstrong, D.B. YOUNT and Miss E.R. CUSHING, both of Augusta county.
Rockingham Register and Advertiser, 25 October 1866 (Thursday), p. 3, c. 3.

YOUTSLER: On Mill Creek, on Thursday evening, the 22nd ult., by Rev. J.J. Harshbarger, Mr. Christian YOUTSLER, aged 73 years, and Miss Mary GRIM, aged 37, all of Rockingham.
Rockingham Register and Advertiser, 20 April 1860 (Friday), p. 2, c. 5.

ZEA: On the 16th ult., by Elder J. Pirkey, Mr. Peter Martin ZEA and Miss Elizabeth B. GAMBRILL, both of Shenandoah county, the former recently from Brunswick, Mo.
Rockingham Register and Advertiser, 1 July 1859 (Friday), p. 2, c. 4.

ZEHRING: On the 21st ult., by Rev. H. St. J. Rinker, Mr. Samuel ZEHRING and Miss Ellen JONEE, all of Shenandoah.
Rockingham Register and Advertiser, 14 March 1867 (Thursday), p. 3, c. 5.

ZIGLER: See entry for MYERS.

ZIGLER: See entry for SHIRKEY.

ZIGLER: On the 13th of February, by Rev. D'l Thomas, Mr. Daniel ZIGLER and Miss Hannah, youngest daughter of Abraham YOUNG, all of Rockingham county.
Rockingham Register and Advertiser, 21 February 1862 (Friday), p. 3, c. 2.

ZIMBRO: See entry for FIX.

ZIMMER: On the 13th inst., by Rev. Thomas Miller, Mr. Simon P. ZIMMER and Miss Eve RIDENOUR, all of Shenandoah.
Rockingham Register and Advertiser, 21 December 1860 (Friday), p. 2, c. 6.

ZIMMERMAN: See entry for ARGENBRIGHT.

ZIMMERMAN: See entry for CLINE.

ZIMMERMAN: See entry for EAVERS.

ZIMMERMAN: On the 24th of December, by Rev. Jacob Thomas, Peter D. ZIMMERMAN, of Rockingham, and Miss Mary CLINE, of Augusta county.
Rockingham Register, 7 January 1869 (Thursday), p. 3, c. 3.

ZIRKEL: See entry for GOOD.

ZIRKEL: See entry for MOORE.

ZIRKLE: See entry for BUSHONG.

ZIRKLE: See entry for CRAWFORD.

ZIRKLE: See entry for McNEAL.

ZIRKLE: See entry for RINKER.

ZIRKLE: See entry for ROSENBERGER.

ZIRKLE: At the residence of Mr. P.B. Moffett, on the 14th inst., by Rev. S. Henkel,

Abraham ZIRKLE and Miss Kate ESTEP, all of Shenandoah county.

Rockingham Register and Advertiser, 28 March 1867 (Thursday), p. 2, c. 6.

ZIRKLE: On Thursday, the 3rd of December, by Rev. Jacob Miller, Benjamin F. ZIRKLE and Miss Fannie J., daughter of David RALSTON, all of Rockingham county.

Rockingham Register, 10 December 1868 (Thursday), p. 3, c. 3.

ZIRKLE: On Wednesday, the 22nd inst., at New Market, by Rev. L. Lenz, Mr. Casper K. ZIRKLE and Miss Kate WINDLE, all of New Market, Va.

The Rockingham Register, 1 May 1863 (Friday), p. 2, c. 5.

ZIRKLE: On Thursday, the 14th of December, by Rev. Jacob Miller, Mr. Henry ZIRKLE and Miss Margaret Hannah, daughter of Isaac McMULLEN, all of Rockingham county.

Rockingham Register & Advertiser, 22 December 1865 (Friday), p. 3, c. 2.

ZIRKLE: On the 8th inst., by Rev. J.A. Snyder, Mr. J.D. ZIRKLE and Miss Susannah C. LLOYD, all of Shenandoah.

Rockingham Register, 18 June 1868 (Thursday), p. 3, c. 5.

ZIRKLE: On the 14th inst., J.F. ZIRKLE, of Rockingham county, and Sarah E. KAGEY, of Shenandoah county.

Rockingham Register, 28 April 1870 (Thursday), p. 3, c. 3.

ZIRKLE: On the 9th inst., near Fishersville, by Rev. C.S.M. See, Jacob B. ZIRKLE, of Shenandoah county, and Miss Sarah M., daughter of Franklin COINER, Esq., of Augusta county.

Rockingham Register, 16 April 1868 (Thursday), p. 2, c. 5.

ZIRKLE: Near Forestville, Shenandoah county, Va., on the 21st ult., by Rev. J.P. Cline, Mr. Jonathan J. ZIRKLE and Miss Elizabeth BRANNER.

The Rockingham Register, 13 May 1864 (Friday), p. 2, c. 5.

ZIRKLE: On the 26th ult., by Rev. Nathaniel

Spitler, Joseph ZIRKLE and Miss Mary A. SOMERS, all of Page county.

Rockingham Register and Advertiser, 26 December 1867 (Thursday), p. 2, c. 6.

ZIRKLE: On the 3rd of February, at his residence, by Rev. A. Henkel, Mr. Lewis ZIRKLE and Miss Lydia TUSSING, all of Rockingham.

Rockingham Register and Advertiser, 18 February 1859 (Friday), p. 2, c. 6.

ZIRKLE: On the 18th ult., by the Rev. G.A. Snyder, Lewis M. ZIRKLE and Mrs. Mary R. WALKER, both of Shenandoah.

Rockingham Register, 2 December 1869 (Thursday), p. 2, c. 3.

ZIRKLE: On the 3rd inst., near Edom, by Rev. R.H. Walton, Dr. Moses S. ZIRKLE and Miss Magdalene, daughter of John BEERY, Esq., all of Rockingham.

Rockingham Register and Advertiser, 12 October 1860 (Friday), p. 2, c. 4.

ZIRKLE: On Thursday, the 29th ult., by Rev. John Kline, Mr. Richard M.J. ZIRKLE and Miss Sarah Jane CORBEN, all of Rockingham.

Rockingham Register and Advertiser, 7 December 1860 (Friday), p. 2, c. 6.

ZIRKLE: On the 2nd inst., at the residence of the bride, by Rev. J.A. Snyder, Mr. Samuel O. ZIRKLE and Miss Julia V. MOFFETT, all of Shenandoah county, Va.

Rockingham Register, 18 November 1869 (Thursday), p. 3, c. 2.

ZIRKLE: On the 11th inst., Solon P.N. ZIRKLE and Mary ESTEP, all of Shenandoah county.

Rockingham Register, 28 April 1870 (Thursday), p. 3, c. 3.

ZOAN: See entry for DOYLE.